LEARNING PLACES

Asia-Pacific: Culture, Politics, and Society
Editors: Rey Chow, H. D. Harootunian,
and Masao Miyoshi

LEARNING PLACES

The Afterlives of Area Studies

Edited by Masao Miyoshi & H. D. Harootunian

Duke University Press   Durham and London 2002

Printed in the United States of America on acid-free paper ∞

Typeset in Trump Mediaeval by Wilsted & Taylor
Publishing Services

Library of Congress Cataloging-in-Publication Data
appear on the last printed page of this book.

In Memoriam: Maeda Ai

Contents

Acknowledgments

Most of the essays included in this volume have been presented in a series of interdisciplinary and collaborative workshops and seminars over the past several years. For making this long and large-scale project possible, we are grateful once again to the University of California, San Diego (Office of the President, the Organized Research Project in the Humanities). We are also indebted to the dean of the School of Arts and Sciences, New York University, and the Center for International and Comparative Studies, Northwestern University.

LEARNING PLACES

Introduction: The "Afterlife" of Area Studies
H. D. Harootunian and Masao Miyoshi

As globalization thickens, the site of research grows increasingly mobile. That means that the sponsors, practices, and products of research, too, are no longer confined to the locale where a given project in area studies is being undertaken. On the other hand, the intensity, extensivity, and velocity of globalization are multiple and variable, requiring a particularized reexamination. The relationship of this revised area studies to other emergent disciplines such as cultural studies, ethnic and gender studies, as well as received disciplines must also be subjected to a rigorous scrutiny. During the past several years newspapers like the *New York Times* and the *Washington Post* have regularly run a number of articles on the funding programs and the roles played by foreign donors who seem all too willing to give money to universities and colleges for curriculum enhancement and research on specific regions of the world. It is embarrassing to read the disclaimers of university administrators and program chairs that the money comes with no strings attached and that its acceptance is necessary for carrying out research. The former is as convincing as those explanations issued by both Republican and Democratic parties that donations do not privilege the special interests of the donors; the latter is always dragged out to serve as a de rigueur response by administrators whose function in life is to orchestrate permanent financial crises in order to induce faculty to search for more funds.

The really important question that must be asked and discussed, in this post–Cold War situation, however, concerns the need of foreign governments, mostly outside of Euro-America, to pay American universities and colleges to teach courses on their histories and societies. With a few exceptions, European governments have not undertaken large-scale funding expeditions in the United States to support the study of their national histories and cultures. In the case of the French, for instance, there has been a regular arrangement where the French government sends distinguished scholars, writers, and artists on what is called *mission* to lecture on French culture in colleges and universities. This tactic, echoing the *mission civilisatrice* of an earlier imperialism, presumably allows the unwashed only the authority of native informants, but does not let them have the privilege of representing France. This program resembles the Japan Foundation's attempt to disseminate Japanese culture throughout the world. It is, however, far less ambitious and generous in the sense that it doesn't supply large cash hand-outs for the training of graduate students in French studies and the augmentation of language and substantive courses in colleges. The same can be said of the Goethe Institute of Germany or the British Council of the U.K.

Not too long ago the Ford Foundation announced the implementation of a new program aimed at encouraging colleges and universities to rethink the mission of area studies. Presumably, it hoped for producing integrated knowledge of areas tailored for a new generation of students whose interest in history and geography is generally far more curtailed than their antecedents. Throughout its history the Social Science Research Council (SSRC) has often embarked upon the reexamination of its area studies committee structure and the organization of the area studies discipline. More recently, the SSRC has considered how it might be altered in an age of accelerating globalization and shrinking funds. The question for the SSRC is how the study and research on areas might be more effectively continued in the absence of large-scale funding. Even the Association of Asian Studies, rarely given to self-reflection, has grudgingly made available space to panels devoted to the discussion of the structure of area studies. In fact, some of the essays in this volume were first delivered in these panels and at a president's roundtable in 1997 that tried to explore the problem of funding and what was to be done in the future.

Any consideration of Asian studies must begin with its enabling structure of knowledge. Historically, area studies programs, as suggested by a number of the essays in this volume, originated in the immediate post-World War II era and sought to meet the necessity of gathering and providing information about the enemy. Later, the investigation was extended to any region of the world considered vital to the interests of the United States in the Cold War. Perhaps unlike other new formations in the social sciences and humanities, area studies relied heavily on domestic extramural funding. Earlier, donations were predominantly from private foundations that would be later replaced by the federal government. The Fulbright Program also began early to encourage American scholars to spend time in foreign countries for purposes of research and teaching. The Fulbright fellowships were not restricted to the Third World but envisaged a comprehensive program that included much of the globe. Along the way, the program became a means of inducing people to research areas outside of traditional

Europe by supplying the necessary resources for travel and long-term residence. One of the purposes of the Fulbright fellowships was to provide the rest of the world with cultural emissaries from the United States who would serve as living examples of American values of democracy and capitalism. By the same measure, the program was also designed to enlist foreign scholars and bring them to the United States where they would have the opportunity to be directly inculcated into the American way of life. The Americans also gathered news, views, and opinions from the visiting scholars to construct a vision of the world as befitted the leader of the Western democracies.

In more recent years, the Japan Foundation and the International Research Center for Japanese Studies in Kyoto (Nichibunken), both sponsored by the Japanese ministry of education (Monbusho) and other government ministries, have expanded upon the Fulbright model by establishing programs that actively seek to encourage people to visit Japan for study and research on Japan. The generosity of such programs has resembled that of the Fulbright, designed to promote national cultural values in foreign visitors. Nichibunken, however, is sharply distinguishable from the Fulbright. There is an unmistakable agenda in the Kyoto institution to influence and control the study of Japanese culture by making grantees intellectually and financially dependent on the resources offered by the center. What Nichibunken and, to a lesser extent, the Japan Foundation have sought to accomplish is both the encouragement of Japanese studies by foreigners and the establishment of the unquestioned primacy of native authority. In this respect, the French *mission*, for example, resembles this cultural conceit, but is carried out on a much smaller scale, as has been already mentioned. In fact, the difference in scale puts the Japanese Foundation in a class by itself. Not only does the foundation offer funding for all of the major regions of the globe but the total sum expended, according to the most recent report, is close to $1.5 billion as of the year 1996; the United States commands nearly 19 percent of this total. The Kyoto center, a smaller operation, simply adds to the hegemony of Japanese funding for the dissemination of Japanese studies. By contrast, the Korean Foundation in 1999 gave only $19 million to the United States and proportionately far less worldwide and pales in significance compared to Japan's "generosity."

Furthermore, the French, unlike the Japanese, Taiwanese, and Koreans, need not fear that without their financial intervention, their national cultures and histories will be forgotten in American colleges and universities. There is an interesting symmetry between the establishment of area programs in the newly imperial United States at the moment of decolonization and the concurrent emphasis upon cultural authority among former colonial empires such as Britain and France as a means of patrolling and controlling interior cultural boundaries.

Again, the French *mission* represents a smaller version of the cultural management which the Japanese, especially, have sought to implement. Even when the French government designates centers of French studies in American universities, as it has in the recent past, the gifts have been minuscule compared to Japan's munificence. But in this difference there hangs a tale: the French and the Germans, who have also funded programs and conferences in the United States, do not really need to fear that the study of their respective cultures and languages will disappear if they are not supported by the metropolitan countries while the Japanese, Koreans, and Taiwanese seem convinced that they must continue this lifeline of assistance or risk the diminution of interest in their cultures in America's colleges and universities. The difference is one between outright subsidization of cultural and language studies and simply support. It is, in any event, in this convergence of forces in history that the problem of foreign sponsorship of the teaching and researching of Asian societies and cultures in American schools must be probed. American schools are unlikely to cease teaching about Asia even if these governments do not supply the cash. But the scale will change and the responsibility for the teaching of cultures and histories may well be, as it already seems to be, assimilated into hyphenated ethnic studies programs that promise students identity in difference. In this regard, hyphenated ethnic studies has, perhaps inadvertently, recuperated the concept of national character that attended and served the formation of area studies programs after World War II, but has renamed it as ethnic identity.

The foreign donations in Asian studies in the United States, especially, but also in the United Kingdom and Western Europe, coincide with the moment Japan, and then South Korea and Taiwan, entered the global stage as serious economic competitors. That is to say, this new cultural offense was inaugurated when Asian economies like Japan and South Korea began to change the terms of their involvement in the global economy, and turned increasingly from being territorially oriented exporters to global competitors in transnational manufacturing and financial activity. The decision by the Japanese, followed by the South Koreans and Taiwanese, to channel large amounts of cash into American colleges and universities for the augmentation of courses on language, culture, and history was linked to this drive for global recognition. It was an effort of these Asian countries to disseminate a favorable image in the United States precisely at the moment when their trade and manufacturing practices were being denounced in the popular press. Thus while these donations were initially directed by government agencies, funding sources came to include private firms. Often corporations would give their gifts directly to the chosen university or college. What is important about this development is that it represented a new stage in the history of area studies by inserting it in an emerging globalizing process that would become dominant once the Cold War ended. One of the ironies of this narrative of development is that area studies has been gradually transformed from the status of supplying information on potential enemies to national interest and security to highly visible public relations services devoted to providing "balanced" (read as uncritical) images of donor societies to an educated segment of the American public, and certainly to that part of the population who will become experts in the formation of public opinion. In the United States, Japanese studies led the way in this transformation and proved itself vital to Japanese donors years ago when influential Japanologists dismissed signs of criticism as "Japan bashing."

The most obvious areas of concentration were the Soviet Union, East Asia, Latin America, the Middle East, and Africa. The last region to be researched as a unit under governmental control was probably Japan's East Asia Co-Prosperity Sphere, which for a short duration studied the peoples and societies within the empire—a practice started earlier by the South Manchurian Railway. In our time, the European Union (EU) supports research among its member states. At any rate, the actual object of study was usually reduced to the unit of a national society, which was politically and strategically more useful, while pedagogically easier to validate and examine holistically, than a heterogeneous region. Today, the nation-state is still the principal agency for raising and distributing money, but increasingly the sponsors are foreign governments rather than the United States, reflecting changes in the world economy. The important feature of this newer project is that these contributions are made to support the study of a specific nation-state so that, for example, the Korea Foundation seldom provides assistance for East Asian studies but nearly always for Korean studies. The same is true of the Japan Foundation and the Taiwanese-based Chiang Ching Kuo Foundation. One of the initial purposes of these new area studies programs was to incorporate the teaching of obscure languages and national cultures into the academic procession, usually finding a place at the rear, where its proponents insisted they had to fight for limited resources. Once this structure was put into place, all that remained were periodic adjustments to the established arrangement of teaching, training, and research to changing political exigencies throughout the globe. This worry was inevitably expressed in the hunt for money, which very early became the principal vocation and justification for area studies, like all other organized bureaucracies.

More than fifty years after the war's end, American scholars are still organizing knowledge as if confronted by an implacable enemy and thus driven by the desire to either destroy it or marry it. Area studies as it was implanted in colleges and universities and their adherents still ceaselessly seek to maintain the received structure of operations with new infusions of cash in a world more global and culturally borderless than the one that existed at the inception of the Cold War. Like those jerrybuilt temporary dwellings thrown up on many campuses during World War II, area studies outlived the original reason for its construction and has become an entrenched structure that maintains the separation of area expertise from general knowledge.

In this, organizations like the Association of Asian Studies stand as empty signs of that missed opportunity to make the study of a specific area part of the general learning of the world. In fact, this separation is inextricable from the fragmentation and isolation of disciplines of knowledge from each other that should be critically and integrally responsive to historical changes. The practice of encouraging the isolation and fragmentation of disciplines, which reinforces their own claims to autonomy, was undoubtedly part of a strategy to control the discipline's subject matter and faculty hierarchy by keeping it free from the interventions by other disciplines. The desire of area studies to offer full disciplinary representation, despite such absence of integral knowledge, is like trying to determine how many swallows make a summer. Throughout, there has never been any attempt to explain why funding is more important than thinking about the reasons for funding. And the obsessive search for cash has resulted in suppressing any genuine concern with thinking through new ways to organize and disseminate the knowledge about Asia or the Middle East, without surrendering such a vocation to business and governmental interests.

These are different days where the student body has undergone a serious change. Although it is in some measure a part of a larger failure of higher education to meet the challenge of people who are convinced they now live in a "post-historical" age, the refusal of area studies to face the changed reality is obtuse and critical. These days the study of languages reflects something of the changed nature of the world that prompts the interests of students in a startlingly new way. Enrollments in Russian have declined precipitously, as have the figures for the study of German, Italian, and French. Spanish recruits more students than any other language, with Japanese and Chinese closing in. The reason for the preference is obviously linked to perceptions of business opportunities. And above all, the invincible confidence in English as the lingua franca of this new world is making nearly all language programs at best halfhearted. Isn't it time that we seriously think about what we do in area studies and the liberal arts structure sustaining it? Should this unexamined compulsion to continue and repeat be allowed to go on? If yes, on what basis, and for what reason? Why don't we seriously examine the reason for continuing to teach areas and regions as if they were remote and unknown yet somehow vital to national interests?

The pursuit of new sources of funding is, in part, driven by the desire to sustain the received structure of organization and the knowledge it is devoted to producing. It should be pointed out that area studies was organized to simplify a region or nation-state into a formula in order to place it in the college curriculum. To this end, it offered a holistic knowledge of the area that, more often than not, was aided by native claims to uniqueness. To insure the legitimacy of area studies, the traditional humanistic and social scientific disciplines were utilized as if they would interconnect an area with the rest of the world and bridge disciplines with all others. Every program therefore was required to have a specialist in history, literature, language, anthropology, economics, sociology, geography, etc. But they never really cohered.

A commitment to this form of organization meant that area studies, despite its claims to be multidisciplinary, actually ended up supporting the retention of disciplinary boundaries, as it still does in the major area studies centers. What else could be expected from a practice that had never thought through the epistemological implications of constituting a subject of inquiry but merely assumed its status as a field and organized the traditional disciplines to subsequently examine what, in fact, was a vacant lot? We must recognize in this designation of a "field" not only a difference from the status of the more traditional discipline of Euro-America, which has never been called "fieldwork." It strikes particular resonance with the ethnographic project that—itself, a product of Euro-American claims to universalism—was conceived as an "outside" study of primitives, natives, simple societies, peoples, and cultures that analogously belonged to the temporality of childhood closely resembling Freud's uncanny. In its beginnings, doing research meant extracting from the field the raw material of pure facticity, literally fieldwork. Since this field was on the outside, it was seen simply as the domain of fact, the object of analysis that would be carried out elsewhere, in the inside, the territory of theory and research. The resemblance of this operation to an earlier imperial practice that saw the world outside of Europe as a vast dominion containing raw materials to be extracted by cheap labor for production in Euro-America is far from being a coincidence and constitutes a historical isomorphism frequently overlooked in even the most critical discourses of postcoloniality. Area studies, despite its arrival with decolonization, thus succeeded in reinforcing this imperial-colonial relationship by maintaining that Euro-America was the privileged site of production, in every sense of the word, while the outside was simply the space for "development" which originated elsewhere.

Paradoxically, area studies has now become the main custodian of an isolating system of disciplinary knowledge, which was originally ranked near the bottom of the academic hierarchy. By the same measure, it is committed to preserving the nation-state as the privileged unit of teaching and study. In this sense it was the perfect, microcosmic reflection of the liberal arts curriculum that since the nineteenth century has been focused on the nation-state as the organizing principle for teaching and research. A new combinatory, meant to integrate the disciplines and opening the way for interdisciplinary study, has become nothing more than a moated wall, insulating the disciplines from the outside world, maintaining boundaries in order to prevent crossings. In retrospect, it now seems possible to conclude that area studies never intended to bring several disciplines together, despite its promise to do so. The reason for this is that it never expunged its own desire to reduce study and research to the manageable dimensions of national character, in spite of its reliance on social science models that often emphasized the centrality of "normative" social systems.

If area studies is contrasted with the newer cultural studies, we can see that while the former has sought to close off the study of a particular national unit from the rest of the world, the latter claims openness as a condition for examining such units in a broader context. While cultural studies has attempted to blur the boundaries of disciplines and even dissolve them, area studies has today become the beleaguered fortress housing the traditional disciplines as if nothing had changed in the last fifty years, a Maginot Line already obsolete before its completion yet determined to protect its domains from infiltration and appropriation. Although quite antiquated now, the strategy of trench warfare is deployed by scholars of area studies as they try to mount an attack on an enemy they scarcely understand. Their obsession has been so intense over the long duration that we must seriously question the psychological as well as political-economic energy driving it.

Humanities scholars over the past several decades have shown a marked loss of interest in the general survey and bibliography of studies in a given field. Once an obligatory reference for all scholars, young or old, such listing and ranking of antecedent scholarly achievements are now infrequently attempted, and seldom respected in most branches of the humanities. The bibliography is after all the mapping and chronology of a discourse. It is difficult to compile at a moment like ours where the required central authority for evaluation has largely vanished from the arena of scholarship. This difficulty may reflect the general skepticism regarding authority, or the recent cultural turn toward poststructuralism, or the simple acceptance of diversity and fracture within disciplinary practice. Still, a bibliography can be either an instrument of centralized surveillance and control on behalf of the established structure (that would deter emerging methods and queries), or a documentation of evolving possibilities and challenges (that would offer a meeting ground for dissenters.) The latter, the oppositionist register, is rarely compiled and sanctioned, while the former, characterized by hierarchism and authoritarianism, the sine qua non of the humanities, is being set aside for now. And yet a total absence of attempts to sort out, interrelate, and map out ideas and analyses could result in a loss of critical scholarship, coherent reference, and articulate knowledge.

The essays collected in this volume, *Learning Places,* would examine the institutions and productions of learning as well as what it takes to learn a place. While the majority of the essays instantiate the national unit of Japan, it is demonstratively evident that the practice of Japanese area studies does not differ significantly from the experience of other culture regions, despite the recognition of local variations that undoubtedly stem from the received culture. As an organized and disciplined practice aimed at extracting knowledge of a specific site, an area studies concentrating on Japan shares more in common with the study of other areas than the often vast differences between cultural formations would seem to imply. In any case, the various articles in this volume review the existing scholarship from the perspectives of the emergent, critical, and, perhaps, oppositional. This anthology is not a bibliography, of course, but it takes its position vis-à-vis what passes today for the standard scholarship in Asian studies in particular.

Take, for example, the recently published *The Postwar Developments of Japanese Studies in the United States,* edited by Helen Hardacre (Leiden, Boston, and Koln: Brill, 1998). A collection of thirteen essays by thirteen hands—each assigned to a scholarly field of recent history, early history, foreign relations, religions, literary studies, anthropology, social science, legal studies, etc. in the United States. The contributions vary, of course, in intelligence, learning, articulation, and general execution. And yet certain remarks must be made regarding the volume as a whole. Scholars who are members of larger and entrenched centers predictably organize the book, obviously meant to be the voice of authority and orthodoxy, according to the received disciplines. Their collective efforts are thus to reinforce, in each of these chapters, the normativity of older practices. The authors by and large discount newer studies they neither seek to understand nor appear to have actually bothered to examine. Often arguments are so simpleminded that it is difficult to avoid concluding that the writers are hiding their discomfort with their novel subjects, which loom as a threat to their ex cathedra position and must feel that their most vital religious principles are being violated. The resistance to newer perspectives is, as everyone knows, often prompted by a reluctance or inability to do the work involved in acquiring an understanding of the unknown, the difficult, the unfamiliar. Updating is hard and exhausting, but that is what is required if one wants to stand side by side with the emergent, the scholars who must examine the world in their own terms here and now. And it is this task that many established scholars are not willing to undertake.

Harold Bolitho's survey of postwar historiography on Japan is no doubt the most symptomatic performance in this book. The author recycles what he wrote twenty years before as if time had not passed. In this survey of current scholarship, Bolitho not only repeats himself, but offers nothing substantive whatever. And yet he dissembles. The title of his paper is "Tokugawa Japan: The Return of the Other," but even this innocuous phrasing not only reveals a desire to appear up-to-date but also confirms the unexceptional observation that the works and authors he denounced years back have had a wider impact than he originally "predicted." The only performance Bolitho attempts in the essay is a dismissal of what he calls "new intellectual history" that "relies on" strange personages that he has never read, that he does not understand, and that are totally irrelevant to Tokugawa Japan or scholars like himself: Louis Althusser, Michel Foucault, John Frow, Hayden White, Paul de Man, Emile Benveniste, Fredric Jameson, Catherine Belsey, Paul Ricouer, Pierre Bourdieu. The list goes on for half a page, mentioning theorists whom graduate, or even undergraduate, students anywhere else would encounter in their required reading list in the humanities and the social sciences nowadays. Bolitho issues his denunciation from a position of authority and privilege that he assumes for no evident reason. He even goes as far as to condemn a younger scholar who has shown sympathies to new interpretative strategies as an "apostate," treason, according to Bolitho, to "conventional intellectual history." Is scholarship still an ecclesiastic practice?

Beyond Bolitho's annoyance with declining control, the volume as a whole is little more than a mechanical list assembled in an age of electronic retrieval systems that have made such activities generally useless today. But if we can recognize the inutility of a now-obsolescent mode of an uncritically cumulative scholarship, we can also see in it another purpose that is still operative. Among the diverse culture regions that make up area studies, Japanese studies has put together more field surveys and state-of-the-field accounts than any other constituency. (This record perhaps attests to the amount of money the Japanese government, by contrast to others, has been willing to invest in the development and maintenance of Japanese studies in the United States.) These lists at the same time claim full and comprehensive coverage, even as they intend otherwise. Driving this comprehensive impulse is, of course, the desire to appear neutral. Yet this apparent neutrality often conceals dismissal, as in the case of those bibliographies that quite deliberately omit certain authors and works and thus make an ideological statement without appearing ideological. What is eschewed, in any case, is theoretic criticism itself, which once was a code for Marxism. Area studies is approaching the end of the road, when it begins identifying heretics and threatens excommunication. These efforts to defend the order of things only succeed in betraying their own irrelevance in a world that scarcely takes note of their presence. Yet the survey also constitutes a sign of a new form of ancestor worship that the larger research centers now practice with religious zeal. Isn't the naming of institutes and research programs after founders, for instance, a new form of the deep-rooted devotional habit in the field studied by American Asianists? Is ancestor worship a function of maintaining the authority and dignity of the institution? What are we to make of the ritual of honoring founders who had been pioneers in establishing the area studies model in larger, national research universities and who subsequently were the procurers of funding from the governments and private corporations of societies they were devoted to studying? Thus we have the Reischauer Institute, the Fairbank Center at Harvard, the Keene Center at Columbia, and who knows what else. At these shrines, the venerated wisdom of the founders is constantly commemorated. But wouldn't naming an institution after a scholar in the field make critical investigation difficult to conduct? Of course, there is the widespread frenzy recently of raising endowments that result in naming anything namable on the campus after the monetary benefactors or political leaders. But the naming of a building after a rich and powerful man or woman is not expected to raise any sense of reverence for his or her academic or intellectual achievement; everyone knows it is the expression of the sheer power of money. The gesture of honoring an intellectual achievement is quite something else on a university campus. That gesture is a long way from the Fermi whose name adorns a scientific research facility outside Chicago and the Reischauer whose involvements with the Japanese have earned him an institute named after him at Harvard University. It sets the standard, the direction, the orientation—in short, the ideology— of scholarship in a powerfully tangible fashion.

These centers are devoted to a knowledge that is believed to be accessible only through the acquisition of the necessary language. In this operation there is the presumption of the transparency of language as an unmediated conveyor of native truths and knowledge, that filter through once the words of another language are understood. With Asian studies, especially the study of China and Japan, this has led to a privileging of the translation as the most perfect means of disclosing the truth of native knowledge, and has resulted in making the translation not only the preferred model of scholarly activity but as the sign of having acquired the only method needed, which is learning the language. On the other hand, it has meant that in the idiographic disciplines the principal technique has not been translation but simple paraphrase of a native scholar properly identified. Much of the work associated with area studies in the heroic days of the Cold War was really a variation on this model of knowledge production (or reproduction, to put it more precisely) and thus a prefiguration of the later identification of area studies programs and the national societies they are devoted to studying and teaching. The relationship is a complex one. In literature, for example, translators were, in fact, editors, covertly "improving" the original native work and shaping the text for foreign publisher and audience. Take Kawabata Yasunari, Junichiro Tanizaki, or even Oe Kenzaburo. Edward Seidensticker quietly emends Kawabata's *Snow Country* and Tanizaki's *Sasameyuki,* while John Nathan condenses Oe's long shosetsu *Atarashi Hito yo Mezameyo* and prints it as a short story with no warning whatever. The authors do not protest the textual abuses. Are English translators of Japanese literature in such short supply that they cannot be challenged? Among historians, Bolitho, again inadvertently, makes the best case when he consolingly concludes his essay in reassuring his congregation of the paradise of paraphrase by pointing to Japanese scholars who will guide the way from theory to real history.

American education has not freed itself from the ideology of a Cold War narrative. There is good reason for this because the Cold War can best be understood as a continuation of capitalism/imperialism that still goes on in the guise of neoliberalism and globalization. It takes various forms such as poststructuralism, cultural studies, and postmodernism, even though it has tried appropriation in the manner of the classic Orientalist tradition. The newer cultural studies has shown greater openness and less commitment to maintaining rigid disciplinary boundaries, and has manifested a greater tolerance for new theoretical strategies. But it has, like the older area studies, often reproduced the same concern for difference (for different reasons), as area studies emphasized cultural uniqueness in its holistic representation of a national society. In this regard, the two have converged to overdetermine the sense of difference and its culturalist dimensions, despite the disclaimers of cultural studies that it seeks to avoid holistic representations. Moreover, they are both still rooted in a culturalism required by the privilege accorded to the organization of area studies, because it was constructed on the principle of the national state.

Here one ought to recall Bill Readings in his observation that culture, separated from the nation-state, is meaningless. The older area studies have failed to take seriously the challenge leveled at it by Edward Said's *Orientalism* to consider the relationship between hegemonic knowledge of an area and colonial power. The newer cultural studies have not always adequately interrogated the relationship of knowledge/power, despite its promise to do so. In its inordinate reliance on the politics of identity, and the ways difference is supposed to empower, it has risked ignoring the genuine political economic conditions that produce relationships of inequity and injustice that such appeals to difference fail to mask. To paraphrase Janis Joplin, difference is all there is when you have nothing else to lose. Too often the enunciation of cultural difference, as we see in current postcolonial studies, slides sadly into claims of authenticity that often mimic the privilege area studies accorded to native knowledge. The circulation of theories of multiculturalism, like the older multidisciplinarism associated with area studies, is little more than a rearticulation of pluralism and the myth of consensus that had been the principal vocation of American studies.

Despite the concentration of these papers on the formation and practice of area studies in the United States, and the changes introduced by postcolonial and cultural studies, especially the attention paid to identity politics, this collection tries to point to the more general problem in higher education and the incapacity of college and university curricula to break free from the Cold War narrative. This does not mean inviting institutions of higher learning to rush enthusiastically to embrace new intellectual agendas signifying either multiculturalism or globalization. These newer perspectives merely reinforce the post-Cold War structure of power, as surely as area studies reinforced the claims of the national security state in the preceding decades. Declarations of globalization and transnationality in business and culture merely disclose that the unit of the nation-state, which had been the focus of the older area studies, is being replaced by larger units such as the globe itself as the proper and supposedly borderless context for business and multicultural identities. What certain scholars such as Homi Bhabha have proposed as a respect for cultural rights, is simply a way of reinforcing capitalism's own desire to undermine fixed subjectivities for producing new ones in order to expand consumption. These papers try to demonstrate the ways area studies and by extension the established disciplinary organization in colleges and universities have been able to maintain their privileged place in pedagogy long after the conditions that had required such resources and arrangements have disappeared. As long as globalization is enabled only by distributive inequity, the site of learning must be particularized to fit the variegated conditions of a specific site. History and geography can never be dislodged from a specific site, although they need to be constantly referred to the forces that drive the whole world, the totality of human existence.

If the papers collected in this volume share a common perspective it is the conviction that it is no longer possible to envisage area studies as a form privileged to structure our knowledge of the world outside of Euro-America. In fact, it is precisely the impossibility of this form and the claims of an unproblematic status, leading, as we have seen, to the reduction of all accounts of itself to mere bibliography, that attests to a unified purpose linking the papers collected in this volume. All of them have been written under the critical sign that acknowledges that the world we now live in has already exceeded the original horizon of area studies programs and that we must begin the labor of reconstituting strategies to securing knowledges of regions of the world that are no longer the outside of Euro-America. Such a task can no longer claim unity, as did the older practices of area studies programs, or even an approach that reduces a region to a cultural whole in time and space. But it is possible to recognize that we now inhabit the space of an "afterlife," as Benjamin once advised, that requires totalizing our relationship to what came before in order to move beyond it. What we mean by referring to the afterlife of area studies is a perspective that has surpassed the older global divisions inaugurated after World War II that informed the organization of knowledge and teaching of regions of the world outside Euro-America but considered essential in the Cold War struggle with the Soviet Union. Just as the older empires moved toward decolonization and a new global order installed after World War II, so we must consider a world no longer dominated by the requirements of the Cold War. It is important, moreover, to factor into this new equation both the logic of global capitalism, which is still misrecognized as modernity, and the Saidian perception that because imperialism once connected much of the world in an integrated network, it is no longer possible to consign the formerly non-West to the borders of Euro-America and its horizon of consciousness.

The afterlife thus refers to the moment that has decentered the truths, practices, and even institutions that belonged to a time that could still believe in the identity of some conception of humanity and universality with a Eurocentric endowment and to the acknowledgment that its "provinciality" must now be succeeded by what Said called "a contrapuntal orientation in history." The former is amply demonstrated in the lead article by Masao Miyoshi, who demonstrates the process by which institutions of higher learning have become committed to the pursuit of intellectual property and the simultaneous bankruptcy of the humanities and its failure to envisage a project of critique and intervention. While the humanistic disciplines have sought to reconstitute their borders to make crossings easier, they have achieved nothing more in the way of critically contesting the new role played by the universities in a corporate role than to confirm students in a menu of subjective identities emphasizing a plurality of differences. In the case of the latter we have both the subject of Tetsuo Najita's meditations on the eighteenth-century Japanese thinker Andō Shōeki and Stefan Tanaka's examination of how Marxist historians in Japan sought, after the war, to imagine a new kind of global history that might in fact satisfy the requirements of a genuine contrapuntal history but which subsequently was aborted by Japan's own Cold War commitments.

In this time of the afterlife, we no longer need to worry about older divisions that had marked the practice of area studies programs, such as premodern/tradition and modern since it is precisely the modern that has become the tradition that must be grasped "contrapuntually." Since the received disciplines have been put into question, we are able to turn to subunits and new combinations that seek to represent the world of decolonization and what we now refer broadly to as the postcolonial moment—ethnic studies and cultural studies. This is the purpose of Rey Chow's article, which examines why those who were at the forefront of theory in literary studies twenty years ago are the most determined opponents of cultural studies. Benita Parry exposes current postcolonial theory's desire to present the "colonial archive" as the place for negotiation. According to her, it is simply a fiction of textual idealism that dramatizes the need for a more historical and materialistically informed approach. And H. D. Harootunian explores how area studies in the United States constituted a prehistory to postcolonial discourse and how it failed to respond to the challenge put to it by Edward Said, which was subsequently taken up by students of English literature.

With ethnic studies, Sylvia Yanagisako traces the boundary between Asian studies and Asian American studies to antecedents in American studies and cultural theory. The purpose of this complex retracing is to show that the "redundant narrative of Asian American history" is transcoded into a history of racist domination and masculinist opposition that only "reinforces the received boundary between Asian Studies and Asian American Studies." In this regard, Richard Okada explores how the efforts to locate ethnicity in American universities and colleges is inevitably yoked to the problem of placement that has haunted area studies. Like Yanagisako, Okada also sees how activism in the service of unformulated political goals leads back to reinforcing the status quo. If ethnic studies in part derives from American studies, American studies, according to Paul Bové, has never functioned to promote the interests of the American state in the way area studies was inaugurated explicitly for this purpose.

Rather, American studies, much like the newer ethnic studies it has generated, "best serves the interests of the nation-state in terms of hegemony and culture rather than policy." Rob Wilson hybridizes American studies by envisaging a new critical space called Asia-Pacific. But in contrast to American studies the new Asia-Pacific paradigm is really an extension of America into the Pacific and a reaffirmation of the utopia of a free-market space that is inscribed in the older model.

Moreover, the new perspective discounts the earlier claims associated with area studies to present a culture holistically. It eschews explicit theorization as it subjects the facticity of native experience to unarticulated theoretical assumptions derived from the social sciences. The provinciality of culturally specific claims of universalism now demands the engagement with theory—as Chow and Harootunian advocate—that must, in some way, account for both the failings of the older approach and disclose newer integrative principles while at the same time considering the importance of the "universality" of the tradition of the modern and coexistence of contrapuntal relationships. Bruce Cumings puts into question the troubled relationship between area studies and social science, and the clash of claims between an idiographic approach that privileges storytelling and model building and the fixation with general laws. Despite the social science dismissal of area studies because of theoretical deficiencies that rely on a historical and ethnographic approach, he demonstrates the utter bankruptcy of rational choice model building (if not its unintelligibility and autoreferentiality) by showing how it fails precisely because, as Adorno observed elsewhere, theory can never be more elegant and orderly than the reality it seeks to explain. The putative "robustness" of a model can never match the totality of a reality marked by inexhaustible contingencies and accidents of history and the apparent appeal to "rigor" and fullness is simply a rhetorical device to conceal the mode's mere dubious heuristic purpose. It is almost as if the purveyors of a noetic social science are so embarrassed by the messiness of reality and its regime of endless contingency that they must devise models that seek order where there is only disorder.

We need not dwell on the political consequences of this form of "science" that, according to Bernard Silberman, is invariably conservative. In the end the insights supplied by an ethnographic methodology are not only more valuable than the non sequiturs of rational-choice economists and political scientists more concerned with the mathematical form of their approaches than the content it wishes to represent and reduce but also its capacity to integrate "areas" into a theoretically informed American intellectual agenda that "is considerably more advanced than the modal type of inquiry in . . . social science, which remains wedded to an obsolescent model how people do their work in the so-called hard sciences." Cumings advises the acceptance of an approach based on knowing one's native land in order to rescue the "unseen" from the recent past before we move into uncharted foreign territory. It is precisely this tack that characterizes Moss Roberts's effort to reread an unfamiliar American past that still remains repressed in contemporary accounts of the Vietnam War that, nevertheless, structured relations with Asia and which must be considered for any adequate understanding of the period of the war's consequences after 1975. Roberts's essay aims to show how a grounding in the specific and concrete history of American-Asian relations over a longer duration is invariably forgotten in both the assessments of principal actors like Robert McNamara, who formulated policy, and newspapers, always hurriedly managing to eliminate history and promote forgetfulness in the interest of the repetitively familiar. But his analysis also reveals how news coverage consistently fails to betray its informing hermeneutic that transmutes the violence of American foreign policy into the instances of morality and humanitarianism.

If Cumings alerts us to the problem of social science in the understanding of "areas," Bernard Silberman specifies how different methodological agendas have been employed to represent Japan. Targeting the specific area of Japan in the United States, Silberman recognizes how in recent years the object of the field—Japan—is beginning to heave and dissolve as a result of retreating funds and new attacks from disciplines like political science. Silberman dissents from prevailing criticism by noting that whatever social science agenda is implemented, its enunciation of views concerning an area invariably disclose a political evaluation. "In the case of Japan," he writes, "the conflict is essentially over the negative and positive evaluation of what constitutes the main axis of Japan's capacity to sustain an integrated culture—one that can be an object of study." While he identifies two prevailing modes of study as "oversocialized" (culture) and "undersocialized" (rational choice) he reminds us that both conceptions are driven by a conservatism when considering the question of social change and uphold constraints on the individual. What is at stake is the preservation of disciplinary boundaries at the expense of area studies in the various social sciences precisely at the moment when the new cultural studies are calling for border crossings and realignments.

In the study of an area such as Japan, the more traditional social science disciplines have, as Silberman attests, junked the concept of the "field" by reinforcing disciplinary optics, whereas the "softer" disciplines like history, literature, and art history have, by and large, remained immune to the challenge of new interpretative strategies. Historians still continue to plow the field of social history with the purpose of microscopic reconstruction. Students of literature write single-author studies seeking to disguise mere biographies, when not appealing to the stale promise of transparency once offered by translation. And art history is still mired in modes of authentication and traditional thematics. In this respect, James Fujii calls attention to how many in the study of Japanese literature continue "their work as if changes in worldly conditions and institutions they helped shape have no bearing on the work they produce." A few, like himself, have turned away from received disciplinary habits and constraints (the text-centered approach) to new intellectual contexts that focus on the logic of the commodity form and the role assumed by "global English" as arbiter of what now constitutes the "unbounded" and "nonhierarchic." He ponders how Japanese literary studies may actually find "a role to play in these contexts." By the same measure, Fujii looks to the precedents established by Japanese scholars like Maeda Ai in the 1970s and 1980s and the exemplarity and appropriateness of their efforts to envisage a cultural studies for our own practices rather than a slavish imitation of models devised exclusively in the Western academy. Mitsuhiro Yoshimoto explores the status of Japanese film studies as a new area of inquiry that was inaugurally housed in the study of literature but which early liberated itself to lead an autonomous but troubled nondisciplinary unbounded existence. Yet, as he observes, Japanese cinema has been, at the same time, instrumental in the formation of film studies in general and is thus inseparable from how it—film studies—has constituted itself as a discipline. Because the study of Japanese film has no clear institutional identity in a well-established discipline today, it has assumed a "free-floating status" that might be used to call into question the autonomy of disciplines. In a sense, Yoshimoto, like Fujii, offers a new perspective for the dissolved object of Japan as an area studies and a new way of reconstituting this "field" in "a postdisciplinary" age that will be "political," by which they mean a tactical intervention in the structures and practices of established disciplines that exceeds the specificity of either cinema or literature, as such. Only in this sense will it be possible to reimagine the true shape of "area studies" as an afterimage that is fully consonant with the vast institutional changes we have undergone in a global age that no longer has any need to be tethered by the identities the older disciplines insist on affirming.

Ivory Tower in Escrow
Masao Miyoshi

Higher education is undergoing a rapid sea change. Everyone knows and senses it, but few try to comprehend its scope or imagine its future. This two-part essay makes some guesses by observing recent events and recalling the bygone past. In the first part I describe the quickening conversion of learning into intellectual property and of the university into the global corporation in today's research universities in the United States—and, increasingly, everywhere else. Part 2 puzzles over the failure of the humanities at this moment as a supposed agency of criticism and intervention.

The Conversion of Learning into Intellectual Property

Richard C. Atkinson, the president of the University of California since 1995, has repeatedly sought to identify the role of the world's largest research university. As he sees it, the goal of today's research university is to build an alliance with industries: "The program works like this. A UC researcher joins with a scientist or engineer from a private company to develop a research proposal. A panel of experts drawn from industry and academia selects the best projects for funding."[1] Thus, although university research encompasses "basic research, applied research, and development," basic research, now called "curiosity research . . . driven by a sheer interest in the phenomena," is justified only because "it may reach the stage where there is potential for application and accordingly a need for applied research."[2] Development—that is, industrial utility—is the principal objective of the research university.

In another short essay titled "Universities and the Knowledge-Based Economy," Atkinson remarks that "universities like Cambridge University and other European universities almost all take the view that university research should be divorced from any contact with the private sector." In contrast to this "culture that eschewed commercial incentives," there has always been in the United States "a tendency to build bridges between universities and industry."[3] This is the background, as he sees it, of places such as Silicon Valley and Route 128, and he proceeds to claim that one in four American biotech companies is in the vicinity of a University of California campus, and that 40 percent of Californian biotech companies, including three of the world's largest, Amgen, Chiron, and Genetech, were started by UC scientists.

How does this marketized university protect its academic integrity? Atkinson is confident: "Our experience over the last fifteen years or so has taught us a great deal about safeguarding the freedom to publish research findings, avoiding possible conflicts of interest and in general protecting the university's academic atmosphere and the free rein that faculty and students have to pursue what is of interest to them."[4] The issue of academic freedom—as well as the conflict of interest and commitment—is in fact complex and treacherous in today's entrepreneurial university, as we will see later. However, in this essay, written soon after he took office, Atkinson dismisses academic freedom as an already resolved negotiation between "academic atmosphere" and personal interest, and he has not touched the subject again since.

Like most university administrators today, Atkinson makes no extensive educational policy statement, not to say a full articulation of his educational views and thoughts, most announcements being scattered among truncated speeches or op-ed pieces.[5] The days of Robert M. Hutchins and Derek Bok, never mind Wilhelm von Humboldt and John Henry Newman, are long gone. It is thus perfectly understandable, if somewhat disquieting to a few, that he should give minimally short shrift to research in the humanities and social sciences in the university.

According to Atkinson, the university does have another role as "the shaper of character, a critic of values, a guardian of culture," but that is in "education and scholarship," which presumably are wholly distinct activities from serious research and development. He thus pays tributes, in his Pullias Lecture at the University of Southern California, to only one specific example each from the two divisions of human knowledge. As for the social sciences, he mentions just one book, *Habits of the Heart*, a mainstream recommendation of American core values, and asserts that the social sciences shape "our public discussion of the values that animate our society." The Humanities Research Institute, at UC Irvine similarly is "an important voice in the dialogue about the humanities and their contributions to our culture and our daily lives." Aside from this reference to one book and one institution, Atkinson has little else to say about the work in the humanities and in the social sciences. He then goes on to assert that the existence of research programs in the humanities and the social sciences at a university devoted to applied science is itself important.[6] Of course, it is possible that I missed some of his pronouncements, but as far as I could discover, there is no other statement concerning the humanities and the social sciences by Atkinson.[7] His listlessness to any research outside of R&D is unmistakable.

A mere generation ago, in 1963, another president of the UC system, Clark Kerr, published *The Uses of the University*, originally given as one of the Godkin Lectures at Harvard University, in which he defined the university as a service station responsive to multiple social forces rather than an autonomous site of learning.[8] These forces, in actuality, consisted mainly of national defense, agribusiness, and other corporate interests. Yet the multiversity was defined as the mediator of various and diverse expectations, however one-sided its arbitration may have been. It was still proposed to be an interventionary agent. The book was reread the following year when the UC Berkeley campus exploded with the demand for free speech by students, many of whom were fresh from the voter registration drive in the South that summer. The students and faculty who took an antimultiversity stand insisted that the university not only produced multiple skills and applications but also "enrich[ed] and enlighten[ed] the lives of its students—informing them with the values of the intellect." Intellectual honesty, political health, and the social vision of a better future were the components of higher education for them.[9] Thus the movement for civil rights, racial equality, peace, feminism—together with free speech—found its place inside the university.

Kerr's multiversity was perhaps the first candid admission of the university as part of the corporate system by anyone in the administration of higher education. It is crucial, however, to realize that his recognition of its multiple functions was yet a far cry from Atkinson's unself-conscious idea of the university as a site dedicated to corporate R&D. Conversely, the antimultiversity view of the students and faculty of the 1960s matter-of-factly countered Kerr's reformulation with the long-established tradition of "liberal education." In the hindsight of the early twenty-first century, this mainstream fable of liberal education as free inquiry also requires reexamination and reformulation. We need to register here, at any rate, that today's corporatized university—which would have been an unspeakable sacrilege for many less than a generation ago—is now being embraced with hardly any complaint or criticism by the faculty, students, or society at large. What is it that has transpired between the university as the mediator and the university as the corporate partner, between the protest of the sixties and the silence of the nineties? Why this acquiescence? We need to return to the beginning of the modern university so that we may see more clearly the institutional changes alongside the unfolding of modern history.

The modern university was built around 1800 to fill the need for knowledge production as Europe and the United States prepared themselves for expansion overseas. Scientific and technological research was its primary program, as it was launched in the name of enlightenment and progress. Together with practical knowledge, however, what is now called the humanities and the social sciences were advanced by the emerging bourgeoisie. But the educational transformation from the ancient regime to the revolutionary bourgeois democracy was not as radical as one might suspect. On the one hand, an old-style university education was the noblesse oblige of the aristocracy, and despite the self-serving devotion to the maintenance of its class position, it claimed to be anti-utilitarian or useless. Erudition, learning for the sake of learning, refinement, intellectual pleasure—such privileged and elevated play constituted the goal of aristocratic education. Bourgeois revolutionary education, on the other hand, was rational, universal, secular, and enlightened. It, too, claimed to be neutral and objective rather than partisan or utilitarian. It is under these circumstances that "liberal" education continued to be a crucial idea of the modern university. There was, however, a more central agenda of founding the modern national state, which demanded the construction, information, and dissemination of the national identity by inculcating common language and centralizing history, culture, literature, and geography. The state promoted national knowledge closely aligned with practical knowledge. Despite its pretense, national knowledge was thus profoundly partisan, and liberal education and national education were often in conflict. They could be, at the same time, in agreement, too: after all, the nineteenth-century state was founded by the bourgeoisie, and it was willing to accommodate the surviving aristocracy, although it was adamant in excluding the interest of the emergent working class. Liberal education was tolerated, or even encouraged, since it promoted bourgeois class interests. It appropriated courtly arts, music, poetry, drama, and history, and, over the years, established the canon now designated as high and serious culture. Liberal education and national education contradicted and complemented each other, as the state was engaged in its principal task of expanding the market and colony by containing overseas barbarians, rivaling the neighboring nations, and suppressing the aspiring underclass. The modern university as envisioned by Johann Gottlieb Fichte, Humboldt, Newman, Charles Eliot, T. H. Huxley, Matthew Arnold, Daniel Coit

Gilman, Thorstein Veblen, Hutchins, and Jacques Barzun contained such contradiction and negotiation of utilitarian nationism and anti-utilitarian inquiry.

Newman had his church, and his university—a separate site—was merely to educate the "gentlemen," Lord Shaftsbury's cultured men, who were aloof to the utility of expertise and profession as well as oblivious to the lives and aspirations of the lower order. Newman's heart always belonged to aristocratic Oxford, even while he was writing *The Idea of a University* for a Catholic university in Dublin.[10] Huxley's scientific research, on the other hand, was devoted to practice and utility, and, unlike the Oxbridge tradition, it was to provide expertise and profession, not Arnoldian culture and criticism. The myth of the university as a site of liberal education, that is, class-free, unrestricted, self-motivated, and unbiased learning, survives to this day. And yet academia has always been ambivalent. In the name of classless learning, it sought to mold its members in the bourgeois class identity. Emerson's "American Scholar" deployed a strategy of defining American learning as non-American or trans-American. In short, it managed to be both American and non-American at the same time, while making American synonymous with universal. This hidden contradiction can readily be compared to Arnold's idea of "culture," free and spontaneous consciousness, which is supposedly free from class bias and vulgar self-interest. To safeguard this culture, however, Arnold did not hesitate to invoke the "sacred state," which will unflinchingly squash any working-class "anarchy and disorder," as he advocated during the second Reform Bill agitation around the late 1860s.[11]

In the United States, Abraham Lincoln signed the Morrill Act in 1862, setting "the tone for the development of American universities, both public and private."[12] This land-grant movement introduced schools of agriculture, engineering, home economics, and business administration. And later, the land-grant colleges and universities were required to teach a military training program, ROTC. Thus no modern university has been free from class interests, and many critical writers chose, and were often forced, to stay outside—for example, Marx, Nietzsche, Rosa Luxemburg, Bertrand Russell, Antonio Gramsci, I. F. Stone, and Frantz Fanon. But perhaps because of the as yet not completely integrated relations of money and power, the university has at times allowed some room for scholars who would transcend their immediate class interests. Such eccentrics, though not many in number, have formed an important history of their own, as we can see in our century in Jun Tosaka, Herbert Marcuse, Jean-Paul Sartre, Simone de Beauvoir, Raymond Williams, C. Wright Mills, and E. P. Thompson. There are others who are still active, yet the university as an institution has served Caesar and Mammon, yet all the while manifesting its fealty to Minerva, Clio, and the Muses.

The three wars in the twentieth century—World War I, World War II, and the Cold War (which includes the conflicts in Korea and Vietnam)—intensified the proclivity of the university to serve the interests of the state. Beginning with weapons research, such as the Manhattan Project, research extended far beyond physics and chemistry, and engineering and biology, to reach the humanities and the social sciences. Following the organization of the intelligence system (the Office of Strategic Services, or OSS), the humanities soon became far more broadly complicit with the formation of state/capitalist ideology.[13] In literature, the fetishism of irony, paradox, and complexity helped to depoliticize, that is, to conceal capitalist contradictions, by invoking the "open-minded" distantiation of bourgeois modernism.[14] The canon was devised and reinforced. In the arts, abstract expressionism was promoted to counter Soviet realism,[15] and in history, progress and development were the goal toward which democracy inexorably marched. In the United States at least, the social sciences have always been directed toward policy and utility. And by compartmentalizing the world into areas, area studies has mapped out national interests in both the humanities and the social sciences.[16] Such nationalization of the university was slowly challenged after the 1960s, and by the end of the Cold War, around 1990, the hegemony of the state was clearly replaced by the dominant power of the global market.

What separates Atkinson from Kerr is the end of the Cold War and the globalization of the economy, two events that are merely two aspects of the same capitalist development. What, then, is this event, and how does it affect the university? Globalization is certainly not new: Capitalism has always looked for new markets, cheaper labor, and greater productivity everywhere, as Marx and Engels pointed out in the Manifesto of the Communist Party in the nineteenth century. The internationalization of trade between 1880 and World War I was proportionately as great as the current cross-border trade.[17] This time, however, expansion is thoroughly different in its intensity and magnitude as a result of the startling technological development and sheer volume of production.

Because of the phenomenal advance in communication and transportation since World War II, capital, labor, production, products, and raw materials circulate with unprecedented ease and speed in search of maximum profit across nations and regions, radically diminishing along the way local and regional differences. The state has always been in service to the rich and mighty, and yet it did, from time to time, remember that it had regulatory and mediatory roles. The state was not always exclusively their agency. Now, however, with the rise of immense multinational and transnational corporations, the state, with its interventionary power, has visibly declined. It cannot deter the dominant downsizing and cost-cutting trends that often produce acute pain and suffering among the workers. It cannot restrain the immense flow of cash and investment in the world. If anything, the state supports the corporate interest, as can be seen in its repeated drives for the North American Free Trade Agreement (NAFTA) and the Multilateral Agreement on Investment (MAI).[18] Untrammeled entrepreneurship and profiteering thus grow. And the extraordinary rejection of the public sector, totality, and communitarianism in favor of privatization, individualism, and identitarianism is pervasive. This results in a fierce intensification of competition, careerism, opportunism, and, finally, the fragmentation and atomization of society.

Environmentally, the earth has reached the point of no return for the human race. There is no longer a square inch left on earth that is not contaminated by industrial pollution. Environmental degradation is now irreversible: The only thing humans can do under the capitalist system is to try to slow down the rate of decay and to attempt a little local patchwork repair.[19]

The most conspicuous social consequence of globalization, however, is the intensification of the gap between the rich and the poor. Globally, 80 percent of capital circulates among two dozen countries. Wealth is concentrated in the industrialized countries, and yet it continues to flow only in one direction, toward the North. To take just one example, Uganda's income per capita is $200 a year—compared to $39,833 of the richest country, Luxembourg. The life expectancy in Uganda is forty-two years—compared to Japan's eighty years—and one in five children there dies before the age of five. Finally, 20 percent of its population is now afflicted with HIV.[20] And yet its annual debt service is twice the government's spending on primary health. There are countries worse off than Uganda.[21] The uneven distribution of wealth is indeed pervasive in every region. Thus 225 of the richest individuals have assets totaling $1 trillion, equal to the collective annual income of the poorest 47 percent of the human population (2.5 billion), and these billionaires, though mostly concentrated in the North, include seventy-eight in developing countries.[22]

The national picture is no better. The inequity in wages and incomes in the United States was widely discussed from 1995 to 1997. Although we don't hear much about it nowadays, it does not mean the discrepancy is narrowing. Everyone knows the epic salary and stock options of Michael Eisner, CEO of the Walt Disney Company,[23] or the assets of Bill Gates. In 1974, CEOs of major American corporations were paid thirty-five times the wage of an average American worker. In 1994, compensation for CEOs jumped to 187 times the pay of ordinary workers. According to a special report in *Business Week* in 1998, the average executive pay is now 326 times what a factory worker earns.[24] This gap is greater than that between Luxembourg and Uganda. Wealth is far more concentrated as the income goes up—that is, between 1979 and 1995, the income of the bottom 20 percent fell by 9 percent, while the top 20 percent gained by 26 percent.[25] From 1992 to 1995, a recent three-year period in which household net worth grew by more than $2.7 trillion, the richest 1 percent boosted their share of the total from 30.2 percent to 35.1 percent. What's more, almost all of that gain accrued to the top half of that segment, a group that saw its average net worth jump from $8 to $11.3 million. On the other hand, the bottom 90 percent of households slipped to just 31.5 percent, down from 32.9 percent.[26] Although the unemployment rate fell dramatically during this time, many jobs were on a contingency basis—that is, part-time or temporary—with no health and retirement benefits, even in the late spring of 1999, after a long period of the so-called booming economy.[27] The state does not intervene: On the contrary, the tax structure, public works programs, defense expenditures, health and welfare policies, and business deregulation are all being reorganized on behalf of the rich and the corporate.[28] The poor are left to the paltry trickle down or simply to their own meager resources.

Such an economy—transnational and all absorbing—obviously has effects on the university. The most fundamental and decisive change is the so-called technology transfer from the university to industry, accelerated with the passage of the Bayh-Dole Act of 1980. I will discuss it fully later, but let me start here with the obvious. In the specific curricula, nation-centered disciplines have been in decline, and area studies, too, has been reexamined since the end of the Cold War. The studies of national literatures and histories, the cornerstone of the humanities for several generations, are visibly losing their attraction. The declining middle class sends its children to land-grant public institutions that cost less, while the rich send theirs to socially elite private institutions that take pride in their rising tuition. The richer students might be more inclined to study the humanities—as they traditionally did before World War II—while the poorer students, who need to support themselves by working at least part-time while in school, are prone to choose practical and useful majors that might lead to careers after graduation. The ruling class always likes to remain useless, while expecting the workers to be useful. And such political economy of student enrollment obviously affects the curriculum. The humanities suffer. Pure science—mathematics and physics, for instance—similarly languishes from diminished support. Thus academic programs are being discontinued, while disciplines in greater demand are being expanded—often regardless of their intellectual significance.[29]

The so-called job crisis in the humanities is not a consequence of an economic downturn as it was, in fact, in the 1970s, nor is it a temporary event resulting from a demographic shift. The basis of national literatures and cultures is very much hollowed out, as the nation-state declines as the hegemonic imaginary. The humanities as they are now constituted in academia are no longer desired or warranted. There is a decisive change in the academic outlook and policy to deemphasize the humanities and to shift resources to applied sciences. Culture—arts and literature—is being driven out of academia, just as in the old days, and has every sign of being reorganized into media, entertainment, and tourism—all consumer activities—that would be assigned a far more legitimate role in the emergent global economy.[30]

Aside from such vicissitudes in specific disciplines, the impact of global corporatization is clearest in the radical change in the general outlook and policy on academic productivity. The university is reexamined in terms of cost and output. Course enrollment, degree production, and Ph.D. placement are closely watched and policed, as if all such figures were industrial statistics.[31] Scholarship is measured by quantified publication and citation record. More importantly, the development office dealing with grants and endowments is one of the most active parts of the university.[32] University presses—which used to publish scholarly monographs for the sake of the autonomous academic enterprise, not for profit but for scholarship—are now reorganizing their inventories to make themselves commercially self-supporting. Once, every university press title had more than one thousand orders in a vanity press setup, where "one group wrote, one published, and one bought the books: a comfortable circuit leading to secure and tenured jobs all around." Library orders have since been radically cut, now averaging below three hundred copies per title and falling. Whole academic areas, such as "literary criticism or Latin American history," are already being eliminated from some university presses.[33] The conventional trajectory of the completion of a doctoral dissertation, followed by its publication for tenure and another monograph for full professorship, is not likely to last much longer. Stanley Fish, professor of English, who also served as the director of Duke University Press, describes/prescribes that university presses "no longer think in terms of a 900 to 1,500 print run" but switch to those that "sell between 5,000 and 40,000 copies." Similarly, the director of the University of Minnesota Press ominously predicts that "in two years there will be hardly any monographs on the market."[34]

Academic downsizing is now accepted as inevitable.[35] Instead of regular faculty, contingency instructors—graduate students and temporary hires without benefits and tenure—are shouldering a major portion of undergraduate teaching.[36] Universities are making use of Internet websites for many undergraduate classes. The California Virtual University (cvu) has now been officially launched, offering hundreds of online courses through extension programs. The cvu involves both public and private institutions of higher education (the UC and California State University campuses, Stanford University, the University of Southern California, among others) to form a "global academic village," as one of its planners calls it. As an instructional supplement, digital programs can, of course, be helpful. But the main objective of cvu lies elsewhere. Although distance learning has yet to replace human faculty and its popularity is indeed far from guaranteed, its money-saving potential is quite obvious. Numerous virtual universities are spreading across the nation and even the world: In addition to cvu, there are New York University's profit-seeking subsidiary; Western Governors University; Pennsylvania State University's "World Campus"; Florida State University; as well as Britain's well-tested Open University.[37] There is also a for-profit behemoth, the University of Phoenix, now the largest degree-granting private university in the United States, which employed, until a few years ago, just seven full-time faculty aided by 3,400 part-time teachers who were paid $1,500 for teaching a course. The profit of the Apollo Group, which owns the University of Phoenix, is rising dramatically.[38] There are resistance movements among the faculty who might be replaced by the growing digital simulacra. Thus nationally, institutions such as UCLA, the University of Maine, the University of Washington, and York University in Canada are testing the strength of faculty opposition.[39]

To remain competitive in attracting students as well as grants and endowments, however, stellar professors are fiercely fought over: A dozen universities now have at least one faculty member who makes more than $750,000 in salary and benefits—very much like corporate ceos who tower over hugely underpaid workers.[40] The policy of forging alliances with industries is firmly in place on American campuses everywhere. Fearful of the disappearance of federal support, universities not only are in search of corporate assistance but are aggressively forming joint research centers. In southern California alone, UC Irvine is building a biomedical center to facilitate the commercialization of university science and to aid the formation of companies. UCLA and USC each received $100 million from an entrepreneur to build a biomedical engineering center.[41] Examples are endless, as we will see below.

Such close alliance unavoidably leads to a clubby intercourse between university and industrial managers. Thus many university presidents and chancellors sit on corporate boards, including the presidents of the University of Pennsylvania (Aetna Life and Casualty Company and Electronic Data Submission Systems); Lehigh University (Parker Hannifin Corporation); Georgetown University (Walt Disney Company); UC Berkeley (Wells Fargo); Drew University (Aramark, Bell Atlantic, United HealthCare, Beneficial Corporation, Fiduciary Trust Company International, Amerada Hess Corporation); the University of Texas (Freeport McMoRan Copper and Gold Inc.); Occidental College (ARCO, IBM, Northrop Grumman Corporation); the University of California system (Consolidated Nevada Goldfields Corporation, Qualcomm Inc., and San Diego Gas and Electric/Enova Corporation), just to name a few. And many of these administrators receive sizable compensation in addition to their academic salaries (for example, the president of Penn received $200,000 in addition to her regular compensation of $514,878).[42] Finally, Robert C. Dynes, who had left Bell Laboratories after twenty-two years of service as a researcher and manager to become the vice-chancellor under Atkinson at UC San Diego, produced a booklet called "Partners in Business" after he replaced Atkinson as the chancellor. At a breakfast meeting in 1996 of the San Diego Biocommerce Association (BIOCOM), Dynes remarked that basic research is no longer being conducted by major corporations and that universities are the source of new technologies. Before this talk, he was introduced by the BIOCOM board member as the "CEO" of UC San Diego. The emcee for the occasion was a UC regent, who also served on the committee that chose Dynes for the chancellorship of UC San Diego.

Conversely, many captains of industry have for generations served on university boards of trustees and regents. Veblen complained about this intrusion of the moneyed and powerful into the academic territory years back.[43] Although there may be a few exceptions, nearly all the trustees and regents of state universities are political appointments, making certain that the corporate interest be securely represented. In more recent days, the selection of the members of the governing board seems to be more blatantly corporation oriented, although systematic studies, reflecting the general apathy of scholars, are not widely available.[44]

More importantly, the CEO has now become the only model for presidents and chancellors of universities. Harold T. Shapiro, president of Princeton University, for one, asserts that "university presidents are their institutions' CEO."[45] The age-old tradition of choosing a college president for his scholarship, vision, character, or even political or military fame is irretrievably gone for now. At least for the foreseeable future, the academic head is a corporate manager who is expected to expand the institutional and corporate base and alliance, build intellectual property, raise funds and endowments, increase labor productivity, finesse the public relations with external organizations, including various governmental agencies, and run the machinery with dexterity. The university-corporation identification cannot be much closer.[46]

Let me turn at this point to the issue that is central to the structural transformation of the knowledge industry, that is, today's practice of university "technology transfer." Atkinson's remarks cited at the beginning of this essay are neither exceptional nor extreme, although they are rhetorically more explicit and less guarded than most in today's academic world. Similar views are being expressed by administrators of higher education—his neighbor, Gerhard Casper, president of Stanford, for one[47]—and they accurately express the policies and practices of most research universities in the United States now.

On 12 December 1980, Senators Birch Bayh and Bob Dole passed a bipartisan bill, the Bayh-Dole Act (Public Law 96–517), the Patent and Trademark Act Amendments of 1980. This law was written in response to the prospects of an intensifying global economic competition, a feared (though not actual) cutback in federal research funding, pressure toward corporate downsizing, including R&D, and the resultant greater need of academic research. During the years of the Reagan-Thatcher economy, the use of public resources for private enterprises was fast gaining respect and significance. The law, as it has been since repeatedly revised, enables universities to commercialize—that is, to own, patent, and retain title to—inventions developed from federally funded research programs. Universities and research institutions could at first commercialize through nonprofit start-ups or small national companies, but later through any businesses, regardless of size or nationality. Prior to 1980, fewer than 250 patents were granted to institutions each year, whereas in FY 1996, over 2,000, and in FY 1997, over 2,740, patents (up by 26 percent) were granted. Since 1980, more than 1,500 start-up companies, including 333 in FY 1997 (up 34 percent from 246 in FY 1996), have been formed on technologies created at universities and research institutions. The revenues, in the form of licenses, equity, options, fees, and so forth, are still relatively small.[48] Total gross license income received from licenses and options of the respondents to the Association of University Technology Managers (AUTM) in FY 1997 was only $698.5 million. (Still, it was up 18 percent from 591.7 million in FY 1996, which in turn was up 19.6 percent from $494.7 million in FY 1995. That is, there has been an "exponential" increase in technology licensing activities.) Although the direct revenues constitute merely a fraction of the total university budget, or even of the university-sponsored research expenditures (from 1 to 5 percent), these small figures belie the actual economic dynamics of university R&D.[49]

University-industry relations are far more conjoined than usually understood. First, start-up companies form a satellite R&D community, providing students and graduates, for instance, with jobs and training, while the companies receive information and technology from the universities. Also, academic licensing is said to have supported 250,000 high-paying jobs and generated $30 billion in the American economy in FY 1997 (compared to 212,500 jobs and $24.8 billion in the previous year). Second, some of the university-related labs and companies grow into corporations that then form industrial research parks such as Silicon Valley, Route 128, Research Triangle (Duke, University of North Carolina, and North Carolina State University), Princeton Corridor, Silicon Hills (Texas), the Medical Mile (Penn and Temple University), Optics Valley (University of Arizona), and the Golden Triangle (UC San Diego). These are the early-twenty-first-century campus landscapes that have replaced the Gothic towers of Heidelberg with their duels, songs, and romance, or Oxford and Cambridge with their chapels, pubs, and booksellers.[50]

The competition among universities for a larger share in R&D resources is fervent in search of both project grants and license incomes themselves and the prestige that comes with being among the top research universities. The UC system is by far the largest research university, with sponsored research expenditures surpassing $1.6 billion, followed by Johns Hopkins University at $942 million and MIT at $713 million in FY 1997.[51] In gross license income, too, UC leads at $67.3 million, followed by Stanford ($51.8 million), Columbia University ($50.3 million), and MIT ($21.2 million). UC is also a major recipient of federal research dollars, attracting over 10 percent of all federal funds spent on research in American universities ($12.3 billion in FY 1996).[52] It must be remembered that these federal funds generate university inventions that are then licensed or contracted to commercial developers. (The corresponding figure for industrial sources in FY 1996 is $1.5 billion, a little over one-tenth of the federal funding.) In the middle of this heightened economic activity, the university faculty ("inventors") earn from 25 to 50 percent—depending on the amount and institutions[53]—of the license royalties from the institutions in whose names the research is conducted and the patents are issued. According to Atkinson, UC is "an $11.5 billion-a-year enterprise. The State of California contributes about two billion of that $11.5 billion, which means that for every dollar the State provides we generate almost five dollars in other funds."[54] Isn't this the source of his conviction regarding the future of the research university of the United States or the world?

Concerning the transfer of federally funded research results to industry, the conversion of nonprofit scholarship to for-profit R&D might well be deemed justifiable on the grounds that inert federal funds are being used and activated by private developers for public benefits. The private sector makes profits, thereby expanding the economic base; students receive direct training, too. Thus the university is made directly serviceable to the public. The high-tech inflow may be said to result in a sharp rise in living standards and the urbanization of an area, benefiting the entire community around the university and the research park, as mentioned above.

There are, however, a number of traps and snares that enthusiastic administrators and policymakers are all too eager to ignore. First, the emphasis on patenting, that is, the conversion of knowledge into intellectual property, means the exclusion of others from sharing the knowledge. The fear of public disclosure that would nullify the commercial possibility of a patent and licensing income hampers the free flow of information that would be facilitated by the conventional means of papers in scholarly journals. Federal sponsorship ought to offer open access to all discoveries and inventions created under it. Patenting delays the dissemination of information, and the principle of free inquiry is compromised. "Communication among researchers suffers, when 'the rules of business precede the rules of science'; colleagues become unwilling to share their data."[55]

Second, the real beneficiaries of academic technological inventions are not consumers and general taxpayers but corporations and entrepreneurs who often reap enormous profits through less-than-equitable pricing. If the Bayh-Dole Act was meant to make federally funded inventions available to the public at large, such an intention is not always fulfilled. Let me cite two instances of the abuse of federal funding. One of the most notorious cases is the 1993 agreement between the Scripps Research Institute and Sandoz, an aggressive Switzerland-based biotechnology multinational corporation. In exchange for a grant of $300 million, Scripps gave Sandoz a major role in its Joint Scientific Council, access to research findings even before notifying the funding agency (the National Institutes of Health [NIH]), and licenses for marketing Scripps's discoveries, all funded by the federal government to the tune of $1 billion. The deal was investigated by a congressional subcommittee, and Scripps and Sandoz were eventually forced to scale down the contract. Scripps may not be strictly a university, but it is a degree-granting academic institution. A very similar agreement was made between Sandoz and the Dana-Farber Institute, a Harvard teaching hospital. For a $100 million grant, Dana-Farber gave Sandoz the rights to colon-gene research that had been funded by the U.S. government.[56] Further, the agreement stipulates that anyone who accepts Sandoz money must give Sandoz licensing rights to their research findings. Corporations are saving a huge amount of money by letting universities conduct research and are reaping the profits by investing a relatively meager amount in fees and royalties. Their funding of some aspects of the research is far from ample or sufficient. Shouldn't a portion of the corporate profit be returned to the public, that is, the taxpayers?

Just as alarming as the uses made of federally funded research is the problem of conflict of interest and/or commitment—inasmuch as it involves the question of academic integrity, free intellectual inquiry, and academic freedom. A case that is not a direct instance of technology transfer and yet is closely related to the topic suggests the risks of the university-industry alliance. In April 1998, a task force was formed by Atkinson to look into the legitimacy of the active UC faculty to pursue professional interests outside the university. The dean of the College of Natural Resources, a professor of business, a professor of economics, and a professor of law, all from the UC Berkeley campus, had together formed a legal and economic consulting firm called the Legal and Economic Consulting Group (LECG). According to the official newsletter of the UC Academic Senate, the *San Francisco Chronicle* discovered that the member of the firm who earned the least stood to own $14 million in LECG stock after the initial public offering, while the member who earned the most received $33 million in stock. Academics from across the country serve as consultants for the firm, and several have significant connections in Washington, D.C. The law professor has been a senior economist on the Council of Economic Advisors, and another law professor from UC Berkeley is a major shareholder who served as the deputy assistant attorney general for antitrust at the Justice Department, a job the economist in the group previously held. One of the firm's principals is Laura D'Andrea Tyson, the dean of the UC Berkeley Haas School of Business. She served, one recalls, in the first Clinton administration, first as chair of the White House Council of Economic Advisers, then as national economic adviser to the president and chair of the National Economic Council. The firm has wide-ranging expertise in areas such as antitrust, environmental and natural resource economics, intellectual property, international trade and policy, and privatization, among many others. The firm's clients include not only large corporations but also the governments of such countries as Argentina, Japan, and New Zealand. The dean, Gordon Rausser, sees no conflict of interest or of commitment, while the university administration announces that "it not only accepts, but encourages outside professional work by its faculty, as such work provides two-way benefits."[57] A conflict of commitment par excellence as I see it, the case divides the jury between those who believe that what one does in one's free time is no one else's business and those who dispute the presumed divisibility of one's commitment.[58] Legally, the distribution of work in an academic employee's time schedule (company time versus private time) is nearly impossible to ascertain (don't the minds wander?), while ethically, the direct and full-scale commercialization of scholarly expertise clearly challenges the idea of a university as a site of free inquiry. In fact, tension is palpable between old-fashioned "pure" scientists and "future-oriented" entrepreneurial faculty in many research universities nowadays.

The second conflict-of-interest case—and another example of technology transfer—also concerns the division of one's interest, time, and energy between nonprofit scholarship and for-profit R&D. Gordon Rausser, the same enterprising dean of the College of Natural Resources, UC Berkeley, is involved in another case, this one concerning Sandoz, which has now merged with Ciba-Geigy and is renamed Novartis Pharmaceuticals Corporation, the world's largest biotech firm. The deal is similar to the Sandoz-Harvard partnership. A new Novartis subsidiary, the La Jolla-based Novartis Agricultural Discovery Institute, Inc., will pay $25 million to UC for research in plant genomics, housekeeping, and graduate-student stipends at the college. In exchange, Novartis will receive first rights to negotiate licenses for 30 to 40 percent of the research products. Research will be guided by a committee of three Novartis scientists and three UC Berkeley faculty members. Another committee, which will determine which projects to fund, will consist of three UC Berkeley faculty and two Novartis scientists. This is the first research agreement ever made between an entire instructional department of a university and a for-profit corporation. Is this university-industry alliance what was intended by the framers of the 1980 act? Is the public the beneficiary of the released research results? Or the Swiss multinational and the UC entrepreneurs? Is the public private, and the private public? At any rate, the cumulative effects of such research preferences will have a profound and lasting effect on the nature of university learning.

It should also be noted that genetically engineered corn produced by Novartis in Germany has cross-pollinated with nearby natural corn, stirring up a storm of protests in Europe. Future problems involving academic freedom are predictable. As if to preempt such fears of infringement, the vice-chancellor for research at UC Berkeley stated, "This research collaboration was arrived at in an open process that was highly sensitive to the public interest and to traditional campus concerns for academic freedom." The CEO of the La Jolla Novartis, on the other hand, expressed his view: "This research is, in my view, the final statement in academic freedom. It's not just the freedom to wish you could do something, it's the resources that give you the freedom to actually do it." It is quite obvious that this man doesn't know that academic freedom is a concept different from free enterprise in academia. As of this writing, a proposed $25 million lab to be provided by Novartis for UC Berkeley and the appointment of Novartis scientists to adjunct professorships at UC Berkeley are still being discussed. Since the negotiation was made public, there have been several protests, including those from graduate students of the College of Natural Resources. The faculty at large, including the Academic Senate, however, have not as yet been heard from.[59]

Universities—presumably nonprofit—are thus now engrossed with forming partnerships with business. They seek greater funds and resources that will generate marketable intellectual property, which will in turn benefit academia and business. The cycle will be repeated by the corporations that repay the universities in grants and funds. Take the example of the University of Chicago. As UC, Stanford, and Columbia compete for the leadership in licensing their technology, Chicago, which has no engineering school, saw its national rank in science funding sink over two decades from among the top ten universities to about the top twenty. To catch up, Chicago launched, in 1986, an in-house venture-capital operation. Called ARCH Development Corporation, it is a joint venture with Argonne National Laboratory to "cultivate an expanded community" of administrators, faculty, "potential CEOS, consultants, associates, and investors." The director of its biomedical operation, hired from Harvard, has replaced 50 percent of his department heads, and the place, according to him, is now staffed "with entrepreneurial people responsible both for raising funds and for turning out actual products." The head of the operation talks of "a new ethic": "I've told the faculty they have an additional responsibility to go beyond the discovery of new knowledge. . . . No longer is the job description to sit in your laboratory and think, and expect me to provide all the resources."[60]

The University of Pittsburgh and Carnegie Mellon University together have formed Innovation Works, Inc. to provide start-up funding grants to help with R&D, marketing, and other business support services.[61] UC has its own BioSTAR (Biotechnology Strategic Targets for Alliances in Research), which similarly seeks to draw private investments for biological studies. It has the MICRO program for microelectronics and the computer industry, and also has plans to establish several more system-wide programs dedicated to engineering and communication technology. Its Office of Technology Transfer, both system-wide and campus-specific, guides the practical application of the results of university research by matching them to active license seekers. "The resulting licensing income provides an incentive to University inventors and authors [i.e., faculty and researchers] to participate in the complex technology transfer process [i.e., sales], funds further University research, and supports the operation of the University technology transfer program."[62] Each campus has its own programs, such as San Diego's Connect, which facilitates the contact and matchup between the campus and local industries. The California State University System, Stanford, USC, and the California Institute of Technology, just to mention Californian institutions, each has a project, and all these ventures show signs of a growing synergic relationship between industry and academia.[63] The bureaucracy reproduces and expands itself, as Pierre Bourdieu would observe,[64] while converting scholars into corporate employees and managers. University administration is now a steady growth industry, far outpacing the conventional scholars in every discipline. "Historically," says the director of industrial partnerships and commercialization for Lawrence Livermore National Laboratory, "we were a closed place until about five years ago. But now we are more interested in maximizing the bang for buck."[65] From the East Coast to the West, from America to Japan, from Australia to Europe, the transformation of academia is indisputable now in nearly all the institutions that are capable of attracting corporate interests.[66]

Not a matter of technology transfer, though certainly related, direct corporate involvement in academic research threatens to intensify the conflict of interest and jeopardize the integrity of scholarly projects and judgments. Sheldon Krimsky, professor of urban and environmental policy at Tufts University, surveyed 789 articles on biology and genetics published in 1992 in fourteen leading journals in the field. The articles were written by life scientists from nonprofit research institutions in the state of Massachusetts. Authors were defined as having a financial interest if they 1) were listed on a patent or patent application; 2) served on a scientific advisory committee of a biotech company developing a related product; or 3) served as an officer or shareholder of a company with commercial ties to the research. Krimsky's discovery was that 34 percent of the articles examined had a financial interest in the described research. Consultancies and honoraria were not included because they are impossible to trace. When these factors are considered, he believes that the percentage is likely to be much higher.[67]

The conflict-of-interest issue is far from clear-cut. Does financial involvement in itself necessarily destroy the validity of a scientific finding? Stock ownership? Should all financial activities be disclosed? There are many scientists who believe otherwise. Kenneth J. Rothman, a professor of public health at Boston University and editor of the journal *Epidemiology*, wrote in the *Journal of the American Medical Association* that "while disclosure may label someone as having a conflict of interest, it does not reveal whether there actually is a problem with the work or whether the implicit prediction is a 'false positive.'" He called it the "new McCarthyism in science."[68] Since 1992, several journals—the *Journal of the American Medical Association*, *Science*, the *Lancet*, the *New En-*

gland *Journal of Medicine*, and the *Proceedings of the National Academy of Sciences*—have adopted a policy of financial disclosure, while others—such as *Nature*—ignore disclosure as unneeded. The latter group insists that the work should be evaluated for itself, not for the author's affiliation, thus virtually erasing the idea of the perceived conflict of interest. Will this interpretation initiate a radical departure from the accustomed legal concept?

There are numerous complex cases involving at least "perceived conflict" that indeed would require minute contractual details just to be nominally accurate. A satisfactory presentation of such cases here will sidetrack this essay from its main thrust, and I would simply refer to the literature listed in the endnotes.[69] A few broad samples might suggest a general picture: A journal editor and university professor accepts and rejects articles evaluating a pharmaceutical product in which he/she is financially involved, and all the rejected pieces question the product, while the accepted ones support it; a researcher praises a drug produced by a company in which he is heavily invested; a climatologist denies global warming while not disclosing that he is paid by oil companies as well as the government of an oil-exporting country; corporate sponsors—pharmaceutical companies, for instance—insist on the rights to review, revise, and approve the research reports. Many pressures are successfully resisted, but not always. After all, the development of effective medicines is extremely costly, and since federal and public funding is not always available, industrial research funds are avidly sought. Some projects will bring huge benefits to public health, as well. Nevertheless, the eventual importance of a final product does not safeguard the project from vulnerabilities to compromise. And while most funds are legitimate and honorable, intensified commercialization of research obviously opens more chances of jeopardy.

Finally, does high-tech corporatization benefit the public around the university? Certainly, the industry enjoys the low-cost R&D, funded by the federal taxpayers and offered by the university. The university managers who often sit on the corporate boards receive some remuneration and satisfaction. True also, a good number of start-ups—one out of four—grow into successful companies, and even those that fail can retry, and their trained employees can find positions elsewhere. But what about outside the "business community"? Science parks undoubtedly generate jobs and incomes. The inflow of high-wage researchers contributes to the growth of shops and markets, in turn creating business in service industries. On the other hand, such rapid urbanization means a steep climb in real-estate values, leading to sprawling housing developments and resulting in traffic congestion. This sets off a vicious circle of further sprawl, traffic jams, and, above all, environmental deterioration. And the infrastructural maintenance for such a development must be entirely funded by the local and state tax-payers. Regarding the corrosive effect of Silicon Valley's indifference toward its surrounding area, an observer has this to say: "The average home price in San Mateo County is more than $400,000; in Santa Clara County, it's nearly that high. Most of the workforce that drives the high-tech engine spends hour after hour commuting to and from another valley—the Central Valley—because that's where the workers can find affordable housing. Polluted air, over-crowded schools and a yawning disparity between haves and have-nots—all are waste products of high-tech's economic internationalism."[70] Unlike some older cities—say, Pittsburgh, Pennsylvania, or Portland, Oregon—which have grown over decades and centuries, repeatedly adjusting economy and civilization to geography, the high-tech research parks lack the needed softening elements of life, such as walks, parks, landmarks, theaters, old shopping districts, plazas—the space for flaneurs. Instead, shopping malls with their sham public spaces offer the only meeting ground to the young and to grown-ups alike. Shouldn't the university provide a place for rethinking all this before it's too late?

The corporatization of a university means its globalization in the current economic situation, since crucial corporations are typically transnational. Universities are networked through countless international ties. It is practically impossible, for instance, to find a scholar in any university in any industrial country who has not spent an extensive period of time in at least one foreign institution, either as a student or as a scholar. Visits, exchanges, and conferences are routines of academic life. Publications are often collaborative and transnational, and their circulation is worldwide. Third World engineers and intellectuals are welcomed in the metropolis. Awards such as the Fields Medal and the Pritzker, Kyocera, and Nobel Prizes are, of course, global, as are, increasingly, key academic appointments. Foreign students, once pursued for geopolitical reasons, are now actively recruited for the tuition they bring from rich families in the Third World. Sources of research funding—institutional funding, project support, endowment of chairs, grants, and fellowships—are often cross-border, as we have already seen. This development obviously contributes to a greater circulation of information and understanding along with capital and technology, helping to erase regional and cultural misapprehension and misrepresentation. And it indeed has salutary aspects.

One danger that cannot be ignored altogether, however, is the emergence of a global academic industry that powerfully attracts and absorbs scholars and students. The industry is far from a "village" envisioned by the administrators of the virtual university; rather, it is a de-territorialized corporation. Transnational scholars, now career professionals, organize themselves into an exclusionary body that has little to do with their fellow citizens, either in their places of origin or arrival, but has everything to do with the transnational corporate structure. As it expands, Novartis is the global model swallowing up administrators, professors, researchers, and graduate students. English, the lingua franca of business, is their standard language. For generations, the goal of the humanities and the social sciences has been advertised as the investigation, interpretation, and criticism of social, cultural, and political relations. But now reality seems to have finally caught up with this facade. The huge impact of the global information and knowledge industry on academic learning that would and should be the most urgent topic of concern was hardly discussed, or even acknowledged, by scholars in the humanities or the social sciences until recent days. Once globalization discourse began, however, terms such as globalization and transnational—together with multiculturalism—have been spreading like any other commodity. In the process, it is being compartmentalized, sheltered, sanitized, and made tame and safe by experts, as if globalization discourse is itself a thriving cultural and intellectual activity. Although some minimal room is still left for serious inquiry and criticism in academia, such space is rapidly shrinking, and the ranks of independent eccentrics are fast thinning. This failure of professors in these "un-applied" divisions of learning to discuss and intervene in the ongoing commercialization of the university is becoming painfully glaring—at least to some observers. What are the intellectual factors that have brought about such a failure? And what are the external circumstances that have promoted this failure? The deafening silence?

The Failure of the Humanities as an Agency of Criticism and Intervention

Recent publications have discussed the link between the global market and the university.[71] The 1995 edition of Kerr's *Uses of the University*, for instance, adds new chapters that are deeply worried about the privatization and corporatization of the university. *Academic Capitalism*, by Sheila Slaughter and Larry Leslie, published in 1998, observes that "the freedom of professors to pursue curiosity-driven research was curtailed by withdrawal of more or less autonomous funding to support this activity and by the increased targeting of R&D funds for commercial research." It even predicts that "faculty not participating in academic capitalism will become teachers rather than teacher-researchers, work on rolling contracts rather than having tenure, and will have less to say in terms of the curriculum or the direction of research universities."[72] And yet these books, solely concerned with the institutional economy, have nothing whatever to say on the humanities, as if this branch of learning had already vanished. On the other hand, books by such humanities scholars as W. B. Carnochan, David Damrosch, William V. Spanos, John Beverley, Michael Bérubé and Cary Nelson, and Neil Postman have hardly anything specific to say with respect to the entrepreneurial transformation of the university and its impact on the humanities.[73] The two sides are oblivious to each other. Slaughter and Leslie prophesy that "the concept of the university as a community of scholars will disintegrate further," but the disintegration has already taken place.[74]

In order to reflect on the circumstances around the retreat of the humanities from the line of intellectual and political resistance, I would like to draw here a thumbnail sketch of the postwar intellectual transformation, keeping a close eye on the gradual rejection of the idea of totality and universality in favor of diversity and particularity among the "progressive" humanities scholars. This ideological shift seeks to rectify enlightenment collectivism, and it is no doubt salubrious. At the same time, it must be recognized that the idea of multiplicity and difference parallels—in fact, endorses—the economic globalization as described in the first part of this essay.

To return to the 1960s, the worldwide student rebellion was obviously not a unified response to cognate historical events. Mexico City, Paris, Berkeley, and Tokyo each had different contingencies traceable to different histories. And yet there were certain circumstances that underlay most, if not all, of the campus uprisings: the pervasive effect of the independence movements in the Third World; anger and guilt over colonialism and racism; a generational challenge by students born after World War II; an intense revulsion to cold war repression both in the East and the West; the newly aroused skepticism about dominant central power, ranging from patriarchy and sexism to statism and straight sex; the growth of the counterculture in defiance of high arts; and, finally, the rejection of Euramerican modernism and enlightenment foundationalism. Such revolts varied in configuration and consequence from society to society, but they were present in some form or other on these strife-torn campuses throughout the world. Further, in a tightening circle of globality, the regional events were interconnected and convergent.

Among the French intellectuals, the consequences of the liberation movements in Vietnam and Algeria were deep and wide, while their historical alliance with Soviet communism was being shattered by Khrushchev's revelation of Stalinism in 1956 and the Soviet intervention in Hungary that same year and Czechoslovakia twelve years later. Marxist humanism was the first to be interrogated after the horrors of postwar discoveries began to sink in to European minds. Such skepticism called into question universality of any kind, including

Eurocentricity, proposing "difference" as the cognitive framework, and "differance" as the strategy. Language was the limits beyond which "reality" was gradually banished as inaccessible. The postmodern turn thus commenced.

After World War II, the preeminent intellectual had been Sartre, whose Marxist commitment to humanism, universality, and collectivism was, in fact, already attenuated by his existentialist rejection of the essence and by his at least dormant structuralism. And yet for Claude Lévi-Strauss, whose ethnology replaced Sartrean existential humanism as the most hegemonic of French thoughts, it was the Saussurean linguistic model of difference that was interpreted as providing the ground for liberation egalitarianism. His perceived abandonment of totality as well as universalism, derived as it was from a profound disillusionment with collectivism, centralism, and enlightenment humanism, was instrumental in generating various schools of structuralism and poststructuralism. According to Lévi-Strauss, "Civilization implies the coexistence of cultures offering among themselves the maximum of diversity, and even consists in this very coexistence."[75] His epistemology of difference that led to the recognition and maintenance of diversity and plurality was powerfully enabling to Third Worldism, Maoism (an alternative Marxism), feminism, antiracism, anti-Orientalism, and antitotalitarianism. More importantly, his challenge to totality and to Eurocentricity had an impact on every branch of learning, from anthropology and sociology, to art, literature, history, politics, and law, among the students and the now dominant poststructuralist theorists, such as Jacques Lacan, Roland Barthes, Louis Althusser, Paul de Man, Jean-François Lyotard, Gilles Deleuze, Félix Guattari, Michel Foucault, and Jacques Derrida.

Lévi-Strauss's structuralism was a response to the rupture of the long-established tradition of Eurocentricity, and it has played an immensely important role in intellectual history not only in France but also nearly everywhere else in the world to this day. However, it also introduced problems of its own, whose culminating aftermath is now beginning to be felt in this age of the global economy. First, Lévi-Strauss's anthropology is, as the title of one of his later books indicates, "the view from afar," because to maintain the diversity of cultures, one should not/cannot intimately identify with any. The result is not only a propensity toward exoticism and superficial knowledge, but uninvolvement, laissez-faire, and indifference regarding the other. Second, diverse cultures are equally unique and autonomous in the sense that there are no common terms in which to compare them: He points out, for instance, "the absurdity of declaring one culture superior to another."[76] Does he mean that cultures, and ages, should be/are always equally desirable or undesirable? Cognitive relativism is unavoidable, and solipsism and randomness ensue. Third, in Saussurean linguistics, which is construed as based on the lexicographic system of difference, a sign is understood in its relation to other signs but not to its referent. In Lévi-Strauss's application, reference is inevitably lost, and thus "truth" is assumed to be unrepresentable. The world is now shifted to texts, and history to narratives. Fourth, every culture or age has its own unique terms and discourses, which are thus judged incommensurable across the cultural and historical borders. Fifth, to the extent that the discreteness of diverse cultures is presumed, each individual subject born into a culture is regarded as inescapably determined by it. This is an impossible contradiction to his basic premise of difference, which denies totality and collectivity (is a given culture an undifferentiated totality?); but, more significantly, the subjectship—the individual agency—is disallowed so as to make any political engagement impossible. Finally, because of this erasure of political agency, the diversity of cultures paradoxically surrenders to the hegemonic center once again—very much as in the so-called global "borderless" economy.

Obviously, this is a simplification, and it might well be called an American literary and critical interpretation of the transmigration of French structuralism/poststructuralism. Also, the rejection of universality, collectivity, reference, and agency in favor of difference, particularity, incommensurability, and structure can hardly be uniform among the poststructuralists. And yet, as seen in the context of the theorists in the United States, there is an undeniable common proclivity among them to fundamentally reject such totalizing concepts as humanity, civilization, history, and justice, and such subtotalities as a region, a nation, a locality, or even any smallest group. As if breathing together the zeitgeist of division and difference, they each believe that foundational ideas and concepts are historical and cultural constructs—as represented by Thomas Kuhn's "paradigm"[77] or Foucault's "episteme"—and that no all-inclusive judgment or causal explanation can be found. The fear of totality as inevitably totalitarian remains unabated. The theory of difference is not limited to history but extends to social and cultural relations. A totality is differentiated as a majority and minorities, then a minority into subminorities, a subminority into subsubminorities, and so on. Differentiation and fragmentation never stop by the sheer force of its logic. Such precise identification is a beneficial calibration in the face of crude generalizations that obliterate the distinctions that exist in any category. It helps to fight marginalization and erasure. Yet if the strategy of division and fragmentation is not contained and moderated with the idea of a totality—its context—it may very well lose its initial purpose and end up paradoxically in universal marginalization.

An individual, a group, or a program requires a totality in which to position itself. Conversely, a totality is not always a monolithic system for the suppression of all differences and marginalities. Specifics and particulars negotiate at all levels with the context and with other specifics and particulars. Likewise, all concepts and ideas may be bound to a specific locale in time and place, but a specific locale in time and place does not produce uniform and identical concepts and ideas. Further, essentialism would be equally present and absent in both totality and particularity.

The contradiction, or antinomy, between totality and particularity is most clearly demonstrated in a debate between Noam Chomsky and Foucault, "Human Nature: Justice versus Power," held in 1974. Their disagreement becomes palpable in the second half of the debate, where they argue about the notion of justice. For Foucault, justice is a historical and social invention "as an instrument of a certain political and economical power or as a weapon against that power," whereas for Chomsky, it should have/has "an absolute basis . . . residing in fundamental human qualities." Foucault disagrees with Chomsky's old-fashioned enlightenment metanarrative on the grounds that it is just one discourse among many. Chomsky speaks not only as a universalist intellectual here but also as one who is committed to the struggle for the suppressed of the world. Chomsky indeed believes that truth and falsehood can be distinguished and that the individual as the subjective agent has a moral responsibility. For Foucault, such claims are merely functions of the desire for power. Chomsky, on the other hand, detects in the Foucauldian abandonment of justice and the truth a cynicism that conceals a moral and political failure behind an elaborate intellectual sophistry.[78]

The theory of difference has been far more enthusiastically embraced in the United States, Canada, and Australia than in European countries because of its long history of a settlement society par excellence, where heterogeneous races and ethnicities have "coexisted" geographically. The university rebellion of the 1960s began, as we have already seen, with the civil rights movement in the late fifties and early sixties, and with the rising protest against the war in Vietnam. Further, the United States was founded on the long history of genocide and slavery, whose effects have not yet been erased even now. More recently, the global economy, as we have already seen, has vastly intensified migration and exchange, and the promise and the problem of difference have been daily encountered and accommodated. Thus multiculturalism is the urgent issue both of pedagogy and political economy in the university in the United States.

Multiculturalism that rejects the discrimination of marginal groups is a democratic improvement over the majoritarian monopoly that had long suppressed all but dominant history and culture. Under multiculturalism, all sections and factions can claim fair inclusion and representation, and there have been signs of success in several actual social programs. Affirmative action is a practical program rooted in a version of multiculturalism that has resulted in an increased participation of women and minorities in both industry and the university. The representation is still far from equitable, and yet one should remember how complete the exclusion of the peripheries was a mere generation ago. Before proceeding to celebration, however, one needs to face the problems. First, there are the revived challenges to the legality of the affirmative action laws that threaten to reduce enrollment of women and minorities once again. Though protected by the present federal laws, the future of such programs of redress is far from assured. And let me repeat once more: The equalization and inclusion of marginals are still far from adequate in any social category.

More crucially, contradictory currents that converge in the program of multiculturalism itself must be noted: the greater recognition of alterities, on the one hand, and the exclusionist reaffirmation of self-identity, on the other. The former is the official line of multiculturalism by which the world is perceived to be diverse and one's place to be within this plurality. The principles of diversity and plurality demand that one's own ethnicity or identity be deemed to be no more than just one among many. If this requirement of equal limitation and discipline were accepted by all members of the "global community," multiculturalism would make great strides toward the realization of a fair and just human community. Self-restriction, however, is seldom practiced for the betterment of general and abstract human welfare—especially when it involves material discipline and sacrifice for the parties involved.[79] Besides, multiculturalism premised on all particularities of all categories—ethnicity to class, region to development, gender to nationality, poverty to wealth, race to age—is infinitely varied, and even in this age of cross-border mobility, no one is expected to know intimately more than an infinitesimal portion of such variety. Picture the variations: aged and impoverished white lesbian women, rich Korean men who speak no English, gay middle-class Lebanese-American males who are newly jobless with no families. However imaginative, sympathetic, or concerned, one is severely restricted in the ability to know and embrace others. The view is bound to be "from afar." When the difference—gap—in wealth is widening, as now, the cross-categorical understanding becomes still more difficult. And the harder the likelihood of coeval encounter proves, the louder the cry for multiculturalism rises. The abstract principle of multiculturalism, an expression of liberal open-mindedness and progressive tolerance, much too often stands in for an alibi to exonerate the existing privileges, inequities, and class differences.

Two other possible perils are inherent in the program of difference and multiplicity. First, very much like industrial globalization, multiculturalism is preoccupied with the facade of internationalism and cosmopolitanism, helping to form a league of the elite in all regions of the world, while ultimately ignoring the multitudes in hopeless economic isolation and stagnancy. Second, multiculturalism has been paradoxically aloof to the establishment of a transidentity affiliation, and this indifference directly inverts itself into the aggressive rejection of any involvement in the affairs of, for, and by the other. Thus multiculturalism amounts often to another alibi: Under the pretext of eschewing the "colonialist" representation of former colonies, it abandons the natives to their "postcolonial" vacuum and disorder of authority, often a direct result of earlier colonialism itself. There are numerous examples of such developments, the most conspicuous of which are the sub-Saharan countries, where starvation, corruption, pillage, and violence relentlessly continue—while the Northern nations merely stand by without offering assistance. At home, inner cities are their equivalents. Supported by the idea of postcoloniality, the positioning of colonialism as a past event, multiculturalism works nearly as a license to abandon the welfare of the unprofitable marginals and concentrate on the interests of the dominant. This is what Slavoj Žižek means when he characterizes multiculturalism as "the ideal form of ideology of this global capitalism."[80]

An oppressed and exploited group has the right and responsibility to defend itself, and it requires the firm establishment of a group identity for self-protection. Once survival and self-defense cease to be a desperate necessity, however, identity politics often turns into a policy of self-promotion, or, more exactly, a self-serving sales policy in which a history of victimization becomes a commodity that demands payment.[81] It can pervert itself into opportunism and cannibalism, be it racial, sexual, national, social, or otherwise. In the name of multiculturalism, one privileges one's own identity, while making merely a token acknowledgment of the other's—whom one proceeds to disregard when an occasion for help arrives. It is as if self-identity were an article of private property, which the group—but more likely its elite leadership—claims to own and guard exclusively. Exclusionism is destructive, whether among the rulers or the ruled. Entrepreneurial self-assertion sunders any possible political alliance with other marginal groups into uncoordinated and fragmented promotional drives, which most likely head toward a disastrous defeat in the hands of the far better organized dominant parties. In this connection, it may do well to reflect on what Tzvetan Todorov suggests as a common human feature: "The context in which human beings come into the world subjects them to multiple influences, and this context varies in time and space. What every human being has in common with all others is the ability to reject these determinations."[82] I do not believe that such freedom is given to everyone, and yet the wish occasionally to alter them, to assume the identity of another, must surely be a very common experience indeed. The borders between beings must remain passable at least in the imagining.

To return to the corporate use of multiculturalism, privatization and entrepreneurship are valorized in globalism. While the corporate system has no reason—or no profit motive—for eradicating racism and sexism, it has similarly little reason—or little profit motive—for always encouraging racism and sexism. In fact, the corporate system stands to gain under certain circumstances by promoting diversity among ethnic and gender groups as it expands its markets, insofar as it can retain class difference and uneven development—the indispensable capitalist condition for cheap labor. Here, identity politics, to which the idea of diversity often irresistibly leads, can easily be played into the hands of corporate management. Every marginal group will be as exclusive and alienated from all others, as it is led by ethnic spokespersons, each working in a self-sealed entrepreneurship, with its identity as a private investment, as capital. Transnational corporatism needs only low-cost labor, regardless of its ethnic origins and geographical roots. Which ethnicities or regions it comes from is of little consequence.[83] In the advocates of exclusionary identity politics, in fact, transnational capitalism, or neocolonialism, finds a soulmate who can stand in as the manager of the group.

In the context of the university's organization, identity politics is bound to create factionalism and fractionalization. But it now has the imprimatur from the philosophy of difference. The multiplicity of perspectives, specializations, and qualifications is intensified with the rage for differentiation. Agreement is ipso facto suspect and unwanted. Internecine disputation is substituted for political engagement. Thus, in a humanities department now, feminists vie with ethnic groups as well as the male of all kinds; among feminists, essentialists contest anti-essentialists; assaults on the "ludic posties" become the career of "postludic" academics; post-Marxists reject orthodox Marxists; conventional disciplinary scholars hold in contempt cultural studies writers; novelists despise theorists who can't sell products; theorists look down on creative writers as ignorant and self-absorbed; empirical historians are convinced that theorists are moonstruck obscurantists; queers believe they are the best because their identities are identity-less; formalists are proud of their purity, while they are the targets of derision as hopelessly out of date and out of touch according to the politically engaged; ethnics are opportunists in the eyes of the whites, whereas the whites are both mindless and heartless troglodytes as the marginals see them.

Factions disagree with each other on nearly every topic, be it the B.A. or

Ph.D. requirements, recruitment and admissions preferences, promotion, tenure, or even the selection of a guest lecturer. The most difficult document to compile in any academic unit nowadays may be the general description of itself, its history and objective, in the form of a handbook or manual. Strife, however, is not the worst of possibilities: At least people are talking to each other—even if they do raise their voices. It is common today to observe a mutually icy-distant silence, which allows everyone to escape into her/his womblike cocoon, talking minimally to the fewest contacts possible. Thus, instead of open discussion and argument at a meeting, perfunctory mail ballots—likely by email—decide issues. Education of undergraduates consists of the mechanical transfer of safe packaged information unsullied by fundamentals and intricacies; graduate education is somewhat more involved, but even that is apt to be left to the students themselves. Uncontaminated as yet, graduate students expect guidance of a general nature in the humanities but often find that the best part of their education is in reading groups they form among themselves rather than in the institutional seminar rooms, where the instructors, full of anxieties over other texts and readings, tend to say nothing of significance. Indeterminacy rules, and it is a poor bargain for those graduate apprentices who must decide on their future in the few years allowed them by the production-dictated rules of their graduate administrators. The administration's pressure toward quantitative production—though no one knows the specifications—heats up the internal mechanics of academia. Nowadays, more frequently than ever, humanities departments are placed in receivership, an academic equivalence of bankruptcy, in which the unit is judged to be incapable of handling itself because of irreconcilable internal dissension.[84]

The faculty would rather do the things that might promote their professional careers. Untenured assistant professors are understandably in panic; they may not make it. Furthermore, they know that a financial downturn—real or fabricated—can legally eliminate the programs they have worked so hard to get into. But before that eventuality takes place, they must first sneak in, even if there is no guarantee of any kind for their long unfathomable future years. Yet the marginalization of the humanities and the social sciences has been terrifying not only the pretenure faculty but also the supposedly securely tenured professors. The same eventualities face them. They still have many years remaining in their careers, and during these long leftover years, they need to appear confident and attractive at least to their students (customers), if not to their colleagues (business competitors). The sad fact is that many aging professors are finding it difficult to conceal the lack of a project that fully absorbs their interest and energy, if not passion and imagination. But most choose to evade it. It is pathetic to have to witness some of those who posed as faculty rebels only a few years ago now sheepishly talking about the wisdom of ingratiating the administration—as if such demeaning mendacity could veer the indomitable march of academic corporatism by even an inch. To all but those inside, much of humanities research may well look insubstantial, precious, and irrelevant, if not useless, harmless, and humorless. Worse than the fetishism of irony, paradox, and complexity a half century ago, the cant of hybridity, nuance, and diversity now pervades the humanities faculty. Thus they are thoroughly disabled to take up the task of opposition, resistance, and confrontation, and are numbed into retreat and withdrawal as "negative intellectuals"[85]—precisely as did the older triad of new criticism. If Atkinson and many other administrators neglect to think seriously about the humanities in the corporatized universities, the fault may not be entirely theirs.

If all this is a caricature, which it is, it must nevertheless be a familiar one to most in the humanities now. It is indeed a bleak picture. I submit, however, that such demoralization and fragmentation, such loss of direction and purpose, are the cause and effect of the stunning silence, the fearful disengagement, in the face of the radical corporatization that higher education is undergoing at this time.

In the macromanagement picture, there is little likelihood here of a return to nation-statism, which enabled the construction of a national history, a national literature, a national culture, and a national economy during the major portions of the last two centuries. Obviously, the nation-state structure will not disappear anytime soon, but this does not mean that it is still the fecund soil for intellectual and cultural imagination now. That time is over, and it is glad tidings in several ways. At the same time, now unchecked by national and regional sectioning, control quietly made pervasive and ungraspable in the global economy is even more powerfully effective. And there is hardly any space for critical inquiry and cultural resistance in academia that might provide a base from which to launch a challenge to this seamless domination of capital. Does this mean an end to all oppositionist politics?

As long as extreme inequity in power and privilege persists, there will be discontent and resentment that can ignite at a propitious moment. The opportunity will not arrive by the call from an intellectual leader, of course. When the workers and underclass find it intolerable to live on with the uneven distribution of comfort and suffering, they will eventually rise up. The humanities as we have known it for many decades have ceased to be of use for now. Critics, however, can still discern signs among people and organize their findings into an argument and program for dissemination. The academics' work in this marketized world, then, is to learn and watch problems in as many sites as they can keep track of, not in any specific areas, nations, races, ages, genders, or cultures, but in all areas, nations, races, ages, genders, and cultures. In other words, far from abandoning the master narratives, the critics and scholars in the humanities must restore the public rigor of the metanarratives. Together with those already mentioned, there are several others whose voices I, for one, would cherish to hearken. As important, we know that in every institution, there are serious minds who quietly keep toiling in their reflection and teaching, often unrewarded and unacknowledged except by their students. They may well be the ones with whom the people will share their future in large measure. What we need now is this powerfully reintegrated concept of society, where diversity does not mean a rivalry of minorities and factions, and resultant isolation. The emerging orientation of scholarship is likely to appear yet opaque and ill-defined for those accustomed to the clear dictates of the nation-state during the colonial, imperial, and Cold War years. It is no mean task in these days to orient one's own scholarship in the university that is being reduced to the exclusive site for R&D. The administrators seem eager to write off the humanities—as an instrument to control minorities, or else merely as a managerial training program in metropolitan manners, style, and fashion, set aside for the socially "elite" institutions. We need a new interventional project with which to combat the corporatization of the university and the mind.

The appellation ivory tower, a translation of *tour d'ivoire*, is a cliché and is as taken for granted as the university itself. Examined closely, however, the designation reveals more than we are accustomed to seeing in it: The modern university is indeed built with ivory, a material robbed from Africa and India, where elephants are now nearly extinct, and thus ivory is contraband.[86] The greatest benefactor of the modern university, upon reflection, may indeed be King Leopold of Belgium, Queen Victoria's uncle, who may have contributed to the extinction of ten million African lives. We should perhaps never talk about the modern university without recalling Joseph Conrad's *Heart of Darkness*. The late Bill Readings's excellent book, *The University in Ruins*, is right in its discussion of the humanities.[87] In other aspects, however, today's university is immensely prosperous and opulent. No longer far from the madding crowd, the university is built increasingly among shopping malls, and shopping malls amidst the university. It is no longer selling out; it has already been sold and bought. The deed has been written and signed, and the check already signed, too. But the deed has not been registered, and the check not cashed as yet. To right the situation, to null the transaction and be just to all on earth, we may have to re-learn the sense of the world, the totality, that includes all peoples in every race, class, and gender.

Notes

I have presented this essay in various stages at the following institutions and confer-ences: the conference on Critical Theories: China and West, at the Chinese Academy of Social Sciences and the Humanities and the Human Normal University; the Border Studies Research Circle, the University of Wisconsin, Madison; the Inter-Asia Cul-tural Studies Conference, the National Tsing Hua University, Taipei; the conference on Aesthetics and Difference: Cultural Diversity, Literature, and the Arts, at UC Riv-erside; the Center for the Study of Race and Ethnicity and the Department of Ethnic Studies, UC San Diego; the Critical Theory Institute, UC Irvine; the Institute for Global Studies, the University of Minnesota; and the Freeman Lecture Series in Ore-gon. I am in debt to the organizers and audiences for their responses. Many friends and colleagues have read the manuscript also in various versions, and I am grateful for their comments and critiques: Marti Archibald, Paul Bové, Chen Kuan-Hsing, Eric Cazdyn, Noam Chomsky, Rey Chow, Arif Dirlik, H. D. Harootunian, Gerald Iguchi, Fredric Jameson, Mary Layoun, Meaghan Morris, Richard Okada, Edward Said, Ro-saura Sanchez, Ulrike Schaede, Don Wayne, Wang Fengzhen, and Rob Wilson. I would like to thank especially Allen Paau, the director of the Office of Technology Transfer, UC San Diego, who spent a generous amount of time with me on this paper.

1   Richard C. Atkinson and Edward E. Penhoet, "Town and Gown Join Forces to Boost State," *Los Angeles Times*, 31 December 1996.

2   Richard C. Atkinson, "The Role of Research in the University of the Future," paper presented at the United Nations University, Tokyo, Japan, 4 November 1997, avail-able at www.ucop.edu/ucophome/pres/comments/role.html.

3   Richard C. Atkinson, "Universities and the Knowledge-Based Economy," paper presented at the California State Senate Fiscal Retreat, 3 February 1996, available at www.ucop.edu/ucophome/pres/comments/senate.html. Actually, Cambridge has been forming an alliance with business by, for instance, developing a science park since the 1960s and forming an internal incubator corporation, Cambridge University Technical Services, Ltd. Though a late starter, Oxford University is also catching up with its Isis Innovation. See Sarah Gracie, "Dreaming Spires Wake Up to Business," *Sunday Times (London)*, 6 June 1999.

4   Richard C. Atkinson, "High Stakes for Knowledge," *Los Angeles Times*, 28 April 1996.

5   While chancellor at UC San Diego, Atkinson, with Donald Tuzin, a professor in the Department of Anthropology, authored an article titled "Equilibrium in the Research University," *Change: The Magazine of Higher Learning* (May/June 1992): 21–31. It is a general statement regarding the missions of the university, of teaching, of general education, and so forth, but, even here, Atkinson and Tuzin barely touch the intellec-tual issues faced by the humanities and the social sciences.

6 Richard C. Atkinson, "Visions and Values: The Research University in Transition," the 19th Annual Pullias Lecture, delivered at the University of Southern California on 1 March 1997, available at www.ucop.edu/ucophome/pres/comments/pulli.html. Atkinson's writing is not always clear. My sentence is a paraphrase of the following: "In each case the fact that these activities unfolded in an institution with research as a central mission has been essential to their nature and impact."

7 Atkinson has another op-ed piece, "It Takes Cash to Keep Ideas Flowing," *Los Angeles Times*, 25 September 1998, which, as the unself-conscious title suggests, repeats what he has been expressing all along. I am grateful to the UC Office of the President for its generous cooperation with my inquiries.

8 Clark Kerr, *The Uses of the University*, 4th ed. (Cambridge, Mass.: Harvard University Press, 1995).

9 Sheldon S. Wolin and John H. Schaar, "Berkeley and the Fate of the Multiversity," *New York Review of Books* 4(3) (11 March 1965): 17.

10 John Henry Newman, *The Idea of a University*, ed. Frank M. Turner (New Haven, Conn.: Yale University Press, 1996).

11 Matthew Arnold, "Conclusion," in *Culture and Anarchy*, ed. J. Dover Wilson (Cambridge: Cambridge University Press, 1932), 202–12.

12 Kerr, *Uses of the University*, 35.

13 See Robin W. Winks, *Cloak and Gown: Scholars in the Secret War, 1939–1961* (New York: William Morrow, 1987). On academic mobilization during the Cold War, see Noam Chomsky et al., *The Cold War and the University: Toward an Intellectual History of the Postwar Years* (New York: New Press, 1997).

14 See Franco Moretti, "The Spell of Indecision," in *Marxism and the Interpretation of Culture*, ed. Cary Nelson and Lawrence Grossberg (Urbana: University of Illinois Press, 1988), 339–46.

15 Serge Guilbaut, *How New York Stole the Idea of Modern Art: Abstract Expressionism, Freedom, and the Cold War*, trans. Arthur Goldhammer (Chicago: University of Chicago Press, 1983).

16 See Bruce Cumings, "Boundary Displacement: Area Studies and International Studies during and after the Cold War," *Bulletin of Concerned Asian Scholars* 29(1) (January–March 1997): 6–26.

17 "One measure of the extent to which product markets are integrated is the ratio of trade to output. This has increased sharply in most countries since 1950. But by this measure Britain and France are only slightly more open to trade today than they were in 1913, while Japan is less open now than then" (see "One World?" *Economist*, 18 October 1997, 79–80).

18 Among the former colonies, nationalism and statism play considerably different roles. For a succinct discussion, see Neil Lazarus, "Transnationalism and the Alleged Death of the Nation-State," in *Cultural Readings of Imperialism: Edward Said and the Gravity of History*, ed. Keith Ansell-Pearson, Benita Parry, and Judith Squires (London: Lawrence and Wishart, 1997), 28–48.

19 For a recent concise survey, see Bill McKibben, "A Special Moment in History," *Atlantic Monthly*, May 1998, 55–78. For a full-scale study of environmental issues,

see David Harvey, *Justice, Nature, and Geography of Difference* (Oxford: Blackwell, 1996).

20 Michael Specter, "Urgency Tempers Ethics Concerns in Uganda Trial of AIDS Vaccine," *New York Times*, 1 October 1998. According to Donald G. McNeil, "AIDS Stalking Africa's Struggling Economies," *New York Times*, 15 November 1998, 9.51 percent of Ugandan adults are infected with AIDS.

21 Mark Weisbrot, research director at the Preamble Center, Washington, D.C., provided the data on Uganda's annual debt service in a telephone conversation, 29 September 1999. As for the poorer countries, examples are, in gross national product per capita, Malawi ($144), Ethiopia ($130), Afghanistan ($111), Tanzania ($85), Mozambique ($80), Somalia ($74), and Sudan ($63) (*The Economist Pocket World in Figures* [London: Profile Books, 1997]). As for the debt-export ratio, Guinea-Bissau is over seven times, São Tomé and Príncipe over six times, and Burundi over five times ("Helping the Third World," *Economist*, 26 June 1999).

22 United Nations Development Programme (UNDP), *Human Development Report 1998* (New York: Oxford University Press, 1998), 30.

23 Eisner's salary was raised by 23 percent to $10.65 million in 1997 (from staff and wire reports, *Los Angeles Times*, 20 December 1997), while he exercised his stock options of $565 million, according to James Bates, *Los Angeles Times*, 4 December 1997.

24 See the special report on executive pay, "The Good, the Bad, the Ugly of CEO Salaries Scoreboard: Executive Compensation," *Business Week*, 20 April 1998, 64–110, with contributions by Jennifer Reingold, Richard A. Melcher, Gary McWilliams, and other bureau reports. The figures for 1974 and 1994 are taken from the website of the House Democratic Policy Committee, available at www.house.gov/democrats/research/6ceopay.html.

What is interesting about this phenomenon is that the raise and option have very little to do with the performance of the companies the executives manage. See Adam Bryant, "Stock Options That Raise Investors' Ire," *New York Times*, 27 March 1998; Adam Bryant, "Flying High on the Option Express," *New York Times*, 5 April 1998; and Adam Bryant, "Executive Cash Machine," *New York Times*, 8 November 1998.

25 David E. Sanger, "A Last Liberal (Almost) Leaves Town," *New York Times*, 9 January 1997.

26 Gene Koretz, "Where Wealth Surged in the 90s," *Business Week*, 25 August 1997, 32. See also Jeff Madrick, "In the Shadows of Prosperity," *New York Review of Books*, 14 August 1997, 40–44.

27 Robert B. Reich, "Despite the U.S. Boom, Free Trade Is Off Track," *Los Angeles Times*, 18 June 1999.

28 "The Disappearing Taxpayer," *Economist*, 31 May–6 June 1997, 15, 21–23; and David Cay Johnston, "Tax Cuts Help the Wealthy in the Strong Economy," *New York Times*, 5 October 1997.

29 The closure of departments is no longer episodic. See my "'Globalization,' Culture, and the University," in *The Cultures of Globalization*, ed. Fredric Jameson and Masao Miyoshi (Durham, N.C.: Duke University Press, 1998), 247–70.

30 In the fall of 1998, the Modern Language Association of America (MLA) published *Profession 1998*, a booklet "covering a range of topics of professional concern." It is, how-

ever, hopelessly out of touch with the changing conditions of the profession and the global culture around it. Its last essay, "Bob's Job: Campus Crises and 'Adjunct' Education," by former president Sandra M. Gilbert, personalizes the historical transformation of today's American culture into a memory of her friend Bob J. Griffin. Profoundly saddening, Bob's death, however, demands a far more clear-headed analysis of the political economy of the United States in the 1990s than the episode of a man with a Ph.D. in English from UC Berkeley who died in his mid-sixties as a part-time composition teacher earning $15,000 without health insurance. The MLA seems committed to evading the real historical situation, thereby perhaps duplicating similar cases in the future as it keeps its operation. As another erstwhile friend of Bob's, I feel the urgency of the need to face honestly the academic-professional situation today.

31 Placement statistics are, of course, indispensable. The question is, what to do with these figures? A recent MLA report finds that of the 7,598 Ph.D.s in English and foreign languages earned between 1990 and 1995, 4,188—55 percent—failed to find a tenure-track job in the year the degree was awarded. The report then compares the job crisis to earlier crises and to those in other disciplines. The report readily recognizes the "pedagogical and professional—indeed, a cultural—crises of great magnitude." It then points out that the current graduate program is mainly "aimed at the major research institution rather than a future in the community colleges, junior colleges, and small sectarian schools that now provide our profession with so large a proportion of its work." Its subsequent recommendations—to cut the size of the graduate program, for instance—should be taken seriously. Yet the report hardly considers the changing nature of the humanities program, or rather of the university itself, which is at the root of this change in higher education. Even if all the funding crises were solved today, the crisis in the intellectual content of learning and teaching in higher education in the United States, or perhaps any other place, would not change. Suppose all the Ph.D.s in the humanities were able to secure tenure-track positions this year. Would this solve the crisis of the content of the humanities teaching? See *Final Report: MLA Committee on Professional Employment* (New York: MLA, 1997). Reproduced in *PMLA* 113(5) (October 1998): 1154–77.

32 "Harvard, with a $12.8 billion endowment, is in the middle of raising $2.1 billion more." An economist asks if the university really needs $15 billion. An endowment, like any other property accumulation, turns into a "habit," whether or not it is needed, and to whatever end. See Karen W. Arenson, "Modest Proposal," *New York Times*, 2 August 1998.

In "Ballooning Endowments Prompt Rich Universities to Loosen Their Belts," *New York Times*, 21 October 1998, Arenson argues that Harvard, Texas, Yale University, and other universities are now spending their soaring endowments in building, maintenance, and financial aid. In a closer look, however, the expenditures seem to be more like an investment for the future: the faculty positions created at these now richer universities are all in biomedical engineering.

33 Phil Pochoda, "Universities Press On," *Nation*, 29 December 1997, 11–16. See also Mark Crispin Miller, "The Crushing Power of Big Publishing," *Nation*, 17 March 1997, 11–18: "Meanwhile, the academic houses are now pressed by cost-conscious university administrators to make it on their own, without institutional subsidies.

Thus those houses too are giving in to market pressure, dumping recondite monographs in favor of trendier academic fare or, better yet, whatever sells at Borders—which, presumably, means few footnotes. Those publishers are so hard pressed there's talk in the academy of changing tenure rules, because it's next to impossible to get an arcane study published—a dark development indeed" (17–18).

34 Judith Shulevitz, "Keepers of the Tenure Track," University Presses supplement, *New York Times*, 29 October 1995. The decline of monograph publication is widely noted. Some efforts are being made to reverse this trend by substituting electronic publication, as by the American Historical Association and some university presses. See Robert Darnton, "The New Age of the Book," *New York Review of Books*, 18 March 1999; and Dinitia Smith, "Hoping the Web Will Rescue Young Professors," *New York Times*, 12 June 1999.

35 George Dennis O'Brien, *All the Essential Half-Truths about Higher Education* (Chicago: University of Chicago Press, 1997), quoted in James Shapiro, "Beyond the Culture Wars," *New York Times Book Reviews*, 4 January 1998. See also William H. Honan, "The Ivory Tower under Siege: Everyone Else Is Downsized; Why Not the Academy?" Education Life supplement, *New York Times* (spring 1998): 33, 44, 46; and Randy Martin, ed., *Chalk Lines: The Politics of Work in the Managed University* (Durham, N.C.: Duke University Press, 1998).

36 "In the Ph.D.-granting [English] departments, graduate student instructors taught 63% of the first-year writing sections, part-timers 19%, and full-time non-tenure-track faculty members 14%, on average." The corresponding figures in foreign-language departments are 68, 7, and 15 percent. See MLA, *Final Report*, 8. A large number of Ph.D.s from literature departments remain jobless, and for them even such temporary lecturerships are highly desirable. See also Seth Mydans, "Part-Time College Teaching Rises, as Do Worries," *New York Times*, 4 January 1995; and Joseph Berger, "After Her Ph.D., a Scavenger's Life: A Temp Professor among Thousands," *New York Times*, 8 March 1998.

37 Such commercial ventures, however, have not proven an immediate success. As of the fall of 1998, most universities—Penn State, SUNY, the University of Illinois, and UC Berkeley—have attracted fewer than five thousand students. To remedy the difficulties, NYU is planning to use a for-profit subsidiary to build its Internet capacity. In "N.Y.U. Sees Profits in Virtual Classes," *New York Times*, 7 October 1998, Karen W. Arenson writes, "Non-profit universities like N.Y.U. have increasingly turned to profit-making ventures to capitalize on their professors' research." See also the same reporter's article, "More Colleges Plunging into Uncharted Waters of On-Line Courses," *New York Times*, 2 November 1998.

38 Lawrence Solely, "Higher Education . . . or Higher Profits? For-Profit Universities Sell Free Enterprise Education," *In These Times* 22(21) (20 September 1998): 14–17. "Because of questions raised by accreditors, the university increased the size of its full-time faculty—it now has 45 full-times on board" (16). The Apollo Group, Phoenix's parent corporation, has increased its revenues more than three times in five years, from $124,720,000 in FY 1994 to $391,082,000 in FY 1998. See also Apollo's website, www.apollogrp.com.

39 See "California's 'Virtual University' Aims to Be a Digital Center for Higher Educa-

tion," *Notice: A Publication of the Academic Senate, University of California* 22(3) (December 1997): 1, 3; and "Notes from the Chair: Course Articulation," *Notice: A Publication of the Academic Senate, University of California* 22(7) (May 1998): 5. See also Kenneth R. Weiss, "A Wary Academia on Edge of Cyberspace" and "State Won't Oversee Virtual University," *Los Angeles Times*, 31 March 1998 and 30 July 1998, respectively. As for faculty opposition to the administrative downsizing via digitalization, see David Noble, *The Religion of Technology: The Divinity of Man and the Spirit of Invention* (New York: Penguin, 1999).

40 Victoria Griffith, "High Pay in Ivory Towers: Star Professors Are Subject of Concern," *Financial Times*, 6 June 1998.

41 James Flanigan, "Southland's Tech Prowess Is in Partnerships," *Los Angeles Times*, 8 March 1998.

42 Kit Lively, "What They Earned in 1996–97: A Survey of Private Colleges' Pay and Benefits: The Presidents of Rockefeller, Vanderbilt, and U. of Pennsylvania Top $500,000," *Chronicle of Higher Education*, 23 October 1998. See also Karen W. Arenson, "For University Presidents, Higher Compensation Made It a 'Gilded' Year," *New York Times*, 18 October 1998.

43 Thorstein Veblen, *The Higher Learning in America: A Memorandum on the Conduct of Universities by Business Men, American Century Edition* (New York: Hill and Wang, 1969). See also Clyde W. Barrow, *Universities and the Capitalist State: Corporate Liberalism and the Reconstruction of American Higher Education, 1894–1928* (Madison: University of Wisconsin Press, 1990).

44 Charles L. Schwartz, professor emeritus of physics at UC Berkeley, singlehandedly studied the conduct of the UC regents over many years, but after a score of detailed reports, he recently gave up his efforts, partly, at least, as a result of lack of support and encouragement.

45 Harold T. Shapiro, "University Presidents—Then and Now," paper presented at the Princeton Conference on Higher Education, March 1996, the 250th Anniversary of Princeton University, included in *Universities and Their Leadership*, ed. William G. Bowen and Harold T. Shapiro (Princeton, N.J.: Princeton University Press, 1998).

46 San Diego Biocommerce Association On-Line, available at www.biocom.org/index. html.

47 Gerhard Casper, "The Advantage of the Research-Intensive University: The University of the Twenty-first Century," presented on 3 May 1998, Peking University, available at www.stanford.edu/dept/pres-provost/president/speeches/980503peking. html. Testifying before the Subcommittee on Technology, the House Committee on Science, during a session entitled "Defining Successful Partnerships and Collaborations in Scientific Research" (11 March 1998), MIT President Charles M. Vest stated, "Universities should work synergistically with industry; they must not be industry" (available at www.house.gov/science/vest_03–11.htm).

48 At least in the context of university research. The research expenditures by federal government sources steadily increased from $8,119,977,073 in FY 1991 to $12,317,829,551 in FY 1996, and $13,040,581,674 in FY 1997. See The Association of University Technology Managers, Inc., *AUTM Licensing Survey, Fiscal Year 1996: A Survey Summary of Technology Licensing (and Related) Performance for U.S. and*

Canadian Academic and Nonprofit Institutions and Patent Management Firms (Norwalk, Conn.: AUTM, 1997), and its FY 1997 version (1998).

49 See the Council on Governmental Relations (COGR) brochure, *The Bayh-Dole Act: A Guide to the Law and Implementing Regulations*, 30 November 1993, available at www.tmc.tulane.edu/techdev/Bayh.html.

50 See, however, note 4 above.

51 AUTM Licensing Survey, FY 1997. See also Richard C. Atkinson, "The Future of the University of California," September 1998, available at www.ucop.edu. The three universities are followed by the University of Washington; the University of Michigan; Stanford; the University of Wisconsin, Madison; SUNY; Texas A&M; Harvard; and Penn in the total sponsored research expenditures in FY 1997.

52 Atkinson, "Future of the University of California."

53 The distribution of license revenues varies from university to university. The University of Michigan gives to the inventor(s): 50 percent up to $200,000, 33 percent above $200,000 (University of Michigan Technology Management Office, "Working with Faculty and Staff" [unpublished document]). The University of California rate is more flexible (UC Office of Technology Transfer, "UC Equity Policy," 16 February 1996, available at www.ucop.edu/ott/equi-pol.html).

54 Atkinson, "Future of the University of California."

55 Seth Shulman, *Owning the Future* (Boston: Houghton Mifflin, 1999), 51. The inside quotation is from an article by Steven Rosenberg in the *New England Journal of Medicine*.

56 Lawrence C. Soley, *Leasing the Ivory Tower: The Corporate Takeover of Academia* (Boston: South End Press, 1995), 41–42. I became aware of the book late in my writing of this essay. Like Soley's virtual university article, the book has good episodic information concerning aspects of the corporatization of the university. Kristi Coale's article, "The $50 Million Question," *Salon Magazine*, 15 October 1998, updates the Scripps deal, reporting that the agreement was detected by the NIH and that Scripps was forced to scale it back to $20 million annually for five years.

57 *Notice: A Publication of the Academic Senate, University of California* 22(7) (May 1998): 1, 3, 4.

58 "Some universities state that the 'academic year salary' covers 80% of the faculty member's time during the nine months of the academic year. Faculty are free to consult 'up to 20% of the time' (usually understood to be one day per week) during the academic year. Payment for the 'summer months' is often under a separate arrangement." See Council on Governmental Relations, "University Technology Transfer: Questions and Answers," 30 November 1993, available at www.cogr.edu/qu.htm.

59 The preceding two paragraphs are based on the following reports: Coale, "The $50 Million Question"; Peter Rosset and Monica Moore, "Research Alliance Debated: Deal Benefits Business, Ignores UC's Mission," *San Francisco Chronicle*, 23 October 1998; Joseph Cerny, "UC Research Alliance," letter to the editor, *San Francisco Chronicle*, 7 November 1998; James Carter, "Concerns over Corporation Alliance with UC College of Natural Resources, *Berkeley Voice*, 19 November 1998; Michelle Locke, "Berkeley Celebrates $25 Million Novartis Grant, but Some Have Questions,"

Associated Press, 23 November 1998, available at www.sfgate.com; "Bay Area Date-
lines," *San Francisco Examiner*, 24 November 1998; Charles Burress, "UC Finalizes
Pioneering Research Deal with Biotech Firm: Pie Tossers Leave Taste of Protest," *San
Francisco Chronicle*, 24 November 1998; Arielle Levine and Susan West, Students for
Responsible Research, Department of Environmental Science, Policy and Manage-
ment, College of Natural Resources, UC Berkeley, letters to the editor, *San Francisco
Chronicle*, 26 November 1998.

60 ARCH Development Corporation, the University of Chicago, "About ARCH," available
at www-arch.uchicago.edu. See also Richard Melcher, "An Old University Hits the
High-Tech Road," *Business Week*, 24–31 August 1998, 94–96.

61 See the article in the University of Pittsburgh faculty and staff newspaper, "Pitt, CMU
Form New Non-profit Corporation, Innovation Works, Inc.," *University Times* 31(7)
(25 November 1998), available at www.pitt.edu/utimes/issues/112598/06.html.

62 UC Office of Technology Transfer, "UC Equity Policy."

63 Kenneth R. Weiss and Paul Jacobs, "Caltech Joins Rush to Foster Biotech Spinoff
Companies," *Los Angeles Times*, 16 September 1998.

64 See Pierre Bourdieu, *The Inheritors: French Students and Their Relations to Culture*,
trans. Richard Nice (Chicago: University of Chicago Press, 1977); *Homo Academicus*,
trans. Peter Collier (Stanford, Calif.: Stanford University Press, 1988); and, with Jean-
Claude Passeron, *Reproduction in Education, Society, and Culture*, trans. Richard
Nice (Newbury Park, Calif.: Sage, 1990).

65 Alex Gove, "Ivory Towers for Sale," *Red Herring*, August 1995, available at www.her-
ring.com/mag/issue22/tech1.html.

66 Sheila Slaughter and Larry L. Leslie, *Academic Capitalism: Politics, Policies, and the
Entrepreneurial University* (Baltimore, Md.: Johns Hopkins University Press, 1997),
is a systematic study on the corporatization of the university in Australia, the United
Kingdom, Canada, and the United States. The book is not concerned with intellectually substantial issues, such as the humanities, the social sciences, academic freedom and political responsibility, although they surface from time to time despite the
book's scheme. See also Jan Currie and Lesley Vidovich, "The Ascent toward Corporate Managerialism in American and Australian Universities," in Martin, ed., *Chalk
Lines*, 112–44. Technology transfer is ordinarily from a university to a corporation.
President John R. Silber of Boston University reverses this direction by investing in a
corporation, Seragen, for its pharmaceutical research. The university as a capital investor, however, may not be as successful as the other way around: Boston University
reportedly invested $84 million over thirteen years, and its value now stands at $8.4
million. See David Barboza, "Loving a Stock, Not Wisely but Too Well," *New York
Times*, 20 September 1998.

67 Karen Young Kreeger, "Studies Call Attention to Ethics of Industry Support," *Scientist* 11(7) (31 March 1997): 1, 4–5; available at www.the-scientist.library.upenn.edu/;
Sheldon Krimsky, *Biotechnics and Society: The Rise of Industrial Genetics* (New
York: Praeger, 1991); and Roger J. Porter and Thomas E. Malone, eds., *Biomedical Research: Collaboration and Conflict of Interest* (Baltimore, Md.: Johns Hopkins University Press, 1992).

68 Cited by Kreeger, "Studies Call Attention." See Kenneth J. Rothman, "Conflict of In-

terest: The New McCarthyism in Science," *JAMA—The Journal of the American Medical Association* 269(21) (2 June 1993): 2782–84.

69   In addition to those listed in note 56, see David Blumenthal et al., "Participation of Life-Science Faculty in Research Relationships with Industry," *New England Journal of Medicine* 335 (1996): 1734–39; Edgar Haber, "Industry and the University," *Nature Biotechnology* 14 (1996): 441–42; Sheldon Krimsky, L. S. Rothenberg, P. Scott, and G. Kyle, "Financial Interests of Authors in Scientific Journals: A Pilot Study of 14 Publications," *Science and Engineering Ethics* 2 (1996): 396–410; Rothman, "Conflict of Interest"; and Daniel Zalewski, "Ties That Bind: Do Corporate Dollars Strangle Scientific Research?" *Lingua Franca* 7(6) (June/July 1997): 51–59.

70   Steve Scott, "Silicon Valley's Political Myopia," *Los Angeles Times*, 4 July 1999.

71   Sheila Slaughter and Philip G. Althach, eds., *The Higher Learning and High Technology: Dynamics of Higher Education Policy Formation (Frontiers in Education)* (Albany: State University of New York Press, 1990); Howard Dickman, ed., *The Imperiled Academy* (New Brunswick, N.J.: Transaction Publishers, 1993); Arthur Levine, ed., *Higher Learning in America, 1980–2000* (Baltimore, Md.: Johns Hopkins University Press, 1993); Ronald G. Ehrenberg, ed., *The American University: National Treasure or Endangered Species?* (Ithaca, N.Y.: Cornell University Press, 1997); Hugh Davis Graham and Nancy Diamond, *The Rise of American Research Universities: Elites and Challengers in the Postwar Era* (Baltimore, Md.: Johns Hopkins University Press, 1997); Donald Kennedy, *Academic Duty* (Cambridge: Harvard University Press, 1997); William G. Tierney, ed., *The Responsive University: Restructuring for High Performance* (Baltimore, Md.: Johns Hopkins University Press, 1997); Roger G. Noll, ed., *Challenges to Research Universities* (Washington, D.C.: Brookings Institution Press, 1998). Although Hanna H. Gray, the former president of the University of Chicago, talks about the crisis in the humanities, her interest is mainly in restoring traditional humanistic scholarship ("Prospects for the Humanities," Ehrenberg, *American University*, 115–27). Donald Kennedy, the former president of Stanford, has a great deal to say about university management, especially technology transfer, but hardly anything to say about the humanities. By no means exhaustive, the list still convincingly indicates the general indifference to the problems of the humanities in the corporatized university.

72   Slaughter and Leslie, *Academic Capitalism*, 211.

73   W. B. Carnochan, *The Battleground of the Curriculum: Liberal Education and American Experience* (Stanford, Calif.: Stanford University Press, 1993); David Damrosch, *We Scholars: Changing the Culture of the University* (Cambridge: Harvard University Press, 1995); William V. Spanos, *The End of Education: Toward Posthumanism* (Minneapolis: University of Minnesota Press, 1993); John Beverley, *Against Literature* (Minneapolis: University of Minnesota Press, 1993); Michael Bérubé and Cary Nelson, *Higher Education under Fire: Politics, Economics, and the Crisis of the Humanities* (London: Routledge, 1995); and Neil Postman, *The End of Education: Redefining the Value of School* (New York: Vintage, 1998).

74   Slaughter and Leslie, *Academic Capitalism*, 243.

75   Claude Lévi-Strauss, *Structural Anthropology*, vol. 2, trans. Monique Layton (New York: Basic Books, 1976), 358.

76 Ibid., 354.

77 See Steven Weinberg, "The Revolution That Didn't Happen," *New York Review of Books*, 8 October 1998, 48–52.

78 Fons Elders, ed., *Reflexive Water: The Basic Concerns of Mankind* (London: Souvenir Press, 1974), 133–97. This important debate deserves to be read and discussed extensively. Edward Said's well-known essay, "Traveling Theory," was the earliest I know to discuss it (in *The World, the Text, and the Critic* [Cambridge: Harvard University Press, 1983], 244–47), followed much later by Christopher Norris's *Uncritical Theory: Postmodernism, Intellectuals, and the Gulf War* (Amherst: University of Massachusetts Press, 1992), esp. "Chomsky versus Foucault," "The Political Economy of Truth," and "Reversing the Drift: Reality Regained," 100–125. Norris's related works, such as *What's Wrong with Postmodernism: Critical Theory and the Ends of Philosophy* (Baltimore, Md.: Johns Hopkins University Press, 1990); *Deconstruction: Theory and Practice*, rev. ed. (London: Routledge, 1991); *The Truth about Postmodernism* (Oxford: Blackwell, 1993); and *Reclaiming Truth: Contribution to a Critique of Cultural Relativism* (Durham, N.C.: Duke University Press, 1996), examine Richard Rorty, Stanley Fish, Jean Baudrillard, and other pragmatic postmodernists, as well as Foucault.

79 Terry Eagleton, "Defending the Free World," in *The Eagleton Reader*, ed. Stephen Regan (Oxford: Blackwell, 1998), 285–93, is suggestive on this point.

80 Slavoj Žižek, "Multiculturalism, or, the Cultural Logic of Multinational Capitalism," *New Left Review* 225 (September/October, 1997): 44. The title is abbreviated on the cover of the issue as "Multiculturalism–A New Racism?"

81 Žižek's *New Left Review* essay is translated into Japanese by Wada Tadashi in *Hihyo kukan*, which has several additional pages that have no counterpart in the English version. In this portion, Žižek makes a very similar point about the victimological use of identity politics. See *Hihyo kukan* 2(18) (1998): 79.

82 Tzvetan Todorov, *On Human Diversity: Nationalism, Racism, and Exoticism in French Thought*, trans. Catherine Porter (Cambridge: Harvard University Press, 1993), 390; emphasis in original.

83 On 24 September 1998, the House approved a measure aimed at bringing nearly 150,000 skilled foreign workers into the United States. The high-tech industry claims that there is an acute shortage of qualified workers, but it is contested by the Institute of Electrical and Electronic Engineers–USA. The applications have no ethnic, national, or regional restrictions. See Jube Shiver Jr., "House Lifts Visa Cap for High-Tech Workers," *Los Angeles Times*, 25 September 1998.

84 See Charlotte Allen, "As Bad as It Gets: Three Dark Tales from the Annals of Academic Receivership," *Lingua Franca* 8(2) (March 1998): 52–59. See also Janny Scott, "Star Professors, as a Team, Fail Chemistry: Once a Model, English Department at Duke Dissolves in Anger," *New York Times*, 21 November 1998.

85 Pierre Bourdieu, "The Negative Intellectual," in *Acts of Resistance: Against the Tyranny of the Market*, trans. Richard Nice (New York: New Press, 1998), 91–93.

86 "Ivory tower" is a translation of *tour d'ivoire*, which was first used in 1837 by Charles-Augustin Sainte-Beuve (according to *A Supplement to the Oxford English Dictionary*, vol. 3), and in 1869 (according to Webster's *Third New International Dictionary*). The

English phrase first appeared (according to the *OED* Supplement) in 1911, in Henri Bergson's *Laughter: An Essay on the Meaning of the Comic,* trans. Cloudesley Brereton and Fred Rothwell (New York: Macmillan, 1911), iii, 135. No explanation is given for the choice of ivory for indicating seclusion from the world or shelter from harsh realities. The fact that no one—as far as I know—has ever detected in the phrase the connection between academia and ivory, the university and colonialism, might reaffirm the devastatingly accurate denunciation implanted in the phrase.

87   Bill Readings, *The University in Ruins* (Cambridge, Mass.: Harvard University Press, 1996).

Andō Shōeki—
"The Forgotten Thinker" in Japanese History
Tetsuo Najita

The radical and eccentric early eighteenth-century thinker, Andō Shōeki, challenges us, through the work of the late Canadian historian and diplomat, E. H. Norman, to reflect on our field of Asian studies, and of Japanese history within this area of study. We are reminded that national and chronological boundaries are not secure, for as Norman wrote as a scholar about Shōeki to call the attention of postwar Japan to its democratic possibilities, he was also to come under the scrutiny of McCarthy in the 1950s for being an enemy of democracy. Norman and Shōeki were subsequently put aside by the "field" in the 1960s that turned its attention to "modernization" as it was reinforced by "high-growth" economics in Japan. This history suggests to me that Andō Shōeki is not merely ignored as a "premodern" eighteenth-century thinker, devoid of influence on the fringe of the Tokugawa polity, and hence irrelevant to Japan's modern history; Shōeki, through Norman, is also part of a more recent history of Asian studies in the United States and Canada. He therefore relates deeply to the problem of criticism and resistance within modernity. Shōeki clearly has been appreciated in this way among intellectuals and scholars in twentieth-century Japan. In the essay that follows, I have tried to situate Shōeki both to the discourse on knowledge within "premodern" Japan and to broad twentieth-century concerns about resistance as they relate to language and ecology. I find Shōeki to be "transnational" and "trans-areal" in significance.

The title of my essay, "The Forgotten Thinker," is drawn from the Japanese translation of E. H. Norman's work on Andō Shōeki (1703–1762). Published as *The Anatomy of Japanese Feudalism* in 1949, the work was translated by Iwanami Press in 1950 as *The Forgotten Thinker—Wasurareta shisōka*, and remains a minor classic in postwar Japanese intellectual history.[1]

The above two titles describe related yet distinct historiographical perspectives. The English version emphasizes the analysis of a historical subject, Norman's explication through Andō Shōeki of the "anatomy" of the old Tokugawa regime as an exploitative political order. The Japanese translation captures another important aspect, which is the value of remembering Shōeki because of the relevance of his ideas for contemporary Japan. This emphasis in translation is also clearly evident in Norman's original narrative. As one of the Canadian representatives to the Allied Occupation of postwar Japan, Norman reflected on the future of democracy in Japan and believed that alongside the liberal and individualistic model, there should also be a parallel one that spoke to equality and egalitarian values, and that textual resources of democracy in this latter sense might be found in Japan's history itself.

Through Norman, Shōeki thus becomes part of Japan's recent intellectual and political history and retains a relevancy because he helps us to recall E. H. Norman in the recent history of Asian studies. We are reminded of the general historiographical point that upon closer reflection "forgotten thinkers" from a distant and obscure Asian history, such as Andō Shōeki in the northeastern regional town of Hachinohe in early eighteenth-century Tokugawa Japan, turn out not to be so far away after all. Through the mediating constructions of historians such as Norman, they come to be closely entwined with the discourses in the present.

To seek fresh perspectives, historians sometimes turn their sights to thinkers who were seemingly distinctive or unique and hence isolated in their own times. Resisting the view that these thinkers were "unrepresentative" of their age and thus irrelevant to the central concerns of historical inquiry, such historians probe the meaning of idiosyncratic thinking and thereby simultaneously clarify the actual nature of authority in that past and, more pertinent to our essay here, raise with a sense of urgency the issue of creative possibilities in the present. In this latter respect, the project of tracing causal influences once upon a time seems less pressing than the issue of creative thinking under trying contemporary circumstance, this being for Norman the quest among citizens in postwar Japan for a democratic future.

I had the honor several years ago to deliver a lecture in Hachinohe, once the castletown where Andō Shōeki lived, as part of a symposium celebrating Shōeki's 290th birthday anniversary. This provided me the valuable opportunity to reflect on Shōeki's ideas and on Norman's effort to call attention to them. I was very much struck by the continuing relativity of the historian who ventures into such an inquiry into the past out of deep concerns with vital issues in the ongoing present. I was reminded too by the philosophical idea expressed by Ernst Cassirer, Paul Ricoeur, Michel de Certcau and others, that historical texts ought not be kept closed on the presumption of their current irrelevance or because their meanings had been fully explicated, for these texts contain ideas that remain in an implicit state to be explored by students of history in another time and place. Such a perspective helped me to focus on the "significance" of the problem expressed by Andō Shōeki and the "implicit" meanings in his text rather than assessing the influence or the immediate political consequences of his ideas in his time. In short, the way in which to remember Andō Shōeki, it seemed to me, was not to reduce him to an inconsequential regional aberration, but to endeavor to keep him open as a text for latent meanings that still resonated with concerns in our modern history.[2]

This latter point is important for those of us who teach Japanese intellectual history in the West, and, in my case, the United States. As a text, Andō Shōeki was initially opened for us by E. H. Norman and presented in a manner directly pertinent to modern Japan. Our field nonetheless chose by and large to ignore and exclude Shōeki in our teaching of Japanese history. It was not so much that we forgot Andō Shōeki; he was never really remembered because Norman himself became something of a "forgotten" thinker, quite unlike his position in the Japanese intellectual world where he is remembered with great respect. I am referring here to the late 1950s and 1960s when Japanese studies made great advances as a profession to a body of American scholars that, unfortunately, was unresponsive to Norman's remembrance of Andō Shōeki. The fate of Andō Shōeki in American historiography on Japan is tied to the fate of E. H. Norman.

In this regard, the observations of Hagihara Nobutoshi and Maruyama Masao, in their published dialogue in *Shisō*'s special commemorative issue on Norman in spring 1977, are worth recalling. Shortly after Norman's death in 1957, Hagihara, on his pilgrimage to Baba Tatsui's gravesite in Philadelphia (Baba being a leading intellectual of the popular rights movement in the 1880s), reviewed the presses thoroughly for scholarly commentary on Norman and recalled:

> The first things I did after arriving in Philadelphia was to visit the gravesite of Baba Tatsui and then, with regard to the death of Norman, to review whenever I had a free moment what sorts of memorials were being written about him by scholars in the United States. I looked in the various places but found nothing at all.[3]

Maruyama reminisced on his year at Harvard, and responded with the following observation:

> While I was at Harvard around 1961, Norman's studies were viewed, how might one put it, as being already out of date; or that things were no longer at Norman's level. This sort of attitude prevailed among the East Asian researchers at all of the east-coast universities.[4]

I was a graduate student at Harvard at just about this time and I can personally attest to the accuracy of Maruyama's observation. There was virtual unanimity in the abhorrence of McCarthyism; and while the tragic death of Norman was lamented, his scholarship was not a subject of central importance. Andō Shōeki thus remained "underground," never really remembered.

Some ten years after Norman's death, Harry Harootunian would review the commentaries on Norman in the following terms: "Yet throughout this literature, much of which today seems like an ancient forgotten past, one will search in vain for an expression of Mr. Norman's achievements in the field of historical scholarship."[5] In the context of the protest over the Vietnam War, interest in Norman was revived, beginning with John Dower's editing of *The Selected Writings of E. H. Norman*.[6] Dower's focus fell on Norman's book, *Japan's Emergence as a Modern State*, and the disregard of this work for ideological reasons, by the Japan studies profession due to Norman's argument about the revolutionary nature of the modern Japanese state, and of the radical and tragic consequences of this transformation. Andō Shōeki remained a side issue in Dower's representation of this thesis. What went undiscussed, therefore, was Norman's attraction to Andō Shōeki within the context of Japan's postwar experience, a matter of central importance to Japanese intellectuals, as pointed out by the various essayists in the aforementioned volume of *Shisō*. Writing in the late 1940s, Norman presented the case of Shōeki to state that democracy and social democracy in Japan could not be realized by authoritative fiat from above and that sympathetic identifications with history were crucial. It was this "modernist" concern that informed Norman's attraction to Shōeki and to Tokugawa thought more generally.

As I reflected on Andō Shōeki in Hachinohe, I could not help but recall E. H. Norman as a historian with a vision of a democratic future for Japan based on Shōeki's values of equality and critical independence. As a discussant of Andō Shōeki, I also reflected on E. H. Norman and his courage to further that vision of democracy for Japan even by focusing his historical lenses on "lesser names," to borrow from Masao Maruyama's eulogy for Norman.[7]

In trying to evaluate Andō Shōeki as a text, we might remind ourselves of the truism that historical memory is often fickle and almost always selective. Shōeki is hardly unusual in falling from the grace of social memory. Aristotle, after all, was forgotten for almost a thousand years before the Renaissance rediscovered him. And although his central place has been secure since then, those scholars, such as Avecinna and Averröes, who kept Aristotle's text alive in the Islamic world, were in turn forgotten in Western historiography.

There are other cases closer to our time. Provocative thinkers who challenged the Cartesian self-object dualism in the mainflow of the Enlightenment were marginalized and all but "forgotten." An example is Giambattista Vico, who denied the knowing self (Descartes' cogito) as a stable philosophical premise, and formulated instead a philosophy based on changing subjectivity and hence potentiality. In the words of Benedetto Croce, Vico "spoke to a century yet to come; and the place in which he cried was a wilderness that gave no answer," and in those of Isaiah Berlin, "a man of original genius," Vico was "misunderstood and largely neglected in his lifetime and . . . all but totally forgotten after his death." As both the modern historians Croce and Berlin make clear Vico was "rediscovered" only in the latter half of the nineteenth century (about the same time as Shōeki, I might add).[8]

Perhaps more pertinent with reference to Shōeki is the case of Baruch Spinoza. Spinoza doubted the validity of the Cartesian philosophical orthodoxy of the day. As outlined succinctly in the opening sections of his *Ethics*, Spinoza built his entire philosophy on monistic materialism. Based on the premise that nature was at once absolute and unlimited, and prior to all political and social forms, Spinoza objected to theological and monarchical absolutism and idealized the natural, communitarian democracy that existed prior to kings and sagely prophets. Spinoza's concept of natural power and motion is akin to Shōeki's "each thing doing" (*hitori suru* and *chokkō*), and I shall return briefly to this theme later; but suffice it to say here that Spinoza was largely "forgotten" for his heterodox view vis-à-vis the mainstream of Enlightenment thought, as Shōeki was in relation to the mainstream Confucian moral philosophy of his day.

Thus I find the metaphorical characterization of Spinoza as "the Savage Anomaly" appropriate in assessing Andō Shōeki. The language is Antonio Negri's, a critic of modern capitalism who wrote from prison these lines that resonate with Shōeki's fate:

> Clearly, Spinozian philosophy is an anomaly in its century and is savage to the eyes of the dominant culture. This is a tragedy of every philosophy, of every savage testimony of truth that is posed against time—against the present time and against the present reality. But the tragedy can open itself powerfully into the future.[9]

Forgotten thinkers are often said to be miserable "losers," even to be lunatics or madmen. In his book *The World Turned Upside Down* the historian Christopher Hill writes of such "losers" on the republican "lunatic fringe" of the English Revolution in the mid-seventeenth century. Such men should not be viewed as lunatics for, in his words, "lunacy, like beauty, may be in the eye of the beholder" and "madness itself may be a form of protest against social norms and the 'lunatic' may in some sense be saner than the society that rejects him." The importance of ideas to historians, Hill emphasizes, as did Norman in his work on Shōeki and the "anatomy" of his political environment, is not their triumphant "influence" but the fact that "they reveal the societies which give rise to them."[10]

Relying on the insights of Negri and Hill, we could characterize Andō Shōeki as a "savage anomaly" and as a "madman." This resonates in my mind with Kanō Kōkichi's reference to Shōeki as a "madman"—*kyōjin*—in announcing the rediscovery in 1908 of this "great thinker."[11]

In turning my attention more specifically at this point to interpreting Andō Shōeki's ideas, I must confess the obvious, which is that I have nothing new to contribute to the basic knowledge of Andō Shōeki, certainly nothing that goes beyond what has been done by Professor Yasunaga Toshinobu or Watanabe Taiko or by the various authors in their insightful essays in the volume on Andō Shōeki (1974). The bibliography in this volume lists some three hundred essays on Shōeki by the most distinguished of scholars. I will not even pretend to approximate the intimate knowledge about Shōeki's historical materials that are found in these essays. I make my comments only as a participant in the international effort to keep Shōeki's text open, to explore meanings in as broad a manner as possible, and thereby suggest something of the comparative and universal in the creative endeavor of a regional thinker. I follow on Norman's path in this regard.[12]

The problem that recurs in interpreting Andō Shōeki is the question of his "originality" or "uniqueness." The question itself is actually deceptive, for if we respond by emphasizing Shōeki's complete uniqueness we isolate him from his intellectual universe and doubt his relevance by picturing him as a solitary eccentric beyond the comprehension of his age. Eccentrics—*kijin*—were quite plentiful in eighteenth-century Japan. Implicit in this characterization of Shōeki's uniqueness is something that I would term modern Japan's "cosmopolitan urge." By this I mean the felt need among Japanese intellectuals in the industrial twentieth century to present something truly unique from within their history to the outside world and especially to the "leading" Western nations. Uchimura Kanzō, Nitobe Inazō, Okakura Tenshin—all important figures of the early twentieth century—were moved by this "cosmopolitan urge." Shōeki thus came to be featured as an original "revolutionary" thinker, or an "anarchist" within indigenous Japanese history. It is even suggested that he was the first to discover modern dialectical theory.

On the other hand, there is the view of Japanese intellectual heroes being, on closer observation, not so original after all. Everything that may be found in the texts can be shown to have been articulated before, and through historical retrogression, this can be taken back to some ancient moment. In Shōeki's case, his ideas are traceable to thinkers dating back to Lao Tzu, and to a dimly lit ancient history in China, thus proving lack of originality. This perspective is not very helpful either for, as Yasunaga Toshinobu has argued convincingly, Shōeki's originality is less in the various parts as in the total construction and the singularity of his critical perspective.[13]

Shōeki's thought places him within an eighteenth-century intellectual discourse. I am inclined to agree with the view expressed by some scholars that Shōeki was deeply engaged in the central philosophical issues of his day, such as those regarding the turn to ancient studies, or medical practice. Shōeki studied to be a physician in Kyoto in the latter part of the 1710s and early 1720s when the ideas of ancient studies propounded by Itō Jinsai and Ogyū Sorai were widely discussed and disputed. Shōeki was also brought up in Sotō Zen, secured the proper qualifications to be a practicing monk, and retained something of the radicalism of this tradition even after he severed his ties with it. These facts do not lessen Shōeki's creativity, but it does situate him within a language and epistemological field of thinking and conceptualization. He shared ideas with other thinkers, even though he took some of them to extreme limits.[14]

Christoper Hill made this important point when he discusses Gerard Winstanley and Thomas Hobbes. Winstanley stood for a communitarian order without a king; Hobbes, for a political order in which a monarch was absolutely essential. What to Winstanley was the ideal of humans living together in terms of nature was to Hobbes pure anarchy. Despite these polar views, Hill observes that these two thinkers shared related ideas, such as their common denial of theological or aristocratic authority to anchor their positions, and their view of nature (close to that of Shōeki, and other eighteenth-century Tokugawa thinkers) as being devoid of religious or superstitious elements. Both saw nature as simply "motion," as in Winstanley's nature as "God is still in motion" and Hobbes's "life itself is but motion."[15]

That Hobbes is credited with being the creator of modern political theory and Winstanley is not, is roughly comparable to the status of Ogyū Sorai and Andō Shōeki as regards Japan. Hobbes and Sorai rested their political theories on a concept of monarchy, Hobbes arguing for the sovereign to regulate human passion; Sorai for the ordered way of the ancient kings (sen'ō no michi) to nourish the little virtue (shōtoku) located in every human being as a heavenly gift. Winstanley envisioned a new world in which humans would "live in community with the globe and . . . the spirit of the globe"; Shōeki for communitarian life in a world of interacting natural energy (*gosei/shizen no yo*). If we follow Hill's interpretive perspective that within a shared universe of ideas, Winstanley was creative as was Hobbes, we may speak similarly of Shōeki in relation to Sorai. Putting this another way, anti-monarchical, or horizontal positions that emphasize equality deserve their proper theoretical places in the history of political philosophy alongside the monarchical, or vertical ones that emphasize the necessity of sovereign agency and authoritative hierarchy.

I find it useful to think in terms of a conceptual "tension" or "disturbance" that might generate creative thinking of the sort we encounter in Shōeki. Of particular relevance in light of Shōeki's upbringing in Zen is the insight offered by Karaki Junzō some years ago when he characterized the turn from "medieval" to Tokugawa intellectual history as a move "from Zen to Ju [Confucianism]"—*Zen kara Ju*. Karaki focused on Fujiwara Seika, a figure not of direct concern to us here. And "Zen" may be taken more broadly to include Buddhist philosophical paradigms.

For five hundred years prior to the Tokugawa era Confucianism, or *Ju*, was housed within Buddhism. By contrast, over these same centuries in China, Buddhism was housed within *Ju*. The turn from Zen to *Ju* in the seventeenth century involved the simultaneous processes of disentangling Confucianism from medieval Japanese Zen, and the removal of Zen from medieval *Ju*. Sung Neo-Confucianism, or *Shushigaku*, was being introduced into Japan as the appropriate moral and political philosophy of the day. We may interpret these conceptual "movements" as being processes of epistemological reduction, or, as we would say today, of "deconstruction."

In the Tokugawa context, we may further see this as the displacement of the life/death (*sei/shi*) dialectic central to Buddhist philosophy with a theory of life/life (*sei/sei*) in which death was to be incorporated within a process of infinite, continuing, Life. Itō Jinsai (*Go-Mo jigi*); Kaibara Ekken (*Taigi roku*); Miura Baien (*Kagen*); Yamagata Bantō (*Yume no shiro*)—all expressed this elemental point of view in their writings. Shōeki shared this basic life-only epistemology with these other thinkers. Death was to be understood within the natural process of infinite life, not as the timeless negation of life. In short, if the Sung Neo-Confucian synthesis may be seen as a grand effort at incorporating Buddhist metaphysics into Confucian ethics, the opposite process was operative in seventeenth-century Japan, in which Buddhist metaphysics were being removed from secular ethics.

A related set of concerns spanned the intellectual spectrum. All of the figures just mentioned in the previous paragraph, including again Shōeki, were concerned with providing a theoretical underpinning for an action ethic—*jissen rinri*—that would lead to saving other people—*kyūmin, saimin*—in the actual world of existence. In other words, what kind of action might be undeniably "truthful"—*makoto* or *sei*. This problem of truthfulness permeated eighteenth century Tokugawa thought, and Shōeki too was deeply concerned with this issue as seen in his idea of truthful action—*katsushin, chokkō*.

Yet, the removal of Zen from *Ju* was a highly problematical process. For if "Zen," or Buddhist philosophy, were taken out of Confucianism it was not at all clear as to what was left in it as an incontrovertible premise for sure knowledge. Indeed, one could argue that without metaphysics there seemed precious little left, except some elementary ethics, which Tominaga Nakamoto, for example, thought of as simply "common sense"—*atarimae*. The "de-synthesization" of Confucianism called for a theoretical redefinition and reduction as to what "remained." Jinsai and Sorai turned to ancient history as the primary focus of study; Tominaga Nakamoto disputed the reliability of all history because of the polemical distortion of language among philosophical schools; Kaibara Ekken and Miura Baien rejected the dualism of spirit and matter, metaphysical and physical and referenced all knowledge to a universal nature.

These thinkers are all roughly contemporaries of Andō Shōeki, and he therefore must somehow be evaluated within the broad discursive pattern in which they were all engaged. Like Tominaga Nakamoto, who studied in Kyoto at about the same time, Shōeki denied the reliability of history and both rejected *Ju* and Buddhism as unreliable positions upon which to rest authoritative claims to knowledge. Unlike Tominaga who relied primarily on the analysis of the changing meaning of language, Shōeki based his thought on a monistic theory of nature. In this regard, Shōeki resembled Jinsai, Ekken, and Baien. Along with these latter thinkers Shōeki, as already noted, displaced the dialectic of life/ death, which Buddhism mediated as a religion in terms of theology and funeral practice, with a monistic life/life theory of infinite Nature. In these thinkers there is the affirmation of human passion as being intrinsic to nature, rejecting accordingly Buddhist ideas about passion and celibacy.[16]

Shōeki may similarly be discussed in relation to Ogyū Sorai, as Maruyama Masao did in his classic work on "nature" and "artifice"—*shizen to sakui*—in Tokugawa thought.[17] When Shōeki spoke out against "music," it was to reject the premise of the ancient classics that music gave order to human emotions, a view of music Sorai repeatedly offered as evidence of the creative genius of the ancient kings and which Shōeki renounced as an artificial device to control humans. Music was no different from language and ideographs upon which Sorai placed great emphasis. Shōeki took pains to show that the teaching of Chinese ideography was a means of controlling the young. In a well-known illustration of his, he depicted a Confucian teacher manipulating the hands of a youngster so as to produce in proper fashion the character for "learning"—*gaku*. And he sharply criticized those who were so enamored with language that they would steal the true, natural meaning of the way—*bun o konomu mono wa michi o nusumu koto o konomu nari*. In each of these points of criticism, he spoke generally of scholars of his day, but it could just as well have been pointed directly at Sorai, who emotionally identified himself with ancient "music," "language," and "learning," as the exclusive source of all sure knowledge.[18]

In the desynthesis of "Zen from *Ju*," the question of the ancient, genetic, basis of society surfaced as a pressing issue. Shōeki agreed with Lao Tzu's view that Confucianism and its moral categories were "artificial," and while Sorai affirmed that view of social artifice as necessary for human history, Shōeki saw artificial constructs as the source of human inequality. One of the key issues involved the idea of the "mean" and, along with it, the significance of truthfulness. To Shōeki, the idea of the mean as a timeless and abstract moral norm was a deception. In this regard he agreed with Sorai for whom the "mean" was simply a relative human "choice"—*yue ni erabu to iu*, as Sorai stated succinctly in his opening section of his *Bendō*, the Discourse on the Way. Shōeki, however, affirmed Lao Tzu's idea of a non-discriminatory natural community. For Shōeki, nature, even if it could not be known in its totality, could be "practiced" and the limits of that practice could be "known" to the particular "self-experiencing" agent—*jikan*, an idea of natural power and natural limitation that Shōeki defined as "each person working"—*hitori hataraku* and *chokkō*; and a natural community could be made to rest on overflowing surplus energies and interactive natural practices—*gosei*. These ideas of Shōeki were dramatically at odds with those of Sorai who insisted that nature could not be known in a detailed and controllable manner as an ultimate principle of knowledge and hence could not be relied upon as a norm for social existence.[19]

In Shōeki, then, the "mean" is not a still and timeless ideal to which all humans ought to aspire, or for that matter even "choose" as a subjective exercise of reason. He expressed it as the "natural mean"—*shizen no chūyō*, a natural and precise extension of oneself within the process of active and dynamic reenactment. Each particular entity practices that which is specific to itself as a natural individual—*hitori*. Shōeki thus read the ideographs for nature—*shizen*—as "oneself doing"—*hitori suru*, meaning each thing acting out what is natural to it. In turn, the ethic of truthfulness, in this active process of realizing the "natural mean" is expressed as "active truthfulness"—*katsushin*.[20]

The contrast here between Shōeki and Sorai is striking. For Sorai, specific human virtues are realized from within the individual, but the conditions for this realization are provided by mediating political constructs dedicated to human nourishment—*yashinai no michi*. Shōeki rejected such a theory of "nourishment" as discriminatory interference from above, the source of exploitation of the natural work of the populace. In his insistence that there is no hierarchic priority in nature beyond "oneself doing," Shōeki theorized an egalitarian philosophy of existence devoid of elites providing "nourishment" for the people. Without exploitation from above that is endemic to hierarchic systems, the people would nourish themselves through the fruits of their own natural labor.

What finally separates Shōeki from other theorists was his rejection of the categories of "heaven" and "earth"—*Ten/chi*, the most fundamental of categories in all of East Asian moral philosophy. They were not even acceptable to him as metaphoric references to a unified natural order. For Shōeki, the idea of "heaven" as the trans-natural source of political mandate to create kings was a total falsehood, whether said of ancient China or ancient Japan. The only source of power was nature as it endowed each particular "individual" with the capacity to realize its "natural mean."

The very concept of heaven and earth for Shōeki was at the basis of discriminating between high and low, the spiritual and the material. As scholars have consistently pointed out, therefore, Shōeki challenged the hierarchic element inherent in the dual concepts of heaven and earth by making the extremely crucial move of using the ideographs of "movement" and "rest"—also pronounced *tenchi*, ideographs that were therefore homophonic with yet radical displacements of heaven and earth.

Shōeki is proposing a fundamental philosophical thought. He placed movement and rest within a nonhierarchical theory of infinite sequence, or infinite replication, one turning into two and two into one, or, more literally, a process that never ended at one nor went beyond two—*fujū ichi fushutsu ji/ichi ni todomarazu ni o idezu*. It is an infinite series that applies equally in the systemic action-process of every natural organism, regardless of size or complexity. By leveling the vertical construction of heaven and earth with motion and rest and infinite sequence, Shōeki rejected dualistic and prejudicial distinctions of every kind. The yin-yang dualism, another central metaphor in Asian philosophy, was supposedly a theory of equal halves becoming one, the "identity of contraries" as posited in Taoism. Shōeki rejected this concept of yin and yang, which was not, actually, two equal halves, but an unequal dualism in which lightness was preferred to darkness, active over passive, masculine over feminine. Nature, for

Shōeki, was but a single process where one becomes two and two turns into one and is not an interactive process of opposites.

From this line of reasoning Shōeki concluded that all things in nature were one "individual"—*hitori*, and, therefore, that men and women were one as human. Alongside the ideographs for "man and woman"—*danjō*, Shōeki inscribed the phonetics for "human"—*hito*, offering thereby an astonishing insight that speaks directly to some of the central social issues of racial and gender discrimination in our day.

Let me continue for a few more lines on Shōeki's use of "language." His "violent" or "savage" bending of conceptual language to produce a text on Nature was informed, in the wording of Yasunaga Toshinobu, by a "mad spirit"— *kyōki*.[21] Shōeki manifests a restlessness with received language and philosophical rhetoric that stemmed from his recognition that language as a social inscription was an ideological instrument, and the challenge to the existing political order must proceed first with an attack on language.

Shōeki's stance vis-à-vis language helps us to understand something of the difficulty of his style. The distinguished sinologist Yoshikawa Kojirō once remarked that had he been a scholar in Shōeki's age, he would not have been impressed by Shōeki's terrible sinographic prose—*kanbun.* "What I mean," Yoshikawa noted, "is that his *kanbun* was very poor. Seeing that prose, I think I would have thought this person is hopeless." Engaged in a dialogue with Yoshikawa, Nakamura Yukihiko commented, "Why did he not write in Japanese rather than in such a difficult to understand and terrible style?"[22] From a somewhat different perspective, Naramoto Tatsuya attested to the difficulty of Shōeki's style. In praising E. H. Norman's linguistic skill in reading Shōeki, Naramoto observed that Shōeki's *kanbun* was distinctive as was his use of concepts: "Without doubt Andō Shōeki's prose cannot be easily read no matter how much in tune one is with the Japanese language. That's because his *kanbun* was distinctive and his grasp of concepts was also unique."[23]

Shōeki's distinctive use of language, however, is central to his critical philosophy. It seems likely that Shōeki retained something of the Zen skepticism toward language. In Zen (as in Taoism) language was "artificial," at best a functional necessity. Any logically constituted mode of communication was deceptive and integral with the world of passion, desire, and suffering. Language was the mediating construct for human ambition in the here and now. It could not explain the true meaning of Enlightenment. Shōeki may be seen as a political extremist at the outer edges of this lengthy historical discourse on the problem of language as fundamentally artificial and deceptive.

Even more broadly conceived, Shōeki's dilemma is that of all those who seek to change human perceptions of social reality by breaking the binding effects of customary norms, which include the conventions of language. To use language as it was received would merely reinforce the pervasive social "prison" —*gyoku*—that "deceives"—*damasu*—human beings and persuades them to accept exploitation from above as normal, as part of the natural order of things.

The fact that he did not write in conventional Japanese, therefore, should not confuse us. Kanbun was the language of intellectual communication and Shōeki was committed to the act of persuasion and was not a romantic recluse who sought solace in nature, as he criticized Lao Tzu and Chuang Tzu of being. We may also surmise that as a skeptic of language, Shōeki was aware that Japanese was not a privileged language. It was not any less deceptive, not any more translucent, than any other language, although *Kokugaku*, National Studies, would seek to demonstrate this transparency with their infusion of the ideal of the naturally sacred in language itself—*kotodama.* The question of style, that is his "poor" command of *kanbun* or his not writing in "Japanese," is far less important than the radical discontent that urged him to write in a "mad spirit." We see in Shōeki, therefore, a relentless tendency to pervert normal meanings, to write violently, to distort and stretch language and thereby to challenge conventional norms.

The interpretive theorist of texts Paul Ricoeur provides helpful insight for our reading of Shōeki. In his essay "Imagination in Discourse and in Action," Ricoeur writes about "semantic innovation" as stemming from the "deviant usage of predicates" to intervene in the flow of grammatical prose, and generating new meaning. Let me quote a line from Ricoeur on the use of bizarre predicates as "metaphor" which is relevant to our discussion:

> The resemblance is itself a function of the bizarre predicates. It consists in the coming together that suddenly abolishes the logical distance between heretofore distant semantic fields in order to produce the semantic shock, which, in turn ignites the spark of meaning of the metaphor. Imagination is the apperception, the sudden glimpse, of a new predicative pertinence, namely, a way of constructing pertinence in impertinence. . . . Imagining is above all restructuring semantic fields.[24]

In the use of "bizarre predicates" is the "shock" that opens to the sudden grasping of the similarity in the multitude of dissimilar things. Thus, in Shōeki, all things are equally engaged in the process of motion and rest, and all dissimilar things are oneself, *hitori,* engaged in practice and work—*hitori suru/hitori hataraku* or *chokkō/katsushin*. The only authority for "all things" being "each thing" is nature, reminding us here of Gilles Deleuze's remark about Spinoza's view of nature in its entirety as an "individual." For both Shōeki and for Spinoza too, nature conceived in this "bizarre" way was to rid the conceptual field of prejudice and hierarchy with a theory of "all things" as "each thing" in infinite process.[25]

Following on Deleuze's reading of Spinoza, I find myself in sympathy with Yasunaga Toshinobu's view that an idea of "freedom" is to be found in Shōeki.[26] It is, in my view, an idea of natural freedom—*shizen ken*—that might be expressed as the autonomous authority or potency of each physical entity or body to extend itself in practice and work, and whose limit is established by the ultimate source of each potency, which is nature. The idea of authority, or *ken*, here is closer to its Tokugawa reading as independent power or authority, rather than as a constitutional "right." In Shōeki, the idea of oneself doing or oneself feeling in work refers to the autonomous physical or sensate body which contains within itself the "authority" and the "limitation" of action. With the acknowledgement of this natural basis of action, "community" becomes possible not as a judgmental or legalistic system but as the interactivity or "interaffectivity" of overflowing energies among equals.

The idea of oneself doing and working—*hitori suru; hitori hataraku*—therefore may be a statement of "freedom" from the interventions of artificial authority; and it is also a definition of the independence of the "power" that is inherent in every concrete physical entity. It is about the power or potency of every organism whose extension is warranted only by nature, and whose limit is similarly determined only by nature. Freedom, in this sense, is not abstract and unlimited. It is not "free will"; nor is it comparable to the political idea of "independent agency." It is not a "right" that can be given away, alienated, as to a nation-state. As an outside authority, the nation-state cannot make a discrete natural entity into something other than what it is naturally. But this same authority can damage and distort by establishing artificial moral and legal limits and thereby cause "illness" among the people.

Thus, to Shōeki the practice of medicine called, first and foremost, for the cure of "politics," not the correction of "nature." His view was out of step with the scientific and experimental medicine that would lead to Dutch medical studies—*Rangaku*. But we cannot deny the truthfulness of his insight about social illness widely evident in our modern day.

Since his rediscovery by Kanō Kōkichi and others in the modern era, it is often said of Shōeki that he was a "utopian" visonary. This view, it seems to me, requires rethinking. His language about nature being oneself doing oneself working does not strike me as being utopian. It was a constant theme of Shōeki of the natural determination of action and freedom that is beyond the conventional division of "good and evil" and other forms of black-and-white moral dualisms.

Shōeki's thinking resonates with fundamental philosophical and practical concerns in our day about the status of nature. The insight of Gilles Deleuze may again be pertinent here. Writing about "Spinoza and Us," Deleuze uses the terms "ethology," "ecophilosophy" and "deep ecology" to characterize these contemporary concerns. These terms refer to the study and care of nature, the "most intense Individual"—Shōeki's *hitori*—and its myriad "bodies." Deleuze explains his understanding of Spinoza's natural body:

> A body, of whatever kind, is defined by Spinoza in two simultaneous ways. In the first place, a body, however small it may be, is composed of an infinite number of particles; it is the relations of motion and rest, of speeds and slownesses between particles, that define a body, the individuality of a body. Secondly, a body affects other bodies, or is affected by other bodies; it is this capacity for affecting and being affected that also defines a body in its individuality.[27]

The idea of nature as life in motion is here articulated by Deleuze through the text of Spinoza as a problem of modernity, not of a utopian dreamer. Shōeki's conception of nature as one, as individual, as *hitori*, in motion, is akin to Spinoza's view of natural things as being ultimately equal in a state of nature.

As I have emphasized in this essay, Shōeki remains very much with us, not as a utopian lunatic, but as a voice within our modern consciousness. Shōeki must be viewed not so much in terms of how modernization came about, but as what resources modern human beings currently have, given the realities of technological innovations, and what will be their impact on nature as *hitori*. Shōeki's natural community—*shizen no yo*—is important as an intellectual resource today. His affirmation of the "power" of nature over all forms of human organization, including military ones—*gungaku wa muyō no gaku*—is a matter that is most pertinent to our view of the globe today.[28]

I was very much intrigued in this regard by the textual linkage of Andō Shōeki and Tanaka Shōzō made by Etō Tekirei, an early twentieth-century writer who was also from the same northeast region as Shōeki and was a practitioner of agrarian communalism. He named his commune on the outskirts of Tokyo the *Tenshinkei*, which incorporates Shōeki's ideas of "movement," "truthfulness," and "reverence" for the natural order. Writing in the 1920s, Etō had strong misgivings about the course of modernization. He also expressed "joy" in having a resource such as Andō Shōeki to refer to and even dedicated his works to him. Etō named his choice of the four great agrarian thinkers: "I choose these four agrarian thinkers of Japan. They are: Andō Shōeki. Satō Shin'en. Ninomiya Sontoku. Tanaka Shōzō."[29]

Etō's referencing here of Andō Shōeki with Tanaka Shōzō is very significant to our interpretive perspective. Through Tanaka Shōzō, Andō Shōeki comes to be linked intellectually with the "ethological" movements in modern and contemporary Japanese history. Unlike the others listed by Etō, Tanaka Shōzō is a figure of the industrializing modern era. Japan's first "deep ecologist," Shōzō gave his life in protest against the copper poisoning of rice fields in the late Meiji era (*Ashio kōzan jiken*). Influenced by the Tokugawa *Ōyōmei* idealistic theory of knowledge as action—*chigyō gōitsu*—and also by Christian idealism, Shōzō provides us with an action "text" that illustrates the ethical ideals of oneself doing, of action as a natural, and hence "truthful," extension of oneself, to challenge the exploitative strategies of large organizational systems.

I might add that Tanaka Shōzō was "forgotten" in the prewar period. A few individuals, such as Kurosawa Torizō who joined Tanaka Shōzō's movement and then lived and worked in Hokkaido to develop the cooperative-based Snow Company, remained loyal to Shōzō's ideas. Shōzō was brought back into social memory by scholars and intellectuals only in the recent decades of high-growth economics. During these times when ecological damage resurfaces along with other serious forms of social "illness," Shōzō regained importance as a valuable visionary well ahead of his times and belongs with Andō Shōeki as historical texts within our ongoing history. In the wording of Kenneth Strong, Tanaka Shōzō was an "Ox against the Storm." The same may be said of Andō Shōeki. Although having lived in totally different kinds of political and economic contexts, one agrarian and the other industrial, they present themselves to us as "savage anomalies" who bravely faced the eye of the storm. They both inform our consciousness about the predicament of modernity.[30]

In closing, I should like to underscore again how valuable it is to remember Andō Shōeki as a thoroughgoing skeptic of language. In particular, his idiosyncratic reading of the term "nature"—*hitori suru*—should caution us against using nature as an extension of "culture," and of viewing nature as an emotional landscape particular to Japan as a privileged site. Shōeki's theory of nature is universal. Shōeki would ask us to question the current ideological language that there is specifically in Japan a unique sense of harmony between culture and nature. There is enough contrary evidence of this in Japan and elsewhere to not find emotional solace in this tenuous relationship. Rather, Shōeki asks us to consider the spaces we have for critical thought and creativity. Shōeki recalls for us the eccentric and creative energies of the regions in Tokugawa times and the potentiality of localities such as Hachinohe, situated far away from the centers of wealth, power, and monarchical symbols.

Shōeki provides us with the opportunity to recall the life and historiography of E. H. Norman in our recent history of Asian studies.[31] Norman set his sights on Shōeki, who pointed to language, especially moral language, as being, finally, political and exploitative, the site of ideology itself, and hence the foe of nature and humanity. Norman's Shōeki has been relegated to the fringe in our field as one who lacked influence and thus, quite appropriately, was forgotten. It is somehow fitting that intellectuals in postwar Japan should have been responsive to Norman's Shōeki by choosing the metaphor the "forgotten thinker" and to mean by this one whose voice belonged within Japan's modernity, and, by extension, all of East Asia's.

Notes

1   E. H. Norman, *Andō Shōeki and the Anatomy of Japanese Feudalism* (Tokyo: Transactions of the Asiatic Society of Japan, 1950) and *Wasurareta shisōka Andō Shōeki* (Tokyo: Iwanami shoten, 1950). The most thorough and serious biography of Norman is Roger Bowen's excellent study *Innocence Is Not Enough—The Life and Death of Herbert Norman* (New York: M. E. Sharpe, 1986).

2   Ernst Cassirer, *Essay on Man* (New Haven: Yale University Press, 1974); Paul Ricoeur, *Interpretation Theory: Discourse and the Surplus of Meaning* (Fort Worth, Tex.: Texas Christian University Press, 1976); Michel de Certeau, *The Writing of History* (New York: Columbia University Press, 1988). This essay is based on my lecture "Andō Shōeki, Gendai shiso o kirihiraku tekisuto," published in *Gendai Nōgyō* (Tokyo: Rinji zokan, 1993), 36–54. I included portions of it in my "Presidential Address: Reflections on Modernity and Modernization," *Journal of Asian Studies* (November 1993): 845–53. The Hachinohe symposium was held on 17 October 1992.

3   *Shisō* 4 (1977): 88–89.

4   Ibid., 101.

5   H. D. Harootunian, "E. H. Norman and the Task for Japanese History," *Pacific Affairs* 4 (1968–69): 545–54.

6   John Dower, ed., *Selected Writings of E. H. Norman* (New York: Pantheon, 1975).

7   Masao Maruyama, "Affection for the Lesser Names—An Appreciation of E. Herbert Norman," *Pacific Affairs* 3 (1957): 545–52.

8   Benedetto Croce, *The Philosophy of Giambattista Vico* (New York: Russell and Russell, 1964), 244; and Isaiah Berlin, *Vico and Herder—Two Studies in the History of Ideas* (New York: Viking, 1976), 3.

9   Antonio Negri, *The Savage Anomaly—Spinoza's Metaphysics and Politics* (Minneapolis: University of Minnesota Press, 1991), 122.

10 Christopher Hill, *The World Turned Upside Down* (New York: Viking, 1972), 13–14, 314–15.

11 Kanō Kōkichi, "Dai shishōka ari," *Naigai kyōikyu hyōron* 3 (1908). Kanō was the headmaster of the most prestigious of higher schools in prewar Japan, the First Higher School or Ichikō, and a fascinating eccentric within the modern political order.

12 Shōeki's collected works are in *Andō Shōeki kenkyūkai*, ed. Andō Shōeki zenshū, 22 vols. (Tokyo: Nōbunkyō, 1984). The various editions of Shōeki's treatises, especially his principal work, *Shizen shin'en dō*, "on the truthful workings of the natural order," are included in these volumes. The Great Introduction or *Daijō* in which Shōeki summarizes his main ideas are in volume 1. An authoritative guide to Shōeki's thought is in volume 22, which I found especially useful in preparing this essay. A detailed textual study of Shōeki's ideas of nature is by Jacques Joly, "L'idée de shizen chez Andō Shōeki," doctoral thesis, University of Paris, 1991. See also Matsumoto Sannosuke, "Andō Shōeki," in *Edo no shisoka tachi*, 2 vols. (Tokyo: Kenkyusha, 1979), 2:3–36; Wada Kosaku, *Andō Shōeki no shisō* and *Andō Shōeki to Miura Baien* (Tokyo: Kōyō shobō, 1992).

13 Yasunaga Toshinobu, *Andō Shōeki* (Tokyo: Heibonsha, 1976), 14–29, 120–25. Also see his *Andō Shōeki: Social and Ecological Philosopher in Eighteenth-Century Japan* (New York: Weatherhill, 1992).

14 See, for example, Miyake Masahiko, "Andō Shōeki no shisō ni okeru keishō to hitei," in *Andō Shōeki*, ed. Nishimura Yoshimi et al. (Tokyo: Iki shōin, 1974), 60–74.

15 Hill, *The World Turned Upside Down*, 313–19.

16 See my *Visions of Virtue in Tokugawa Japan* (1987; Honolulu: University of Hawai'i Press, 1997), especially the chapters on Goi Ranju and Yamagata Bantō.

17 Masao Maruyama, *Studies in the Intellectual History of Tokugawa Japan*, trans. Mikiso Hane (Princeton: Princeton University Press), and also my *Tokugawa Political Writings: Ogyu Sorai* (Cambridge: Cambridge University Press, 1998).

18 Watanabe, *Andō Shōeki to shizen shineidō* (Tokyo: Keisō shobō, 1940), 162.

19 Translations of Sorai's *Bendō* and *Benmei* appear in my *Tokugawa Writings*.

20 Watanabe, *Andō Shōeki*, 36, 141–45. These ideas are all spelled out in Shōeki's *Daijō* or Great Introduction (*Andō Shōeki kenkyūkai*, vol. 1).

21 Yasunaga, *Andō Shōeki*, 69.

22 Nakamura Yukihiko, ed., *Nihon no shisō*, vol. 18: *Andō Shōeki, Tominaga Nakamoto, Miura Baien* (Tokyo: Chikuma shobō, 1971); see "Taidan."

23 Naramoto Tatsuya, "Norman to Andō Shōeki," *Shisō* 4 (1977): 108.

24 Paul Ricoeur, *From Text to Action* (Evanston: Northwestern University Press, 1991), 173.

25 Gilles Deleuze, *Spinoza: Practical Philosophy* (San Francisco: City Lights Books, 1988), 122–30.

26 Yasunaga Toshinobu, "Andō Shōeki no shisō to jidai," in *Andō Shōeki*, ed. Nishimura Yoshimi et al., 44–62, esp. 58.

27 Deleuze, *Spinoza*, 123; and also Negri, *Savage Anomaly*, 111.

28 Watanabe, *Andō Shōeki*, 145–47.

29 Tsukidate Kinji, "Andō Shōeki no shisō keishōsha to shite no Eto Tekirei," in *Andō Shōeki*, ed. Nishimura, 145–71, esp. 149.

30 Kenneth Strong, *Ox Against the Storm* (Tenterden, U.K.: Paul Norbury, 1977).

31 I should like to call attention here to Peyton Lyon's letter to the *Ottawa Citizen* (4 April 1997), "Isn't it time to let Herbert Norman rest in peace"; and his article "Robert Bryce and Herbert Norman: A True Friendship," *Ottawa Citizen* (8 July 1997). A former diplomat for the Canadian government, and adjunct professor of political science at Carleton University, Lyons was appointed in 1990 by the foreign minister to review the Norman case based on full access to the files. His report completely vindicated Norman, whom he characterized as a leading scholar of Japanese history and brilliant servant of Canada. Also of note is a recent "open letter" from Roger W. Bowen in the *Globe and Mail* (21 June 1997), "Seeking answers to the death of Herbert Norman." The author of the biography on Norman, *Innocence Is Not Enough* mentioned in note 1 above, Bowen's letter is addressed to the CIA requesting access to classified documents that might shed light on Norman's tragic death.

Objectivism and the Eradication of
Critique in Japanese History
Stefan Tanaka

Japan's surrender in 1945 and the subsequent occupation by American forces created the potential for the termination of Japan's history as it developed in the early twentieth century and the opening for a different history. Indeed, stories of students blacking out line after line of their history textbook suggest the possibility for something quite different.[1] Central to this questioning of pre-World War II history was the interrelation between the nation-state and historical knowledge. Ogura Yoshihiko writes, "When entombed in a non-critical stance toward the logic of the Japanese 'nation-state' (*kokka*), no matter how one conducts research on Asia, one will never see 'Asia.'"[2] Ogura raises questions about the possibility of accurate research on other societies (as well as Japan) when one does not also interrogate the discursive structure of one's own position, especially within the unit of the nation-state. He raises as one of the troubling problematics of modern society the role of history in the separation of knowledge from life.

In post-World War II Japan it was clear to American occupiers and many Japanese that the history that had been practiced and taught was an ideological mystification that though "based upon real life" also "disguised or transposed that real life."[3] A number of historians, such as Tōyama Shigeki, Inoue Kiyoshi, and Ishimoda Sho, who were connected to the Rekishigaku kenkyūkai (Rekiken), a Marxist historical association, imagined a different modern. They sought a reconfigured past where history no longer served as one of those ideologies and mystifications that maintained that separation between knowledge and life.

While reading materials from this period, I have been struck by their conceptual sophistication—that is, the understanding of many of the problematics of a history in and of modern society—and their commitment to the centrality of history to political life. Yet until recently, such conceptual debates and historical issues have been virtually absent from Japanese studies in the United States. Despite their stature and centrality to history and the historical profession, these historians are infrequently discussed or cited, and when mentioned are usually summarily dismissed as "Marxist." I have also been surprised at the difficulty of finding many of the writings of these historians. Perhaps it is because I am in a corner of the United States; but computer databases, even though I am mindful of their incompleteness, have shown a paucity of citations of the Reki-ken historians during the 1950s. No doubt there are problems with the framework of these historians, but we must also remember that many of the critical approaches that we use today are also grounded in an understanding of Marx. In writing this paper, I have often fantasized how our field might have evolved had the issues these historians raised been included—not necessarily accepted—in the historiographical training of Japanese history as taught in the United States.

From the end of the war through the 1950s and 1960s these historians debated widely from what today is called "theory" to the exegesis and significance of specific historical moments. Their efforts to reconfigure history, especially the relation between historical knowledge, national ideology, and (mis)understandings of Asia (especially China) parallel our inquiry into area studies in the United States. Their importance was not in connecting history to ideology—that was clear to most people in the immediate postwar period. They reintroduced the performative nature of history and also offered an alternative vision. History, they argued, is more than a descriptive discipline, it also enables, transforms, and restricts individuals and social units. They examined how objectivistic historical knowledge often reinforces a reality that is more linked to an ideological structure rather than the objects they purport to describe. Moreover, they proposed an alternate vision that, while fully located within a modernist project, sought to reaffirm the historicity of many modern categories, thereby bringing process and human agency back to historical studies.[4]

I hope that by raising some of the issues debated during the postwar years and by pointing to many of the reasons for their gradual elision in the 1960s, I will stimulate others to revisit—not resurrect—the writings of these historians. The end of the Cold War makes it imperative that we reexamine Japanese historiography during this period when, despite a strong, critical framework, history returned to the noncritical stance of which Ogura warns.

The Recovery of Time

On 11 January 1946, elementary school classes on ethics, national history, and geography were suspended. This act forewarned of the *Report of the United States Education Mission to Japan* which was submitted to the Supreme Command of Allied Powers (SCAP) on 30 March 1946, which asserted that the history and geography curriculum played a "major role in political and militaristic indoctrination" largely because "Japan's recorded history has been consciously confused with mythology, and its geography protectively and even religiously self-centered."[5] Here, the ideology that guided those who made history is questioned, covered up (in the blackening out of texts), and a potential is opened for eradication. But ultimately (to get well ahead in my narrative), the connection is only covered up, hidden by a facade. The Ministry of Education quickly followed this report, proposing reforms to the curriculum that would correct the nationalistic history of prewar Japan (that had been considered objective and scientific). The ministry sought a 1) scientific and objective perspective, 2) a history, not only of royalty and nobility, but also of people (jinmin), 3) a history from a world history (sekaishi) perspective, and 4) a history of industry, economics, and culture rather than wars and political transformation.[6]

In October provisional textbooks were approved; the first elementary history textbook, compiled by the Monbushō (Ministry of Education), was *Kuni no ayumi* (Ienaga Saburō was one of the authors). The major (and significant) change was to alter the temporal markers, changing them from national eras symbolized by emperors and the glorious nation-state to historical eras within Japan's past. For example, the 1943 textbook divided Japan's modern period into "Emerging world," "Rising Japan," "Defending East Asia," "The shifting world," and "The glorious reign of Showa." The same period in *Kuni no ayumi* is "The decline of the bakufu," "Meiji restoration," "The world and Japan," and "From Meiji to Showa." The subchapters shift from imperial reigns and glorious events (such as the Imperial rescript and wars) to political, economic, and social changes.[7] Even though the authors were criticized for not going far enough, of "old authoritarian ideas," "mistaken emperor-centrism," and "defense of militarism,"[8] it is an indication of hope, of a new history that does not glorify the nation-state.

Historians at this time focused on authoritarianism and the failure of democracy. The principal issues were why didn't a more democratic government emerge in Japan, despite the creation of modern political and economic systems; and how can history help understand how a more democratic, modern society might be created. The debate among historians covers a wide range of issues, from which data to include and exclude to a concern over the level of reflexivity, a questioning of methods—especially the notion of pure research—and epistemological concerns. A central group of critical historians associated with Rekiken sought to reenvision the spatial and temporal parameters of historical studies.[9] These historians were influenced by a translation that was published in 1947 of Marx's manuscripts that form the basis of his *Grundrisse*.[10] This debate on the structure of history itself revolved around the third of the Monbushō proposals, to write history from a world historical perspective (*sekaishi*). They viewed *sekaishi* as a global historical perspective that would interrogate the conflation of history with the nation-state, a collusion that facilitated the concentration of power in the state. Their goal was to refocus history away from the nation-state toward peoples, using socioeconomic structures and modes of interaction as the principal criteria for creating temporal categories to measure change.

In 1949 Inoue Kiyoshi proposed that Rekiken focus on the "fundamental contradictions of various societies (later changed to social structures)."[11] Thus, even though the lineage to prewar Marxism is apparent, this marks a departure from the previous focus on modes of production and absolutism. In that year Rekiken made the "basic laws of world history" (*sekaishi no kihon hōsoku*) the theme of their annual meeting. The themes for the following years were related: the stages of nation-state power (*kokka kenryoku no shodankai*, 1950); the national problem in history (*rekishi ni okeru minzoku no mondai*, 1951); on national cultures (*minzoku no bunka ni tsuite*, 1952); and Asia in the world (*sekai ni okeru ajia*, 1953).[12] The 1949 meeting began what many have considered the "golden years" of Rekiken that lasted until 1953.

Second, Rekiken paralleled this conceptual reformulation of history into abstract temporal categories—primordial and ancient, medieval, and modern (*gendai*)—with a structural reorganization that better fits this framework. These periods were defined by socioeconomic conditions, for example, primitive, slave, feudal, capitalist, and socialist societies. I should note that there was no agreement on the exact meaning and content of these periods.[13] Regardless of what we think of this Marxist framework, the prioritization of temporal categories over national or regional entities has the potential at minimum to historicize the spatial categories we use in writing history and about history (connected to Japan as well as more generally).

The historical profession in Japan up through World War II was (and still is) divided into discrete geographic histories—Japan (*kokushi*), the Orient (*tōyō-shi*), and the West (*seiyōshi*). In this structure, the nation-state is naturalized; in all three "fields" it becomes the referent, the often unspoken norm by which others (*tōyō*) and (*seiyō*) have been studied. *Kokushi* turns the referent into an object as well.

This "new" periodization has the potential to recognize one of the major limitations of history. Rekiken historians correctly identified and sought to correct a site of slippage in modernist histories, where the unit of analysis, the nation-state, becomes simultaneously diachronic and synchronic. Tōyama is quite explicit that an antithesis to their proposal is the focus on a single country (*ikkoku;* he does not use the word for nation-state, *kokka*). The privileging of the nation-state as the primary unit of analysis elides critical data and problems about the transformation of societies and the relation between people and structures. Through claims to science and objectivity such histories incorporate critique: criticism is allowed as long as it does not destabilize the myth of the referent. Usually scientific and critical histories assume the nation-state; it is part of that common sense of the historical profession that naturalizes historical forms into immanent categories. It recalls Koselleck's invocation of Hegel in a description of *Geschichte,* in contrast to *histoire,* which works through—and creates and maintains—a unity, the collective singular of the nation-state. According to Koselleck, this collective singular "made possible the attribution to history of the latent power of human events and suffering, a power that connected and motivated everything in accordance with a secret or evident plan to which one could feel responsible, or in whose name one could believe oneself to be acting."[14]

Tōyama argues that in histories that presuppose the nation-state (in his later writings he extends this to regions), the historicity of a unilinear narrative of development (à la Hegel, Guizot, Buckle, etc.) is elided. He argues that national histories too often overemphasize the uniqueness of the nation, looking for data for differentiation rather than the relationship to general trends. Indeed, this is so evident that we regularly frame questions and use subcategories that presume that differentiation is the goal of history. Moreover, once the spatial form is defined, a linear progressive framework reinforces the naturalness of that space. This national space is reinforced by chronologies of political epochs codified as objective history in the late nineteenth and early twentieth centuries that pretend that the nation-state has always existed. Japanese history, for example, has usually been divided by political change that feigns progress while essentializing the nation-state: Nara, Heian, Kamakura, Muromachi, Tokugawa, etc. Moreover, because the nation-state is the primary unit of analysis, the human dimension is deemphasized and only used as examples for the development of the national unit as if it speaks for the human.

One of important aspects of the Rekiken proposal is this historicization of spatial units that have become naturalized and institutionalized. They argue that the history of all societies should be described not by political epochs unique to that place, but by conditions that affect all societies, albeit in different ways. In a recollection written in 1967, Tōyama gives a sense of this world history in a rather long passage:

The structure of world history that we want is not one that enumerates the historical phenomena of each nation (*minzoku*) intersecting them with the same temporal eras that connect them through a history of intercourse. It is not a mode of grasping development where the history of all nations, divided into advanced and late developing, follow the same developmental path; thus under the influence and leadership of the advanced countries the late-developers follow in their wake. The world history we want is a world history with a uniform (*ittei*) structure with laws of development. Today, the nations (*minzoku*) of Asia, Africa, and Latin America possess both unique (*dokuji*) values and codes of behavior (*undō hōsoku*); they occupy particular positions, serve particular roles, and are conjoined with the forward drive of the developmental laws of world history. The people (*jinmin*) of imperialist countries, of socialist countries, and of newly independent countries, while each are at different developmental levels and strive to resolve different issues, can be connected by a common theme where they share an autonomous and equivalent issue of overcoming imperialism and colonialism and achieving peace, independence, and democracy.[15]

The reorganization of history into these universalistic categories of conditions that all societies (will) experience maintains the progressive movement of post-Enlightenment history. This temporal structure was considered scientific (as an antithesis to nationalist histories). At this point, both an alternative history and one reduced to a variation of the same, a return to bourgeois history, are possible. The important difference between the different historical visions is an inversion of the relationship between the particular and the universal. By turning to temporal moments rather than the nation-state as the referent of historical inquiry, this framework possesses the potential to bring out one of the secrets at which Koselleck hints, the naturalization of temporal categories within the nation-state, where chronologies or epochs enable the elision of the myriad temporalities that might coexist; for example, time of the body, seasonal time, eschatological time, as well as different horizons of expectations.

It is important to point out that *sekaishi* did not provide a different temporal horizon as the modernist history that Rekiken historians criticized. It is still based on a universalistic ideal—that of development—that unfolds from some primitive form to an ideal (not yet known) future. The periods themselves are a modification—via Marx—of the Hegelian primitive, classical, and modern. Their historiographical debates sought to locate the moment of transition from one socioeconomic condition to another where different data are located within these modified categories. Their history was one that argued that this is science, the other, despite claims to objectivity, is not. They, too, were looking for that authentic past, that altar of history that historians believe can be retrieved when others' problems are corrected. But they underestimated the power of such positivistic history that also made claims to science, but one based on simplistic biological metaphors;[16] and they were often blind to the ways that their own conceptual structure could become equally static within a vision of a scientific history.

As is implicit above, these historians did not deny the importance of histories of the particular, nor did they deny the centrality of nation-states in the twentieth century. To do so would be folly. They were seeking to problematize the historicity of these historical forms as well as the primary unit of analysis, the nation-state, in which such progress had been deployed. Tōyama, for example, emphasizes the relation of the laws of world history (the universal) to the particular, not vice versa. To understand specific relations of the various people to the noninstitutional and fluid socioeconomic forms used in *sekaishi*—social structure, economic development, and class—nations (*minzoku*) provided that delimited, but fluid, unit of analysis.

The theme of the 1951 annual meeting was "problems of nation in history" (*rekishi ni okeru minzoku no mondai*).[17] *Minzoku* provides the data through which these historians tried to recover experiences of the many, the "real" and concrete, in a history that had devalued the human world in favor of the objectivity and certainty of politicoeconomic institutions.[18] Tōyama explains the centrality of *minzoku*: "The perspective of the nation was both a quest to grasp concretely and developmentally the dialectic relationship between the universality and particularity of the historical laws of one country and a problematic that, by locating the history of one country into a world history, sought to understand through the subjectivity of the respective nations the connection between the developmental laws of one country with the developmental laws of world history."[19] The use of the nation provides the historical particularities that had been occupied by the nation-state while simultaneously working in a framework that deemphasized the nation-state. Moreover, an emphasis on nation, the various peoples, diverted the principal topic of history from the political institutions to the mobilization and utilization of various resources for political (and economic) purposes.

One possibility opened up through this framework is the recognition of the problematic of nonsynchronism—that different nations, people, groups, etc. at the same moment have different temporalities. Here Tōyama is attempting to recover the historicity of history, that the categories, objects, and forms that we use today are not necessarily apposite for descriptions of earlier moments. The positivism of bourgeois history insists on the representation of pasts according to fixed temporal categories that render difference into a hierarchical unit. Koselleck calls this temporalization of society a new time, *Neuzeit*.[20] It is an apt word, for it forces us to recognize the historicity of the very concepts we commonly use in historical discourse. For Rekiken historians, by exposing the historicity of concepts and structures, such as the nation-state, they found it possible to locate the areas where modern society has elided (or naturalized as an essential characteristic) the very contradictions of its own system. History was not to be described through abstract concepts, such as progress, mechanical time, etc., but through processes and interactions of peoples. It was an attempt to recover experience in modern society. For example, in their hands, *minzoku* is reconfigured from its national-socialist ties to a liberatory concept. Toma Seita writes in 1951:

> Until now, the emperor-system government has completely substituted statism and anti-foreignism for Japan's ethnic national consciousness; thus the development of both an ethnic national consciousness with a populist foundation and a concept of international solidarity has been greatly hampered. Moreover, modernism, which has had such a strong influence over our intellectual class, has arrested the development of ethnic national consciousness and worked to encourage cosmopolitanism.[21]

Minzoku in this framework was an attempt to recover the time of nations, the multiple temporalities as a constantly changing (in dialectical relationship with the historical laws), rather than eternally fixed, form.[22] The use of *minzoku* here recognizes the fluidity of the history of contemporary political units. Tōyama, for example, points out that in the ancient period the earth was divided into many worlds: Greece and Rome, the Orient, the subcontinent, and the East, centered around China. The latter, he argues, was not an "East Asia" (an idea that is today institutionalized in many universities); it did not exist, nor did a Japan, China, or Korea as nation-states. Instead, these peoples existed in a world centered by a Chinese imperium. Differentiation of these three entities emerged only with the rise of mercantile capitalism. Rekiken historians did not deny a *minzoku* that can be identified using today's terms, Japan, Korea, China, but that the nature of their interaction to other places differed in interaction with the historical laws. In other words, while there is clearly a Japanese nation-state in the nineteenth century, it is a mistake to find the same unit (albeit with a different level of development) in an earlier period when the idea of a Japanese *minzoku* was much weaker. Tōyama is arguing for the recognition of both the differences of the local, the *minzoku,* where the particulars of interaction with capitalist markets differ by time and region, and of the relations among the capitalist nations: the nature of their competition, when each entered different regions, and who entered which place.

The inversion of universal and particular brings up the power relation embedded in discursive structures of world development, an issue that has only recently (since Said's *Orientalism*) become commonly acknowledged. It was an attempt to discuss contemporary issues and recent histories of formerly colonized places outside of a conceptual framework that reinforced the colonial hierarchy but while also recognizing the centrality of modernity. Rekiken historians pointed to the failure of comparative studies in the way it reinforces the nation-state by emphasizing the characteristics of one place as normative by highlighting the differences of another.[23] Inoue went further; he pointed to those "illusions" of connection and interaction through, "convenient words"—intercourse (*kōryū*) and transmission (*denpa*)—that mask the preeminence of the particularities of the nation-state as well as the asymmetry of the global capitalist system. The problem, he argues, is not in the linearity per se but in the merging of linearity with cultural types. In Hegel, who Inoue identifies as the first to write a world history that unifies Asia and Europe into a global historical framework, he finds some commonality in spirit and freedom (Inoue conveniently overlooks Hegel's religiosity). But, he points out, it evolved into a history that rejected the principle of development in favor of asymmetric classifications, the division of peoples into fixed cultural spheres or types (*ruigata*) (he cites Weber's cultural spheres as an example) located along various points of a developmental scale. Thus, on an international level, variation is relegated to differentiated but hierarchically fixed typologies. By foregrounding the temporal structure, this framework is attempting to bring back the formerly naturalized developmental process (and categories) as objects of inquiry. Only after historicizing those categories and frameworks can one then restore history of the particular through those connections of the local to different historical moments and sociopolitical forms.

The Recovery of History: The Elision of Time

The year 1953 marked the end of the "golden years"; much of the momentum of the previous five years began to wane. Rekiken historians continued to write quite actively. Historians such as Inoue, Tōyama, and Ishimoda are among the best-known in the profession. Yet the drive to refocus history dissipated. No doubt much had to do with the changing political and international scenes. But as Tōyama points out, commitment was tepid and, more important, there was insufficient understanding of the principals of *sekaishi* to overcome the habits and infrastructure of an academia that privileged the nation-state as the primary unit of analysis.[24]

But perhaps a more important problem, one that confronts us today, is the similarity between Rekiken and orthodox histories, where attempts at critique often supported that which was criticized. In this case, the similarity of the Marxist framework to the modernist historiography, especially the two principal components, unilinear development and *minzoku*, made the transformation even more difficult. They lend to a rather simplistic reading of problematics in ways that reduce the oppositional possibility to variations of the whole.

Linearity shorn of its processual dynamic could easily (and would be) reintegrated into discussions that assumed geocultural integrity. For example, in seeking those moments of transition, the precise boundaries of one era and another (ancient to feudal and feudal to modern), these historians reified a different category, that of the temporal era rather than the nation-state. In commenting on historiographical debates such as the transition from ancient (slave) to feudal societies or whether the Meiji Restoration was a bourgeois revolution, Tōyama points out that the seemingly major differences among authors were often rather narrow.[25] The study of process gave way to categories which served as markers of process; feudal and modern merely replaced tradition and modern. Moreover, because this new history was "more" scientific, objective data was critical. But because the data which focused on socioeconomic change was very close to institutions of the early states, the differences between state, nation-state, and nation were easily blurred. In these modern histories, though the nation-state was supposed to be problematized, each utterance bore a connection to some part of the history of the nation-state, the meaningful presence. The nation-state (*kokka*) has sufficiently incorporated (or co-opted) elements of the nation, the *minzoku*, or Volk, to obfuscate the unpacking of rhetoric, politics, and history, thereby returning discussions on *minzoku* to a category of immanence. As we have seen today, it is very difficult to separate the idea of nation from histories and the ideology of the nation-state.

A different problem was linearity itself. Though Rekiken historians were critical of modernity as it evolved in a liberal-capitalist mode, they were much more sanguine about a Marxist variation. But in the latter, despite the efforts to build in a heterogeneity into the universalist framework, they did not eliminate the hierarchies that restricted the subjectivity of colonized places. Part of the problem, as Tōyama recognized in a retrospective, was that they did not then see the possibility of a bidirectional interchange. Discussions on imperialism and capitalism focused on the effect of these forces on Japan or Asia; they did not investigate processes in the other direction.[26]

Perhaps most important was the reemergence of orthodox historians. The renewed confidence of these historians can be illustrated in the annual reviews published in *Shigaku zasshi,* the journal of the Japanese Historical Association. In contrast to a besieged mentality in a lament about the historical discipline in 1948, the review of 1950 celebrates the revival of different fields. But more important, this review was organized by region—Oriental, Western, and Japanese—and employs a chronology through political eras (in the case of China, dynasties) and subregion as natural categories. The section on Oriental history (written by Wada Sei, the senior *tōyōshigakusha* [Orientalist] at Tokyo University) is further divided by epochs and national group along virtually the same lines as prewar Japanese academia; for example, Chinese history is divided into pre-Qin; Qin and Han; Wei, Jin, and Tang; Song and Yuan; Ming and Qing; late Qing and Republican. Regional/national categories follow: Manchuria and Korea; Mongolia and Inner Asia; and Southeast Asia and India. In a high school social studies text on world history by the title *sekaishi,* probably written in 1952 (the introduction was written in January 1953), Wada and Yamanaka Kenji write within a framework of progress, recognize that modernity, the civilization of the West is dominant, point out problems with a unilinear time, and argue for the variance of civilizations (*bunmei*) and human experience. In this sense, they are in line with Rekiken. But the principal point of difference is the nature of variance as it is produced in a historical framework. Wada and Yamanaka argue, perhaps unconsciously, that this difference is both the base and the goal of historical research. They write, "It is critical to know the development of these heteronomous cultures in order to investigate the essence of human cultures. This knowledge is more important than even thinking about the history of the development of Western civilization."[27]

On the one hand, this statement can be read as a plea to incorporate the history of the Orient (*tōyōshi*) into any account of world history—a prewar line. But they recognize that it is not a matter of incorporation, but the mode of incorporation. They prefer separate accounts that presume the integrity of cultural and national units. There is an oblique criticism to the Rekiken version of *sekaishi;* they argue that a deterritorialized history that combines East and West into synchronic forms fosters confusion: "One cannot understand the conditions of historical development, it unnecessarily complicates a complex past, and it fosters unease and confuses readers."[28] They propose to discuss the history of the West and the history of the East separately until the modern period when a single world and world history emerges. Thus in the chapters on *tōyō,* China centers a discussion that is organized through its dynastic changes and relations with peripheral peoples. The history of the West begins with ancient Greece and moves through Rome, the Middle Ages, early modern (Renaissance), revolutionary period, and the formation of nation-states in the nineteenth century. Text on Japan is virtually absent; its history is to be discussed in courses on Japanese history. Yet Japan is present in this text, forever the referent by which other histories are evaluated.

Even though they recognize intercourse between the Occident and Orient in the ancient and medieval periods, the "conditions of historical development" mask a presupposition of spatial, cultural, and national divisions—Orient and Occident, and subdivisions, China, India, and Southeast Asia—as primary categories over social or ideational forms. The categories proposed by Rekiken, because they do not use those units of analysis, are depicted as overly complicated and fostering confusion. Instead, history for Wada and Yamanaka should use the naturalized categories of the present to discuss the past.

This structure illustrates the response of the orthodox historians, especially those who held positions in the major universities and research institutions through the war. Despite the soul-searching during the 1960s, this structure has continued until the present. It is the "commonsensical," i.e., objectivist methodology, that elevates fact over theory. Enoki Kazuo explained this common sense:

> Historical theory (*riron*) and perspective are certainly essential in investigating historical facts and grasping historical development. However, facts are not born and history is not formed from theory. Theory is induced from historical facts, and theory is abstracted from history. Historical theory acquires the support of historical facts and then everybody pays attention to it. Facts are synthesized through the historical perspective of the investigator and then given structure. Certainly one area of growth and advancement of our postwar historical profession is the understanding and integration of such a commonsensical methodology and the recognition of the necessity of a "rich and fruitful" historiographical structure. In any event, 1951 was the fruitful year that our historical profession gradually regained composure and equanimity and inaugurated new advances.[29]

Enoki is reasserting the primacy of the historical fact, that is, concrete data over conceptual structure. Of course, in his mind the division by areas and political periods are "natural"; they are not conceptual. He ignores Droysen's sage statement, that facts are stupid without interpretation, in favor of a naive reading of Ranke's *wie es eigentlich gewesen* (Inoue's reading of Ranke that recognizes his rhetoric and the referent in the German nation or Protestantism is overlooked). It is here that the historicity of history is occulted. Time is rendered as periods, irrespective of the conditions that gave rise to such divisions; nation-states become those timeless vessels as if they always existed in the current (albeit more primitive) form that allow for a chronology that stands for time; and cultural areas take on conditions of a chronologically fixed place. They become part of that "secret or evident plan" that Koselleck describes (or what Enoki calls the "commonsensical") that pulls all heterogeneity to the collective singular and supports the conviction (though illusory) by which people act. But the claim to common sense is quite devious. Categories and statements of intent make many of the same claims as Rekiken historians. Problematics they raised are incorporated as variations of the natural process of development. Though (or because) organized chronologically, these periods efface the problematics of process and transformation in favor of finite units where dates suffice for process and transformation. By reducing one's vision to a narrow moment of an immanent nation, positivistic historians such as Wada were eliminating the possibilities for heterogeneity—what was called unnecessarily complex—and gaining more control over their object of study. Wada has reaffirmed a property of modern historical methodology, to avoid chance wherever possible.[30]

Celebration: Effacement of Critique

Throughout the 1950s and into the 1960s debates continued on the relation between history and the possibilities for a less hegemonic and homogeneous history, thus the nation-state. Despite the lack of agreement over the exact narrative as well as the methodological issues, the majority of Japanese historians operated within the general framework proffered through Rekiken. We must remember that the new elementary and high school textbooks generally followed this *sekaishi* framework.[31]

In the 1960s Rekiken confronted a formidable challenge. In 1960 John W. Hall and Edwin Reischauer convened a conference at Hakone, one of the initial meetings of the Conference on Modern Japan, more commonly known through the edited series published by Princeton University Press. The conference was a special project of the Association for Asian Studies and supported with a grant from the Ford Foundation. And in 1962 the Asia and Ford Foundations sought to invigorate the study of China in Japan through grants to the Tōyō Bunko.

Both events must be seen in relation to the Cold War and the buildup of area studies programs in the United States. In the first case, the study of Japan's transformation shifted from a historical problematic that sought to understand the relation between institutions *and* inhabitants as a way to expose and correct structural imperfections, to an exegesis of the transition as a "case study" (actually model) of a worldwide, i.e., universalistic, transformation of a non-Western place to a modern nation-state. In other words, Japan became historical data to describe the process of modernization. In the second case, the support of Japanese research on China using the considerable body of expertise of Japanese researchers (especially those connected to the elite prewar institutions) would provide the data that simultaneously highlighted Japan's "success" (in comparison to an intransigent and "traditional" China) and provide prescriptions of American policy to foster liberal capitalism in East Asia.[32]

In Japan these events gave renewed focus to Rekiken historians and awakened memories of especially those China historians whose own research was connected to Japan's imperialist policies in Asia.[33] Historians again questioned the separation of past from present as a pretense for claiming objectivity, the role of theories and methods, and the relation between scholarship and national policy. These debates are remarkable for the candor, sophistication, and openness in which many historians sought to transcend arbitrary but institutionalized boundaries. In many ways, the issues that confront area studies today were rehearsed at this time. In both cases, the central issue or target was the application of modernization theory (with its lineage to Hegel and especially Weber) through area studies. Ōta Hidemichi's criticism is common; he criticized the hidden values in the emphasis on rationality and mechanization and discerned its convergence with supporters of the Pacific War in the tendency to pardon Japan's invasionary path from the Meiji to the Pacific war.[34]

Most Japan specialists are (or should be) familiar with the Hakone conference held from 29 August to 2 September. In a sense, this is the originary moment (not a beginning) for Japanese studies in the United States. But it also marks the effacement of much of the Japanese historiography written between 1947 and the early 1960s. In short, it sets in motion a shift from Japanese historians determining the contours of their history to American academics setting the agenda. I will not rehearse the conference here. Summaries are readily available.[35] Appraisals, written by Tōyama, Ronald Dore, and Reischauer, were published in Japanese newspapers.[36] Here I would like to think about this conference not for what emerged, but for what was ignored. In reading the preconference materials and published reports in English and Japanese I have been struck by the naivete and arrogance of most American participants and the quite sophisticated critiques by many Japanese participants that contrasts with the impression in the Princeton series. My lament is that Japanese studies today would be conceptually much stronger had a dialogue emerged rather than a silencing of difference. Also surprising is the active interaction of Japanese participants, perhaps because public discussion was conducted in Japanese but more likely from recognition that the proposed conceptualization would efface a substantial portion of historiography over the previous fifteen years. But even though the con-

ference itself overcame a common stereotype that Japanese are not active participants, Hall's English report uses that stereotype to localize and diminish the
criticisms and issues that Japanese scholars raised.[37]

Even though participants were rather evenly balanced, the meeting was
structured and took place in a way that minimized the influence of Japanese
scholars on the conceptual construct of modernization.[38] First, the meeting
was structured to authorize modernization theory as proposed by Hall and Reischauer. Hall suggests the following agenda in a memo: first-day discussion—
"'Modernization' in terms of general principles," focusing on the issues raised
by Dore, Hall, Reischauer, and Levy; second day—discussion of modernization
in Japan; and third day—the study of Japan's modernization. While this does not
necessarily set priorities, Hall ends with the following request to Japanese participants: "It will be noted that the papers prepared by American participants are
largely directed toward the problem of the first day's discussion. It will be most
helpful if the Japanese participants will direct their thought to the more specific
problem of the modernization process in Japan proper."[39]

Even though the essays of Japanese scholars were also directed toward the
general principles of modernization, the structure proposed by Hall is consistent
with an Orientalist stereotype: the conceptualization is that of North American
scholars (Dore was then at the University of British Columbia), while the natives, the Japanese, serve as the informants. The relegation of Japanese scholars
to native informants is described by Kawashima Takeyoshi in his complaints
that American scholars curtailed discussion on critical issues, such as democracy, capitalism, and feudalism as value-laden and not directly related to the
topic. On occasion when Japanese participants brought up these issues, they
were abruptly dismissed with what he called "emotional responses" by several
American participants, no doubt an exasperation at the subjectivity and "ideology" of the Japanese participants. Such condescension was felt by a number of
the Japanese participants.[40]

Despite the tension, strong words, and often sharp disagreements, there was
considerable agreement over the principal issues and problems. Proceedings in
the Japanese language encouraged their participation, but it did not overcome
misunderstandings when words and concepts bore different contexts and legacies; the American "open approach" sought objectivity using rational and mechanistic criteria; Japanese questioned the absence of democracy and socioeconomic transformation (from feudalism to capitalism and socialism); and
both sides operated within a universalistic paradigm that envisioned the development of societies along a modernist trajectory. Hall writes, "It is in this context that the concept of modernization has been brought into being as some-

thing more inclusive of the total range of changes affecting the world in modern times."[41] Hall's "total range of changes" is similar to that of *sekaishi*. Both modernization theory and *sekaishi* claimed to be universal, scientific, and interdisciplinary.

One of the fascinating issues about the limits of science when applied to humans that this conference demonstrates is the extent to which their modern scientific methods obscured a shared ideal, in this case, democracy. The surprising curtailment of any discussion of democracy, dismissed as value-laden, reflects less a disinterest than an unbridled optimism.[42] But Japanese scholars, especially Tōyama and Kawashima were right to focus on this moment. It is at this point that Koselleck's warning that "the determinations of experience are increasingly removed from experience itself."[43] Hall writes, "The attempt to devise a unified and objective conception of modernization is not a light task, for it calls upon the scholar first to detach himself from the actual flow of history around him and secondly to give up any preconceptions he may have had about the values upon which modern society might rest."[44] For Hall, this means a detached objectivity. This, of course, is disingenuous for the very separation of experiences, American and Japanese turns American values into norms and transposes, as subjective, those concerns of the Japanese scholars into subjective and value-laden issues. Kawashima aptly points out that such empirical methods have been used in history by an orthodoxy against something considered heterodox. This elision of experience becomes clear in Reischauer's explanation of the difference between the two sides:

> Because Japanese scholars have experienced the whole process of Japan's modernization there is a strong tendency to consider Japan's modernization through their values (*kachi*). In other words, in Japan they think about desired results. On the other hand, because westerners have not experienced modernization to the same extent, they view it objectively. They try merely to record and analyze events of a century ago and defer value judgments.[45]

Reischauer presupposes that the past is separable from the present, but only concerning the object of study. He has simultaneously effaced the Cold War as a framing event (i.e., the subjectivity of American scholars, especially Reischauer) and the recent experience of these Japanese historians having lived through a fascist period. Tōyama's paraphrase of an American retort to his critique of modernization theory exposes this myopia, "Japanese scholars emphasize the distortions and slowness of Japan's "modernization," but we evaluate Japan, as a part of Asia, as an example that has rapidly succeeded."[46] In other words, Japan has now become a successful model in Cold War Asia.

Hall's report in the Jansen volume attempts to encompass the range of discussion; he does acknowledge Tōyama's critique. But rather than engaging these issues, he describes Tōyama's voice as one that substitutes "chaos for order, of a 'no-system' approach instead of one based on conceptual certainties."[47] Hall's comments echoes Wada's criticism of sekaishi, of unnecessary complications and confused readers. Hall's chaos is the multiple and contradictory possibilities in history, a part of modernity itself, while his conceptual certainties is that property of modern history that seeks to avoid chance.

Tōyama's critique of modernization theory questions its simplicity, what Inoki Masamichi called seductive (mirokuteki) but limited, and exposes the conceptual poverty that permeates area studies today. His criticism of modernization theory follows the general problematics raised in sekaishi. First, he points how categories and norms are too often defined through the particular; by using England and France as the implicit norm, peculiarities (impediments to modernization) are found in tradition—the very nationalistic characteristics that were celebrated in Japan's imperialistic and fascistic periods—not in the process whereby past forms are both destroyed and employed for different but modern purposes. Second, he points out that the emphasis on an objectivity guided by mechanization and rationality fosters a fragmentation of the object of study despite professions to interdisciplinarity. For Tōyama, the avoidance of capitalism, especially its effects on society and politics in favor of exegeses that measure successful growth, both supports and is supported by fragmented studies within various disciplines that use mechanistic criteria to determine change. In area studies, interdisciplinarity becomes a mask for empirical studies where culture obviates the need for disciplinary rigor. And last, he argues that modernization theory conflates time; it flattens the many and considerable changes that occurred from the eighteenth century through the twentieth century into this category of modernization. Indeed, one of the problems of area studies today is the tendency to reduce temporality into two categories, the modern and traditional. Even newer studies that profess to bring out the invention of traditions often operate within a flattened notion of time.[48]

We can only speculate where Japanese historiography might be today had we engaged with these issues in the 1960s. To Hall's credit, he did acknowledge Tōyama's critique (though as an afterthought); but in postconference reports, the subsequent seven conferences, and recent historiography, those who were most critical have been virtually elided from recent historiography.[49] The pattern by now should be clear, Marxist historiography is reduced to economics or dismissed as value-laden.[50] Hall (and others) dismiss these issues as simply a different "problem consciousness," one that he depicts as declining (therefore anachronistic)—he describes Inoue Kiyoshi and Eguchi as younger scholars who are moving away from their Marxism. The presumption here is that Marxism is unchanging, and the critiques of Inoue and Eguchi support his proposal for a different history.[51] This view should be placed within the organizational structure of the conference, where Japanese participants were native informants and any criticism of those "certainties" (here undefined) can only be those of the less sophisticated.

While most summaries note the differences between Americans and Japanese, there was also considerable differences within each side, especially the Japanese participants. These variations provided Hall with the opening to incorporate a "Japanese" point of view. Some, like Maruyama Masao who focus on the individual psyche rather than structural issues of capitalistic society, were retained for their interest in how individual Japanese did or did not make the transition to the modern. Maruyama's focus on individuation touches on questions of democracy, but only as long as cause can be localized in the culture or past (tradition or the individual), not the system. In the last essay of the first volume of the modernization series, Maruyama divides the Japanese participants into two groups: the Marxists—Tōyama and Ōuchi (we should also add Kawashima)—are those who focused on "limiting the notion of modernization to a particular historical process, that is, the process from feudalism to capitalism."[52] The second group comprised those (unspecified) who were willing to work within the modernization approach, but one more broadly conceived to include "ethos" and "ideology." Maruyama, too, trivializes the breadth and alternatives of *sekaishi*, reducing it to the process from feudalism to capitalism and contrasting it to a broad and universalistic modernization theory. Maruyama, of course, has become well known among American Japan specialists; he became a native informant in two senses: the Japanese scholar who is somewhat critical but willing to work amidst the modernization framework; and the intellectual historian who brings ethos and qualitative issues to Japanese studies.

So in the name of a framework that professes breadth and universalist methods we have seen the institutionalization of hermetic fields of study that vigorously defend their particularity. We now have a study of Japan that emphasizes national particularities, as both a positive (that of uniqueness) example for what it was able to accomplish, as well as an impediment—those traditions and legacies, the past, that hinder modernization. Positivistic data dominates, approaches that question the framework are rendered as too difficult, chaotic, and "theory." Japanese historians, such as Tōyama Shigeki, Ishimoda Sho, Inoue Kiyoshi, Eguchi Bokurō, Uehara Senroku, etc., were not only virtually effaced from the Conference on Modern Japan, but their historiography is removed from American Japanese studies.

An Epitaph

The accounts of the Hakone meeting by Dore and Tōyama in *Mainichi shinbun* indicate the road taken by subsequent conferences was a lost opportunity for dialogue between the different approaches. This is apparent in the titles: that of Tōyama's suggests hope despite quite different backgrounds, "Possibility for Scholarly Cooperation Despite a Different Present and Traditions," while that of Dore suggests difficulty and closure, "Difference of Problem Consciousness: A World Perspective and an Ethnic Perspective." Tōyama in recognizing the differences suggests that such a conference bears an important similarity with domestic meetings, the need to recognize that agreement is not always forthcoming and that one can learn from others. Dore's assessment of the conference indicates the arrogance of Western scholars. He attributed the differences to the cosmopolitan experiences and wealth of the Western scholars in comparison to the provincial Japanese. He writes, "American scholars can travel throughout the world with support of foundations, etc. and there are many who participate in the plans to support overseas economies. Japanese scholars are surrounded by a major impediment, that is, language and lack of resources, and with the exception of the natural sciences, the taint—of course not to the extent as Russia—of a provincialism (*shimaguni*) remains strong."[53]

These concluding paragraphs serve as a metaphor for activities that followed the Hakone conference. The Conference on Modern Japan continued, with carefully selected Japanese participants (or by omitting those who were critical of this version of modernization theory).[54] Meanwhile, in Japan—a long way from Bermuda and Puerto Rico—academia took up the challenge of modernization theory and had to confront a new issue. In 1962 the Asia and Ford Foundations proposed to use their considerable riches to invigorate the study of modern China, i.e., to make Japanese scholars less provincial. The plan to support the Tōyō Bunko—resources, graduate student fellowships, and institutional support—paralleled the Ford Foundation's support of area studies, especially of China, in American universities. But in Japan this proposal along with the Hakone conference awakened memories of those whose research was tied to Japan's imperialist policies in Asia. *Rekishigaku kenkyō* responded with special issues on modernization, Japan, and history in May 1961, on academic freedom and responsibilities in November 1962, and on the subjectivity and duty of historians in September 1963. In October and November 1963 *Shisō* published special issues on Weber and modernization theory. Tōyama, too, revised *sekaishi* taking area studies into consideration.[55]

Tōyama's "new" version of *sekaishi* highlighted the international aspect of Western capitalism by dividing history into the following categories: the age of ancient world empires; the age of the dissolution of ancient world empires; the age of formation of world markets of capitalism; the age of imperialism; and the collapse of imperialism. The purpose of this history was to conceive of a historical framework that corrected a bourgeois history that exoticized the Orient by placing the experience of peoples and countries into meaningful, autonomous positions within history.[56] He did not find the problem in the identification of bourgeois history with the West (to do so pretends that history as practiced today is universal). He acknowledges that the historical unification of the world took place at a particular moment in Western (he identifies Hegel) writings. But he criticizes the way that this history stratifies societies and areas into fixed categories. Tōyama argues instead that world history should be "a history of all nations (*minzoku*) as a structural composites that differ by developmental levels and social structure. That composite structure changes over time and one can establish autonomous temporal divisions of world history as an indicator of fundamental transformation of that structure."[57]

The strength of this proposal is in the centrality of processes and interactions as the central feature in the transformation of peoples. Categories and characteristics of time, region, or nation-state are temporal—that is, fluid. Tōyama recognizes the heterogeneity of different peoples, attempts to account for different temporalities, recognizes the separation between nation and nation-state, and does not shy away from the centralizing and homogenizing tendencies of modernity as well as its contradictions.

Tōyama's work is not a panacea, but he reminds us that history is both a discourse and a practice. He points us in a direction that will help us recover experience, the human that was written out of modernization theory in the name of objectivity. It is that area of which Michel de Certeau warns us, "we have to stay out of the virgin forest of History, a region of 'rich fuzziness' in which ideologies proliferate and where we will never find our way. Perhaps, too, by holding to the idea of discourse and to its fabrication, we can better apprehend the nature of the relations that it holds with its other, the real."[58] We would be well served to exhume an important body of writings that has been occulted beginning in the 1960s.

Notes

1 See for example, Carol Gluck, "The Past in the Present," in *Postwar Japan as History*, ed. Andrew Gordon (Berkeley: University of California Press, 1993), 64–95.

2 Ogura Yoshihiko, *Ware Ryūmon ni ari* (Tokyo: Rōkei shoten, 1974), 55.

3 Henri Lefebvre, *Critique of Everyday Life*, trans. John Moore (London: Verso, 1992), 146.

4 For a discussion on problematics of history, see Michel de Certeau, *The Writing of History*, trans. Tom Conley (New York: Columbia University Press, 1988).

5 United States Education Mission to Japan, *Report of the United States Education Mission to Japan* (Washington, D.C.: U.S. Government Printing Office, 1946), 15.

6 Tōyama Shigeki, *Sengo no rekishigaku to rekishi ishiki* (Tokyo: Iwanami shoten, 1968), 15.

7 Kimura Shigemitsu and Konno Hideharu, "Rekishi kyōiku to jidai kubun," *Nihonshi kenkyū* 400 (1995): 101–4.

8 Tokutake Toshio, *Kyōkasho no sengoshi* (Tokyo: Shin nihon shuppansha, 1995), 46.

9 For an overview of this period as well as other groups involved, see Gluck, "The Past in the Present." She refers to this group as the progressive historians. For an account of debates on subjectivity, see J. Victor Koschmann, *Revolution and Subjectivity in Postwar Japan* (Chicago: University of Chicago Press, 1996).

10 "Shihonsei seisan ni senkō suru shōkeitai," *Rekishigaku kenkyū* 129 (1947). Selected portions were translated into English in 1971; *The Grundrisse*, trans. David McLellan (New York: Harper, 1971).

11 Inoue Kiyoshi, "Sengo no rekiken no ayumi ni tsuite," *Rekishigaku kenkyū* 212 (1957): 50.

12 I have learned much from Kevin Doak's work on *minzoku*, which he translates as ethnic nationalism: "What Is a Nation and Who Belongs? National Narratives and the Ethnic Imagination in Twentieth-Century Japan," *American Historical Review* 102 (1997): 283–309; and "Ethnic Nationalism and Romanticism in Early Twentieth-Century Japan," *Journal of Japanese Studies* 22(1) (1996): 77–103.

13 See for example, Ōta Hidemichi for a criticism of the overly general categories, "Shisō to shite no sekaishizō," in *Minzoku no mondai*, ed. Rekishi kagaku kyōgikai (Tokyo: Azekura shobō, 1976), 261–87.

14 Reinhart Koselleck, *Futures Past: On the Semantics of Historical Time*, trans. Keith Tribe (Boston: MIT Press, 1985), 31.

15 Tōyama Shigeki, "Sekaishi ni okeru chiikishi no mondai," in *Minzoku no mondai*, ed. Rekishi kagaku kyōgikai (Tokyo: Azekura shobō, 1976), 250–51.

16 This version of progress drew from philosophers, such as Condorcet and Comte, and historians, such as Guizot. See for example Keith Michael Baker, *Condorcet: From Natural Philosophy to Social Mathematics* (Chicago: University of Chicago Press, 1975).

17 For analyses of the use of *minzoku* by these historians in the postwar period, see Doak, "What Is a Nation."

18 See Lefebvre, *Critique of Everyday Life*, 59.

19 Tōyama, "Sekaishi ni okeru chiikishi no mondai," 247.

20 Koselleck, *Futures Past*, xxiv.

21 Quoted in Doak, "What Is a Nation," 303–4.

22 See Henri Lefebvre, *The Production of Space*, trans. Donald Nicholson-Smith (Oxford: Blackwell, 1991), 95, for a discussion in this interaction between time and space.

23 Ibid., 247.

24 Tōyama Shigeki, "Sen kyuhyaku gojūsan nendo taikai no kekkan wa naze umareta ka?" in *Tōyama Shigeki chōsakushū*, vol. 9 (Tokyo: Iwanami shoten, 1992), 111–18.

25 Tōyama Shigeki, "Jidai kubunron," in *Nihon rekishi, bekkan I* (Tokyo: Iwanami kōza, 1963), 213.

26 Tōyama, "Sekaishi ni okeru chiikishi no mondai," and "Sen kyuhyaku gojūsan nendo taikai no kekkan wa naze umareta ka?"

27 Wada Sei and Yamanaka Kenji, *Sekaishi* (Tokyo: Nihon shoin, 1954), 1.

28 Ibid., 2.

29 Quoted from Ogura, *Ware Ryūmon ni ari*, 48–49.

30 Koselleck, *Futures Past*, 117.

31 According to Kimura and Konno, 1956 marked the beginning of a gradual erosion of this framework into a more nation-state-centered history. "Rekishi kyōiku to jidai kubun," 104–5.

32 See, for example, the comparison in Edwin Reischauer, *Japan Quarterly* 10 (July-Sept. 1963): 298–307.

33 For example, in a special issue devoted to modernization theory, Eguchi Bokurō stated that *sekaishi* is at a crossroads. "Sekaishi ni okeru 'kindaika' no mondaiten," *Shisō* 473 (1963): 1521.

34 Ōta Hidemichi, "Shisō to shite no sekaishizō," 271. See also Inoue Kiyoshi, " 'Kindaika' e no hitotsu no apurōchi," *Shisō* 473 (1963): 1455–63.

35 See John Whitney Hall, "Changing Conceptions of the Modernization of Japan," and Masao Maruyama, "Patterns of Individuation and the Case of Japan: A Conceptual Scheme," in the first volume of the Conference on Modern Japan, in *Changing Japanese Attitudes toward Modernization*, ed. Marius Jansen (Princeton: Princeton University Press, 1965). For a rather different account in Japanese see Kawashima Takeyoshi, "Kindai nihon no shakai kagakuteki kenkyū," *Shisō* 442 (1961): 483–88.

36 Essays by Tōyama and Dore were part of a series entitled "Kokusai kaigi no muzukashisa," *Mainichi shinbun*, 8 and 10 Sept. 1960; the individual titles were "Genjitsu to dentō wa chigau mo gakusha no kyōroku wa kanō" and "Mondai ishiki no sōi: sekaiteki na kenchi to minzokuteki na kenchi to"; and Reischauer, "Tōsai 'kangaekata' no kōkan," *Asahi shinbun*, 11 Sept. 1960.

37 I recognize that there were many differences among the American and Japanese "groups," yet all summaries concur that debate generally divided among these groups.

38 Tōyama mentions the limited understanding of the contextual and discursive meaning of words. "Kokusai kaigi no muzukashisa."

39 Memo, John W. Hall to Participants in the Hakone Conference on Modernization. A copy of preconference memos and preliminary papers are bound in the International House of Japan library.

40 Kawashima, "Kindai nihon no shakai kagakuteki kenkyō." For Hall's disappointment and dismissal, see his "Changing Conceptions of the Modernization of Japan," 26–28.

41 Hall, "Changing Conceptions of the Modernization of Japan," 11.

42 Robert Ward later explained that sometimes authoritarian and oligarchic rule is a necessary expedient to get to the ultimate end of a liberal government (i.e., democracy), a chilling reminder of Naitō Kōnan's metaphor of an irrigation ditch, arguing that sometimes violence is a necessary expedient to correct obstinate (and ignorant) obstacles. Robert E. Ward, "Epilogue," in *Political Development in Modern Japan*, ed. Robert E. Ward (Princeton: Princeton University Press, 1968), 588. For Naito's statement see his *Shinshinaron*, in *Naitō Kōnan zenshō*, vol. 5 (Tokyo: Chikuma shobō), 514.

43 Koselleck, *Futures Past*, xxiv.

44 Ibid., 14.

45 Reischauer, "Tōzai 'kangaekata.' "

46 Tōyama, "Kokusai kaigi no muzukashisa."

47 Hall, "Changing Conceptions of the Modernization of Japan," 38.

48 See above for his work in *sekaishi* which did attempt to address the multiple temporalities present in global change.

49 A similar elision seems to be occurring today, where the work of Harootunian and Najita seem to be overlooked in historiography of modern (not premodern) Japan. See Narita Ryuichi and a recent article in *Le Monde* (March 14, 1997), Pierre-François Souyri "Dynamisme de l'historiographie japonaise aux Etats-Unis."

50 For a critique of Marxist historiography that is limited to economics, see Kozo Yamamura.

51 He did not respond directly to Inoue's quite critical (and one should add much more sophisticated) comments on modernization theory in the following years.

52 Maruyama Masao, "Patterns of Individuation and the Case of Japan: A Conceptual Scheme," in *Changing Japanese Attitudes toward Modernization*, ed. Marius Jansen (Princeton: Princeton University Press, 1965), 490–91.

53 Ronarudo P. Dōa, "Kokusai kaigi no muzukashisa," *Mainichi shinbun*, 10 Sept. 1960.

54 The following meetings and their organizers were: Marius Jansen, January 1962, Bermuda; William W. Lockwood, June 1963, Colorado; Ronald P. Dore, January 1963, Bermuda; Robert E. Ward, January 1965, Bermuda; Donald H. Shively, January 1966, Puerto Rico; James W. Morley, January 1968, Puerto Rico. An "informal meeting" which today is called a workshop was held in January 1967 in Bermuda as a follow-up to the conference. This meeting led to the formation of the Joint Committee on Japanese Studies of the American Council for Learned Societies and the Social Science Research Council.

55 Tōyama, "Sekaishi ni okeru chiikishi no mondai."

56 Ibid., 251.

57 Ibid., 252.

58 de Certeau, *The Writing of History*, 21.

Theory, Area Studies, Cultural Studies: Issues of Pedagogy in Multiculturalism
Rey Chow

I would say that there is no future for literary studies as such in the United States. Increasingly, those students are being taken over by the astonishing garbage called "cultural criticism."—Harold Bloom, cited in Shulman 1994: 75

Unfortunately, the negative view toward cultural studies expressed by Harold Bloom is not unique to him. It is shared by many teachers of the humanities in North America, in particular the United States. What is perhaps peculiar about such openly negative sentiments toward cultural studies is that they often come from those who, during the 1960s and 1970s, were staunch promoters and defenders of what is called "theory," when theory itself was derogated and attacked by reactionary humanists as some metaphysical garbage that found its way from continental Europe to the higher education sectors of North American society.[1] Arguments against theory then sounded similar to the arguments against cultural studies today, not in the least by way of the charge that theory, by paying attention to the ideological assumptions that lie behind language, text, and discourse, was introducing issues that were, properly speaking, not about (the intrinsic qualities of) literature itself but instead about philosophy, sociology, and so forth. Twenty some years later, many of those who took pride in the race for theory are precisely the ones who back away from cultural studies. Why?

Genealogical Affinities between Theory and Cultural Studies

The brief history of cultural studies—its origins in the class-conscious analyses of popular culture in England, in particular the work undertaken at the Centre for Contemporary Cultural Studies at Birmingham; its subsequent migration to the United States and elsewhere, a migration that is accompanied by the concomitant forces of "French theory" and "Anglo-American" feminism; and its

many recurrent elements—has already been well elaborated by many of its practitioners.[2] As a literary and cultural theorist whose work straddles cultural studies and theory, what I would like to highlight in this first part of this essay is
hence not a recapitulation of that history but rather some of the prominent types
of analyses that have been developed in cultural studies in North America in the
past fifteen years or so. Four of these are especially worth mentioning because
of the tremendous impact they have in shaping discussions from multiple disciplines.

The first prominent type of analysis is the critique of Orientalism—of Western representations of non-Western cultures—that follows from Edward Said's
(1978) groundbreaking book. Even though Said's book has been under attack
from all kinds of directions since its first publication and even though many
refuse to acknowledge their indebtedness to it, the conceptual model of
Orientalism-critique has proven to be the kind of critical intervention with
which one cannot not come to terms. But if *Orientalism* alerts us to the pernicious effects of an ongoing ideological domination of the West by way of *culture and representation*, it does not exactly offer viable alternatives. Said's work
leaves us with an impasse in which the issue of a subordinated otherness and
with it, the other's right to participate in the representation of itself, has irrevo-
cably been raised, without being followed by any practicable notion of how such
representation could go beyond the parameters of Orientalism. Instead, because
the issue of otherness is delineated by Said on the premise of a racial dyad—
namely, the white West as opposed to the non-white non-West—his logic seems
to foreclose the possibility of the non-white non-West ever having its own "culture." Said's work begs the question as to how otherness—the voices, languages,
and cultures of those who have been and continue to be marginalized and silenced—could become a genuine oppositional force and a useable value.

In the context of an irreversibly demystified West and the uncertainties of
representation that follow from such demystification, the racial dyad of Said's
conceptual model requires a kind of supplementation that would juxtapose
other types of hierarchical discriminations with issues of racial injustice. It is in
such a context that Gayatri Chakravorty Spivak's (1988) essay "Can the Subaltern Speak?"[3] emerges as the second prominent type of analysis in cultural studies. While the issue of otherness remains for Said an issue of race, Spivak's essay astutely displaces the essentialism of purely racial considerations onto the
equally crucial considerations of class and gender. In Spivak's analysis, the female subaltern from an underprivileged "third world" nation—the composite
of gendered, class, and racial subordination—becomes the ultimate silent/si-
lenced bearer of the burdens of centuries of Western imperialist history. Because

for Spivak, "speech" and self-representation signify, by definition, access to the symbolic and to political power, her conclusion is a pessimistic one: the subaltern cannot speak. If the subaltern can speak, Spivak adds later in an interview, then she is not a subaltern any more.[4]

Between Spivak's radically unsentimental pronouncement, which devolves from the deconstruction of language as law (whose function is to prohibit rather than to enable), and the more humanistic idealism of those cultural critics who continue to assert that the subalterns have spoken, an enormous discursive dimension unfolds. This discursive dimension, which constitutes the third prominent type of analysis in cultural studies, is that of "minority discourse." As elaborated by critics such as Gilles Deleuze, Félix Guattari, David Lloyd, Abdul JanMohamed, and others,[5] theories of minority discourse share Spivak's criticism of Western ideological domination but not her conclusion. Because this difference amounts to the significant opening up of possibilities, whereby coming to terms with otherness means making attempts to seek and listen for the voices of the subordinated others, minority discourse has become arguably the most prevalent and most productive conceptual model in U.S. cultural studies. Unlike the absolute certainty of a negative conclusion such as "the subaltern cannot speak," "minority discourse" analyses offer hope: their recognition of subordination (as evidenced in the word "minority" as opposed to "majority" or "mainstream") is accompanied by a persistent belief in the possibilities of expression, articulation, and agency (as evidenced in the word "discourse"). In terms of its capacity for understanding cultural diversities as discursive practices, "minority discourse" is an eminently *enabling* conceptual model. Under its rubric, "otherness" finds a variety of infinitely expanding and changing expressions—as differences performed by way of class, gender, sexual preference, religion, and so forth. Articulated together, these multifarious minority discourses could potentially become an effective coalition against the domineering legacy of the white Protestant heterosexual man of property.

As soon as different minority discourses begin to mushroom, however, it becomes clear that "otherness," as the site of opposition, alternative subject formation, and alternative value, is hardly a unified essence. Otherness-as-diversity soon becomes recognized not only from outside the West, in the margins of mainstream representation, but from within the apparatuses of Western imperialist domination as well. The cultures of imperialism as much as the cultures of the West's others, the white Protestant heterosexual man of property as much as the subaltern, are now considered anew as so many different kinds of "hybrids"—as the work of Homi Bhabha, among others, suggests.[6]

Even though these four types of analyses—Orientalism-critique, investiga-

tions of subaltern identities, minority discourses, and culture-as-hybridity—
have generated a phenomenal variety of contents, what they demonstrate collec-
tively is cultural studies' close relation to "theory" in the poststructural sense.
To cite what is perhaps the most evident instance in that relation, an essay such
as Jacques Derrida's (1970) "Sign, Structure, and Play," which deconstructs the
metaphysics of the "center" as a kind of indispensable but ever-shifting function
in human signification, could now be seen as a document that maps out, in theoretical terms, the potentialities that arise with the displacement of the West as
the universal "center." Between the philosophical underpinnings of deconstruction's imperative to undo the West from within its own logocentric premises and
cultural studies' insistent orientation toward pluralism, the structural affinities
are more than obvious. One could go as far as arguing that cultural studies' chief
characteristic, summarized by Simon During (1993: 16) as the "affirmation of
otherness and negation of metadiscourse,"[7] is genealogically made possible and
necessary by the dislocation of the sign that inaugurated the "structuralist controversy"[8] of three decades ago. Cultural studies as we know it today would not
have been conceivable without the radical reformulations of language and discourse, of the relation between high and low culture, and of the relation between
representation and politics, that were enabled by poststructuralist theory. Even
at its most empirical, therefore, cultural studies contains within its articulations this fundamental *theoretical* understanding of the need to challenge the
center of hegemonic systems of thinking and writing.[9] And yet, if poststructuralist theory is, at least in the United States, in part what triggers the "new cultural politics of difference"[10] that has become such a global movement, why is it
that so many of those who raced toward "theory" are now among the harshest
critics of cultural studies and cultural criticism?

It seems to me that the answer to this question lies in cultural studies' status as, in effect, a kind of dangerous supplement to poststructuralist theory. For
all its fundamental epistemological subversiveness, the dislocation of the sign
as philosophized in the heyday of "high theory" could still be contained within
a more or less European tradition. One could, for instance, trace the work of
Derrida back to Lévi-Strauss, Saussure, Husserl, Heidegger, Nietzsche, and ultimately to Kant. This explains why, for nearly two decades in North America, an
act as avant-garde and as radical as dislocating the sign was paradoxically practiced in the most elitist educational institutions, such as Yale, Johns Hopkins,
and Cornell, where the followers of deconstruction enjoyed the best of both spiritual and material worlds, as mental radicals and as well-paid Ivy League professors. But that period was an Indian summer. The implications unleashed by the

dislocation of the sign were soon no longer confinable within Europe or within Ivy League institutions. Soon, what teachers and students felt needed to be dislocated included Europe and the Ivy League institutions themselves, and the culture and pedagogical disciplinarity they represented.

Moreover, the turn toward otherness that seems to *follow* from the theoretical dislocation of the sign is, strictly speaking, the very historicity that *precedes* the poststructuralist subversion: the supplementary look at Europe's others reveals anew the violence that was there, long before the appearance of "theory," in the European imperialism of the past few hundred years. This violence that is now disturbingly unleashed in academic institutions is thus a kind of retroactive replay, a re-membering of the history of racial and cultural imperialism that lies at the "foundations" of the theoretical dislocation of the sign.[11] Because this violence can no longer be safely contained within the folds of a purely European tradition, it also renders the (illusory) articulatory self-sufficiency of that tradition untenable. Cultural studies, by its dogged turns toward the other not only within language and text but also outside language and text, in effect forces poststructuralist theory to confront the significance of race—and with it the histories of racial discrimination and racial exploitation—that is repressed in poststructuralist theory's claim to subversiveness and radicalism. By so doing, *cultural studies challenges poststructuralist theory's own position as the "other" of Europe, as the "other" within the European tradition.* And this, I think, is cultural studies' most significant threat to the once avant-garde theorists who, like Bloom, must literally junk it.

Culture and Area Studies

Once racial difference is introduced into the picture, it is possible to argue that the study of what is called "culture," in particular the cultures of the non-West, is in fact not a novel event, at least not in North American universities. Since, after the Second World War, the United States has inherited Western Europe's former role as military-aggressor-and-cultural-imperialist-cum-savior around the world, the study of non-Western cultures has always been part of its universities' function as the support for United States foreign policy. Through "fieldwork," teaching in the classroom, and language training, social science disciplines such as anthropology, economics, and political science, and humanistic disciplines such as history, linguistics, and literature, have long participated in the massive information retrieval that constitutes the study of non-Western cultures under the establishment known in the U.S. as "area studies." In such study, what are continually being observed and analyzed by the mainstream practitioners of the various disciplines are not only monuments, documents, rituals, customs, practices, and narratives, but also the "peoples of color."[12]

Area studies, in other words, has long been producing "specialists" who report to North American political and civil arenas about "other" civilizations, "other" regimes, "other" ways of life, and so forth. To the extent that such "others" are now often also the objects of investigation for cultural studies, one could perhaps argue that cultural studies as a "new" discipline (or counterdiscipline) is merely a belated institutional form, a new name for certain well-established pedagogical practices. If, for area studies, the information target field is defined by way of particular geographical areas and nation states, such as South Asia, the Middle East, East Asia, Latin America, and countries of Africa, then for cultural studies, the information target field is something called "culture" or "ethnicity."

There is, however, a major difference: whereas the study of "culture" in the area studies establishment is frequently undertaken in the name of scientific objectivity, knowledge acquisition, cross-cultural understanding, and other such humanistic ideals which continue to belie the racist underpinnings of the establishment itself, cultural studies cannot similarly pretend that its tasks are innocent ones. However much the practitioners of cultural studies might subscribe to similar humanistic ideals, they are compelled by the theoretical premise of cultural studies—the affirmation of otherness and the negation of metadiscourse that are genealogically derived from or affined to poststructuralism—to acknowledge, if not directly address, the exploitative, asymmetrical relations inherent in the Western studies of non-Western cultures, relations that continue to be deemphasized if not altogether denied by many area studies specialists. Once these relations are acknowledged, the paths of inquiry taken by cultural studies toward its "objects" are bound to be different from those historically adopted in area studies. Meanwhile, because area studies and cultural studies do seem to overlap in terms of their objects, cultural studies, in order to demarcate its own pedagogical goals, must remain on the alert toward this persistent denial of racial inequities coming from area studies specialists. Otherwise, since such denial tends to reproduce and perpetuate itself, it could easily turn cultural studies into a reification of culture. This potential of cultural studies for turning against its own critical capacity is, I think, the foremost danger against which students of cultural studies must be repeatedly warned. To understand this point fully, we need, once again, to return to the relationship between cultural studies and theory, and show how this problem of (potential) culture-reification, too, is implicated in that relationship.

"Theory" against "Culture" — "Monolith" against "Pluralism"?

In spite of the disavowal of cultural studies' relation with theory, a disavowal that comes *both* from many of cultural studies' critics (who dislike cultural studies for being "untheoretical," "empiricist," and "garbage") and many of its supporters (who dislike "theory" for being "elitist," "abstract," and "universalist"), the mutual implications between theory and cultural studies are, as I mentioned in the foregoing pages, tenacious.[13] Accordingly, the position of those who feel they need to defend theory against cultural studies is a hypocritical one. When theory is upheld as some pristine, ultimate ideal that cannot be soiled by the "garbage of cultural criticism," or when multiculturalism is dismissed *en bloc* as a "cloud-cuckooland of egalitarianism and euphemism" (Gates, 1994: 73), the shape of the opposition to cultural studies inevitably resembles that of reactionary patriarchal attacks on feminized mass culture. In this instance, "theory" stands against "culture" as "mind" against "matter" or "masculinist" against "feminist," complete with all the repressive coercions typical of attempts to adhere to what has become historically defunct. However, even though such reactionary attacks on cultural studies are annoying, they are not, to my mind, its major problem. What is much more problematic is the disavowal of cultural studies' relation with theory that comes from the other direction— namely, the direction of those supporters of cultural studies who think that the study of "culture" means that there is no longer a need to engage with "theory."

At this point, my own experience as a teacher and writer provides some help in illustrating my arguments. As someone who is officially affiliated with the discipline of comparative literature and whose work has much to do with Asian cultures and literatures, my position contains within it major aspects which seem to contradict each other in the age of cultural studies: on the one hand, comparative literature is the hotbed of "theory" and the bastion of Eurocentric views of literature;[14] on the other, by virtue of the fact that I teach and write about the non-West, my work also unavoidably intersects with the "culture" study that is undertaken by the area studies establishment. Perhaps because of these two at times incompatible anchorings of my professional life, I tend to be more vigilant than some of my colleagues in either field against any kind of irresponsible dismissal of either "theory" or "culture," and more invested than most in pursuing the affinities between them. As a discipline, comparative literature is currently faced with a challenge both in terms of the form and content of its disciplinarity—form, because the question as to what kinds of comparative *relations* should be introduced and what kinds of media should be "compared" can no longer be taken for granted; content, because the kinds of literatures that need to be addressed have far exceeded the traditional Eurocentric parameters of the discipline.[15]

For those engaged in the study of comparative literature, then, this is a moment of opportunity, a moment when cultural studies has very interesting alternatives to offer in terms of the study of non-Western cultures and literatures, and of other kinds of media.[16] Instead of the traditional Eurocentric frameworks of the nation-state, national language, and geographical area that constitute area studies, cultural studies offers modes of inquiry that require students to pay attention to the cultural politics of knowledge production. Instead of reinforcing the kind of Orientalist methodology that is deeply entrenched in area studies, cultural studies would emphasize how the study of non-Western cultures as such cannot proceed as if modernity and tradition were simply a matter of "indigenous" continuity without taking into consideration the ideological consequences of Western imperialism or without addressing the asymmetrical relations between "master discourses" and "native informants."

On the other hand, precisely because of the obstinacy of the methods of area studies, this is also a moment of danger because the turn toward "other" cultures that is espoused in the name of cultural studies could easily be used to refuse and replace rather than strengthen the theoretical modes of inquiry that remain a valuable part of comparative literature. For instance, it is disturbing to hear a kind of claim that is now often made about the study of non-Western cultures in the age of multiculturalism: "Now we can go back to the study of indigenous cultures and forget all about 'Western theory'!" Even though this is a caricatural paraphrase, I believe it accurately sums up the sentiments that are involved in the *anti-theoretical clamor for cultural studies.* Let me be more specific about why such sentiments are problematic.

In the age of the general criticism of Western imperialism, the study of non-Western cultures easily assumes a kind of moral superiority, since such cultures are often also those that have been colonized and ideologically dominated by the West. For the same reason, "theory," for all its fundamental questioning of Western logocentrism, has easily but effectively been lumped together with everything "Western" and facilely rejected as a non-necessity. This is evident in the manner in which the following type of question, for all its illogicality, continues to be in vogue among some practitioners of Asian studies: "Why should we use Western theory to study Asian cultures?" In the climate of multiculturalism, such practitioners find in cultural studies' obligatory turns toward pluralism a kind of rhetorical justification that works to their own advantage—for what better "reason" is there for the rejection of "Western theory" than the widely advocated study of "other" cultures? In the name of studying the West's "others," then, the *critique* of cultural politics that is an inherent part of both poststructural theory and cultural studies is pushed aside, and "culture" returns to a coherent, idealist essence that is outside language and outside mediation.[17] Pursued in a morally complacent, anti-theoretical mode, "culture" now functions as a shield that hides the positivism, essentialism, and nativism—and with them the continual acts of hierarchization, subordination, and marginalization—that have persistently accompanied the pedagogical practices of area studies; "cultural studies" now becomes a means of legitimizing continual conceptual and methodological irresponsibility in the name of cultural otherness.

One prominent instance of such legitimation is the argument for returning to "indigenous" origins. As Spivak points out, the notion of a return to pure "indigenous theory" is not a viable one because of the history of imperialism: "I cannot understand what indigenous theory there might be that can ignore the reality of nineteenth-century history. As for syntheses: syntheses have more problems than answers to offer. To construct indigenous theories one must ignore the last few centuries of historical involvement. I would rather use what history has written for me" (Spivak, in Harasym 1990: 69).

To add to Spivak's point, it should be emphasized that the advocacy for a return to indigenous theory and culture usually masks, with the violence of "the West," the violence of the cultural politics that is *within* an indigenous culture.

Furthermore, the same untheoretical espousal of non-Western cultures leads some to think that cultural studies is something that can be conveniently localized and nationalized, and, by the same token, globalized and internationalized. We have, for instance, the new formula of "X cultural studies," with X being a nation, a place, or a particular group, the study of which is always simultaneously held to be "international" and "global" in its implications. If one of the major tasks of cultural studies is that of bringing the entire notion of "culture" into crisis rather than simply that of assembling different cultures for their mutual admiration, then a localizing and nationalizing strategy as such, which returns culture to the status of some origin, property, or set of attributes—such as "Chinese," "French," "American"—that everyone owns prior to language and discourse, would precisely put an end to the critical impetus of cultural studies. As Fazal Rizvi (1994: 60) puts it in a different context:

> while multiculturalism may be viewed as intrinsically oppositional in nature, all cultural practices are thought to be valid within their own terms.

These culturalist presuppositions support a rationalist pedagogy that is both ahistorical and depoliticised. Ahistorical because it treats culture as something fixed, finished or final and depoliticised because it obscures the inherently political character of pedagogical practices.[18]

It is only because the gestures toward localism and pluralism—the two are virtually synonymous in this context—are ultimately essentialist and positivistic that the study of culture could be imagined as a way of putting an end to "Western theory." Ironically, thus, a new rhetorical/pedagogical situation has arisen: at academic conferences and research gatherings as well as in print, very conservative practitioners of area studies can now safely endow their own retrograde positions with the glorious *multiculturalist* aura of defending non-Western traditions. Even those whose work has only to do with the most culturally chauvinistic, canonical issues and nothing to with gender, class, or race, are suddenly able to claim not only for their objects of study but also *for themselves* the subject position of an oppressed, marginalized minority simply because they are the so-called "specialists" of a non-Western culture; because they are, as they always have been, straightforward Orientalists! In the words of Spivak (1993: 279), such specialists of non-Western cultures in fact help legitimize the position of those to whom they think they are opposed:

> There is a lot of name-calling on both sides of the West-and-the-rest debate in the United States. In my estimation, although the politics of the only-the-West supporters is generally worth questioning, in effect the two sides legitimize each other. In a Foucauldian language, one could call them an opposition within the same discursive formation. The new culture studies must displace this opposition by keeping nation and globe distinct as it studies their relationship, and by taking a moratorium on cultural supremacy as an unquestioned springboard.

In sum, in contrast to the hostile critics who defend "theory" against cultural studies, the friendly supporters who applaud cultural studies on the moral high ground of recognizing diverse "contexts" and "histories" present a very different, and to my mind much more insidious, kind of problem. This time, we are confronted not with the forgetting of the racial origins of theory (and their multicultural implications) but rather with the reification of culture in the name of opposing "theory" and opposing reification. For those who see in cultural studies the critical potential for examining and transforming institutionalized intellectual disciplinarity itself, the necessity to mobilize against such foreclosures of that potential by many enthusiastic supporters of "curriculum-diversification" cannot be sufficiently emphasized. Otherwise, in the name precisely of sponsoring the "marginal," the study of non-Western cultures would simply contribute toward a new, or renewed, Orientalism:

> As this [marginal] material begins to be absorbed into the discipline, the long-established but supple, heterogeneous, and hierarchical power-lines of the institutional "dissemination of knowledge" continue to determine and overdetermine its conditions of representability. It is at the moment of infiltration or insertion, sufficiently under threat by the custodians of a fantasmatic high Western culture, that the greatest caution must be exercised. The price of success must not compromise the enterprise irreparably. In that spirit of caution, it might not be inappropriate to notice that, as teachers, we are now involved in the construction of a new object of investigation—"the third world," "the marginal"—for institutional validation and certification. One has only to analyze carefully the proliferating but exclusivist "Third World-ist" job descriptions to see the packaging at work. It is as if, in a certain way, we are becoming complicitous in the perpetuation of a "new orientalism." (Spivak 1993: 56)

Culture and Power

Beyond the institutional boundaries of theory, area studies, and cultural studies, the much larger question that is lurking behind multiculturalism remains, finally, that of the relation between culture and power, between representation and social equality.[19]

Multiculturalism is, in many ways, the result of the putative end of metanarratives, an end that Jean-François Lyotard (1984) calls the "postmodern condition." The apparent absence of metanarratives gives rise to the impression that every kind of expression, every kind of representation, and every kind of culture is as valid as others. This is one reason why the variety of objects that can be studied in cultural studies seems infinite and the criteria for judgment seem increasingly arbitrary. At the same time, if indeed multiculturalism is intent on promoting a liberalist politics of recognition, recognition is still largely a one-way street—in the form, for instance, of *white culture recognizing non-white cultures only.*[20]

For those groups on the side of non-white cultures, the problem presented by multiculturalism remains one of tactical negotiation. Negotiating a point of entry into the multicultural scene means nothing less than posing the question of rights—the right to representation and the right to culture. What this implies is much more than the mere fight (by a particular non-white culture) for its "free-dom of speech," because the very process of attaining "speech" here is inextrica-bly bound up with right; that is, with the processes through which particular kinds of "speeches" are legitimized in the first place. To put it in very sim-ple terms, a non-white culture, in order to "be" or to "speak," must: 1) seek le-gitimacy/recognition from white culture, which has denied the reality of the "other" cultures all along; 2) use the language of white culture (since it is the dominant one) to produce itself (so that it could be recognized and thus legiti-mized); and yet 3) resist complete normativization by white culture.[21]

If this example using racial inequality is but one among the many many kinds of tactical negotiations that inevitably take place in multiculturalism, then the issue of "culture" in cultural studies cannot in effect be divorced from the issue of power—of rights, laws, and justice. And unless such fundamental power relations are carefully articulated alongside the politics of recognition, the "equality" principle of multiculturalism would simply be exploited to cover up the perpetuation of certain kinds of power. As Rizvi (1994: 63) writes, a multi-culturalism that preaches a "harmonious multicultural society in which all cul-tural traditions can be maintained" is

> really about a politics of assimilation concerned with domesticating egali-tarian demands. By invoking the universalist ideal of a society governed by a set of social principles for a common humanity, in which we can all partic-ipate happily without reference to class, ethnicity, race or gender, multi-culturalism obscures the issues of power and privilege. A curriculum based on these assumptions can only deal with differences by making them mar-ginal; by being tokenistic.

For the practitioners of cultural studies to address these issues of power, a type of theoretical intervention that continues to critique the legitimating structures inherent in the production of knowledge is absolutely necessary, es-pecially at a time when everything seems equivalent and we could all happily return to our own "cultures," "ethnicities," and "origins." To put it in a different way, it is precisely at the time of multiculturalism, when "culture" seems to be liberalized in the absence of metanarratives, when "culture" seems to have be-come a matter of "entitlement" rather than struggle, that we need to reempha-size the questions of power and underscore at every point the institutional forces that account for the continual hierarchization of cultures. Instead of simply per-petuating what Spivak (1993: 284) terms the "revolutionary tourism" and "cele-bration of testimony"[22] that seem to characterize so much of what goes on under the name of cultural studies these days, it is the meticulous investigation of such legitimating structures of power that would, in the long run, give cultural studies its sustenance and integrity as a viable pedagogical practice.

In the classroom, this means that students should not be told simply to reject "metadiscourses" in the belief that by turning to the "other" cultures—by turning to "culture" as the "other" of metadiscourses—they would be able to overturn existing boundaries of knowledge production that, in fact, continue to define and dictate their own discourses. Questions of authority, and with them hegemony, representation, and right, can be dealt with adequately only if we insist on the careful analyses of texts, on responsibly engaged rather than facilely dismissive judgments, and on deconstructing the ideological assumptions in discourses of "opposition" and "resistance" as well as in discourses of mainstream power. Most of all, as a form of exercise in "cultural literacy," we need to continue to train our students to read—to read arguments on their own terms rather than discarding them perfunctorily and prematurely—not in order to find out about authors' original intent but in order to ask, Under what circumstances would such an argument—no matter how preposterous—make sense? With what assumptions does it produce meanings? In what ways and to what extent does it legitimize certain kinds of cultures while subordinating or outlawing others? Such are the questions of power and domination as they relate to the dissemination of knowledge. Old-fashioned questions of pedagogy as they are, they nonetheless demand frequent reiteration in the climate of cultural studies.

Notes

This essay was first published in *A Question of Discipline: Pedagogy, Power, and the Teaching of Cultural Studies*, edited by Joyce E. Canaan and Debbie Epstein (Boulder, Colo. and Oxford: Westview Press, 1997), 11–26. With slight modifications, it is reprinted here.

1   This is a point made by Gabriele Schwab in her presentation in the forum "Why 'Comparative Literature'?" at the University of California–Irvine, April 1994. For those who are less familiar with the controversies of "theory" in the United States, the term has been used generally to refer to the debates about language, signification, and discourse in literary and humanistic studies that began in the 1960s with the introduction of French poststructuralist thinkers such as Jacques Derrida, Jacques Lacan, Roland Barthes, and Michel Foucault into the English-speaking world. Over the decades, even though those who attack "theory" invariably speak from specific theoretical positions—in other words, even though there are no positions, not even antitheory ones, which are not implicitly theoretical—the term "theory" continues to be used more or less exclusively to refer to poststructuralist theory and deconstruction.

2   See, for instance, the introductions in Grossberg, Nelson, and Treichler (1992), and During (1993). See also the historical and critical accounts in Inglis (1993), which discusses, in addition to the British background, the significance of certain continental European thinkers for the conception of cultural studies.

3   See my discussion of Spivak's essay in the chapter "Where Have All the Natives Gone?" in Chow (1993a: 27–54).

4   Again, see my discussion of Spivak's essay, in particular of the problem of *naming* (the subaltern) in postcolonial cultural politics in the chapter "Against the Lures of Diaspora" in Chow (1993a: 99–119) and in Chow (1993b).

5   See Deleuze and Guattari (1986), Lloyd and JanMohamed (1990). The latter was originally published as *Cultural Critique* 7 and 8 (1987–88).

6   For Bhabha's most influential essays, see those collected in Bhabha (1993). I am, as I have indicated elsewhere, skeptical of the larger implications of Bhabha's formulations of hybridity; see my discussion in "Where Have All the Natives Gone?" in Chow (1993a).

7   Similarly, Grossberg, Nelson, and Treichler (1992: 6) write that "cultural studies offers a bridge between theory and material culture."

8   See the essays in Macksey and Donato (1970).

9   I should emphasize here that my argument *for* the theoretical significance of cultural studies is made from the perspective of those working in the United States. Ironically, to those who work outside the United States, American cultural studies can appear to be—contrary to the charge that it is too empirical—already too theoretical. Stuart Hall, for instance, attributes to American cultural studies what he calls "theoretical fluency," by which he means that cultural studies tends to be so institutionalized in the United States that it runs the risk of constituting power and politics as exclusively textual and discursive matters. See Hall (1992: 286).

10 See West (1993: 203–17). This is a version of an essay that appears in Ferguson et al. (1990).

11 I will cite here merely a handful of the many important works that have been done to delineate the workings of this violence: Hulme (1986); Retamar (1989); Viswanathan (1989); Suleri (1992); Pratt (1992); Sharpe (1993).

12 For a related discussion, see the chapter "The Politics and Pedagogy of Asian Literatures in American Universities" in Chow (1993a: 120–43).

13 See also Chow (1994).

14 For a detailed argument about the Eurocentrism of comparative literature, see the discussion of the modern novel in Said (1994).

15 For a set of responses from comparative literature teachers to the challenge posed by cultural studies, see the essays in Bernheimer (1994).

16 See my discussion in Chow (1994).

17 This is what Charles Bernheimer (1994: 9) means when he writes: "On the face of things, it would appear that multiculturalism, inherently pluralistic, would have a natural propensity toward comparison. But this propensity has been checked by the mimetic imperatives of an essentialist politics." Bernheimer's word "comparison" could easily be substituted with the word "theory."

18 This essay offers a succinct argument about the contradictions inherent in multicul-
    turalism.
19 See for instance the discussion of this point in Bennett (1992).
20 This is a point made by Rizvi (1995).
21 I am indebted to Judith Butler for my formulation of the problem here. For a related
    discussion, see West (1993), in particular the section "The Existential Challenge"
    (214–16), in which he describes the options available to people of color who are inter-
    ested in representation.
22 Spivak is referring specifically to certain practices of "transnational feminism."

References

Bennett, T. 1992. "Putting Policy into Cultural Studies." In Grossberg, Nelson, and
    Treichler, 23–37.
Bernheimer, C., ed. 1994. *Comparative Literature in the Age of Multiculturalism.* Balti-
    more and London: Johns Hopkins University Press.
Bhabha, H. 1993. *The Location of Culture.* New York and London: Routledge.
Chow, R. 1993a. *Writing Diaspora: Tactics of Intervention in Contemporary Cultural
    Studies.* Bloomington: Indiana University Press.
——. 1993b. "Ethics after Idealism." *diacritics* 23(1) (spring 1993): 3–22.
——. 1994. "In the Name of Comparative Literature." In Bernheimer, 107–16.
Cultural Critique. 1987. Volume 7.
Cultural Critique. 1988. Volume 8.
Deleuze, G., and F. Guattari. 1986. *Kafka: Toward a Minor Literature,* trans. R. Bens-
    maïa. Minneapolis: University of Minnesota Press.
Derrida, J. 1970. "Structure, Sign, and Play in the Discourse of the Human Sciences." In
    Macksey and Donato, 247–72.
During, S., ed. 1993. *The Cultural Studies Reader.* New York and London: Routledge.
Ferguson, R., et al., eds. 1990. *Out There: Marginalization and Contemporary Cultures.*
    New York: New Museum of Contemporary Art; Cambridge Mass.: MIT Press.
Gates, D. 1994. "It's Naughty! Haughty! It's Anti-Multi-Culti!" *Newsweek* (10 October):
    73–75.
Grossberg, L., C. Nelson, and P. Treichler, eds. 1992. *Cultural Studies.* New York and Lon-
    don: Routledge.
Gunew, S., and F. Rizvi, eds. 1994. *Culture, Difference and the Arts.* St. Leonards, Austra-
    lia: Allen and Unwin.
Hall, S. 1992. "Cultural Studies and Its Theoretical Legacies." In Grossberg, Nelson, and
    Treichler, 277–94.
Harasym, S., ed. 1990. *The Post-Colonial Critic: Interviews, Strategies, Dialogues.* New
    York and London: Routledge.
Hulme, P. 1986. *Colonial Encounters: Europe and the Native Caribbean, 1492–1797.* Lon-
    don and New York: Routledge.
Inglis, F. 1993. *Cultural Studies.* Oxford and Cambridge, Mass.: Blackwell.
Lloyd, D., and A. JanMohamed, eds. 1990. *The Nature and Context of Minority Dis-
    course.* New York: Oxford University Press.

Lyotard, J.-F. 1984. *The Postcolonial Condition: A Report on Knowledge,* trans. G. Bennington and B. Massumi. Minneapolis: University of Minnesota Press.

Macksey, R., and E. Donato, eds. 1970. *The Structuralist Controversy: The Languages of Criticism and the Sciences of Man.* Baltimore and London: Johns Hopkins University Press.

Nelson, C., and L. Grossberg, eds. 1988. *Marxism and the Interpretations of Culture.* Urbana: University of Illinois Press.

Pratt, M. L. 1992. *Imperial Eyes: Travel Writing and Transculturalism.* New York and London: Routledge.

Retamar, R. F. 1989. *Caliban and Other Essays,* trans. E. Baker. Minneapolis: University of Minnesota Press.

Rizvi, F. 1994. "The Arts, Education and the Politics of Multiculturalism." In Gunew and Rizvi, 54–68.

——. 1995. "Trajectories of Racism and Australian Multiculturalism." Paper presented at the Conference on Multicultural Critical Theory: Between Race and Ethnicity, University of Victoria, Canada, January.

Said, E. 1978. *Orientalism.* New York: Random House.

——. 1994. *Culture and Imperialism.* New York: Vintage.

Sharpe, J. 1993. *Allegories of Empire: The Figure of Woman in the Colonial Text.* Minneapolis: University of Minnesota Press.

Shulman, K. 1994. "Bloom and Doom" (an interview with Harold Bloom). *Newsweek* (10 October): 75.

Spivak, G. C. 1988. "Can the Subaltern Speak?" In Nelson and Grossberg, 271–313.

——. 1993. *Outside in the Teaching Machine.* New York and London: Routledge.

Suleri, S. 1992. *The Rhetoric of English India.* Chicago: University of Chicago Press.

Viswanathan, G. 1989. *Masks of Conquest: Literary Study and British Rule in India.* New York: Columbia University Press.

West, C. 1993. "The New Cultural Politics of Difference." In During, 203–17.

Signs of Our Times: A Discussion of
Homi Bhabha's *The Location of Culture*
Benita Parry

Prefatory Note: September 1999

Times have changed since this essay was written in 1994. The vigor and volume
of work advancing Marxist/Marxisant positions within postcolonial studies is
now so evident that rebuttal of a thesis assuming the intellectual defeat of the
left may no longer appear so urgent. Moreover, the prestige of "reconciliatory
postcolonial thought," described by a skeptical critic as fusing "postcolonialism
with postmodernism in [its] rejection of resistance along with any form of binar-
ism, hierarchy, or telos,"[1] has now been undermined by practitioners of historical materialist analysis. With the return of capitalism, social division and class
struggle to the discussion of colonialism and contemporary globalism, the axi-
omatically governed readings of the colonial archive directed at re-presenting
colonialism as the site of negotiation emerge as textual idealism, while the celebration of a liberated postcolonial condition appears as mindlessly idealistic.

Despite these changes in the intellectual climate, republication of the piece
seemed to me justified because books and essays reiterating Bhabha's notions
without examination of their premises continue to appear, while students routinely reproduce his pronouncements in manifest ignorance of their theoretical
context and ideological implications. I have made a few alterations in presentation, while leaving intact the substance and structure of the argument advanced
in the original essay.

Bhabha's essays,[2] written over more than a decade and in circulation for some
time before their collection as a volume in 1994, are a strong articulation of the
linguistic turn in cultural studies. The book, which is distinguished by Bhabha's
insistence on the absolute primacy of discourse, appeared at a time when there
were already signs of a challenge to critical modes predicated on the autonomy

of signifying processes and privileging the means of representation as the sole progenitor of meaning. One symptom of this move away from a practice that had been ascendant for some years, although never uncontested, was the growth of interest in Pierre Bourdieu's work on cultural production, where the textual idealism of transferring the Saussurean language model to social and literary analyses is repudiated.[3] Another was Christopher Norris's censure of "facile textualist thought" that "contrives to block the appeal to any kind of real-world knowledge or experience," a criticism made on ethical as well as cognitive grounds by one who has been a prominent exponent of deconstruction.[4] There was also reason to anticipate a more widespread and closer attention to Marxist/ Marxisant theories of culture and history, since, as any competent clairvoyant could have foretold, Derrida's lectures and writings on Marx,[5] were destined to persuade susceptible epigone that their preparations for the burial of an explanatory system they had declared moribund, too often without observing the protocols of scrupulous examination, should at least be deferred.

As regards Bhabha's stipulations of what constitutes "*the* colonial condition" and "*the* postcolonial experience/ perspective/critique" (emphasis added to suggest a totalizing tendency that Bhabha would ordinarily eschew), these have been disputed in discussions that follow other theoretical procedures and are producing different objects of knowledge from the same archival material.[6] Thus when Bhabha buoyantly claims that "a shift within contemporary critical traditions of postcolonial writing" (241) is heralded by the methodologies that he and like-minded critics have devised, this prediction of a new and unassailable hegemony—whose preeminence could already be in the past tense—depends on disregarding alternatives to the methods he espouses; and indeed it is noticeable that while Bhabha militantly combats a putative "left orthodoxy," he gives scant attention to the often searching questions that have been asked of his own work.[7]

Bhabha's evident scorn for his left detractors makes it all the more imperative for his critics to venture an assessment of his confident, ambitious, and influential theoretical program. This seeks to examine the translation of Western discourses from the disjunctive and displacing sites of "postcolonial" perspectives that, Bhabha maintains, provide a form of writing cultural difference that is inimical to binary boundaries, and effects the relocation of Western modernity (251). Such an undertaking may appear to have affinities with Edward Said's "contrapuntal" readings of the colonial archives, which in mapping the overlapping territories and intertwined histories of metropolis and colony, and noting the mixtures of cultures and identities on a global scale consolidated by imperialism, claim to restore to the history of modernism "the massive infusions of non-European cultures into the metropolitan heartland."[8] It also seems to resemble Paul Gilroy's contention that the doubleness of the black experiences in the West constitutes the counterculture of modernity.[9]

Bhabha's work however, preoccupied as it is with the generation of meaning within textual forms and functions, is situated within other theoretical spaces and manifests an agenda and trajectory that sets it apart from the writings of theorists such as Fanon, Ranajit Guha, Said, and Fredric Jameson whom he generously attempts to enlist as allies in his own project. The substance of this assignment, which is signaled by Bhabha's well-known "taste for in-between states and moments of hybridity" (208) and exceeds a concern to make known a postcolonial condition of displacement and diaspora, or to narrate a postcolonial transgression of boundaries, is amply evident in his usage of paradoxical and open-ended words: ambivalent, borderline, boundary, contingent, dispersal, disjunction, dissemination, discontinuity, hybridity, in-between, incommensurable, indeterminate, interstitial, liminal, marginal, negotiation, transitional, translational, and uncertain. This preference for terms that condense the play of difference, the instabilities of enunications or the elements of undecidability within any system of communication, registers Bhabha's affiliation with a critical practice that undertakes to reveal how the uncertainties of textual meaning are produced/undermined as permutations on a chain of signification. It also denotes an adherence to Foucault's recommendation that difference be freed from an oppositional and negative system, to operate as "thought without contradiction, without dialectics, without negation"[10]—a stance that brings to mind Fredric Jameson's remark that at stake in such moves "is the rolling back of Hegel and Marx by way of a conceptual discrediting of contradiction and dialectical opposition."[11]

The implications of rewriting a historical project of invasion, expropriation, and exploitation in the indeterminate and always deferred terms Bhabha proposes and implements, are immense, and for me immensely troubling, since his elaborations dispense with the notion of conflict—a concept that certainly does infer antagonism, but contra Bhabha, does not posit a simplistically unitary and closed structure to the adversarial forces. But before I embark on the discussion of Bhabha's work, a word of self-exculpation is necessary: the matter of his wayward style is not one on which I will dwell, other than to observe that an enchantment with troping, punning, and riddling all too often sends the signifier into free-fall, rendering arbitrary the link between word and signified. To mean what you say is not the same as to say what you mean, and because for this reader Bhabha's unruly and indeed obfuscatory prose presents the hazard of inadvertent misconstruction, I have taken the precaution of illustrating my gloss with extensive citations from his writing.[12]

Given the difficulty of exegesis replete with the specialized terminology of linguistic and psychoanalytic theory, its density thickened by improbable juxtapositions and innumerable, fleeting allusions to the incommensurable comments of critics, thinkers, and writers, it may seem remarkable that Bhabha's writing has been so readily and widely redeployed by others working in cognate areas. The extent of his influence suggests the importance of Bhabha's rethinking culture "as an uneven, incomplete production of meaning and value" (172), his insights into the hierarchy retained by the liberal ethic of multiculturalism, his attention to the differential historicities of races, nations, and peoples, his innovative work on the inflections of colonialism within Western thought, and his contributions to opening up the categories of identity, culture, and nation to their heterogeneity. However it is also apparent that when critics cite his key concepts in order to authorize their own propositions, they do so without necessarily indicating a grasp of, or interest in, the problematics within which Bhabha is writing. I will therefore attempt to discuss his work as generated by multiple determinations in the form of both theoretical modes and social location. In doing so I must declare that while appreciative of the ground Bhabha has broken in asking new questions of old problems, I am uneasy about his disposal of the language model to explain both colonialism's pasts and contemporary "postcolonial" situations; and what I will be proposing is that Bhabha's many fecund insights into cultural processes are paradoxically denatured by the theoretical modes that inform his work.

In Bhabha's usage "postcolonialism" does not indicate "sequentiality," its gestures to a "beyond" denoting a disjunctive relationship with that anterior condition by which it is indelibly marked, and which, it is claimed, enables a critique displacing the language and precepts of both colonialist and anticolonialist writing. As is now well-known, the problems with the connotations of "postcolonialism" are legion: Anne McClintock contends that its *singularity* "effects a re-centering of global history around the single rubric of European time . . . reduces the cultures of peoples beyond colonialism to *prepositional* time . . . [and] signals a reluctance to surrender the privilege of seeing the world in terms of a singular and ahistorical abstraction." Drawing attention to its "depoliticizing implications," Ella Shohat has observed that by alluding to colonialism as "a matter of the past," the term shuts out "colonialism's economic, political, and cultural deformative traces in the present." For Laura Chrisman, who observes its metropolitan coinage, " 'postcolonial' . . . occludes or erases the overtly political dynamics contained in the term "anti-colonial,' " allowing or implying "the interchangeability of material . . . with aesthetic and interpretative processes," and liberating those practitioners naming themselves postcolonial "from the messy business of political alignment and definition."[13]

Both Masao Miyoshi and Arif Dirlik find that the deployment of the postcolonial serves as a license for ignoring the contemporary actuality of global politics within a capitalist world-system. Miyoshi views its use as a device to conceal the operation of a continuing and even more active colonialism by transnational corporatism: "Ours is not an age of *post*colonialism but of intensified colonialism, even though it is under an unfamiliar guise" ("A Borderless World?" 728, 750); while for Dirlik, the word "mystifies both politically and methodologically a situation that represents not the abolition but the reconfiguration of earlier forms of domination" ("The Postcolonial Aura," 331). Furthermore, Dirlik maintains, those forms of postcolonial criticism that repudiate all master narratives and disclaim foundational historical writing, must also reject capitalism as a determinant category, and with it the capitalist constitution of the world, thus occluding the changing structural position within this system of the "Third World"—which he insists is not an essentialist but a relational category. As against Gyan Prakash who contends that we cannot thematize colonial history in terms of development of capitalism, since this would entail accepting the homogenization of the contemporary world by capitalism,[14] Dirlik argues that while no stark dichotomy of economic and social form between First and Third Worlds can now be asserted,[15] the globalism of capitalism effects the *uneven* insertion of heterogeneous and discrepant histories and *differential* economic formations into a world system.[16]

The implications of the above strictures are far-reaching for a project that privileges postcoloniality not only as the position from which to deconstruct colonialism's past legitimizing strategies, but also as the unproblematic location of contemporary globalized intellectual and cultural discourses. As if heedful that "a postcolonial critique" in welcoming the arrival of a "transnational" culture could seem to ignore the world-wide material conditions of division and exploitation inhibiting its realization, Bhabha notes the "conflictual, contradictory locutions of those cultural practices and products that follow the "unequal development" of the tracks of international or multinational capital" (241). It is true that Bhabha understands postcoloniality to be "a salutary reminder of the persistent "neo-colonial" relations within the "new" world order and the multinational division of labor; moreover, he goes on to suggest that "such a perspective enables the authentication of histories of exploitation and the evolution of strategies of resistance" (6). All the same, these allusions to a concern with the material conditions, institutions, and practices of colonialism and the neocolonial are not pursued in his efforts to derive social explanation from enunciative modalities, or the "activity of articulation as embodied in the language metaphor" (177).

Bhabha's agenda is starkly evident in his rewriting of "radical maroonage"; that is, the guerrilla wars waged by runaway slaves against their erstwhile masters.[17] Here a practice involving tactics and maneuvers designed and conducted by subjects-as-agents on contested territory, repeated and embellished in folk memory as cherished stories of downtrodden ancestors moved to resistance, and rewritten by contemporary critics recuperating signs of enacted disobedience, is translated into a set of discursive moves: "From this liminal, minority position where, as Foucault would say, the relations of discourse are of the nature of warfare, the force of the people of an Afro-American nation emerge in the extended metaphor of maroonage. For "warriors" read writers or even "signs" (145). As I read Bhabha's revision, an endlessly reworked narrative that renders the experiential realities of slave resistance intelligible is overwhelmed by the nominalism of the language metaphor, and in the interests of establishing the autarchy of the signifier, the narrated event is existentially diminished.

This demur does not entail questioning the linguistic turn in all its possible registers; indeed it is now surely impossible to conceive of cultural or historical analyses working within a realist paradigm that do not address the tropological ruses and effects of their archival sources; are unaware that systems of meanings are animated and borne by signs, metaphors, and narratives; or are indifferent to the constitutive role of these in articulating social relationships. In its "weak" form, which does not of course imply weak theory, this disposal of the language model actively reads texts against the grain, alert to silences, gaps, disjunctions, aporia. Recognizing that all language is figurative, such commentaries are attentive to the rhetorical strategies and effects of enunciations, which in the process of naturalizing prevailing precepts and categories in order to create their objects of knowledge, displace meaning and escape or exceed self-conscious intentionality—thus marking the disjunction between program and performance, between aspiration and actualization. Among the many instances of this mode, Bhabha's deconstructions of the fissures and ruptures in colonial texts are exercises of great subtlety, seeming to share with other studies a recognition of the *instrumentality* of colonialism's utterances.[18]

The elaboration of Bhabha's project has, however, taken quite other directions, and because his work is situated within that theoretical mode that rather than conceiving language as signifying reality, allots ontological priority to the semiotic process, the generation of meaning is located in the enunciative act, and not in the substance of the narrated event:

The erasure of content in the invisible but insistent structure of linguistic difference does not lead us to some general, formal acknowledgement of the function of the sign. The ill-fitting robe of language alienates content in the sense that it deprives it of an immediate access to a stable or holistic reference "outside" itself. It suggests that social signification's are themselves being constituted in the very act of enunciation, in the disjunctive, non-equivalent split of *énoncé* and *enunciation*, thereby undermining the division of social meaning into an inside and an outside. (64)[19]

Arif Dirlik, who is Bhabha's most disobliging critic, has charged him with "a reduction of social and political problems to psychological ones, and of substituting poststructuralist linguistic manipulation for historical and social explanation" ("The Postcolonial Aura," 333 n.6). Bhabha's claim of course is that his theorizing is providing *different* explanations derived from the premise that social agency is performed, and is therefore recuperable, at the level of enunciation; and since the testimony of history is invested in the *mode* of its writing, "the social specificity" of the "productions of meaning" is hence understood as the circulation of "signs within specific contextual locations and social systems of value" (172). All the same, Bhabha's procedures subordinate the cognition and explication of social forms, institutions, and practices, which are ultimately dependent on empirical inquiry, to deconstructions of the signifying process, while the structure of linguistic difference and the vicissitudes in the movement of the signifier are invested with the power to alienate and overwhelm content. These moves register Bhabha's affiliation with the language model in its "strong" form, one that surpasses a statement of "the obvious, that there is no knowledge—political or otherwise—outside representation" (23).[20]

Rather than positing the capacity of theories to constitute multiple understandings of reality, and which in turn inform diverse plans for human action, Bhabha's methodology renders this reality dependent on the knowledge produced by critical discourse. Thus although he wittily warns that "the rule of empire must not be allegorized in the misrule of writing," what he offers us is the World according to the Word: "Our task remains . . . to show how historical agency is transformed through the signifying process" (12); "history is *happening*—within the pages of theory, within the system and structures we construct to figure the passage of the historical" (25); "It is the horizon of holism, towards which colonial authority aspires, that is made ambivalent in the colonial signifier" (128); "The people are not simply historical events or parts of a patriotic body politic. They are also a complex rhetorical strategy of social reference" (145).

The distinction Bhabha makes between the "pedagogical" and the "performative" in "writing the nation" could appear to indicate the disjunction between a discursive construct and historical practice, since he notes that the "performative" interrupts to confront us "with the nation split within itself, marked by difference and articulating the heterogeneity of its population" (148)—from which observations few would dissent. But the machinery of his argument is geared to other ends, which is to warn against "the intellectual appropriation of 'the culture of the people' (whatever that may be) within a representational discourse that may become fixed and reified in the annals of History" (152):

> Such a pluralism of the national sign, where difference returns as the same, is contested by the signifier's "loss of identity" that inscribes the narrative of the people in the ambivalent "double" writing of the performative and the pedagogical. . . . The nation's totality is confronted with, and crossed by, a supplementary movement of writing . . . the heterogeneous structure of Derridean supplementarity in *writing* closely follows the agonistic, ambivalent movement between the pedagogical and the performative that informs the nation's narrative address. (154)

When language is taken as a paradigm of all meaning-creating or signifying systems,[21] and human practice is consequently perceived as mimicking Writing, the definitive disparities between construing the structure of language and explaining the forms of social and cultural practice are collapsed, the inference being that these latter also operate as a hermetic encoding of discursive differentials within a regime of phrases, and also follow the agonistic and ambivalent movement of writing.[22] Unless I have misconstrued the course and consequences of Bhabha's argument, let me cite the gloss of Gyan Prakash, who offers Bhabha's work as exemplifying an exemplary postcolonial critique. According to Prakash, Bhabha's understanding of how "colonial discourses operated as a structure of *writing*," and were therefore ambivalent, enables him to reveal that "the structure of their enunciation remained heterogeneous with the binary oppositions . . . colonialism instituted in ordering the discursive field to serve unequal power relations." From this premise, Prakash continues, the critic can deduce that "the implacable logic of oppositionality" in colonialist thought, whose aim was "to suppress the other as different and inferior," is always and necessarily disrupted, since writing produces a structure of differences and disjunctive meanings that veers away from the given order of priorities, breaking down the violent hierarchy which the discourse installs. Cognition of this immanent movement in writing, according to Prakash, then enables a contemporary critical practice to mark the interstitial space *opened*—note, not registered—by the text, and thus to provide different accounts of how colonialism operated ("Postcolonial Criticism and Indian Historiography," 16, 17).

Prakash's commentary seems to me true to the deductive process pursued by Bhabha. In "the specific 'interruption,' or the interstices through which the colonial text utters its interrogations, its contrapuntal critiques" (174) in the enunciative equivocations displacing the axes of power, Bhabha discerns the spontaneous generation of an auto-critique that disables colonialism's will to power. For, he contends, since the act of colonial enunciation as a text of power is doubly inscribed, split between historicity and fantasy (108), and afflicted by uncertainty (113), the ambivalence of its address is a threat "to the authority of colonial command" (97). Thus "the effect of colonial power" can be seen as "the production of hybridization rather than the noisy command of colonialist authority or the silent repression of native traditions" (112). What Bhabha appears to infer from textual indeterminacies is colonialism as a political event in which the *exercise* of authority was rendered uncertain, or as Prakash's gloss has it, where "the *functioning* of colonial power" was disjunct from its founding oppositions (17). If by this is meant that discursive instabilities acted to inhibit colonialism's drive to mastery, undermined its programs of domination and endangered its magistracy—a claim that is different from the proposition that discursive equivocations *registered* colonialist doubts and unease—then it is an astonishing assertion which contradicts countless narratives of the dispossessions the West visited on other worlds, is at variance with the audible violence in its many colonialist utterances, and is perversely indifferent to explaining the success and longevity of colonialism.

"The reason a cultural text or system of meaning cannot be sufficient unto itself is that the act of cultural enunciation—the place of utterance—is crossed by the *différance* of writing" (*Location of Culture*, 36). A reader concerned with the inner coherence of Bhabha's thesis would observe that since the ambiguities of discourse are attributed to the semiotic process, then this is a sufficient condition for *all* inscriptions to be *always* fractured and equivocal,[23] no input of social tension and contradiction being required to render enunciation indeterminate. Yet it is around the doubleness of colonialist inscription and its contradictory belief—that is, around an uncertain writing produced under *specific* conditions —that Bhabha has produced important insights into "the anomalous discourse of colonial governmentality" where the civil state is continually put under erasure (97). Moreover if, as Bhabha contends, enunciation as such is rendered discontinuous by an inner dissonance at the core of its own utterance, then this would seem to threaten his thesis on the *particular* circumstances producing what he calls "a colonial contramodernity at work in the matrices of Western modernity":

> My growing conviction has been that the encounters and negotiations of differential meanings and values within "colonial" textuality, its governmental discourses and cultural practices, have anticipated *avant la lettre*, many of the problematics of signification and judgement that have become current in contemporary theory—aporia, ambivalence, indeterminacy, the question of discursive closure, the threat to agency, the status of intentionality, the challenge to "totalizing" concepts. (173)

My interest, however, is in a theoretical reconstruction which in adhering to the rules of the language model, rewrites, or rather writes over, the inscriptions of conflict within the real world. This is effected by using "a language of critique" that "overcomes the given grounds of opposition and opens up a space of translation . . . conceiving of the time of political action and understanding as opening up a space that can accept and regulate the differential structure of the moment of intervention, without rushing to produce a unity of the social antagonisms or contradiction" (25).

By subsuming social realities to textual representation, Bhabha represents colonialism as transactional rather than conflictual—a version that should be distinguished from the study of how the colonized *negotiated* colonialism, and which has been investigated by Bhabha in essays on "mimicry" and "sly civility," where the "native's refusal to satisfy colonial command" (99) is revealed in the interstices of the colonial texts. It is also distinct from the recognition that the exercise of power is heterogeneous and never total, that subordinate groups cannot be wholly subordinated, that equivocal exchanges between ruler and ruled do occur, that collaborators always emerge to play a mediatory (often treacherous) role, and that domination and resistance are hostile interlocutors.

The partial qualification Bhabha makes in conceding the legitimacy of using the language of political economy "to represent the relations of exploitation and domination in the *discursive* division between the First and the Third World, the North and the South" (20; emphasis added) is eroded by the iteration of "the ambivalence of the presence of authority, particularly visible in its colonial articulation" (110). For Bhabha's concern is with establishing that the hierarchical division set in place by colonial discourse was unsustainable *because* the loci of inscription, or the dynamics of writing, always display a "difference" within the signification—a contention distinct from the proposition that colonial discourse *inscribed* the continual transgression of boundaries between colonizer and colonized, the assumption here being that the text *signifies* such traffic.

Integral to Bhabha's revisionist work on colonialism is a concern to effect the "break-up of a binary sense of political antagonism" (206), thereby displacing the received perception of dichotomies in conflict, with the "in-between" space of negotiation:

> As a mode of analysis [the postcolonial perspective] attempts to revise those nationalist or "nativist" pedagogies that set up the relation of Third World and First World in a binary structure of opposition. The postcolonial perspective resists the attempts at holistic forms of social explanation. It forces a recognition of the more complex cultural and political boundaries that exist on the very cusp of these often opposed political spheres. . . .
>
> The contour of difference is agonistic, shifting, splitting, rather like Freud's description of the system of consciousness which occupies a position in space lying on the borderline between outside and inside. . . .
>
> The contingent and the liminal become the times and the spaces for the historical representation of the subjects of cultural difference in a postcolonial criticism. (173, 110, 179)

In refusing to replicate the colonizer/colonized divide integral to received accounts of both colonial authority and anti-colonialist opposition, Bhabha seeks to undo a given order of priorities by displacing the system of conceptual oppositions making that order possible. Advising that "the margin of hybridity . . . resists and binary opposition of racial and cultural groups . . . as homogeneous polarized political consciousness" (207) and proffering an "analysis of ambivalence [that] questions dogmatic and moralistic positions on the meaning of opposition and discrimination" (67), Bhabha undertakes to demonstrate colonialism as "a mode of authority that is agnostic (rather than antagonistic)" (108). The small difference in these signifiers, marked by three letters, is incommensurate with the chasm between their significations: whereas "agonistic" pertains to ancient Greek athletic contests, "agon" being derived from "a gathering" and denoting "a public celebration of games, a contest for the prize at games," "antagonistic" specifies "the mutual resistance of two opposing forces, physical or mental; active opposition to a force" (*Shorter Oxford English Dictionary*). I have argued that Bhabha reads social processes according to the rules of writing, refuses the nondiscursive specification of subjects, and dismisses notions of determinate relations between different interests. In rejecting "antagonistic" in favor of "agonistic," is he then positing colonialism as a competition of peers rather than a hostile struggle between the subjugated and the oppressor?

Theoretical moves directed at erasing inscriptions of inequality and conflict in the material colonial world are evident in Bhabha's disdain for that anticolonialist tradition that perceived the struggle in terms that were antagonistic rather than agonistic, and construed the colonial relationship as generically— rather than "often," as Bhabha would have it—one between competing political groups and goals. Consider Aimé Césaire's question and response: "Has colonization really *placed civilizations in contact?* . . . Not human contact but relations of domination and submission";[24] or Fanon's stark definition: "Decolonization is the meeting of two forces, opposed to each other by their very nature."[25] It would seem that the contestation of colonialism's claims in an idiom avowing a struggle between polarized interests, fought against a decidable opponent across binary battle lines, makes present-day postcolonialist theorists embarrassed by anticolonialist forebears who failed to conform to their rules about discursive radicalism,[26] and who by projecting the making of an insurgent subjectivity, committed what Bhabha considers the solecism of introducing "restrictive notions of cultural identity with which we burden our visions of political change" (38).[27] Perhaps these perceived errors in the writings of theorists immersed in the struggles against colonialism prompted Bhabha's appropriation of Fanon to his own mode, a procedure whose validity I and others have disputed.[28]

Because Bhabha has written about "hybrid" cultural articulations when glossing the novels, poetry, and films of postcolonial writers and artists, critics have readily interpreted his use of this concept as denoting culture's multiple and incongruous accents, cross-cultural inventions, and transnationality—that is, as descriptive of subject positions and social conditions traversed by heterogeneous cultural inflections. Yet an examination of Bhabha's usage belies an easy identification with that notion posited long ago by Caribbean and Latin American writers and intellectuals as creolization, métissage, or mestizaje. It is also distinct from both Paul Gilroy's insistence on the inescapable intermixture of ideas and forms in neologistic transitional cultures, or Stuart Hall's account of the disjunctive, displaced, and unstable postcolonial identities constituted in representation but which relate to real sets of histories. (I will return to Bhabha's place on the spectrum of concepts around identity posited within black British theory.)

Although familiar with the innovative idioms deployed by such multiply located subjects, Bhabha's concern is with the production of hybridity through the *process* of a colonial and postcolonial relocating and reinscribing, or the translating and transvaluing of cultural difference "in the Third Space of enunciation," where it is reiterated differently from its prior context:

Hybridity is the revaluation of the assumption of colonial identity through the repetition of identity effects. It displays the necessary deformation and displacement and domination. . . . For the colonial hybrid is the articulation of the ambivalent space where the rite of power is enacted on the site of desire, making its objects at once disciplinary and disseminatory.

The hybrid object . . . retains the actual semblance of the authoritative symbol but revalues its presence by resisting it as the signifier of *Entstellung—after the intervention of difference* . . . the theoretical recognition of the split-space of enunciation may open the way to conceptualizing an *inter*national culture, based not on exoticism of muticulturalism, or the diversity of cultures, but on the inscription of culture's *hybridity.*" (112, 115, 38)

As I read it, Bhabha "hybridity" is a twin term for the "catachrestic reinscription" of "cultural difference" in the disjunctive postcolonial discursive space—that is, it is descriptive of the textual processes and effects held to constitute social forms and conditions, and not of those forms and conditions as articulated in social practices. For when contesting "the consensual, ethnocentric notion of the pluralistic existence of cultural diversity" (177) with "the ambivalent process of splitting and hybridity that marks the identification with culture's difference" (224), Bhabha postulates cultural difference as an analytic strategy, a discursive product:

Cultural difference . . . is not the acquisition or accumulation of additional cultural knowledge; it is the momentous, if momentary extinction of the recognizable object of culture in the disturbed artifice of its signification, at the edge of experience.

Cultural difference must not be understood as the free play of polarities and pluralities in the homogeneous empty time of the national community. . . . The analytic of cultural difference intervenes to transform the scenario of articulation. . . . The aim of cultural difference is to rearticulate the sum of knowledge from the perspective of the signifying position of the minority that resists totalization . . . producing other spaces of subaltern signification. (126, 162)

This shift from the concept as a context-dependent category deployed to legitimate discriminatory practices, or as a counter-device of political affirmation, subdues the charge immanent in "difference" as a marker of social inequalities and a sign of resistance to oppression. In Norris's telling phrase when discussing a "nominalist (or textualist) stance which denies any possible grounds of appeal in the realities of oppression as *known and experienced* by members of the relevant class, community, or interest group," what is ignored is "the stubborn *facticity* of . . . difference . . . the manifold differences—the real and material (not just 'discursive') differences of interest" (*The Truth About Postmodernism*, 23, 24).

It is such differences that engender political and ethical collectivities;[29] for while it is now well-known that our class subjectivities are crossed and modulated by diverse and competing identifications, the *structural* relations of capitalism-as-transcontinental-imperialism continue to provoke situations that demand that plurally constituted and positioned subjects, with multiple associations, different proclivities, and diverse enthusiasms, mobilize around class conceived either as a socioeconomic category or as a community engaged in struggle. This very notion of solidarity is resisted by Bhabha, whose reply to the question he rhetorically poses, "Do we need to rethink the terms in which we conceive of community, citizenship, nationality, and the ethics of social affiliation?" (174) must be, given his premises, to posit difference, incommensurability, and dispersal as rendering traditional constructions of communality unsatisfactory and unsafe: "Can such split subjects and differentiated social movements, which display ambivalent and divided forms of identification, be represented in a collective will that distinctively echoes Gramsci's enlightened inheritance and its rationalism?" (29). Implicit in Bhabha's critique of identitarianism and his valorizing of difference is a recommendation of coalition politics and rainbow alliances, but one that foregoes the necessary examination of their operations, hazards, consequences, and failures.[30]

To question the deployment of "difference" as a counter to the negatively perceived "totalization," is not to deny the fecundity of a notion which insists on subjectivity as polymorphous, community as heterogeneous, social formations as mutable and culture as vagrant. It is to recognize that "difference" has been diverted by a postmodernist criticism as a theoretical ruse to establish a neutral, ideology-free zone from which the social dissension and political contest inscribed in the antagonist pairing of colonizer/colonized, have been expelled. A policy statement defining difference in terms of bland variations on a placid continuum, unhinged from the planned inequalities of actually existing social regimes and political struggles, can be found in the writing of the film director and critic, Trinh T. Minh-ha: "I have often been asked about what viewers call the lack of conflicts in my films . . . Conflicts in western contexts often serve to define identities. My suggestion to the 'lack' is: let difference replace conflict. Difference as understood in many feminist and non-western contexts, difference as foregrounded in my film work, is not opposition to sameness, nor synonymous with separateness."[31]

Here "difference" is used to deny both class contest and anti-imperialism in the thought of practice of "non-Western" histories and societies, while also eliminating the incompatible agendas and goals at work within "feminist contexts." Norris has observed how poststructuralism "operates on an abstract, quasi-systemic model of "opposition" and "difference" whereby those terms are deprived of all specific historical or experiential content, and treated, in effect, as linguistic artifacts or products of "discursive definition"; (182) and he goes on to insist that "*difference* can only be a fashionable buzzword . . . so long as it is conceived in ideal abstraction from the contexts of real-world experience or the lived actualities of class or gender oppression" (26, 24)—to which can be added "colonialist and imperialist domination."

If it is conceded that the structure of colonial power was ordered on difference as a legitimating strategy in the exercise of domination, then it could be argued that the construct of binary oppositions retains power as a political category. This is repudiated by Bhabha, whose theoretical urge to displace division with interjacency is elaborated in his version of agency and resistance. Directed at exposing "the myth of the 'transparency' of the human agent" (24) and disposing of the discourse of the intentional subject or collectivity, this narrative is once again predicated on the performative role of the signifying process, historical agency being located in sign and symbol, while subaltern as well as postcolonial agency is discovered in interrogative, contestatory, catachrestic procedures performed on the prior text through relocation and reinscription:

> My contention, elaborated in my writings on postcolonial discourse in terms of mimicry, hybridity, sly civility, is that the liminal moment of identification—eluding resemblance—produces a subversive strategy of subaltern agency that negotiates its own authority through a process of iterative "unpicking" and incommensurable, insurgent rethinking. (184–85)

Bhabha's notion of agency as enacted at the level of enunciation and discernible in the indeterminate moment of narrating the event, falls outside the longstanding debate between structural explanations that foreground the determinate constraints of ideological construction, and those paradigms privileging the conscious, self-reflexive actor; it is also distinct from that other famous account of how history is made by human subjects, but not under conditions of their own choosing.

When exploring "the question of agency as it emerges in relation to the indeterminate and the contingent" (183) in "the negotiation of meaning that is . . . a *time-lag*" or temporal break, between the signifier and the signified (184), Bhabha turns his attention to the Indian Mutiny, examining the "cultural strategy and political confrontation constituted in obscure, enigmatic symbols, the manic repetition of rumor, panic as the uncontrolled, yet strategic effect of political revolt" (199), and specifying "the politics of agency" as embedded in the rumor transmitted through the circulation of chapatis:

> The indeterminacy of rumor constitutes its importance as a social discourse. Its intersubjective, communal adhesiveness lies in its enunciative aspect. Its performative power of circulation results in the contagious spreading. The chain of communication in the rumour, its semantic content is transformed in transmission . . . the messages syntactically contiguous. (200)

Thus far we have the sign as the bearer of rebel agency—and when Bhabha congratulates the historical agency of the *sipahi* (*sepoy*) for succeeding by stratagem and not arms, he somehow omits to recollect that the rebellion issued as an armed struggle, and was disarmed and repressed by exorbitant military force. The effect of moving agency from the subject-as-insurgent-actor to textual performance is to defuse resistance as practice directed at undermining and defeating an oppressive opponent—a practice that also effected experiential transformation in the colonized[32]: "Resistance is not necessarily an oppositional act of political intention. . . . It is the effect of an ambivalence produced within the rules of recognition of dominating discourses as they articulate the signs of cultural difference and reimplicate them within the deferential relations of colonial power—hierarchy, normalization, marginalization and so forth" (110–11).

This construction of resistance as an *effect* of the aporia in the inscriptions of empire that are seized and reinscribed by the subaltern, marks the difference of Bhabha's concept from Said's representations of a "culture of resistance" (see *Culture and Imperialism*, especially chapter 3, "Resistance and Opposition") where a language of the subject is deployed. In attending to written and remembered stories of insubordination and revolt, Said acknowledges the energies of the colonized's self-affirmation, especially commending the work of the Subaltern Studies collective for recuperating agency as performed by conscious human subjects, the rebel in Ranajit Guha's work being conceived as "an entity whose will and reason constituted the praxis called rebellion."[33]

The consequences to Bhabha's narrative of agency are yet more extensive: by discerning the adhesiveness of "its enunciative aspect" it contrives to connect subaltern to colonialist in a move that is directed at breaking down the received division between the Indian peasant and the Raj, and displacing the "binary sense of political antagonism" with a perception of the middle ground between colonial authority and colonial resistance:

> The iterative action of rumor, its *circulation* and *contagion*, links it with panic—as one of the affects of insurgency. . . . The indeterminate circulation of meaning as rumor or conspiracy, with its perverse, psychic effects of panic, constitutes the intersubjective realm of revolt and resistance. . . . What kind of agency is constituted in the circulation of the chapati? Time, I believe, is of the essence. For it is the *circulation* of the chapati that initiates a politics of agency negotiated in the antagonisms of colonial cultural difference. . . . Panic spreads. It does not simply hold together the native people *but binds them affectively, if antagonistically—through the process of projection—with their masters* . . . the organizing principle of the *sign* of the chapati is constituted in the transmission of fear and anxiety, projection and panic in the form of circulation *in-between* the colonizer and the colonized. . . . A contingent borderline experience opens up *in-between* colonizer and colonized. . . . The margin of hybridity, where cultural differences "contingently" and conflictually touch, becomes the moment of panic which reveals the borderline experience. (200, 203, 206, 207; emphasis added)

In Bhabha's rewriting of agency, the deliberated juxtaposition of incommensurable terms is intended to complicate relations between domination and resistance. That transactions between colonizer and colonized occurred and influenced the practices of the parties is not in question. What concerns me is the configuration produced by "link," "intersubjective realm," "bind," "in-between," and "borderline," which I read as reiterating Bhabha's interest in representing the colonial encounter as a complicit relationship. Undoubtedly it was an entangled event; but Bhabha, who brings a psychoanalytical discourse of desire to bear on the realities of colonial power, and speciously ties "affectively" to "antagonistically," also claims that the critical operations he exercises on his sources ruins the representation of colonialism as a combat. Yet the interlocution within the "in-between" he has construed is a conversation scripted by the critic, and is remote from what could properly be described as a dialogue, where a minimum prerequisite is surely that each party perceives the other as an agent of knowledge. That colonialism and now imperialism inhibit such colloquy is graphically evoked by Jameson's comment: "What the First World thinks and dreams about the Third can have nothing whatsoever in common formally or epistemologically with what the Third World *has to know* every day about the

First. Subalternity carries the possibility of knowledge with it, domination that of forgetfulness and repression."[34]

To retrieve colonialism's transactions as "contrapuntal" may be designed to shift the position of the colonized from victim to participant. Christopher Miller has observed that in response to "the messy history of hegemony and conflict," recent trends in anthropology have turned to a "far more congenial model of interpretative practice," which by drawing on Bakhtinian criticism, is concerned to show how "dialogue and polyvocality can be uncovered within apparent hegemonies." While Miller acknowledges dialogue to be "the most compelling *ethical model* for the representation of cultures," he cautions that "such a fantasy depends on a complete rewriting (or ignorance) of the material conditions of history . . . that vitiate dialogism within the substance of history."[35] The tendency to introduce dialogic paradigms is apparent in contemporary studies of colonialism; consider Sara Suleri's *The Rhetoric of English India*,[36] which construes a mutual narrative of complicity, dubiety, and guilt linking the imperial power with the disempowered cultures, creating, she argues, a counterculture not explicable in terms of an allegory of otherness.

It is possible that the Indian materials that are the sources for Suleri and Bhabha offer opportunities for discovering a middle ground, given the long histories of communication between the colonizer and regional and national elites, and the consequent commerce between dominant and marginalized knowledges. Yet although these exchanges should not be allowed to obscure the brutality of colonialism's territorial expropriations in the Indian subcontinent, or the murderous punishments inflicted on opposition, and which persisted until British withdrawal, there is now a vogue for rewriting British rule in India as a hegemony—which I understand as coercion significantly tempered by reciprocity and consent, or consent fortified by coercion. This is a version of the relationship between rulers and subaltern classes disputed by Ranajit Guha, who represents the situation as one of domination and resistance.[37] Furthermore, other contexts, such as plantation colonialism and genocidal settler regimes, or the atrocities attendant on violent territorial expropriation in North and sub-Saharan Africa, confront us with narratives of physical force and economic compulsion, from which the elite natives' peaceable colloquies with the invaders' cognitive systems are wholly absent, and where the construing of affective linkages would introduce a grotesque romanticism into annals of physical, institutional, and discursive violence.[38] Thus even while Bhabha announces that the "testimony of colonial dislocation . . . refuses the ambition of any total theory of colonial oppression" (41), the testimony of colonial oppression renders Bhabha's construct of a collaborative colonialism nugatory.

If for no other reason, colonialism's *differential* histories render suspect the metanarratives being written by critics who otherwise fiercely refuse grand narratives, and whose stories feature mutuality rather than conflict as the *norm* of colonial encounters. That model has, I think, to be distinguished from Said's call for readings of the colonial experience as "interactive and embroiled." His own nuanced accounts of these interconnected histories are haunted by visitations of schism, the affirmations of congruence being repeatedly interrupted by the recognition that colonialism installed a radical discontinuity in terms of human space, preserved "absolute geographical and cultural boundaries" and "fundamental ontological distinctions" between the West and the native, "withheld mutuality," and exercised an "almost total control" that placed the parties to the encounter in "devastating continuous conflict." And indeed against the grain of his own optimistic vision, Said in the last pages of *Culture and Imperialism* makes this melancholy observation: "History . . . teaches us that domination breeds resistance, and that the violence inherent in the imperialist contest—for all its occasional profit and pleasure—is an impoverishment for both sides" (348). The tensions inherent in the working out of Said's lateral strategies may reside in his perception that aggression and supremacy are indeed carved into the colonialist archive, and that the critical effort to superimpose a tale of complicities will not obliterate the prior inscriptions.

What then is the relationship of Bhabha's theoretical model to the record of colonialism as violent dispossession achieved by military force and sustained by institutional power? Does it succeed in challenging and displacing received perceptions of the quotidian colonial world as a place of economic exploitation, social divisions, and political conflict? The perceptions of colonialism as a spatial or geographical enterprise now offered by historical-materialist geographers brings into view how, in the words of David Harvey, "the world's spaces were deterritorialized, stripped of their preceding significations, and then reterritorialized according to the convenience of colonial and imperial administration."[39] As both Edward Soja and Neil Smith have argued,[40] the global spatial integration initiated by colonialism and completed by imperialism entailed the uneven insertion of the colonies into a world economy as the underdeveloped sector, and instituted an international division of labor effecting a transfer of value that flowed from periphery to core. To speak then of metropolis and colony as inhabiting the same in-between, interstitial ground ignores that this territory was differentially occupied and that it was contested space, being the site of coercion and resistance and not of civil negotiation between evenly placed contenders. If we follow Harvey in wanting to give "an account of space and time in social life" that will "highlight material links between political-economic and cultural processes" (201), then our readings of colonial texts will seek to uncover those inscriptions of epistemological differentiations that Johannes Fabian has named as the West's "denial of coevalness" with the colonial worlds.[41] In directing his energies at erasing "a politics of binary opposition," Bhabha intimates that while theory and the real are not enemies they can be strangers.

I alluded earlier to the determinations of social habitat on theoretical stances, and I want now to bring the resonances of the book's title to a consideration of how Bhabha situates himself, from which position he speaks, and who the implied addressees might be—matters that can be seen to converge in his engagement with questions of identity/subjectivity, a discussion in which black British theorists have actively participated. For all his castigation of binaries, Bhabha posits essentialism or difference, nativism or cosmopolitanism, the claim to a purity of origins or the immersion in transnational cultural flows, as the only possible positions for a postcolonial perspective. During the 1980s it was those critics attesting to the overdetermined nature of identity and eager to repudiate "essentialism" who made inroads into a totalizing theorization of the heterogeneous. An essay by Kobena Mercer in a collection exemplifying the age of "the politics of articulation," commended "the rearticulation of black" as "a political rather than racial identity among Asian, Caribbean, and African people . . . thus creating a new form of symbolic 'unity' out of the signifiers of racial difference."[42] At the same time, Stuart Hall proposed "ethnicity" as the concept which recognizes that the black subject is "constructed historically, culturally politically," maintaining that this notion enables "a new cultural politics which engages rather than suppresses *difference*."[43] Subsequently, Paul Gilroy negotiated a position between "anti-essentialism" and "anti-anti-essentialism," rejecting not only exceptionalist and mystical claims to an ethnic essence of blackness, where the inner differentiation of black cultures are overlooked, but also contesting the arguments of radical constructionists that fail to acknowledge that black identity "is lived as a coherent (if not always stable) experiential sense of self. Though it is often felt to be natural and spontaneous, it remains the outcome of practical activity: language, gesture, bodily significations, desires" (*The Black Atlantic*, 102).

In the pages of *Third Text*, which pointedly identifies itself as providing "Third World Perspectives on Contemporary Art and Culture," many and competing understandings of cultural identity have been posited over the years. Among these, Rasheed Araeen, who urges the necessity "of recognizing the critical and historical roles of autonomous individuals from non-European cultures," proposes "cultural identity" as "both fiction and necessity," finding that it gives "a cutting edge to question and interrogate many of the assumptions of Western culture by which it claims its superiority and supremacy"; while Geeta Kapur has dissented from a postmodernism that "seems to accommodate otherness as never before in the history of capitalist culture," but does so "through a process of such infinite differentiation that all questions of identity are destroyed . . . along with the normative function of culture."[44] It is apparent then that the empowering effects of a placed identity have not been relinquished by the critical community. What is more, there are those who have advised that the cost of the "hybridization" attendant on colonialism and accenting the post-colonial should not remain uncounted. In glossing Edward Brathwaite's definition of creolization "as one's adaptation to a new environment through the loss of parts of oneself and the gain of parts of the Other," Manthia Diawara—who cautions that the question of hybridity "as *the* correct way of being Black in the West has enabling elements as well as uncanny moments"—has observed: "One must be aware of the fact that in fusing Whiteness with the seductiveness of hybridization, one is sacrificing not only a part of Blackness, but certain Black people" ("The Nature of Mother in *Dreaming River*," *Third Text*, 82).

These "certain Black people" are too often forgotten in the euphoria of celebrating the arrival of the postcolonial. It is true that Bhabha does eloquently specify "the demography of the new internationalism" in terms of "the history of postcolonial migration, the narratives of cultural and political diaspora, the major social displacements of peasant and aboriginal communities, the poetics of exile, the grim prose of political and economic refugees" (5). This account acknowledges that "the transnational dimension of cultural transformation—migration, diaspora, displacement, relocation—makes the process of cultural translation a complex form of signification" (172). Yet Bhabha's vista emerges as narrower than the above comments promise; for while this does encompass diverse "narratives where double-lives are led in the postcolonial world, with its journeys of migration and its dwellings of the diasporic" (213), what is foregrounded by Bhabha in prose that can be translucent but is often purple (see, for example, 1 and 139) is "the poetics of relocation and reinscription" (225) known by the cosmopolitan artist, writer, intellectual, professional, financier, and entrepreneur in the metropolis, rather than the "grim prose" of low-waged workers in Western capitals, and contract laborers in the Gulf states or other centers of capitalist growth within the Third World. Moreover, the claim that "the contingent and the liminal become the times and the spaces for the historical representation of the subjects of cultural difference in a postcolonial criticism" (179), emphasizes the "affective experience of social marginality"—which by intimating the circulation of emotion and desire, registers the experience as one of unmitigated pleasure. Indeed assertions about the "unhomely" as paradigmatic of postcolonial social and cultural displacement, or "the liminality of migrant experience," "the migrant culture of the in-between," and the "indeterminacy of diasporic identity" (224) now constitute the near-consensual opinion: consider Bruce Robbins's commendation of Bhabha's essay "DissemiNation" as providing "a portrait of trans-national hybridity as an increasingly unavoidable condition of emotional and intellectual life."[45]

It is, I would suggest, a configuration in urgent need of unpacking. In representing the productive tensions of its own situation as normative and desirable, the privileged postcolonial is prone to denigrate affiliations to class, ethnicity, and emergent nation-state that continue to fashion the self-understanding and energize the resistances of exploited populations in the hinterlands of late imperialism, as well as of immigrant laborers living on the outskirts of one or another metropolis. The stance of the elite thus further severs their modes of cognition from those of communities that, while themselves also inhabiting cultural spaces that are multiply inflected and impure, do not share in the freewheeling pleasures of commuting between cultures available to the privileged postcolonial.

Such different situations are starkly noted in the inventory compiled by Neil Lazarus: "In Mozambique, Nigeria, Korea and El Salvador, the question of the nation-state has never before seemed so pressing or so central. In Brazil, Jamaica, Ghana, and Malaysia, the concepts of 'diversity,' 'mobility' and 'communication' are of practical significance only to foreign elites and indigenous comprador classes" ("Doubting the New World Order," 99).

In a related register, Masao Miyoshi, who has voiced concern that the new cultural configurations of transnational corporate capitalism threaten the survival of local cultures, is acerbic about those critics who rejoice at the imagined camaraderie of an amalgamated world culture. Remarking that " 'multiculturalism' is a luxury largely irrelevant to those who live under the most wretched conditions" Miyoshi moves from the preoccupation in cultural studies with "recognizing different subject-positions from different regions and diverse backgrounds" to urging the need for a project that will address political and economic inequalities as differences that must be erased ("A Borderless World"). With this he turns the discussion in the direction of political economy and international class politics, toward which Bhabha's writings, enclosed as they are in a theoretical mode that subdues the continuing exploitation of the Third World and the growing disparities of resources and opportunities within the First, can do no more than gesture.

Although Bhabha situates himself within French critical theory, his translations of an expatriate postcolonial location have been deeply inflected by the particular modulations of the theoretical discussion conducted within Britain during the past two decades. The presence of Marxism as a current in British intellectual and academic life, together with socialism's established place on the political spectrum and the existence of a small but important tradition of anti-colonialism[46]—to both of which colonials living in the metropolis contributed —may have prompted Bhabha to associate his writing with "the materialist mode," and offer his work as an effort both "to enhance understanding of political struggle" (208), and to "historicize the event of the dehistoricized" (198). Perhaps more significantly, the course of his work displays affinities with the particular trajectory of British poststructuralism, which in drawing on French critical theory, redeployed both psychoanalytic writing and Marxism-via-Althusser. Francis Mulhern has suggested that

> semiotics, developing through a critical ingathering of modern scientific initiatives in poetics and linguistics—formalist, structuralist and other— offered concepts and taxonomies that bore the promise of a post-aesthetic, materialist analysis of textual forms and functions. Psychoanalysis appeared not merely as a potent analogy but as a decisive contributor to the understanding of subjectivity. Marxism furnished terms of historical understanding and defined the politics of text and subject.[47]

During the 1970s, according to Antony Easthope, the film journal *Screen*— to which Bhabha later contributed—"set out to theorise 'the encounter of Marxism and psychoanalysis on the terrain of semiotics,'" the commitment to materialism manifested in the thesis that "the semiological determination of film was realized in its specific materiality and that this presented itself at the level of the signifer." For Easthope, the "intervention of poststructuralism in cultural studies" was exemplified in *Language and Materialism: Developments in Semiology and the Theory of the Subject* (1977), which its authors, Rosalind Coward and John Ellis, offered as performing the meeting of psychoanalysis with Marxism, and which proposed that "the subject is an effect constituted in the process of the unconscious, of discourse, and of the relatively autonomous practices of the social formation.[48] Even if Bhabha's implementation of materialist methods could be considered as at least eccentric, it is apparent that those traces of a putative materialism that survive in his work, conform to the forms devised by British poststructuralism.

The subsequent elaboration of Bhabha's work is further accented by the British version of post-Marxism disseminated during the 1980s. In Bhabha's valorizations of decentering, dispersal, and dissemination, although spoken in his own inimitable voice, echoes can be heard of *New Times* celebrating the effects of post-Fordist productive modes in "flexibility, diversity, differentiation, mobility, communication, decentralization and internationalization." (Curiously, the thinking of *Marxism Today* closely followed a base/superstructure model, unproblematically deriving perceived shifts in consciousness and ideology from changes in the mode of production.) These processes, as Neil Lazarus points out in "Doubting the New World Order," were hailed as rendering the old conceptual paradigms, political identities, and political strategies obsolete, and heralding the arrival of "culturalism"—a move tracked in a scathing essay by A. Sivanandum, where he attacked the dissociation of the economic and political from the cultural, and lambasted those intellectuals who located the political struggle in the discursive.[49]

An intellectual environment in which Marxism circulated as an important current, a trend that was subsequently, and it nows seems temporarily, diverted by the denigrations of "post-Marxism," provided Bhabha with targets who without being named are casually assembled as a "left orthodoxy." By attaching disqualifying clauses that render suspect the concepts of alternative explanatory categories, Bhabha represents his unspecified antagonists as manichean dualists, identitarian mystifiers, diverse peddlars of class, people, nation, and gender as unified and uniform sets, and dialectical materialists bent on defusing energizing disjunctions through sublation. "Monolithic category" is joined to "community," "essentialist identities" to "communal," and "homogenized" to "national culture"; "a simplistic sense of intentionality" characterizes notions of "collective agency"; "polarities" are "primordial"; leftist forms of writing history are "historicist," "transcendent and teleological"; "holistic form" deforms "social explanation."

Bhabha has produced work opening up the categories of culture and nation to reveal their inner differentiations and disjunctions, and his case surely does not require that he traduce those who insist on the political and experiential uses of constructing insurgent identities around notions of communalities, and of retaining class as a primary conceptual category.[50] Indeed his polemic against "the left" is marred by a levity only available to that generation who arrived at post-Marxism without ever having occupied the anterior position, and superceded "anti-imperialism-in-itself" (241) without participating in the struggles which this stance animated:

> Political positions are not simply identifiable as progressive or reactionary, bourgeois or radical, prior to the act of *critique engagée*, or outside the terms and conditions of their discursive address. It is in this sense that the historical moment of political action must be thought of as part of the history of the form of its writing. (22)

Instead of "identikit political idealism" demanding that critical discourse produce "a pure ideology of analysis whereby the prior principle is simply augmented . . . its identity as socialist or materialist . . . consistently confirmed in each oppositional stage of the argument," Bhabha is concerned to stress the fully historical and discursive *différance* between them; instead of "a primordial and previsionary division of right or left, progressive or reactionary," Bhabha argues for "language of critique . . . which . . . overcomes the given grounds of opposition and opens up a space of translation" (25)—thus returning us to his abhorrence of concepts of conflict and his undertheorized notions of an ubiquitous middle ground and coalition.

Bhabha's theories mark his distance from a black British legacy that is still manifest in the continuing significance of *Race and Class* as a forum for discussions in the Marxist mode. In his chapter on "C. L. R. James and the Black Radical Tradition,"[51] Cedric Robinson places James among a community of expatriate intellectuals from the British Empire who as internationalists participated in the communist and labor politics of the metropolis and who, as Tim Brennan notes, were subsequently written out of the history of the British left by the British New Left.[52] It was in Britain too that many of the programs for the anticolonial struggle were devised, as well as it being the place from which countless students from all corners of the then empire returned to their native lands as doctors, lawyers, and teachers—and as Marxists of one or other denomination who participated in the liberation struggles of their communities. That *this* vibrant narrative of transnational intellectual exchange is now being forgotten in the annals of postcoloniality can only impoverish its revisionist chronicles. There are numerous critics who for long have urged as a moral imperative that theory engage in the struggle against the arrogance of capitalism's international power; and if rather than citing their compelling arguments I choose Derrida's words on "the foreign debt," it is because these articulate the calculated absence in the utterances of so many of his followers:

> With this name or with this emblematic figure, it is a matter of *interest* and first of all of the interest of capital in general, an interest that, in the order of the world today, namely the worldwide market, holds a mass of humanity under its yoke and in a new form of slavery. . . . Now, these problems of the foreign debt—and everything that is metonymized by this concept—will not be treated without at least the spirit of the Marxist critique, the critique of the market, of the multiple logics of capital. (*Spectres of Marx*, 93–94)

Derrida's disparagement of those who evangelize in the name of the ideal of liberal democracy is made on the firm grounds of specifying actually existing conditions, and may disturb the convictions of those who reprove the error of representing facts as transparent and outside the form of their writing: "Never have violence, inequality, exclusion, famine, and thus economic oppression affected as many human beings in the history of the Earth and of humanity." His reluctance to celebrate "'the end of ideologies' and the end of the great emancipatory discourses" will make the postmodern scorn for metanarratives appear as yesterday's argot, and could even persuade some critics that it is fitting to associate their work with the still-unfinished global emancipatory project. Above all, Derrida's appeal to the principle of hope animating political action in the interest of constructing a different future must surely reveal the poverty of theories which by refusing a Marxist eschatology, turn and turn in the gyre of an eternal present:

> Now, if there is a spirit of Marxism which I will never be ready to renounce, it is not only the critical idea or the questioning stance. . . . It is rather a certain emancipatory and *messianic* affirmation, a certain experience of the promise that one can try to liberate from any dogmatics and even from any metaphysico-religious determination, from any *messianism*. And a promise must promise to be kept, that is, not to remain "spiritual" or "abstract," but to produce events, new effective forms of action, practice, organization. (89)

Notes

1   Simon During, "Postcolonialism and Globalisation: A Dialectical Relation after All?" *Postcolonial Studies* 1(1) (1998): 31–47.
2   Published by Routledge, 1994.
3   See for example V. Y. Mudimbe, "Reading and Teaching Pierre Bourdieu," *Transition* 61 (1994): 144–60; Anthony Arnove, "Pierre Bourdieu, the Sociology of Intellectuals, and the Language of African Literature," *Novel* 26(3) (spring 1993): 276–95; Toril Moi, "Appropriating Bourdieu: Feminist Theory and Pierre Bourdieu's Sociology of Culture," *New Literary History* 22 (1991): 1071–1149; Nicholas Thomas, *Colonialism's Culture: Anthropology, Travel and Government* (Oxford: Polity Press/Blackwell, 1994).
4   *The Truth about Postmodernism* (Oxford: Blackwell, 1993).
5   *Spectres of Marx: The State of the Debt, the Work of Mourning and the New International*, trans. Peggy Kamuf (London: Routledge, 1994).
6   As examples, see Abdul JanMohamed, "The Economy of Manichean Allegory: The Function of Racial Difference in Colonialist Literature," *Critical Inquiry* 12(1) (1985); Laura Chrisman, "The Imperial Unconscious? Representations of Imperial Discourse," *Critical Quarterly* 32(3) (1990): 38–58; Neil Lazarus, "Disavowing Decoloni-

zation: Fanon, Nationalism, and the Problematic of Representation in Current Theories of Colonial Discourse," *Research in African Literatures* 24(4) (winter 1993): 69–98; Arif Dirlik, "The Postcolonial Aura: Third World Criticism in the Age of Global Capitalism," *Critical Inquiry* 20 (winter 1994): 329–56; Masao Miyoshi, "A Borderless World? From Colonialism to Transnationalism and the Decline of the Nation-State," *Critical Inquiry* 19 (summer 1993): 726–51. Also the papers of Chrisman, Miyoshi, and Lazarus given at the conference "The Politics of Identity, Secular Criticism and the Gravity of History: The Work of Edward Said," Warwick University, March 1994, and collected as *Cultural Readings of Imperialism: Edward Said and the Gravity of History*, ed Keith Ansell-Pearson, Benita Parry, and Judith Squires (London: Lawrence and Wishart, 1995).

7   For critiques addressing Bhabha, see Lazarus, "Disavowing Decolonization"; Ania Loomba, "Overworlding the 'Third World,'" *Oxford Literary Review* 13(1–2) (1991): 164–91. Loomba also cites the criticisms of Bhabha made by Suvir Kaul in "The Indian Academic and Resistance to Theory," 174. See also my "Problems in Current Theories of Colonial Discourse," *Oxford Literary Review* 9(1–2) (1987): 27–58; Manthia Diawara, "The Nature of Mother in *Dreaming Rivers*," *Third Text* 13 (winter 1990/91): 73–84; Thomas, *Colonialism's Culture*; Alex Callinicos, "Wonders Taken for Signs: Homi Bhabha's Postcolonialism," in *Post-ality: Marxism and Postmodernism*, ed. Masud Zavarzadeh, Teresa L. Ebert, and Donald Morton (Washington, D.C.: Maisonneuve Press, 1995); Lawrence A. Phillips, "'Lost in Space' Siting/Citing the In-Between of Homi Bhabha's *The Location of Culture*," *Scrutiny* 23(1) (1998): 16–25; Geeta Kapur, "Globalization and Culture: Navigating the Void," in *The Cultures of Globalization*, ed. Fredric Jameson and Masao Miyoshi (Durham N.C.: Duke University Press, 1998).

8   *Culture and Imperialism* (London: Chatto and Windus 1993), 292.

9   *The Black Atlantic: Modernity and Double Consciousness* (London: Verso, 1993).

10 "Theatricum Philosophicum," in *Language, Counter-Memory, Practice*, trans. Donald F. Bouchard and Sherry Simon (Ithaca: Cornell University Press, 1977), 185.

11 *Postmodernism, or, The Cultural Logic of Late Capitalism* (London: Verso 1991), 344.

12 A harsher estimate of the implications to this style is offered by Dirlik, who finds Bhabha to be "a master of political mystification and theoretical obfuscation," observing that while the same tendencies are apparent in much postcolonial writing, these are rarely evident "with the same virtuosity (and incomprehensibleness) that he brings to it" ("The Postcolonial Aura," 333 n.6).

13 See Anne McClintock, "The Angel of Progress: Pitfalls of the Term 'Post-Colonialism,'" and Ella Shohat, "Notes on the 'Post-Colonial,'" *Social Text* 31/32 (1992): 84–98 and 99–113; Laura Chrisman, "Inventing Post-Colonial Theory: Polemical Observations," *Pretexts* 5 (1–2): 205–12. Shohat suggests that "post-colonial theory" should articulate itself as "'post-anti-colonial critique,' as a movement beyond a relatively binaristic, fixed and stable mapping of power relations between 'colonizer/colonized' and 'center/periphery'" (105, 108). I would dispute Shohat's designation of "Third World nationalist discourse"; see my "Resistance Theory/Theorizing Resistance," in *Colonial Discourse/Postcolonial Theory*, ed. Francis Barker, Peter Hulme, and Margaret Iversen (Manchester: Manchester University Press, 1994). It is Lazarus's contention that Bhabha uses the concept of postcoloniality *against* the nationalism or

nationalitarianism of liberation discourses, thereby repeating the move prevalent amongst radical critics to disavow nationalism *tout court* by positioning nationalist discourses, both metropolitan and anticolonial, "as coercive, totalizing, elitist, authoritarian, essentialist, and reactionary," and hence obscuring these "as the open site of political and ideological contestation" ("Disavowing Decolonization," 70).

14 "Writing Post-Orientalist Histories of the Third World: Perspectives from Indian Historiography," *Comparative Studies in Society and History* 32 (1990), and "Postcolonial Criticism and Indian Historiography," *Social Text* 31/32 (1993): 8–19.

15 See Aijaz Ahmad, *In Theory: Classes, Nations, Literatures* (London: Verso 1992); and Michael Sprinker, "The National Question: Said, Ahmad, Jameson," *Public Culture* 6(1) (fall 1993): 3–29.

16 "Post-Socialism/Flexible Production: Marxism in Contemporary Radicalism," *Polygraph* 6/7 (1993): 133–69.

17 See Houston A. Baker Jr., *Modernism and the Harlem Renaissance* (Chicago: University of Chicago Press, 1987), 75–79.

18 See, for example, V. Y. Mudimbe's discussion of Africanist discourse, *The Invention of Africa: Gnosis, Philosophy and the Order of Knowledge* (London: James Currey, 1988); Mary Louise Pratt, *Imperial Eyes: Travel Writing and Transculturation* (London: Routledge, 1992); and Laura Chrisman, *Rereading the Imperial Romance: British Imperialism and South African Resistance in Haggard, Schreiner, and Plaatje* (New York: Oxford University Press, 2000).

19 Eagleton's critique of the "anti-realist" position in the work of post-Marxists, which rejects

> the kind of classical epistemology which assumes some match or "correspondence" between our concepts and the way the world is. Rather, objects should be considered not as external to a realm of discourse which seeks to approximate them, but as wholly internal to such discourses, constituted by them through and through . . . as well as merely inverting the relation between signified and signifier. Hindess and Hirst . . . also effect a fatal semiotic confusion between *signified* and *referent.* . . . The relation between an object and its means of representation is crucially not the same as that between a material practice and its ideological legitimation or mystification. . . . Discourse for them "produces" real objects; and ideological language is therefore just one way in which these objects get constituted. But this simply fails to identify the specificity of such language, which is not just any way of constituting reality, but one with the more particular function of explaining, rationalizing, concealing, legitimating, and so on. . . . With Laclau and Mouffe, what Perry Anderson has called "the inflation of discourse" in poststructuralist thought reaches its apogee. Heretically deviating from their mentor Michel Foucault, Laclau and Mouffe deny all validity to the distinction between "discursive" and "non-discursive" practices, on the grounds that a practice is structured along the lines of a discourse. . . . A way of *understanding* an object is simply projected into the object itself . . . The category of discourse is inflated to the point where it imperializes the whole world, eliding the distinction between thought and material reality. (*Ideology* [London: Verso, 1991], 209, 219)

20 This does not prevent Bhabha from belaboring the point: "It [the function of theory] makes us aware that our political referents and priorities—the people, the community, class struggle, anti-racism, gender difference, the assertion of an anti-imperialist, black or third perspective—are not there in some primordial, naturalistic sense. Nor do they reflect a unitary or homogeneous political object. They make sense only as they come to be constructed in . . . discourses" (26).

21 Saussure's concept of language as a system of arbitrary and conventional signs, each defined not by essential properties but by its difference from other signs, maps the relational nature and inner operations of the linguistic system. As Christopher Norris has argued, Saussure's lack of interest in the referential aspect of language, justified as "a matter of convenience or methodological priority," does not provide "a warrant for extending the strictly heuristic principle to the point where any mention of the referent—any appeal beyond the self-enclosed domain of signification—is regarded as a lapse into naive ('positivist' or 'metaphysical') ways of thought" (182).

22 In "Doubting the New World Order: Marxism, Realism, and the Claims of Postmodernist Social Theory," *Differences: A Journal of Feminist Cultural Studies* 3(3) (1991): 94–138, Neil Lazarus argues that the "post-Marxist" position prematurely "extirpates *realism* in the course of its campaign against *empiricism,* reverting to an epistemological conventionalism that shaded almost inevitably into idealism, pragmatism, and, citing Roy Bhaskar, 'judgmental relativism' "; while postmodernist theorists following Foucault insist that discourse "is not a language about the social; on the contrary, it is not to be thought of as any kind of signifying practice exercised upon the social. *There is no social; there is only discourse*" (115, 123–24).

23 This problem is noted by Robert Young in his otherwise positive reading of Bhabha: see "The Ambivalence of Bhabha," in *White Mythologies: Writing History and the West* (London: Routledge, 1990).

24 *Discourse on Colonialism,* trans. Joan Pinkham (1955; New York: Monthly Review Press, 1972), 11.

25 *The Wretched of the Earth,* trans. Constance Farrington (1961; London: MacGibbon and Gee, 1965), 30.

26 For a development of this argument, see my "Resistance Theory/Theorizing Resistance."

27 See Stuart Hall's generous estimates of these and other anticolonialists in "Cultural Identity and Diaspora," in *Identity: Community, Culture, Difference,* ed. Jonathan Rutherford (London: Lawrence and Wishart, 1990), 223.

28 See my "Problems in Current Theories of Colonial Discourse" and Cedric Robinson, "The Appropriation of Frantz Fanon," *Race and Class* 35(1) (1993): 79–91. That Bhabha's "catachrestic" rewriting is untrue to the language and spirit of Fanon's text has since been forcefully argued by Neil Lazarus in an extensive critique where he contends that "Bhabha's textualism and his theoretical idealism prevent him from engaging adequately with the vastly differential thrusts, effects, and modes of domination/ subjection as practiced at different times by different powers in different parts of the world, or even with single colonies subject to the vicissitudes of uneven development. The problem derives, arguably, from the fact that although Bhabha predicates his theory of colonial discourse upon the work of Fanon, he contrives to read him 'back to

front'—that is from *The Wretched of the Earth* to *Black Skin, White Masks*—thereby falsifying the testimony of Fanon's own evolution as a theorist." By reading *Black Skin, White Masks* "not merely tendentiously but more specifically *against* Fanon's subsequent intellectual production, Bhabha uses it "to disavow Fanon's political commitments and his theorization of 'the African revolution' " ("Disavowing Decolonization," 87).

29 See David Harvey, "Class Relations, Social Justice and the Politics of Difference," in *Principled Positions: Postmodernism and the Rediscovery of Value*, ed. Judith Squires (London: Lawrence and Wishart, 1993), 85–120.

30 For a believer's view, see R. Radhakrishnan, "Poststructuralist Politics—Towards a Theory of Coalition," in *Postmodernism/Jameson/Critique*, ed. Douglas Kellner (Washington, D.C.: Maisonneuve Press, 1989).

31 "Not You/Like You: Post-colonial Women and the Interlocking Questions of Identity and Difference," *Inscriptions* 3/4 (1988): 71–77.

32 This is an argument I elaborate in "Resistance Theory/Theorising Resistance."

33 See "The Prose of Counter-Insurgency," in *Selected Subaltern Studies* (Oxford: Oxford University Press, 1988), 46.

34 *The Geopolitical Aesthetic: Cinema and Space in the World System* (Bloomington: Indiana University Press, 1992), 199.

35 *Theories of Africans: Francophone Literature and Anthropology in Africa.* (Chicago: University of Chicago Press, 1990), 27, 28.

36 Published by University of Chicago Press, 1992.

37 "Dominance without Hegemony and Its Historiography," *Subaltern Studies* VI (Delhi: Oxford University Press, 1989), 210–301.

38 Chrisman on "the neglect or marginalization of those geographical regions which experienced a different form of colonialism"; "Inventing Post-colonial Theory."

39 *The Condition of Postmodernity: An Enquiry into the Origins of Cultural Change* (Oxford: Blackwell, 1989), 264.

40 *Postmodern Geographies: The Reassertion of Space in Critical Social Theory* (London: Verso, 1989); and *Uneven Development: Nature, Capital and the Production of Space* (Oxford: Blackwell, 1984).

41 *Time and the Other* (New York: Columbia University Press, 1983).

42 "Welcome to the Jungle," in *Identity: Community, Culture, Difference*, ed. Jonathan Rutherford (London: Lawrence and Wishart, 1990), 55.

43 "New Ethnicities," in *Black Film, British Cinema* (London: ICA Document 7, 1988), 27–31.

44 "How I Discovered My Oriental Soul in the Wilderness of the West," *Third Text* 18 (spring 1992): 85–107; "Contemporary Cultural Practice: Some Polemical Categories," *Third Text* 11 (summer 1990): 109–17.

45 "Review Essay: Colonial Discourse: A Paradigm and Its Discontents," *Victorian Studies* 35(2) (winter 1992): 209–14.

46 See Stephen Howe, *Anticolonialism in British Politics: The Left and the End of Empire, 1918–1964* (Oxford: Oxford University Press, 1993).

47 "Althusser in Literary Studies," in *Althusser: A Critical Reader*, ed. Gregory Elliott (Oxford: Blackwell, 1994), 166.

48 *British Post-Structuralism since 1968* (London: Routledge, 1988), 34, 35, 72.

49 "All that Melts into Air Is Solid: The Hokum of *New Times*," *Race and Class* 31(3) (1989): 1–30.

50 For a powerfully argued case on the continuing need for forms of class politics, see David Harvey, "Class Relations, Social Justice and the Politics of Difference," in *Principled Positions*.

51 In *Black Marxism: The Making of the Black Radical Tradition* (London: Zed Books, 1983).

52 "Black Theorists and Left Antagonists," *Minnesota Review* 37 (fall 1991): 80–113.

Postcoloniality's Unconscious/Area Studies' Desire
H. D. Harootunian

It is hard to know what more can or even should be said about the status of post-colonial discourse and theory these days. So many books, articles, journals, criticism, and countercriticism devoted to it have appeared in recent years, at such a staggeringly dizzy pace, that it is a full-time job to simply keep up with the flow of paper, much less maintain a mastery of the field. In the United States, and I suspect elsewhere, it has seized control of English departments and along with its ally identity politics redefined the character of cultural studies. As a growth industry, it has probably peaked; its "inventories" have already exceeded the capacity for much further consumption. One of the lesser noted paradoxes of the practice of postcolonial studies is the volume of production and apparent ambiguity, if not outright invisibility, of the object upon which so much industry has been lavished in describing. In this regard, postcolonial studies resembles the older practices of area studies programs with their intellectual and scholarly divisions of labor into regional subsets like East Asia, Middle East, South Asia, Africa, geographical markers whose substantiality was realized only in maps. A sign that the status of the object itself and its uncertain decidability might be at the heart of so much activity is the splitting of postcolonial theory into the practices of discourse and criticism, both, apparently, claiming lives of their own. But this division may yet be only another manifestation of the effort to give further definition to an object that continually seems to be sliding and avoiding the stability usually associated with other objects of research. This nervousness over the uncertain status of its object has, it seems, prompted many of its adherents to take quite defensive stands in the face of what they consider hostile criticism (any criticism, I've discovered, is considered hostile) and appeal, no doubt anxiously, to both the relevance of criticism, yet to an indeterminacy that supposedly will answer critics and allow postcolonial studies to have it both ways.[1] Bart Moore-Gilbert's recent *Postcolonial Theory* is only the most recent reminder of this self-defensiveness, where he both accepts criticism but tries to turn critics on their head, so to speak, in the same gesture that he concludes his study on the resounding note of indeterminacy (where have we heard this before?) that solidly anchors him in mid-air.

I would like to suggest here that this anxiety may in fact stem from the rumblings of postcoloniality's unconscious and the resurfacing of a repressed history that refuses to remain buried. That history is, of course, the role played by area studies and its several practices, which was the way the non-European world was first studied and taught in universities and colleges at the beginning of the Cold War. In the United States, its formation and implementation had everything to do with the Cold War and the demands of the national security state. Yet despite the confidence attending the establishment of area studies programs and its promise to grasp the totality of a region, its inaugural moment was marred by the absence of a definable object. Asia was simply an age-old cartographer's fantasy, reinforced by the necessities of World War II, referring only to itself in the expectancy that something out there will eventually correspond to it or be made to align with it. Vast professional organizations, college curricula, graduate training programs, and research institutes were organized around this substanceless something, as if it were an object, pledged to disseminating a knowledge even as the object vanished once it seemed we had a grip on it. (Postcoloniality has sought to avoid this embarrassment by disavowing totalities altogether but it has not solved the problem of the vanishing object.) With area studies Asia, for instance, was simply a process of naming but the names were as lifeless as the social science—geography—that once declared its reality and named its presence. The best-kept secret in the practice of area studies was the fact that nobody ever questioned the directional tyranny that names as east the place we go to study. But where is it that we really start from, where is the place that enunciates this itinerary? By restoring this history—an unconscious—to the discourse on postcoloniality, an understandably unwanted history, we might learn something about the disappearance of an object and how a phantom and a fantasy mobilized immense intellectual resources and structured institutional programs to produce its "knowledge."

It should not be surprising that area studies and postcoloniality are historically yoked. For it was postcolonial discourse's canonical text, Edward Said's *Orientalism*, that fixed the relationship between the formation of colonial discourse as politically empowered knowledge and the then established practice of area studies, especially Middle East studies programs.[2] Toward the end of the book, Said turned to area studies programs devoted to Middle East and Islamic studies and observed how their own informing claims to knowledge of people of the area were imbedded in Orientalist assumptions. Despite his own penchant for stereotyping those whom he accuses of stereotyping, it was logical for Said to relate his analysis of Orientalist knowledge to institutionalized area studies programs. But what is puzzling is why and how this move to link an incipient colonial discourse to area studies was almost immediately overlooked, ignored, and forgotten in the subsequent formation of a field of postcolonial studies. While Said clearly referred to area studies as a current example of how Orientalist knowledge had been recoded, there is little in his original account to suggest that colonial discourse, seen from the perspective of decolonization, was more than a chronological marker and a mode of knowing that shaped and voiced the other during the long period of European colonization in the Middle East. If Said's *Orientalism* sensitized us to the practices of Europeans who were in a position to construct knowledges and identities of non-Europeans, invariably the colonized, and spoke for them as master ventriloquists, it did not, at the same time, propose the establishment of a new epistemology capable of authorizing a methodology devoted to elucidating its objects. (Said's book showed an astonishing indifference to the rest of the colonial world, the diversity of colonial experiences and those regions that were being classified as Third World, which may have had a prior colonizing experience that ended in the nineteenth century —Latin America—or none at all, like Thailand or Japan.) What I mean is that though he identified for us how knowledge about the Orient was constituted, he also showed that it had derived directly from received systems of knowledge already in practice in nineteenth-century Europe. It was thus one thing to alert us to how Europeans constituted the figure of the colonial other; it was an entirely different thing to leap to the assumption that colonial discourse opened the way to a new epistemology identified with the field of postcoloniality and its objects, one that would transform a chronological moment into an epistemological program promising a different way of looking at the world. With Said, the importance of linking his observations on the formation of colonial knowledge to area studies signaled the time and occasion to rethink the practice of area studies, revitalize it and put it on another, less politically mediated, basis of knowledge. In this regard, Said's book represented an important intellectual challenge to the mission of area studies which, if accepted, would have reshaped area studies and freed it from its own reliance on the Cold War and the necessities of the national security state. What Said's book disclosed to area studies for a short moment was its desire for theory, which it had displaced by privileging language acquisition as both all the theory and method needed for understanding a region. Hence, the challenge was never accepted, perhaps for the very reasons of instrumentality that had implanted such programs in colleges and universities in the first place, cumulatively constituting stakes and investments that made change too high a price to pay. Instead, Said's critique migrated to English studies to transform the study of literature into a full-scale preoccupation with identity and its construction.

Although writers like Peter Hulme and Stuart Hall understandably have not recognized this relationship, owing, perhaps, to the underdeveloped role played by area studies in the United Kingdom, they have focused on the "tension" between the two moments of chronology and epistemology inscribed in the "post" of postcoloniality, its temporality rooted in viewing the colonial experience from the perspective of its aftermath, and its putative critical ambition to figure a new field of knowledge.[3] As suggested above, this division was absent in Said's earlier work (but is made to appear as natural in *Culture and Imperialism*) and explains why he linked colonial knowledge to area studies, rather than envisage a new epistemology pursuing a knowledge of different objects. There is nothing in the temporality of colonialism and indeed its decolonizing aftermath to authorize the leap to an image that, in Benjamin's idiom and example of translation, constituted not a copy but another original, an afterlife and afterimage. The consequences of the colonial experience for the period of decolonization did not necessarily require a new mode of knowledge designed to grasp what after all was still a problem of modern temporality. But what is missing in the narrative of postcolonial studies is its massive institutional expansion in the 1970s and the subsequent transformation of English departments and its traditional curriculum. Because of this transmutation of English studies, especially in the United States, postcoloniality was forced to jettison its more modest associations as chronology and temporality—as a historical subject—to acquire a new identity as a critical knowledge serving an entirely new or different field of study and research, as an evaluative concept rather than a descriptive term. While I will say more about this transformation and expansion later, it is important to suggest that it was necessitated by enlargement of graduate training and a job market that simply couldn't accommodate the numbers of new Ph.D.s within the older paradigm of literary studies.

It is important to remember that area studies suffered from the same absence of an object in its aspiration to represent the totality of a country/region as plainly as postcoloniality strove to be more than a chronological marker in order to become a global theory of knowledge. Just as area studies inaugurally and lastingly suppressed the role of capital in its curricular and research paradigms, so postcoloniality has insisted upon rejecting the totalizing force of capitalism—seen merely as another Western narrative—in order to avoid structuring essentialisms and foundationalism. Area studies early appealed to functionalist social science and its total system as a model for grasping a region and ultimately relied upon a number of structuring principles that fixed the identity of a particular group or region. By the same measure, postcoloniality, wedded to the Saidian critique of a politically empowered knowledge, was faced with its alternative, implicit in Said but obviously resisted, which was the allure of native knowledge. This is not to say that postcoloniality slipped into a defense of native knowledge and experience but only to suggest that there are moments when it, in discourses like subaltern studies, risks resembling earlier plaints protesting the loss of native culture and knowledge before the eroding assault of capitalist modernization. Fanon was one of the earliest to observe how capitalism destroyed cultures of reference wherever it established its regime and recognized the necessity of finding a way to construct a new national culture that was able to preserve elements from the received tradition without being assimilated to the culture of colonizers and capitalism. Moreover, he insisted on the importance of the specificity of historical location in any effort to envisage a new national culture. Japanese thinkers in the 1920s and 1930s, as only one among a number of historical examples, invariably turned away from the performative present to a cultural experience in an indeterminate past in order to recall what it had meant to be Japanese before the coming of capitalism. Yet when a writer like Partha Chatterjee wonders whether the former colonized are to become nothing more than mere consumers of modernity, in the interest of trying to locate an anticolonial nationalism uncontaminated by the force of a colonizing presence, we come very close to embracing the claims of cultural authenticity an earlier generation promoted in order to rescue heterogeneity and the cultural exceptionalisms Japanese and others still make audible. But in the absence of capitalism, as Arif Dirlik has so forcefully reminded us in his critique of postcolonial discourse, both area studies and its postcolonial successor have been forced to appeal to culturalism, area studies to explain a region as a total system that privileges the outer world as the subject/agent and postcoloniality to an experience emphasizing the identity of subject as the putative structuring force. This turn to culture has inevitably led to both a supercession of history, and to the articulation of formalist exceptionisms where history seems to have been completed in archaic times. Where area studies has privileged the region/national origin, postcoloniality has valorized the formation of subjectivity and a politics of identity rooted in location. Yet this move echoes earlier programs, already noted, of thinkers and writers who appealed to an authentic ground as the unassailable domain of native interiority free from the corrosions of the outside world, that is to say, the West.

When, for example, Japanese native ethnologists in the 1920s and 1930s sought to contest the consequences of capitalist modernization, they invariably positioned place and its relationship to a specific subject formation. But in either case, politics disappears and culture appears as a constant in subject formation. If area studies, clinging to an older culture/personality social science, envisaged a fixed and unchanging subject traversing all of historical time, postcoloniality has presented figures of the colonized as equally fixed in their hybridity, virtually encased in their fractured composition, as if they were necessary to the smooth working of a functionalist social system. If, for example, Ruth Benedict's earlier *Chrysanthemum and the Sword* defined for area studies a holistic social science that presumed to represent Japanese or Chinese (I am thinking of Francis Hsu's *In the Ancestor's Shadows*) for all time to come, the move by postcolonial studies in depriviliging the role played by history (and capital as its most recent social formation), the stereotyping that Said and Homi Bhabha (respectively the indeterminate "subaltern" and the performer of "sly civility" and "mimicry") produce while protesting against it in others differs only in the slightest degree and shares the same indifference to history. Where area studies and postcoloniality differ is in the temporality each occupies and in the choice of epistemologies each has sought to align itself with: in area studies the epistemology and methodology of choice was generally functionalist social science while in postcoloniality it has been the literary/semiotic disciplines (textuality). Despite this difference it is surprising that the two strategies are as closely related to each other in their produced effects.

It is understandable why postcoloniality has repressed its historic relationship to area studies. It should be well known by now that area studies had grown out of service language schools in the United States that had been established to train young men and women in the languages of the enemy in order to serve as interrogators of Japanese initially, then Koreans, Chinese, and Vietnamese. In time, this inaugural gesture was reinforced by the Cold War and the necessity of understanding not only the enemy but potential enemies among the nonaligned. Any reader of Ruth Benedict's *Chrysanthemum and the Sword* will recall her acknowledgment that the book was commissioned by the Office of War Information and its stated purpose was to better understand the behavior of the enemy the United States was fighting. The systematic formation of area studies, principally in major universities, was thus a massive attempt to relocate the enemy in the new configuration of the Cold War. This relocating was made possible by large infusions of cash from private corporations, scholarly organizations like the Social Science Research Council "brokering" (actually pimping) for both government and private funders, and businesses.

But this intervention was not simply limited to American universities. The

Rockefeller Foundation poured in a lot of money into the reorganization of the social sciences in France to give the French a new and more scientific social science capable of combating the claims of Marxism. During the Vietnam War, the Ford Foundation was seen trying to support the study of Southeast Asian studies at Kyoto University and for years has been active in both India and Indonesia. In fact, the Cold War easily replaced the experience of wartime necessity to learn the enemies' language and customs by establishing a more comprehensive and integrated link between the task of identifying the enemy and gathering knowledge—intelligence—about it. As a field of inquiry finding its own place at the end of the academic procession in colleges and universities, area studies was a response to the wartime discovery of the paucity of reliable information concerning most of the world outside of Europe. In the United States, deficiency of knowledge also included Latin and Central America, long regions subjected to American financial and commercial exploitation, constituting yet another example of how imperialism and colonialism blot out history.

In the immediate postwar period, recognition was made more urgent by the military and political expansion of the United States in its effort to reconfigure the world. Underscoring this new urgency and giving it force were a number of reports issued by official and semi-official commissions that called for the rapid installation of multidisciplinary programs, comprised of specialists in a variety of disciplines, to train a postwar generation as area specialists and provide policy making and business strategies with informed, socialized knowledge of specific regions. These commissions called for ill-conceived programs that emphasized the need for "integrated" approaches that privileged the present, suggesting that interest in historical cultures was no longer useful to government and business. Corporate sponsorship was early recruited and reflected in large-scale grants from the Rockefeller, Carnegie, and Ford Foundations to programs at Yale (Far Eastern studies), the University of Washington (Far East and Russia), Columbia University (Soviet and East European studies), Harvard (Russia studies), the University of Michigan (Japanese Studies), the New Nations Program at the University of Chicago, and the modernization of societies program at Princeton. While the government took over this responsibility with the passage of the National Education Defense Act in 1958 (the "Sputnik" effect), private foundations continued to pour money into established area studies program, which in time was supplemented by overseas foundations associated with foreign governments and private foundations.

It should be pointed out that the establishment of area studies programs promised to "transcend" disciplinary boundaries-partitioned knowledge to provide holistic and integrated accounts of different regions. (This was the purpose of the massive Human Relations File project undertaken at Yale University in the early years of the Cold War.) But because of the relentless kinship area studies formed with strategic policy making, serving national interests and "contract research," it was never able to free itself from the pursuit of a knowledge bonded to the necessities that had given it shape. In a 1970 report on the status of Japanese studies in the United States for the Social Science Research Council, John W. Hall, formerly of Yale University, saw Japanese area studies programs and its personnel as a national resource. During the Vietnam War, Professor John K. Fairbank of Harvard, literally the last emperor of Chinese studies in the United States, constantly hammered on the instrumentalist theme that the war showed how little Americans knew about Asia and why it was important for both government and private business to support Asian (Chinese) area studies programs. Yet it was precisely this division of intellectual labor marking area studies—its service to the state and business and even to foreign governments, as we've seen recently—that has militated against realizing an integrated knowledge of areas and encouraged its continuing partitioning and fragmenting.

In the late 1940s, reports calling for the establishment of new area studies programs invariably revealed the kind of knowledge that should be secured. William Fenton's influential *Area Studies in American Universities* of 1947 proposed that the very methodology of integrated studies constituted a new challenge. "In taking the functional view of contemporary civilizations," he wrote, "it jeopardizes the strong position which the historical method holds in academic thinking." The new functional approach concentrates on the present situation with its "latent historicity, in place of long developmental curricula running from Aristotle to modern times." And "its calls on the method of the cultural historian to develop major themes in the civilization, delving deep enough into the past only to make the present understandable."[4] In time, this was an invitation to abandon history altogether, to ignore the effects of power in order to simply identify the structural parts that functioned to make possible an orderly social system. Needless to say, this was the "end of ideology," utopian dream of functionalist social science which camp followers in area studies would seek to instantiate in countless studies throughout the 1950s and 1960s. While an older social science focusing on the interaction of culture and society in the formation of a modal (national) personality, dramatized at war's end by Benedict, Geoffrey Gorer, and Francis Hsu, cooperated with this recommendation to eliminate the long duration of history or any temporality but the present, not to mention historical specificity as such, it could not supply an adequate account for explaining change and development so vital to Cold War policy strategies aimed at winning the hearts and minds of the free and unaligned world. Because of this deficiency, it risked making modern social groups appear as identical with their stone age predecessors. Owing to this epistemological failure, a different kind of social science capable of explaining development and change was required, especially one that might offer an alternative to Marxian conflict models and its conception of revolutionary transformation. This was provided by structuralist-functionalism, which in the 1950s rearticulated the Social Darwinist conception of evolutionary adaptation and development and was reconfigured into an export model of growth that was called modernization and convergence theory. What eventually would be offered as both a representation of and a prescription for development was an evolutionary model of growth, against a putative revolutionary one that, if followed, would promise the realization of the peaceful development of capitalism and, presumably, political democracy in nonaligned societies, precisely the staging place of decolonization and the subsequent installation of postcolonial studies. Claiming normative status but appearing more as a lavish idealization scarcely reflecting any recognizable American society on which it was supposed to be based, the theory was inspired by Talcott Parsons's theoretical patternings and Marion Levy's unusable applications. Its theory and claim to knowledge rested on a number of ideal typical traits: society as coherently organized systems whose subsystems were interdependent; historical development (periodized into traditional and modern) that determined social subsystems; modernity meant rational, scientific, secular and Western; the process of modernization was historically evolutionary; and, lastly, traditional, nonmodern societies could successfully modernize if evolution had already demonstrated a process of adaptive upgrading of social and cultural values. What modernization theory seemed to share with Marxism, and later postcolonial discourse, was a refusal to recognize modernity as a specific cultural and temporal form and thus a failure to acknowledge a consciousness of lived historical time that differs according to differing social forces which rely on experience of place as much as they do on time. In the scholarly world of the 1950s, 1960s, and 1970s, this interpretative strategy dominated research agendas related to area studies, as they still do, as an unquestioned common sense, even though the Cold War has ended. Yet in this period of time, marked by the ending of the Vietnam War and the explosion of colonial discourse, its most spectacular success was supplied by the example of Japan and the singularity of the national model, which area studies invariably reinforced. Modernization theory was seemingly able to validate the category of national society more easily than a heterogeneous area like East Asia and show how a country like Japan was able to reproduce the necessary patterns successfully when others like India and Turkey were apparently failing. It was for this reason that Japanese political arrangements have consistently been represented as democratic and consensual when, in fact, they are still driven by a single party and a bureaucracy devoted to managed capitalism rather than the "free play" of the market. Japan was made to inhabit a narrative free from conflict and contradiction, where traditional values were able to adapt to new exigencies and perform as rational agents. But it is important to notice that the category of the nation is made to stand in for the area or region and the efforts to present a coherent East Asia invariably appeal to the binding power of a religion or an ethic as they fuse with capitalism, which stretches the imagination as much as it insults the intelligence. The force of muscular national or ethnic metonyms seems also to have migrated to postcolonial studies where Bengal is made to stand in for the subcontinent.

One of the real effects of modernization theory was to transmute a prescriptive into a descriptive, the putatively rational into the real, an ought into what is. One consequence of this tactic in the study of societies like Japan has been to discourage the importation of newer theoretical approaches (sensitive to knowledge/power, cognizant of colonial experiences, etc.) in order to defend the representation of what has been naturalized as a sign of empirical research. What I mean is that a particular representation of Japan, driven by the demands of modernization theory, is made to appear as the natural result of empirical research unmediated by theory. But in fact, the Japan and China fields, more than most, have never shown much inclination to "validate" theoretically or methodologically the "field," as such, which itself never questions the conceptual status of a "field" called "Japan," other than to assume its status as a race-nation without further explanation. Japanese studies, as practiced today in the English-speaking world (United States and the United Kingdom), for the most part, has remained riveted to serving a national interest, first in the United States, United Kingdom, or Australia and then Japan. Organizations like the SSRC, especially, and the Japan Foundation, presumably devoted to "cutting edge" methodology, have made sure that the national committee structures directing their respective activities (distributing funding and controlling the nature of research) serve as sole custodians and vigilant guard dogs against precisely the kind of theoretical and methodological innovations they purport to promote. Instead of encouraging greater integration of differing knowledges and new intellectual agendas, they have managed only to produce partitioning and dispersion, which the reproduction of received views of a region promise to secure. This jealously guarded defense of a particular view of the area, say Japan, is matched by the reproduction of institutional and organizational structures (composition of committees distributing funds for fellowship and research) that go the distance to reinforcing claims of normativity. It is here that the negative desire for theory at the heart of area studies is defined and repressed.

Apart from the vast institutional and financial inducements that encourage the study of an area through the optic of the nation, the nation as a category often determines how people will study it. Many who rush to a study for one personal reason or another (missionary connection, service experience, delayed exoticism, etc.) usually seek to mask such emotional attachments behind appeals to empirical and "scientific" authority. The early generation of Americans who raced to study Japan after the war, for example, showed how the nation's history disclosed the rule of reason and how closely the modernizing experience resembled the example of the United States. (In this project, they received inestimable assistance from the experience of the U.S. military occupation, which had envisaged Japan as a laboratory for social democracy and a window of opportunity for improving upon the American experience and removing its defects.) This fantasy was projected by the work of modernization studies, sponsored by the Ford Foundation, that effectively worked to transform former foe into friend and trading partner. Yet it went further to disguise or misrecognize the semi-colonial status of Japan after the occupation ended. The real consequences of this transformation was to show in teaching and research that Japan most nearly replicated the developments of the capitalist and democratic West, despite its brief and disastrous interlude with fascism. In the case of China, study was dominated by the paradigm of challenge and response (actually an old Toynbeean chestnut recycled by Fairbanks and his personal army of students) that saw China responding to the West and failing, owing to retrograde institutions and intellectual traditions, often described negatively as the "non-development of science" and the "non-development of capitalism." Early interpreters of South Asia (what used to be called "Empire Studies") easily and enthusiastically overlooked colonialism and attributed all of India's problems as a fledgling democratic order to the dead hand of religion and overpopulation, as if, in fact, the subcontinent had never been colonized. With South Asia, the approach to the region seemed to still be shadowed by Hegel's dim assessment concerning the negativity of Indian life.

If the identity between professional area specialists, say, Japanologists, and the field of study appears more prominent and thus overdetermined than in other area studies, it is, I believe, because of the overwhelming production of native knowledge and thus self-consciousness that has marked the path of Japan's own modernity. By contrast, the development of subaltern studies as a form of native intervention came comparatively late and related more to the development of postcolonial studies than the maintenance of South Asian studies. This valorization of native knowledge is, in any case, an occupational handicap that dogs the study of Asia especially and parts of the non-European world. Area interest is powered by a mix of exoticisms, however displaced, and the desire for nearness, closing the distance, being there rather than here, pursuing the promise of difference. During my first trip to Japan, I encountered all kinds of Americans (and some French) fulfilling their exotic and erotic fantasies for re-identification, ranging from obsessive *kanji* sharks (obsession with learning many stroke ideographs rarely used) as they were called, to those who wore baskets on their head, carried wooden rice bowls, and pretended they were itinerant Buddhist pilgrims. We might call this the Pierre Loti effect, which is easily recognizable as a mode of making contact with otherness even though it relies on costume and performance. Since then, only the objects promising instant identity with the other have changed. (The latest example is a male American who, after a brief stay in Japan, has written a novel from the viewpoint of a geisha about to be made into a movie by Spielberg!) With China, there was the "helping hand," the vanished missionary vocation transmuted into modern Chinese studies, the feigned outrage over the loss of high culture and the empty nostalgia for what never existed and the seeming helplessness of the Chinese people before Japanese aggression. Later, for only a moment, it was the romance of revolution. In the case of Japan, there is the legacy of the American Occupation and the romanticization of this inaugural partnership to rebuild a free and prosperous Japan.

When I was a graduate student studying history, I was puzzled by the way Japan, and indeed most of Asia, was presented as a field where one went to do fieldwork, even if one's purpose was archival rather than ethnographic. People were always off to the field or just returning from it. (The University of Michigan actually had a "field station" outside of Okayama.) By the same measure, I knew that France, Italy, and England were countries where people went for study and research; Japan—Asia—and Africa were simply fields that required first-hand observation, recording, and, in some instances, intervention. Perhaps this sense of the field revealed the deeper relationship of these areas to a colonial unconscious, where they were still seen as spaces occupied by "natives" that needed to be observed and thus represented. What this differentiation between field and country, the present and the past, suggested was both distance, physical and figural, and the existence of different temporalities marking the boundary between modern and premodern. As students, we were enjoined to spend time in the field to observe societies who lived in a different temporality, even though we all inhabited the time of the present, the now. Its most important effect was to classify the field as inside and native and we as visitors from the outside and non-native, driven by the desire to gain entry in order to penetrate and thus grasp the concealed secrets of native knowledge and sensibility, which always remained out of reach, until the last, lonely instant. The conceit of transforming a place into a field was a custom long practiced by anthropologists and ethnographers, who saw the field as code for laboratory; now it became a commonplace among historians, political scientists, economists, sociologists, and students of literature. Encouraged therefore to view Japan (or China, which was closed off to Americans, who were thus forced to settle for surrogates like Taiwan and Hong Kong) as an ethnographic site, students were required to complete intensive language work and gather experience living among the natives. These two conditions were inevitably seen as more than adequate substitutes or replacements for theory and methodology, as they still are; in fact, they were seen as functional analogs to theory and method. Moreover, trainees since the end of World War II have regularly acquired wives who could double as native informants and stand in for the field experience in those long durations away from the field. If this often constituted a kind of passage in the rite of training, it also sealed an identity with Japan (or the area) that worked to further foreclose the possibility of critique. It became an integral part in the process of acquiring identity with the area.

What this relationship revealed was a deeply imbedded hermeneutic that had always promised to promote the immediacy of empathy and identification as the most appropriate and authentic mode of studying Japan and, I suspect, Asia in general. This unspoken epistemological assumption inevitably betrayed its own racialist conceit in the recognition that only natives are able to stand in the place of the native. (I recall colleagues who were specialists in China and Chinese always calling into question the capacity of the non-Chinese to truly understand the Chinese language and, by extension, China.) But it is important to remind ourselves that this conception of a hermeneutic, based on the primacy of and experience in the field ("field-time") and the desire for native or near-native language proficiency has marked both the way regions are studied and the conditions that inhibit the practice of theory in the construction of research and intellectual agendas, which are dismissed out of hand and even hysterically denounced in "field" journals like the *Journal of Japanese Studies, Harvard Journal of Asiatic Studies,* and *Monumenta Nipponica.* In fact, the punctual exercise of terrorist denunciation has become the principal vocation of such field journals today, which notoriously act solely as self-arrogated custodians of what can only be described as the authenticity of native knowledge and native concepts, as if native experience anywhere, much less Japan, remained immune from the threat of what Chatterjee identified as the consumption of modernity. The recent attack on James Hevia's *Cherishing Men from Afar* in *Modern China,* under the supposed occasion of assessing "The Uses of Theory in Modern

Chinese History Research," was more a gang bang enacted by some of the leaders of the field than a critical engagement of a work that tries to appeal to new interpretative strategies. What was staged was a call to return to the sources and the facts so venerated by Chinese scholars, as if native knowledge itself, not to mention either the "sources" and facticity, the archive, were untroubled and unproblematic concepts capable of revealing their own reason of theory, with little effort. Years ago the *Journal of Japanese Studies* orchestrated a similar panic attack against E. H. Norman's older *Japan's Emergence as a Modern State,* where the writer dug into the footnotes to show how Norman had fudged, even though the real issue was Norman's putative Marxism, which, of course, the critic and the journal only understood in the worst idiom of the Cold War. That the journal is housed at the University of Washington, which once employed Karl Wittfogel, who denounced Norman to a House Un-American Activities Committee as a communist were, of course, passed over in the review and by the editors of the journal, as if it were unrelated. While no work is free from error and mishaps, one has to wonder why sewer-based scholarship is always leveled against those on the left but exempts those on the right.

Nevertheless, the appeal to native knowledge, even by those who do not qualify as natives as such holds the promise of retaining the sense of immediacy capable of resisting all mediations. In this way, the desire for native knowledge promised by a hermeneutics of identification became the principal epistemological and methodological agenda lodged in the heart of area studies. Years ago the sociologist of Japan R. P. Dore observed (more like fantasized) that area specialists acquire the characteristics of the areas they study. Paul Cohen's recent call for a sinocentric history (one that would undoubtedly and enthusiastically please the editors of *Modern China* and its bestiary of tried-and-true contributors) simply reaffirms this desire but does not persuasively explain how it can be satisfied. It is an attempt to redress the imbalance produced by Fairbank's conception of "response" that privileged the West as the first term in an uneven and asymmetrical binary, which always saw the second term as lack and incomplete. If the claims of this unstated hermeneutic rejects theory out of hand for the "facts" and thus the authority of native knowledge and experience, it has also forced its adherents to repeat native pieties and serve willingly as its amanuenses, faithfully conveying the dictations produced on the so-called native ground of cultural authenticity. But this appeal, which still prevails among students of Japan and China, if not other areas, contrasts dramatically with the traditions of studying regions like Europe and Latin America that are geographically and culturally closer to our own national experience of history. Recently, Jonathan Culler has called for the reorganization of European studies along the lines of the area studies model and thus a repackaging of pedagogy and research in terms of discrete national entities.

Area studies as a model has produced a theory of knowledge and a practice based on the authority and authenticity of native experience in a world where the native is simply no longer on the outside, as once imagined, but rather subjected to the same political-economic processes and structures all of us encounter in our everyday lives. If the native were outside, as desired by those who call for native-centered knowledge and a return to the sources, there would be no possibility whatsoever for retrieving them for representation. (One has to wonder about those ancient Romans and Greeks that generations of British schoolboys were made to "understand" as if they shared a common identity.) The distinction between West and non-West and the geopolitical identification between modernity and a specific place is simply a Western concept that has been used to establish and maintain Western unity and superiority and can no longer be taken for granted. If area studies has produced a theory, as I believe, based on this differentiation, it has also unwittingly incorporated both the imperial and colonial aspirations of the West, even as it sought to ignore these empowering structures in the effort to envisage a total knowledge of a region. Any critique must now be positioned not inside or outside the "West," since the West can no longer be thought of as a geographical concept privileged to structure the non-West or to differentiate the place of Asia. But rather it must be located imminently within the temporality of modernity that embraces new cultural forms developing in what used to be called the non-West and which now offer the occasion for dialectical encounter.[5] Owing to its own desire to identify with native knowledge, area studies has strangely run the risk of forming a link with all those more recent efforts to elevate identity and cultural difference as the true vocation of a cultural studies seeking to succeed the study of the area. Finally, the most important consequence of these patterns of identification with the "field" has been to prevent its practitioners from reflecting on themselves as specialists in the field, from seeing the field as a practice itself as an object of knowledge production. Instead, it has relied on the natural identification with the native's knowledge and fluency in the cultural idiom—as a more than adequate substitute for theoretical self-reflection. But, as I've suggested, this was a desire, not a method, which concealed the absence of theory and method that postcolonial studies has more than satisfied. This resistance to theoretical self-reflection has been signified in the overdetermined effort of area studies to recruit funds from any willing source, domestic or foreign, without asking too many questions and worrying too much about finding new ways to think through the more difficult task of constructing a knowledge of Asia and teaching it. Far from this purpose, the real intention of this craze to find funding seems to have no other reason than sustaining the structure of area studies and maintaining what can only be described as a dinosaur whose head can longer support its body.

If the search for funding, aimed at sustaining the received organization of area studies, its structures of knowledge, and curriculum, still characterizes its principal vocation, it has also reinforced further resistance to the incorporation of new cultural strategies capable of offering a solution to the deficiencies of an approach driven obsessively by the search for money. The retention of this approach only recuperates the lost historical world of its own origins as a program of study, research, and teaching. While the newer cultural studies promises to open ways to a more productive understanding of how to integrate local experiences into the larger world, it might also help restore the relevance of national societies by alerting us to models competent to resituate the role of critique and instate diverse local experiences as instantiated inflections of larger processes. The importance of cultural studies lays in the recognition—completely overlooked by area studies, of seeing knowledge as production that demands an abandoning of what Louis Althusser once referred to as the "mirror myths of immediate vision." If earlier area studies employed a strategy driven by a holistic conception of knowledge that emphasized the primacy of enduring cultural values ("core values") and the claims of political and social normativity, the method it privileged to realize this putatively innocent description was based on a multidisciplinarism that too often was misrecognized as interdisciplinarism. What it has managed to accomplish was the maintenance of disciplinary domains as hallowed precincts and boundaries as inviolable dividers. This means that an understanding of the area as a totality is possible only when and if the disciplines are all accounted for. Yet this approach has never really been questioned for its enabling assumption of understanding the whole so long as the disciplinary parts are all lined up like ducks ready to speak their partial truths. But the one truth area studies never spoke was the operation of its conditions of empowerment that produced a particular knowledge of an area or region to serve the national interest, whether it was the security state or multinational corporations.

By contrast the new cultural studies has tried to break with both holism and its concern for core values and an approach that has consistently disavowed considerations of knowledge/power for one that explicitly centers the operations of power and domination. Moreover, it has worked to break down disciplinary barriers to better understand not just the locus of power but its migrating habits, even though it has not always managed to replace an earlier and discredited multidisciplinarism. Where this obsessive Foucauldianism has often led to locating power everywhere, it also finds the opportunity for resistance everywhere. Too often this has resulted in lavish declarations of resistance among the powerless, the weak, and consumers who are made to appear as if they are exercising choice when buying a commodity or surfing TV channels. Sometimes, the mere enunciation of cultural difference and thus identity is made to appear as a political act of crowning importance when it usually means the disappearance of politics as such.

The politics of identity based on the enunciation of cultural difference is not the same as political identity whose formation depends less on difference than on some recognition of equivalencies. Yet all of this is still a vast improvement over an approach that has led its practitioners to acquire the characteristics of the field they study, without for a moment thinking about what it means to invade, inhabit, and "snatch" the body of an other. Because of the implementation of a Foucauldian desire to locate power everywhere but nowhere in specific, the appropriation of a Gramscian conception of hegemony to disguise the status quo or a Habermasian dependence upon the installation of a public sphere nobody seems to inhabit yet, the new cultural studies risks recuperating a similar reluctance noted earlier in area studies to explicitly link power and domination in specific configurations to the role played by capital and the state. If the older area studies aimed at promoting descriptions that masked a prescriptive for development in order to export American capitalism and its system of values to the Third World and to defeat the Second, the new cultural studies often risks reaching the same place by concentrating on microtechnologies of power and displacing state and capital to indeterminate loci of power and its local inflections. This is accomplished by emphasizing discourses of power and their slippage, splitting subjectivities and charting their subsequent dissemination, as if the movement constituted a natural function of an unnamed conception of social order that already exists, though its proponents disavow totalities. In more recent efforts to imagine a "globalization" process to account for the local yet diminish the importance of the category of the nation, we see what often appears as a rearticulation of modernization theory in a different register. This neomodernization celebrates cultural difference enthusiastically, very much in the manner of the united colors of Benetton, yet fails to recognize that production of plural identities is fully consistent with the propensity of global capital to undermine all fixed positions for a fetishized "narcissism of small differences." Which brings us back to postcolonial theory as the natural successor of area studies by virtue of both genealogy and geography.

In a certain sense, area studies missed the opportunity first made available when Said argued that its knowledge of region was already mediated by the power/knowledge considerations of colonialism and colonial discourse. Said, correctly I believe, wanted to assimilate the practice of area studies to colonial discourse, which would have ultimately endowed it (postcolonialiality) with a desire to account for the complex relationship between colonizer and colonized, metropole and colony, a world shaped by the forces of Western imperialism, as well as the all too often forgotten observation of Franz Fanon that hegemonic cultures also colonize the mind. As for this significant but missed opportunity, it is important to say here that the indifference of area studies to Said's strategic observation meant that it would remain locked in its own enclaves of knowledge and that the work of rethinking the mission of regions outside of Europe, what had become marked as the Third World, would pass to English studies and the humanities. Although there was activity in response to the publication of *Orientalism* among Asianists (the *Journal of Asian Studies* published a symposium of three papers on the book from the predictable perspective of China, Japan, and South Asia), it soon dissipated into general indifference and ultimate forgetfulness.

We must try to imagine the reasons why the institutional proponents of area studies were so eager to miss the occasion provided by Said's critique. The best guess is that the Saidian critique called into question the neocolonialist origins of area studies (its inaugural reason for existence) and its conception of knowledge that, by the mid 1970s, was deeply imbedded in American schools and colleges. The investment in training programs (assisted by the federal government), faculty recruitment, and curriculum seemed too great to leave to the uncertainties of a critique that was now calling for the overhaul of a system of knowledge. This missed opportunity was seized by English studies especially, undoubtedly owing to Said's own disciplinary affiliation and professional reputation, which quickly transmuted colonial discourse into a critique of the received canon and as an occasion for rethinking and expanding both established curriculum and its intellectual focus. One of the genuinely consequential effects of this overlooked opportunity and the monopolization of colonial discourse by English studies and its gradual transformation into postcolonial theory is that the migration of colonial discourse to English studies meant that its emphasis would be textual, semiotic, and generic, whereas if area studies had confronted the challenge posed by the Saidian critique, there would have been greater concern for the social sciences and the role played by political economy, that is to say, materiality. It is also because of this association with British literature, especially nineteenth-century writing, that explains why so much of postcolonial discourse has instantiated South Asia, especially Bengal, rather than other parts of the Empire or indeed the empires of other nations. One of the genuine ironies of postcolonial studies is the observable fact that some of the principal, pioneering theorists—Fanon, Cesaire, Senghor, Memmi—came from the French empire, Africa, and the Caribbean, yet none of these founding texts developed into a full-scale theory or discourse of postcoloniality in either France or Western Europe. In fact, some of our leading theorists of postcoloniality are from Britain's former South Asian colony, who have been trained principally, or at least inaugurally, in English studies. The exception are the historians, to be sure, Guha's stable of subaltern specialists whose major focus, nevertheless, concentrates more on Bengal than India.

While the critical literature on postcoloniality concentrates on the qualitative side of this transformation, calling into question its epistemological claims, it has almost entirely neglected the quantitative impact it has on English studies and cultural studies in the United States. What I mean is that Said's *Orientalism* enabled English studies, and by expansion departments, to remake themselves precisely at that moment graduate schools were being overpopulated with students with few prospects for either viable subject matters for research (how many books on Keats do we need and what's left to edit?) and fewer jobs in the canonical fields and authors. In the process by which English studies became postcoloniality, it acquired the tropes and subject matters of a number of disciplines, organizing them into new combinations, in the effort to expand traditional subjects for dissertation research and to open up new positions where none existed before. English studies seemed to eagerly ape both imperialism and colonialism themselves, inasmuch as the immense expansion was virtually global, and the tropic appropriations often resembled the violence of outright seizure. Like Cecil Rhodes, English studies would have annexed the stars, if it could. And like the grateful citizens of Santa Ana in Southern California, who erected a statue of John Wayne in front of the airport to commemorate what the "Duke" did for the community of Orange County, English departments everywhere should raise monuments and statues to Said for having saved English studies by giving it a new (imperial) lease on life. This expansion has marked not just the bloating of the curriculum but also the movement of English departments in colleges and universities—virtually becoming a stand-in for the now discredited programs in area studies devoted to revealing how literature, and ultimately culture, was deeply complicit in imperial and colonial oppression even as it is behaving like an imperial and colonial power. This irony has probably been lost on those armies of enthusiasts who catapulted onto the bandwagon or, more appropriately, got onto the gravy train.

In its postcolonial inflection, this sense of imperial expansion and colonial entitlement has been even more discernible. It has concentrated on typifying a putative relationship between the English and their Bengali subjects and made it into muscular trope promising to stand in for the relationship between colonizer and colonized everywhere, marked by psychoanalytical ambiguity that owes much to Hegel's description of master and bondsman and the desire for recognition of the former that only the latter can supply. The privileging of novelistic narratives as the principal body of data (and symptom?) of both nationalism and modernity works simply to retain the older disciplinary privilege of studying the modern novel in new dress and forgetting about the materiality of political economy which, in earlier thinkers, constituted the only way to understand imperialism and colonialism. Benedict Anderson forged this connection between novel, modernity, and national formation in his influential *Imagined Communities*, but it was taken to extremes by the edited volume of Homi Bhabha (*Nation and Narration*) where the English model was not only forcefully restated and the act of writing the nation and modernity itself was made to look inconceivable without appealing to the novelistic narrative. Yet both Anderson and Bhabha, to name only the most prominent, have, by resorting to a generic and textual form now elevated to the privileged status of norm, merely overdetermined the role of culture over other considerations. In this regard, postcolonial studies has strangely converged with area studies in recuperating the privilege of culture and cultural values. Moreover, it is not simply privileging culture but rather the achievements of a particular culture that has expressed its own aspirations in the form of the novelistic narrative, as if the indigenous forms of writing of other societies can have no equivalent valence in our understanding of the postcolonial moment. In fact, the presumption that the novelistic narrative supplies the privileged means to grasp the postcolonial encounter can only confirm the structure of colonialism itself, rather than dramatize the various ambivalences and hybridities theorists wish to emphasize as complicating the relationship between colonist and colonizer. In this regard, postcoloniality has simply managed to reinforce the primacy of textuality and reaffirm the older disciplinary claims of English studies.

We can and should applaud this sensitivity to both the dominated and the margin (nowhere to be found in the older, scientifically "neutral" area studies) to what Fanon sadly recognized as the devastating "sacking of cultural patterns, or at least the conduit of such sacking."[6] In this regard, postcolonial theory's promise to supply a critique of Eurocentric conceptions of knowledge and provide a forum for the hitherto excluded to speak their own voice from the margins where domination and power has held them silent since the beginning of modernity, now reread as colonialism, stands as the true successor of area studies which, as I've argued, can be seen as its prehistory. Yet the search for the excluded voice often leads to the dead-end pursuit for authenticity and restores precisely the Eurocentric claims of the sovereign subject it wishes to eliminate. In this sense, it discloses its own quite explicit historical myopia and consequent incapacity to see beyond the horizon of a specific colonial encounter and the retrospective illusion that comes with occupying a position now post to the actual, historical colonial moment. A survey of the longer duration of history elsewhere would have supplied examples of different kinds of colonizing and deterritorializing experiences (exceeding the tropic claims of British India) and how the loss of cultural reference, as experienced by the Japanese, even as they remained exempt from the physical seizure of territory, signified a relationship between colonization and capitalist modernization. Capitalist modernity was seen by Japanese between the wars as a totalizing process that was affecting every part of society. This historical experience is crucial to an understanding of precisely the colonial episode postcolonial currently wishes to theorize as a knowledge. If this consideration were taken into account, it would have shown the actual impossibility of imagining what some have insisted on identifying as an "anti-colonial nationalism" and the availability of uncontaminated autonomous cultures at the heart of colonialism. What this reveals is the conviction that the disempowered seemed to have involuntarily recuperated the space of non-reification Lukacs once invested in the proletariat because they were involved in manual, not mental labor. In making this move, adherents of postcolonial theory misrecognize an identity between capitalism and its masking claims of universalism; they elide homogeneity with universalism even more than the most enthusiastic capitalist. The point seems to be, according to Pierre Vilar, that capitalism has "universalized" history inasmuch as it has established systematic relations of social interdependence on a global scale that have eventually encompassed noncapitalist societies. In this regard, it has managed to fix a standard of measurement—world time—produced by a "single global space of co-existence," within which action and events are subject to a single, quantifiable, chronology. But because there remains different social practices outside of this abstract measure, capitalism has not "unified" history.[7]

But what for postcolonial theory became the sign of an authentic anticolonial nationalism, uncorrupted by the West, had been for others—Japanese, Chinese, Indians, French, Germans, and Italians—the irreducible mode of a modernist critique against the devastation caused by capitalist modernization and the need to find a location for historical difference capable of forestalling further destruction. The appeal to native culture was, in fact, the very sign of capitalist modernity and its modernist ideological inflection rather than active resistance to it (even though it enunciated resistance), the appearance of the uncanny out of time, the revenant, a ghostly repetition that has erupted from the surplus of what has been suppressed to trouble the stable boundaries between past and present, demonstrating the degree to which these societies, despite their colonial and semi-colonial political forms, were modern because there appeared to be no other alternative to the vast deterritorializing wealth of capital and labor power of the deterritorialized worker. The appeal to such autonomous resources, immune to the encroachments of capitalism, even in the colony, is a fiction not worth "delving into" Fanon recognized long ago: "A national culture is not a folklore, nor an abstract populism that believes it can discover the people's true nature. It is made up of the inert dregs of gratuitous actions, that is to say, actions which are less and less attached to the ever-present reality of the people."[8] In mapping this image of authentic knowledge onto an earlier moment—the colonial era—postcolonial proponents like the subaltern historians risk becoming seekers of the authentic, yearning for the silent cultural space of an unaffected interior accessible only to native sensibility and everything else that such a gesture implies politically. Moreover, this return to the pursuit of cultural authenticity loops back to form a symmetry with the desire of an earlier area studies program to stand in the place of the native.

It has been often observed that postcolonial theorizing slips into a necessary ambivalence and indeterminacy that, in the case of Homi Bhabha and Gayatri Spivak, grows out of a methodological desire to exploit the splits and contradictions imbedded in the discourse on rationality.[9] While such a strategy aims to unsettle readers and turn them away from the promise of epistemological certainty, because it is critique that has put into question consciousness and experience, it is hard to know, unlike the texts of Fanon and Said, who is being targeted and the location of its enunciatory platform.[10] But by resorting to a division stamped by the colonial experience and its afterimage, it has created a binary no more productive and exempt from the charges of epistemological certainty than the older polarities it has held up for derision. We can recognize in the working of this binary precisely all of those categories constructed by Homi Bhabha to explain the encounter between colonizer and colonized and to mark its complexity. While he is undoubtedly correct to show that this relationship between colonizer and colonized was not simply an instance of a hegemonic discourse representing the other, and this relationship was a two-way street filled with anxiety and the possibilities for slippage, the terms informing the encounter still expressed a self and other recast now as pedagogy and performance. With this move, Bhabha has given a new lease on life to a functional conception of the social that he refuses to name. Although postcolonial theory has promised to restore history as a mediation capable of accounting for differences older strategies had overlooked, it is, because of its own circulation of binary terms, as ahistorical (anahistorical?) and blind to the temporal and spatial differences lived and experienced by those voiceless, excluded, marginalized peoples it seeks to redeem. The chronology of the colonizer is not always the same for the colonized; Bengal under British rule is different temporally and spatially from Korea under the Japanese even though they are contemporary to each other; and the forms of colonial domination differ widely from Africa to Asia, demanding sensitivity to the specific political and economic histories postcolonial theory rarely, if ever, manages to address. Only history is capable of showing the vast range of differences that help us to avoid the essentialisms and exceptionalisms postcolonial theory produces in lifeless stereotypes. In its desire to turn away from the global forces of capitalism, another suspect Western narrative that works to hegemonize, it trades in stereotypes and holism and the fantasy of locating a genuine, anticolonial nationalism uncontaminated by either the colonial epoch or capitalist penetration. One of the weirder effects of this strategy is the recuperation of a Gandhian vision of agrarian self-sufficiency in a world linked by electronic networks of communication. Hence, postcolonial theory moves restlessly from cultural essentialism to an indeterminate social system that is never named, and whose subjects are grasped through a psychoanalytic framework that itself is culturally specific to the oppressive culture the colonized are supposedly trying to resist and overcome. With this vacillation, postcolonial theory has, according to Aijaz Ahmad, "become transhistorical, always present and always in process of dissolution in one part of the world or another, so that everyone gets the privilege, sooner or later . . . of being colonizer, colonized, and postcolonial all at once." Not quite, perhaps. The point he wishes to emphasize is how the postcolonial "levels out all histories, so that we are free to take up any of a thousand available micro-histories, more or less arbitrarily, since they all amount to the same thing, more or less."[11]

What, then, can we hope from postcoloniality? An innocuous "cultural respect," postcolonialty's response to human rights? In this time, when its initial theoretical splash has turned into a puddle, when researchers have found theory and criticism outside of their endless self-referrals, postcoloniality might return to its prehistory in area studies as a step toward enriching both (but hopefully dissolving the latter). This would mean coming to grips with its epistemological claims and rewinding them through its original chronological identity. By returning to its incipient origins in area studies, postcoloniality might recover the moment when the Third World was envisaged from its colonial past but not necessarily its unwanted heritage—the apparent price of decolonization. This reunion might enforce upon postcoloniality memories of uneven development and the reminder of a powerful presence of capitalism as the principal deterritorializing agent and the determinant of a narrative that knows no boundaries. By the same measure, postcoloniality might infuse into a moribund area studies the memory of a desire for theory which, as I've suggested, was early repressed in the scramble to recruit funds rather than ideas. What all this points to is how postcoloniality might be refigured into an act of memoration, rather than just a chronology or critique masquerading exceptionalism and unnamed theories of the social, one that might help us to avoid the confusion of history and memory and restore to each their own order of knowledge and experience. Beyond this move to memoration, we might look to a new candidate for cultural studies that would, along the way, incorporate postcoloniality within the larger framework of capitalist modernity and its transformations. Such a study might redirect our attention to the role played by capitalism throughout the globe and to the relationship between the experience of everydayness and the relentless regime of the commodity form. Everydayness, as a consideration for cultural studies, refers to the experience of the lived reality that marks the appearance and expansion of industrial and finance capitalism and their propensity to install similar conditions everywhere they establish their regimes. In this switching of codes, the difference produced is seen in the transmutation of postcoloniality's emphasis on hybridity into the unevenness lived and experienced in the everyday.[12] Pierre Vilar has reminded us that capitalism was "born out of colonization and the 'world market,' " and has subsequently universalized history, even though we confront the task remaking history, *tout court*.[13] Henri Lefebvre early called attention to the distinction between what he called the "exceptional" and the "everyday" (later recoded by Bhabha as "temporal caesura" and "epochal 'event' " or pedagogy and performative) where the latter breaks or splits off from the former in order to negotiate the meaning of the modern. It is in this time lag, which a universalized history fails to unify but seeks to mask a corrosive unevenness driven by capitalism's power to deterritorialize and reterritorialize, that the everyday is lived and experienced and where it must write its history.

Notes

1 See Stuart Hall's attempt to respond to Arif Dirlik's "Postcolonial Aura" in "When Was the Postcolonial?" in *The Post-colonial Question: Common Skies, Divided Horizons*, ed. Iain Chambers and Lidia Curti (London: Routledge, 1996), 256–59.
2 Edward Said, *Orientalism* (New York: Vintage, 1979), 201–352.
3 In Hall, "When Was the Postcolonial?" 246.
4 In Ravi Arvind Palat, "Fragmented Visions," unpublished ms., 62–63. Also W. N. Fenton, *Area Studies in American Universities: For the Commission on the Implica-*

tions of *Armed Services Educational Programs* (Washington, D.C.: ACLS, 1947), 81–82.

5   Peter Osborne, *The Politics of Time* (London: Verso, 1995), 1–68.

6   Frantz Fanon, *Toward the African Revolution* (Harmondsworth: Penguin, 1970).

7   In Osborne, *Politics of Time*, 34. Also, Pierre Vilar, "Marxist History: A History in the Making Towards a Dialogue with Althusser," in *Althusser: A Critical Reader*, ed. Gregory Elliott (Oxford: Blackwell, 1994), 41.

8   Frantz Fanon, *The Wretched of the Earth* (New York: Grove Press, 1968), 233.

9   Robert Young, *White Mythologies* (London: Routledge, 1990), 174.

10 Ibid.

11 Aijaz Ahmad, "Postcolonialism: What's in a Name?" in *Late Imperial Culture*, ed. Román de la Campa, E. Ann Kaplan, and Michael Sprinker (London: Verso, 1995), 33.

12 H. D. Harootunian, *History's Disquiet: Modernity, Cultural Practice, and the Question of Everyday Life* (New York: Columbia University Press, 2000).

13 Vilar, "Marxist History," 41–42.

Asian Exclusion Acts
Sylvia Yanagisako

This essay considers some of the conceptual forces behind the acts of exclusion through which scholars in Asian studies and Asian American studies have constructed and maintained the boundary between their respective fields of study. I trace these Asian exclusion acts to their antecedents in the disciplinary practices of sociocultural anthropology, because as an anthropologist I am interested in the role my discipline has played in promoting theories of culture and society that have shaped our understanding of area studies, ethnic studies, and the border between them. My hope is that my exploration will stimulate scholars from other disciplines to undertake an archeology of the practices through which their disciplines have contributed to the academic division of labor between area studies and ethnic studies and to assess their intellectual and political implications.

The academic institutionalization of area studies has built upon and promulgated a typology of culture areas in which subjects—including individuals, local communities, and nation-states—appear to be distributed among distinctive geopoliticocultural spaces. Area studies relies on an implicit assumption of the analytic power and parsimony of lumping together an array of social units that are characterized by diverse political, economic, ethnic, linguistic, and religious practices, as well as by different locations in international hierarchies of power. Although I do not have the time to develop this argument here, I suggest also that the constitution of areas such as Asian studies commonly relies on the metonymic extension of the politicocultural character of its politically dominant nations to the area as a whole. Building on Bruce Cumings's argument (in this volume) that the logic of area studies entails the identification of particular places as the location for the study of particular processes, I suggest that area studies characterizes large regions of the globe as particular kinds of politicocultural "fields of study."

The academic credibility of area studies would appear to require the patrolling of the borders between these geopoliticocultural spaces. Individuals and groups that do not fit into this typology—that is to say, those whose politicocultural features do not conform to the alleged distinctive features of their area location—are potential threats to the analytic coherence of the area and, consequently, to the broad knowledge claims of its experts. Likewise, subjects that move across the borders of areas may challenge the typology of politicocultural spaces by blurring the boundaries between them. When, for example, people who are defined as Asian, because they are seen as having been constituted as subjects in Asian politicocultural space, move into other politicocultural spaces such as Latin America, Africa, or North America, they present a problem of academic containment. This problem has been met, for the most part, by representing these people as particular kinds of subjects caught up in particular processes which, in turn, require the expertise of specialists in a particular "field of study." In the case of Asian studies, the emergence of Asian American studies as an interdisciplinary field with its own distinctive subjects and social processes has drawn upon and further institutionalized a typology of politicocultural spaces.

In the first part of this essay, I trace the boundary between Asian studies and Asian American studies to its antecedents in the theory of culture and society employed in ethnographic "field" studies. By comparing John Embree's classic ethnography of a Japanese village, *Suye Mura*,[1] with his less well-known monograph *The Acculturation of the Japanese of Kona, Hawaii*,[2] I show how a structural-functional theory of culture and society informs his characterization of these two communities as different kinds of politicocultural places in which different kinds of social processes are at play. In the second part of the essay, I show how Asian American studies defined its project in opposition to the acculturation model exemplified by Embree's study of the Kona Japanese Americans. I argue that the redundant narrative of Asian American history as a history of racist domination and masculine resistance reinforces the boundary between Asian American studies and Asian studies and reaffirms the typology of geopoliticocultural spaces and the structural-functional theory of culture and society that has shaped both fields of study.

Suye Mura: A Field Study of Natives in Their Native Habitat

John Embree was among the few anthropologists to study people in what might be deemed both their "native" and "alien" habitats. His research in 1935 and 1936 on a rice-growing village in the prefecture of Kumamoto, Japan, produced what is widely touted as "the first detailed anthropological study of Japanese life."[3] Embree described his study as "an attempt to present an integrated social study of a peasant village in rural Japan. While Suye Mura, the village described, cannot be claimed to represent all rural Japan any more than can any single village, it is at least representative in many respects."[4] By this Embree meant that Suye Mura, like most Japanese villages in the 1930s, depended economically primarily on a single product, in this case rice, with the raising of silkworms as a secondary source of income.

In his foreword to the 1964 edition of *Suye Mura*, the anthropologist Richard Beardsley praised Embree for his deep appreciation of "the reciprocity and collective sentiment that bound the villagers together as equals," but faulted him for not understanding the "nuances of class structure" that derived from the deep-reaching, hierarchical structure of power based on landholding, wealth, and inherited family status.[5] Beardsley attributed this failure to Embree's Chicago training in peasant community studies, out of which also emerged Redfield's influential model of peasant village culture and society. This training, Beardsley claimed, "did not prepare [Embree] to seek historical data which would have shown him . . . how much carry-over of class feelings from the Tokugawa period still governed affairs in his time."[6] As a consequence, Embree overlooked the hierarchical inequality that divided the village into two main divisions: the mass of ordinary farmers and tenant cultivators and the upper stratum of families with power and influence.

Embree himself, however, credited the British social anthropologist A. R. Radcliffe-Brown with providing him with most of his "formal training in searching out the rules of a society."[7] Radcliffe-Brown's rule-focused model of society came to dominate British social anthropology between the two world wars and extended its hegemony to the United States during the period of Embree's training at Chicago in the 1930s, when Radcliffe-Brown taught there. Initially fashioned to capture the social order of stateless, "tribal" societies, it projects a legal framework on all societies, ferreting out and granting structural primacy to the normative "principles" and "rules" that most closely resemble the state-enforced laws of Western European nations. It assumes, moreover, that people follow the rules because they have internalized them as a result of their socialization in families and other institutions of cultural reproduction. In other words, it assumes a harmonic compatibility between individual subjectivity (personality), collective subjectivity (culture), and institutions (social structure). Hence, even where social structures entail domination and exploitation, a stable equilibrium is posited. Having construed the "natives" as cultural subjects located in their natural habitat, the model incites little interest in investigating how they have been made to follow the rules. The Durkheimian collective conscious that people, especially members of small-scale, local communities, are assumed to share obscures the analytic recognition of the coercive forces operating to enforce the "rules of society."

Suye Mura is rife with the tension between Embree's commitment to Radcliffe-Brown's structural-functional, equilibrium model of society and his recognition that the village had been undergoing significant changes since the emergence of Meiji and modern nation-state control. On the one hand, he concludes, "The basic pattern of life in Suye Mura is evidently an old one. It has survived a long and varied history and probably dates back at least to the time of the introduction of Chinese civilization in the sixth century. One of the reasons for the stability is perhaps that Kuma has always been off the main line of travel, being as it is a dead-end valley surrounded by mountains."[8]

On the other hand, Embree notes that changes have been taking place in both the internal and external relations of the village—including the role of the government in directing and controlling those changes. While he is well aware of the strong arm of the state and its interventions, Embree does not address the issue of whether and how villagers question or attempt to resist state policies and programs. Neither does he view the decline in the forms of cooperation, which he attributes to villagers' increasing integration into a money economy, as generating any social or cultural tensions. Instead he maintains his commitment to the thesis of harmonic compatibility between subjectivity, culture, and social structure, concluding that state control of the Westernization process has been useful because it has facilitated change without breakdown.

Kona Japanese Americans: A Field Study of Natives in an Alien Habitat

In 1941 Embree published his second monograph, *Acculturation among the Japanese of Kona, Hawaii*, based on research he had conducted in Kona, Hawaii, for a six-month period from August 1937 to February 1938. The community seemed ideal for a study by Embree, as forty percent of the coffee farmers of Kona came from the Japanese prefecture of Kumamoto, where Suye Mura was located. In Embree's own terms, "this monograph is a study of acculturation among Japanese farmers in Kona, Hawaii. To be more specific, the study is concerned with change in the social organization, the network of social relations, which have taken place in rural-Japanese society, when transplanted from Southern Japan to the island of Hawaii."[9]

Where his research on Suye Mura was guided by a search for the rules of society, Embree's research on Kona was guided by an interest in social and cultural change. Throughout the monograph—as he works through the topics typical of peasant village studies of that era of ethnographic research (e.g., village organization, the household, the local group, death, birth and marriage, associations and clubs, religion)—Embree's constant concern is with the processes of adjustment to an alien environment. His use of the botanical metaphor of transplantation is repeated throughout the monograph, although what is alien shifts. At times it is the environment that is characterized as alien—as, for example, when he includes among the forces bringing about change in Japanese society in Kona "the exigencies of having to recreate a new social group in an alien physical and social environment.[10] At other times, it is the Japanese themselves who are alien: "It is the first generation alien group with which this study is chiefly concerned."[11]

Whereas *Suye Mura* demonstrates the influence of British social anthropology on Embree, the theme of cultural loss and degradation that pervades his monograph on the Kona Japanese Americans bears the traces of Embree's training in American cultural anthropology—where a history of research on displaced American Indian tribes had made the search for cultural tradition and authenticity central to the theoretical nostalgia of the discipline. Having observed the Japanese of Kumamoto in their natural environment, Embree could not resist the temptation to constantly judge the customs observed among the Japanese of Kona by the standard of their authentic origins in Japan. The result is a pervasive sense of loss and deviancy. In Kona, "there are not enough relatives to perform a proper funeral, so close friends and kumi [members of neighborhood associations] also participate"[12] and "breaches of traditional etiquette not to be found in the rudest mountain hamlet of Japan"[13] are observed. As a final indignity, the dead are laid out in flat coffins and face north instead of in a kneeling position facing west.[14]

In his final chapter, Embree concludes that the fundamentally cooperative peasant society of Japan has changed into a fundamentally competitive one. These changes are due in part to acculturation through "continuous firsthand contact" with modern American culture and in part to pioneer conditions and settling in a new environment lacking the associations and tradition of an old Japanese village.[15] As is common in acculturation studies, what the Kona Japanese Americans are acculturating *to* is assumed rather than investigated. There are no ethnographic observations of the Kona Japanese Americans' "continuous firsthand contact with modern American culture" in Embree's monograph —only an occasional passing reference to the social institutions that are the presumed forces for change, such as the public school system, the Christian churches, and the economically and politically dominant "haole" (white) culture. This glaring lacuna of ethnographic evidence in a field study focused on the process of acculturation is not peculiar to Embree; it was commonplace in acculturation studies. It is merely rendered more obvious because of the community's location in pre-World War II Hawaii, which lies outside the continental borders of what was commonly assumed to be the space of "modern American culture." For Embree, however, the political and economic dominance of white Americans over the territory to which the Japanese had been "transplanted" was sufficient to define it as American politicocultural space.[16]

Yet, Embree's assumptions about the generalized white American culture with which the Kona Japanese Americans were having "continuous firsthand contact" appear shaky when we consider that the local representatives of this culture constituted a small racial and cultural elite whose cultural practices were, one suspects, significantly shaped by their location at the top of a quasicolonial hierarchy of race and class. His failure to interrogate local structures of culture and power flows logically, however, from his commitment to a study of acculturation. For when people migrate out of their natural habitat into an alien environment, the model of harmonic compatibility among personality, culture, and society is replaced by one of disharmonic incompatibility. Construed as a state of social disequilibrium, the situation is inherently unstable and, consequently, something must change. That something is the personality and culture of the immigrants, for the institutional structures of the alien social structure are viewed as stable, if not entirely fixed, because they are assumed to be in harmonic and functional congruence with the dominant cultural system; i.e., in this case, with "modern American culture." In conformance with the typology of places and processes promoted by area studies, the Japanese Americans of Kona inhabited an alien politicocultural space in which cultural change was inevitable. It never occurred to Embree, nor to other students of acculturation, that the political, social, and cultural institutions of the alien society might themselves be altered by the immigrants. Hence, what was to be studied was the immigrants' acculturation to these dominant political, economic, and cultural institutions.

In spite of Embree's clear differentiation between Suye Mura and Kona as types of politicocultural spaces characterized by particular social and cultural processes, however, the fact that he undertook both studies demonstrates that, at least until the end of the 1930s and before the post-World War II establishment of area studies, Japanese Americans could be studied by a scholar who had conducted research in Japan. The border between the ethnographic study of a Japanese village and a Japanese American immigrant community was still permeable. In the following section, I consider how, three decades after Embree's research, the institutionalizaton of Asian American studies contributed to the closing of this border. I leave it to others to investigate the ways in which the establishment of Asian studies in the intervening years constructed the border between these "fields of study."

Asian American Studies and the Closing of the Border

Asian American studies, like its counterparts in African American and Chicano studies, emerged in the late 1960s in response to student demands for ethnic studies courses. From its inception, Asian American studies has been a self-consciously political and pedagogical practice aimed at raising the ethnic consciousness of Asian American college students.[17] Courses on Asian American history have occupied a central place in that practice. By teaching students about the omission of Asians, as well as the history of race and class oppression they have experienced, from the grand narrative Americans are taught about how "we" became to be who "we" are today, Asian American history courses challenge the hegemony of "American history." Yet, like all histories, Asian American history is itself a selectively constructed narrative through which a collective historical memory is created which renders the present meaningful in terms of the past. The excavation of the "buried past" constructs Asian American historical experience and with it Asian American ethnic consciousness. In short, Asian American history does for an ethnic group what American history does for the nation.

Since the 1970s, the Asian American history courses that have been taught in universities and colleges in the United States have shared a common narrative structure, including a high degree of uniformity as regards the topics covered, the periodization of time, the linkage between periods and topics, and the core required readings.[18] The usual chronology begins with the mid-nineteenth-century international and domestic political economy that shaped Chinese labor migration and the discriminatory laws passed in the United States to control Chinese immigration, prohibit naturalized citizenship and racial intermarriage, and restrict the movement and enterprises of immigrant Chinese. The violent racism of the nineteenth-century anti-Chinese riots, which led to the concentration of Chinese into segregated Chinatowns, is described along with the symbolic violence committed by that era's virulent racial stereotypes of Chinese. Courses then jump to Japanese immigration at the end of the nineteenth century. Once again the early experiences of the first-generation immigrants are presented within the context of the political economy of labor immigration and the discriminatory legislation against Japanese. The early labor history of Japa-

nese Americans as agricultural workers is followed by coverage of their uproot-
ing experience during World War II, when all Americans of Japanese descent on
the West Coast were imprisoned in concentration camps. Attention then shifts
to the Filipino immigrants who arrived during the Depression years and, in particular, to their experiences as migrant workers on the West Coast. In the post-
World War II period, the focus is on the new immigrants (in particular the Southeast Asians), their problems of economic and social adjustment, and their need
for social services. Courses commonly include a section on the resurgence of
anti-Asian racism in the 1980s, often linking it to resentments spawned by the
increased flow of Asian immigration and the expansionist success of Japanese
business.

The chronology of immigration from different Asian countries provides
Asian American history courses with a seemingly logical succession of subjects—from Chinese to Japanese to Filipino to Korean and Southeast Asian. In
each historical period a new group of immigrants is seen struggling against the
tide of white racism to gain a foothold in the new land. The exception is World
War II, when the imprisonment of first, second, and third-generation Japanese
Americans yields a different drama of racism and struggle for survival. A concern
with "origins" and "ancestors" endows this chronology, in which each historical period bears the stamp of a single immigrant group, with a compelling narrative logic. It seems commonsensical to ask what was happening to Chinese
Americans in the nineteenth century, to Japanese Americans during World
War II, to Filipino Americans in the 1930s, and to Vietnamese Americans in the
1980s. At the same time, it seems reasonable *not to ask* what was happening to
Chinese Americans during World War II, to Japanese Americans in the 1930s
and to Filipino Americans in the 1980s. Just as an immigrant group or its children begins to experience significant social mobility, Asian American history
courses shift their gaze to more recent immigrants. As a consequence, an amaz-
ingly uniform succession of historical experience—a collective narrative—is
constructed out of the diverse histories of Asian American communities.

This practice is mirrored in the some of the comprehensive volumes on
Asian American history recently published. Takaki's *Strangers from a Distance
Shore: A History of Asian Americans*[19] best exemplifies this narrative strategy.
Not only are the first 400 of the 491 pages of his book devoted to the period up
until the end of World War II, but the two chapters concerned with the postwar
period are devoted primarily to the second wave of recent Asian immigration—
those who Takaki labels the new "Strangers at the Gates Again."

Even more striking than the degree of uniformity in course content and
structure is the agreement as to the core readings in Asian American history

courses. In the late 1980s, for example, a small number of books were used so commonly as to qualify as the canonical texts of Asian American history. The three books that almost invariably appeared as required readings were *America Is in the Heart* by Carlos Bulosan, *Longtime Californ'* by Victor Nee and Brett de Barry Nee, and *Pau Hana: Plantation Life and Labor in Hawaii, 1835–1920* by Ronald Takaki.[20] *America Is in the Heart* is the "autobiographical" account of the Filipino American poet Carlos Bulosan, which is perhaps more accurately described as the mythic, collective biography of the Filipino men who came to the United States during the 1930s to work as cannery workers, domestic servants and migrant field laborers. *Longtime Californ'* is a compilation and interpretation of oral histories collected from inhabitants of San Francisco's Chinatown in the early 1970s. Finally, *Pau Hana* chronicles the development of the sugar industry in Hawaii and the plantation labor force into which it inducted an ethnically diverse, but predominantly Asian (Chinese, Japanese, Korean, and Filipino) immigrant population.

Together these three core texts celebrate the working-class past of Asian Americans. The heroic figures of that past are the men who struggled to survive the lean years of hard labor, racist violence, and class exploitation. Although women are not entirely absent, the laboring past has an unmistakably masculine cast to it.[21] The pedagogical privileging of a masculine, working-class past along with the earliest period of each immigrant group's experiences molds a uniform ethnic, gender, and social class consciousness out of more divergent historical realities. In one sweep, the experiences of women, farmers (as opposed to farm laborers), and petty bourgeoisie are pushed to the margins of the collective past. That the occupational past of Asian Americans was much more diverse and dynamic than its representation in these courses is documented in a wide range of articles and books—all of which are accessible to college undergraduates.[22] Lacking too is a discussion of the relationship between Asian American social mobility and their economic and political organizations in the post–World War II era. For example, Takaki's book *Pau Hana,* in which Japanese Americans are one of the key groups in the Hawaiian plantation labor force, is not followed by an account of how second-generation Japanese Americans (Nisei) came to dominate the Democratic Party and state government in Hawaii after statehood. Nor does it discuss the key role they have played in linking U.S. mainland and overseas capital to local real estate development.[23] Likewise, studies of Japanese American agricultural workers in California do not evolve into studies of Japanese American farms and agribusiness, their ethnic business organizations (such as the Nisei Flower Growers Association), and their labor practices (for example, the latter's conflicts with the United Farm Workers Union).

My point is not simply that Asian American studies courses suppress the histories of social class mobility and economic success of Asian Americans, but rather that they deny the constitutive character of these experiences. In other words, the past that constitutes Asian American subjectivity—their collective conscious and sense of being and acting in the world—is deemed a working-class one. It is also masculine and resistant.

The acts of exclusion and redundancy in meaning of Asian American history courses reflect the issues and dilemmas, at once political and pedagogical, which the instructors of these courses feel compelled to address. Not surprisingly, they feel compelled to correct the erroneous but prevalent assumption that all Asian Americans arrived at these shores with slide rules in hand and surplus capital to invest in business enterprises. Most Americans, including some Asian Americans, after all are ignorant of the working-class history of many Asian Americans and their struggles against class exploitation and racial discrimination. In addition, the redundant narrative and exclusions of these courses reflect the instructors' attempts to construct a unifying and politically mobilizing ethnic identity.

One of the dominant themes guiding Asian American student activism as well as other student movements in the 1960s and 1970s was a critique of U.S. imperialism. Asian American immigration and labor history was located within the context of American imperialism and labor exploitation of Third World peoples, both at home and abroad. According to Nee and Nee, the student activists in the San Francisco community in the early 1970s,

> feel that as victims of racism and economic exploitation, American Chinese share a similar experience with blacks and other minority groups in the U.S. as well as third world people in Asia, Africa, and Latin America. They see themselves as standing in solidarity with these people and the international workers' movement in a broadly based political struggle against a common oppressor which they have identified as American imperialism.[24]

Emerging as it did out of this student movement, Asian American history courses became the pedagogical practice through which this analysis was inscribed in the collective historical conscious of students for whom that past had been lost in more ways than one. The result is the narrative construction of Asian America as a particular kind of cultural-political space that calls for the study of a particular kinds of processes: namely, the modes through which people at odds with hegemonic cultural institutions resist cultural and political domination.

The masculine character of that resistance is understandable as a reaction to the themes of cultural loss and political accommodation of acculturation studies like Embree's and to hegemonic Orientalist representations of Asians as "female" and "passive" in opposition to a "male" and "active" West. Said's critique of "Orientalism" enables us to see that to be labeled an "Oriental" in the United States is to be identified as having origins in a cultural tradition that is antithetical to that of the West and inferior to it. It was this system of representations and the power relations inscribed in them that student activists in the late 1960s rejected along with the label "Oriental" when they redefined themselves as "Asian Americans." The emphasis on the active agency of men in Asian American history is a conscious attempt to challenge the metonymic equation of Asians with the feminine. To celebrate male ancestors characterized by an "indomitable spirit, fiercely hopeful and resilient"[25] is to undermine the symbolic equation that East is to West as female is to male.[26]

Asian American studies has also been shaped by a political history of demands for exclusive national allegiance from people whose experiences, families, and commitments often cross the borders of a single nation-state. The confinement of Japanese Americans in prison camps during World War II was accompanied by the coercive confinement of their allegiance to a single country. First-generation Japanese Americans (who had only Japanese citizenship because they had been barred by U.S. law from becoming naturalized citizens) and their U.S.-born children (most of whom had only U.S. citizenship) were asked to declare exclusive allegiance to the U.S. government and forswear any allegiance to Japan and its emperor at the risk of deportation. This precipitated both great distress and intense conflict within families. Many second-generation Japanese Americans found themselves in bitter disagreement with parents; siblings chose opposing sides and the government's segregation of the "loyal" from the "disloyal" Japanese Americans broke up families, some of which never reunited after the war. Following all too quickly upon the heels of this Japanese American nightmare was the Chinese American one of the Cold War and the demonization of Communist China.

The demand that Japanese Americans and Chinese Americans confine their political loyalties within the borders of the nation has led to a suppression of relations that cross-cut national spaces. Not only did World War II and the Cold War cut off the flow of people, goods, and information across national borders but it stigmatized and silenced talk about relations with people defined as political enemies. In addition, in the case of Japanese Americans, the government suppression of Japanese language schools during World War II resulted in the loss of the linguistic means among the third generation of reestablishing those relations and recovering their histories through Japanese texts even after the end of overt political hostilities.

In spite of its emergence as a counterhegemonic practice, Asian American studies has responded to this demand for exclusive national allegiance by including within its field of study only those people, relations, communities, and institutions located on U.S. soil. This has led to the confinement of historical memory to spaces inside the nation. "Asian American experience"—in other words, the collective experiences that are constitutive of Asian American ethnic subjectivity—is located exclusively within the borders of the nation rather than viewed as a transnational process involving individuals, families, communities, events, and sociopolitical structures which cross-cut these borders.[27]

The constitution of Asian American studies as an interdisciplinary field of study with its distinctive subjects and social and cultural processes affirms the distinctiveness of "Asian American" space from "Asian" space, thus reaffirming the typology of geopoliticocultural spaces of area studies. In envisioning Asians in the United States as cultural subjects who share something beyond their political location in a particular national space, moreover, Asian American studies risks affirming an essentialist representation of Asian culture. For without an assumed cultural unity or similarity among Asians, the rationale for lumping together, for example, Filipino Americans with Chinese Americans and Japanese Americans rather than with Mexican Americans or other Latin Americans immigrants is lost. The latter, after all, share with Filipino Americans a history of Spanish colonialism as well as a similar subject position in the U.S. In addition, Asian American studies tends to represent Asian America in a manner that parallels and reproduces the metonymic representation of Asia in Asian studies. In both fields, those who are economically and politically dominant (China and Japan; Chinese Americans and Japanese Americans) play an inordinate role in defining the area as a particular kind of politicocultural space in which particular processes are to be studied.

My focus in this essay has been on the ways in which Asian American studies contributed to the institutionalization of the boundary between itself and Asian studies, rather than on the ways in which Asian studies has done so. I suspect that the contributions of the latter field are similarly easy to chart and its analytic consequences readily demonstrable. Certainly, the antecedents I have traced to John Embree's pre–World War II monographs suggest that any exclusionary practices entailed in the institutionalization of Asian studies had precedents in the theories and methodologies of sociocultural anthropology. My interest here has been in demonstrating that the unspoken gentlemen's agreement of mutual exclusion between Asian studies and Asian American studies betrays their mutual commitment to a structural-functional theory of personality, culture, and society. This model of cultural and social integration justifies the boundary between Asian studies and Asian American studies, treating it as a natural geographic feature in a topography of academic spaces. Conversely, an insistence on the distinctiveness of Asian studies and Asian American studies as academic fields of study affirms the vision of the two areas as characterized by different processes of cultural reproduction and transformation.

If we are to critically assess the analytic implications of the academic division of labor between area studies and ethnic studies, we must also interrogate the hegemonic disciplinary and interdisciplinary practices that have contributed to their construction. In the absence of such a critique, we risk reproducing these practices and, along with them, the forms of knowledge they have generated.

Notes

1   John Embree, *Suye Mura: A Japanese Village* (1939; Chicago: University of Chicago Press, 1964).
2   John Embree, *Acculturation among the Japanese of Kona, Hawaii,* American Anthropological Association Memoirs no. 59 (Washington, D.C.: American Anthropological Association, 1941).
3   Richard Beardsley, Foreword to the 1964 edition of *Suye Mura,* vii.
4   Embree, *Suye Mura,* xix.
5   Beardsley, Foreword, x.
6   Ibid., x.
7   Embree, *Suye Mura,* xxiii.
8   Ibid., 300.
9   Embree, *Kona, Hawaii,* 5.
10 Ibid., 151.
11 Ibid., 6.
12 Ibid., 59.
13 Ibid., 69.
14 Ibid., 59.
15 Ibid., 143–44.
16 When Embree conducted his research in the 1930s, Hawaii was a territory of the United States.
17 According to Russell Endo and William Wei, "the first goal [of most programs] was related to the socialization of Asian American students and involved increasing their ethnic consciousness and self-awareness" (Russell Endo and William Wei, "On the

Development of Asia American Studies Programs" in *Shattered Windows: Promises and Prospects for Asian American Studies,* ed. Gary Okihiro [Pullman: Washington State University Press, 1988], 7).

18 This assessment of Asian American history courses is based on my examination of the course syllabi and reading lists of nine introductory Asian American history courses taught at four West Coast universities in 1988 and 1989 (University of California at Berkeley, University of California at Los Angeles, University of Washington, and San Francisco State University). Each of these campuses has a well-established Asian American studies program. A more complete study would have entailed observation of class lectures and discussions, as well as interviews with students and instructors. I note that there are already indications that these courses, as well as Asian American studies scholarship in general, have begun undergoing a significant transformation for the first time since their inception twenty years ago.

19 Ronald Takaki, *Strangers from a Different Shore: A History of Asian Americans* (New York: Penguin, 1989).

20 Carlos Bulosan, *America Is in the Heart: A Personal History* (1943; Seattle: University of Washington Press, 1973); Victor G. and Brett de Barry Nee, *Longtime Californ':
A Documentary Study of an American Chinatown* (1972; Stanford: Stanford University Press, 1986); Ronald Takaki, *Pau Hana: Plantation Life and Labor in Hawaii, 1835–1920* (Honolulu: University of Hawaii Press, 1983).

21 I do not mean to claim that materials by and about Asian American women are entirely excluded from courses on Asian American history. All the courses I reviewed included some materials on Asian American women although there was nothing close to a "gender balance" in them. The readings on women, however, tend to avoid the issue of sexual inequality *among* Asian Americans. Instead, they either present a "woman's version" of the past or they show how Asian American women have been doubly burdened by the racism and sexism of white society. Noticeably absent from the reading list are books such as Evelyn Nakano Glenn's *Issei, Nisei, War Bride: Three Generations of Japanese American Women in Domestic Service* (Philadelphia: Temple University Press, 1986), which discusses sexual inequality and physical abuse by husbands in Japanese American marriages, and articles like Lucy Cheng Hirata's "Free, Indentured, Enslaved: Chinese Prostitutes in Nineteenth-Century America," *SIGNS* 5 (1979): 3–29, on the exploitation of Chinese women as prostitutes in Chinatown.

22 See, for example, Shotaro Frank Miyamoto's study of the predominantly petite bourgeois Seattle Japanese American community in the 1930s, *Social Solidarity among the Japanese of Seattle* (Seattle: University of Washington Press, 1939); Embree, *Kona, Hawaii;* James W. Loewen's study *The Mississippi Chinese: Between Black and White* (Cambridge, Mass.: Harvard University Press, 1971), who were imported as agricultural laborers but quickly became retail store owners (and who strove successfully to change their racial classification from black to white); and Edna Bonacich and John Modell, *The Economic Basis of Ethnic Solidarity: Small Business in the Japanese American Community* (Berkeley: University of California Press, 1980), a study of small business among Japanese Americans before and after World War II.

23 See George Cooper and Gavan Daws, *Land and Power in Hawaii: The Democrat Years* (Honolulu: University of Hawaii Press, 1985).

24 Nee and Nee, *Longtime Californ,'* 355–56.

25 Takaki, *Pau Hana*, 178.

26 Unfortunately, in the case of some Asian American writers such as Frank Chin, the rejection of an emasculated Asian American image of "sissiness" entails the wholesale adoption of a (white) American cowboy image of manly ruggedness or a tough, aggressive "adolescent sexuality and aggression" appropriated from a caricature of black and Chicano working-class males. See Michael J. Fischer, "Ethnicity and the Post-Modern Arts of Memory," in *Writing Culture: The Poetics and Politics of Ethnography*, ed. James Clifford and George Marcus (Berkeley: University of California Press, 1986), 194–233.

27 See Sylvia Yanagisako, "Transforming Orientalism in Asian American Studies," in *Naturalizing Power: Essays in Feminist Cultural Analysis*, ed. Sylvia Yanagisako and Carol Delaney (New York: Routledge, 1995), 75–298, where I argue that the marginalization of women in Asian American history is part and parcel of the suppression of a history of transnational relations that threatens to disrupt the narrative of an ethnic history neatly encompassed within the borders of the nation and the working class. I show how the women disrupt these seemingly exclusive, natural boundaries of class, nation, and ethnic identity by signaling the boundary crossings that have occurred.

Areas, Disciplines, and Ethnicity
Richard H. Okada

An incident that occurred a few years ago spurred the following thoughts on the subject of area studies, disciplines, and ethnic studies in our post-Cold War world. I'm referring to a sit-in staged by Asian American and Latino students at Princeton University in the spring of 1995 in which the office of the president was occupied for thirty-six hours. The students demanded a full-time Asian American studies professor, increased library holdings, four to five courses a year in relevant subjects, and an ethnic studies center. The upshot of the protest was that the administration agreed to fund a full-time professor of Asian American studies and library holdings were increased, but no center was established. After a series of job searches came up empty, a professor was finally appointed and began teaching the next spring semester. The appointment is a joint one between the American studies program and English, with the former designated the institutional "home."

In order to gain a foothold within an institutional framework, it seemed to the students necessary to take political action. Political activism, however, usually assumes some sort of ground of identity upon which the action is based, in this case the clearly bounded identity of the "Asian American." The action can perhaps be justified if we take it to fall within the practice of what some have called, following Gayatri Spivak, "strategic essentialism." It is a strategic move given the apparent impossibility of not being essentialist. Thus, "one can self-consciously use this irreducible moment of essentialism as part of one's strategy," to employ an "impossible totalization" in order to rectify an intolerable situation.[1] Although one wants to sympathize with the students and their dilemma, it is thoroughly problematic whether the grasping of agency by recourse to such methods based on identity, even as a temporary strategy, is valid or ultimately effective in the context of an examination of both ethnicity and politics.

The practical question of where to "house" the Asian American studies professor, who must speak for "ethnicity," was the first problem the hiring process faced. The "home base" designated for the person was the American Studies Program, but as its program status proclaims it is only a virtual department consisting of professors from various "disciplines." Since the appointment was to be a joint one with American Studies, disciplinary departments such as English, Sociology, and History participated in the search. East Asian Studies, an area department, also participated in the search but the possibility of a joint appointment there met with considerable resistance from in-house faculty. In the case of disciplinary departments, the new professor's specialty needed to be monitored so that any overlap with existing faculty specialization could be at least kept to a minimum. In the case of East Asian Studies, faculty members raised objections by appealing to the standard of linguistic competency, i.e., will the prospective professor be conversant in a language taught in the department (Chinese, Japanese, or Korean) in order to carry out "original" research in the field?

The protest students had demanded a professor to teach Asian American studies but had not specified any particular discipline. The institutional organization of knowledge based on disciplinary parameters, however, required that the professor of Asian American studies be, so to speak, disciplined. In the East Asian area studies department, which focuses on language teaching and includes the disciplines of history, literature, and linguistics, the question of language competence was as important as discipline (presumably because the subject matter was considered sufficiently different).

Keeping the above incident in mind, what I would like to do now is to consider further the relations between area, discipline, and ethnicity, especially as they pertain to Japan and the teaching of Japanese literature after World War II.

The teaching of Japanese literature after World War II took place in "language and literature," or regionally defined, departments that effectively kept the enterprise segregated from other, western literature departments as well as from a direct relation to issues of "discipline" per se. The East Asia area grouping arose, of course, out of strategic requirements following the war and with the advent of the Cold War. In those days and until very recently, a nation like China or Japan was taken to be an unquestioned "presence" insofar as its integrity as an object of knowledge was simply assumed. It is the very installation of an "area," however, that produces the entities that are predicated on literal grounds (for example, geographical location) as unproblematically foundational to what are actually realms of "imagined communities," whose discursive construction results in the illusion of a plenitude that we call the nation-state. Following a constructivist argument, one can argue that rather than nations existing as clearly bounded entities prior to the establishment of the strategic area or area studies department, it is the establishment of the department that creates the effect of a preexisting, wholly definable object. At the same time, that invented object, in the case of the Far East, was coded as inscrutably "other" to the "West," accessible only to those properly trained to understand it.[2] It is not the case that a "Japan" is "simply" a discursive construct but the argument marks the beginning of a rethinking that takes seriously the "constitutive force of exclusion, erasure, violent foreclosure, abjection and its disruptive return within the very terms of discursive legitimacy."[3] It is, ultimately, a question of the operation of power. As Judith Butler puts it, "power also works through the foreclosure of effects, the production of an 'outside,' a domain of unlivability and unintelligibility that bounds the domain of intelligible effects."[4] Teaching about the area without problematizing the consequences of its constructedness further confirms its seemingly safe "ontological" status, which then serves as the basis on which literary, historical, cultural, or other information can be disseminated.

A similar situation obtains with disciplines, for the integrity of their objects of knowledge (such as "literature") is not something that exists prior to the establishment of the discipline but it is the latter that gives the illusion of the former as its effect. Once a field of study is institutionalized, the enabling exclusionary acts must be forgotten as disciplinary practice proceeds along naturalized lines of autonomous inquiry. As Samuel Weber notes, "[the university] instituted areas of training and research which, once established, could increasingly ignore the founding limits and limitations of the individual disciplines. Indeed the very notion of academic 'seriousness' came increasingly to exclude reflection upon the relations of one 'field' to another, and concomitantly, reflection upon the historical process by which individual disciplines established their boundaries."[5]

Whether taught within area studies or disciplinary departments, therefore, conceptions of the nation-state and the academic subjects that pertain to it exist in an exceedingly problematic relation to their founding assumptions and within the institutional settings in which they are placed. For my purposes, the construction of an area within which a discursive object like "Japan" is located produces ipso facto a body of material that gets subsumed under "content" categories, such as "Japanese literature." The boundary situation that obtains for areas and disciplines, furthermore, is also inextricably connected to the question of ethnicity since the location of a nation within an area creates an exclusionary demarcation in which questions of ethnicity get displaced on to a discourse of difference and otherness. Ethnicity comes to stand internally for the marked "other" within the nation as distinct from an assumed "mainstream" or, externally, as part of a diasporic or immigrant community living abroad. Issues pertaining to ethnicity then come to be viewed as appropriate objects of knowledge "for themselves" primarily within ghettoized ethnic studies departments or as marginal topics within slightly larger institutional frameworks (such as American studies). That mark also governs the choice of literary texts to be used in teaching either about the "home" area or the diasporic community.

The "discipline" of literature, as in the case of English, occupies a special place in the humanities. It is not simply one subject among many but a site where scholarly and pedagogical practices merge in particular ways with discourses of the nation-state. A nation's soul or cultural essence is considered to be embedded inside its literary texts (especially premodern texts) so that as one reads the works of a foreign nation that metaphysical subtext, at times expressly articulated, becomes operative, consciously or not, in the minds of readers and teachers. Universalizing tropes of modernity often deflect attention away from localized discussion but ideologies of the nation-state continually haunt the teaching of literature.

It is not surprising, then, that the teaching of literature at many colleges and universities in America, despite attacks from different theoretical perspectives over the past few decades, is still dominated by a pedagogical unconscious supremely suited to the requirements of the modern nation-state: the New Criticism.[6] Its heralded emphasis on a strictly delimited object of study, the autonomously construed "verbal icon," and its banishment of elements (author, history, society, etc.) believed to be external to the analysis, are well-known. It was also inextricably implicated in a notable feature of modern discourse, the concern with identity and difference. As Paul Bové notes, the New Critics "tried to discover whatever it was that made for the identity of one sort of language as opposed to another . . . [and carried on] the post Renaissance business of making distinctions and marking identities about such things as genre. . . . [Further] it helped to constitute an entire field of knowledge about language; it helped discipline the judgment, and thereby the response of students and teachers." Bové thus marks the establishment of "professionalized academic literary criticism" as New Critical procedure became institutionalized and served to hierarchize "not only poetry and prose but, implicitly, identity and difference, authority and subservience, taste and vulgarity, and continuity and discontinuity as well."[7] The position of the reader vis-à-vis its exclusionary maneuvers, which aim to keep its object of study isolated by focusing on "internal" forces like "tension" and "ambiguity," mimics the position of the researcher vis-à-vis the nation and the disciplinary subjects mentioned above. In both, the reader/researcher is installed in a position of dominance over a bounded body of material. And, true to its patriarchal genealogy, its position need never be inflected by gender, class, ethnicity, or historical specificity.

In the configuration I am attempting to trace, the place of "Japan," for example, becomes concomitant with the nature and position of the "verbal icon." And, as many have pointed out, the New Criticism and its practitioners played a vital role in World War II, thereby demonstrating its affinity with military strategy that is perhaps not unrelated to the role of "Japan" in the postwar period. Its participation in military and Cold War engagements has been examined by a number of writers, including Donald Pease, Richard Ohmann, William Spanos, Robin Winks, and William Epstein. I cite here in particular Eptsein's essay, "Counter-Intelligence: Cold War Criticism and Eighteenth-Century Studies," which details not only the analogs between Cold War military counterintelligence and formalist criticism but also the active participation of literary scholars (particularly those from Yale University) and the manner in which they put to use their academic training in reading English texts to assist the war effort, specifically in regard to the Office of Strategic Services (OSS), Research and Analysis (R&A), and Counter-Intelligence (x-2). Epstein shows how, in his words, "literary scholars served as cold warriors in both communities [intelligence and academic], and also how both the New Criticism and the old historicism (specifically, the historical scholarship of eighteenth-century studies) were collusive with and indeed crucial to the OSS/CIA at its founding in the early months of World War II."[8]

According to Epstein, features of the Cold War legacy evident in literary study include the attempt to isolate poetry and criticism from social context, the valorization of objectivity, the expunging of the emotive or psychological effects of literature, especially from poetry, and the erasure of ideology. Among the features familiar to us today, the emotive, in particular, was feared because its perceived instability and unreliability made it susceptible to being taken over by rival programs and ideologies and thereby parallels the Cold War fear of a take over of American democracy by Communism. That fear, Epstein writes, "produced . . . a post-war liberalism which, eschewing extremes, sought an 'end of ideology' through a pragmatic 'politics of consensus' that was located in a 'vital center,' supervised by interactive cultural elites, and safeguarded by a controlled, counter-espionage surveillance program."[9] Epstein also notes that throughout *The Verbal Icon*, one of the founding texts of the New Criticism written by one of its forefathers, William K. Wimsatt, there appears a "combative rhetorical strategy," deriving from a "pragmatic textual politics and fear of subversion." Many of the features Epstein enumerates were prevalent in prewar scholarship.

Epstein goes on to make the following comments on the OSS and, in particular, a division of R&A called CID (Central Information Division). The CID was put in charge of "gathering and organizing . . . specialized knowledge and strategic information about and from the entire world."[10] The model for the "gigantic research project" was the Yale Walpole edition, which was "the largest publishing project ever carried out through private resources." The reorganization of knowledge accomplished by the CID catapulted American scholarship especially in the humanities and social sciences from a position believed to be inferior to Europe at the start of the war to one "predominant on the world scene" by the 1950s.

Referring to the rise of postwar areas studies, Epstein states, "McGeorge Bundy and others have pointed out that this R&A-inspired reorganization of the world's knowledge also induced the 'area study programs developed in American universities in the years after the war.'"[11] These programs "were 'manned, directed, or stimulated by graduates of the OSS' and supported directly, or indirectly, by CIA, State Dept, and other federal agencies," and he notes that "this American academic recolonization of the post-war world is perhaps the classic instance of [the] Cold-War alliance of government and education."[12] It is crucial to keep in mind this enabling context when we examine area studies programs and present-day scholarly research on Asia.

Obviously, vast changes have occurred since the 1960s, the period where Epstein's account ends. We are nevertheless in many ways still in the grip of the institutional apparatuses and academic paradigms set in place during those early years of the Cold War. The changes that have occurred since then—including the urgent need for remasculinization and cultural retrenchment felt after America's defeat in Vietnam, the debates on and establishment, notably at Harvard (from 1974 to 1978), of a core curriculum, and the rise of the right and its attacks on "political correctness" during the Reagan-Bush years, the effects of which are still being felt in many quarters today—have continued the trend toward what one writer has called the "unprecedented depoliticization of American culture and scholarship." Touching on the intimate connection between education and the war effort, the writer goes on to state that "the whole history of literary theory . . . since World War II can be read as an exorcism of the earlier influence of Marxism, with one theoretical school after another gaining popularity precisely because each has afforded yet another avenue for evading radical politics."[13]

The establishment and preservation of Japan as a pure, homogeneous, and othered object of study marked postwar scholarship as America moved after the Occupation to reconstruct its former enemy from military aggressor into an entity palatable to America and the West. Toward that end, the reconstructing narrative focused on two traits in particular: an indomitable work ethic and an essentialized aesthetic propensity. Speaking to the latter, I would argue that scholars of Japan, in accord with Cold War agendas, faithfully reproduced in relation to their object of study the iconic, exclusionary reading practiced by the New Criticism. One influential example was the pronouncement by Sir George Sansom, an eminent historian, that the culture of Heian Japan (794–1192) was "unique" precisely because it was "almost entirely aesthetic"[14] and governed by a "rule of taste."[15] The move encouraged postwar scholars to ignore the political aspects of the texts of all periods as they employed positivistic historical methodology to buttress the aesthetic emphasis. The aestheticizing posture was widely evident as the work of translating Japanese literature became depoliticized exercises that neatly cleansed Japanese literary texts of sociopolitical and ideological concerns thereby effecting an erasure both of the operative circumstances surrounding the texts' emergence as well as the broader implications of readerly subject-positions within postwar scholarly practice. Texts accorded canonical status in Japan (*Taketori monogatari*, *Kagero nikki*, *Ise monogatari*, *Genji monogatari*, "court poetry" collections, and *Heike monogatari*, etc.) were duly taken up by American translators and located within the aestheticizing frame.

Literary studies exhibited a similar tendency. In a 1961 study, *World of the Shining Prince*, the writer finds, on the one hand, the polygamous tendencies of the main male character (and by extension the society in general) in *The Tale of Genji* reprehensible. He rescues the character by portraying him as a savior precisely because his behavior can be seen as restraining what to the author are equally unacceptable promiscuous tendencies in the women of the time, especially a woman like Sei Shōnagon.[16] Heian aristocracy, then, in Morris's words, although "marked by a curious mixture of depravity and decorum," is prevented from "degenerating into something crass and sordid" by "the dominant part played by the rule of taste" and, we might add, one of its main representatives, Hikaru Genji (227). There also appeared around the same time the now standard study of Japanese court poetry, in which the co-authors relied heavily on the New Criticism for their analytical perspectives as they ushered the study of the thirty-one syllable *waka* into the age of modern literary criticism.[17] The aestheticizing process reached a plateau of world acceptance when the Nobel Prize for literature was awarded to Kawabata Yasunari in 1968. Even though he wrote

politically motivated stories and maintained an uneasy coexistence with proletariat writers of the day, the works highlighted were ones that lent themselves
to an aesthetic reading: *Snow Country, Sound of the Mountain,* and *A Thousand
Cranes.* The prize consolidated the designation of Japanese culture as "aesthetic" at its essentialist core, a culture that for all practical purposes inhabited
a transcendent realm not to be trespassed or adulterated by criticism, "theory,"
or "politics," all of which were delegitimized as irrelevant or reductive.[18]

The actual teaching of "Japanese literature" (especially premodern literature) at major institutional centers, at least from the late 1960s, assumed as their
founding principle the coherent integrity of "Japan" mentioned above and often
viewed its scriptive texts as consisting more of codes to be broken rather than as
"literary" texts to be critically analyzed.[19] Graduate education at an institution
like what was then called the Oriental Languages Department at UC Berkeley
was purportedly based on "rigorous linguistic training," which itself implied a
marginalization of "literature." The most common pedagogical method, however, instituted under an overdetermination of the difficulty of Japanese language, hardly amounted to more than an alibi for translation, an activity that
marked the primary raison d'etre for many scholars and masked an almost complete ignorance or dismissal of theoretical perspectives. The ability to trans-
late the difficult Japanese language, like the ability to break military codes, was
viewed as reflecting an innate intelligence that implicitly validated the authority of the translator who was privy to the secret essence of the literary text and,
by extension, of the nation and people being studied. Of course, many scholars
were returnees from Occupation duty in Japan. As in the case of the New Critical protocols, the text itself remained the valorized object while the critic assumed a position as neutral observer or transmitter of the essence of the target
text. In fact, however, the pose of neutrality concealed the translator's or critic's
position of supreme authority, an authority warranted not by appeal to any val-
idating source (like historical or theoretical methodology, or even discipline)
but by an assumed talent that was itself beyond criticism. For Japanese literature
in North America, as for military intelligence as noted by Epstein,[20] the practice
of translation and its handmaiden, commentary—until fairly recently, Japanese
literary study often took the familiar form of a translation with its predictable
introduction and commentary—derived from the New Criticism (and a version
of the old historicism).

The production of "Japan" as a bounded and coherent object of study, in accord with the New Critical unconscious, simultaneously enacted the exclusionary procedures that mark much of Japanese literary study today. With some
exceptions, Japanese literature courses still tend to feature predictable texts by

predictable authors. Even when they include texts by writers marked somehow by "otherness," however, courses subscribe to a basic framework that remains tied to the idea of a reified "Japan" to which embodiment certain marginalized texts (whether written by a non-mainstream Japanese writer, an Okinawan, a Korean living in Japan, or a Japanese abroad) constitute an addendum. Without a thorough-going reconfiguration of that framework, the addition of texts marked by "otherness" only provides a non-threatening element of "diversity," a situation governed by the seemingly inclusionary logic of pluralism that, while ostensibly a laudable move, effectively preserves the status quo. In a similar manner, and given current configurations of our objects of knowledge and institutional practices, it would not really matter where an Asian American professor were housed. The hiring, while accommodating the protestors, simply meant the addition of one more faculty member and one more subject area to be covered by coursework.

What, then, can be done? Is there a way both to effect inclusivity and speak to the demands of a global century without resorting to identity politics?

First of all, issues relevant to the postwar construction of the bounded identity at the bottom of Asian American and Asian studies and also the question of ethnic identification need to be reexamined as part of an ongoing pedagogical and analytical practice. We can begin with this statement by Rey Chow: "In North America, . . . the study of Asian literatures cannot be divorced from the knowledge of the history of Asian immigrants."[21] She is speaking mainly about modern Asian literatures but the presence of the displaced-from-roots "native" and the process of her/his subsequent ethnicization, produces concomitant positivities (in our case "Japan" and "United States") that function as the stabilized "homes" of "classical" national literatures. As the establishment of the modern nation-state required the invention of a "past" as a timeless presence that was always there, so too does the question of ethnicity immediately conjure up dual traditions, a homeland from which she/he is forever sundered and a foreign land always already in place that she/he must accommodate—the familiar narrative of loss and assimilation. And, it can be argued, just as both can be theorized only from our perspective in the modern nation-state, premodern or "home" literary traditions (as well as modern literatures and the "home," i.e., Japan itself) can be theorized effectively only by being constantly subjected to interrogation in relation to the positioning and status of ethnicized and diasporic issues. Since it is the excluded "ethnic" element that enables the constitution of the "pure" homeland in the first place, the teaching of premodern as well as modern Asian (here, Japanese) literature cannot be divorced from either "the knowledge of the history of Asian immigrants," or the enabling positions and perspectives that constitute them. The problem of ethnicity, then, is always already a problematization of the "home." Here is Rey Chow again: "Ethnicity signifies the social experience which is not completed once and for all but which is constituted by a continual, often conflictual, working out of its grounds."[22] For me, the notion of a continual destabilization of the grounds of ethnicity is highly productive since it puts into question the "grounds" of any identity, be it that of "Japan "or the "United States," the very grounding of which must now always be newly (re)-negotiated in the constitutive terms of "ethnicity." In order to effect an intervention in the teaching and study of "Japan," then, the process of "working out" would seem to be a neverending one.

I want to ask further at this point whether it is possible to think differently about the logics of identity and difference in which the assumption of ethnicity (as an entity distinctively different from a "mainstream") remains embedded. In other words, is it possible to think community without identity, to conceive of any kind of alliance or social bond with others without participating in the exclusionary logics that continually produce bounded, autonomous individuals? As Bill Readings has asked, "If community is grounded neither upon some fundamentally shared ethnic bond (the premodern community of blood and soil) nor upon modernity's assumption of a shared possibility of communication, how is it even possible to form?"[23] One promising avenue that challenges the usual notions of self-other and community, that tries to think community without identity, has been pursued by thinkers like Giorgio Agamben, Jean Luc-Nancy, and Bill Readings. It has been characterized as a "politics of singularity,"[24] which names the attempt to construct "a form of knowledge that respects the other without absorbing it into the same,"[25] and posits not a community of "subjects" but of "singularities."

Such a community would not be based on the desire for individual autonomy and freedom since that would continue the current exclusionary status quo. Current conceptions of community result from the idea of a civil society constructed in terms of the state, which becomes the foundation for relations among its members: "Modern community is founded upon the autonomous decision of individuals to communicate with each other as subjects of a state. . . . The state positions individuals as subjects subject to the idea of the state as an instance of community. . . . The singularity . . . of others is reduced, since community with others becomes possible only insofar as those others are, identically with oneself, civil subjects."[26] Moreover, the universalizing logic of membership in modern civil society creates individuals for whom communication is rendered transparent. The presumption of the state-authorized social bond among autonomous individuals cannot be questioned because it is the unrepresentable horizon in which free discussion reaches its consensus. Here Readings notes, "Hence all problems of communication, any differences of idiom, must be presumed to be merely secondary to, or parasitical upon, a fundamental clarity—an ideal speech situation."[27] The marking of an otherness within such a society, as in the case of ethnicity—the rise of an "idiom"—can only become an equally transparent and marginalizing move made against the self-identical whole.

In contrast to the state-centered community, what has been called the "coming community" (Agamben's term) would make "the singularity of others" irreducible. The new community would not be, in Readings's words, "organic in that its members do not share an immanent identity to be revealed; the community is not directed toward the production of the universal subject of history, to the cultural realization of an essential human nature."[28] It would be based, if we follow Agamben's discussion of singularity, on his notion of the "example," which "escapes the antinomy of the universal and the particular."[29] "Pure singularities," he argues, "communicate only in the empty space of the example, without being tied by any common property, by any identity."[30] Here we begin to deal with a crucial concern for properties, commonalities, and belonging, which are usually thought to be natural components of individuals in relation to any type of alliance or coalition. In Agamben's case, however, the "whatever" (his term for an existence not of "indifference" as the word suggests but of "being such that it always matters"[31]) is constituted not by the indifference of common nature with respect to singularities, but by the indifference of the common and the proper, of the genus and the species, of the essential and the accidental. "Whatever is the thing *with all its properties*, none of which, however, constitutes difference. In-difference with respect to properties is what individuates and disseminates singularities."[32] A community constituted by singularity, then, would be political not in the usual terms, which lead to a struggle against the state or to protest movements that assume a collective identity in opposition to state authority or its representatives (the Princeton protest), but would present, in Agamben's reading, what "the State cannot tolerate in any way": for "singularities [to] form a community without affirming an identity, that humans co-belong without any representable condition of belonging (even in the form of a simple presupposition). . . . For the State, therefore, what is important is never the singularity as such, but only its inclusion in some identity, whatever identity (but the possibility of the *whatever* itself being taken up without an identity is a threat the State cannot come to terms with)."[33]

Such a conception of community provides a critique of the institution of Asian American studies courses the Princeton students were demanding and the installation of ethnic identity that ensued. For, as Agamben prefigures it, the "coming community," "is mediated not by any condition of belonging (being red, being Italian, being Communist) nor by the simple absence of conditions (a negative community, such as that recently proposed in France by Maurice Blanchot), but by belonging itself."[34] In other words, to make belonging the result of a condition, such as ethnicity, is to preserve the exclusionary violence of discrimination, whereas the idea of a "belonging itself" suggests that there exists no property common to each person aside from the space that is shared. It is useless, Agamben argues, to search for or try to preserve a "proper identity in the already improper and senseless form of individuality . . . [if] humans were to succeed in belonging to this impropriety as such, in making of the proper *being*—thus not an identity and an individual property but a singularity without identity, a common and absolutely exposed singularity . . . then they would for the first time enter into a community without presuppositions and without subjects."[35]

Of crucial importance is that it will be a community without a unifying ethical idea. Embracing the inability of singularity to know in advance how persons will be aligned, it would aim at demystifying the notion of "a self-legitimating, autonomous society" by positing a community that lives within what Readings has called "the horizon of dissensus" where there can be no answers to the question of the social bond because "no rational consensus can decide simply to agree on an answer."

> To preserve the status of the social bond as a question is to tolerate difference without recourse to an idea of identity, whether that identity be ethnic ("we are all white, we are all French"), or even rational ("we are all human"). It is to understand the obligation of community as one to which we are answerable but to which we cannot supply an answer.[36]

Readings's discussion of obligation makes explicit a necessary ethical horizon constituted by an ethics which "remembers that the singularity of the 'I' or the 'you' is caught up in a network of obligations that the individual cannot master."[37] It will be a community in which its participants take seriously "the network of obligations" that each member owes to another even though such obligations are not transparently available to the subjective consciousness of any one member. If they were transparent, as is usually assumed, a person would be able to repay all of her/his debts to others and to society thus freeing her/him from further obligations and allowing him, as a model citizen, to stand for the community as a whole. No one person can represent the whole because the "whole" itself, in terms of obligations, is unknowable as any possible consensual or unifying by-product.

What the above gestures toward is a community that is neither based on identity nor dependent on a social bond produced out of any unifying idea, but one committed to honoring the property-less singularity of its members and scrupulous in its remembrance of the unpayable nature of obligations. Such a community based on singularity would not come to constitute any bounded community (Asian American) that would authorize the self-identity of any of its members and that can be positioned against another bounded community (mainstream America). Moreover, no member of the community would be able to "stand for" any other member or the community as a "whole." It would thus render meaningless discussions about assimilation to a normative mainstream as well as of individuals somehow caught "in-between."

I want to conclude with a few remarks on the status of the "political" and its relation to "literature," since a thorough reconsideration of both politics and ethnicity is necessary in order to create a community as discussed above. The postwar invention of Japanese literature and literary studies as apolitical signals a double marginalization: of literary study and of Japan. The marginalization of literature stems in part from its characterization as "merely fiction," or rhetoric, which forms a common binary with its externalized other, "reality" or the literal, the latter pair serving to ground the former. The "political" (and often the "historical") is commonly viewed as inhabiting a literal, real-world ground, where agency and action are situated and from where it can oppose the literary as marginal or otherwise politically impotent. As critical work has shown in recent decades, the fictive and the real are not self-identical, mutually exclusive entities.[38] The desire to read literary texts as apolitical stems from their essentialized cultural function mentioned earlier where borders of texts are made to form an analog with the borders of a nation-state within which an essential core is assumed to exist. The defense of the interior from transgression is then undertaken by an external force, either the "political" as represented by the state or, in the case of the New Criticism, the political as always masked by some other, neutral-seeming position of authority.

As long as the literary and the political are conceived of in this polarized way, no amount of "politicizing" literary texts will effect a change in the basic institutional structures since the move simply transfers an internalized "literary" to an external, prediscursive ground called the "political," and therefore keeps it mortgaged to the political writ large, i.e., the State.[39] What we need to do at this point is not to abandon literary texts (or any texts for that matter) but to displace their appropriation by pedagogic practices harnessed to nation-state agendas and to the literal in its various guises. Literary texts are actually useful sites for the work of displacement because the interrogations of the relation of the "fictional" to the "real" characteristic of certain kinds of critical and theoretical work can be extended productively to other realms in order to displace the hold of entrenched binary conceptions. If the fictive is a structural part of all constructions of the real, for example, then the literary or textual can be seen as constitutive of all conceptions of the political, at which point the notion of bounded, foundational identities would have to undergo a radical destabilization. Thus, to return to the question of ethnicity, the lesson to be learned from the Princeton protest is perhaps that the suppressed "other" will always return to haunt the "self" as long as the self persists in assuming a stability and wholeness that can only be captured at tremendous cost. The creation of a community of singularity and dissensus may ultimately be impossible to achieve since the desire for stasis, answers rather than questions, may continue to prove too powerful. It would seem, however, that the stakes involved are just too high not to make a concerted attempt.

Notes

1 Gayatri Chakravorty Spivak, *The Post-Colonial Critic*, ed. Sarah Harasym (New York: Routledge, 1990), 107; Judith Butler notes that Spivak herself has more recently cast doubt on the strategic use of essentialism. See *Bodies That Matter* (New York: Routledge, 1993), 281.

2 Cf. "This definition [of geographical areas in terms of international political relations rather than distinctive historical affinities and coherence] conceives of these entities as, for investigative purposes, culturally more homogeneous than diverse, and as *irretrievably 'other'*" (emphasis added). Anne Middleton, "Medieval Studies," in *Redrawing the Boundaries*, ed. Stephen Greenblatt and Giles Gunn (New York: Modern Language Association of America, 1992), 22.

3 Butler, *Bodies That Matter*, 8.

4 Ibid.

5 Samuel Weber, *Institution and Interpretation* (Minneapolis: University of Minnesota Press, 1987), 32.

6 The genealogy of the New Criticism's twentieth-century instating and its relation to the schemes of I. A. Richards and to the needs of U.S. mass education (not unlike the British experience in India) is beyond the scope of this paper. I want to thank Paul Bové for his helpful comments regarding the genealogy of the New Criticism. See, also, among his many essays relating to the subject, Bové's *Destructive Poetics: Heidegger and Modern American Poetry* (New York: Columbia University Press, 1980), especially chap. 3, and his discussion of I. A. Richards in chap. 4 of *Intellectuals in Power* (New York: Columbia University Press, 1986).

7 Paul Bové, "Discourse," in *Critical Terms for Literary Study*, ed. Frank Lentricchia and Thomas McLaughlin (Chicago: Chicago University Press, 1995), 50–52.

8 William Epstein, "Counter-Intelligence: Cold-War Criticism and Eighteenth-Century Studies," *English Literary History* 57 (1) (spring 1990): 68.

9   Ibid., 74.

10   Ibid., 82.

11   Ibid.

12   Ibid., 83.

13   Donald Lazere, "Cultural Studies: Countering a Depoliticized Culture," in *After Po-
     litical Correctness: The Humanities and Society in the 1990s*, ed. Christopher New-
     field and Ronald Strickland (New York: Westview Press, 1995), 350; what "radical pol-
     itics" means in this case, however, remains problematic.

14   George Sansom, *Japan: A Short Cultural History* (New York: Appleton-Century-
     Crofts, 1962), 238.

15   George Sansom, *A History of Japan to 1334* (Stanford: Stanford University Press,
     1958), 178. Sansom was perhaps not coincidentally echoing Motoori Norinaga's
     proto-nationalistic, eighteenth-century valorization of *mono no aware* as the key to
     The Tale of Genji.

16   See Ivan Morris, *The World of the Shining Prince* (New York: Alfred Knopf, 1964),
     242.

17   Robert Brower and Earl Miner, *Japanese Court Poetry* (Stanford: Stanford University
     Press, 1961).

18   Translation was a neutral activity needed for the dissemination of knowledge about
     Japan so is justified; native critical studies could be used because native scholars had
     studied the proper texts and contexts. Criticism, however, was a foreign element
     deemed improper to the native text: the basic fact was that some scholars simply be-
     lieved that Japanese literature was not good enough to warrant criticism. On the "for-
     eignness" of theory, see Bill Readings, "Why Is Theory Foreign?" in *Theory Between
     the Disciplines: Authority/Vision/Politics*, ed. Martin Kreiswirth and Mark A. Chee-
     tham (Ann Arbor: University of Michigan Press, 1990).

19   Speaking of the schools of "new" critics in France and the United States, Edward Said
     remarks, "Texts were to be unlocked or decoded, then handed on to anyone who was
     interested." "Opponents, Audiences, Constituencies, and Community," *Critical In-
     quiry* 9 (1982): 6. Also quoted in Middleton, "Medieval Studies," 21.

20   Many postwar Japan scholars, of course, actually served as U.S. intelligence officers in
     that country during the Occupation.

21   Rey Chow, *Writing Diaspora* (Bloomington: Indiana University Press, 1993), 140. The
     chapter "The Politics and Pedagogy of Asian Literatures" presents a major statement
     of the issues of teaching Asian literatures.

22   Ibid., 143.

23   Bill Readings, *The University in Ruins* (Cambridge, Mass.: Harvard University Press,
     1996), 185.

24   Lawrence Grossberg, "Identity and Cultural Studies," in *Questions of Cultural Iden-
     tity*, ed. Stuart Hall and Paul du Gay (London: Sage, 1996), 102.

25   Robert Young, *White Mythologies*, quoted in Grossberg, "Identity and Cultural Stud-
     ies," 103.

26   Readings, *The University in Ruins*, 181–82.

27   Ibid., 182.

28   Ibid., 185.

29 Giorgio Agamben, *The Coming Community* (Minneapolis: University of Minnesota Press, 1993), 8.

30 Ibid., 10–11.

31 "Whatever" is from the Latin *quodlibet*, which Agamben takes not as "being, it does not matter which [i.e., it does not matter which, indifferently], but rather as "being such that it always matters," 1.

32 Ibid., 18. Emphasis in the original.

33 Ibid., 84.

34 Ibid., 85.

35 Ibid., 64. Emphasis added.

36 Readings, *The University in Ruins*, 187.

37 Ibid.

38 Although deconstruction, for example, has been vigorously criticized as being apolitical and unable to countenance political agency, writers have shown that keeping the distinction between the rhetorical and the literal clearly divisible is itself a thoroughly political move. See Bill Readings, "The Deconstruction of Politics," in *Reading de Man Reading*, ed. Lindsay Waters and Wlad Godzich (Minneapolis: University of Minnesota Press, 1989), 223–43.

39 "I would argue that American pluralism is as totalitarian as Stalinism, in that both seek to elide the possibility of differing (politics, in the sense in which I wish to use it) from the state, either by inclusion within, or exclusion from, a real that is the totality of the state determined as the literal ground of political existence" (Readings, "The Deconstruction of Politics," 239).

Can American Studies Be Area Studies?
Paul A. Bové

The simplest answer to this question is "No." Area studies has existed to provide authoritative knowledge to the state, specifically the government and its policy-makers, to enable the state to expand its power and to defend its interests geopolitically. Area studies has an essential link to the operations of foreign policy, and area studies experts tend to be knowledge workers with skills particularly valued by their sponsors who are also their readers. Particularly, the United States (and affiliated foundations) sponsors area studies research focused on the actions as well as culture and history of other nation-states. Throughout this essay, I make use of essentially realist theories of the state to make distinctions between American studies and area studies, especially to explain that the U.S. state has neither need nor desire for an organized study of the American state system.

Generally, among progressive humanist scholars in the academy, conventional thinking about the state rests upon a rather specific constellation of left-wing thinkers from Marx and Lenin to Gramsci and Althusser. In particular, versions of Althusserian thinking about ideology and Gramscian notions of hegemony allow leftists to extend thinking about the state to almost all areas of culture and economy which come to be seen as part of the state's ideological apparatus—as opposed to the state's monopoly upon legitimate force. These are valuable modes of work and they allow for deep analyses of connections between knowledge forms and interest—precisely a mode of analysis which acknowledged state intellectuals would do well to study. Nonetheless, for my purposes in this essay, the theory of the extended state as the entity including schools, families, churches, and other ideological institutions and formations must be set aside so I can make a specific analytic claim: the U.S. state sustains area studies on a realist model of power.

Fareed Zakaria's much-debated book *From Wealth to Power* has one essential idea relevant to this discussion—i.e., his elaboration of a modified version of realism: the national power does not make policy decisions; state power makes those decisions—specifically, the government makes those decisions. It is the government, particularly the executive branch, that funds and consumes the knowledge produced within area studies because that knowledge, the government believes, enables success in competition with other states. Area studies exists to serve the foreign policy interests of American state power directly and specifically. American studies, on this model and by contrast, can best be understood as a mechanism by which the state purchases domestic tranquility to facilitate its deployment of real and symbolic economic resources better to position itself for its fundamental task, competition with foreign agents. There is little evidence that the state reads American studies as an essential or necessary part of maintaining or controlling its own power in relation to foreign competitors or resources within its own borders. The state already knows what it needs of American studies and arranges its functions and draws on its products; by contrast, the state feels it needs the knowledge it demands of its area studies workers and while it arranges the institutions to produce that knowledge, the state must also read that production for its own success.

Yet the social sciences, so important to domestic policymakers, play a much more important role in serving the needs of the state than traditional American studies. Parsonian models more effectively influence actions of the government than humanistic studies of national narrative or cultural studies of enfranchisement. Humanists would like to argue that their work in studying the large cultural forms of society gets at the bases of knowledge, ideology, and ruling interests; no doubt this is so. The state, however, commissions and hires social scientists and statisticians to guide its actions in policy. The work produced by NEH-funded projects, for example, results from governmental policy decisions manifest in the selection of executives and programs—often at the behest of political parties and their pollsters; NEH-sponsored work does not itself guide policy but is constrained by and made possible by decisions already taken by politicians and bureaucrats. By contrast, careful, learned, sophisticated documents produced by area studies people (often passing through the SSRC) can indeed redirect the forms of state action on issues ranging from environmental policy to finance and trade to nuclear weapons and war fighting decisions.[1]

Were American studies to become an area studies project, its primary consumer or reader would have to become the state itself. From an Althusserian perspective, one would argue that universities in particular, as the special home of American studies, functioning as part of the ideological state apparatus, always and already have inscribed American studies within the state regime. On its surface, however, such a view is meaningless insofar as all knowledge produced within universities falls within the same category. A more precise question must be asked to understand the function of these different fields and forms of knowledge: does American studies have the state and its policymakers as its immediate consumer, its first reader?

It goes without saying, as we have all known for many years now, that the work of the extended state occurs in the spheres of culture, of narrative, and symbolic production. Following Gramsci and others on the question of hegemony, interrogating the role of culture in the domain of nation formation, we can say easily that the interpretation of U.S. culture by Americanists (such as the consensus historians) to construct what are called "national narratives"—such efforts come together with the work of the state in creating the United States as a nation-state form. But, it must also be said that this sort of academic intellectual work does the business of the state precisely in its extended spheres and does it not by directing policy decisions but rather by making available as a knowledge-form symbolic systems politicians and state players can manipulate and deploy. Examples of this practice are too numerous to name.

To put it reductively, we could say that there is no "U.S. desk" in the state department. I deny neither that the work of American studies helps form both the political unconscious of policymakers about the United States; nor that, at times, the government calls upon Americanists' expertise to deal with a problem; nor the ideological and cultural materiality of the work American studies does or has done in confirming the basic arrangements of the U.S. state regarding citizenship, national unity, the creation of dominants, marginals, and so on. Rather, at the risk of repetition, I insist on a specific and simple point: area studies was created to meet a policy need to allow the state greater success in its own expansion and development. American studies, insofar as it has existed in the twentieth century, did not come into being for these reasons. Of course, to enhance its own position, the state needs to draw upon the resources of the nation and American studies plays a role in allowing the state to deploy the symbolic values and signifying practices of various cultural elements within the nation—which the state and its political agents come to know in their own ways. No doubt these resources matter when the state attempts to enhance its own interests in ways sometimes (as many would argue in Vietnam) not in the national interest. But even if we can show that American studies has not been a form of area studies, another question remains: can American studies be transformed into an area studies? Even if one can show that American studies has not had the U.S. state as the primary consumer of its knowledge, the remaining question itself has policy implications: can American studies thrive as an area studies program; would the state be wise to preserve American studies by transforming it into an area studies and so allying it with older forms—such as "East Asian Studies"—which many feel are themselves increasingly irrelevant in a post-Cold War world.

My general claim would be "no" precisely because, at this moment, the state has no policy interests in such a reformed American studies and, equally important, because American studies best serves the interests of the nation-state in terms of hegemony and culture rather than policy.[2] If the state comes to be willing to make available area-studies-type resources to American studies to transform it into an apparatus for producing knowledge essential to policy, this would require a revised American studies whose existence would reflect an entirely new and perhaps more troubled relation to state power than the one currently existing within the nation. Implicitly, state power would have come to the point where it sees "the nation," or whatever one wants to call the "objects" of American studies, as both a competitor and alien about which it needs specialized and authoritative knowledge on the basis of which it can direct its own policy toward that object. It is not hard to imagine this case coming into being; indeed, many on the left and far right would already claim this is our reality and would point to ever-increasing incarceration of criminals and to incidents like Waco as evidence. More subtle and perhaps more relevant would be the claim, already partly true, that New Americanism,[3] with its multiculturalist agendas, produces knowledge about population fractions relevant to policymakers, but of a sort capable, in itself, of reorganizing for consumption and party organization potentially rebellious fragments of the population that can be managed hegemonically, short of violent state intervention.

If a reader wants a simple definition of what American studies has been, this is not the place to look. American studies cannot be defined although some of its functions can be described. Generally it has been quite variable in its appearance; it has undergone a number of changes from the earliest days of its concerns with "American myths"—the stories and unities underlying and forming U.S. identity, doing the cultural work of Americanization, as it were, on a population of immigrants. It has at times attempted to turn itself into a mimic of social science and left the realms of art and literature for the more easily mathematized realms of social questions. But at its center American studies has had history and literature treated hermeneutically and culturally, not the social sciences' quantitative and rhetorical ideals. Of course, there are social scientific studies of the United States; and American studies programs sometimes involve social scientists studying U.S. government or social actions. Nonetheless, the defining acts of American studies rest in the literary historical investigations into the questions of what forms American subjects, cultures, and institutions. Although many of these studies, especially the studies of origins, of the founding of the United States, speak of American relations to European ideas and cultures, the emphases always center on the uniquely American transposition or revolution upon what was; they insist upon the effect of circumstance upon inheritance, upon the invention of the new—in this way, America has become a metonym of the modern.

A social history of the origins of American studies would have to begin with the problems of population and immigration, as well as with issues of enfranchisement, which means issues of race and gender. Literary historians in particular have done an excellent job of unearthing the effects of American studies efforts to produce useful knowledge about, to create representations of, the qualities and characteristics of American, citizen, identity, and so on. American studies has had, I believe, two important moments of flourishing growth—each stands in an important relation to war and migration, to the intrusion of new populations into the public spaces and institutions. These two periods, roughly speaking, are the 1930s and 1947–1966. Space does not allow a detailed treatment of the materials produced in these periods (although I will return to some of them later in this essay), yet one point can be made clear: American studies, in both cases, set itself around literature and history in opposition to the increasing power and prestige of the state-sponsored social sciences. The issue, in a word, was territorial: which disciplines, which modes of knowledge production, would define knowledge of America? Would it be Talcott Parsons or the criticism of the greatest of Harvard's cadre of literary historians and critics, F. O. Matthiessen?[4] Such a pairing simplifies and, in a sense, each of these great scholars wins the battle. Parsons developed knowledge for policymakers, but Matthiessen, with his great book, *The American Renaissance,* dominated a central portion of American studies. Indeed, the literary historical dominance remains in effect even after World War II when, for example, the massively influential Lionel Trilling occupies the space of knowledge production in the spheres of (elite) cultural value, attempting to define, as Jonathan Arac has shown definitively, the space of U.S. race relations and American national character by writing on *Huck Finn* at the very time when innumerable social scientists took American race relations as their topic to offer advice—often ignored—to U.S. policymakers.[5] Until very recently, as critical Americanists have begun to reflect upon the history of American studies, the relations between activities on both sides of this political divide between policy and cultural value have been left unexamined.

There is no formal reason why American studies could not take on the protocols of an area studies program. One could conceive of it or imagine how it would look, give it a curriculum and requirements. There are, however, historical and theoretical reasons, related to the nature of knowledge production, why this is most unlikely to happen. For one thing, Cold War mandarins were not educated in American studies but in law or, as with George Kennan, in diplomatic history, or, as with Henry Kissinger, in schools of government. Generally, educational and cultural but not governmental or political elites work in American studies and most often in alliance with, sometimes as friendly critics of, and on occasion in open opposition, to U.S. policy on such matters as civil rights and foreign adventures.

If we accept the hypothesis that the primary consumer of knowledge produced in the traditional area studies programs in the United States—Asian studies, European studies, Soviet studies—was and is the American state apparatus, then the primary difference of area studies from American studies appears theoretically and so politically. While the United States may well have done much to fund the expansion of American studies, especially after World War II in founding centers for American studies abroad, and while the orthodoxy of these centers was relatively carefully policed, there was no sense in which the state needed the knowledge produced by American studies for its own executive purposes. (The United States did not encourage a critical study of the U.S. state—for knowledge of that state was already held and kept in-house.) Those centers and the knowledge they reproduced and distributed served collateral purposes in the domains of culture and ideology, sometimes "at home," but often "abroad," supporting and expanding the interests of U.S. hegemony in a competition with third-world nationalism or Soviet or Chinese expansionism. Indeed, functionally it served to maintain and blur the distinction between "home" and "abroad" in ways essential to a global state power. It maintained it by insisting—notoriously—on the necessity of dealing with things "American" in noncomparative terms, producing relatively nationalist narratives of exclusion and privilege— unlike, for example, U.S. historians of the nineteenth century. But it also blurred the distinction by establishing the America as a subject-agent uniquely placed and largely self-determined and determining, an agent for which the world was "naturally" the field of action. In this sense, the United States occupies the principle position of "knower of the world" in contrast to all other competitive entities that either remain ignorant of the United States—for lack of resources or understanding—or study it under U.S. influence.[6] (The great Soviet-era centers for the study of the United States and Canada were an important exception to this generalization.)

Nonetheless, American studies had little direct effect upon state policy—

rather, it was an instrument of the state; F. O Matthiessen, the author of *The American Renaissance*, whose name is more important to the history of American studies than any other humanistic scholar, no more "brought about" the policies of the Cold War than Perry Miller's foundational text, *The New England Mind*,[7] produced northern housing segregation or the discrimination against immigrants or their exploitation by urban democratic parties. Although others have analyzed the ideological and cultural work done by the symbolic constructions emanating from American studies—we know a great deal more about the American studies injunctions to marginalize women, homogenize race, deny the existence of class, erase the memory of genocide, circulate the symbolic resources of consensus formation, and so on than we did not long ago—these powerful analyses of the American studies mythologeme machine prove that the state was not its primary consumer or reader. What I mean by this is simple: even these critical New Americanist studies depend upon the fact that the public sphere or, if we prefer, civil society is the space of production within which readers of American studies exist. I say this despite both Hegel and Althusser's arguments about the inevitable subsumption of civil society into the extended state. Even after Reagan, most of the work to delegitimate and defund the disciplines that underlie American studies has been carried out in "civil society," especially in and by the media and involves church and civic groups, journalists, foundations, and corporations as prominently as political parties. The defunding and refocusing of the NEH, for example, has been forced by an orchestrated public relations assault, led by Reagan-era neoconservatives (such as its former director, William Bennett), think tanks, the Christian Right, talk radio, Eurocentric academic combatants in the canon wars, and so on. The state has cooperated with this defunding effort precisely because the state does not rely on American studies for authoritative knowledge to guide policy within the United States and does not need it as much as it did in the days of the Cold War as a weapon in competition with foreign adversaries for cultural legitimacy. To the degree that the Clinton administration resisted this defunding, its policy was to use the NEH and, to whatever degree possible, the NEA, to encourage regional, populist, and multicultural agendas—protecting these agencies to some degree from claims that they destroy American values. These new NEH projects are ideologically "safe" in electoral terms and do not aim to produce knowledge essential to the decision making of state policy—although it is a knowledge with potential instrumental value within globalism represented by the U.S. ruling elites as threatened by dissensus. Politically the sorts of Americanist projects encouraged by the Clinton coalition seem often to stand in opposition to rightist positions on culture and politics; tactically, they seem to reflect both the most that can be done to preserve these funding agencies and the attempt to co-opt the conservative impulses within a milder center-right coalition that benefits from this form of commodification of "culture" as a product for consumption and export. (This is to acknowledge merely the journalistic consensus on Clinton's political skills.)[8]

Taken together with the continuing decline in employment possibilities—in history and literary studies—for American studies scholars, this defunding of public institutions central to the production of aesthetic and humanistic knowledge workers suggests how inessential the American studies projects are to the state's policy-making processes and expansionist ambitions. These defunding efforts go hand in hand with means of knowledge production alternative to the university bases of traditional American studies.[9] The far right wing of the ruling coalition carries the day in its attacks on the funding agencies not merely as a matter of political strength or expediency, but because the state has little need for the knowledge the funding agencies produce in American studies; nothing essential to the state is at stake. The governing coalition chooses to allay its right wing with a hegemonic compromise that not only defunds the American studies bases, but also enables private, ideological alternatives to those bases for talking about the United States—a talking about more important for its journalistic public relations value within the political program of any one faction than for its actual value to the state as it itself struggles with any competitor.

An example of some of how this works appears in the efforts of the now moribund Christian Coalition. In its *Contract with the American Family*, the Christian Coalition took a devastating, revealing, and largely effective position under the slogan "Privatizing the Arts": "The National Endowment for the Arts, National Endowment for the Humanities, Corporation for Public Broadcasting, and Legal Services Corporation should become voluntary organizations funded through private contributions."[10] More of this document makes clear some of the cultural right's avowed reasons for defunding the endowments:

> The National Endowment for the Humanities (NEH) also would be improved by privatization. Lynne Cheney, the NEH Chairman from 1986 to 1992, testified in January in support of ending federal funding for the agency. During her testimony she explained, "The humanities—like the arts—have become highly politicized. Many academics and artists now see their purpose not as revealing truth or beauty, but as achieving social and political transformation. Government should not be funding those whose main interest is promoting an agenda." The controversial national history standards, which NEH funding assisted in bringing into existence, are one such example.

William Bennett cites another example of the NEH's use of taxpayer dollars: "[T]he NEH provides funding for the Modern Language Association (MLA). Their annual convention attracts over 10,000 professors and students and reveals the type of agenda that NEH grants make possible. Past panels include such topics as 'Lesbian Tongues Untied;' 'Henry James and Queer Performativity;' [and] 'Status of Gender and Feminism in Queer Theory.'" It is clear that at a time when 24 percent of the average American family's budget goes to the federal government in taxes, we can find a better use for these tax dollars than through continued funding of the NEH.

There are, of course, important reasons why the political right has struggled to defund these endowments and often-affiliated university programs and faculty.[11] There are two points worth stressing: first, the right insists that knowledge produced by so-called liberally biased academic disciplines ruled by "campus radicals" produces no knowledge about society, but merely causes trouble by circulating ideas that unsettle the sense of "traditional American values" and lead to intolerable demands upon resources, especially upon state resources; second and more important, the right has decided to destroy the university as a place of intellectual work significant to society openly substituting activist politics as a replacement for anything approaching rigor or, if you will, disinterest in the production of knowledge about U.S. society. In so doing, the right merely follows a path already well marked out by the history of its involvement with think tanks. Amos Tevelow shows how increasingly, from around 1970, the statist ideal that think tanks would produce expert knowledge of a managerial sort "beyond ideology" gave way to advocacy think tanks the principle aims of which were to generate new naturalizing representations of a predatory transnational capital and to produce new kinds of public relations intellectuals always ready and available to operate in the media, on TV, in op-ed pages, and, when necessary, in government and foundations.[12] To the extent that these policies "weakened the state," they in fact de-democratized the state, reducing the ability of the people to demand resources and paradoxically, as in the case of the Reagan arms build-up, enhanced the state's ability to compete.[13] This means, for example, that rather than look to careful research of a sociological, economic, linguistic, or cultural sort into the workings of racism in contemporary U.S. society (a meritocratic professional approach), especially as this has been transformed and reactivated by transnational capital working upon demographics and employment needs (for instance, in attempting to close the middle class to African Americans by ending affirmative action), policymakers in the present ruling coalition rely upon the representations of race advanced by intellectual creatures of their own making who, post facto, provide the circulating legitimation for withdrawing the state—often against the law and the constitution itself—from the task of promoting employment and educational opportunity.

I spend time sketching these political skirmishes to show some reasons why the U.S. state has no need and, indeed, no desire to transform American studies into an area studies.[14] Rather than generate knowledge about America that, derived from the literary and historical traditions, might open space for knowledge contrary to the ambitions of the state, the government and its intellectuals—in this case, the cadre represented by the extreme right whose ideological claims have influenced state policy—would rather rely upon alternative centers of knowledge production and distribution. Dinesh D'Souza's book, *The End of Racism: Principles for a Multiracial Society*,[15] is a fine example of this strategy and its success. Similarly, transnational capital and its mandarins— who are not usually the same as the cultural rightists—have their own intellectual producers of junk science and stand on both sides of the putative left-right divide of U.S. politics. In *Pop Internationalism*, Paul Krugman makes a convincing argument for the state's disinterest in academic economic science.[16]

At just about the same time as the right-wing intellectuals wage these jeremiads against their enemies, traditional American foundations programmatically embrace a sort of counter-agenda, one predominantly promoting multiculturalism at home and abroad—with "diversity" as its key term. While it is true that the likes of the Olin Foundation busily align themselves with the overtly politicized think tanks of the right and support conservative tactics on university campuses, the likes of the Rockefeller and Ford Foundations support efforts, largely multicultural, on both national and international levels, to enhance— often within area studies—cultural knowledge and liberal tolerance.

One example of this can be found on the web site of the Ford Foundation, which sponsors a minority grant program administered by the NRC; Ford's program supports and sustains diversity as its mission statement makes clear: "A fundamental challenge facing every society is to create political, economic, and social systems that promote peace, human welfare, and the sustainability of the environment on which life depends. We believe that the best way to meet this challenge is to encourage initiatives by those living and working closest to where problems are located; to promote collaboration among the nonprofit, government, and business sectors; and to assure participation by men and women from diverse communities and at all levels of society. In our experience, such activities help build common understanding, enhance excellence, enable people to improve their lives, and reinforce their commitment to society."

The foundation explains that it currently has three fields of interest: "Grants and PRIS are given in the Foundation's fields of interest through a program division encompassing three broad areas: Asset Building and Community Development; Education, Media, Arts, and Culture; and Peace and Social Justice." In the culture areas, the Christian Coalition would have no trouble identifying the foundation's work as multiculturalist and potentially un-American: "A new area of activity concerned with belief systems, values, and pluralism supports projects that explore ethical questions underlying many of the Foundation's major program areas. . . . The program also supports projects that advance understanding about cultural identity and community." The Rockefeller Foundation is, if anything, more explicit about this part of its aims. It heads its section on "Arts and Humanities" with the following remark, urging the strategy upon grant seekers: "Support efforts to understand diversity and bridge differences in culture, class, ethnicity and tradition."

I have spent time drawing the far right and centrist wings of current ruling elite opinion together on these topics to suggest that no matter the place on the narrow political spectrum within the ruling U.S. coalition, the state, for two reasons, has no interest whatsoever in forwarding an American studies agenda that will take state policy—as conceived by realists—as part of its investigation: first, the state would not welcome and will not fund careful critical examination of its own policies and powers; second, it finds American studies intellectuals already producing knowledge for the most part instrumentally valuable to the state's agenda.[17] To put it simply: American studies intellectuals both continue to produce knowledge the state's policymakers do not need to enhance the competitive resources of the state and they do not study the state at the level of policy in ways that would make their knowledge significant to the state or its opponents. American studies will not become a form of area studies, then, because American studies will not have the state as the primary consumer of its product; and, without this market, American studies intellectuals will not take state policy as its principal object of investigation with the idea of affecting that policy.

American studies scholars have principally focused on matters of culture and history, the areas of "civil society" or "the public sphere," acting as if, in this way, they were accessing the U.S. state through its extensions; but the ruling sub-disciplines forming American studies have been largely anthropological in the Kantian sense. Anthropological scholarship focuses on human activity to construct society; largely ethnographic, the traditional techniques of American studies do not make central the study either of the largest forces of history, the inhuman elements of market, capital, and so on; nor do they take the fact of the U.S. state as itself an agent that must be confronted, in itself, by means of detailed, concrete, material and theoretical analyses. This is evident from such foundational titles in American studies as *The New England Mind, The American Renaissance,* or *The American Jeremiad;* such competing and seemingly more materialist titles as *The Machine in the Garden* or *No Place of Grace* barely depart from the consensus.[18]

Recently, scholars have revised and redirected American studies toward the examination of the multicultural diversity and multiplicity not only of the peoples and cultures present in the United States, but their histories, positions, trajectories, and everyday practices. Indeed, these studies have shown the victimization and strengths of marginal groups—both facts previously obscured by national narratives and their Americanist reconstructions. We see newer titles dealing with ethnicity, transvestitism, passing, border communities, and so on. American studies finally begins to move away from the habit of studying the United States as an exceptional and isolated entity; this means not so much a look at the place and function of the United States in a global order, though, as it does a tendency to compare U.S. forms of culture to those of other usually national or subnational groupings from Canada to Chile; often there is a special interest in those thought of as subaltern.[19] Although there are mentions of NAFTA, WTO, and the Mexican bailout,[20] the focus of American studies teaching and research, especially at the most elite universities, is culturalist and local.[21]

In their fascination with the cultural domains of multiplicity and the politics of justice and injustice, American studies assumes a close and continuing link between the state and civil society.[22] This essentially Hegelian notion, important to any thinking about the state's reach into society, should not be allowed to obscure the fact that the U.S. state, as Admiral Mahan's study of sea power was among the first to make clear, increasingly functions as an independent agent mostly interested in its own empowerment, an agent whose nature and identity cannot be understood unless its critics recognize that it understands itself and acts as the state theorized by realism. American studies' instrumental value for the state depends upon American studies *not* taking the state, as an entity different from the nation or its "culture(s)," as a subject of knowledge. Indeed, the current arrangements of intellectual practice operates in such a way as to assure that, concerned with multiculturalism and economic survival in the shadow of the Democratic Party, it will not be able to think the independence of the American state from society despite the increasingly obvious evidence of its autonomy.

American studies has undergone an intra-academic revision, as have most other cultural disciplines, that is, it has felt the pressure of post-Cold War economic cutbacks, ideological critique of its role as an agent of U.S. hegemony, and it has seized the opportunity to give critical attention to the multiplicity of histories that belong to the various peoples and groups of U.S. society.[23] This revisionist effort strengthens populist and melodramatic politics and tends to make all intellectual work into a commitment to will alone, into a politics of truth defined totally by representative and representational categories of struggle. There is profound intellectual and political irresponsibility in this. In essence it makes violence the chief criterion of truth and, in so doing, not only allows violence to remain unexamined as a category productive of value, but it obscures the proper role of the intellectual which, as Edward W. Said repeatedly reminds us, is to speak truth to power. Importantly, it avoids a discussion of the state which is defined, quite precisely, by its control of the means of violence. In other words, violence, in this reform of American studies, has been de-realized into the activities of "cultural domination" active within social hegemony.

If a reformed American studies progresses under the impact of multicultural cultural studies—a possibility inherent in the interdisciplinary history of American studies—then it might well expect support from foundations interested in directing research and teaching into these areas. Furthermore, it will find potential allies among those in traditional fields committed to similar tasks. Indeed, they will all agree that the time has more than come to do away with the basic ideological positions of American studies: exceptionalism, example to the world, bastion of democratic values, and so on. In their place will come studies in what was once forgotten; studies of the discursive forces that "construct" realities of ethnicity, race, gender, and so on; as well as some objection to the idea that the United States can be studied alone as a discrete object in the world. These are the kinds of studies the NEH and the foundations might support; the resources for knowledge production are in these areas—not in the study of the state nor in the producing of knowledge about the American state for its policymakers. Allocating resources in these areas will keep American studies from becoming an area studies.

Neither academic scholars nor their right-wing critics will question the possibility of justifying a field called American studies as such. Many of those who are now among the most progressive practitioners of American studies were themselves formed in an era before historical changes ended the classic decorum. Their dissertation directors were, at least figuratively and in many cases actually, the grand old men of the field. Moreover, there is a broad, relatively rich, widely marketed body of scholars whom we might call "Americanists" who teach at all levels from small colleges to large research universities, who publish big books, get newspaper reviews, and reproduce themselves. This is an institutional reality and it forms the context in which American studies conducts itself. The constant point of reference for the work done in this context is still within the national boundaries of the United States as a political entity that, oddly but increasingly, is administered by a state that has fewer and fewer "organic" relations or obligations to its population.[24]

To most of those who think about these issues, especially in the literary humanities, the very construction of American studies and the terms America and American are at stake in the maelstrom of shifting forces defunding and repositioning what they do. This is a familiar way of asking questions, of thinking and talking within the American studies fields. Such ways of thinking and talking belong to the hope that important political resistance and perhaps social "empowerment" might come from the alignment of academic work of this kind with subaltern groups within the United States and crossing its borders. My hypothesis is that critics cannot fulfill this hope.

Rather than argue directly for this hypothesis let me try to identify certain kinds of work that do not belong to American studies, the absence of which not only prevents it from being area studies but from fulfilling the best hopes of its friends. More severe, we could say, is the fact that it is a kind of work that, were it included, would prevent it from remaining American studies.

Let me take as evidence examples from the work of two scholars, one central to this collection and the other an influential figure whose primary work matters to America's relations with other parts of the world. Bruce Cumings and Edward Said have made major contributions to the understanding and judgment of the U.S. state by their work on the policy consequences (and origins) of the representational devices of U.S. knowledge systems and media.[25] From Cumings's "Time to End the Korean War," for example, we come to see that the vaunted American intelligence system—including the universities and think tanks—promotes state policy based on ignorance; that the U.S. media is "blindly imitative, fundamentally ignorant," sustaining racist demonizations; and that all this is due to an asymmetry of power that, ironically, could lead the United States to its own downfall as an empire.[26] Along the way, Cumings details how antidemocratic policy making is; how elites act on often ill-considered mythologies that are the common sense of their circles; and how the regime of U.S. intelligence, especially in the form of its experts, will cement the necessity, the naturalness of the elite's ignorant and dangerous biases.

I submit that this is the sort of knowledge about the United States that cannot circulate as a form of American studies.[27] First of all, to produce such knowledge requires work in materials and languages completely outside the purview of Americanists; it is a kind of work that U.S. elites will not fund since in its truth lies their own delegitimation; and, in essence, it assumes the United States cannot be understood nor its best interests recognized without breaking the very mold of American studies and insisting that knowing the United States means studying its state form realistically, putting it into the world, into its deployed sets of power relations, all of which are precisely off limits to the universities under both the papal-like denunciations of the right and the culturalist populisms of the foundations. Above all, Cumings proposes something other than an intellectual politics of representation which is all that "progressive" American studies has come to be—such a politics, we see, places the intellectual within a hegemonic position in relation to the represented; more precisely this sort of intellectual mediates the subaltern's relation to the hegemony and acquires legitimated leadership as a result. Paradoxically, such an intellectual comes to occupy something like a parody of the position of the reduced welfare state itself. Cumings's knowledge steps away from such a self-legitimating play of specularity that encompasses and enables the succeeding waves of market fashions in cultural studies: there is no claim to representation but rather an analysis of the formations and forces of power.

As such, it is similar to Edward W. Said's work from *Orientalism* to *The Politics of Dispossession*.[28] Said's writing is very much an analysis of the American deployment of power in the world and, as such, of the American institutional arrangements for producing "knowledge"—which in this case consists merely in systematic representations guided by the interests of its producers. This means that the critique of Orientalism as the fact of U.S. state policy replacing the European empires of the last century, precisely because it is a study of state policy and its affiliated cultural regimes, defines an example of American study that, despite the efforts of some, has found no home in American studies. In presenting a statement that summarizes a career of experience in dealing with this American system and of how to oppose it, Said, in reply to a question from René Backmann of *Le Nouvel Observateur*, makes the following statement:

L'un des grands problèmes que doivent affronter les intellectuels américains, c'est en effet la prolifération de ces gens qui se définissent eux-mèmes comme des experts et qui vendent leur expérience dans les médias. Je doies admettre que j'ai remporté sur ce terrain quelques succès pendant l'Intifada, en devenant une sorte de référence. En faisant entendre, face au statu quo, au discours dominant, une autre voix. Mais je sais qu'on ne peut tenir ce rôle trop longtemps sous peines de devenir un simple poin et d'être absorbé par le système. Il faut être d'une grande vigilance pour voir à chaque instant où vous pouvez communique, expliquer, clarifier. J'ajoute que l'intellectuel ne doit pas se contenter de jeter de temps en temps une bouteille à la mer, si c'est possible, rassembler ses messages, publier des livres, constituer une œuvre, donner un sens à son travail.[29]

This is Said's effort to describe how the intellectual must form his speech against power. Putting aside, for the moment, the definitions of power, the point made has to do with defining the shape work on the United States must take if it is not to be wasted. Fascinatingly, while academic Americanists might accept a Saidian critique of the knowledge formations that have to do with Islam or the Orient, they are little willing to worry the question of their own expert status. At most they seem to feel that shifting the line of criticism from the idea of the American Renaissance to the critical representation of either the "experience" of the subaltern or the analysis of how particular subalternities have been "constructed"—they feel that this "cultural poetics" relegitimates their work and revives American studies as a "new Americanist-ism."[30]

Of course, private foundations seem willing to support the effort to carry out this reforming project as a form of multiculturalism. Absent the sort of formed work Said recommends, American studies will not, easily, get past this. To become area studies would require not only that American studies shift its object, its point of view, and the shape of its career trajectory; it would also require finding a way to entice the state to buy the knowledge it produces. The effort to achieve this would be fruitless because the state is not buying.

The appetite for multiculturalist Americanist knowledge lies, if anywhere, in the jaws of the transnationals for whom such culturalist knowledge, whether intended to be subversive or oppositional or not, is knowledge only of and for a market. Often, since such culturalist work crosses borders, it functions in relation to emerging transnational groups (as, for example, the English novel written in Singapore) who consume it for their own purposes and which, as a form of representative knowledge, aligns the producers of such culturalist work as representative for and within the hegemony of transnational capital. It is hard to see how American studies could (be allowed to) redefine itself as an area studies given the absence of the necessary conditions, especially the possibility of imagining alternative paradigms to the present transnational-dominated combinations of power and capital that stand in a mutually dependent relation with a powerfully independent U.S. state.

If we take Cumings and Said as representing work and knowledge of a sort that an American area studies would need, we cannot imagine it as the sort of work the state needs, wants, or would buy. If we imagine American studies without such work, then it is only the same old American studies reformed but not changed. In each case, we must keep in mind the increasingly important role transnational capital plays in influencing the deployment of state resources not in the interest of nation or national capital, as such, but in the interest of the transnationals themselves and the world market. This last fact raises an interesting question: what would an area studies that takes the world market as its subject look like? Where would it stand? Should we not expect that in the face of the world market's increasingly evident power—recall Marx had already theorized it in the *Grundrisse* and Mahan technologized it in his science of logistics—area studies itself is not only defunded but challenged by global modeling based on rational choice and game theory? Furthermore, would there not be something supremely ironic in attempting to reimagine American studies as a scholarship of the globe, the stage on which the last remaining superpower acts? We should recall that the sort of work Said and Cumings represent rests on a strong anti-imperialism. Alfred Mahan's studies of sea power and his work on logistics are more than objects of antiquarian interest. Looking at them again gives us a sense of America's self-construction as inherently imperial and expansionist. Mahan's analysis of British hegemony and his development of logistics as a science early on model a state system inseparable from the project of an empire attempting to be at one with the world market itself. The logic of Mahan's position has become increasingly evident with the end of the Cold War, not only in the Middle East and Korea, but in the expansion of NATO, the undeclared struggle against France in Central Africa, and the debates about China.

We might know this to be some of the truth of America, but it is not that knowledge which the state requires—not especially since, as in the case of Mahan, the state has already produced the theory of its own globalizing action, a theory we critics can only hope to rush to catch. If America has had this structured intent to be identical to the world—for what else can it mean to be the world's only remaining superpower?—then where can American studies people stand to get a view of all this if they continue to commit themselves to study within the purview of putative "American culture(s)," rather than from a more cosmopolitan position that stands willfully apart from any remaining illusions that the anthropological study of civil society brings them any nearer to understanding power and the United States.

These are hypotheses for discussion since it is important how intellectuals study the United States and how knowledge of the United States circulates and reproduces. Just how intellectuals theorize the United States in the age of openly dominant world market agents of transnational capital—this is a question with geopolitical consequences that exceed the borders, crossed and transgressed as they already are, of the United States and its intelligentsia. But it is a question that needs to begin with a look at the U.S. state itself. Non-American intellectuals sometimes have knowledge of the U.S. state; we must find ways for this to circulate in the United States; and where intellectuals do not produce this knowledge, then we should encourage it. Simply because the United States has power is not itself reason for this statement; but because the United States is the instrument for enhancing the world market, knowledge of it is necessary to everyone. This means that Americanists, with their native assumptions about territorial identity, commonality and difference, sovereignty and citizenship, must give way to cosmopolitans unafraid to think the U.S. state, its power, its instrumentalizations, and its alienations from its people and society.

Appendix: Dissertations Completed in American Studies at Yale, 1988–1995

1988

Ferraro, Thomas J., III. *Ethnic Passages: The Mobility Narratives of Yezierska, Miller, Puzo, and Kingston* (Director: JC Agnew)

Frank, Dana L. *At the Point of Consumption: Seattle Labor and the Politics of Consumption, 1919–1927* (Director: D Montgomery)

Johnson, Dianne A. *For the Children of the Sun: What We Say to Afro-American Youth Through Story and Image* (Director: RB Stepto)

MacDonald, Bonney. *In the Making: Acts of Creation in the Writing of William and Henry James* (Director: RWB Lewis)

Rosenthal, Joel. *Righteous Realist: Perceptions of American Power and Responsibility in the Nuclear Age* (Director: G Smith)

Stock, Catherine M. *Main Street in Crisis: The Old Middle Class in the Great Depression* (Director: HR Lamar)

1989

Brown, David H. *Garden in the Machine: Afro-Cuban Sacred Art and Performance in Urban New Jersey and New York* (Director: HR Lamar)

Ibarguen, Raoul Richard. *Narrative Detours: Henry Miller and the Rise of New Critical Modernism* (Director: A Trachtenberg)

Scobey, David M. *Empire City: Politics, Culture, and Urbanism in Gilded-Age New York* (Director: A Trachtenberg)

Watts, Linda S. *"The Moment of Recognition": A Feminist Approach to Religious and Artistic Creation in the Writings of Gertrude Stein* (Director: A Trachtenberg)

Ye, Wei-li. *The American Experience of Chinese Students in the Early Decades of the Twentieth Century* (Director: JD Spence)

1990

Beavers, Herman. *Wrestling Angels into Song: Coherence and Disclosure in the Fiction of Ernest J. Gaines and James Alan McPhearson* (Director: RB Stepto)

Bruce, Marcus C. *The Unfinished Universe: William James, Pragmatism, and the American Intellectual* (Director: J Butler)

Morrissey, Katherine G. *Mental Territories: Environment and the Creation of the Inland Empire, 1870–1920* (Director: HR Lamar)

Myers, Kenneth. *Selling the Sublime: The Catskills and the Social Construction of Landscape Experience in the United States, 1776–1876* (Director: J Prown)

1991

Cartwright, Elizabeth. *Physiological Modernism: Cinematography as a Medical Research Technology, 1895–1960* (Director: A Trachtenberg)

Glasser, Ruth. *Que Vivio Tiene la Gente Aqui en Nueva York: Music and Community in Puerto Rican New York, 1915–1940* (Director: D Montgomery)

Nickerson, Catherine R. *The Domestic Detective Novel: Gothicism, Domesticity, and Investigation in American Women's Writing, 1865–1920* (Director: A Trachtenberg)

Oberdeck, Kathryn. *Labor's Vicar and Variety Show: Popular Religion and Cultural Class Conflict* (Director: D Montgomery)

Stein, Sally. *The Rhetoric of the Colorful and the Colorless: American Photography and Material Culture between the Wars* (Director: A Trachtenberg)

Tal, Kali. *Bearing Witness: The Literature of Trauma* (Director: RB Stepto)

Wallach, Glenn. *Obedient Sons: Youth and Generational Consciousness in American Culture, 1630–1850s* (Director: DB Davis)

1992

Ballard, Barbara. *Nineteenth-Century Theories of Race, the Concept of Correspondences, and Images of Blacks in the Antislavery Writings of Douglass, Stowe, and Browne* (Director: DB Davis)

Casper, Scott E. *Constructing American Lives: The Cultural History of Biography in Nineteenth-Century America* (Director: RH Brodhead)

Goldberg, Michael L. *"An Army of Women": Gender Relations and Politics in Kansas Populism, the Woman Movement, and the Republican Party, 1879–1896* (Director: NF Cott)

Grasso, Christopher D. *Between Awakenings: Learned Men and the Transformation of Public Discourse in Connecticut, 1740–1800* (Director: HS Stout)

Griffin, Farah J. *"Who Set You Flowin'?" Migration, Urbanization, and African-American Culture* (Director: RB Stepto)

Haltman, Kenneth. *Figures in a Western Landscape: Readings in the Art of Titian, Ramsay Peale from the Long Expedition to the Rocky Mountains, 1819–1820* (Director: J Prown)

Phillips, Kimberley. *Heaven Bound: Black Migration, Community, and Activism in Cleveland, 1915–1945* (Director: NF Cott)

1993

Brekus, Catherine A. *Let Your Women Keep Silence in the Churches: Female Preaching and Evangelical Religion in America, 1740–1845* (Director: HS Stout)

Den Tandt, Christophe. *The Urban Sublime in American Literary Naturalism* (Director: A Trachtenberg)

Desmond, Jane. *Physical Evidence: Bodies in Contemporary American Performance* (Director: BJ Wolf)

Dilworth, Leah C. *Imagining the Primitive: Representations of Native Americans in the Southwest, 1880–1930* (Director: BJ Wolf)

Dudziak, Mary L. *Cold War Civil Rights: The Relationship Between Civil Rights and Foreign Affairs in the Truman Administration* (Director: DB Davis)

Fisher, Paul. *Itineraries in the Art-World: The Cult of Europe and Transatlantic Careers in High Culture, 1865–1920* (Director: RH Brodhead)

Forbath, William E. *Law and the Shaping of American Labor* (Director: D. B. Davis)

Hartman, Saidiya V. *Performing Blackness: Staging Subjection and Resistance in Antebellum Culture* (Director: HV Carby)

Murolo, Priscilla. *Working Girls' Clubs, 1884–1928: Class and Gender on the "Common Ground of Womanhood"* (Director: D Montgomery)

Rachman, Stephen. *Narrative Pathology: Plagiarism, Exhaustion, and Obscenity in the American Renaissance* (Director: RH Brodhead)

Satter, Beryl E. *New Thought and the Era of Woman, 1875–1895* (Director: NF Cott)

Schnog, Nancy J. *Inside the Sentimental: The Psychological Work of Nineteenth-Century American Women's Writing* (Director: RH Brodhead)

Sellers, Christopher. *Manufacturing Disease: Experts and the Ailing American Worker* (Director: WJ Cronon)

Shannon, Christopher. *Conspicuous Criticism: Tradition, Autonomy, and Culture in American Social Thought, from Veblen to Mills* (Director: J-C Agnew)

Shen, Xiao Hong. *Yale's China and China's Yale: Americanizing Higher Education in China, 1900–1927* (Director: J Butler)

Stowe, David. *Swing Changes: The Transformation of Jazz in American Culture, 1935–1950* (Director: M. Denning)

Wickberg, Daniel. *The Sense of Humor in American Culture, 1850–1960* (Director: J-C Agnew)

Wescott, Brian. *Freed to Be Something New: Native American Journey into the Performing Arts* (Director: H Lamar)

1994

Deloria, Philip. *Playing Indian: Otherness and Authenticity in the Assumption of American Indian Identity* (Director: H Lamar)

Gedge, Karin. *Without Benefit of Clergy: Women in the Pastoral Relationship in Victorian American Culture* (Director: J Butler)

Reid-Pharr, Robert. *Conjugal Union: Gender, Sexuality, and the Development of an African American National Literature* (Director: H Carby)

Richard, Yevette. *My Passionate Feeling about Africa: Maida Springer-Kemp and the American Labor Movement* (Director: D Montgomery)

Schoelwer, Susan. *Painted Ladies, Virgin Lands: Women in the Myth and Image of the American Frontier, 1830–1860* (Director: B Wolf)

Viehmann, Martha. *Writing across the Cultural Divide: Images of Indians in the Lives and Works of Native and European Americans, 1890–1995* (Director: A Trachtenberg)

Waldstreicher, David. *The Making of American Nationalism: Celebration and Political Culture, 1776–1820* (Director: DB Davis)

Yoo, David. *Growing Up Nisei: Second-Generation Japanese Americans* (Director: H Lamar)

1995

Belgrad, Daniel. *The Social Meaning of Spontaneity in American Literature, 1940–1960* (Director: J-C Agnew)

Cleghorn, Cassandra. *Bartleby's Benefactors: Toward a Literary History of Charity in the Antebellum South* (Director: R Brodhead)

Gilmartin, Katie. *The Very House of Difference: Intersections of Identities in the Life Histories of Colorado Lesbians, 1940–1995* (Director: NF Cott)

Green, Amy. *Savage Childhood: The Scientific Construction of Girlhood and Boyhood in the Progressive Era* (Director: W Cronon)

Filene, Benjamin. *Romancing the Folk: Public Memory and American Vernacular Music in the Twentieth Century* (Director: RB Stepto)

Lassonde, Stephen. *Learning to Forget: Schooling and Family Life in New Haven's Working Class* (Director: J Demos)

Lepore, Jill. *The Name of War: Waging, Writing, and Remembering King Philip's War* (Director: J Demos)

Rotella, Carlo. *October Cities: The Redevelopment of Urban Literature* (Director: RB Stepto)

Swinth, Kristen. *Painting Professionals: Women Artists and the Development of a Professional Ideal in American Art, 1870–1920* (Director: NF Cott)

Townsend, Gretchen. *Protestant Material Culture and Community in Connecticut, 1785–1854* (Director: J Butler)

Notes

1 Needless to say I am aware of how careerism and ideology, for example, combine with ruling discourses within knowledge-producing apparatuses to assure that most area studies knowledge confirms rather than redirects power. The fact is, though, that the state funds this knowledge production, erroneous as much of it may be, with the idea that it enhances state power against competitors.

2 Needless to say this distinction requires clarification beginning with the statement that the distinction is not absolute. But it is functional. As a matter of convenience, I rely on Fareed Zakaria's articulation of these issues in *From Wealth to Power* (Princeton: Princeton University Press, 1998).

3 By New Americanist I refer not only to the massively influential series of books edited by Donald E. Pease under that title for Duke University Press; nor to the claims Pease and others have made for the critical agenda of New Americanism—attention to minority cultures, critique of unifying historical narratives, the study of socially symbolic acts of resistance; I refer also to the broader alliance—increasingly criticized by

Pease—between New Americanism and the anti-theoretical impulses of the so-called New Historicism, which, having arisen in the age of Reagan and calling itself "cultural poetics," undergirds the facile careerism and marketability that comes from aligning elements of Americanism in the university with both multicultural projects of the center-right of the Democratic Party and uncritical practitioners of identity politics in the cultural arena.

4   F. O. Matthiessen, *The American Renaissance* (New York: Oxford University Press, 1941).

5   Jonathan Arac, *Huckleberry Finn as Idol and Target* (Madison: University of Wisconsin Press, 1997), 118–32.

6   This is an argument Edward W. Said developed often specifically when he discussed the imbalance in the knowledge/power relations between the U.S. and the Arab world. See, for example, *Covering Islam: How the Media and the Experts Determine How We See the Rest of the World* (New York: Pantheon Books, 1981), 154ff.

7   Perry Miller, *The New England Mind: The Seventeenth Century* (New York: Macmillan, 1939), followed by *The New England Mind: From Colony to Province* (Cambridge, Mass.: Harvard University Press, 1953).

8   For some sense of what I mean by this, see the collection of essays in *boundary 2* 26(2) (summer 1999) gathered by Ronald Judy under the title "Reasoning and the Logic of Things Global," 3–74.

9   See, for example, Edward Wyatt, "Investors Are Seeing Profits in Nation's Demand for Education," *New York Times,* 4 November 1999, 1f.

10   I take this quotation from the Christian Coalition's Web site listing of their magazine the *American Christian:* http://www.fopc.org/politics/index.html.

11   Indeed they have set up foundations and provided training documents to enable conservative faculty to defund these programs from within the university. The language of Cheney and Bennett is too explicit to require much comment, although Bennett's obsession with matters of queer sexuality might require psychoanalytic as well as political analysis.

12   Amos Tevelow, "Globalism and '70s Intellectuals," paper presented at the International Communication Association Convention in Montreal, May 1997. See also Tevelow, "Maintaining the Order of Things: Class, the Gospel of Scientific Efficiency, and the Invention of Policy Expertise in America, 1865–1921," in *Turning the Century: Essays in Media and Cultural Studies,* ed. Carol Stabile (Boulder, Colo.: Westview Press, 2000).

13   By degrading the welfare state these ideologically charged think tanks have strengthened the state by reducing the number of claims made upon it and by freeing it to act as state on a geopolitical stage defined as globalization—as "the one remaining superpower."

14   Another essay would be needed to explain why the state might not want to establish a relatively independent body of scholars whose object was the study of the U.S. state itself. One can imagine how, for example, work of this sort done by Chomsky might create complications. At the same time, it might draw attention to the quite direct and revealing writing often done by U.S. state intellectuals themselves who often are quite explicit articulating their aims for and within the state. Historically, of course,

Alfred Thayer Mahan comes to mind as a good example of such state intellectuals from the study of whose career a great deal might be learned about the U.S. state.

15 (New York: Free Press, 1996.)

16 *Pop Internationalism* (Cambridge, Mass.: MIT Press, 1996). In his introduction, Krugman explains that this small book came into being as a result of an epiphany he had while a guest at one of President Clinton's economic fora prior to taking office. Krugman's discovery is worth quoting in full to make a certain point: "In other words, all the things that have been painfully learned through a couple of centuries of hard thinking about and careful study of the international economy—that tradition that reaches back to David Hume's essay, 'On the Balance of Trade'—have been swept out of public discourse. Their place has been taken by glib rhetoric that appeals to those who want to sound sophisticated without engaging in hard thinking; and this rhetoric has come to dominate popular discussion so completely that someone who wanted to learn about world trade without reading a textbook would probably never realize there is anything better" (viii–ix).

17 Noam Chomsky: "Power in the Global Arena," *New Left Review* 230 (July/August 1998) might be taken as an example of how American studies transformed into the study of the U.S. state might look. Chomsky makes particularly telling use of state sources in writing this essay.

18 These texts are all authored by leading or dominant figures in the fields of American studies with Harvard University's Department of English and American Language and Literature. Sacvan Bercovitch, *The American Jeremiad* (Madison: University of Wisconsin Press, 1978); Leo Marx, *The Machine in the Garden: Technology and the Pastoral Ideal in America* (New York: Oxford University Press, 1967); Jackson Lears, *No Place of Grace: Antimodernism and the Transformation of American Culture* (New York: Pantheon, 1981).

19 This term, derived perhaps from Gramsci, has become a familiar term in the last two decades, finding its most frequently cited existence in the work of a famous group of Indian historians who call themselves "the Subaltern Studies group." The term has been extended to refer to all those marginal peoples within even advanced societies who are denied representation and the possibility of self-representation. In the last decade, scholars have attempted to apply subaltern studies models to the United States and to see it as preferable even to New Americanism as a mode of investigation. See, for example, Ranajit Guha and Gayatri Chakravorty Spivak, eds., *Selected Subaltern Studies* (New York: Oxford University Press, 1988); and Eva Cherniavksy, "Subaltern Studies in a U.S. Frame," *boundary 2* 23(2) (summer 1996): 85–110.

20 The U.S. Treasury organized a $20 billion bailout of the Mexican economy around February 1995, despite Congressional (Republican) unwillingness.

21 As evidence, I attach a list of recent dissertations from Yale's distinguished program in American Studies (see appendix). Let me also detail the titles from a recent American studies colloquium at the University of Pittsburgh: "Place Your Bets: Risk and the Eclipse of Security in the 1970s" (to avoid confusion, let me say this paper created a genealogy of the category "risk" in mass discourse and did not treat security in terms of state policy); "The Method Born of James's Madness, or, Hamlet's Solution in the Making of Pragmatism"; and "Habitual Authenticity: Reframing the Fantasy of Crossover in American Popular Music."

22 Cf. Paul A. Bové, *The End of Thinking*, Centro de Semiótica y Teoría del espectáculo, Universitat de València (València, Spain: *Eutopías, 2a época*, 1994).

23 Let me offer titles of some recent dissertations from Yale as examples of how American studies has changed its rhetoric and objects of study under this pressure: "The Very House of Difference: Intersections of Identities in the Life Histories of Colorado Lesbians, 1940–1995"; "Growing Up Nisei: Second-Generation Japanese Americans"; and "Playing Indian: Otherness and Authenticity in the Assumption of American Indian Identity."

24 The Personal Responsibility and Work Opportunity Reconciliation Act of 1996 is perhaps the most convenient example of how even anti-government conservatives can strengthen the state, in this case by reducing demands made upon the state's resources at a time of massive budget surpluses.

25 In his book *Huckleberry Finn*, Jonathan Arac, in his final chapter before the coda closing the study of the hypercanonization of Twain's novel, turns to the work of Edward Said precisely because Said is an outsider in at least two ways: first, he is not an Americanist nor is his work central to Americanist criticism; second, Said is not a native-born son: "I draw on Edward Said's *Culture and Imperialism* (1993). In reflecting on American nationalism, it is salutary to bring in a writer who is an American citizen not born in the United States" (203). In Arac's dynamic critique, Said comes in to offer a look askew at a tradition of Huck adoration begun, we should recall, by Said's great Columbia predecessor, Lionel Trilling. Arac leaves us with the strong sense that American studies, even when its concerns are in the hands of the strongest critic of the mid-century, cannot be trusted to produce knowledge "beyond" the canonical; breaking such repetition would require a willingness to think the United States as those engaged, like Said, with the foreign consequences of U.S. state power and so can see the very realities Americanists purchasing domestic tranquility cannot. It is the deep purpose of Arac's text to reveal the effort made in canonizing Huck to purchase tranquility as a massive error: it churns up dissensus and it turns critique away from its proper targets. Worse, it sustains, as it must, the existence of the very horror it finds repulsive—both to repeat itself in relation to that horror and to keep eyes focused on it.

26 *Atlantic Monthly* (February 1997): 71–79. See also Bruce Cumings, *Korea's Place in the Sun: A Modern History* (New York: W. W. Norton, 1997); *Parallax Visions* (Durham: Duke University Press, 1999), especially chap. 7, "Boundary Displacement: The State, the Foundations, and International and Area Studies during and after the Cold War."

27 It goes without saying that such knowledge cannot circulate as area studies knowledge either. This, after all, is the basis of Cumings's book. There is a more specific point here: if area studies always takes the policy actions of states under study as part of their object of knowledge, an American studies become area studies would need to take the U.S. state as its object and so it would need to know the kinds of things Cumings knows. It is crucial that Cumings produces such knowledge about the U.S. state and not an American studies scholar.

28 Edward W. Said, *Orientalism* (New York: Pantheon, 1978); *The Politics of Dispossession: The Struggle for Palestinian Self-Determination, 1969–1994* (New York: Pantheon, 1994).

29 I cite this from the Web page archives of the *Nouvel Observateur* http://frigor-ix.sdv.fr/nouvelobs/archives/voir_article.cfm?id=11505&mot=Backmann. It appears in print in 16 January 1997 under the title "Interview."

30 Donald E. Pease, "Negative Interpellations: From Oklahoma City to the Trilling-Matthiessen Transmission," *boundary 2* 23(1) (spring 1996): 1–34.

Imagining "Asia-Pacific" Today: Forgetting Colonialism in the Magical Free Markets of the American Pacific
Rob Wilson

South Seas, turquoise green skies, the archways of a bazaar, the mysterious house—all of this Oriental scenery surrenders to the fairy-tale wish [for some imagined utopia] with great affinity and absorbs it. . . . The land of wishes from the [European] medieval South Seas, so to speak, has remained.—Ernst Bloch, *The Utopian Function of Art and Literature*[1]

James Clavell, who just died, made the Far East a less mysterious place.
—National Public Radio reporter, on the death of *Shogun*'s author, September 6, 1994

Courting the Asia-Pacific Yacht People

Nobody quite knows what "Asia-Pacific" means these days in terms of specific ingredients or future directions, but one thing remains clear: many forces are trying to court and construct it into a transnational identity as a meta-geographical "region."[2] To cite one localized example, the Democratic Governor of Hawai'i, Benjamin Cayetano, in May of 1997 led a delegation of businessmen, Realtors, and Pacific educators on a ten-day trip to Taiwan to promote business, tourism, and investment opportunities in Hawai'i. As the self-appointed and state-like base of the "Asia-Pacific Operation Center" (APROC), Taiwan seemed a likely place to make such a pitch as a site that is competing with Hong Kong and Singapore to become "the space of [transnational] flows" across the Pacific.[3] Going beyond his pro-tourism rationale, Cayetano sought to inform Taiwan's people about Hawai'i's "Immigrant Investor Program," which has become one of the most popular programs for immigrant investors seeking permanent residency in the United States. "This program gives immigrant investors the opportunity to stay in the U.S. with an investment of one million dollars," Cayetano boasted, adding that it has already been implemented throughout the United States.[4] Cayetano's mission was not just interested in luring Taiwanese investment from the Pacific Rim: he had already led similar trips to the Philippines, Korea, Japan, and China. (Canada and Australia are also making money-for-passport offers and, at the same time, trying to fight off backlashes of "white only" nationalism and the reactive rise of Hansonism.)[5] The call across the Pacific to the markets of Asia these days is not so much to the "boat people" but to the "yacht people" of some vast—and, at times, threatening—"Greater China."[6] The rise of nationalism and protectionism in post-crisis Asia since 1997 and 1998 has generated renewed calls for U.S. intervention in promoting, shaping, and guiding Asia-Pacific as a transnational region (more on this below).[7]

As a U.S. literary scholar working in the Pacific, I could only recall the gloomier "Asia-Pacific" region portrayed in Maxine Hong Kingston's memoirs of the modern Chinese diaspora, *The Woman Warrior: Memoirs of a Girlhood among Ghosts* (1976) and *China Men* (1980): generations of uprooted stowaways contracted to years of labor in Cuba, New York, Bali, and Hawai'i: plantation workers, railroad men, day laborers working long hours in restaurants, clothing factories, and laundromats, struggling for livelihood while surviving on mythic self-constructions as they confront social exclusion among the taunting "ghosts" of Gold Mountain. Or recall, as well, Joy Kogawa's portrait of generations of Japanese Canadians in *Obasan* (1982), three generations unjustly uprooted from the Northern Pacific coast region and forced to relocate several times in remote areas of Canada as wartime "Yellow Peril" discourse on the coast (as in California) reached phobic extremes: their property confiscated; citizenship questioned; families broken; long ties to the land, language, and nation denied.[8] Kingston, interviewed in Taiwan in 1995 (in her own uncanny words, "a country made up of exiles, misfits, and outsiders" and "like America, a country where immigrants have taken over the land and dominate the indigenous, primal people") revealed the trauma of her own family's U.S. immigrant experience and the necessity to distort it by means of mythic imagination: "Now that my father has died, I can tell you that he actually came to the U.S. as a stowaway on a ship from Cuba, and he made the journey not once but three times. He was caught twice by immigration police and deported twice. I had to tell many legal and magical versions of my father's entry in case immigration authorities read my book and arrest and deport him again, and my mother too."[9]

Kingston's memorable portrait of such a traumatized Chinese immigrant is that of her dreamy middle-class aunt, Moon Orchid, who comes from Hong Kong to the U.S. in the 1970s looking to meet her by-now-diasporic family and connect with her doctor husband, who has illegally taken a second wife in Los Angeles and does not want her to interfere with his prosperous medical practice or new family. To quote *Woman Warrior*: "Brave Orchid [Maxine's quite worldly mother] looked at this delicate sister. She had long fingers and thin, soft hands. And she had a high-class city accent from living in Hong Kong. Not a trace of village accent remained; she had been away from the village [Sun Woi, Canton] for that long. Brave Orchid would not relent; her dainty sister would have to toughen up. 'Immigrants also work in the canneries, where it's so noisy it doesn't matter if they speak Chinese or what. The easiest way to find a job, though, is to work in Chinatown. You get twenty-five cents an hour and all your meals if you're working in a restaurant.' "[10] Moon Orchid cannot adjust and slowly goes crazy imagining that Mexicans, Filipinos, and Washington, D.C. "ghosts" were coming to take her family and turn them into ashes (156–60) —multicultural immigrants and white immigration officials merging into one paranoid vision of North America as a land of symbolic disintegration, harm, language loss, death. Crossing Asia-Pacific for Kingston's aunt had become a space of fractures, disjuncture, traumas, confusion, and disappointments— this is quite another vision of exchanging money and labor for the passport to the "Gold Mountain" the United States is supposed (by diasporic Chinese) to stand for.

What is this "Asia-Pacific" region anyway, who gets to define it, in what kind of language games, and towards what shared ends? In effect, I will be discussing and estranging (in various modes of discourse from literary figuration to journalistic and policy statement) what it now means *to regionalize a space:* that is to say, (a) to make it more porous to the cross-border flows of information, labor, finance, media images, and global commodities; (b) to shrink the distances of space, culture, and time; and (c) to cross and fuse the older national borders of the dirty, yet somehow vast and magical Pacific. To use Lawson Fusao Inada's title phrase, from his parodic mock-tourist poem "Shrinking the Pacific," what does it mean *to shrink the Pacific*—that is, to compress and fuse (displace, confuse, disorient) these various and diverse Asian/Pacific cultures and peoples into an imagined single or unified zone of "space-time compression"?[11]

Such questions of construction and purpose in Asia and the Pacific region have taken on greater and boom-and-doom urgency after the currency and "asset bubble" crisis of 1997 and 1998 that has now caused many U.S.-based economists and their journalist pundit allies to heap recriminations upon the so-called Asian way of capitalist expansion and, thus, to question the whole process of state-driven liberalization regimes which had seemingly failed to protect the region and its nation-state players (especially Indonesia, South Korea, and Thailand) from high volatility and the global dynamics of boom-and-bust investment.[12] Even advocates of transnationalization and the patchwork liberalized economies in the Asia-Pacific region have come to recognize "the perils of globalization for small open economies" in the wake of the Asian currency (called in the U.S. press, in a metaphor latent with yellow-perilous implications of inferiority, "the Asian flu") since the plundering and disorienting summer of 1997.[13] To be on the (uneven) road toward transnational globalization still remains a perilous task for the makers of materials, forms, and outlets affiliated to national culture. Whatever the perils of nationalism, racism, inequality, and protectionism, the goal of forging Asia-Pacific into a transnational region remains (in the words of New Zealand's Prime Minister Jenny Shipley to the Asia-Pacific Economic Cooperation meeting in 1999) one of "opening markets and keeping them open, as well as reducing barriers to trade and investment within and between our economies."[14]

To mean anything trenchant, these days, "Asia-Pacific" has to be situated and unpacked from within distinct cultural-political trajectories to disclose what this signifier stands for in its present ambivalent implications. Aiming to provide a U.S.-situated national and overtly politicized notion of "imagining" as an act of wary social fantasy, I want to play the more dominant APEC-like constructions of Asia-Pacific as region of imagined capitalist co-prosperity and market-driven bliss, as measured against the region as it is now being imagined in literary and cultural works by American, and Asian American, novelists (and, in other chapters, poets) that would challenge these neo-liberal formations and suggest a different cultural-political way of reading "Asia-Pacific" as space of identity construction. Doing cultural studies against the grain, as it were, *inside APEC.*

More specifically, I want to examine and provide a critical genealogy for the term "Asia-Pacific" as a cultural-ideological signifier, especially as this sign/banner has been constructed from within a distinct U.S. cultural trajectory, looking into its power-laden connotations as the U.S. Pacific goes on emerging from more overtly "orientalist" images of vast Asian markets and "yellow peril" threats, through the phobic sublimity of Melville's whale and Jack London's Social Darwinist slime; down into the neo-frontier of global cyberspace where a tousle-headed Seattle multi-billionaire, Bill Gates of Microsoft, would welcome the global village, with open smiles and innocent American arms, to what he rather naively enthuses is the system of "friction-free capitalism" (sic) taking place, these days, in what he calls (recalling the Gold Rush fury of mines and rails that built up California in 1849) "the Internet Goldrush."[15] As a point of contrast, I will later evoke the way that a lesser and ever-mobile regional power, Taiwan, is thickening this Asia-Pacific cultural-political imaginary into its own loaded signifier of promises, goals, and dreams inside the global/local city of Taipei where capitalism is not so unregulated and not by any means friction free.

The commonplace, taken-for-granted assumption of "region" implied by a signifying category like "Asia-Pacific," entails an act of social imagining that has had to be shaped into coherence and consensus, in ways that could call attention to the power politics of such unstable representations. To be sure, the everyday imagining of "Asia-Pacific" reeks of the contemporary (transnational / postcolonial) situation we are living through, here and there on the Pacific Rim and Basin so to speak, and can barely conceal the uncanny traumas and social contradictions that haunt its very formation. All but replacing warier Cold War visions of the "Pacific Rim" as the preferred global imaginary in the discourse of transnationalizing and de-nationalizing corporate Americans, that is to say, "Asia-Pacific" has become a discourse of liberal sublimation that has surfaced, in the late 1980s and throughout the 1990s, to trumpet neo-liberal market forces and regimes and thereby to forget Cold War traumas and to get beyond the stark geopolitics of imperialism and colonialism that had marked the region's long history.[16]

"Asia-Pacific" has already become a utopic discourse of the liberal market, an emerging signifier of transnational aspirations for some higher, supra-national unity in which global/local will meet in some kind of "win-win" situation and the opened market will absorb culture and politics into its borderless affirmative flow. Still, the postwar Asia-Pacific region is haunted by the "race hates" and "race wars" that deformed the prior vision of inter-Asia as a region of mutual co-prosperity and co-existence just half a century ago, and we need to guard against the emergence of "provocative racial and martial idioms" in a new, transnational key.[17] Northern and southern tensions, as well as lurking racialized binaries of residual orientalist frameworks, haunt the region and continue to return in uncanny ways on the U.S. home fronts.

As interlocked global players in the region, at least since the late 1970s if not throughout the Cold War era of East-West demonization and in relation to the Japanese entanglement in imperial expansion during the 1890s, the United States and Taiwan have been caught up in the (neo-liberal or "postnational") *Asia-Pacific restructuring game*. Still, who best shapes and defines this "Asia-Pacific" region these days, and toward what ends? What does this discursive fusion of region into a higher unity imply for the diverse cultures, spaces, and "identity politics" of this region? Does "Asia-Pacific" mean anything more than the utopic dream of a "free market"; that is, the post-Cold War trope of First World policy planners and market strategists, all doors flung open to the free flow of the commodity form? In short, can this signifier of "Asia-Pacific" be wrested away from the discourse of APEC (for more on this, see below) to serve other functions and to open different cultural and critical possibilities?

"Imagining Asia-Pacific" as Region

By "*imagining* Asia-Pacific" as region, I am working with a discourse of "imagining" that is not just another act of liberal consensus, cosmopolitan expression, or the shapely postcolonial construction of transnational "hybridity" discourse.[19] In the wake of anti-colonialist cultural critics of mongrel "contact zones" like Edward Said (*Orientalism; Culture and Imperialism*) or Mary Louise Pratt (*Imperial Eyes*) and creative cultural authors of "minority literature" inside English (like the above-mentioned Kingston and Kogawa; or the critically diasporic Japanese/Brazilian postmodern novelist, Karen Tei Yamashita; or the trans-Pacific revolutionary Korean/Pacific novelist from Hawai'i, Gary Pak), the verb "imagining" means articulating *a situated and contested social fantasy.* "Imagining Asia-Pacific" thus involves ongoing transformations in the language and space of identity by creating affiliated representations of power, location, and subject; in effect, expressing the will to achieve new suturings of (national) wholeness within "the ideological imaginary" of a given culture. In our era of transnational and postcolonial conjunction, that is, the very act of imagining (place, nation, region, globe) is constrained by discourse and contorted by geopolitical struggles for power, status, recognition, and control.[20] What cannot be imagined, as Wittgenstein once urged, cannot even be discussed, or in my terms, worried ("reimagined") into the language of political negotiation and affiliated spaces of social embodiment.

The "sublime object of ideology," as Slavoj Žižek formulates it (in theorizing from a Lacanian-Marxist perspective the imagining of "sublime objects of desire" as diverse as the *Titanic,* capital, the dead body of Stalin, and the Cold War psychodramas of Alfred Hitchcock), is haunted by *lack* and riddled with traumas of incompletion and pained social struggle, antagonisms of class, gender, and nation in the (all-too-"phallic") language of imagining: "Ideology is not a dreamlike illusion that we build to escape insupportable reality; in its basic dimension it is a [social] fantasy-construction which serves as a support for our 'reality' itself: an illusion which structures our effective, real social relations and thereby masks some insupportable, real, impossible kernel," as Žižek contends.[21] Imagining is an act of semi-joyous signifying that both props up ("structures") and distorts ("masks") the materials of social reality, and works (through the production of some symbolic "excess" to cover up the holes) to conceal and reveal (via sublimation, displacement, and other defenses) those social traumas and antagonisms haunting its very creation.[22] (Uneven and unjust, the memory of *immigration* and *war* is just such a traumatic Asian-Pacific "kernel" being worked through in Asian/American fiction as in other genres of cultural criticism.)[23]

When reading a nature poem by Wordsworth or a self-drenched essay by Emerson, we need not just admire the tropes but work to resist the layers of romanticism that would claim autonomy for the transcendental "identity" of the U.S. poet for whom, as Emerson puts it in "Self-Reliance," during the expansionist moment of Manifest Destiny on the continental frontier, "Vast spaces of nature, the Atlantic Ocean, the South Sea—long intervals of time, years, centuries—are of no account."[24] For a social-historical reading of such poetic "imagining" to take place, as Charles Bernstein has written in defense of more identity-blocking poetic languages like those of the Language poets, "absorption / of the poem's ideological imaginary must be / blocked."[25] That is, in confronting the U.S. poet's "artifice of absorption," the reader must *refuse* full absorption into the lyric trope: (here) the Emersonian language of sublime transcendence by means of which Atlantic and Pacific spaces and peoples are mastered into ciphers and history into a diary of national (and private) self-empowerment. Simply put, the trauma or "lack" that Emerson is facing is his own professional and class diminishment, as literary scholar and theological heir, in an era of annexation, frontier expansion, mass immigration, industrial take-off, slavery, and ongoing Indian removal—to mention just a few traumatic issues of his day. Emerson's poetics of the American sublime serve, in part, as his own majestic attempt to maintain illusions of self-mastery ("self-reliance") and democratic autonomy within this "joint-stock company" of a culture, staying at home and conquering his own Pacific as it were.[26]

We can recall here as well the way that the great novelist Herman Melville, following more skeptically down Emerson's Manifest Destiny expansionist path, turns the American Pacific whale named "Moby-Dick" into a creature not just of *economic* but of *symbolic* excess and, thus opening the Pacific for American commercial usage, shows the quasi-imperialist danger of such a symbolizing process in the nature-destroying language of Captain Ahab on the transnational whaling ship, the *Pequod*. Ahab's very ship is named to commemorate the destruction of the Pequot Indians in Connecticut in 1637, which later led to the wholesale destruction of native peoples. To suggest its imperial globality, interestingly enough as well, this doomed multicultural ship of American commerce named the *Pequod* is also transnationally masted with pine wood from "double-bolted" and "impenetrable" Japan, "cut somewhere on the coast of Japan, where her original ones were lost overboard in a gale."[27] A piece of Pacific timber from pre-Perry and Dutch-influenced Japan—that mysterious nation of typhoons, racial phobia, managed ports, and closed markets. As Melville puts it, via Ishmael erotically delighting in the opening of these same sleepy Asian-Pacific markets and "all the millions in China" (77) to American commerce from Nantucket to Formosa (448) and Japan, "Penetrating further and further into the heart of the Japanese [whale] cruising ground, the Pequod was all astir in the fishery" (463).

Feminized "oriental" markets, slavishly asleep in centuries of feudal tyranny, land-locked wealth, and modes of animistic pre-Enlightenment superstition ("long Chinese ages" of pre-democratic speechlessness [467]), must be liberated for purposes of global commerce and, to be sure, American expansion westward (across the vast Pacific, which Melville maps) to the mysterious Orient. At times in the text, Melville's pro-imperialist tone is ominous, foreboding in the past (and read into the present moment of APEC): "Let America add Mexico to Texas," he writes in chapter 14 praising the enterprising whalers of "Nantucket," "and pile Cuba upon Canada; let the English overswarm all India, and hang out their blazing banner from the sun; two thirds of the terraqueous globe are his. For the sea is his; he owns it, as Emperors own empires; other seaman having bought a right of way through it. . . . The Nantucker, he alone resides and riots on the sea; he alone, in Bible language, goes down to it in ships; to and fro ploughing it as his own special plantation" (77). Melville links and crosses the Pacific as an oceanic American plantation, and the whale ship as factory via an international division of labor in which "native American [meaning New Englander] liberally provides the brains, and the rest of the world as generously supplying the muscles" (127): such is Melville's ominous vision. Disavowing more Spanish or French forms of overt colonialism in the liberal-commercial takeover of the Pacific region, Americans supposedly always come to liberate the frontier and save the peoples from their own worst enemy, themselves.[28]

As such literary passages can remind us, representing Asia-Pacific as a region—not to mention the troubled crossing of the Atlantic Ocean into New World real estate or the "middle passage" into creolized creativity of the "Black Atlantic"—was never just an act of private freedom, but loaded with geopolitical overtones, subaltern trauma, and spooky nationalist fervor. For over four hundred years, the "Pacific" region has been a contested construct from various socio-historical angles, a site of trade, conversion, conquest, and an East-West and Center-Periphery struggle in which native peoples and sites have been rudely subordinated. As Richard Higgott has remarked, in a useful essay from 1995 in Australia (the early home of APEC) called "APEC—A Skeptical View,"

"Competing definitions [of "the Pacific" or, later, "Asia-Pacific"] are often inclusive or exclusive exercises in the politics of representation."[29] Whose "Asia-Pacific" is a question that always needs to be asked, as we enter the uncertain and uneven waters of the New Millennium.

"The sublime" remains an uncanny U.S. trope to represent *sublimated immensity*, not so much of the ocean as such but (in displaced form of desiring) for the transnational free-market: sublime immensity, as an image of national self-identity, has haunted American culture from the era of Manifest Destiny and the movement westward across continental vastness, via frontier settlement and Indian dispossession, towards the "illimitable" Asian markets of the Pacific Ocean. The ideology of this American sublime at once suggests some continental vastness of resources in the land and ocean, and a transcendental selfhood and imagined national community, that frees up longings for liberal infinitude and democratic possibilities of freedom but blocks closure and certitude with the trauma of some excess "savagery" that may be lurking at the borderlands or "frontier" and refusing easy representation. This conviction of the American sublime is what the mystical Emerson called, in his essay "The Over-Soul," and courted as ground of personal (and national) self-identification, "an immensity not possessed and that cannot be possessed."[30] The sublime is exactly that U.S. trope used to represent the post-colonial pursuit of global immensity and the vision of expanding markets that now haunts Asia-Pacific as a transnational frontier in which the local, paradoxically, is said to win a newfound share of hegemony, and the traumas of colonial occupation, regional fracturing, and world war will be washed away in the dirty, magical waters of the Pacific.[31]

Social Darwinism in the Asia-Pacific: From Sea-Wolf to Cyberspace

Caught up in the racialized politics of the "Yellow Peril" era of U.S. imperialism he helped to popularize and invent, Jack London portrayed the American outreach into the "illimitable Pacific" as space of vast natural resources, international geopolitics, and primordial struggle. The muckraking novelist staged a battle for commercial (and male-psychological) possession of this frontier-like space of the Pacific by means of a power-crazed crew of seal hunters in *The Sea-Wolf* (1904): "And north we traveled with it [the great seal herd]," London writes with macho savor for the hunt, "ravaging and destroying, flinging the naked carcasses to the shark and salting down the skins so that they might later adorn the fair shoulder of the women of the cities. It was wanton slaughter, and all for woman's sake. No man ate of the seal meat or the oil."[32] If the Pacific proved to be the origin and end of Jack London as representative U.S. novelist, as the suicidal contradictions and longings for capitalist egress of *Martin Eden* (1909) exposed, this ocean was the "frontier" staging ground for an imperial virility London advocated and embodied in strange, new ways as the "American Kipling" of his era.[33]

London's *The Sea-Wolf* is set in 1893 during the "Open Door" era of imperial annexation as the United States reached out "into the great and lonely Pacific expanse" (29) via an over-extended Monroe Doctrine into the peripheral spaces of Hawai'i, Cuba, and the Philippines. In this hyperbolic novel, a seal-hunting schooner named the *Ghost* is commanded from private yacht into commercial venture by a power-hungry force of imperial virility named Wolf Larsen. As his name suggests, "Wolf" is a domineering American who rules over lesser moral forces and compels submission of his motley English / Irish / Scandinavian / Pacific Islander crew of international outcasts hunting seal skins from San Francisco and the Farillon Islands to Japan. A literary intellectual named Humphrey Van Weyden is forced into service ("involuntary servitude to Wolf Larsen" [26]) as wage-beast laborer after being shipwrecked near the Golden Gate Bridge and bullied by Captain Larsen to undergo physical abuse and slap-punctuated lessons in Darwinian social survival until this scholar emerges into a macho Robinson Crusoe. Van Weyden's toughened ego becomes capable of founding and settling (colonizing in implicit battle with the Japanese in their part of the Pacific) his own island in the Pacific, as he defeats Wolf in the struggle for possession of woman (a shipwrecked poetess named Maud Brewster), ship, and deserted island ("Endeavor Island," an "undiscovered" seal rookery waiting to be colonized somewhere between Japan and "the bleak Bering Sea").

Troped into a "terrible sea" (224) of struggle, cruelty, and relentless "awfulness" (29), London's American Pacific is portrayed as a traumatic element of ooze and slime and cold indifference, threatening the ego with domination, abjection, and death like so many seals: "And I was alone, floating apparently in the midst of a gray primordial vastness" (7), Van Weyden screams out like a drowning woman, shipwrecked and unable to swim. The Pacific is the arena of "the sea-wolf," meaning not just Wolf Larsen but all forms of power seeking to dominate or be destroyed on ship, land, or sea.

As "industrial organization gave control" of capital over labor across the region (53), there is already in place a vast "division of labor" (2), London argues, between the strong and the weak, meaning those who can control force and plunder profits and those who submit to such energy and are humiliated, exploited, devalued by indifferent laws of supply and demand. In such battles, Emersonian self-reliance is counted as "a cipher in the arithmetic of commerce" (53), only later to be resurrected in the Defoe-like circumstances on Endeavor Island where the American strong self of Van Weyden can assert itself in an "unpeopled" wilderness of seals and ocean. The Pacific region is portrayed, from the perspective of this death-dealing schooner, as a space of seal hunting, murder, mutiny, and plundering, with market endeavors "ranging from opium smuggling into the States and arms smuggling into China to blackbirding and open piracy" (87). "Force, nothing but force obtained on this brute ship" of imperialism (38), Van Weyden realizes, as he is turned from a literary gentleman of idealist pretensions into his nickname of deformed matter, "Hump": "I was known by no other name, until the term became a part of my thought processes and I identified it with myself, thought of myself as Hump, as though Hump were I and always had been I" (32). The interpellation of the Pacific space into a symptom of Darwinist identity struggle is all but complete, as London himself came to be known by his predatory nickname, "Wolf."

Rewriting Melville's vision of the Asia-Pacific as space of transcendentalized commodities and romance quest, London enforces a more "brute materialist" vision of the Pacific region with metaphors of de-sublimated matter drawn from biology and zoology and applied to humanity, society, and the market. Thus, Wolf's vision of human "piggishness" and "the way of the wolf" is naturalized as a primordial struggle to survive via energy and will to domination over the maternal Thing itself: "This yeasty crawling and squirming which is called life" (67). "I believe that life is a mess," Wolf argues, and would prove it by becoming-animal like pig or wolf, or even more so, becoming-yeast: "It is like yeast, a ferment, a thing that moves and may move for a minute, an hour, a year, or a hundred years, but that in the end will cease to move. The big eat the little that they may continue to move, the strong eat the weak that they may obtain their strength. The lucky eat the most and move the longest, that is all" (42). Humphrey Van Weyden has become a battered Hump who realizes, fists and knife drawn: "I was becoming animallike myself, and I snarled in his face so terribly it frightened him back" (72). For London, writing from within the age of Yellow Peril and native overthrow, the Pacific is a region of deformity, brutality, disease, the national ego moving down on the evolutionary scale towards savagery, force, and virus: as the Cockney British cook, Tommy Mugridge puts it, "I near died of the scurvy and was rotten with it six months in Barbados. Smallpox in 'Onolulu, two broken legs in Shanghai, pneumonia in Unalaska, three busted ribs an' my insides all twisted in Frisco" (104). Torn between socialist compassion and Nietzschean power visions, the Pacific became the space of London's tensions: a "double Pacific," at once a space where white men regressed into savage beasts and where a paradise of instinct and primordial power could still be found.

In Alexander Besher's "novel of virtual reality" and cyberpunk business-as-usual set in transnational cyberspace called *RIM* (1994), the Social Darwinism of the transnational capitalist free market, with all its lurid games of macho competition and corporate killing, has gone inward: the Asia-Pacific now internalized into the space-time compression of cyberspace. The year is 2027, and Sartori Corporation (owner of a virtual reality entertainment empire based in a kind of virtual "Neo-Tokyo" inside Tokyo) is embroiled in cutthroat corporate warfare to preserve market share. The Asia-Pacific is the space of the Keiretsu wars, white-collar crime and Tibetan mystical quests for the digitalization of consciousness and the discovery of a "new Matrix" frontier being the order of the day. Frank Gobi is the American romance-quest hero (Besher's idealized self-image as "consulting futurist on Pacific Rim Affairs for Global Business Network" in Japan?) trying to save the Japanese corporations from destruction and "data muggings" and free cyberspace for open libidinal usage.[34] A professor moonlighting as cybernetic Bogart, Gobi teaches a course in "transcultural corporate anthropology and organizational shamanism" at UC Berkeley, now a Tokyo University extension, of course (15). He studies "the business culture that was emerging in the region" and has written an interactive textbook called "TransRim Customs 3.0."[35]

The scenery is of *RIM* is sheer phobic and techno-orientalist Pac Rim (and, elsewhere in cyberspace, Tokyo, and Berkeley, much quasi-orientalist sexuality with Japanese corporate princesses): "Rowdy groups of wealthy Greater Chinese businessmen milled about in front of glitzy Hong Kong-style hotels with atrium lobbies, preparing to head down to the Grant Avenue restaurants in New Chinatown" (65). Hong Kong to San Francisco, Los Angeles to Tokyo: the Pacific Rim has merged into one border-fusing culture of cybernetic capitalism. As he notes an array of "Rim carpetbaggers and keiretsu types," the scenery gets even more ominous, suggesting the reign of gangsterism and warfare in the region: "There were a couple of Greater China arms dealers, noticeable in their shark-skin suits of gray shantung silk. Flaunting jade rings the size of Kowloon and Seiko-Rolexes loaded with the latest Hsinchu Park circuitry on their pudgy wrists, the GCs looked more like rich uncles on holiday than they did merchants of death. . . . One of the North Koreans on board, a traveling salesman from Pyongyang, judging from his Kim Jong Il memorial bouffant hairdo—was already drunk and getting red in the face" (131–32). You get the picture: a kind of neo-orientalism directed against the Greater Chinese and Third World peoples of

Asia, while global Japanese and American corporate forces try to outwit each other to control Asia-Pacific cyberspace as a vast market of entertainment and profit.

In *RIM*, the Asia-Pacific geography has turned phobic and regressive: the U.S. and Japan align themselves for domination of the Internet frontier and exclude the "invisible empire" of the Overseas Chinese who practice clannish forms of gangsterism and subterranean capitalism as they belatedly seek to become, as one British journalist of social science puts it, "Lords of the Rim": "Thousands of middle-class Chinese immigrants have returned [from North America] to work in Asia this [back-and-forth the Pacific] way, earning them the sobriquet 'astronaut,' because they spend so much time in orbit. They have become Overseas Chinese in reverse—living overseas and sojourning in Greater China."[36] Indeed, these Overseas Chinese again threaten to become the master of Pacific waters and offshore moneys, that space of transnational flows where mobility is everything and secrecy has gone cybernetic, back-and-forth astronauts and opportunists of instability—"financial pointmen of the new age of borderless global capitalism," as Sterling Seagrave puts it with all the loathing (and resentful admiration) this biographer of the Song family (and KMT machinations) can muster.[37] The vast multitudes of Asia are coming again—this time not from Japan but from "Greater China"—they have mastered the latest capitalist technologies and speculative regimes of the West, and their powers to become "Lords of the Rim" are as inscrutable, occult, and sinister as ever.

APEC's Transnational Dream of "Asia-Pacific"

Mobilizing a range of ancient energies and new possibilities, "Asia-Pacific" is used in all kinds of ways as signifier: we speak of "Asia-Pacific cuisine"—it's a hit at gourmet restaurants like Roy's in Hawai'i Kai and Indigo in Honolulu, and on menus at the Lai Lai Sheraton in Taipei; and there are array of "Asia-Pacific" art magazines, architectural symposia, fashion and interior design spreads, and literary journals to be found from Tokyo and Hong Kong to Los Angeles using the cachet of this term. Cultural styles of "Asia" and "the Pacific" promise to fuse into some expressive hybrid synergy called "Asia-Pacific," and no harm will be done except to purists of cultural borders or canon-mongers, who refuse to dream fusion (and "shrink the Pacific") over the world's biggest ocean. More than just stylistic promise or commercial slogan, "Asia-Pacific" serves as a signifier to bespeak the push towards the creation of what is called "an open regionalism." This trope of *Asia evenly yoked to Pacific* is used to mobilize economies in the region, which, without such a signifier, does not yet exist in anything like a coherent framework; spaces and lives inside the creativity of the Pacific are being shaped, coded, and reorganized under this "Asia-Pacific" banner, and this demands critical interrogation.

Started up in 1989 during a ministerial meeting in Canberra, APEC serves as the most powerful shape this desire for regional coherence, shared direction, and unity as tied to a narrative of a co-prosperity sphere now takes in the Asia-Pacific of the 1990s. Fearing a round of conflict between the United States and Japan and discriminatory arrangements between Europe and North America, APEC came into a kind of slow, ad hoc existence into what one political economist calls a "capitalist archipelago."[39] Uneven and fluid at the core, this disjunctive signifier of "Asia" and the "Pacific" threaten to unhinge concentric "East-West" binary visions of superpower governance and Cold War teleology.[40] At the outset, the United States opposed APEC, but under Clinton it was a strong promoter of its expanding formation. One of the earliest visionaries of a new post-Cold War Pacific was Mikhail Gorbachev (at a speech in Vladivostok in 1986), but history turned otherwise and Russia has yet to be included in APEC although it has a long Pacific coast and a history of entanglement in the region.[41]

As the organizing frameworks for the current use of "Asia- Pacific," as this vision of region is circulated by the economies around the Pacific Rim, APEC refers to "Asia-Pacific Economic Cooperation." Linking North America and Mexico to the export-driven dragons of East Asia , Tokyo, and the Pacific ex-settler states of Australia and New Zealand, APEC was formed to ease trade barriers and to liberalize markets in the region in some kind of consensual, patchy, culture-conscious, quasi-systematic way. At this point, though the dollar, yen, and nuclear weapons refuse casual governance, APEC gathers eighteen "economies" for regional forums and policy prodding: Australia, Brunei, Canada, Chile, mainland China, Hong Kong, Indonesia, Japan, Malaysia, Mexico, New Zealand, Papua New Guinea, the Philippines, Singapore, South Korea, Taiwan, Thailand, and the United States.

If you wondered what "Asia Pacific" means and what ingredients are to be included, this is *one* way of defining the will to regional unity. The user-friendly identity term used to describe these diverse APEC players—as so many loose "economies" linked around and within the Pacific Ocean—suggests a de facto way of overriding problems and bypassing political tensions without resolving them in such a market-driven forum. Imagined into shape by some user-friendly trope of Pacific "community," APEC would fuse disparate units small and large, from city-states, superpowers, and Third World entities into a vision of coherence, teleological optimism, and regional "cooperation." This vision of "Asia-Pacific" is premised upon some commitment to the mandates of free-market capitalism and a vague sense of Asia-Pacific cultural heritage and allure of "Pacific Century" destiny.

Under the post-orientalist regionalism of "Asia-Pacific," the unresolved Chinese polities of Taiwan, Hong Kong, Singapore, and mainland China can talk. Big and small assume symbolic equivalence around the bargaining table, players smiling with President Clinton and President Ramos in Asian-Pacific shirts at the same photo sessions. *Pacific regionality* here suggests some post-political cultural bonding, or at least underlying geographical linkage, that can network across the polities of Asia-Pacific. As this trope of transnational community would have it, colonial history, world wars and Cold War trauma may be washed away in this Asia-Pacific. "Everything flows toward the Pacific, no time for anything to sink, all is swept along" is how Marguerite Duras uncannily describes this quality of Pacific waters to dissolve the traumatic past of colonial memory and to loosen capitalist class-suffering (in her case, growing up semi-poor and white in French colonial Indochina) into some perpetually flowing oceanic present where the spirit of optimism might be renewed and memories of war and poverty dissolved in these (seemingly) post-imperial waters.[42] Colonialism, imprisonment, and internment apparently can be erased in the magical waters of the Pacific Ocean.[43]

In the skeptical (if schizophrenic) words of Malaysian scholar-activist Chandra Muzzafar, which still resonate today for lesser powers (connected to ASEAN) in the region who fear U.S. encroachment on their common ("Asian") identity: "As a concept, 'Asia-Pacific' makes little sense. Unlike East Asia or South Asia or Southeast Asia, it has no shared history or common cultural traits. Asia-Pacific is not even an accepted geographical entity. The U.S. has vast economic ties with Europe but is not part of the European Community which jealously protects its historical, cultural and political identity. Similarly, Japan is deeply involved in the U.S. economy but it is not part of the North American Free Trade Agreement. It is only in the case of Asia, more specifically East Asia that there is a concerted attempt to suppress its common identity and thwart its legitimate quest for a common identity."[44]

On the other hand, we can invoke the postnational vision of Kenichi Ohmae, who relentlessly argues for an expansive "borderless" new regional order, where "nation-states are eroding as economic actors [and] region-states [like Taiwan, Guangdong, and Singapore] are taking shape," a new order that recognizes linkages with the global economy.[45] To survive, he says, these entities of borderless capitalism must "put global logic first" to interact locally and thrive globally: places of Asia-Pacific identity must retool their industry and reshape their conceptual and social geography to fit the contours of this transnational push. In

Ohmae's trilateral (Japan/United States/Europe) arrangement of the "borderless economy," to meet the mandates of globalized production it is no longer the nation-state but the "region-state" which becomes the agent of political-economic change.

In today's liberal-popular vision of the inter-Asia Pacific, APEC is the most broadly circulated framework for conceptualizing this restructuring move towards open borders, market-driven teleology, and social interlinkage.[46] Formed in the shadow of global capitalism, APEC's vision of the "Asia-Pacific" is, in truth, *culturally and politically naive,* ignoring, bypassing, or suppressing the cultural complexity, historical issues, and symbolic profusion of the region in order to form this regional identity. One Filipina scholar has described the "Pacific community" idea as "a baby whose putative parents are American and Japanese and whose midwife is Australian."[47] This kind of *regionalism* can be as dangerous as nationalist interpellation, even if taking place at a higher (and more sublimated) level in which the absent others against which APEC is forging its identity in relation (like the economies and cultures of Southeast Asia and the Pacific Islands) are silenced and bypassed. As Kuan-Hsing Chen has warned about this will to Asian-as-region (whether under a Japanese or Chinese banner), in a forum on "Multiculturalism and Multilingualism—Critical Limits of the Nation-State" held in Kyoto in July of 1996: "One has to be extremely careful with the celebrating side of regionalism; the imperialist 'Greater East Asia Co-Prosperity Sphere' project launched in the 1930's was able to operate precisely under the name of regionalism."[48] If in this era of global culture, as Milan Kundera put it, the European is "one who is nostalgic for Europe," the Asian as well may be one who is nostalgic for Asia as a civilizational and cultural unity.[49]

The assumption of some shared Asia-Pacific regional unity is, after all, the invention and construct of those globalizing powers (especially the United States and its military-industrial and tourist apparatus) who stand to benefit most by the borderless circulation of peoples, goods, and symbols within its framework.[50] As a multicultural fate in more localized senses, the "Asia-Pacific" imagined by authors as diverse as Melville and Epeli Hau'ofa, Maxine Hong Kingston and Patricia Grace, Haunani-Kay Trask and Li Ang, John Dominis Holt and Vilsoni Hereniko, Kenzaburo Oe and Lois-Ann Yamanaka remains a riddle and a maze, a rim and a charm, a struggle and a curse, both dream and slime, an ocean with ancient contents and cyborgian futures all cast into one strange regional poetic. It seems offensive to bring together so many cultural constructions under the same frame, "Asia-Pacific." For this *transnational* commitment of APEC's vision of "Asia-Pacific" unity reveals the future in which cultural and literary studies will take place in the Pacific. If disorganized by the flux, we must come to terms with this reconfigured situation in which nations and localities are coming unglued at local and global levels.[51] The one-way gaze and "the whole catalogue of colonial platitudes" that propped up and mapped the region (as did the British in "meretricious" Hong Kong) are no longer adequate to the scene.[52]

Perhaps post-communist Yugoslavia is a worst-case scenario for subnational fragmentation into ethnic heteroglossia and disidentification at this time.[53] And yet, in the Asian/Pacific Rim hub city of Los Angeles alone, L.A. city schools are already four-fifths non-white (Mexican, Korean, Vietnamese, Samoan, Chinese, El Salvadoran, Filipino, Iranian, and others) and must teach kids who speak something like 150 different native languages inside deteriorating conditions of economic polarization, lost promise, racial backlash, lean-and-mean budgeting in which more money is going to build state prisons than to universities, and conditions of postindustrial deskilling.[54] Perhaps this is *not* what APEC intends to mean by its trope of Asian-Pacific peoples "working together" inside some late-capitalist eternity of "Asia-Pacific Cooperation."

Isn't "the Asia-Pacific" emanating from the Pacific Rim tigers and Japan/ U.S. superpowers just a more loosely hegemonic vision of the region taking shape along the following lines: *too much Asian dynamism unevenly hyphened together with too little Pacific content to beat the world system?*

Moving from modes of literary imagining to journalistic and public policy modes of discourse, I bring up these *extra-literary* matters haunting APEC's "imagined community" because, if there is to be an Asia-Pacific signifier worthy of its peoples, symbolic heritages, and cultures, then one of the tasks for such a cultural poetics is to challenge and critique these liberal master formations of the Pacific region. Cultural criticism needs to locate such stories and mastertropes within history, pushing to unmask and expose the contradictions of such representations: "Asia-Pacific" as a unified, user-friendly, anti-socialist, and seamless region where the culture of global capitalism will come home to roost.[55] While contemporary cultural studies works to provide genealogies and critiques of dominant cultural forms and social frameworks of locality and national identity, propped up as they often are by literary canons and the spread of academic discourses like that of "postcoloniality," it can also study these competing traditions and put them in critical dialogue in the present rather than keeping them apart or confined to the past.

More affirmatively considered, the public invention of an "Asia-Pacific"– based poetics demands border crossing, conceptual outreach, nomadic linkages, and interdisciplinary originality; its birth at this moment is mired in cultural politics and the global political economy. Much needs to be done to intervene as well in contexts and genres that dominate the airwaves with APEC-like stories and Pacific Rising images: media events, international forums, daily journalism and so on, nurturing alternative spheres and counter-narratives inside public culture. We can begin articulating a "critical regionalism" in the Asia-Pacific region, respectful of Asian and Pacific heritages, diasporas, and communities but wary of hegemonic designs upon these diverse localities and groupings, as well as to begin interlinking globally these local struggles.[56]

The meaning of "Asia-Pacific" has to be struggled for in specific cultural locations and institutional settings. For definitions of the "Asia-Pacific" will mean different things to rival nations, racial and gender groupings, and hegemonic class agents. Global dreams of the Pacific region must be situated to bring out their contradictory social meaning, bringing them down to earth and cultural politics, placing master narratives of the local and small in their social communities, nearer to what Maxine Hong Kingston once called "those little stories of Chinese culture you learn from your mother."

On his way from Washington to the APEC meeting in Manila in 1996, where he would be greeted with "APEC Go Home" and "Say No to APEC" protest signs, President Bill Clinton stopped in Hawai'i to play some golf, rest, and prepare for the trip through what his policy planners now call "Asia-Pacific." Why stop in multicultural Hawai'i? "Because he wanted to see what APEC people look like!" or at least that is what Dr. Seiji Naiya told listeners of ICRT (International Radio of Taipei) on May 28, 1997, as he accompanied Governor Cayetano on his passports-for-dollars mission to Taiwan. "Hawai'i is a real Asia-Pacific state," an important "linking place between North American markets and the large Asian-Pacific markets," Dr. Naiya added, with all the wonder and missionary zeal of a Columbus or Balboa in the New World Pacific. Yes, come all ye transnational citizens to the magical new waters of Asia-Pacific! You'll like it there; in fact, you are already there working the territory inside the heart of Asia-Pacific, so let us now begin to describe, critique, and analyze what it is as "region" or (better yet) imagine what it could be as a different, non-imperialist future.[57]

Taiwan's Asian-Pacific Imaginary

Underspecified and full of utopic longing for regional power, "Asia-Pacific" has become a code term for internationalization in the transnational era. Used with a mobile liquidity that befits its oceanic origins, "Asia-Pacific" serves as an organizing frame to marshal the global dreams and local tensions of regional centers like Taiwan into a dynamic trope refiguring the political economy in inventive ways.

The complex "Asia-Pacific" locality of Taiwan looks at once forward to the high-tech and culturally commodified market of Japan and backward to its own primordial Pacific inhabitants whose languages and tribal visions make new claims upon the Han-based nation which emerged in differential defiance. In this sense it is truly "Asia-Pacific" in its tension and ties to Asia and the Pacific: torn between Hong Kong and Tokyo and Beijing and Washington, as well as called back by the conjuring of primordial memories older than the urban mode and the nation-state the KMT represented as collective common sense to its tribal inhabitants from mountain and sea.

From my own informal survey of the *China Post* and *China News* in the spring of 1995 and 1997, it is clear that "Asia-Pacific" is a frequently used signifier to express Taiwan's regional insertion in a furiously globalizing economy, although what it means seems, to my Americanized ears, *peculiar:* "Asia-Pacific" means the transnational capitalist culture of Asia for the most part, and dominantly Hong Kong and Southern China, perhaps Japan; but there is no mention of any internal or island Pacific country or location, and the United States seems to figure in only as one huge export zone.[58] "Asia-Pacific" is a much-used term in Taiwan and serves as a key organizing signifier for this borderless regionality, evoking the Pacific Rim location of Taiwan as some kind of "hub" or "center" of fluid spatiality, a region open to transnational flux and to local linkages. Exemplary of the Asia-Pacific dynamics constructing and reforming the Pacific Rim, Taiwan is envisioned (by political policy and in its own English press) as a regional "hub" of Asia-Pacific transport, business, media, and exchange. Liberalization and increased deregulation in the 1990s have led to a freer flow of goods and people into and out of the island, which competes with more-established business hubs like Hong Kong and Singapore for regional primacy as "Asia-Pacific center" of exchange.[59]

Island of complicated locality, caught between discourses of the fake and the essential, Taiwan remains an Asian-Pacific space of unresolved ambiguities, part nation, part "Asia-Pacific" region of transnationalization, part Chinese province; some have even called it the 51st U.S. state. The complicated "name game" of fixing/slashing together identity—is it independent and sovereign Taiwan, "the Republic of China in Taiwan," Formosa, or some other new compound signifier?—has crucial consequences for international, national, and local domains and for how the "Asia-Pacific" region will be imagined and installed at the everyday level. This "Taiwan" of Asian-Pacific longings remains an *un-*

stable entity situated flexibly ("ambivalently" as they say) between region, nation, locality, and what the mainland Chinese regard rather ominously as "renegade province" of the Rim. The undefinedness, fluidity, and multiplicity may be, at this point in the unstable global economy, an advantage.

Shrinking the Pacific in Taipei: Unlovable, Chinese-Monumental, Multi-lingual, Global/Local Taipei

"The brief period of Taipei's existence [moving 'from colonial backwater to world city'] has created a remarkably rich diversity of architectural styles and features. . . . The architectural mix of Taipei has been subject to frequent derision. For example, [Michael] Herr ['Taipei: Wicked Cities of the World,' *Holiday* 43, 1968] has opined that 'no matter how you come to love Taipei, you will never think of it as beautiful.' W. Glenn ["Growing like Topsy," *Far Eastern Economic Review* 61, 1968] has disdainfully referred to the built landscape as a 'mongrelizing.' He cites the negative aspects of Taipei's environment: its hills are too far off, it has no port, no spacious parks, and few imposing buildings."[60]

"Many accounts of the city point out that Hong Kong does not look very different from other Asian cities with its indiscriminate mix of drab and grandiose buildings. However, all we have to do is compare Hong Kong with a city like Taipei, which is quite as affluent, to see the difference. Taipei also displays a mixture of architectural styles, but the overall feeling is not quite the same. One of Taiwan's strongest claims to political legitimacy has always been to present itself as the true custodian of 'Chinese culture.' As a result, there is a kind of hesitancy in its employment of contemporary architecture forms, which stems from the implicit ideological interference of its image of Chinese identity. Hong Kong has neither a fixed identity nor the inhibitions that come from it. . . . The Chiang-Kai-shek cultural complex is a pastiche of Chinese architectural styles, while the Hong Kong cultural center is committed to contemporaneity."[61]

Taipei, the magic postnational center where all roads lead and crisscross: a maze of unlicensed buildings, unregulated traffic, hazardous sidewalks, unsightly this and unruly that, but alive with the energies of construction and labor, impure mixtures of languages, speeds, messages. Beyond zoning, beyond rules, postmodern if not postcolonial Taipei swarms and creeps, amalgamates, grungy and grimy and full of signs and textures, mixes business and pleasure, life and cash:

this neo-sublime of mixed commercial-residential uses, makes Tokyo and Seoul seem tame like Hilo. There's that ICRT radio ad for Pacific Rim survival (partly in English and Mandarin) when it's summer in the city: *"It's gridlock in Taipei. Oh no, I have another headache. Take Bufferin!"*

As a space of flows and textures perpetually under construction, and increasingly open to the creative forces of democratization in fluid new ways, Taipei, to zoom in on this urban maze of off-the-shelf vitality, barrages the senses of the visitor as an impure, dynamic, and unevenly interwoven mixture of the traditional and modern, postmodern and primitive, high-tech and agrarian residual.[62] As a fate of transnational and local intermixture, Taipei incarnates all the expressive synergy of the global meeting the local, meaning the unstable global/local dialectic. Thus, there is cultural substance to the claim of an English-speaking FM station in Taipei, "Here's your chance to think globally, while you tune in locally to ICRT, and find out what's really hot on a global scale!"

Pacific Rim hub of globalized/localized contact and mishmash fertility, the "global city" that is Taipei confronts the contemporary as a space of uneven modernity, uneven sidewalks of odd materials, overloaded textures of ceramic and textuality, where well-gentrified streets collide into Third World hovels, the clash of cultural capital and sheer trash and industrial grunge, "pigsty" to some Germans—modernity, premodernity, postmodernity all at once in some collage not clearly accountable to the colonial-to-transnational "global city" paradigm set up (on the London / New Delhi axis of European core / Asian periphery) by Anthony King, though the Japanese colonial legacy of built-forms, bureaucratic infrastructure, and class-divided spaces is there as spatial palimpsest.[63]

Consider this global/local item in all its splendid mixture as a geopolitical strategy of adaptation to local and transnational flows into the "global city" of capitalist culture: "The Taipei City Government is considering adopting English as a third 'common language' alongside Mandarin and Hokkien (Taiwanese) as part of efforts to become a world-class metropolis and a major business hub in the Asia-Pacific region. . . . [The goal is] to expand the use of English into all levels of society to come in line with the city's development into a more international city" (*The China Post*, April 5, 1995). Thus, in one move, the triple pulls of the *local* (Taiwanese) and the *transnational* (World English) upon the *national* (Mandarin) would be pragmatically legitimated and brought by the city government into heteroglossic circulation and public ratification, as they already are to some degree in the Pacific Rim city of flows and abodes that is Taipei.

Taipei floats along the Pacific Rim as a place of work, under construction, embodying a fetching swarm and maze of interconnected neighborhoods and

Chinatowns not just made for sightseeing. The motorbikes, stopping, starting, swerving, nearly colliding, accelerating at their own interactive unregulated rhythm track the nerves of this Pacific Rim city. As mentioned, from certain European angles of urban vision, Taipei has been described as "the pigsty" of East Asia, scorned and derided despite its buildings of mainland-like imperial grandeur, its sweepingly situated grand memorials and vista-strong hotels (the Grand Hotel still has the best urban feng shui, overlooking the urban landscape of Taipei as it spreads outward, with cloudy rivers in front and green mountains in back) all somehow invoking the physical monumentality of the mainland and its courtly sublime. You may get disoriented in Taiwan, but when you do you will know you are lost and turned around in an ever-porous region of "Asia-Pacific," where space is shrunken and the diverse cultures collide, as borders are flung open to the future of creativity and risk.[64]

Notes

1   Defending the utopian function of wish and dream as projections of the narrative imagination worth preserving, even within the bleak dialectics of late capitalism, Ernst Bloch saw the "oriental" South Seas, from the medieval carnivals to the imperial fantasies of Rudyard Kipling in India, to be a key site of Western dream-projection and social wish: see "Better Castles in the Sky at the Country Fair and Circus, in Fairy Tales and Colportage," in *The Utopian Function of Art and Literature: Selected Essays*, trans. Jack Zipes and Frank Mecklenberg (Cambridge: MIT Press, 1988), pp. 176–79, p. 158.

2   As substantiated below, "region" in my usage means less a self-evident unit of geography or civilizational culture than some kind of (imagined) mutual co-prosperity zone of our U.S. transnational moment. An historically informed approach that makes for critical wariness about the way the world has been divided into "metageographical" constructs drenched in power and ideology—like "East" and "West," Europe and the Orient, "North" and "South," First/Second and Third World and so on down to this quasi-deconstructive era of "civilizational" thinking—is offered in Martin Lewis and Karen E. Wigen, *The Myth of Continents: A Critique of Metageography* (Berkeley: University of California Press, 1997), esp. chapters 2 and 3. ASEAN, for example, is seen to construct Southeast Asia into a "residual and artificial category" that will give the regional players a better sense of "coherence" more than it ever had in the past, and thus a better grip on the future direction of the region as such (176); APEC, a larger-scale area projection of cultural and economic "coherence," is not dealt with in this important study.

3   I speak here of the "informational" or "global city" of transnational capitalism in which money, information, transportation, media images, and commodities can flow with maximum speed in a site of space-time compression: on Hong Kong's materialization of this fate in the 1980s and its threat of "disappearance" under Chinese rule

in 1997, see Ackbar Abbas, *Hong Kong: Culture and the Politics of Disappearance* (Minneapolis: University of Minnesota Press, 1997), pp. 2–25.

4   "Hawai'i Seeking Investors," *China Post*, May 23, 1997, p. 5.

5   After years of stressing how its future was linked to the growth of Asia Pacific as a capitalist region, Australia is reversing the geopolitics of Labor Prime Minister Paul Keating and beating a hasty retreat from the crisis of Asia: "Australia is geographically part of the Asia-Pacific region, no doubt about that," Treasurer Peter Costello recently said in New York, "but that doesn't mean our economy follows the paths of East Asian economies" ("Australia Distancing Itself from Asia Woes," *Honolulu Advertiser*, May 26, 1998, B6).

6   On the Canadian version of this ambivalent call to Hong Kong—"we want your money, but we may not want you"—see Katharyne Mitchell, "The Hong Kong Immigrant and the Urban Landscape: Shaping the Transnational Cosmopolitan in the Era of Pacific Rim Capital," *Asia/Pacific as Space of Cultural Production*, ed. Rob Wilson and Arif Dirlik (Durham, N.C.: Duke University Press, 1995), pp. 284–310. On Koreans as insiders and outsiders to the "American Dream" of social mobility and capitalist trajectory across the transnationalized Pacific Rim in Los Angeles, see Nancy Abelman and John Lie, *Blue Dreams: Korean Americans and the Los Angeles Riots* (Cambridge: Harvard University Press, 1995).

7   "U.S. Sees Critical Role for APEC in Post-Crisis Asia," *Korea Herald*, August 5, 1999, p. 1.

8   Joy Kogawa, *Obasan* (Boston: David Godine, 1982).

9   "An Interview with Maxine Hong Kingston," by Shan Te-Hsing, *Tamkang Review* 25 (1995), pp.6, 9.

10 (New York: Vintage International, 1989), p. 127

11 See Lawson Fusao Inada, "Shrinking the Pacific," in *Asia/Pacific as Space of Cultural Production*, pp. 80–81, on the huge problems of displacement that result as Japan flows back into Oregon; the Pacific Northwest region (as in British Columbia) is where the Japanese citizens were racially marked as outsiders during the relocation and internment traumas of World War II. (Inada's own poetry continues to come to terms with this via narrating his own family's experience of internment and relocation, his own traumatic and re-symbolized version of Pacific Rim "regional" culture.)

12 For a reading of this "Asian crisis" as global in its characteristics and interlinked solutions, see Manuel F. Montes, "Global Lessons of the Economic Crisis in Asia," *Asia Pacific Issues*, No. 35, March 1998, East-West Center, Honolulu; and, more specifically, Richard W. Baker, "Indonesia In Crisis," *Asia Pacific Issues*, No. 36, May 1998, East-West Center, Honolulu.

13 Lee Kuan Yew, "Fix the Global Financial System," *Time*, Asia edition, Feb. 1, 1999.

14 Shipley is quoted in "U.S. Sees Critical Role for APEC in Post-Crisis Asia," *Korea Herald*, August 5, 1999, p. 1.

15 See Bill Gates, *The Road Ahead* (New York: Penguin, 1996), chapter 8, "Friction-Free Capitalism." To quote from David S. Bennahaum, who sees a new East/West division arising along English/Cyrillic alphabet lines erupting cyberspace markets: "Cyberspace is the ultimate distillation of what the Information Age is meant to be

—a home for 'friction-free capitalism,' the end of nation-states, and a state of being where matter is 'demassified' into bits and electrons, which form the bricks and mortar of a new world" [of transparent free-market exchange]. In "Freedom's Just Another Name for WYSIWYG" (MEME 3.03, a journal on the Internet, June 1997), section 5, "The WYSIWYG Society."

16   On U.S. discursive framing of the region circa 1970–1990, see Christopher L. Connery, "Pacific Rim Discourse: The U.S. Global Imaginary in the Late Cold War Years," *Asia/Pacific as Space of Cultural Production*, pp. 30–56. On the mythic poetics of U.S. geopolitical imagining in the post-Cold War framework, also see Christopher L. Connery, "The Oceanic Feeling and the Regional Imaginary," in *Global/Local: Cultural Production and the Transnational Imaginary*, ed. Rob Wilson and Wimal Dissanayake (Durham, N.C.: Duke University Press, 1996), pp. 284–311. Also see John Eperjesi's probing study of Asia and Oceania's formation into a region of policy concern by the American Asiatic Society in 1898, in the context of U.S. imperial entanglements with Japan and China, in "Imaginary Circulation: The American Asiatic Association and the Creation of an American Pacific," which forms part of his doctoral dissertation being written in the English Department at Carnegie-Mellon University. On the rival imperialisms and economic expansionist visions that generated Japanese and U.S. outreach into the Pacific region in the late nineteenth and early twentieth centuries, as well as counter-traditions of anti-imperial nationhood that such social Darwinian visions evoked, see the powerful diplomatic histories of Akira Iriye, *Pacific Estrangement: Japanese and American Expansion, 1897–1911* (Cambridge: Harvard University Press, 1972); and *Across the Pacific: An Inner History of American–East Asian Relations* (Chicago: Imprint Publications, 1997); as well as his edited collection on phobic and enchanted images, policies, and discourses, *Mutual Images: Essays in American-Japanese Relations* (Cambridge: Harvard University Press, 1975)

17   See John W. Dower, *War without Mercy: Race & Power in the Pacific War* (New York: Pantheon Books, 1986), p. 314. As Andrew Mack and John Ravenhill remind us, in a collection they have co-edited called (against evidence supporting the instability of any long-term "hegemony" in the Pacific region) *Pacific Cooperation: Building Economic and Security Regimes in the Asia-Pacific Region* (Boulder: Westview, 1995) "For four decades following the end of World War II, the politically divided Asia-Pacific was the principal battleground on which global Cold War rivalries were fought. Wars first in China, then Korea, Vietnam, and Cambodia pitted the United States and its allies against nationalist movements that, assisted by the two great communist powers, fought under the banner of revolutionary socialism" ("Economic and Security Regimes in the Asia-Pacific Region," p. 22).

18   My own reading of Asia/Pacific will here be doubled, situated yet ambivalent, skeptical and utopic by turns, miming the language of imperial expansion and the capitalist-state but turned back upon itself. For, as I now see it, "Asia/Pacific" it is not *just* an ideologically recuperated term, but represents those situated aspirations and shared promises of mixture and contradiction worth exploring and as these go on clamoring into (uneven) existence.

19   On the dialectics of imagining a new cultural geopolitics beyond national or inter-ethnic frames, see the probing collection of Pheng Cheah and Bruce Robbins, eds.,

Cosmopolitics: Thinking and Feeling beyond the Nation (Minneapolis: University of Minnesota Press, 1998).

20 *The Woman Warrior* is such a contested and politicized imagining: the despised Chinese daughter becoming "woman warrior" and "American-feminine" to free herself from stereotypes and her family from social disintegration.

21 Slavoj Žižek, *The Sublime Object of Ideology* (London and New York: Verso, 1989), p. 45.

22 Strong claims to aesthetic autonomy (as in the "pure poetry" of Poe or Mallarme) reflect a willed version of social abnegation and the all-too-romantic delusion by the lyric artist (which bourgeois society desperately needs) of "having escaped from the weight of material existence" and having achieved freedom from reigning practices of utility and commodity exchange. See Theodor W. Adorno, "On Lyric Poetry and Society," *Notes to Literature*, vol. 1 (New York: Columbia University Press, 1991), p. 39.

23 In Kingston's narrative, "talking story" is a way for the immigrant to master social reality in "the terrible ghost country of America" (99) via a skillful mixture of revealing and concealing, infusing history with myth, speech with "unspeakable" silence: "There were secrets never to be said in front of the ghosts, immigration secrets whose telling could get us sent back to China" (*Woman Warrior*, p. 183). On "exclusion acts" directed against Asian immigrants baring them from U.S. citizenship and assimilation, see Lisa Lowe, *Immigrant Acts: On Asian American Cultural Politics* (Durham, N.C.: Duke University Press, 1996); David Palumbo-Liu, "The *Bitter Tea* of Frank Capra," *positions: East Asia Cultures Critique* 3 (1995): 759–89; and David Palumbo-Liu, ed., *The Ethnic Canon: Histories, Institutions, and Interventions* (Minneapolis: University of Minnesota Press, 1995).

24 Ralph Waldo Emerson, *Self-Reliance and Other Essays* (New York: Dover, 1993), p. 29.

25 Charles Bernstein, "Artifice of Absorption," *A Poetics* (Cambridge: Harvard University Press, 1992), p. 21.

26 "Performing the immigrant" (immigrant acts of heterotopia or ethnographic self-fashioning, for example) also raises the tricky "postcolonial" ruses for Asian American immigrants of what Kuan-Hsing Chen (see below) has called "diasporic opportunism" as the threat of U.S. professional/class positioning of an elite self as a perpetual "subaltern" of racial exclusion yet class superiority. On Emerson's troubled relation to the expanding U.S. market and its annexationist policies in Texas and Mexico, see Rob Wilson, "Literary Vocation as Occupational Idealism: The Example of Emerson's 'American Scholar,'" *Cultural Critique* 15 (1990): 83–114.

27 Herman Melville, *Moby-Dick* (New York: Signet, 1980), p.82. Further references will occur parenthetically. In the Persian Gulf War, the Patriot missile was constructed in the media and by President George Bush as an icon of national might, but upon closer examination it can be seen (like the *Pequod*) as a transnationally constructed and globally manned object. These same Patriot missiles now watch over the peace and security of the Asia-Pacific region, especially in troubled sites like South Korea and Taiwan with their unresolved Cold War tensions towards the north.

28 As Richard Drinnon summarized the wisdom of Melville to his own generation of empire-building Americans crossing the continent to confront, via Manifest Destiny,

the natives of Asia and the Pacific with latter-day Puritanical visions of higher possession, "As the author of *Moby Dick* well knew, such [frontier writers and explorers] as
James Kirke Paulding and Charles Wilkes already had come to regard the Western Sea
[the Pacific] as an extension of the American West. Melville had the unsettling gift of
seeing that when the metaphysics of Indian-hating hit salt water it more clearly became the metaphysics of empire-building, with the woodsman-become-mariner out
there on the farthest wave, in Melville's words, riding 'upon the advance as the Polynesian upon the comb of the surf'" (*Facing West: The Metaphysics of Indian-Hating
and Empire Building* [New York: New American Library, 1980], p. 215).

29 In *Pacific Cooperation*, p. 68. For the foundational contradiction between Euro-
American cognitive and commercial mappings of the Pacific region, and internal
Asian and Pacific forces of settlement and diaspora, see Arif Dirlik, "The Asia-Pacific
Idea: Reality and Representation in the Invention of a Regional Structure," *Journal of
World History* 3 (1992): 55–79.

30 *Self-Reliance and Other Essays*, p. 53.

31 See Rob Wilson, *American Sublime: The Genealogy of a Poetic Genre* (Madison: Uni-
versity of Wisconsin Press, 1991) for my semi-affirmative critique of this national ide-
ology as it worked itself out in a romanticized cultural form of continental possession.
On the "colonialism" of our transnational (and supposedly "postcolonial") era, see
Masao Miyoshi, "A Borderless World? From Colonialism to Transnationalism and the
Decline of the Nation-State," *Critical Inquiry* 19 (1993): 726–51.

32 Jack London, *The Sea-Wolf* (New York: Tor, 1993), p. 128. Further references to this
novel will occur parenthetically. On the 1941 "classic" Pacific wartime movie of
crazed males, *The Sea Wolf*, directed by Michael Curtiz and starring Edward G. Robinson as Wolf Larsen, see *Jack London's* The Sea Wolf: *A Screenplay by Robert Rossen*,
ed. Rocco Fumento and Tony Williams (Carbondale: Southern Illinois University
Press, 1998).

33 See Colleen Lye's superb study of London and related figures in her 1998 Columbia
University dissertation, "Model Modernity: Representing the Far East"; and Donald
E. Pease, "*Martin Eden* and the Limits of the Aesthetic Experience," *boundary 2* 25
(1998): 139–160. On London's self-fashioning as act of market expansion and form of
masculine self-empowerment caught up in U.S. frontier expansions into the Pacific
Northwest and Asian markets, see Jonathan Auerbach's (overprivatized) study, *Male
Call: Becoming Jack London* (Durham, N.C.: Duke University Press, 1996), esp. chapter 2, "Between Men of Letters: Homoerotic Agents in *The Sea-Wolf*."

34 *RIM: A Novel of Virtual Reality* (London: Orbit, 1994), p. 57. Further references to
this novel will occur parenthetically. On the devious workings of transnational culture and "cultural capital" flowing back and across the cybernetic Pacific from Asia to
the U.S., see David Palumbo-Liu and Hans Ulrich Gumbrecht, eds., *Streams of Cultural Capital: Transnational Cultural Studies* (Stanford: Stanford University Press,
1997).

35 Besher himself is the author of such a business guidebook called *The Pacific Rim Al-
manac* (New York: Harper Perennial, 1991). On such "Rim speak" works of corporate
business culture, see the cautionary and rich analysis by Christopher Connery (see
note 12 above).

36 See Sterling Seagrave, *Lords of the Rim* (London: Corgi Books, 1996), p. 321, who offers

a phobic-sublime image of the Overseas Chinese as an "invisible empire" in Asia-Pacific, a globalized community of up to fifty-five million expatriates with two trillion dollars in assets and a vast network of influence, favor, and crime.

37 Ibid., p. 272. On Taiwan as a postwar economy compounded of dynastic intrigue and strategic measures of U.S. anticommunist support, via global media like *Time Magazine*, see *Lords of the Rim*, chapter 17, "The Fall of the House of Chiang."

38 These are the orientalist aspects of the "Yellow Peril" syndrome which John Dower traces back through pre-war American journalism, popular culture, and mass media forms in *War without Mercy*, pp. 162–63.

39 Bruce Cumings, "Rimspeak; or, The Discourse of the 'Pacific Rim,'" in Arif Dirlik, ed., *What Is in a Rim? Critical Perspectives on the Pacific Region Idea* (Boulder: Westview, 1993), p. 25. Japanese economists, speaking in international forums at the East-West Center in Hawai'i and other such sites in Australia in the Cold War era, had formulated such visions of "economic and cultural cooperation" as early as the 1960s, and Australian and American policy planners in the region long cultivated these broad links to Asia and what came to be called the Pacific Rim.

40 Even as U.S. policies are being disoriented in the region and the East-West Center of knowledge/power is threatened with extinction, to give one example of institutional and conceptual *instability* in the region, an "Asia-Pacific Center for Security Studies" has opened in 1995 in Honolulu, with substantial federal funding. To articulate a post-Cold War rationale for the East-West Center in order to defend it from lean-and-mean Republican budget cuts, Hawai'i's Senator Daniel Akaka declared that this postwar center of cross-cultural knowledge production was "one of the most respected and authoritative institutions dedicated to promoting international cooperation throughout Asia and the Pacific."

41 See text of speech by Gorbachev in Vladivostok, July 28, 1986, reprinted in *The Soviet Union as an Asian Pacific Power*, ed. Ramesh Thakar and Carlyle Thayer (Boulder: Westview, 1987), p. 223.

42 Marguerite Duras, *The Lover*, trans. Barbara Bray (New York: Harper, 1992), p. 22. The globally successful novel/movie by Duras, *Hiroshima Mon Amour*, tries to figure this new post-Hiroshima utopia in the troubled love match of the Japanese journalist and the French nurse who cannot forget the traumas of world war and the Cold War legacies of military and nuclear terror.

43 Another such romantic dreamer of this post-traumatic Pacific is the American banker wrongly accused of murder in the Stephen King-based movie, S*hawshank Redemption* (1994), played by Tim Robbins. He longs to escape the Maine prison where he has been placed for a life sentence and get down to a little blue hotel by the Pacific where he can finally forget the brutal humiliations, capitalist crimes, and hellish degradation he has been through in prison: "*This ocean*, as the Mexicans say, *it has no memory.*"

44 "APEC serves interests of U.S. more than others," *New Strait Times*, July 29, 1993, p. 13. Quoted in Richard Higgott, "APEC—A Skeptical View," p. 91.

45 Kenichi Ohmae, "Putting Global Logic First," *Harvard Business Review* 73(1) (1995): p. 125.

46 In "Regionalism and Nationalism," portraying various versions of local and global regionality in the Pacific, Richard A. Herr notes the shift from decolonizing visions of

Pacific Islands regionalism to those today which are more transnationally driven: "The emerging international order is likely to propel the islands towards further engagement with the rest of the world, particularly the countries of the Pacific rim" (298), in *Tides of History: The Pacific Islands in the Twentieth Century*, ed. K. R. Howe, Robert C. Kiste, and Brij V. Lal (Honolulu: University of Hawai'i Press, 1994), pp. 283–99.

47 Valera Quisumbing, in Jose P. Leviste Jr., ed., *The Pacific Lake: Philippine Perspectives on a Pacific Community* (Manila: Philippine Council for Foreign Relations, 1986), p. 81.

48 "Multiculturalism or Neo-Colonial Racism?," *Ritsumeikan Linguistics and Cultural Research Journal* (spring, 1997): 373. In this respect, see John Dower's exemplary discussion of racial and economic exploitation of Asia by Japan, in "Global Policy with the Yamato Race as Nucleus," *War without Mercy*, pp. 262–290. In "yellow peril" discourse propagated by Jack London et al., "Orientals" are feared for their military-industrial potential challenging the West (Japan), their inscrutable antidiscursive mystique and kung fu ways (China), as well as vast laboring hordes threatening white labor and national purity (India, China, Korea).

49 Milan Kundera, *The Art of the Novel* (New York: Harper & Row, 1988), p. 128.

50 *Globalization* of the local into some higher-level regional configuration has become the mandate of the transnational cultural critic/class tracking the transcultural cash in supple ways, as the news reeks of identity politics, racial violence, ethnic strife, religious antagonism, and gender suppression, not to mention structural imbalances of labor and profit all along the "global assembly line" from New Jersey to Manila.

51 For a related discussion of what "cultural studies" might begin to look like "inside APEC" in places like Hawai'i, Hong Kong, and Taiwan, see Rob Wilson, "Towards an 'Asia/Pacific Cultural Studies': Literature, Cultural Identity, and Struggle in the American Pacific," *Studies in Language and Literature* 7 (August 1996): 1–18, a journal of National Taiwan University. On a localist/nationalist note, also see Ross Gibson, *South of the West: Postcolonialism and the Narrative Construction of Australia* (Bloomington: Indiana University Press, 1992).

52 See Richard Mason, *The World of Suzie Wong* (Hong Kong: Pegasus Books, 1994 [1957]), pp. 188–89, who was at least able to risk miscegenation and an affirmative portrait of Eurasian offspring, despite his overall allegorizing of Hong Kong as a spunky, meretricious prostitute who remained occult and innocent despite her violations by sailors and an array of neurotic businessmen from China, England, America, and Australia.

53 See Arjun Appadurai on what he calls "the Bosnia fallacy" of reducing such ethnic and nationalist conflicts to "primordial" or "tribal" antagonisms immune to modernization (*Modernity at Large*, pp. 21). He credits the American mass media with such misreadings.

54 Richard Walker, "California Rages against the Dying of the Light," *New Left Review* 209 (1995): 42–74.

55 "Asian-Pacific Cultural Studies" needs to nurture, support, and teach the literatures and narratives of those subordinated and less powerful in the region, I would urge, whose complex claims upon the *Pacific* (many of whose contemporary works are

written not in indigenous languages but in World English) and *Asia* (which, as we all know except for Samuel Huntington) was not and will never be a *single* Confucian "Orient") have too long been tokenized or ignored in the interests of settler peoples and *their* nation-state.

56 On the forging of a locally situated yet globally interconnected cultural studies as a critical knowledge formation, see the powerful and situated analysis of Kuan-Hsing Chen, "Voices from the Outside: Towards a New Internationalist Localism," *Cultural Studies* 6 (1992): 476–84; and "Positioning *positions:* A New Internationalist Localism of Cultural Studies," *positions* 2 (1994): 680–710. On the intensifying formation of Asia-Pacific networks wherein Britain and Europe are hardly as important as "East-West" binaries once implied, see Jon Stratton and Ien Ang, "On the Impossibility of a Global Cultural Studies: 'British' Cultural Studies in an 'International' Frame,'" in *Critical Dialogues: Cultural Studies, Marxism, and Postmodernism in the Writings of Stuart Hall*, ed. Kuan-Hsing Chen and David Morley (London and New York: Routledge 1995), pp. 361–91.

57 During the November 14–16, 1997, meeting of APEC in Vancouver—at which point Russia, Chile, and Vietnam were added to the expanding roster of APEC players in the Pacific—the indigenous peoples of the Pacific issued a "Pacific Peoples Declaration on APEC" (representing 12 nation-states, 16 first nations, and over 50 organizations present) resisting and eloquently countering policies of "trade liberalization and other mechanisms for economic globalization" in the region as "undemocratic," disadvantaging to many, dislocating, as well as culturally and environmentally damaging. In short, the statement goes, "APEC is not viable for Pacific Peoples."

58 The slogan "Go South," used by President Lee Teng-hui's Taiwan government to mobilize and diversify investment strategies (in places like Vietnam, where Taiwan leads foreign developers) takes on credible weight as an unfulfilled linkage with the other Pacific, and not just the migrant labor of the Philippines. This focus on "North/South" dynamics, thus, can have disturbing potential and help to unhinge the often-deceptive "East/West" colonial binary imagination. This is the complex terrain an emerging Asian-Pacific cultural studies must help to figure. Taiwan's "Go South" strategy was of course a way to divert investment from mainland China, where Taiwan investors have poured some U.S. $30 billion in the last decade. It can be linked, as well, with a push towards economic (and political) independence in the long-run, and this is also a threat to imperial imaginings of the region as a Chinese-bound co-prosperity sphere.

59 The regional context is suggested in the following news item on APROC within APEC: "The 'Asia-Pacific Regional Operations Center Coordination and Service Office' [APROC] officially opened its doors amid fanfare yesterday, marking a major step towards developing Taiwan into a major regional hub for multinational corporations," especially as "other hubs in the region [Hong Kong facing 1997, Singapore after the Barings fiasco] are losing their charm to foreign investors." *China Post*, March 7, 1995.

60 Roger Mark Selya, *Taipei* (Chichester, England: John Wiley, 1995), p. 39.

61 Ackbar Abbas, *Hong Kong: Culture and the Politics of Disappearance*, p. 80.

62 To register a negative evaluation of same, from an international and local viewpoint: "Taipei, according to some people, is the least inviting city in Southeast Asia, if not

the world. It is filthy, chaotic, and the argument says, like a huge garbage dump with its 2.7 million residents breathing seriously polluted air, and drinking contaminated water. . . . The city has been described as a 'pigsty' by the German magazine *Der Spiegel*" (*China Post* editorial, "Make Taipei Livable Again," Feb. 14, 1995).

63 Anthony D. King, *Global Cities* (London: Routledge, 1990). As King remarks of such imperial-to-global spaces of cosmopolitan mixture, "All cities today are 'world cities'" (p. 82); but not all of them like their new face where global capital meets and defaces the textures of the local-nation, where some sense of cultural identity had been constructed in the pores of empires and global flows. On imperial Japanese construction of China and Taiwan as pre-modern and non-white primitive spaces, see Leo Ching, "Yellow Skins, White Masks: Race, Class, and Identification in Japanese Colonial Discourse," in *Trajectories: Inter-Asia Cultural Studies*, ed. Kuan-hsing Chen et al. (London and New York: Routledge, 1998), pp. 65–86. As Chen warns in his introduction on "The Decolonization Question," if wary of neo-imperialism in the region by financial superpowers of transnational outreach, we have to resist surrendering "the power of geographical imagination to the super states" such as the regionalization project of APEC (p. 5).

64 Linkage between Taiwan and peoples of Asia/Pacific may not be all that capricious or merely postmodern. Recent high-powered DNA research suggests that ancestors of New Zealand's Maori and other Polynesian peoples (like the Hawaiians) came from China, specifically from Taiwan: "The DNA study [of Geoffrey Chambers at Victoria University] shows that, starting from Taiwan, they island-hopped their way through the Philippines and Indonesia to West Polynesia, on into the islands of East Polynesia and then to New Zealand." Maori oral mythologies identify Hawai'i ("Hawaiki" in Maori) as the Pacific home from which ancestors of New Zealand Maori set out on sea-faring voyages of discovery and migration to Aotearoa. Here are the makings of a diasporic, interactive, and inventive Asia/Pacific of precolonial origins and native feats of Pacific crossing. See "DNA Tests Trace Polynesians to China Origins," *Honolulu Advertiser*, August 11, 1998, A1. On the plight of Taiwan's Pacific "mountain people" and "ocean people" within the KMT Chinese nationalist hegemony, see Fred Yen Liang Chiu, "From the Politics of Identity to an Alternative Cultural Politics: On Taiwan Primordial Inhabitants' A-systematic Movement," in *Asia/Pacific as Space of Cultural Production*, pp. 120–46. On the conflicted nationalisms of Taiwan, also see Marshall Johnson, "Making Time: Historical Preservation and the Space of Nationality," *positions* 2 (1994): 178–249; and, on diasporic linkages and opportunistic breaks of "Greater China" across the postcolonial Pacific, see Aihwa Ong and Donald Nonini, eds. *Ungrounded Empires: The Cultural Politics of Modern Chinese Transnationalism* (New York: Routledge, 1997).

Boundary Displacement: The State, the Foundations,
and Area Studies during and after the Cold War
Bruce Cumings

It is a curious fact of academic history that the first great center of area studies
. . . [was] in the Office of Strategic Services. . . . It is still true today, and I hope it
always will be, that there is a high measure of interpenetration between universities with area programs and the information-gathering agencies of the government.—McGeorge Bundy, 1964[1]

The late Mr. Bundy would know what he was talking about. At a time when he
was dean of Arts and Sciences at Harvard, making life difficult for young scholars with political backgrounds that he or the FBI found suspect, he was also
working closely with various Central Intelligence Agency projects.[2] The declassification of American archival materials on the service to the state provided by
many prominent academics during the Cold War has barely begun, but there is
enough to suggest that Bundy was not the exception, but rather the rule—a rule
particularly evident at the most prestigious American universities. It is now fair
to say, based on the declassified evidence, that the American state and especially
the intelligence elements in it shaped the entire field of postwar area studies,
with the clearest and most direct impact on those regions of the world where
communism was strongest: Russia, Central and Eastern Europe, and East Asia.
A surge of opposition to the Indochina War in the 1960s directed some light into
this academic-intelligence nexus, but by no means enough to disrupt the ongoing dailiness of its exchanges. But the collapse of Western communism and the
end of the Cold War have set major changes in motion, ones that have threatened
existing area programs and that have called into question the connection between the state's need for information and academe's capacity and willingness
to provide it. If we are not in a new era, we are in a time when the consumers
of area-studies knowledge are fewer, the provisioners of its ongoing funding
are stingy, and scholars with competing paradigms of analysis claim pride of
place.

In this essay I propose to examine the displacement and reordering of the boundaries of scholarly inquiry in the postwar period, in two phases: the first determining burst of academic work that began during World War II but vastly expanded in the early years of the Soviet-American confrontation, which is the necessary prelude to understanding the second phase, namely the contemporary revaluation of American studies of the rest of the world occasioned by the watershed changes since 1989. If space permitted I would also examine the interim period, the war of movement on the campuses that began around 1965 and continues today between hegemonic and counter-hegemonic forces; here I simply want to acknowledge its existence and its role in making tenuous any claim that the intelligence-university nexus is determining of the work that scholars do (depending on the university or the field, academics who work with the intelligence arms of the state may feel beleaguered or even marginalized over the past thirty years).[3] I would still argue that the ultimate force shaping scholarly studies of what used to be called "the non-Western world" is economic and political power; this power is concentrated in the central state, but the most interesting effects of such power are often the least observed, at those local points or "ultimate destinations" (in Foucault's phrase) where power "becomes capillary,"[4] like universities and academic departments, and the organizations that mediate between academe and the foundations—for example, the Social Science Research Council (SSRC). A Foucauldian understanding of power also helps us understand that conscious agency is not always, or even usually, the point in these relationships; people do things without being told, and often without knowing the influences on their behavior. In observing power "going capillary" in newly rearranged rivulets, we can discern both the origin of the "area" boundaries that expanded and contracted academic knowledge, the disordering occasioned by watershed changes in power politics and the world economy, and in the 1990s, emergent new relationships between power and knowledge.

If the first phase (the 1940s) has been much studied, it is still rare to find an acknowledgement of the often astonishing levels of collaboration between the universities, the foundations, and the intelligence arms of the American state that accompanied that phase.[5] If the second phase unfolds intermittently before our eyes (and with only partial information, much as in the late 1940s), it is remarkable how central the intelligence function has been to it. Since I propose to offer an assessment of such relationships, among others, let me say that in this essay I do not assume a moral position, nor do I wish to indict individual academics or take to task the foundations or the SSRC, nor am I involved in "conspiracy theory." In earlier public presentations of versions of this paper,[6] such comments have predictably come up: I must be trying to single out and blame scholars who worked at some point in their careers for the government, and in so doing I must be asserting an evil conspiracy. Rather, what I wish to do is evaluate contemporary boundary displacements in the unblinkered light of what we now know about the early years of area and international studies.

Perhaps I should also make clear my position on academics in government service. In an earlier draft of this essay I stated that working for the government against Hitler was different from doing the same thing during the Cold War: the difference, it seems to me, is that between a crisis that drew nearly every American to the effort against the Nazis and Japan in conditions of total war, to Washington and overseas posts distinct from campus positions, as opposed to the very different requirements placed upon scholars and universities in peacetime: to uphold their independence and academic freedom, and to make full disclosure of possible biases deriving from clandestine sponsorship and privileged access to research funds.[7] To join, say, an Office of Strategic Services (OSS) inhabited by Paul Baran, Cora DuBois, John King Fairbank, Hajo Halborn, Charles Kindleberger, Wassily Leontif, Herbert Marcuse, Barrington Moore Jr., Franz Neumann, and Paul Sweezy,[8] was almost to be asked to join the best faculty the United States could assemble, thus to defeat Hitler. (The luminous names do not provide their own justification for such service, of course; Charles Beard set a different sort of example by resigning from Columbia University in protest of Woodrow Wilson's drafting of college students in World War I, and then interrogating Franklin Roosevelt's pro-war policies in publications written both before and after World War II.)

One commentator argued that by saying such things I had given up a principled position of academic independence: working for the state was always wrong. I disagree; to offer one's expertise to the Research and Analysis (R&A) Branch of the OSS does not compromise academic integrity, in my view, if we stipulate that (1) the war is one of total mobilization against an enemy clearly determined to take away all our freedoms, including academic ones; (2) one takes a leave of absence from the classroom to serve this war effort, establishing a clear difference between the two domains of the state and the university, and (3) classified work does not continue after re-entry to the university. These same principles, of course, argue for a complete separation of the intelligence and the academic function in ordinary times. Nothing should be more sacred to faculty offered tenure-to-the-grave security and full legal protection for their viewpoints, however heretical, than honesty and full disclosure before their colleagues and students—something unavailable to those who sign agreements never to speak or write about what they do for intelligence agencies.[9] But then, what are "ordinary times"—would the Cold War struggle against the Soviet

Union qualify? The oss "faculty" in R&A appear to have split over that question; Herbert Marcuse and Paul Sweezy were not, to say the least, enlisted in that cause. If we nonetheless stipulate that the Cold War fit the first criterion above, doing intelligence work during the four decades of the Cold War's life clearly did not meet the second and third criteria. Instead such activities compromised academic freedom.

These prefatory points are necessary because it was the oss Director, William "Wild Bill" Donovan, who in 1941 enunciated the rationale for employing the nation's best expertise "to collect and analyze all information and data which may bear upon national security;" present at this creation were representatives of the SSRC and the American Council of Learned Societies (ACLS), who helped Donovan come up with "a slate of [academic] advisors" for the oss.[10] Donovan's relationship to left-leaning academics was similar to General Leslie Groves' collaboration with Robert Oppenheimer on the Manhattan Project (i.e., nothing in common), but it yielded a political spectrum in oss from an anticommunist like Philip Mosely to the Marxist founders of *Monthly Review*, Baran and Sweezy. The Research and Analysis branch was widely thought to be the most successful program in the oss. It thus presented a model for postwar collaboration between intelligence and academe, and influenced the division of the Central Intelligence Agency into separate research and operations branches. In many ways it also helped to create the basic division between the academic disciplines and something else, a catchment area for interdisciplinary work that soon came to be called "area studies."[11]

For a generation after the Second World War, the bipolar conflict between Moscow and Washington and the hegemonic position of the United States in the world economy drew academic boundaries that had the virtue of clarity: "area studies" and its sister called "international studies" had clear reference to places or to issues and processes that became important to study, backed with enormous public and private resources. The places were usually countries, but not just any countries: Japan got favored placement as a success story of development, China got obsessive attention as a pathological example of abortive development. The key processes were things like modernization, or what was for many years called "political development" toward the explicit or implicit goal of liberal democracy.

East Asian studies are what I and the contributors to this volume know best, and will be my main focus. The Association for Asian Studies (AAS) was the first "area" organization in the U.S., founded in 1943 as the Far Eastern Association and reorganized as the AAS in 1956. Before 1945 there had been little attention to and not much funding for such things; but now the idea was to bring contemporary social science theory to bear on the non-Western world, rather than continue to pursue the classic themes of Oriental studies, often examined through philology.[12] Political scientists were often the carrier of the new "theory" (modernization), and they would begin talking to Orientalists. In return for their sufferance, the Orientalists would get vastly enhanced academic resources (positions, libraries, language studies)—and soon, a certain degree of separation which came from the social scientists inhabiting institutes of East Asian studies, whereas the Orientalists occupied departments of East Asian languages and cultures. This implicit Faustian bargain sealed the postwar academic deal—and meant that the Orientalists didn't necessarily have to talk to the social scientists, after all. If they often looked upon the latter as unlettered barbarians, the social scientists looked upon the Orientalists as spelunkers in the cave of exotic information, chipping away at the wall of ore until a vein could be tapped and brought to the surface, to be shaped into useful knowledge by the carriers of theory.

So, which "areas" did we study, and how did we do it? Countries inside the American hegemonic system, like Japan, and those outside it, like China, were clearly placed as friend or enemy, ally or adversary. But national boundaries were not sufficient to the task. A part of Korea and a part of Vietnam had one epistemology, and the other parts, a totally different one. In both direct and indirect ways the American government and the major foundations forged these boundaries by directing scholarly attention to distinct places and to distinct ways of understanding them: in academe, communist studies for North Korea, North Vietnam, and China; modernization studies for Japan and the other halves of Korea and Vietnam; on the National Security Council, one expert to cover China and North Korea and a different one for Japan and South Korea. To be in "Korean studies" or "Chinese studies" was daily to experience the tensions that afflicted Korea and China during the long period of the Cold War. Over the decades of the Cold War this revaluation by power gave us two tropes, yielding an entire inventory of East and Southeast Asia. The first trope was "Red China," yielding a red blotch on the map that spilled over to the northern part of the DMZ in Korea; the second was "Pacific Rim," a trope bequeathed by the Nixonian transition in response to defeat in Vietnam (opening relations with China, etc.). Each trope valued and revalued East and Southeast Asia, as Westerners (mostly Americans) recognized and defined it, in ways that highlighted some parts and excluded (or occluded) others. This change happened in the 1970s, and most of the area scholars came trundling along in its wake.

When East Asia was "painted Red," it held an apparent outward-moving dynamic whose core was "Peiping": 400 million Chinese armed with nuclear weapons, in Dean Rusk's 1960s scenario, threatened nations along China's rim with oblivion: South Korea, South Vietnam, Taiwan, Indonesia, Thailand, and the big enchilada, Japan. "Pacific Rim" was the post-1975 artistry, an era of forward movement and backward occlusion, as Americans sought to "put Vietnam behind us." The new trope looked forward: suddenly the Rim became the locus of a new dynamism, bringing pressure on the mainland of Asia. Organized into the new inventory were "miracle" economies in Japan, South Korea, Taiwan, Hong Kong, Malaysia, and Singapore, with honorable mention for Thailand, the Philippines, Indonesia, and post-Mao (but pre-Tiananmen) China—signified by "Beizhing," which is the Ted Koppel-approved way to pronounce Beijing. But "Pacific Rim" also heralded a forgetting, a hoped-for amnesia in which the decades-long but ultimately failed American effort to obliterate the Vietnam revolution would enter the realm of Korea, "the forgotten war." The many working-class and anti-systemic movements of the East Asian region in the past decades remained poxes, irrationalities that illustrate immature "political development" in the Rim. The constant element was that Rimspeak, like modernization theory, continued to look with curiosity if not disdain upon anyone who did not privilege the market. And the centerpiece in the region was still Japan, a newly risen sun among advanced industrial countries—indeed, "Number One" in Ezra Vogel's perfectly timed book,[13] published in 1979. From the 1950s through the late 1980s it was almost heretical to utter a critical word about postwar Japan, or to point out that in the midst of the Korean "miracle" Park Chung Hee and Chun Doo Hwan were beating the brains out of thousands of workers and students, bivouacking their troops on elite university campuses and jailing and torturing professors.

When the Cold War ended and Western communism collapsed in 1989–91, a third revaluation unfolded. One set of rationales for studying "areas" (or areas in particular kinds of ways, namely communist studies) collapsed, while another—"development," whether economic or political—deepened. In effect the previous boundaries disappeared as the framework of inquiry distended to approximate the reach of the world market; the dawning "world without borders" collapsed area studies into international studies. Even "Pacific Rim" gave way to a new globalism, as Japan's economic bubble burst and the U.S. emerged finally as the mature hegemonic power of the century. It turned out that we were now living in a world economy, something that radicals had written about for decades but that now materialized as the essential domain of American activity and academic endeavor.

The state and the foundations were the quickest to sense this displacement and to redirect practical and scholarly efforts. The Clinton administration moved toward a major emphasis on foreign economic policy, spinning off one alphabet-soup organization after another (NAFTA, APEC, etc.). Lacking a clear enemy and worried about their budgets, forces within the national security state sought to re-position China as another Soviet Union requiring "containment." But they were vastly weaker than the enormous weight of the multinational business forces wanting to "engage Beizhing." The foundations moved to attenuate their support for area studies, emphasizing instead inter-regional themes (like "development and democracy"). The SSRC and the ACLS, long the national nexus for raising and administering funds for area studies, found their very existence threatened and began a major restructuring for the first time in more than thirty years. The source of power had shifted in the 1990s, from the state's concern with the maintenance of Cold War boundary security to transnational corporations that, as the organized expression of the market, saw no geographic limit on their interests. Sponsors' expectations of area experts likewise changed quickly: a Kremlinological opinion about "China after Deng" was less interesting than informed judgements on "China's economic reforms: whither the old state sector?" and the like. The entire field of communist studies found itself alone with the intelligence agencies and the Pentagon, searching for a function after the object of their desire had rolled itself back to nothing. A government publication that had exemplified the age now exemplified the transition: to change *Problems of Communism* to *Problems of Post-Communism* delimits and even announces a certain post-Cold War marginality.

As postwar history unfolded, in other words, scholars caught up in one historical system and one discourse that defined discipline, department, area, and subject suddenly found themselves in another emerging field of inquiry, well in advance of imagining or discovering the subject themselves. To put a subtle relationship all too crudely, power and money had found their subject first, and shaped fields of inquiry accordingly. But I have given you my conclusions, without the evidence. I will now revisit in more detail the origins of area and international studies in the early Cold War period, examine how both changed with the end of the Cold War, and suggest how we might rethink boundaries (of area and discipline) and reengage our minds with the task of understanding the world outside American boundaries.

Area and International Studies in the Early Cold War

The channel is more important than that a lot of water should be running through it.
—McGeorge Bundy

After World War II ended, the new area programs and associations (like the AAS) instantly confronted the existing boundaries of the social science and humanities disciplines; this often made for interesting intellectual confrontation as well. William Nelson Fenton was present at the creation of area studies, and in 1947 he wrote that area programs

> faced fierce resistance from the "imperialism of departments" since they challenged the fragmentation of the human sciences by disciplinary departments, each endowed with a particular methodology and a specific intellectual subject matter.[14]

The anthropologist Cora DuBois thought that the OSS' collaborative work during the war was the prelude to a new era of reformist thinking on an interdisciplinary basis: "The walls separating the social sciences are crumbling with increasing rapidity. . . . People are beginning to think, as well as feel, about the kind of world in which they wish to live."[15] Area studies, much maligned as the precinct for atheoretical navel-gazing and Orientalia, was beginning to challenge the parochialism of the disciplines in the name of an interdisciplinary work or even unified knowledge.

Still, these were not the power lines that counted. The state was less interested in the feudal domains of academe than in filling the vacuum of knowledge about a vast hegemonic and counter-hegemonic global space, and it was the capillary lines of state power that shaped area programs. This was effected in the first instance by the relocation of the OSS' Soviet division to Columbia University, as the basis for its Russian Institute which opened in September 1946, and in the second instance by a Carnegie Corporation grant of $740,000 to Harvard to establish its own Russian Research Center in 1947.[16] Soon the Ford Foundation put in much more money, a total of $270 million to thirty-four universities for area and language studies from 1953 to 1966.[17]

This munificent funding created important area programs throughout the country, and provided numerous fellowships that allowed scholars to spend years in the field acquiring difficult languages and other forms of area knowledge. McGeorge Bundy, however, was much closer to the truth in linking the underpinnings of area studies to the intelligence agencies—the OSS, and subsequently the CIA. William Donovan may have directed the wartime OSS and then returned to Wall Street, but he was also in many ways the founder of the CIA.[18] In his papers, combed through by the CIA and then deposited at the Army War College, there is a brief account of the original development of "foreign area studies," in which Donovan, George F. Kennan, and John Paton Davies played the major roles. Davies had a plan to transform area studies and bring enormous amounts of government and foundation funding into American universities, through what was originally to be an Institute of Slavic Studies, but which subsequently became a model for the organization of studies of the communist world and threatened Third World areas.

Donovan, who was then with the Wall Street firm Donovan, Leisure, was at the center of this effort, working with Davies in 1948 and helping him to get foundation funding. The organizers specified that the government was not to be involved publicly in developing area studies, thus to allay suspicions that such programs were little more than "an intelligence agency." Their work should be "impartial and objective," clear of conflicts of interest, and so on. (Indeed, the files on this project are full of concern with academic independence and proper procedure.) However, in a letter to Donovan, Clinton Barnard of the Rockefeller Foundation—which with the Carnegie Corporation funded this effort at the beginning—wrote, "the most compelling aspect of this proposal is the intelligence function which the Institute could perform for government."[19]

Sigmund Diamond greatly expanded our understanding of the establishment of area studies centers during the early years of the Cold War in his book *Compromised Campus*. Diamond paid particular attention to the Russian Research Center at Harvard, which, following upon Columbia's Russian Institute and Davies' Slavic studies institute, became a model for other area programs on Eastern Europe and China. It was also a model of cooperation with the CIA and the FBI. Although Diamond's government documents on Harvard in this period have been greatly expurgated—and Harvard's own papers remain closed to scholars under a fifty-year rule—he was able to document that the Harvard's Russian Research Center was based on the wartime OSS model (like Columbia's); that the Center was deeply involved with the CIA, the FBI, and other intelligence and military agencies; that several foundations (Carnegie, Rockefeller, Ford) worked with the state and the Center to fund projects and, in some cases, to launder CIA funding; that the same scholars who undertook this activity often were subjects of FBI investigations themselves; that some of these scholars, in turn, were responsible for denouncing other scholars to the FBI; and, finally, that these academics were major figures in the postwar development of Russian area studies in the nation as a whole.[20] By 1949 Harvard and the Center had established a mutually satisfactory relationship with the local FBI office: indeed, results of the Russian Research Center's work were

> made available to the Bureau officially through contact with President James B. Conant of Harvard University, who has on occasion indicated his respect for the Bureau's work and his understanding for its many and varied interests in connection with internal security matters.

At roughly the same time, Conant also negotiated basic arrangements between Harvard and the CIA.[21]

I frequently chide myself for running afoul of what I might call the fallacy of insufficient cynicism. I had not, for example, thought that J. Edgar Hoover enjoyed being wined and dined by major figures in organized crime, or that the Mafia had blackmailed him (either because of his closet homosexuality or his gambling debts) into refusing for years to investigate organized crime, even into denying that there was such a thing.[22] Nor had I imagined the lengths to which the FBI would go to investigate even the most trifling aspects of life in academe in the early Cold War period. It is only a bit of an exaggeration to say that for those scholars studying potential enemy countries, either they consulted with the government or they risked being investigated by the FBI; working for the CIA thus legitimized academics and fended off J. Edgar Hoover (something particularly important for the many scholars born in foreign countries, or the many one-time communist émigrés now engaged in anti-communist research).[23]

Diamond's papers contain large files of FOIA material on FBI investigations of academics in the early 50s, throughout the country. Although most of the files are still thoroughly blacked out by "declassification" censors (in truth there has been hardly any declassification on this issue), there is enough to indicate that any hearsay, any wild charge, any left-of-center organization joined, any name entered on a petition for whatever cause unacceptable to the FBI (like peace or racial integration), any subscription to a magazine the FBI didn't like (e.g., the *Nation* or the *New Republic*), was enough to get an entry in the file. The FBI routinely checked the credit records of academics, tailed them around, monitored their lectures, questioned their colleagues and students, and sought out reliable campus informants (William F. Buckley Jr. distinguished himself at Yale by becoming an important source for the FBI, as did Henry Kissinger to a lesser degree at Harvard).[24]

One FBI memorandum on Harvard goes on for forty-two detailed pages with a detailed account of its courses on the USSR, complete with syllabi, teachers, and the content of the courses.[25] Another has extensive reports on lectures at

Harvard sponsored by the John Reed Club (which future Japan scholar Robert Bellah chaired, and which had as its members future China scholars Albert Feuerwerker and Franz Schurmann).[26] Academics working on East Asia, of course, were particularly vulnerable to FBI harrassment; those working on the USSR were as well, but for reasons deeply involved with the history of those fields (e.g., the USSR never inspired much sympathy among academics in the postwar period, but China, pre- and post-1949, did) more Asianists seemed to have come to the FBI's attentions. The Korean War, for example, had an immediate impact on Harvard's policies toward the John Reed Club. Two months after the war began Harvard banned the club from using Harvard facilities, unless it went through a lot of formalistic procedures (membership lists, sources of funds, etc.) not required of other groups. In the same period Harvard security people blocked China-hand Israel Epstein from speaking at a club gathering. An FBI informant in the John Reed Club reported that the war in Korea was the cause of this new policy, and that some club members did not want to register with Harvard for fear that their names would be turned over to the government.

Mosely at Columbia

If Harvard's Russian Research Center were the only place where such intelligence ties and government interference went on, it could be dismissed as an aberration. Unfortunately, it was a central model for area programs around the country, as was the one at Columbia University (to which OSS R&A transferred its Soviet division, as we have seen). Philip Mosely ran Columbia's Russian Institute for many years; an R&A branch veteran, he was one of the most important figures in Russian studies and American foreign policy in the 1950s. In addition to directing Columbia's Center, he was head of the Council on Foreign Relations from 1952 to 1956, a member of various boards and committees at the Ford Foundation, and a prominent leader of the American Political Science Association. His papers raise the same question Sigmund Diamond did in his book: why did so many of the major figures in academe and the foundations, and particularly the leaders of area centers, have CIA ties and background?

Although Mosely's papers contain little formerly classified material, they document his nearly constant involvement with secret government agencies from the late 1940s through his retirement from Columbia in the late 1960s.[28] The sketchy and incomplete nature of his papers make it impossible to know exactly what he did for the CIA and other agencies, or whether he had such clearances at all times. But his continuing relationship with intelligence groupings is clear. One example would be his communication with W. W. Rostow in

1952 about which portions of Rostow's "classified project" on the "dynamics of Soviet society" should be released for publication, a project for which Mosely was an advisor.[29] Another would be Frederick Barghoorn's letter to Mosely in the same year, asking for Mosely's help in getting government work for the summer:

> In addition to some sort of official interview project or intelligence operation, it has occurred to me that perhaps I might obtain some connection with the State Department's educational exchange project.[30]

In 1955 John T. Whitman of the CIA wrote to Mosely, asking that Mosely schedule recruitment interviews for him with students at Columbia's Russian Institute, "as you so kindly did for Messrs. Bloom, Bradley and Ferguson last year." Mosely was happy to oblige.[31] Mosely was also an active partisan in the politics of the McCarthy era. He testified before the Subversive Activities Control Board in 1953, for example, that an unnamed "respondent's" views and policies "do not deviate from those of the Soviet Union." This testimony was part of the Justice Department's attempt to get the CPUSA to register under the McCarran Act, whereupon its members could be jailed.[32] The McCarthy era, of course, produced the most widespread wave of political repression in American history, according to Ellen Schrecker, a wave that was especially effective in eliminating dissent over America's role in the world.[33]

Mosely was a central figure at the Ford Foundation throughout the formative years of American area studies centers, which Ford supported to the tune of $270 million. On May 5, 1953, Ford's Board on Overseas Training and Research approved an agenda for implementing a program of "Coordinated Country Studies." Shortly thereafter Paul Langer wrote to Mosely, stating that the first item in regard to implementation would be consultation with CIA Director Allen Dulles. After suggesting that a person high in the Foundation should consult with Dulles, the other items to be discussed were listed as follows:

> (b) In what terms are the projects to be presented to the CIA?
> (c) To what extent will the Foundation assume responsibility toward the government in regard to the political reliability of the team members?
> (d) Should mention be made of the names of persons tentatively selected?
> (e) Should the directors of the proposed study projects be informed of the fact that the CIA has been notified?[34]

Another memorandum from the Ford Foundation concerning "implementation of the proposed country studies,"[35] said in the second paragraph that "Carl Spaeth [of Ford] offered to call Allen Dulles to explain in general terms the nature of the proposed studies," to be followed up by a more detailed presentation of the projects in a meeting between Cleon Swayze, also of Ford, and Allen Dulles. (Here, however, the purpose of these contacts with the CIA was said to be "merely to keep interested government agencies informed.")

Other memoranda in Mosely's files show that plans for these "country studies" spawned some of the most important works later published in the field of comparative politics; for example, Langer recommended Lucian Pye for work on guerrillas in Malaya, and suggested "a broadly conceived" study of Burmese government and politics" (which Pye also did somewhat later, although he was not recommended for it in this memorandum). Langer also wanted a study of Turkey as "a special case in the Near East" of "smooth development toward democracy" and immunity "to the appeals of communism." Among other scholars, he thought Dankwart Rustow would be good for the task; Rustow, together with Robert Ward, later published a central work on how Japan and Turkey modernized successfully.[36] (There is no evidence in these memoranda that Pye or Rustow knew that they were under consideration for such tasks.)

Later in 1953 the Ford Foundation sponsored the Conference on Soviet and Slavic Area Studies to discuss a program of fellowships in that field. Major academic figures in Soviet studies like Mosely, Merle Fainsod, Cyril Black, and Frederick Barghoorn attended; also attending was China specialist George Taylor. Government figures present included George Kennan, Paul Nitze, Allen Dulles, and several CIA officials. Pendleton Herring of the SSRC also attended.[37] Among other things, the conferees fretted about "loyalty" checks on fellowship grantees, and therefore suggested denying fellowships to "partisans of special Soviet movements and recognized supporters of political parties inimical to the best interests of the United States." Although this stricture was directed primarily at the CPUSA, the language was broad enough to include, say, supporters of Henry Wallace's Progressive Party. The Carnegie Corporation also applied such concerns to a variety of liberal academics.[38]

One apparent result of this program was a CIA-sponsored study entitled "Moslems of the Soviet Central Asia" done by Richard Pipes, a well-known Harvard historian of Russia and who eventually became responsible for Soviet affairs on Ronald Reagan's first and most ideologically committed National Security Council.[39] Langer, Mosely, and others also sought in 1953 and 1954 to develop Chinese studies along the lines of their previous work in Russian studies.[40] The Ford Foundation's decision in the late 1950s to pump at least $30 million into the field of China studies (to resuscitate it after the McCarthyite onslaught, but also to create new China watchers) drew on the same rationale as the Russian programs examined above:

The investment strategy was based on the model designed just after World War II by cooperation on the part of the Carnegie Corporation of New York and the Rockefeller Foundation in supporting Soviet studies, initially and principally through grants to Columbia and Harvard Universities.[41]

That Mosely provided a working linkage among Ford, the CIA, and the ACLS/SSRC well into the 1960s is suggested by Abbot Smith's 1961 letter to him, referring to lists of possible new CIA area studies consultants whom he wished to clear with Mosely, William Langer, and Joseph Strayer. (Smith was described as the director of the CIA's "consultants' group.")[42] In Mosely's response, he recommends among other people China scholar John M. Lindbeck of Columbia, A. Doak Barnett (China-watcher then with the Ford Foundation but soon to join the Columbia faculty), and Lucian Pye of MIT ("my first choice").[43] In 1962 Mosely told James E. King of the Institute for Defense Analyses (IDA, an academic arm of government security agencies), who had proposed a three-year program of some sort to Ford, that "of the major foundations, only Ford has shown a willingness to mingle its money with government money, and even it is rather reluctant to do so"; Mosely counseled King that "the question of 'end-use,' i.e., whether classified or publishable, is important to the foundation."[44] Other evidence suggests that Columbia professors like Mosely and Zbigniew Brzezinski worked closely with the IDA, both in supporting students completing dissertations, like former CIA employee Donald Zagoria, and in bringing IDA people into Brzezinski's Research Institute on Communist Affairs.[45]

This incomplete but important evidence from the Mosely papers suggests that the Ford Foundation, in close consultation with the CIA, helped to shape postwar area studies and important collaborative research in modernization studies and comparative politics that were later mediated through well-known Ford-funded SSRC projects (ones that were required reading when I was a graduate student in the late 1960s).[46] According to Christopher Simpson's study of declassified materials, however, this inter-weaving of foundations, universities, and state agencies (mainly the intelligence and military agencies) extended to the social sciences as a whole:

> For years, government money ... not always publicly acknowledged as such—made up more than 75 per cent of the annual budgets of institutions such as Paul Lazarsfeld's Bureau of Applied Social Research at Columbia University, Hadley Cantril's Institute for International Social Programs at Princeton, Ithiel deSola Poole's CENIS program at MIT, and others.

Official sources in 1952 reported that "fully 96 per cent of all reported [government] funding for social sciences at that time was drawn from the U.S. mili-

tary."[47] My own work in postwar American archives over the past two decades
has taught me how many books central to the political science profession in the
1950s and 1960s emerged first as internal, classified government studies.

Allen and Taylor at Washington

The University of Washington in Seattle has one of the oldest area studies centers, with parts of it established well before the Second World War. But the Cold
War transformed it as well, beginning with a case that made headlines all over
the country. In January 1949 the Board of Regents of the University of Washington fired three tenured professors for their political views: two because they initially denied and then later admitted membership in the Communist Party, and
one—Ralph Grundlach, a national figure in the discipline of psychology—who
was not a party member but a radical who was uncooperative with University
and state legislature inquiries. Ellen Schrecker wrote that this decision "had na-
tionwide repercussions," not only as the first important academic freedom case
in the Cold War period, but one that also established a model for purges at many
universities thereafter. President Raymond B. Allen was the prime mover behind this influential case; Schrecker takes particular note of how careful Allen
was to assure that proper academic procedure be followed in all political cases.[48]

There is no suggestion in Schrecker's definitive account, however, or in the
more detailed study of this case by Jane Sanders,[49] that Allen had extensive contact with J. Edgar Hoover and his close aides in the FBI as the case unfolded, or
that he was advised by William Donovan on the crucial matter of how to construct a model argument against these professors, an argument that would make
it possible to fire them and still be consistent with contemporary doctrines of academic freedom, one that would stand up in a court of law.[50] By far the most disturbing aspects of this case, therefore, begin at the top: not in what this president
did in the early Cold War period to protect academic freedom and threaten faculty or to arouse the suspicions of the FBI, but in what he did to facilitate such
suspicions and deliver up such faculty.

I came across Donovan's role in shaping Allen's argument in the former's papers,[51] but the FBI's involvement was much greater. For unknown reasons the FBI
file on the University of Washington (hereafter UW), is relatively unexpur-
gated.[52] This relationship apparently began with President Allen's request to
meet with Hoover or a top assistant in May 1948,[53] to express his concern that
the so-called Canwell Committee (Washington state's early and vicious version
of the House Un-American Activities Committee), was not abiding by agreements he had made with it. Allen had instructed UW faculty to assist in Can-

well's investigation, and to speak with Everett Pomeroy, one of Canwell's chief investigators (whom Allen wrongly believed to be a former FBI agent). In return, Allen said, Canwell had agreed to turn over the names of faculty to be hauled before his committee, so that UW could carry out its own internal investigation first (thus to avoid public embarrassment).

Allen was also interested in an arrangement that he thought obtained at UCLA, whereby an on-campus FBI representative "cooperates with university officials;" he wished to have a similar arrangement at the University of Washington, so that he could get current FBI information on UW faculty, and check the names of potential new faculty with the FBI. Hoover scrawled on this document, "make sure this isn't being done" at UCLA, apparently a comment for the file since the FBI proceeded to set up for Allen what can only be called the arrangement Allen asked for—the one he persistently thought existed at UCLA in spite of FBI denials, and in any case one which provided him the information he wanted on UW faculty. By November 1948 an FBI agent was seeing Allen weekly, and Allen in return was giving him privileged information on what the relevant faculty committee and the Board of Regents were likely to do about politically suspect professors. Allen even provided to the FBI the entire transcript of the University's internal proceedings, including privileged testimony assumed to be strictly confidential.[54]

In a case of particular interest to the Korean field at the University of Washington (an area that it has specialized in since 1945), Allen told the FBI that "although Harold Sunoo appeared to be an innocent dupe of the Party, he [Allen] was not entirely satisfied with the information available with respect to Sunoo," and asked for more from the FBI.[55] Dr. Sunoo taught at the University in the early Cold War period, and subsequently was forced to resign. Many years later he told me that he thought George Taylor, for decades the director of the Russian and Far Eastern Center at the University, had turned him in to the FBI as a security risk because of his membership in a small faculty group critical of the Syngman Rhee regime.

I later verified that information independently with another Korean employed by the University of Washington at the same time, who participated in the same group, and who said that Taylor's denunciation of him to the FBI was responsible for getting him fired (from a department having to do with the arts and thus utterly unrelated to any possible security problem). For nearly two decades thereafter he was unable to obtain a passport. Worse happened to other Koreans who ran afoul of the FBI in other states: according to Dr. Sunoo and other Korean Americans from that era with whom I have spoken, some Koreans who were active politically in the U.S. were deported to South Korea where they were subsequently executed. (FBI files on these cases were still closed when I sought access to them several years ago.)

Declassified documents demonstrate that George Taylor did indeed collaborate with the FBI. An example is a conference he helped to organize in 1955 (the same year that, in a celebrated case, the University of Washington cancelled a speaking invitation to Robert Oppenheimer[56]). At first the conference was to be titled "World Communism and American Policy." Taylor invited a local FBI agent to attend while assuring him that "there would be no improper interference from the presence of the agent," and offering to synopsize the conference for the FBI. Subsequently the name of the conference was changed to "American Policy and Soviet Imperialism," with the public invited to attend and with verbiage such as this in conference fliers:

> DO YOU KNOW that over half your income taxes are due to the aggressive nature of Communist imperialism?
> DO YOU KNOW what Lenin and Stalin intended regarding world domination?
> ... DO YOU KNOW the kinds of private American Cold War operations and what they are doing?[57]

One only begins to understand the early Cold War period by learning that Taylor and his colleague Karl Wittfogel were also attacked as left-wingers or communist sympathizers, by right-wing groups who noted Wittfogel's past communist affiliations and Taylor's presence alongside China-hand John Service in the Office of War Information, and Taylor's membership in the Institute for Pacific Relations. President Allen chose to stand by them, however, and shortly Allen accepted the directorship of the Psychological Strategy Board, a CIA position Taylor had turned down in 1950.[58] (Once again, one senses that in this period you either consulted with the CIA or got investigated by the FBI.) Meanwhile Taylor and Wittfogel offered hostile testimony against Owen Lattimore in the McCarran inquisition.

Nikolai Poppe also taught for decades at the University of Washington and also testified against Lattimore. Originally a specialist on Mongolia, he defected from the USSR to the Nazis on the first day that they arrived in his town in 1942, and "actively collaborated" with the quisling government in the Karachai minority region in the Caucasus—the first acts of which consisted of expropriating Jewish property, followed by a general roundup of Jews for gassing. He later worked at the Nazi's notorious Wannsee Institute in Berlin, which involved itself primarily in identifying ethnic peoples of the USSR and Eastern Europe. He was picked up after the war first by British intelligence, and then by American intelligence as part of "Operation Bloodstone" to make use of Nazis who might aid the U.S. in the developing Cold War struggle.

Poppe was brought to the U.S. in 1949 as part of the same area studies "Institute" program presided over by John Davies and George Kennan, described above. Placed first in Harvard's Russian Research Center (where sociologist Talcott Parsons had been his big backer), he soon went to the University of Washington. There, George Taylor introduced him to Benjamin Mandel—chief investigator for the House Un-American Activities Committee, and then for the subsequent McCarran inquisition of the China field; Mandel at the time was preparing a perjury indictment against Lattimore. None of this came out at the time of Poppe's testimony against Lattimore, and Lattimore's role in blocking an American visa for Poppe until 1949 (on the grounds that he had been a Nazi ss officer) also remained unknown.[59]

International Studies during the Cold War

"International studies" has been a more muddled field than area studies, although for many the two labels are synonymous.[60] One can count on most members of area programs to have competence on those areas, but international studies is such a grabbag that almost any subject or discipline that crosses international boundaries can qualify for inclusion. The annual meetings of the International Studies Association have an extraordinary range of panels, with political scientists predominating but with a profusion of disciplines and subfields typically represented on the program. It is anything and everything, perhaps with a bias toward international relations and policy-relevant research. International studies is an umbrella under which just about everything gathers, from fine work and fine scholars to hack work and charlatans.

Among the earliest and the most important of international studies centers was MIT's Center for International Studies, or CENIS; it was a model for many subsequent international studies centers, and it was a model of CIA involvement—in its early years in the 1950s, the CIA underwrote this Center almost as a subsidiary enterprise. CENIS grew out of "Project Troy," begun by the State Department in 1950 "to explore international information and communication patterns." It later broadened its agenda to "social science inquiry on international affairs,"[61] but narrowed its sponsorship mostly to the CIA. This is evident in the transcript of a visiting committee meeting at MIT in May 1959, attended by MIT faculty W. W. Rostow, Ithiel deSola Poole, Max Millikan, and James Killian (president of MIT for several years); the visitors included Robert Lovett,

McGeorge Bundy, and several unidentified participants.[62] One assumes there must be many similar CENIS transcripts; in any case this one offers a vintage example of CIA-university collaboration, and the problems such affiliations raised.

Queried as to whether the Center served just the CIA or a larger group of government departments, Millikan remarked that over the five years of the Center's relationship with the CIA, "there has been some continuing ambiguity as to whether we were creatures of CIA or whether CIA was acting as an administrative office for other agencies." He also admitted that the Center had "taken on projects under pressure" to have work done that the CIA wanted done (these were among "the least successful projects" from MIT's standpoint, he thought). At one point in the transcript Millikan also says that "[Allen] Dulles allowed us to hire three senior people," suggesting that the CIA director had a hand in CENIS' hiring policies. The Center provided an important go-between or holding area for the CIA, since "top notch social scientists" and "area experts" had no patience for extended periods of residence at CIA headquarters: "A center like ours provides a way of getting men in academic work to give them [sic] a close relationship with concrete problems faced by people in government."

This transcript predictably shows that the two big objects of such work were the Soviet Union and China, with various researchers associated with the Center doing internal, classified reports that subsequently became published books —for example Rostow's *Dynamics of Soviet Society.* The primary impetus for this, of course, was the professorial desire to "get a book out of it." But Millikan also noted another motivation:

> In an academic institution it is corrosive to have people who are supposed to be pursuing knowledge and teaching people under limitations as to whom they can talk to and what they can talk about.

One way to remedy that problem was to take on no project "whose material we can't produce in some unclassified results [sic]." McGeorge Bundy, however, thought that the value of classified work was not in its "magnitude" or in the number of books produced, but in the connection itself: "The channel is more important than that a lot of water should be running through it."

Lovett acknowledged that there could be "very damaging publicity" if it were known that the CIA was funding and using CENIS, since the CIA provided "a good whipping board"; he thought they could set up a "fire wall" by making the National Security Council (NSC) "our controlling agent with CIA the administrative agent." Killian responded that "I have a strange animal instinct that this is a good time to get ourselves tidied up. We shouldn't take the risk on this." Another participant named McCormack said he had always thought "that others would front [for] the CIA"; a participant named Jackson said that the NSC could be "a wonderful cover." In the midst of this discussion (which recalls Hollywood versions of Mafia palaver), card-carrying "Wise Man" Robert Lovett provided the bottom line: "If this thing can be solved you will find it easier to get more money from the foundations."[63]

Area and International Studies after the Cold War

Perhaps there is enough detail above to convince independent observers that several major American centers of area and international studies research came precisely from the state/intelligence/foundation nexus that critics said they did in the late 1960s—always to a hailstorm of denial then, always to a farrago of "why does this surprise you?" today; CIA-connected faculty were so influential that they made critics who stood for academic principle look like wild-eyed radicals in the 1960s, if today critics merely appear to be naifs who didn't know what was going on.[64]

If we now fast-forward to the 1990s, we find that the first proponents of the state's need for area training and expertise (thus-to-meet-the-challenges-of-the-post-Cold-War-era, etc.) decided to put the intelligence function front and center, with a requirement that recipients of government fellowships consult with the national security agencies of the same government as a quid pro quo for their funding. I refer, of course, to the National Security Education Act (NSEA, also known as the Boren Bill, after former Senator David Boren). Several area associations went on record in opposition to this program, and it nearly fell beneath Newt Gingrich's budget-cutting axe in 1995.

In a useful summary[65] of the issues that scholars raised about the NSEA, the administrator in charge of the program in 1992, Martin Hurwitz (whose background is in the Defense Intelligence Agency, an outfit that makes the CIA look liberal and enlightened by contrast), suggested that everyone should be open about the intelligence aspects of the program: even though "the buffer approach is 'traditional clandestine tradecraft,'" Hurwitz thought that "aboveboard is the way to go" for the NSEA in the 1990s.

The NSEA was something less than "aboveboard," however, since its public board was supplemented by a "shadow board"; some also complained that "aboveboard" was not quite descriptive of the Defense Intelligence College that was to house the NSEA. People worried about such affiliations therefore hoped to find a non-Pentagon house and call this new office, with a certain ineffable predictability, "The David L. Boren Center for International Studies" (with no substantive changes otherwise). On February 14, 1992, three area associations (not including the Association for Asian Studies) wrote to Senator Boren, expressing worries about "even indirect links to U.S. national security agencies." Each of those three organizations had extant resolutions on their books urging members not to participate in defense-related research programs.

The Secretary-Treasurer of the AAS, L. A. Peter Gosling, introduced the issue to the membership as follows:[66]

> The goal of our continued discussions about and with the NSEA [*sic;* he refers to discussions with Martin Hurwitz] has been to make it as useful and acceptable to the scholarly community *as possible,* which in turn involves insulating it *as much as possible* from the Department of Defense where it is funded and located [my emphasis].

Gosling went on to fret that "there are *no* [*sic*] other sources now, nor in the immediate future" for funding international or area studies, and that although the NSEA only supplemented Title VI funding, "there are those who fear that the traditional Defense Department/intelligence community whose support has so often saved Title VI funding from extinction may [now] be less motivated to do so." Gosling thought the program would benefit Asian studies at both the undergraduate and graduate levels and noted that all Asian languages were included in the NSEA's list of priority languages (and isn't that wonderful, etc.). Even though the NSE Board "sets the priorities for the program," this could be mitigated, Gosling thought, by "the use of re-grant organizations" in administering parts of the program, such as the Fulbright program; through such modalities the program might escape from Defense Department control. Gosling closed his statement by saying that the AAS has "made clear the desirability of distancing this program from Department of Defense design and control."

At least three major area associations (for the Middle East, Latin America, and Africa) refused participation in this program, as we have seen. Anne Betteridge, an officer of the Middle East Studies Association, had argued that "academic representatives do not wish to obscure the source of funding, but do wish to assure the integrity of academic processes." Others commented that some academics worry that students in the program "may appear to be spies-in-training," and that the program would compromise field research in many countries around the world.

A fair reading of these statements, it seems to me, suggests that Betteridge and the area associations from Latin America, Africa, and the Middle East raised important objections to the NSEA, whereas the Secretary-Treasurer of the Association for Asian Studies seemed concerned primarily with (1) getting the money, (2) showing AAS members how important the NSEA would be for Asian studies, and (3) evincing no concern whatever for the "traditional clandestine tradecraft" that makes "re-granting agencies" mere window dressing—perhaps because of a different "tradition" in Asian studies: that of intelligence-agency support for Title VI funding, a tradition that I, for one, had never heard of before Gosling brought it to my attention.

Important changes have also come to SSRC and the ACLS in the 1990s. These organizations have been the national, joint administrative nexus of American academic research since the 1930s. The SSRC has not been a center of social science research as most social scientists would define it (the Survey Research Center at Michigan, for example, would come much closer), but a point at which the existing disciplines find meeting ground with "area studies." (I have walked on that ground many times myself, as a member of various SSRC committees and working groups over the years.) As such, of course, it is a more important organization than any of the area associations. Therefore we can hearken to how the SSRC vice president, Stanley J. Heginbotham, appraised the NSEA.[67]

First, he welcomed it by saying that "new forms of federal support for higher education" have been "extremely difficult to mobilize" in the recent period of spending cuts, budget deficits, and the like. Senator Boren, he explained, wanted the NSEA to facilitate area studies education at the graduate and undergraduate levels, and had hoped the program would be part of an independent governmental foundation. However the Office of Management and Budget blocked this, and instead ruled that for defense funds to be disbursed for the NSEA under the 1992 Intelligence Authorization Act, it would have to be located in the Department of Defense. Heginbotham added in a footnote that Boren decided further to strengthen "the credibility of the program in academic circles" by putting the administration of the program under the Defense Intelligence College; "few observers were reassured by this provision," Heginbotham wrote, but the Defense Intelligence College retained what he called a "nominal" role in the program.

Heginbotham expressed particular concern about "merit review" provisions in the NSEA:

> The academic and scholarly communities need firm assurance that selection processes will be free from political or bureaucratic interference beyond assuring compliance with terms of reference. . . . It would not *seem* acceptable [my emphasis], for example, to have candidates screened on the basis of their political views . . . [or] their ability to obtain security clearances.

Heginbotham went on to recommend that grants to individuals be made by "independent panels of scholars," that the academics on the "oversight board" be selected by a means "transparently independent" of the state agencies making up the same board. But "most worrisome," Heginbotham wrote, were the service requirements of the NSEP. He described the post-grant requirements for individuals as follows:

> Finally, the legislation includes important but ambiguous 'service' requirements for individuals who receive funds. . . . Undergraduates receiving scholarships covering periods in excess of one year, as well as all individuals receiving graduate training awards, are required either to serve in the field of education or in government service for a period between one and three times the length of the award. The legislation also prohibits any department, agency, or entity of the U.S. government that engages in intelligence activities from using any recipient of funds from the program to undertake any activity on its behalf while the individual is being supported by the program.[68]

Heginbotham suggested that the post-grant term be limited to a year, and limited not just to positions in "government and education," but enabling any employment that used the training to benefit the nation's international needs.[69]

Heginbotham's analysis is similar to Gosling's in three respects but superior in others: first, the analysis and recommendations are almost entirely procedural; neither Heginbotham nor Gosling defend international and area studies as important apart from what the state (let alone the "intelligence community") may want. Both also leave the impression that any funds of such size are ipso facto worth having, regardless of provenance, assuming that the procedures can be "as good as possible" in Heginbotham's words. And of course, the guarantees that Heginbotham asks for have not only been routinely bypassed by the state and area studies academics that we examined above (and used as a cover), but even powerful senators complain that the very "oversight" committees responsible for monitoring the CIA have been ignored and subverted—especially in the most recent period (I refer mainly to the revelations of the "Iran/Contra" scandal and the murders of Americans by CIA-associated militarists in Central America).

The SSRC's Heginbotham, however, seems both more responsible and more concerned than the AAS' Gosling about "re-granting agencies" being little more than laundries for DOD funding; his calls for merit review, academic independence, recognition of the difference between scholarship and government "service," etc., would seem to be basic principles for any kind of fundraising, and were the ones I observed in action on several SSRC committees. Heginbotham should be praised for enunciating them again—even if few seem to be listening, as sources in South Korea, Taiwan, and Japan have become major funders of Asian studies in this country, usually without proper peer and merit review.[70] Subsequently the Social Science Research Council decided to have nothing to do with the NSEP, a welcome if belated decision.

The *Bulletin of Concerned Asian Scholars* provided periodic coverage of the NSEA, whereas (so far as I can tell) the other alternative journal in the field—*Positions: East Asia Cultural Critique*—has been silent.[71] Mark Selden argued correctly that the NSEA "poses anew the issue of scholarship and power that lay behind the origin" of the Committee of Concerned Asian Scholars and its *Bulletin*, and noted that unlike earlier such activities, this one "saw no reason to conceal the military and intelligence priorities and powers shaping the field." The *Bulletin* drew particular attention to article three of the "purposes" section of the NSEA, calling for it

> to produce an increased pool of applicants for work in the departments and agencies of the U.S. Government with national security responsibilities.

The *Bulletin* also noted the similarity between the issues posed by the NSEA, and those that the Columbia chapter of CCAS took up in regard to the contemporary China committee of the SSRC, in a controversial set of articles in 1971.

As a graduate student I participated in preparing that report, the main author of which was Professor Moss Roberts of New York University. We were interested in Ford Foundation funding of the China field, the SSRC's Joint Committee on Contemporary China (JCCC), and an organization formed in the State Department in 1964 to coordinate government and private area studies research, called the Foreign Areas Research Coordinating Group, or FAR. From our inquiry it appeared that FAR played a role in shaping the field of contemporary Chinese studies, in line with the state's needs and with Ford Foundation funding.[72] It did this by suggesting appropriate research and dissertation subjects, in hopes that, together with Ford funding, the expertise of the government's China-watching apparatus would be enhanced (with obvious benefits also to China watchers in academe).

We were able to establish that FAR had grown out of the army's concern for the "coordination of behavioral and social science" in and out of government, which had long been sponsored by the Special Operations Research Office of Johns Hopkins University. FAR had been in contact with the JCCC, which had been one of many beneficiaries of the Ford Foundation's decision to reconstitute the China field. Our report also drew attention to the first chair of the JCCC,

George Taylor of the University of Washington, who, we argued, was a partisan in the McCarthy-McCarran inquisition that had nearly destroyed the China field, and therefore a strange choice to preside over a committee hoping to heal wounds and reconstitute the field. We questioned as well why non-China scholars like Philip Mosely were included on the first JCCC.[73]

The report brought a vituperative response from John Fairbank of Harvard which evokes in me today the same emotions it did in 1971: it is a political attack, designed to ward off such inquiries, rather than to provide a sincere and honest response to the many questions of fact that we raised. He began by saying our report "raises an issue of conspiracy rather than an issue of values," and ended by accusing us of offering "striking parallels to the McCarran Committee 'investigation,'" that is, we were left-McCarthyites. In between, precious few of our questions were answered.[74] Ultimately a precise specification of the relationship to and responsiveness of FAR and the JCCC to government or intelligence agendas could not be judged in the absence of access to classified materials. But the issues are strikingly similar to those raised by the NSEA today.

In November 1994 the cunning of history gave us the "Gingrich Revolution," and a chainsaw approach to cutting budgets: thus the NSEA appeared to get what it deserved, namely, a quick burial. No doubt Newt thought the NSEA was just another boondoggle for academia (and maybe he was right). At first Congress cut all its funds, but then restored some of them—or so it seems, since NSEP scholarships were again available to students in early 1996. Still, the NSEA is limping along into the post-Gingrich era.

If government funding for area studies seems to be drying up, so is that from the foundations. One result is the contemporary restructuring of the Social Science Research Council. For forty years SSRC and ACLS committees have been defined mostly by area: the Joint Committee on . . . China, or Latin America, or Western Europe; there were eleven such committees as of early 1996. That is all changing now, under a major restructuring plan.[75] The SSRC has justified this effort by reference to the global changes and challenges of the post-Cold War era, the "boundary displacements" that I began this essay with. These include (1) a desire to move away from fixed regional identities (i.e., the area committees), given that globalization has made the "'areas' more porous, less bounded, less fixed" than previously thought;[76] (2) to utilize area expertise to understand pressing issues in the world that transcend particular countries, which is the real promise of area studies in the post-1989 era; (3) to reintroduce area knowledge to social science disciplines that seem increasingly to believe that they can get along without it (this is an implicit reference to the rational choice paradigm and to "formal theory" in economics, sociology, and political science); (4) to integrate the U.S. into "area studies" by recognizing it as an "area" that needs to be studied comparatively; and (5) to collapse the SSRC and ACLS projects themselves, given the increasing cross-fertilization between the social sciences and the humanities. (I do not know if the restructuring will actually yield just one organization, but refer only to the justifications I have seen for the new plans.)

Major funding organizations like the Mellon Foundation and the Ford Foundation have recently made clear their declining support for area studies and their desire to have cross-regional scholarship, so in that subtly coercive context item one in this plan becomes obligatory (some say that the SSRC has been teetering on the edge of bankruptcy for several years). Item two is no different from the original justification for area studies. Items three and four are laudable, however, for anyone conversant with the daily life of the social sciences in American universities in the 1980s and 1990s.

Rational choice theory is the academic analogue of the "free market" principles that Margaret Thatcher and Ronald Reagan represented in the 1980s, and that are now offered to the "world without boundaries" as the only possible paradigm of economic development. Like the putative free market, "rational choice" collapses the diversity of the human experience into one category, the self-interested individualist prototype that has animated and totalized the economics profession in America. As this paradigm now proposes to colonize political science and sociology, it has no use for (and indeed views with deep hostility) anyone who happens to know something about a "foreign area," or, for that matter, the United States: they are all threats to the universality of this model, which can explain everything from how Japanese Diet members control the Ministry of Finance to why Indian widows throw themselves onto funeral pyres—with every explanation contingent on the listener knowing little or nothing about the subject itself. So-called formal theory takes this paradigm one step further: if "soft" rational choice seeks to verify the claims of its model empirically, through the collection and testing of data, the estimation of regression coefficients and the like, "formal theory" is a simple matter of the researcher staring at the game-theoretic mathematical formulas that appear on the computer screen, thus to determine how the real world works. If the theory does not explain political, social, or economic phenomena, it is the real world's fault.

The rise of these two paradigms of social science inquiry have put at risk the sub-fields of economic history, historical sociology, and comparative politics, and the entire area studies project. Why do you need to know Japanese or anything about Japan's history and culture, if the methods of rational choice will explain why Japanese politicians and bureaucrats do the things they do?[77] If some recalcitrant research problems nonetheless still require access to Chinese or Swahili, why not get what you need from a graduate student fluent in those languages, rather than an academic expert on China or Africa? The "soft" rational choice practitioner may in fact have language and area training, or if not, will still find value in the work of area specialists; once again they are the spelunkers who descend into the mysterious cave to mine a lode of "facts," which the practitioner will then interpret from a superior theoretical vantage point. The formal theorist, however, has no use for either of them.

This is hardly an idle matter of one paradigm contesting another in the groves of academe. Rational choice people are determined to have the social sciences their way, to dominate them and exclude those who disagree. This is evident in Harvard political scientist Robert Bates' injunction to the profession concerning which young scholars should get tenure: political science departments ought to "re-think their approach to evaluating junior personnel," he wrote; and, further,

> unless fortunate enough to be a native speaker of a foreign language or to possess an unusually strong mathematical background, most junior faculty will not be able to consolidate both area and analytical skills prior to facing the tenure hurdle, much less to produce research demonstrating a confident command of both. In making promotion decisions, therefore, rather than focusing purely on product, attention will have to be placed on investment.[78]

Rational choice proponents have no idea what "area specialists" actually do, but ritually caricature and cubbyhole their scholarship anyway. A scholar like Barrington Moore is certainly an expert on an "area"—originally, Russia. He is also a theorist of the first order. But his best-known work, *Social Origins of Dictatorship and Democracy*, is a classic of the comparative method precisely because of his deft mix of abstract theory and thoroughly known and thought through history. Scholars who work on Japan, India, China, France, the United States, and England—his six "case studies"—have all been required to come to grips with his analysis for the past three decades, whether they agree with it or not. But above all it is the modern experience of Germany that breathes through this work, and yet there is no German chapter. There need not be, since Moore's analysis of lord and peasant in the modern world is also a social science meditation on how the greatest catastrophe of modern times could possibly have occurred. Rational choice has never produced, and will never produce, a book that holds a candle to Moore's *Social Origins*. Yet Barrington Moore came out of the same oss/Ford Foundation/"area studies" nexus that I discussed earlier. If it is a choice between the slim pickings of contemporary rational choice and the oss-spawned likes of Moore, Cora DuBois, John Fairbank, Franz Neumann, and yes, Philip Mosely, I say gimme the oss old boys' network any day of the week.

Item four in the ssrc's new program proposes to turn the U.S. into an "area," and were it ever to succeed it would also transform the disciplines. Research on the United States is indeed an "area study" just like any other; but then it's our country and has all manner of idiosyncrasy and detail that the non-expert or foreigner could never possibly understand—and following upon that insight, you arrive at the dominance of Americanists in almost any history, political science, or sociology department. That they might be as blithely ignorant of how the world beyond American borders influences the things they study as any South Asian area specialist, makes no dent on their departmental power. Much more important, the ancient injunction to "know thyself" and the doctrine that there is no "thing in itself," makes comparative study obligatory. So, to have a "Joint Committee on the United States" under the ssrc/acls rubric would be a big step forward.

Kenneth Prewitt, president of the ssrc, wrote that for all the aforesaid reasons, and no doubt others that I am not aware of, the ssrc/acls has come to believe

> that a number of discrete and separated "area committees," each focused on a single world region, is not the optimum structure for providing new insights and theories suitable for a world in which the geographic units of analysis are neither static nor straightforward.[79]

Instead of eleven committees, the new plan will apparently constitute three, under the following general rubrics: area studies and regional analysis; area studies and comparative analysis; area studies and global analysis. There may also be a fourth comittee designed to support and replenish the existing scholarly infrastructure in the U.S., and to develop similar structures in various other parts of the world. Nonetheless Prewitt still envisions an important function for area specialists:

> If scholarship is not rooted in place-specific histories and cultures, it will miss, widely, the nuances that allow us to make sense of such phenomena as international labor flows, conflicting perspectives on human rights, [etc.].[80]

As this restructuring project got off the ground (before Prewitt became president in 1996), the ssrc's Heginbotham sought to justify it by reference to the unfortunate Cold War shaping of area studies in the early postwar period and the need for "rethinking international scholarship" now that the Cold War is over.[81] This odd return of repressed knowledge stimulated a sharp response: several scholars associated with Soviet and Slavic studies weighed in to deny that political pressures deriving from the Cold War agenda of U.S. foreign policy had much effect on their field, which often produced scholarship "strikingly independent of assumptions driving U.S. political preferences." Various area institutes may have been formed "partially in response to the Cold War," but nonetheless were able to conduct scholarship "without compromising their academic integrity." The authors also argued that the new ssrc framework

> will tear international scholarship from the rich, textured empirical base that has been assiduously developed through decades of research, moving it instead to a nebulous "global" framework for research.[82]

This is a nice statement of the likely outcome of the current ssrc/acls restructuring, but as we have seen Heginbotham is clearly right about the state's role in shaping the study of "foreign areas"; honest and independent scholarship was possible in the early area institutes, but the academic integrity of the institutes themselves was compromised by a secret and extensive network of ties to the cia and the fbi. It is a bit much, of course, for the ssrc to acknowledge this only now by way of justifying its new course, when it spent all too much time in the 1960s and 1970s denying that the state had any influence on its research programs.[83] More important, however, is the contemporary denial of the same thing, and here the ssrc's critics had a point.

If the current American administration has one "doctrine," it is a Clinton doctrine of promoting American-based global corporations and American exports through the most activist foreign economic policy of any president in history. Clinton's achievements in this respect—nafta, apec, the World Trade Organization and many other alphabet-soup organizations, and the routine, daily use of the state apparatus to further the export goals of U.S. multinationals—are all justified by buzzwords that crop up in the new ssrc plans: a world without borders, increasing globalization, the wonders of the Internet and the World Wide Web, the growth of multiculturalism, the resulting intensification of sub-national loyalties and identities, etc. Furthermore the ssrc drafts of its restructuring plan make clear the concern not just for scholarship, but for policy relevance and encouraging better capacities for "managing" the new global issues of the 1990s—a clear rationale for scholarship and "area expertise" to be at the service of national security bureaucrats.

I am by no means a purist on these matters, and I see nothing particularly wrong with scholars offering their views on policy questions, so long as the practice is not openly or subtly coerced by funding agencies and does not require security clearances (as the NSEA clearly does). The post-1960s SSRC, in my limited experience, has managed the nexus where state power and scholarship meet about as well as could be expected, assuming that there is some necessity to do it in the first place if the organization hopes to be funded as a national organizer of social science research. Many SSRC research projects and even a couple of its joint committees (notably the Latin American group) have had clear counter-hegemonic agendas and produced scholarship of enormous relevance to political struggles around the world.[84]

The SSRC/ACLS area committees have also been fertile ground for inter-disciplinary scholarship: for decades they offered a rare venue where one could see what a historian thought of the work of an economist, or what a literary critic thought of behavioralist sociology. Meanwhile my own experience in the university has led me to understand that an "area specialist" is as unwanted in the totalized world of Friedmanite economics as a *zek* from the Gulag would be at a meeting of Stalin and Beria. To the extent that the more diverse discipline of political science has produced any lasting knowledge about the world beyond our shores, it has almost always been done through the contributions of area specialists to the subfields of comparative politics and international relations.[85]

In 1994 Northwestern University won a grant from the Mellon Foundation to run two year-long interdisciplinary seminars in the hopes that they would bridge the areas and the disciplines. I participated in writing that grant proposal, and I directed the first seminar in 1995–96, "The Cultural Construction of Human Rights and Democracy." The results of this effort are not completely in yet, but it seems to me that this funding succeeded in providing a useful and important forum for interdisciplinary work, getting people to talk to each other across areas and disciplines, and I hope that the book that grew out of it will be valuable.[86] To the extent that the Mellon Foundation supports such seminars as an addition to the funding of existing area programs, it is a great service. To the extent that they represent a redirection of funding away from area studies, the seminars are no substitute for the training of people who know the languages and civilizations of particular places. You win with people, as football coach Woody Hayes used to say, and had there not been people already steeped in the regions we studied, inventing them would have been impossible—or at least forbiddingly expensive, when compared to the level of funding provided by Mellon.

In one of the SSRC restructuring plans there is this sentence: "There is no making sense of the world by those ignorant of local context-specific issues; and there is no making sense of the world by those indifferent to cross-regional and global forces." I think this is true, even if I would phrase the point differently. Although "area programs" trained many scholars and made possible a rare interdisciplinary intellectual program, the sad fact is that most area specialists were not interested in it. There is no reason, of course, why a person working on Chinese oracle bones should have anything in common with an expert on the Chinese communist politburo; their common habitus in a Chinese studies program was the result of an historical compromise between the universities and the state in the early Cold War period. In return for not complaining about the predominance of Kremlinologists or communist politics specialists, the oracle bone or Sanskrit or Hinduism specialist got a tenured sinecure and (usually) a handful of students in his or her classes. The state, the foundations, and the universities supported scholars who spent their entire lives translating the classics of one culture or another into English, often with next to no interaction with their colleagues. Many were precisely as monkish and unyielding to the intellectual life outside their narrow discipline as a micro-economist. I have never thought it too much to ask that a person like this find something to teach that would attract enough students into the classroom to pay the bills, but it happens all the time and now the area studies programs are paying the price; often representing enormous sunk costs, the faculty and the sinecures are very expensive now and unlikely to be sustained at anything like current levels in the future. If we end up having no Sanskrit, no Urdu, no oracle bones, and no Han dynasty history, it will not just be due to the ignorance of the foundations, the government, and the university administrators, but will also reflect the past privilege of the hidebound, narrow scriveners themselves.

Perhaps the most disappointing aspect of the new SSRC/ACLS restructuring and the apparent new direction of the major foundations is the absence of any reference to the basic motivation for so many of the new tendencies in the 1990s world that they hope to adapt themselves to, namely, the global corporation.[87] This is the motive force and modal organization for "globalization" and the technologies that speed it. Bill Gates' Microsoft is as dominant in this new sphere as John D. Rockefeller's Standard Oil was a century ago; and no doubt our grandchildren will vote for various governors and senators, if not presidents, named Gates—and the ones who become academics will go to the "Gates Foundation" for their research grants. Another symbolic American corporation, Coca-Cola, has become the first U.S. multinational to place overall corporate management in the hands of its world office rather than its historic national center in Atlanta. In that sense, SSRC is merely following Coca-Cola's lead by making the United States of America just another subsidiary, just another "area committee." All the globally competitive American corporations are all-out for multiculturalism, multiethnic staffs, a world without borders, and the latest high technology no matter what its impact on human beings, something evident in their media advertising: "Oil for the Lamps of China" may have been Standard Oil's slogan for selling kerosene worldwide, but now Michael Jordan as the high-flying, globe-trotting logo for Nike might as well be the logo for America, Inc. (Jordan and his Chicago Bulls have been particularly popular in "communist China"—just as in my household.)

This is not a matter of the ssrc raising a challenge to the global corporation, which is hardly to be expected, but it is a matter of not abandoning hardwon scholarly knowledge and resources that we already have—and here I am not speaking simply of the existing area programs. Because of the ferment of the 1960s, social science scholarship of the 1970s met a high standard of quality and relevance. In political science, sociology, and even to some extent economics, political economy became a rubric under which scholars produced a large body of work on the multinational corporation, the global monetary system, the world pool of labor, peripheral dependency, and American hegemony itself. A high point of this effort was Immanuel Wallerstein's multi-volume *Modern World-System*, but there were many others.

I would say that one of the shocks of my adult life was to see the alacrity with which many social scientists abandoned this political economy program, especially since the abandonment seemed roughly coterminous with the arrival of the Reagan and Thatcher administrations. Often the very social scientists who produced serious scholarship in political economy in the 1970s became the leaders of a march into the abstractions of rational choice and formal theory in the 1980s. One of the ssrc committees that sought to sustain this 1970s agenda was the States and Social Structures Committee (my bias: I was a member); it was summarily eliminated by a new ssrc president in 1991. Be that as it may, there remains a fine body of work in American political economy that could be the basis for a revival of scholarship on the global corporation and the political economy of the world that it creates before our eyes.

Conclusion

What is to be done? Immanuel Wallerstein recently offered some useful, modest suggestions, which I fully support:[88] encourage interdisciplinary work by requiring faculty to reside in two departments, bring faculty together for a year's work around broad themes, reexamine the epistemological underpinnings of the social sciences in the light of the eclipse of the Newtonian paradigm in the hard sciences, and re-invent a university structure still strongly shaped by the conditions of the 18th and 19th centuries. I have some additional modest suggestions, in the interest of continuing discussion and debate:

1. Abolish the social sciences and group them under one heading: political economy (if economics will not go along, connect it to the business school).
2. Regroup area studies programs around a heterodox collection of themes that allow us all to stand "off center"[89] from our native home and the (foreign?) object of our scholarly desires.
3. Raise funds for academic work on the basis of the corporate identity of the university as that place where, for once, adults do not have to sell their souls to earn their bread but can learn, write, produce knowledge, and teach the young as their essential contribution to the larger society.
4. Abolish the CIA, and get the intelligence and military agencies out of free academic inquiry.

Several commentators on earlier versions of this essay thought I was being much too hard on the social sciences. Actually, I was being satirical; I hardly expect anyone to follow my injunction. Of course there is much scholarship of lasting value in the social sciences, and the sub-fields of historical sociology, comparative politics, and economic history are eminently worth preserving, from my point of view. But economic history has been abolished from most economics departments, and the formalist hounds are hot on the heels of the other two subfields. The point I would stress is not my likes and dislikes, though, but rather that the historically limited and contingent theory of the rational, interest-maximizing individual is colonizing all the social sciences—and in so doing is abolishing them as creators of worthwhile knowledge whether we like that outcome or not.

If we began this paper with McGeorge Bundy, it is best to close it with words from one of the few scholars to speak out against the FBI purge in the early postwar period—and for his efforts, to suffer his due measure of obsessive FBI attention: historian Bernard A. DeVoto. In 1949 he wrote words as appropriate to that era as for the "National Security Education Act" and the "globalized" world of today:

The colleges . . . have got to say: on this campus all books, all expression, all inquiry, all opinions are free. They have got to maintain that position against the government and everyone else. If they don't, they will presently have left nothing that is worth having.[90]

Notes

1   Bundy's 1964 speech at Johns Hopkins, quoted in Sigmund Diamond, *Compromised Campus: The Collaboration of Universities with the Intelligence Community* (New York: Oxford University Press, 1992), p. 10.

2   For ample evidence of Bundy's intimidation of young scholars, see Diamond, *Compromised Campus*, pp. 3–6, and passim; on Bundy's contemporaneous CIA work, see Christopher Simpson, *The Science of Coercion: Communications Research and Psychological Warfare, 1945–1960* (New York: Oxford University Press, 1994). Bundy was particularly involved in the "Soviet Vulnerabilities Project" that W. W. Rostow ran for the CIA, along with Philip Mosely, Adam Ulam, and several other well-known Soviet studies scholars.

3   Robin Winks shows how the nexus between area programs and the state broke down in the 1960s, as (some) specialists on Southeast Asia condemned the American intervention in Vietnam. On the one hand, he writes, "the dog bit the hand that fed it," leading to a predictable decline in support for area studies programs; on the other, it was not and is not "the function of a university to be supportive" of state policies. (Winks, *Cloak and Gown: Scholars in the Secret War, 1939–1961* [New York: William Morrow, 1987], pp. 447–49.)

4   Michel Foucault, *Power/Knowledge: Selected Interviews and Other Writings, 1972–1977*, ed. Colin Gordon (New York: Pantheon Books, 1980), p. 96.

5   Barry Katz has written an informative, well-researched book that nonetheless barely scratches the surface in examining the problems inherent in professors doing intelligence work; furthermore he ends his story in the late 1940s. See *Foreign Intelligence: Research and Analysis in the Office of Strategic Services, 1942–1945* (Cambridge: Harvard University Press, 1989). Robert B. Hall's seminal study done for the SSRC in 1947 still makes for interesting reading, but Hall, of course, would not have had access to classified intelligence documentation on the government's relationship to area studies. (Hall, *Area Studies with Special Reference to Their Application for Research in the Social Sciences* [New York: Social Science Research Council, 1947]).

6   I presented some of the ideas in this essay at the Association for Asian Studies (AAS) in 1993, on a panel held in honor of the 25th anniversary of the *Bulletin of Concerned Asian Scholars*. I presented a much-revised version at the 1996 AAS meetings, and then published an earlier version in a symposium in this same *Bulletin* (vol. 29, no. 1 [Jan-March 1997], pp. 6–26). Various other people offered comments on my essay in this symposium, comments to which I responded in the subsequent issue (vol. 29, no. 2 [April-June 1997], pp. 56–60). As I said in the latter essay, my work on these matters is in no sense definitive, nor could it be. The subject is not what I am working on, nor is it part of my ongoing research, nor could it be. Why? Because we are nowhere near the truths of our profession and its relation to power, or the evidence that would allow us to assess and debate that relationship. The evidence that I have gathered is incidental to archival research on other subjects; my choice was to leave the information in the files, or find a way to get it out so that it could be discussed in hopes that others will come forward with more information. Moreover, that evidence was just a frag-

ment of what exists in the unmoving bowels of the national security state, especially the Central Intelligence Agency, which still declassifies next to nothing of real importance on the events of the postwar period (e.g., the destabilization of Mossadeq in Iran in 1953, the overthrow of the Arbenz regime in Guatemala the following year, the Bay of Pigs). Thus, it is simply not possible in 1997 to offer definitive answers to questions about the relationship of area studies to the state in the past half-century. Because some foundations (like Ford) and some universities (not Harvard) have opened their archives to varying degrees, it may be possible to look at one or two sides of that triangle. But the most important side would still be missing. For their helpful comments on the different versions of my essay I would like to thank Arif Dirlik, Bill and Nancy Doub, Harry Harootunian, Richard Okada, Moss Roberts, Mark Selden, Chris Simpson, Marilyn Young, Masao Miyoshi, and Stefan Tanaka. Obviously I am responsible for the views presented herein.

7 My ambivalence, it appears, was shared by Confucius. In the *Analects*, book 18, his judgement is *wu ke, wu buke,* namely, "no [absolute] acceptance or rejection" of serving the state. I am indebted to Moss Roberts for bringing this to my attention.

8 Katz, *Foreign Intelligence,* pp. 11, 29, 99, 115.

9 The CIA, for example, enjoins its employees from ever writing about anything to do with their work for the Agency without a prior security vetting, and prosecutes or hounds forever employees who write about their experiences anyway (like Frank Snepp and Phillip Agee).

10 Katz, *Foreign Intelligence,* pp. 2–5.

11 Ibid., pp. 159–61; see also Winks, *Cloak and Gown,* pp. 60–115.

12 Immanuel Wallerstein, "Open the Social Sciences," *Items* 50(1) (March 1966): p. 3.

13 Ezra F. Vogel, *Japan as Number One: Lessons for America* (Cambridge: Harvard University Press, 1979).

14 William Nelson Fenton, *Area Studies in American Universities: For the Commission on Implications of Armed Services Educational Programs* (Washington, D.C.: American Council on Education, 1947), paraphrased in Ravi Arvind Palat, "Building Castles on Crumbling Foundations: Excavating the Future of Area Studies in a Post-American World," University of Hawaii, February 1993. (I am grateful to Dr. Palat for sending me his paper.)

15 Cora DuBois, *Social Forces in Southeast Asia* (Minneapolis: University of Minnesota Press, 1949), pp. 10–11, quoted in Katz, *Foreign Intelligence,* p. 198.

16 Katz, *Foreign Intelligence,* p. 160.

17 Ibid.; also Palat, "Building Castles on Crumbling Foundations;" also Richard Lambert et al., *Beyond Growth: The Next Stage in Language and Area Studies* (Washington, D.C.: Association of American Universities, 1984), pp. 8–9.

18 See Betty Abrahamson Dessants, "The Silent Partner: The Academic Community, Intelligence, and the Development of Cold War Ideology, 1944–1946," Organization of American Historians annual meeting (March 28–31, 1996). Katz (*Foreign Intelligence,* pp. 57–60) argues for a break between the anti-fascist politics of the OSS and the anti-communist politics of the CIA, but a close reading of his text suggests many continuities into the postwar period, in the persons of Alex Inkeles, Philip Mosely, W. W. Rostow, and many others; an alternative reading would be that the anti-fascists, many

of them left-liberals, were either weeded out or fell by the wayside, distressed at the turn taken by American Cold War policies after 1947.

19   The letter is dated Oct. 28, 1948. Those who wish to pursue this matter can find additional documentation in the William Donovan Papers, Carlisle Military Institute, box 73a. Others included in this effort were Evron Kirkpatrick, Robert Lovett, and Richard Scammon, among many others. Christopher Simpson terms this same operation "the Eurasian Institute," listing it as a special project of Kennan and Davies, in which Kirkpatrick participated. See *Blowback: America's Recruitment of Nazis and Its Effects on the Cold War* (New York: Weidenfeld & Nicolson, 1988), p. 115; Diamond also has useful information on this matter in *Compromised Campus*, pp. 103–105.

20   Diamond, *Compromised Campus*, chapters three and four. Diamond also has several chapters on Yale. Robin Winks (in *Cloak and Gown*) also documented in some detail the extraordinary role that Yale played in providing faculty participants and student recruits for America's clandestine services, a phenomenon with which he is considerably more comfortable than a critic like Diamond. Like other analysts, Winks locates the origin of area studies in wartime intelligence work, especially for the R&A branch of OSS:

> It is no exaggeration to say that the rapid growth of area studies programs . . . grew out of the structure of the foreign service, the OSS, and the work of ancillary groups. . . . One finds the alumni of the OSS scattered throughout typical area studies programs. (pp. 114–15)

21   Boston FBI to FBI Director, Feb. 9, 1949, quoted in Diamond, *Compromised Campus*, p. 47; see also pp. 109–110.

22   Anthony Summers, *Official and Confidential: The Secret Life of J. Edgar Hoover* (New York: G. P. Putnam's Sons, 1993). Summers' evidence on Hoover's cross-dressing homosexual encounters is thin and offered mainly to titillate, but his extensive information on Hoover's suborning by organized crime seems undeniable.

23   For example, the Sigmund Diamond Papers (at Columbia University) contain an enormous file on Raymond A. Bauer's inability to get a security clearance to consult with the CIA in 1952–54, because he had once been an acquaintance of William Remington, whom the FBI thought was a communist. (See box 22.)

24   Diamond Papers, box 15.

25   Memo from SAC Boston to J. Edgar Hoover, 3/7/49, Diamond Papers, box 13.

26   Boston FBI report of 2/1/49, ibid.

27   Boston FBI report of 11/1/50, ibid. Box 14 also has an extensive file on Robert Lee Wolff's security check before he became a consultant to the CIA in 1951.

28   Mosely's files show that he worked with the Operations Research Office of Johns Hopkins on classified projects in 1949; that he had a top secret clearance for CIA work in 1951 and 1954; that in 1957 he had CIA contracts and was a member of the "National Defense Executive Reserve" assigned to the "Central Intelligence Agency Unit," and that he renewed his contracts and status in 1958; that he worked on an unnamed project for the Special Operations Research Office of American University in 1958; that he was cleared for top secret work by the Institute for Defense Analysis (IDA, a major academic arm of government security agencies) in 1961; and that in the same year he

kept Abbot Smith of the CIA informed about his travel to the USSR in connection with ACLS/SSRC work on academic exchanges with that country. See Philip Mosely Papers, University of Illinois, box 13, Operations Research Office to Mosely, Feb. 28, 1949 and Nov. 2, 1949 (the latter memo refers to "the optimum use of the social sciences in operations research"); also "National Defense Executive Reserve, Statement of Understanding," signed by Mosely 12/19/57 and renewed, 6/26/58 (the latter memo also refers to a "contract" that Mosely has with the CIA, separate from his activities in the "Executive Reserve"); also Mosely to Abbot Smith, March 10, 1961. (Mosely begins the letter to Smith, "In accordance with the present custom I want to report my forthcoming travel plans.") Smith, an important CIA official and colleague of Ray Cline and William Bundy among others, is not here identified as a CIA man. But he is so in Ludwell Lee Montague, *General Walter Bedell Smith as Director of Central Intelligence* (University Park: Pennsylvania State University Press, 1992), pp. 138–39, where information on Abbot Smith's CIA work can be found. In 1961 Mosely worked with the IDA on a secret project on "Communist China and Nuclear Warfare" (S. F. Giffin, Institute for Defense Analysis, to Mosely, Nov. 24, 1961, and Mosely to Giffin, Dec. 6, 1961). See also various memoranda in box 2, including a record of Mosely's security clearances. Mosely was an American of Bulgarian extraction; unlike most Bulgarians, he hated the Soviets.

29 Ibid., box 4, letter from W. W. Rostow, MIT, to Mosely, 10/6/1952.

30 Ibid., Frederick Barghoorn (Yale University) to Mosely, 1/17/1952.

31 Ibid., Whitman to Mosely, 10/5/55; Mosely to Whitman, 10/10/55.

32 Ibid., box 13, Nathan B. Lenvin, U.S. Department of Justice, to Mosely, April 20, 1953.

33 Ellen Schrecker, *The Age of McCarthyism: A Brief History with Documents* (Boston: Bedford Books of St. Martin's, 1994).

34 Mosely Papers, box 18, Langer to Mosely, May 11, 1953.

35 Ibid., Paul F. Langer to Mosely, Carl Spaeth, and Cleon O. Swayze, May 17, 1953.

36 "Report Submitted by Paul F. Langer to the Director of Research, Board on Overseas Training and Research, the Ford Foundation," April 15, 1953, ibid. The books Pye later authored were *Guerrilla Communism in Malaya* and *The Spirit of Burmese Politics.* One could also include in this group Daniel Lerner's *The Passing of Traditional Society* (New York: The Free Press, 1958), another central text in comparative politics; Lerner had worked with Pye, Ithiel deSola Poole, and other political scientists at MIT's CENIS on projects dealing with communications and society, insights from which were later used in the CIA's Phoenix program in Vietnam. Much of this research was funded under CIA or government contracts for psychological warfare. On this see Christopher Simpson, "U.S. Mass Communication Research and Counterinsurgency after 1945: An Investigation of the Construction of Scientific 'Reality,'" in *Ruthless Criticism: New Perspectives in U.S. Communication History,* ed. William S. Soloman and Robert W. McChesney (Minneapolis: University of Minnesota Press, 1993).

37 The conference was held October 9–10, 1953. See the list of those who attended, Mosely Papers, box 18.

38 Ibid., box 18. As Diamond shows, such considerations extended to Carnegie's acknowledged policy of excluding scholars who were "way to the left," which at one point led to worries about Derk Bodde and Arthur Schlesinger Jr., and major fretting

about Gunnar Myrdal; however these cases paled before Carnegie's concerns about the Institute for Pacific Relations and Owen Lattimore (*Compromised Campus*, pp. 299–301.)

39 Mosely Papers, box 18, George B. Baldwin to Mosely, Dec. 21, 1954.

40 Ibid., Swayze to Mosely, Oct. 21, 1954; Langer said he was involved in developing Chinese studies, in Langer to Mosely, Spaeth, and Swayze, May 17, 1953.

41 JCCC, *Report on the Conference on the Status of Studies of Modern and Contemporary China* (SSRC, New York, March 1968), quoted in *ibid.*, p. 98.

42 Ibid., box 13, Smith to Mosely, February 28, 1961; see also notations on Mosely to Smith, March 10, 1961.

43 Ibid., Mosely to Smith, March 16, 1961.

44 Ibid., Mosely to King, April 17, 1962.

45 Ibid., Mosely to John R. Thomas (of the IDA), July 19, 1963, where Mosely refers to RAND funds going to help Zagoria complete his dissertation, and IDA funds that helped support Zagoria for a post-doctoral project; see also Mosely to Brzezinski, August 20, 1963.

46 I refer for example to the "Studies in Political Development" series, sponsored by the Committee on Comparative Politics of the Social Science Research Council, yielding by my count seven books, all published by Princeton University Press in the mid-1960s and all of which became required reading in the political science sub-field of comparative politics: Lucian W. Pye, ed., *Communications and Political Development*; Joseph LaPalombara, ed., *Bureaucracy and Political Development*; Ward and Rustow's *Political Modernization in Japan and Turkey*; James S. Coleman, ed., *Education and Political Development*; Joseph LaPalombara and Myron Weiner, eds., *Political Parties and Political Development*; Lucian W. Pye and Sidney Verba, eds., *Political Culture and Political Development*; and Leonard Binder (along with Pye, Coleman, Verba, LaPalombara and Weiner), eds., *Crises and Sequences in Political Development*.

Gabriel Almond and James S. Coleman authored the ur-text in this literature, *The Politics of the Developing Areas* (Princeton: Princeton University Press, 1960). Almond also was an academic participant in intelligence projects at the time. Documents in the Max Millikan Papers at MIT show that Almond was a member of a classified "Working Committee on Attitudes toward Unconventional Weapons" in 1958–61, along with Air Force Gen. Curtis LeMay, Harvard academic Thomas Schelling, and MIT's deSola Poole among others. The committee studied "a variety of types of unconventional weapons, nuclear, biological, and chemical, for use in limited war." The social scientists were expected to find ways of "minimizing" unfortunate reactions by target peoples to the use of such weapons—or as Millikan put it in his letter to Almond inviting him to join the committee, the committee would discuss measures to be taken that "might reduce to tolerable levels the political disadvantages of the use of a variety of such weapons," and how to use weapons of mass destruction and still have "the limitability of limited conflict." (Millikan to Almond, Nov. 3, 1958, Max Millikan Papers, box 8.) Millikan's long memorandum of Jan. 10, 1961, to the committee stated clearly that use of such weapons might include crop-destroying agents that would cause general famine; the covert use of this and other unconventional weapons would be accompanied by overt denial that the U.S. had used them. The key case he mentioned would be use of such weapons against a conventional Chinese attack on a country in Southeast Asia (Millikan Papers, box 8).

47 Simpson, "U.S. Mass Communication Research and Counterinsurgency." Simpson has long lists of social scientists who worked for the oss and other intelligence agencies during the war: they include Harold Lasswell, Hadley Cantril, Daniel Lerner, Nathan Leites, Heinz Eulau, Elmo Roper, Wilbur Schramm, Clyde Kluckhohn, Edward Shils, Morris Janowitz, and many others; after the war, "a remarkably tight circle of men and women" continued to work for the state, including Lasswell and Lerner, Cantril, Janowitz, Kluckhohn, and Eulau.

48 Ellen Shrecker, *No Ivory Tower: McCarthyism and the Universities* (New York: Oxford Univesity Press, 1986), pp. 97–104, 125.

49 Jane Sanders, *Cold War on the Campus: Academic Freedom at the University of Washington, 1946–64* (Seattle: University of Washington Press, 1979). She has two entries for J. Edgar Hoover and three for the fbi in her index, none related to the 1949 case.

50 Allen's influential argument—"soon [to] be embraced by the academic world"—was, in Schrecker's presentation, "that academics 'have special obligations' that 'involve questions of intellectual honesty and integrity.' Communism, because of its demand for uncritical acceptance of the Party's line, interferes with that quest for truth 'which is the first obligation and duty of the teacher.' . . . [Thus] Allen concluded that . . . 'by reason of their admitted membership in the Communist Party . . . [the two teachers were] incompetent, intellectually dishonest, and derelict in their duty to teach the truth' " (ibid., p. 103).

51 See Donovan's advice to President Allen in Donovan Papers, box 75a, item 889, handwritten notes dated Feb. 3, 1949 (the advice was given earlier than this date). George Taylor also worked with Allen in devising an effective strategy for firing communists and radicals. See Sanders, *Cold War on the Campus*, p. 79.

52 See Diamond Papers, box 15.

53 Diamond Papers, box 15, Lew Nichols to Charles Tolson, May 18, 1948.

54 Diamond Papers, ibid.; see also other memos in this file in May 1948, and fbi Seattle to Hoover, 11/4/48. Allen met with Hoover on May 6, and made several subsequent visits to the fbi in 1948 and 1949. According to Clyde Tolson's memo to Nichols of May 19, 1948, a Los Angeles fbi agent named Hood had no special relationship with ucla, but was "personally friendly with the Dean and just a few days ago the Dean wrote him regarding an individual and wanted certain information." The memo says Hood didn't give him the information. When President Allen later asked the local fbi agent responsible for contacts at uw to furnish information on six professors, however, Tolson told the agent to give it to him. (See Tolson to Nichols, June 21, 1948.) Allen also asked the fbi for information on Melvin Rader, a stalwart radical whom I remember from when I taught at uw, and who was never accused of being a cp member—although as fbi information shows, Allen told the fbi he thought Rader was "closely connected with the Communist Party"—while offering no evidence. Later it developed that the Canwell Committee had faked evidence on Rader. (Sanders, *Cold War on Campus*, p. 86.)

55 Diamond Papers, box 15, Seattle fbi to Director fbi, 1/26/49.

56 On that episode, which tarnished UW's reputation among scientists for years thereafter, see Sanders, *Cold War on Campus*, pp. 138–42. Oppenheimer had been invited to lecture at both Washington and the University of Oregon; he arrived in Portland and was told two things: (1) Einstein had died while he was en route; (2) the University of Washingon had rescinded its invitation.

57 Ibid., Seattle FBI to Director, FBI, 6/8/55; Seattle FBI to Director, FBI, 8/24/55. The invited conference guests included representatives from the State Department, the Voice of America, and Radio Free Europe; Alex Inkeles was a featured speaker, as were Taylor and historian Donald Treadgold.

58 Sanders, *Cold War on Campus*, p. 94. The best study of the Psychological Strategy Board is Gregory Mitrovich, "The Limits of Empire," unpub. ms., 1997. I am grateful to Dr. Mitrovich for letting me read his manuscript, which shows that McGeorge Bundy and Walt Rostow were deeply involved in the CIA's psychological warfare programs, one of which was Radio Free Europe, a CIA covert program in which the Ford and Rockefeller foundations were also heavily involved (pp. 70–71).

59 Simpson, *Blowback*, pp. 118–22; Robert P. Newman, *Owen Lattimore and the "Loss" of China* (Berkeley: University of California Press, 1992), pp. 363–64. On Taylor's introduction to Mandel, see Diamond, *Compromised Campus*, p. 308. (Poppe has always denied that he was an ss officer, saying that as a foreigner he could not have joined the ss; he also claimed that his "research" had nothing to do with the "final solution"—which was announced at the Wannsee Institute in January 1942 by ss leader Reinhard Heydrich, with Adolph Eichmann in attendance. See Simpson, *Blowback*, p. 48n.)

60 See for example Richard D. Lambert, *Points of Leverage: An Agenda for a National Foundation for International Studies* (New York: Social Science Research Council, 1986).

61 Guide to the Max Franklin Millikan Papers, MIT.

62 This transcript was provided to me by Kai Bird, who got it from David Armstrong, who is writing a dissertation on the Rostow brothers. I am grateful to Kai for alerting me to the transcript. The first few pages of the original document are missing, so some of the participants are hard to identify; furthermore their statements were truncated and paraphrased by the transcriber. The meeting was held on May 18, 1959. (All quotations in the text come from this transcript.) Millikan was an assistant director of the CIA in 1951–52, and director of CENIS from 1952 to 1969, the year in which he died.

63 Ibid.

64 Professor Diamond begins each of his chapters on Harvard's Russian Research Center with the "official stories" given out to the public about its activities: "We have no classified contracts," "all our research is generated out of our own scholarly interests," the various centers and institutes were established by disinterested foundations, and that, in general, all views to the contrary reflect some sort of conspiracy theory (Diamond, *Compromised Campus*, pp. 50–51, 65).

65 The summary is by Anne Betteridge, Executive Officer of the Middle East Studies Association, and is to be found in *Asian Studies Newsletter* (June/July 1992), pp. 3–4.

66 *Asian Studies Newsletter* (June/July 1992), pp. 4–5.

67 "The National Security Education Program," *Items* 46(2–3) (June-September 1992): pp. 17–23.

68 Ibid., p. 19.

69 "Area scholars are extremely sensitive to the damage that can be done to their personal reputations and to their ability to conduct scholarship abroad when they come to be perceived as involved with intelligence or defense agencies of the U.S. government" (ibid., p. 22).

70 See Amy Rubin, "South Korean Support for U.S. Scholars Raises Fears of Undue Influence," *The Chronicle of Higher Education* (October 4, 1996), pp. 10–11.

71 Mark Selden, James K. Boyce, and the *Bulletin* editors, "National Security and the Future of Asian Studies," *Bulletin of Concerned Asian Scholars* 24(2) (April-June 1992): pp. 84–98. See also the updated information in *Bulletin of Concerned Asian Scholars* 24(3) (July-September 1992): pp. 52–53.

72 See the report of our work, a response by John Fairbank, a further response by Moss Roberts, and David Horowitz's essay, "Politics and Knowledge: An Unorthodox History of Modern China Studies," in *Bulletin of Concerned Asian Scholars* "Special Supplement: Modern China Studies," 3(3–4) (summer-fall 1971): pp. 91–168.

73 Ibid., p. 127.

74 Ibid., p. 105.

75 I have seen drafts of the restructuring plan and some of the various joint committee responses, all dated in late 1995 and early 1996, but cannot cite the documents under the terms of their provision to me; this is not because of secrecy so much as the provisional and evolving nature of the restructuring itself, as ssrc administrators respond to suggestions and complaints about their new plans. I will also refer to Kenneth Prewitt's "Presidential Items," in the March 1996 issue of the ssrc's newsletter called *Items*, which reflected the essence of the restructuring drafts I have seen.

76 Prewitt, ibid., p. 15.

77 See Chalmers Johnson and E. B. Keehn, "Rational Choice and Area Studies," *The National Interest*, no. 36 (summer 1994): pp. 14–22.

78 Robert Bates, contribution to *PS: Political Science and Politics* 30(2) (June 1997): p. 169. This is the newsletter of the American Political Science Association.

79 Prewitt, "Presidential Items," p. 16.

80 Ibid.

81 Stanley J. Heginbotham, "Rethinking International Scholarship: The Challenge of Transition from the Cold War Era," *Items* (June-September 1994).

82 Robert T. Huber, Blair A. Ruble, and Peter J. Stavrakis, "Post-Cold War 'International' Scholarship: A Brave New World or the Triumph of Form over Substance?" *Items* (March-April 1995).

83 Heginbotham wrote: "Those who shaped the emerging institutions of international scholarship in the early years of the Cold War should have been more attentive to a range of issues involving the autonomy and integrity of scholars and scholarly institutions." The response of Huber, Ruble, and Stavrakis to this truth was to ask Heginbotham to name names: "Which individuals were inattentive to scholarly autonomy and integrity?" they ask, since such people should have "an opportunity to defend themselves."

84 One good example is a book that grew out of a conference sponsored by the Latin American committee: David Collier, ed., *The New Authoritarianism in Latin America* (Princeton: Princeton University Press, 1979).

85 Heginbotham's critics refer to "the damage done by the exceptionally strong behavioral wave that swept through the social sciences in America thirty years ago," but the damage has been at least as great from the rational choice wave of the 1980s–90s.

86 Bruce Cumings and Meredith Woo-Cumings, eds., *Contending Cultures of Human Rights and Democracy* (Rowman and Littlefield, forthcoming).

87 Also noteworthy is the similarity between the rhetoric of globalization that Ken Prewitt uses to justify the new SSRC course, and rhetoric that was used a decade ago by Richard Lambert in his *Points of Leverage* (for which Prewitt wrote the preface; see for example pp. 1–2, 7, 27–31). "Globalization" may be the new mantra, but maneuvering to find ways to meet the needs of our global corporations is getting old by now.

88 Wallerstein, "Open the Social Sciences," pp. 6–7.

89 I use Masao Miyoshi's phrase in his *Off Center* (Cambridge: Harvard University Press, 1993), suggestive of a stance placing the scholar neither in his native country nor on the ground he studies but in a place "off center," yielding a parallax view essential to new knowledge—about anything. Miyoshi made his scholarly reputation as a literary critic of Victorian novels, and now writes about Japan (and the U.S.) with a rare insight born of a rare experience.

90 Quoted in Diamond, *Compromised Campus*, p. 43.

The Disappearance of Modern Japan:
Japan and Social Science
Bernard S. Silberman

For academics one of the more interesting, if not completely surprising, aspects of the post-World War II period was the evolution of the almost complete dominance, if not hegemony, of global social science by American practitioners. By the late 1950s American practice had become the standard in all the social sciences. New paths were broken—behavioral studies based on surveys and structured experiments in political science and psychology, developmental studies, quantitative analysis and modelling in political science and sociology, formal mathematical analysis and modelling in economics, and "interdisciplinary" studies, whose most prominent offspring was area studies, all made their appearance in this period. The total nature of the war that had recently ended and to which was now added the possibility of an even more encompassing disaster with the rise of the Cold War, lent great weight to the notion that an understanding of the culture of past and future enemies and allies was important. With government participation and subsidies area studies flourished. At the heart of the area concept was the commitment to the notion of culture as an integrated holistic entity which constrained individuals to achieve social order.

In recent years, however, area studies have come under attack from several directions and appear to be in the process of dissolution.[1] This essay is an attempt to understand the nature of these attacks on area studies through a discussion of the stresses and conflicts faced by Japanese studies in recent times. Indeed, area studies appears to be in the process of dissolution as pressure has come to be applied to and by the Social Science Research Council to reorganize the area studies committees into more functionally oriented ones.[2] Thus, for example, Stanley J. Heginbotham, vice president of the council in 1994, reported receiving a letter from the Andrew W. Mellon Foundation announcing a new program "largely intended to replace the Foundation's support for area studies, as they are traditionally defined."[3]

These committees might well have disappeared much earlier if not for continued although declining foundation and government support. This support has produced a fragile solidarity among the recipients. This essay, then, is an attempt to understand the increasing impatience of much of social science with the idea of societies such as Japan being the object of integrated holistic analysis —that is, as a *field*.

Some of the impatience with area studies no doubt arises from the stresses of a harsher fiscal climate for universities. When money is short those areas of university life that are not firmly anchored in a departmental structure are the first to be accused of intellectual shallowness. Surely the criticism that area studies is somehow inferior in methodology and conceptual rigor to social science disciplines falls considerably short of the mark. The social science disciplines are, after all, arbitrary constructions arising from the eighteenth-century Enlightenment fascination with categorizing and the nineteenth and twentieth-century economic incentives and compulsion to draw professional boundaries. The fragility or arbitrariness of the disciplines is revealed by the fierceness and swiftness of their defense of their boundaries. Fundamentally, the problem of Japanese and area studies generally—how they are described, whether they are useful in any fashion as a concept or whether they are, on the contrary, a bafflement, a source of bemusement—is both an academic and a political problem.

A variety of social scientists have sought to make area studies an autonomous field. In the process there has been a progressive fractionation of each of the area studies into a number of different camps. It is accurate to say, for example, that presently there are now at least several or, perhaps, as many as three Japanese studies—a sign or symptom of the meaning of Japan as an object of study. Each of these has become autonomous and sports its own experts. Their expertise has produced abstractions which, I believe, distances them from society at large and robs it of an intelligent lay public constituency.

Once upon a time, possibly, it *could* be said that there was something one could indeed call "Japanese studies." That time might be seen as an age of innocence when American social scientists, influenced very powerfully by German romanticist and idealist thought, had a singular view of what constituted the object of study—those unique patterns of behavior and language evoked by history which seem to confirm the universal presence and patterns of unique identities rather than universal similarities. But for some time now there has not been sufficient agreement on a single view of what those patterns mean or where they fit in with the persistence of what we continue to recognize, for example, as Japanese society or, for that matter, whether such patterns exist outside of our own interests and purposes. Rather, what we have instead are a number of Japans and a number of Japanese studies. That is, we can say that presently in the social sciences Japan is observed, dissected, and constructed through several quite different lenses. But whatever position is taken it can, I believe, be shown that they enunciate views of the area under study as the object of political evaluation. In the case of Japan the conflict is essentially over the negative and positive evaluation of what constitutes the main axis of Japan's capacity to sustain an integrated culture—one that can be an object of study.

The first of these positions might be termed "oversocialized"; a second, "undersocialized"; and a third might be categorized as postmodernism or perhaps, for want of a better label, might be called contingent (these terms are used here in a critical but not pejorative sense).

What I mean by "oversocialized" is an approach that we often find in the disciplines of anthropology, political science, sociology, and history.[4] My contention here is that area studies was created out of these "oversocialized" views of individuals. Viewing it in these terms leads us, I believe, to an understanding of the weaknesses of this view which have made it vulnerable to the undersocialized and postmodern critiques.

For shorthand purposes, the oversocialized view can be crudely summed up in the word "culture." The essential weakness of this concept is an inherent tendency to make "culture" the sufficient cause of institutional formation and individual constraint.[5] In the other direction the "undersocialized" conception is most evident in the recently popular expression "rational choice." This approach counters and critiques cultural constraint with the notion that individuals are constrained by subjective rational calculation, which is thus at the bottom of all institutional formation. This view sees culture as lacking contingency or eliminating options and therefore not a sufficient cause for the emergence and transformation of institutions. This latter view leaves the way open for postmodern epistemological freedoms of choice in deconstructing and devaluing norms and social constructs, which in turn also leads to the dissolution of holistic stable structures like "Japan." The result of this clash of views is to break down the power of "culture" as a concept by which institutions may be explained—in effect, accusing this conception of being one in which individuals are constrained by social facts over which they have little or no control—there are no individual choices, only social ones.

The oversocialized view has its origins in the nineteenth-century romantic/idealist notion that reason resides in history rather than in human rationality. This view rejected the Enlightenment idea that reason was in some sense autonomous. Thinkers like Herder and, later, Hegel sought to show that reason was different with each age and place—that it worked its way forward and upward and was reflected in ever-more complex orders of unique social institutions.[6] More important for our purposes here is that this view emphasized that the facts of each time and society were the means of coming to some general understanding of the state of reason at any particular time. Reason was historical and autonomous but not individual and free floating.

Out of this idea rose, as the nineteenth century wore on, the concept of social facts. In the face of a shifting and fluid world there were attempts by people like Durkheim, Mauss, Tonnies, Spencer, and even Weber to provide a stable foundation for the understanding of social behavior by organizing observed social behavior into categories, "social facts," which were not reducible to individual rational choices. In doing so they sought to establish the fact that it was not subjective reason or will that brought order to human behavior. Rather, there were exogenous continuing social forces at work.

The discovery of the social by such figures as Comte, de Maistre, and DiBonald who transformed the Cartesian *cogito* to "I think, therefore I am from somewhere; by exercising my powers of reflection, I do not affirm my sovereignty, I betray my own identity."[7] The counter-enlightenment of which these were formidable representatives sought to provide stability and order out of the transformation and flux of society in two ways: through providing categories of social facts which persisted in each society or through narrative ordering of social facts. The latter sought underlying immutable forces in history—those which underlay the constant flux. This mode is best reflected in Marx's wonderful analytical narrative of the *Eighteenth Brumaire of Louis Bonaparte.*[8] Despite himself, Marx's structuralist bent was overwhelmed by this splendid analytical narrative. Here the particular *French* social facts of class, of the social relations rising out of the dominant mode of production, were constructed into an analytical narrative of a very high order, but one which explained a very particular event. The narrative seemed to deprive the event of its universality even though it came to be viewed as an analytical model for examining the bourgeois seizure of power. Bonapartism, as Marx described it, was to be used as a way of examining and explaining seizures of power in the modern bourgeois world.

This tradition was carried on in Japan by the *ronoha* and *kozoha* schools of marxist interpretation. For the West this tradition was perpetuated by E. H. Norman's eclectic adaptation of *ronoha* and (with somewhat greater emphasis) on *kozoha* schematic narratives. In his classic *Japan's Emergence as a Modern State*[9] Norman refashioned elements of *rono-kozoha* analyses after the *Eighteenth Brumaire* and produced a compelling analytical narrative that also established a set of particular Japanese social facts of class that produced an equally particular event (the Meiji Restoration) and a uniquely Japanese set of consequences. The uniqueness of Japanese "social facts," however, made it extremely difficult to shape the Japanese experience as a typical example of a universal condition produced by rational individual responses to the constraints of the mode of production. It was precisely this difficulty which has produced a seemingly endless controversy over what the Restoration meant in terms of the social relations arising from a dominant mode of production.[10]

Another side of this mode was formulated by Ruth Benedict's *Chrysanthemum and the Sword*.[11] She created a set of behavioral categories based on the "social facts" of everyday behavior. Out of this emerged a schema of cultural identity in which the polarities of obligation and shame played major roles. In doing so, she achieved two significant things: she created the archetype of the oversocialized individual, and she constructed an order of everyday life that appeared to be a seamless coat that enclosed Japanese society.

Although not explicit, one cannot read *Chrysanthemum and the Sword* without realizing how constantly in the present and non-historically based Benedict thinks these norms and values are. More important, Benedict leaves us with the view of the Japanese as individuals almost totally constrained by internalized social norms which provide the basis for the social facts that make up an integrated holistic Japanese culture. It is easy to see here how this view—that the social facts of culture dominate individual choices and ideas of appropriateness—can elicit a specific conception of identity. To a considerable degree *Chrysanthemum and the Sword* is as much about American identity as it is about Japanese norms and values. Each of the norms and values catalogued by Benedict has its spoken or unspoken polar opposite in the stereotypical conception of American values: individual pragmatic market relations vs. group network obligations; individual internalized conscience vs. external shame determining appropriate behavior.[12]

These two works, perhaps more than any others, shaped the character (and identity) of much of Japanese studies in the United States and to a considerable degree in Europe and Japan as well. At several levels these two constructions of "social facts" sought to restore order to a world which had lost its unity within living memory under the ceaseless hammering of modernity. From 1868 to the present an enormous mass of intellectual energy has been aimed at Japan, by Japanese as well as non-Japanese, in the attempt to find some stability beneath the flux of modernity and industrial capitalism. In the case of Norman it set off a whole series of attempts by American scholars in the late 40's, through the 50's and into the early 60's to construct alternative narratives.[13] This, of course, occurred within the context of an emergent Cold War—a war which sought to field a victor in defining the configuration of modernity and twentieth-century history. Benedict's book became the touchstone for explaining not only Japan's capacity to undertake major wars but also Japan's ability to acquire the accoutrements of modern society.

Very soon indeed the modes of analysis in these works became part and parcel of the modernization constructs which came to dominate much of comparative political science, sociology, and anthropology in this period. These narratives sought to show that Japan had been merely derailed in the process of modernization. The problem with Japan, these narratives unfolded, was that she was too enthusiastic about catching up to the West, and this led to a mismatching of cultural norms and modern institutions—a kind of cultural dyspepsia.[14] Getting back on the rails was and had to be accomplished exogenously—by defeat in wwii—the obverse of Marx's characterization of the Eighteenth Brumaire (the first time farce, the second tragedy, instead of the obverse). What followed was Japan's economic success within the confines of a democratic regime. However, this success could not be laid to the democratic political regime. It was more than evident even to the most casual of observers that the groundwork for this economic success had been laid prior to the war.

There was rather startling agreement here between marxists and structural functionalists (who, between them, dominated the discourse on Japan's development well into the 1970s) that the groundwork for economic development had been laid in the nineteenth century. However, since economic success and modernization had occurred under several different governmental regimes since the Restoration, it could not reasonably be laid to any specific political regime. The only alternative explanation which emerged and could emerge from these modernization narratives was that culture, springing out of the cunning reason of history, was responsible. This success was thus laid to the cultural norms which allowed, in Nakane Chie's (and many others) structuralist conception, new wine to be poured into the old bottles which made up Japanese society and identity.[15]

The neat thing about this explanation was that it restored order to Japanese history. Japan's history was not to be characterized by successive breaks and bewildering events and catastrophic wars. Rather, in this view Japan was characterized by *procedure*. The whole body of seemingly immutable *Nihonteki* norms and values were procedural rules without substantive goals—they were instrumental means for achieving any set of goals whether it was modernization or imperialism—Nakane Chie's new wine in old bottles.[16] This procedural view of Japanese society restored wholeness to Japan's history and identity.

It was, as we shall see, the perfect companion to the democratic structure created under the Occupation. That structure was also a procedural one. As the Political Section of scap soon discovered, democracy could not be simply a function of American values. Democracy had to be a procedural solution to the problem of social order and a just society or it could not be exported as an answer to communism.

Nor were the marxist versions devoid of similar ironies. To put the argument crudely, Japan's development was a consequence of its historical marginality in the process of the emergence of industrial capitalism. Japan's unique history and placement in the development of national structures produced a unique response—a response that produced violent discontinuities. These discontinuities were, however, papered over and perpetuated by the persistence of feudal structures which "feudalized" the Japanese middle classes, and thus provided a continuity which was not dialectical.[17]

Perhaps more striking is the degree to which cultural anthropology in its Boas/Kroeber/Benedict genealogy came to serve as the basis for the creation of area studies in the post-WWII era. The concept of a holistic culture was adopted by the major consultants to the creation of a post-surrender policy. Concerns about the emperor's key place in the web of Japanese values led to a policy of imperial retention but, perhaps, not emasculation.[18] The desire of the early Japanese post-war Japanese specialists to retain the basic core elements of Japanese society which might make it easier to govern and transform the society led, ironically, to encouragement of the view that Japanese culture was unique. But what was unique about it? Increasingly the view that Japanese uniqueness rested on its ability to copy and to emulate rather than create and invent was traced to the unique quality of its cultural norms which emphasized, so to speak, structure over content. Emphasis on structure removed the moral or at least ethical baggage of content. The Japanese, in effect, are able to copy without endangering their value structure because "there is no there there."

This holistic view of Japanese culture as an almost seamless web of norms and values centered around relationships was, in a sense, not only echoed in the Boasian stream of social anthropology and its *volksgeist* tradition but was also confirmed by it.[19] Benedict's book reverberated on several levels. The most immediate and concrete was perhaps the creation of centers like the Center for Japanese Studies at the University of Michigan. Michigan's Center, founded in 1947, was created and dominated by anthropologists and geographers—so much so that the history and political science students were often required to do field work in the anthropological tradition. Following from this emerged the tradition, powerfully present still (try to get a degree in comparative politics, for example, without going to the "field"), that training in any kind of social science (with the exception of economics in the last several decades) concerning another society requires presence and research in the field.

This is completely distinct from the Sinological model which had dominated in the prewar period. The Sino-Japanological tradition emphasized the knowledge of classical languages and texts as a means of understanding the enduring unique character of a society. One did not need to engage in "fieldwork." The essence of a society was present in its great texts—the colloquial was merely a dim and diluted reflection of this essence. Arthur Waley, after all, did not step foot in Japan—nor did he ever really feel the need to do so.

At another level, Benedict's work on Japan came at a propitious time for both the Japanese and the Americans. Published immediately after the war at the nadir of modern Japanese history it provided an authentication for the Japanese which the defeat in war had seemingly destroyed. There could be few happier circumstances than this one. Benedict's version of Japan provided the basis for reauthenticating a Japanese identity. Moreover, and perhaps most important, it was an identity which Benedict showed was not irretrievably attached to any particular political system. Her schema might show why the Japanese were able to sacrifice themselves or subjugate themselves to social authority, but it could not show why prewar Japan had the politics it did. This made it possible to transform the emperor from a political fact into a cultural one and to separate culture from politics.

This had two unexpected consequences. The first was that the egalitarianism of culture would displace the demand for equality. Democracy and hierarchy could thus exist side by side—"We are, after all," the slogan might go, "all Japanese together, bound by strong ties of cultural norms." These norms of hierarchy become the only means of access to society. Hierarchy provides a place for everyone and everyone knows their place. Anarchy is thus avoided. Democracy as procedure did not require equality outside of the realm of the ballot box in Japan any more than it did in the United States in the nineteenth and twentieth centuries. So long as majorities dominated, third-generation Japanese of Korean descent and *buraku-min* could continue to be placed at the lowest levels of hierarchy. It goes without saying that women could be placed here as well since it is culture that consigns them to their places.

The second consequence of separating culture from politics was the ability to separate *economics* from politics and attach it to *culture.* The Occupation's desire and hope to construct a liberal democratic regime was fortuitous and became another happy coincidence. The regime the Occupation sought (and by and large was successful in creating) to construct was a version of liberal democracy which was founded on the idea of procedure. That is to say, members of the Political Section of SCAP were largely of the view that the essence of democracy as a political system inhered in its capacity to provide a form of fairness and equality. Through the use of appropriate rules and procedures which would give equal weight to each individual's desires and link this to the accountability of those selected to achieve those desires, Japan would not again rise to imperial military might.[20]

All else would follow from this. In this conception democracy is not there to create a system of achieving or possessing individualism. These things might or might not emerge. The point, as Japanese politicians came to see, was that there was nothing inherent in procedural democracy that precluded what they believed to be the unique character of Japanese society. At the same time, if politics was procedure and thus relatively without particular cultural content, then it was easy to see how it was that Japan had developed so rapidly despite an "evil" authoritarian prewar political system. Economic development, as the postwar period showed, could roll along just as merrily under a democratic regime as under a fascist or absolutist or limited constitutionalist regime—all of which Japan experienced between 1868–1945 and none of which had seriously hindered economic development. Even the Pacific War turned out to be less than disastrous since it cleared away an increasingly obsolete technology and laid the groundwork for capital renewal.

The flowering of the Cold War at this time made the whole idea of an authentically unique Japanese culture even more appealing to Japanese and American political leaders. The notion of unique cultural identities had a kind of elective affinity for the Western market-oriented polities. The idea of cultural uniqueness could be directly opposed to the universalist cocnceptions of the communist world. American Cold War ideology stressed the notion that cultural identity need not be lost under procedural conceptions of liberal democracy. Each society could thus make its unique contribution—democratic institutions would not homogenize societies.[21] So powerful (or threatening) was the appeal of this idea that late-Stalinist and post-Stalin policy regarding the nationalities increasingly came to emphasize national uniqueness and constructed boundaries to authenticate that singularity of identity. Needless to say, it was a policy which did much to undermine the universalism of the communist regime(s).[22]

In the dense atmosphere of the Cold War of the 1950s and 60s the idea of cultural uniqueness and identity provided sustenance and legitimation for the receding American Occupation and conservative Japanese politicians to resist the demands and visions of the left, which were labeled as "un-Japanese."[23] Culture was transformed into ideology, or maybe it was really ideology being transformed into culture. This made it possible, as I have suggested earlier, for politics to be made into the administration of the economy. The economy became the true place or representation of an authentic Japaneseness. It was in the economy and its organizations that the so-called core Japanese values of loyalty, obligation, strong ties, consensus, and the like were to be found and sustained. Japanese-style management and industrial relations dispossessed politics as the focal point of Japanese identity.

All of this, perhaps, gives an exaggerated impression of the influence of Benedict's *Chrysanthemum and the Sword*. And to some extent it is so. My intention, in this hyperbolic presentation, is to indicate the degree to which this one genealogy of the American anthropological tradition became a means for "understanding" the "enemy" and, then, how this oversocialized understanding came to be used in a startlingly efficient manner by American and Japanese political leaders and intelligentsia. It is not coincidental that the trail stretches from wartime purpose through Cold War utility.

This tradition has produced a wide range of social science work on Japan. Others have continued this tradition in sociology and anthropology, as well as in political economy and political science generally. Recent work on Japanese identity also hearkens back to this tradition. One can see it in the political science literature in the constant reference to Japanese values of consensus. Thus, for example, a recent work edited by Kumon Shumpei and Henry Rosovsky[24] leans heavily on the notion of the individual constrained by a set of internalized norms kept in place by a combination of self-monitoring and the monitoring of those around them.

In more recent years this view has come increasingly to be tempered by attempts to resolve the problem of individual autonomy. Building on the structural slack indicated by Nakane (by this I mean the structuralist conception that the frame is what counts and can be filled with anything, and the frame will make sense of it more or less), recent work in anthropology has sought to clarify how language acts to mediate between individual desires and cultural norms. This, it is argued, allows the individual the ability to negotiate the social context within the frame by contesting meanings others seek to impose on the frame. The problem here is how to account for boundaries. That is, what can be said to be the constraining frame in any specific situation? Unless the frame can be specifically determined or defined then the argument must be forced back upon some idea of essential culture and identity which maintains the frame in the face of constant renegotiation. Thus, the oversocialized conception of the individual cannot avoid an essentialism that rejects any pluralist view of culture, society, and identity.

The second approach—the "undersocialized view"—has its roots in Enlightenment classical economics. Individuals, in this view, are seen to make choices and organize strategies unhampered by social relations. This is a view which stems from the self-referential rationality (subjective rationality) so characteristic of the modernist view as it emerged in the nineteenth century. The observation of true social facts was seen to be restricted to those acts of choice which produced prices and, thus, markets. Both classical and non-classical (marxist, utopian, syndicalist) economists sought to explain "social facts" as part of an orderly metasocial and metahistorical orderly process. The non-classical economists saw choice as a function of internalized class roles; i.e., objective class rationality as opposed to subjective individual rationality. The classical economists saw choice as rational as well, but this was a rationality that was individual and self-referential. Social facts, as opposed to random ones, were the consequence of many *individuals* ordering their priorities and seeking to fulfill them. The choices of a multitude of individuals with similar priorities imposed constraints which were reflected in the structure of prices which was described metaphorically as a market. Prices were determined sytematically by the interaction of many choices and, thus, were no mystery. Prices were the consequence of an underlying order—the ubiquitous "invisible hand."

In this view markets are seen as metasocial structures of order which depend on choices regardless of culture. That is, the same mechanisms are at work everywhere where there are large numbers of individuals seeking to fulfill their desires. It is a system in which the global individual becomes the basis for political and cultural agency. It is clear that this is also a metatheory which seeks to construct order out of subjective rationality. So long as everyone is free to "truck and barter" as Adam Smith would have it, order would prevail. Priorities would become self-evident and aggregrate choices would produce institutions. The clue to order here is the self-regarding individual.

As Hirschman has put it,

> [because idealized markets involve] large numbers of price-taking anonymous buyers and sellers supplied with perfect information . . . [they] function without any prolonged human or social contact between the parties. Under perfect competition there is no room for bargaining, negotiation, remonstration or mutual adjustment and the various operators that contract together need not enter into recurrent or continuing relationships as a result of which they would get to know each other well.[25]

Or to put it slightly differently:

> The solution of . . . classical economics is antithetical: [to the Hobbesian solution of autocratic authority] repressive political structures are rendered

unnecessary by competitive markets that make force or fraud unavailing. Competition determines the terms of trade in a way that individual traders cannot manipulate. If traders encounter complex or difficult relationships, characterized by mistrust or malfeasance, they can simply move on to the legion of other traders willing to do business on market terms; social relations and their details thus become frictional matters.[26]

In the "undersocialized" view the problem of finding an underlying or immutable order governing the structure of choice is resolved by elevating self-regard to the basic principle of social behavior. Decision-making is, thus, a function of rational choice—individuals pursuing their own best interests regardless of what others may do. Since markets, whether for commodities or social relations, do not always "clear" the social outcomes of such behavior, they produce problems that are referred to as collective-action problems. Individuals under these circumstances are seen as attempting to resolve such problems with least harm to themselves. The result of clearing markets or of collective-action problem resolutions is seen as an equilibrium; that is, a condition in which no one has an incentive to abandon the present or existing outcomes.

From this point of view the concept of a holistic order (embodied in the idea of culture) that constrains choices seems subsumed under the notion of equilibrium. That is, culture is merely symptom and epiphenomenon of an equilibrium produced by self-conscious and self-regarding individuals who understand that they are better off under existing choice mechanisms than any other of which they might conceive. Equilibrium and integrated culture are thus seen as the outcomes of situations where large numbers of individuals are free to make choices. Culture is thus the product of market conditions where individuals through their aggregate experience and behavior can establish appropriate behaviors and rules for social relations.

In terms of Japan we can see this approach in recent work by Ramseyer, Rosenbluth, McCubbins and others.[27] Here, Japanese behavior is seen as integrated by rules of rational individual choice—rules which are essentially universal or global in character. We are left to infer, with some ease, that equilibrium failed to appear in post-Meiji Japan, for example, as a consequence of the failure to overcome the Prisoner's Dilemma. As Ramseyer and Rosenbluth write in their conclusion:

> Armed with simple assumptions about self-serving behavior and simple theories of how institutions constrain action, we explored the choices successive generations of political leaders made between 1868 and 1932. The oligarchs, we suggested, collectively wanted neither to concede popular

representation, nor to grant military independence; their internal strife left them no better option.

Finally, we used Japanese history to reflect back on the theoretical literatures. Institutions, we found, may long outlive their framers. These framers, moreover, may not select an institutional arrangement that maximizes their collective interests. Even political leaders with sufficient resources to rig the rules of the game may be unable to do so effectively—because they fail to collude. For all the weight of Japan's so-called "consensus-building" culture, the oligarchs just could not figure out how to get along. And that, we argued, turned out to be of no small consequence.[28]

This quotation, I think, makes it clear that in this approach the universal character of self-regarding rationality displaces culture as the axis along which Japanese society arranges itself.

What is interesting about both the "oversocialized" and "undersocialized" conceptions represented here is that they are essentially conservative when it comes to social change or constraints on individual choice. Why is it then that someone like Chalmers Johnson has expressed his views of the rational choice approach with open and quite fervid contempt?[29] The rational choice arena is essentially a conservative one also, and the views of Ramseyer and others in the rational choice domain are quite evident. Why, then, the conflict?

This perhaps can be explained by their intellectual genealogies. Underlying Johnson's understanding of Japan seems to be a belief in the unique cultural structure of Japan with its integrating and constraining norms and values as the major source of Japan's success as a "developmental state."[30] In short, he seems to hold an "oversocialized" view. Like many whose genealogy hearkens back to a functionalist view of society, Johnson appears to believe that culture is functional and in the case of Japan is the source of a social equilibrium—this is basically, it seems to me, a conservative view. From this position, knowledge of the society and culture are essential if there is to be any serious discussion of what occurs. Culture is an independent variable: a set of macro constraints that are important in helping to explain the kind of collective-action resolutions that emerge. Area studies thus is treated gently and encouraged.

Those committed to a rational choice approach are grounded in a nineteenth-century liberalism with its emphasis on methodological individualism and the concept that the market provides an equilibrium. Area studies is thus evaluated from the political stance of methodological individualism and its conservative outlook.

Culture in this schema is not an independent variable but a dependent one.

Rather, the independent variables are the variance in interests of individuals and the obstacles to choice in achieving interests. Where interests or desires have a narrow variance and there are few obstacles to choice, the chance for resolving collective choice problems and producing equilibrium ("clearing the market") is high. The persistence of this condition is what produces culture (institutions). When the variance is narrow and obstacles to choice are many, the outcome is politics (decision-making rules). Where the variance is high and obstacles to choice are few, the outcome is a free market (contract rules). In a situation where variance is high and obstacles to choice are many, instability is immanent and when it persists structural decline and conflict are the consequence. Thus, it comes as no surprise that the highest value is likely to be accorded to an equilibrium where the greatest number of interests and choices are available. Surely this must be the case where self-regarding interest is seen as the highest value for individuals in the pursuit of everyday affairs. It follows from this that rational choice outlooks are inimical to area studies which stress macro constraints as the determining factors in the emergence of culture and institutions.

Recently there has been, especially in anthropology, a return to Mead's conception of social order emerging as the consequence of a dynamic relationship between the individual and the social context. Thus,

> at stake here is a constitutively oriented approach toward social life. In other words, the organization of self or society is not reducible to a "core" of patterns or structures; or even a "core" of person that is found "behind" its participants. Nor is order itself discarded as a concept. Instead, the approach to order is embedded in social conext, and includes the process by which participants constitute social situations, *and thereby participate in a dynamic that includes the mutual process of their constituting and being constituted by social order.* This process *is* the order, and this order includes the organization of self and society, since it is mutually constitutive of both.[31] (italics in the original)

Here there is clearly a rejection of the global character of the individual—of methodological individualism. At the same time there is a disaggregation of culture. The two poles of universalist conceptions are here abandoned. The modernist impulse toward universalism is suppressed by an emphasis on the particular. In place of modernist universalism there is a conception that has strong elements of pragmatism combined with a distaste for the universal and a commitment to the particular. Despite overtones of Bourdieu, Heidegger, and others this position tends to operate on a conception of embeddedness in which the individual is in a constant bargaining process with the central elements of social order. There is not only a criticism of essentialism but also of the idea of a stable and unchanging metaorder. This attack on holism and methodological individualism carries with it a political stance as do these positions. From a certain point of view this, in some ways, postmodern conception also denies the possibility of area studies. One can look at particular societies and seek to discern along what axis the individual situates him or herself with regard to social order. The *process* (procedure) is universal, the substance is not. Area studies begins with notions of fixed substance and cannot provide us with a real understanding of what goes on in the lives of the Japanese. Japan is not a fixed entity of any sort. There is no essential personality nor is there an essential Japaneseness. What is incontrovertibly Japanese is the axis along which the "bargaining" takes place. The axis doesn't require a genealogy, it is there and understood to be the product of a historical but not a substantive *process*.

The emphasis on process recalls us to our understanding of liberal democracy. It is precisely because liberal democracy views the individual as seeking to fulfill desires within a context of social order that procedure—*process*—is central to its conception. At the heart of liberal democracy is the understanding that process is the social order. Rather than the European phenomenologists to which the postmodern or contingent view in American social science seeks to trace its genealogy, its true(er) genealogy lies with the typically American strain of pragmatic conception of individual and social order represented by individuals such as George Herbert Mead, William James, and John Dewey. These are, in many ways, the bearers of a conception of individual and social order that is, ironically enough, incontrovertibly American. It is American and liberal in the sense that past, present, and future are constantly in the process of change—it is the tradition of no tradition. This too has the defects of its advantages. The commitment to process and procedure too often creates pressures for conformity, but it is a conformity that after all provides the means by which our society hangs together. In this sense this postmodern view is really the last gasp of modernism. Procedure and process are the metaphysical basis on which we hang our hopes for order and stability.

Conclusion

Under the impact of these different conceptions, the modern Japan we once knew has disappeared. In its place there are now several Japans, each masking a political stance that makes any unity of understanding impossible and improbable. These conflicting views and politics have become endemic to all area studies. The political/methodological conflicts which now rage in the social sciences provide us with little in the way of guidance. One thing is clear, however, given these conflicts and regardless of their outcome, area studies may be viewed as a Cheshire cat—little left but the smile, and that too will disappear shortly. Instead, these conflicts will take place within disciplinary boundaries. Cultural/macro, rational choice/micro, and contingent/micro-macro explanations have become the protagonists in the struggle for dominance in American social science. Underlying these manifest conflicts over method is a struggle over what are the means for achieving social order—community, market, or self-conscious process. Each of these is veiled behind a rhetoric of methodology—a rhetoric which has escalated in heat and tendentiousness. We are each of us now left to the tender mercies of our disciplines where we must legitimate our field of analysis by our commitment to a methodological position. In this dynamic the scientism of rational choice has made it appear that it alone follows a scientific paradigm and therefore ought to hold a privileged position. In return the oppositional methodologies view rational choice methods as basically uncultured (in both senses of the word). This, of course, raises the question of whether area studies as we know it is worth the struggle. Given its weak institutional base, area studies does not seem worth the struggle unless you have a commitment to an ideological-political position. If this is the case then the relationship of these methodological stances to political ones must be discussed openly and not through the surrogates of methodologies and methodological debates.

Notes

1 The vigor of this attack is especially noticeable in political science. See, for example, Robert H. Bates, "Letter from the President: Area Studies and the Discipline," *APSA-CP: Newsletter of the APSA Organized Section on Comparative Politics* 7(1) (1996): 1–2. Also, Robert H. Bates, "Area Studies and the Discipline: A Useful Controversy?" *PS: Political Science and Politics* (30)2 (June 1997): 166–69.

2 Stanley J. Heginbotham, "Rethinking International Scholarship: The Challenge of Transition from the Cold War Era," *Items: Bulletin of the Social Science Research Council* 48(2–3) (June-Sept. 1994): 33–40.

3 Ibid., 36.

4 In the use of the terms "oversocialized" and "undersocialized" I have depended on Mark Granovetter, "Economic Action and Social Structure: The Problem of Embeddedness," *American Journal of Sociology* 91(3) (November 1985): 481–510.

5 Margaret S. Archer, *Culture and Agency: The Place of Culture in Social Theory*, rev. ed. (Cambridge: Cambridge University Press, 1996), pp. 1–9.

6 Charles Larmore, *The Romantic Legacy* (New York: Columbia University Press, 1996). See especially pp. 38–49.

7　Alain Finkelkraut, *The Defeat of the Mind* (New York: Columbia University Press, 1995), p.25.

8　Karl Marx, *The Eighteenth Brumaire of Louis Bonaparte* (New York: International Publishers, 1964).

9　(New York: Institute of Pacific Relations, 1940).

10　Some sense of the longevity of this argument can be obtained from Germaine A. Hoston, *Marxism and the Crisis of Development in Prewar Japan* (Princeton: Princeton University Press, 1986).

11　(New York: Houghton Mifflin & Company, 1946).

12　See, for example, pp. 95–96; 112–15; 150–57; 181–87; 228–35; 253–56.

13　Perhaps the most ambitious of these was the Princeton University Press series entitled *Studies in the Modernization of Japan*. The series included the following volumes: Marius B. Jansen (ed.), *Changing Japanese Attitudes toward Modernization* (1965); William W. Lockwood (ed.), *The State and Economic Enterprise in Japan* (1965); Ronald P. Dore (ed.), *Aspects of Social Change in Modern Japan* (1967); Donald H. Shively (ed.), *Tradition and Modernization in Japanese Culture* (1971); Robert E. Ward (ed.), *Political Development in Modern Japan* (1968); James W. Morley (ed.), *Dilemmas of Growth in Prewar Japan* (1971).

14　As Edwin O. Reischauer put it:

> Growth in any society is likely to be uneven, thus producing new imbalances. This seems to be true even when growth has been a relatively slow, evolutionary process, but imbalances are more likely to become dangerously pronounced when growth has been artificially forced, as in Meiji Japan, by a strong leadership utilizing the experience and patterns of more developed societies. Japan's very success in changing her technology and institutions in the nineteenth century seems to have contributed to what had become dangerous imbalances by the 1920's and 1930's.

"What Went Wrong? in James W. Morley, ed., *Dilemmas of Growth in Prewar Japan* (Princeton: Princeton University Press, 1971), p. 509.

15　Nakane Chie, *Tateshakai no ningen kankei: Tanitsushakai no riron* (Tokyo: Kodansha, 1967). This has been translated under the title *Japanese Society* (Berkeley: University of California Press, 1970).

16　Nakane, *Japanese Society*, pp. 102–3; 114–15.

17　See Kojima Hinehisa, *Nihon shihonshugi ronsōshi* (Tokyo: Arisue, 1976), pp. 148–62.

18　Robert E. Ward, "Presurrender Planning: Treatment of the Emperor and Constitutional Changes," in *Democratizing Japan: The Allied Occupation*, ed. Robert E. Ward and Sakamoto Yoshikazu (Honolulu: University of Hawaii Press, 1987), pp. 4–10.

19　See Matti Bunzl, "Franz Boas and the Humboldtian Tradition: From *Volksgeist* and *Nationalcharakter* to an Anthropological Concept of Culture," in *Volksgeist as Method and Ethic: Essays on Boasian Ethnography and the German Anthropological Tradition*, vol. 8: History of Anthropology, ed. George Stocking Jr. (Madison: University of Wisconsin Press, 1996), pp. 17–78.

20　Robert E. Ward, "Conclusion," in *Democratizing Japan*, ed. Ward and Sakamoto, pp. 407–8.

21　See for example the summation by Sidney Verba of the the extensive and influential workshops sponsored by the Committee On Comparative Politics of the Social Science Research Council resulting in the nine-volume Princeton University Press series entitled *Studies in Political Development*. Sidney Verba, "Sequences and Development," in *Crises and Sequences in Political Development*, ed. Leonard Binder et al. (Princeton: Princeton University Press, 1971), pp. 310–12. Also in the same volume, see Lucian W. Pye, "Identity and Political Culture," pp. 101–34.

22 Ronald G. Suny, *The Revenge of the Past: Nationalism, Revolution, and the Collapse of the Soviet Union* (Stanford: Stanford University Press, 1993).

23 John W. Dower, *Empire and Aftermath: Yoshida Shigeru and the Japanese Experience, 1878–1954* (Cambridge, Mass.: Council on East Asian Studies/Harvard University Press, 1988), pp. 316–68.

24 *The Political Economy of Japan. Volume 3: Cultural and Social Dynamics*, (Stanford: Stanford University Press, 1992).

25 Albert Hirschman, "Rival Interpretations of Market Society: Civilizing, Destructive, or Feeble?" *Journal of Economic Literature* 20(4) (1982): 1463–84.

26 Mark Granovetter, "Economic Action and Social Structure: The Problem of Embeddedness," *American Journal of Sociology* 91(3) (November 1985): 481–510.

27 Mark J. Ramseyer and Francis McCall Rosenbluth, *Japan's Political Marketplace* (Cambridge, Mass.: Harvard University Press, 1993). Matthew McCubbins and Francis McCall Rosenbluth, "Party Provision for Personal Politics: Dividing the Vote in Japan," in *Structure and Policy in Japan and the United States*, ed. Peter F. Cowhey and Matthew McCubbins (New York: Cambridge University Press, 1995).

28 Mark J. Ramseyer and Francis McCall Rosenbluth, *The Politics of Oligarchy: Institutional Choice in Imperial Japan* (Cambridge, Mass.: Harvard University Press, 1995), p. 172.

29 Chalmers Johnson, "Perception vs. Observation, or the Contributions of Rational Choice Theory and Area Studies to Contemporary Political Science," *PS: Political Science and Politics* (30)2 (June 1997): 170–74, is an excellent example of the genre.

30 Chalmers Johnson, *Japan: Who Governs?: The Rise of the Developmental State* (New York: W. W. Norton, 1995), pp. 109–10.

31 Jane M. Bachnik and Charles Quinn Jr., *Situated Meaning: Inside and Outside in Japanese Self, Society, and Language* (Princeton: Princeton University Press, 1994), p. 5.

Bad Karma in Asia
Moss Roberts

In a rare instance of power speaking truth, former U.S. Secretary of Defense Robert Strange McNamara confessed that in Vietnam, "We were wrong, terribly wrong. We owe it to future generations to explain why."[1] With the evasive candor commonly affected by high-level bureaucratic managers, McNamara expressed only anguish; he did not acknowledge any responsibility to "past generations" nor did he propose any measures to right the wrongs "we" had done. His powerfully subjective outburst—really more "I" than "we"—thus lacks objective moral dimension: he speaks for no other war leader, much less for the American nation.

Confined to simple past tense, McNamara's assessment leaves unaddressed the post-1975 consequences of the Vietnam War, the still-exploding land mines, the lingering defoliant poisons, the covert Sino-American war against Cambodia's people, and above all the unassuaged grieving of the survivors in all the countries of the former Indo-China, as well as in America. Looking *backward* at the war is now McNamara's main interest. Together with high-level Vietnamese military officials, McNamara is searching for missed moments when a different "we" (*their* leaders and *ours*) might have seized an opportunity for peace. In his new work, *Argument without End*, McNamara hopes to find Vietnamese of his rank and station to share his sense of guilt, having found so few Americans to do so.[2]

Contrition was far from the minds of U.S. political authorities and their spokesmen as the Vietnam War was coming to an end in April 1975. Disavowal of responsibility was the more common theme. Representative of such thinking is this passage from a *New York Times* editorial from 4 April 1975, entitled "Earthquake Vietnam":

> Vietnam now has to be seen as an earthquake, not a battlefield; our moral commitment must be to its victims. . . . The fate of millions of displaced

persons in South Vietnam, Cambodia, and Laos depends on humanitarian assistance [from the United States through the United Nations and voluntary agencies]. . . . America's future in this corner of the world depends on its contribution to restoring lives brutalized by the war in which we were so deeply enmeshed.

The editorial transforms illegal acts of war into acts of god or natural violence, and the U.S. role, virtually an afterthought to the editorial writer, is treated as a passive if not accidental involvement. Appealing for "moral commitment" and "humanitarian assistance," as if these were the priorities of "our" foreign policy, this *Times* editorial speaks weightily of the "fate of millions," and for the Vietnamese war victims the editorial uses the obsolete World War II term for international refugees, "displaced persons," as if the year were 1945. (How often have wars the United States has fought in Asia been draped with the mantle of sanctity that World War II is assumed to possess?)

Protestations of moral commitment notwithstanding, the U.S. government organized no postwar humanitarian assistance to benefit the people in Vietnam, Cambodia, or Laos; though later, individuals and private groups (veterans among them) did try to help war victims in the region. Revenge, not healing and reconciliation, was the real U.S. policy in 1975—revenge in the form of fomenting war in Cambodia in collusion with the Chinese. Thus the evils that McNamara wrought lived on.

To review the unfolding of these evils I have chosen to work backward in time, moving from present effects to past causes. U.S. involvement in all three nations of Indo-China was at all times subordinate to the primary problem of U.S. relations with China. Therefore, to contextualize and illustrate events in Indo-China, this essay addresses the changing pattern in U.S.-China relations by focusing on these questions: (1) How did China factor into U.S. policy toward Cambodia during and after the Vietnam War? (2) How did the United States and China, after two decades of enmity, become "friends" in the early 1970s, and how did this policy change relate to the Vietnam War? (3) How did the United States and China, allies against Japan in World War II, become "enemies" after World War II, and how was this change part of a broader pattern of colonial restoration in Asia? (4) How did U.S. favor in Asia shift from Japan to China beginning in late 1938, and how did this switch set the stage for future (post-World War II) entanglements of U.S. policy in Asian affairs?[3]

Cambodia and the China Factor

Last to be freed from the ordeal of war, Cambodia sprang back into news headlines in June 1997 as the Khmer Rouge (KR) insurgents under Pol Pot disintegrated, and Pol Pot himself was captured and put on trial by his own men, with his death reported soon after. Much about Pol Pot and his movement remains unknown. What *is* known has been presented in the media in a slanted and reductionist manner so that the U.S. public could hardly learn the extent and complexities of outside involvement in his movement. The media also ignored earlier contributing factors to the genocide that Pol Pot's forces launched soon after they entered Cambodia's capital, Phnom Penh, in April 1975.

1975–1979

Once in power the Pol Pot regime continued to pursue a policy of civil war. Committed to a program of primitive nationalism in the guise of "Maoist" revolutionism, the KR liquidated many "foreign" and elite sectors of Cambodian society. Cambodia's Vietnamese minority was a salient target. The KR's civil war policy quickly evolved into one of war against Vietnam itself. Estimates of the overall death toll appearing in the U.S. press have fluctuated widely, with numbers presently running between one and two million.[4] This was a period when Sino-U.S. global military cooperation was developing rapidly, and both governments wanted to encourage the KR to undertake military action against Vietnam.

The Khmer Rouge moved covertly against Vietnam until early 1977, and overtly thereafter. Pol Pot's 1978 raids on southern Vietnam's western borders compelled the war-weary Vietnamese to invade and install a new government in Cambodia in December of that year, a month after signing a treaty with the USSR. Pol Pot retreated to conduct guerrilla and sabotage operations with ever-larger and more-public military, economic, and diplomatic backing from China and the United States.

The January 1979 Vietnamese counter-invasion of Cambodia brought KR rule, after less than four years, to an end. The Vietnamese put in power a new Cambodian government, with Heng Samrin as president and Hun Sen as foreign minister. Official atrocities ended but the Cambodians knew little peace. Khmer Rouge forces went over to armed insurgency, conducting terrorist campaigns against the new government. In this, the KR won increasing support and sponsorship from the United States and China, who for "strategic" reasons of their own had decided to keep the Cambodian civil war going and prevent the new Cambodian government from stabilizing and sharing in the newly established general détente in East Asia.

Coverage of Cambodia in the U.S. press pictures the Americans virtually as bystanders during this period, with connections between U.S. agencies and the Khmer Rouge usually handled in a tangential and evasive fashion. Yet the salient facts about U.S. involvement are universally available. Commenting on U.S. actions in the post-1979 period, Cambodia scholar Ben Kiernan writes: "For eleven years after [the] overthrow [of the Khmer Rouge] Washington has supported the occupation of Cambodia's UN seat by those very genocidists [Pol Pot's KR], while opposing their opponents [Vietnam, USSR] and providing military aid to their allies [China, Thailand, domestic factions]."[5]

Pinpointing the origins of Sino-American collaboration with the Khmer Rouge remains difficult. The documents are at present secret and may one day be illegally destroyed by the CIA (as they have already shredded the Iran files). Context and circumstance, however, support the conjecture that the collaboration was formed around 1975. Chinese support for the Khmer Rouge was visibly formalized in August 1975, two months after Pol Pot made a secret visit to China.[6] At that time China promised the new regime one billion dollars in military aid over several years while denying Vietnam's pleas for assistance with its postwar reconstruction effort.[7] It is unlikely that a sum of this magnitude came solely from China. Future declassification of U.S. government documents should reveal an American contribution, and judging by the context of 1975 it may have been large. Jay Peterzell has reported that "according to Jack Anderson, the financial burden of this [China's] support has been shared by the United States. . . . Anderson described a CIA planning document which said the agency had been channeling money through China to Pol Pot's Khmer Rouge."[8]

Prominent among the rationales for backing Pol Pot was the desire of both the United States and China to prevent Vietnam from consolidating Cambodia (and Laos) into its sphere of influence and thus reestablishing the former Indo-China (Vietnam-Cambodia-Laos) as a Soviet ally. Achieving this "strategic" goal by means other than war—by a peace process, for instance, or by the offer of U.S. aid in rebuilding what it had destroyed in Vietnam, Cambodia, and Laos— was never seriously attempted. But the "strategic goal" may actually have been no more than a rationalization for a cruder, crueler goal: continuing the Vietnam War through proxies. The truth, as is often the case, may have been the reverse of appearances: that is, that the United States and China wanted to isolate Vietnam by driving it into alliance with the USSR.[9]

In an article written in the *Far Eastern Economic Review* in 1981, Derek Davies questioned "why. . . the Heng Samrin regime [installed by Vietnam] excite[s] such bitter opposition that Asean, China and the United States prefer to back Pol Pot and his bloodstained henchmen of the Khmer Rouge? The official answer," Davies noted, "is that, as a matter of principle, those nations refuse to recognize a government put in place by an occupying army. This argument is not altogether convincing." Davies speculated about another motive—one perhaps more on the United States's side than on the Chinese—namely, "an element of vengefulness against the country which had the temerity to beat the Americans." Part of the U.S. tactic was to dangle "normalization" in front of the Vietnamese. Foreign Minister Nguyen Co Thach traveled to the United States in October 1978 with hopes of negotiating a normalization of U.S.-Vietnam relations. Davies reports that U.S. officials made "Thach [wait] in New York for three weeks. Instead of flying back to Hanoi via Paris with normalization agreed as he had hoped, he flew instead to Moscow where, on November 3, 1978, . . . he signed the Vietnam-Soviet Treaty of Friendship and Cooperation which finally impaled Vietnam on the Soviet hook."[10]

1969–1975

In most U.S. reportage the story of the Cambodian "killing fields" is casually dated from April 1975, when KR forces overthrew Lon Nol and entered Phnom Penh, shortly before the final evacuation of U.S. forces from Saigon. However, that is only part of the story, part of the truth. More of the truth is to be found in the parts of the story that have gone unmentioned.

The origin of the genocide that gripped Cambodia from 1975 to 1979 lay in large measure in the years when the U.S. war in Vietnam was at its height: 1969 to 1975. In this earlier period Cambodia passed through the equivalent of a holocaust at the hands of the American war leaders as they tried desperately through massive bombardment to regain some initiative in their war against Vietnam (and to keep the Air Force bureaucrats and their suppliers profitably occupied). Bombing was continual from March 1969 to August 1973; the worst stretch was the last (between February and August 1973), when "American bombers dropped 257,465 tons of bombs on Cambodia . . . 50 percent more than the total tonnage dropped on Japan during World War II."[11] In July 1973 Congress belatedly and indecisively put a stop to the bombing (allowing the U.S. Air Force to continue its aerial onslaught during a six-week grace period).

Tactically, the American leaders were trying to stave off the collapse of their "ally" Lon Nol, titular ruler of Cambodia. "Strategic" explanations for the bombing included convincing Hanoi of Washington's determination, demonstrating support for U.S. satellite regimes in the region, destroying networks and bases that aid the "enemy," and making an object lesson of anyone who defied American imperatives. One must not overlook, however, the banal mercenary motive of profits resulting from the consumption of ordnance and equipment.

There was continuous pressure at the highest levels of U.S. authority for maximum utilization of air power. When bombing in North Vietnam was halted, greater bombing in South Vietnam followed; when bombing in South Vietnam was halted, bombing in Cambodia rose. "American bombing in Indochina was like an insane game of musical chairs," writes Vietnam historian Marilyn Young. "As a region was removed from the list of acceptable targets, the total tonnage was simply shifted to the remaining allowable areas."[12]

In the postwar period, U.S. domestic reportage redesigned the historical record, ritually underplaying the effects of five years of massive U.S. aerial bombing of Cambodia.[13] One of the little-noted effects was the fact that the magnitude of this bombardment, its willfully indiscriminate destructive intent, and its contempt for the rules of military conduct helped set the stage for the subsequent horrors under Pol Pot.[14] "The longer the bombing continued, the stronger Pol Pot's faction grew," writes Marilyn Young.[15] Ben Kiernan agrees that U.S. bombing was a major cause for the growth of the KR: "From the ashes of rural Cambodia arose Pol Pot's Communist Party of Kampuchea (CPK). It used the bombing's devastation and massacre of civilians as recruitment propaganda and as an excuse for its brutal, radical policies and its purge of moderate communists and Sihanoukists."[16]

1969

Nineteen sixty-nine was a pivotal year for Asia and America. As U.S. war policy in Vietnam was coming under increasing criticism in the year after TET, U.S.-China relations were on the verge of a turnaround.[17] It may take a bit of effort to remind ourselves that prior to 1969 U.S. domestic propaganda had defended the U.S. government's every military act in Asia as a preventive measure against Red Chinese or Maoist "aggression." Indeed, the U.S. war in Vietnam was justified as a preventative measure against China. Author William Shawcross notes that "as Dean Rusk claimed that the war [in Vietnam] kept 'a billion Chinese armed with nuclear weapons' at bay, so Nixon campaigned in New Hampshire in February 1968 on grounds that the Vietnam effort was 'the cork in the bottle of Chinese expansion in Asia.'"[18] The "Chinese aggression" myth of the 1950s and 1960s was seldom challenged in the mainstream media or in academia. Throughout the 1960s the line was officially embodied in the person of Dean Rusk, secretary of state under presidents Kennedy and Johnson, a man as close to the pro-Taiwan "China Lobby" as a high American official could get without appearing blatant. Rusk was the forger of the peculiar formula that Communist China was Russia's Manchukuo. No open approach to China itself was possible with a mind-set clinging to World War II at the State Department. A glimpse of the inner workings (and the inner man) is revealed in a memorandum of a State Department meeting held on 26 October 1949. Citing the memorandum, Gordon Chang says: "Rusk, as paraphrased in the minutes, provocatively suggested 'arms for some [KMT anticommunist] guerillas as a form of payment' and 'employ whatever means were indicated . . . in the furtherance of our interests—arms here, opium there, bribery and propaganda.'"[19]

This was the backdrop against which the events of 1969 unfolded. Frustrated by its diplomatic isolation, stung by worldwide and homefront condemnation of its wanton military violence, and stalemated on the battlefield, the American war leadership desperately needed a breakthrough. Deciding that Cambodia's long-reigning Prince Norodom Sihanouk was not collaborating enough in their war in Vietnam, the U.S. government conspired to overthrow the prince and install in his place a long-time American asset, Lon Nol.[20]

Lon Nol gave the U.S. military the latitude that Sihanouk never agreed to. Over the next five years U.S. air power put helpless and innocent Cambodian peasants to fire and sword. Conspiratorial concealment of the crimes by the Nixon war leadership with the full cooperation of the U.S. press had succeeded—temporarily.

In public discourse the part not told about Pol Pot is the American part, the "we" element. If an account of the U.S. role in the creation of Pol Pot is missing, or if that role is concealed, distorted, or diminished, then precisely the facts most relevant to Americans have been covered up.[21] The usual approach is to pass over U.S. agency and to pin responsibility on one or two of the "them" components—Pol Pot, for example. Depicting Pol Pot as a Maoist radical tied to China was another way that the causal role of the U.S. air bombardment in the preceding period was minimized.[22]

The United States and China Become Friends

In contrast to fears about a Sino-American war that sporadically threatened to break out in the 1950s and the 1960s, the present quasi-"friendly" relationship between China and the United States has allowed a measure of economic development in the region and offers the potential for a longer-term peace in Asia. Moreover, the political evolution of South Korea and Taiwan—from military dictatorship to partial democracy—owes more than is generally acknowledged to U.S.-China détente. But the realization of these positive prospects depends equally on the stability and growth of the world economic system and on whether U.S. leaders can learn to treat China as an equal.

Taking their historical bearings from the history of Japan's integration into the world economy, future historians may compare Deng Xiaoping to Emperor Meiji as a way to measure the project of bringing China into the world economy after a period of exclusion. The disasters that Japan caused and suffered in the process of *its* integration (1868–1945) were as much the result of the global context as of Japan's political order itself. The global context will powerfully affect the kind of role China plays in the twenty-first century. This brings us to our second question, how did the United States and China become "friends" in the early 1970s?

As we will see in detail below, China-U.S. hostility dominated Asian (and American) politics during the two decades prior to 1969. What factors account for the sudden démarche in 1969, at a time when both protagonists were dealing with crises that were then at their height: for the United States the war in Vietnam, and for China the Cultural Revolution?

The structural factor is not difficult to identify: the Western economies had surpassed their pre-World War II levels of strength and were ready to expand further. The tactical factors are also clear: to squeeze the Russians and upstage Japan. But the immediate, catalytic factor is often underemphasized: U.S. defeat in Vietnam (and its worldwide and domestic ramifications).

How the Vietnamese factor influenced the growth of U.S.-China "friendship" is seldom talked about by either the Americans or the Chinese. By containing the U.S. military threat in Asia, the Vietnamese had helped to prevent a China-U.S. war from developing and thus facilitated the creation of a new order of relative peace in East Asia, if not immediately for themselves. For their contribution, however, the Vietnamese were as seldom recognized, much less rewarded, as the USSR was for its role in defeating fascism.[23] Mao Zedong, however, acknowledged the debt that the Chinese and the Americans owe to the Vietnamese. In November 1971 Mao is reported to have told Vietnam's Prime Minister Pham Van Dong: "Your victory has forced Nixon to come to Peking."[24] Had the Vietnamese resistance not been strong enough, who knows how far into an Asian land war the lust for power would have driven the American leaders.[25]

The immediate conditions that gave rise to U.S.-China "friendship" in the early 1970s were several: exhaustion of the United States in its Asian wars, the winding down of the Cultural Revolution, the completion of China's break from the USSR, and the realization of the successful recovery of global capitalism (especially in Japan, Taiwan, and South Korea). Mao (always ambivalent at best about working with the Russians) may have seen the significance of these changing realities even before the Americans. But the war stood in the way. The United States may have been ready for a relationship with China in economic terms but politically it was not yet ready.

The spring of 1968 brought the "Tet Offensive" in Vietnam, followed by President Lyndon Johnson's declaration that he would not run for a second term. Hearing from eminence grise Clark Gifford that he no longer had support for a wider war, President Johnson refused General Westmoreland's demand for another 200,000 U.S. servicemen in Vietnam. Washington's war policy had gone to hell, and the new war leadership under Nixon came into office waving peace plans at the electorate. (Indiscriminate bombing of military targets and noncombatants was not affected, however.) The discredited Vietnam policy had discredited the China policy that had rationalized the U.S. war in Vietnam. Domestically cornered, Nixon and Kissinger were desperate for a reversal of fortune. A China-U.S. deal, they thought, would partly defuse the Vietnam war issue and reassure the U.S. public that their government could still conduct foreign policy. More immediately, Nixon wanted the Chinese to urge Hanoi to reduce the level of combat; Mao may have obliged, but his urging had little effect on the Vietnamese.

Despite U.S. propaganda about China's isolationism, the Chinese had always wanted in. In 1970–71 China was beginning to recover from factional campaigns (the ordeals of the Cultural Revolution), a period of both anarchic movement and virtual martial law. Through the Cultural Revolution, China was also completing its separation from the USSR, a course to which it had been intermittently committed since the late 1950s. This was one of Mao's shrewder if underappreciated policies. To the Chinese the détente meant the end of the U.S. economic embargoes, covert operations, and nuclear blackmail against its cities; it also meant admission to the United Nations, which would facilitate and legitimate China's reintegration into world politics and economics.

As early as 1939 Mao had written that "the objective of the imperialist powers in penetrating China is certainly not to transform a feudal China into a capitalist China; on the contrary, their objective is to transform China into their semi-colony or full colony."[26] Yet, in 1971, it was Nixon who went to the mountain and dined with Mao. The Chinese had waited a long time for this moment, and the world breathed a sigh of relief as fears about the possibility of the Vietnam conflict spreading into a general war in Asia all but evaporated. Among the nations, and even in U.S. forums of public opinion, support for the changed policy was strong. Twenty years of anti-Chinese ideological rhetoric (purveyed by most high-level officials, journalists, and academics) was silently flushed away. Slogans like "Friendship has a history" (referring to Sino-U.S. cooperation against Japan in World War II) were floated around.

The relationship that the Americans and Chinese created in the 1970s thus answered a mutual need. The only bit of plastic surgery required was to cut away the tie-in with the Vietnam War itself—by the United States and China as well (see note 9). Another generation passed before Vietnam and Laos, largely thanks to their Asean neighbors and India, joined in the common development of East Asia.

The United States and China Become Enemies

The logic of how Sino-American friendship was formed in the late 1960s is clear enough, but how the two nations became enemies after World War II is not clear at all. To address this, our third question, requires going back to the fall of 1944 when President Roosevelt recalled General Joseph Stilwell from China at the behest of Chiang Kai-shek, leader of the Nationalist regime. Stilwell had been trying for years to create an effective Chinese land force against the Japanese, but his efforts kept running afoul of the smoldering civil war in China between the Communists and the Nationalists. Despairing of getting the Nationalist leaders (whom he despised as corrupt and feckless) to shape up, Stilwell wanted to explore military cooperation with the Communists. But Nationalist leader Chiang was determined that no American aid go to the Communists, no bonds be formed; and in the end, out of respect for Nationalist sovereignty, Roosevelt gave in to Chiang and recalled Stilwell. The recall of Stilwell meant that there would be no landing of U.S. forces in China, and therefore no land ally against Japan. To make up for the lost China theater, the Americans needed Russia in the war. Russia was induced to break the neutrality pact it had with Japan and to join the Allied campaign. Its entry into the war in the Far East was agreed upon at Yalta in February 1945. By attaching themselves to the side of the Nationalists in China, the Americans forfeited the chance seen and urged by farsighted foreign service officers like John S. Service (Stilwell's aide) to work with the Communists against Japan, and perhaps lay a foundation for fruitful relations with China after the war.[27]

With no Chinese ally in the field, Roosevelt at Yalta could not but agree to much of what Stalin wanted in Asia in return for his pledge to send Russian forces in against the Japanese. August 8 was to be the date for Russian entry into the war against Japan. Hiroshima was bombed August 6; Nagasaki, August 9. In late July and early August of 1945 Russian forces saw some action in Manchukuo but the end of the war came swiftly. The American Pacific campaigns had been decisive in winning the war against Japan.

As World War II in the Pacific ended, the Truman administration wanted unilateral dominion in order to attain the two objectives for which the United States had waged war in Asia: control over the Japanese state and economy and predominance in China. With Japan defeated and the occupation authority in place, Truman pursued the second objective as he plunged into China's civil war, giving the Chiang regime military, economic, and diplomatic support in their anticommunist crusade. Opponents of this strategy such as Owen Lattimore, who had been a high-level wartime consultant to Chiang Kai-shek, were swept aside:

> My position had always been that it would be disastrous for the United States to get involved in the Chinese civil war supporting one side against the other. Even before the end of the Pacific War, seeing the increasing involvement of the United States only on the side of Kuomintang, I wrote to President Truman presenting my view. Truman received me on 3 July; but this interview did not last more than three minutes. . . . Truman told me that there were well-informed experts in the State Department and they knew what they were doing. Thank you, Mr. Lattimore. Good-bye.[28]

By intervening in China's civil war, Truman effectively restarted World War II in Asia, prolonging the sufferings of the Chinese people and winning for the United States decades of justly deserved enmity. In the latter half of 1949, like Odysseus and Telemachus returning to Ithaca to rescue home and country, the Communist forces began to rout the "suitors," the Nationalists and their American backers. Swept ignominiously from China, the Americans could hardly admit to themselves or to the world how badly they had misplayed their hand. As 1949 drew to a close, through political shallowness and ideological conceit, the American war leaders would in effect lose half of the spoils of World War II in Asia, unless they could come to terms with China's new government.

The narcissistic pique of American (and British!) leaders is captured in a comment of the British consul general in Shanghai on 3 August 1949: "The United States has been the prima donna in China since the war . . . [but now] she has flown into a tantrum and is kicking the footlights out."[29] The darker depths of the fury of the American leadership, almost Ahab-like in its fanatic pride, are suggested in the above-mentioned cameo notes citing Dean Rusk's four horsemen of foreign policy: "Arms, opium, bribery and propaganda." The Truman policymakers had cornered themselves and could not or would not follow what seemed the sensible course to, say, England (which recognized the new Chinese government in January 1950) or India: recognize the new Chinese government and normalize relations. The policymakers had nothing but contempt for such a rational choice. One senses under the surface the racial issue as well; the "restless ghost" of American history. Could an America that had defaulted domestically on its central claim—equality—treat a nation of color as an equal?

What if by some measures (culture, political self-confidence) that nation should prove to *be* an equal (or even superior to the United States)? Having come through their century-long ordeal owing the American rulers nothing, the Chinese were quite unlike the dependent, humbled, and seemingly grateful Japanese. Like Moby-Dick, China became an object of obscure anxiety to many Americans with bureaucratic or academic authority because it existed free and independent, beyond the waves of the Pacific and the bidding of American power. In addition, its very existence exposed repressed, unpleasant truths about the nature of American power.

Attempting to deal with this historical moment, most American writings explain away the recognition issue. Some lead the reader to the unreal side of the mirror where, it is blithely claimed, the cultural and ideological fixations of China's new leaders would have elicited a negative response to American offers of recogniton. Others argue that the Chinese were too committed to the USSR to strike a deal with the Americans. Typically these claims accentuate the "them" element, not the "we." In fact, Chinese Communist leaders had, especially in the spring of 1949, shown serious interest in normalization.[30] Nonetheless, it has become a reiterated assumption that the Chinese one-sidedly isolated themselves from the rest of the world until the détente of the 1970s. In diplomatic history circles much effort is still expended to repress or confuse the rather awkward-to-explain actualities of the late 1949 to early 1950 period and Washington's abnormal and provocative refusal to recognize the new government of China.[31]

This "designer history" is evident in a symposium published in *Diplomatic History* in 1997 entitled "Rethinking the Lost Chance in China."[32] The academics who participated in the symposium claim to show what in reality can only be an untested hypothesis; namely, that the U.S. leaders did not "lose the chance" to establish normal diplomatic relations with China after October 1949 because it was impossible to make such a deal with the Communists. Clearly unwilling to assign any responsibility to the American leaders for the conflict, Warren Cohen writes, "U.S. archives reveal that the Truman administration did precisely what lost chance critics wanted it to do, to no avail."[33] Maybe so, depending on which critic he means. But the Truman administration did not do what was precisely necessary for China: offer recognition. That's the legal norm. Diplomatic recognition is the only real point at issue, the point so many (and all the symposium participants) are so careful to avoid.

One of the participants, Chen Jian, describes the Chinese position in May-June 1949 (essentially refuting his own arguments) as follows: "Unless the Americans were willing to sever relations with the GMD [Kuomintang, or Nationalist Party] and to treat China equally, the CCP [Communist Party] would not consider having relations with the United States."[34] But of course; and such a position was just and reasonable for any government to take.

Neither Mr. Chen nor any of the other participants were able to challenge analytically the American leadership on its refusal to sever relations with the Nationalist Party, nor were they able to confront the fact that the United States was a belligerent—i.e., militarily engaged—in China, not a neutral outsider with clean hands. Chen himself acknowledges that "there is no doubt that Washington's continuous support of the GMD during China's civil war played an important role in the CCP's anti-American policy."[35] Suddenly, we have a moment of near candor, but only a moment. In the next sentence candor is dropped and instead of probing the problem the author shifts into what I would call platitudes from Chi Civ 101: "But America's pro-Jiang [Chiang] policy alone does not offer a comprehensive explanation of the origins of the CCP-American confrontation . . . we must explore the historical-cultural environment in which it emerged."[36] This digression into the untested and irrelevant tries to dehistoricize the actual moment, which was an extremely fluid one—anything really was possible, and to speculate on what China's response *might* have been to an offer never put forward. As they say, you never know until you ask.[37]

Whatever anti-Western rationalizations the Chinese Communists proffered to their followers and allies, or to world opinion, whatever moods and rhetoric they indulged in, whatever their relations with the USSR, it is doubtful that Mao and his group would have turned down a serious offer of recognition, one that would have severed U.S. colonialist (unequal) relations with the Nationalists.[38] The ball was in the American not the Chinese court. The U.S. government had far greater military and economic power, and it also had amends to make.

In the spring of 1949 U.S. Ambassador John L. Stuart conveyed to the Chinese Washington's concerns that "the CCP might attach itself to the side of the Soviet Union in a confrontation with the United States . . . , and that the CCP, after unifying China by force, would stop its cooperation with the democratic figures and give up democratic coalition government."[39] The ambassador's approach was ill-advised. Chiang Kai-shek himself might have balked at such pressure tactics, judging from his remarks to Lattimore. No, with the experience of invasive Japanese demands fresh in memory, no leadership of an independent China could accept such U.S. interference in its foreign relations and its internal organization, any more than the American leaders would have accepted a Chinese demand that it create a democratic coalition in Vietnam and not restore French colonial rule there, or prevent the Dutch from returning to power in Indonesia, or that it do away with the colonial state structure inherited from the

Japanese in Korea, or that it not attach itself to the side of Emperor Hirohito, or that it create a democratic coalition of blacks and whites in Mississippi or in Cuba. Diplomatic recognition is not properly concerned with such things because it simply formalizes equality on the state level and protects the state-to-state relationship from other considerations. The interests of the people of the United States were ill served by Ambassador Stuart's crude maneuvering in pursuit of unequal—hence improper—advantages all too familiar to the Chinese. This is not to say that recognition alone would have solved all the problems. Recognition is no more than a reasonable way to create a context for addressing problems. Irresponsibly, the American leadership chose (as it later chose to do with Vietnam in 1975) not to take the path of comprehensive peace in Asia that victory over Japan, with all its sacrifices, had made possible. "Arrogance of power," Senator William Fulbright's apt phrase for U.S. behavior in Vietnam, applies here too.

The end of World War II presented the American leaders with a golden opportunity to disentangle themselves from China's political affairs and get the sticky Chiang Kai-shek off their hands. The Truman administration lost that chance and pursued the destructive meddling that fed into the chain of causes leading to the wars in Korea, Laos, Vietnam, Cambodia, and Indonesia.[40] Indeed, the American war machine was picking up where the Japanese Imperial Army had left off. Perhaps one may think of this as the Japanization of American foreign policy in Asia, the dark side of the Americanization of Japan. Is this what Allied troops had fought for? Is this what Roosevelt's aspirations for the end of colonialism had come to?

From the Chinese vantage point, the geographical arc that encircles China —from Burma to Korea—is a graphic representation of U.S. desires to reestablish colonial rule throughout Asia. Support for Chiang and for waging low-intensity war ("arms, opium, bribery and propaganda") against the new Chinese government fit into that broad program. Once we factor in the ever-elusive "we" element, the picture becomes fairly clear. Author Ronald McGlothlen quotes Dean Rusk as saying: "Our general attitude in those days was that it was important for the United States to have control of every wave in the Pacific Ocean. . . ." "From the early 1930's through the end of World War II," McGlothlen writes, "Japan aggressively pursued economic ascendancy in the Far East under the guise of creating a 'Greater East Asia Co-Prosperity Sphere.' In the postwar years, [Secretary of State Dean] Acheson sought a surprisingly similar ascendancy for Japan. . . . 'We used to joke a little,' Dean Rusk candidly recounted, 'about this revival of the Greater East Asia Co-Prosperity Sphere.'"[41]

Many millions of Chinese perished at the hands of the Japanese aggressors. I doubt that Rusk's little joke would have amused many Chinese. I *do* think they got his point, however.[42]

Shift in U.S. Favor from Japan to China

We now move back another decade in time to take up the fourth and final question, how did the United States and China become friends and then allies against Japan?

In the international context of the 1930s China was a virtual colony with many would-be masters. England and Japan both had major economic interests in China, but Japan was making a bid to bring China under its exclusive control. In the period 1939–1941, President Roosevelt began to maneuver toward cooperation with China against Japan. He sensed the limits of both Japanese and British power, and that the United States—which had a smaller business stake in China—might supplant both. Since the Chinese republican revolution of 1911, U.S. foreign policy had not been particularly friendly to China, and Roosevelt's move was more a tactical exception than the norm.[43]

Accurately establishing the time line is critical in dealing with the late 1930s. Wartime Sino-American friendship does not apply prior to late 1938. The norm, historically speaking, was Anglo-American cooperation with Japan in order to dominate China. As Bruce Cumings observes, "In a sense, Japan got the empire that the United States and England wanted it to have."[44]

Stretching the time line back to the beginning of the century brings into consideration the working relationship that Great Britain, the leading Western nation before World War II, had developed with Japan between 1895 and 1902. Formalized in 1902, the Anglo-Japanese Alliance was directed primarily against China, Russia, and Korea. The Japanese had proved worthy of this recognition by defeating China in the Sino-Japanese War of 1894–95. From then on Japan turned its back on its traditional mentor (China) to join the (dysfunctional) family of Western nations. In the foreign repression of the Boxer Rebellion of 1898–1900 the Japanese again distinguished themselves in their exceptional service to the West by slaughtering Chinese. Their reward—the Western seal of approval—was the alliance with England. For its part, England was following its own interests: weakened in the Boer War and overextended in India, England needed the help of a subimperialist in East Asia.

Successful as a subimperialist power, Japan yearned to become a regular imperialist force. With Britain its model and mentor, the Japanese imperial state sought an India of its own, and that meant making China the jewel of its empire. Having annexed Korea in 1910, with British and American approval, Japan during World War I next tried to create for itself a special position in China by making its "21 Demands" on the recognized Chinese warlord government in Beijing (in 1915). Japan's gambit succeeded only in part; after World War I the Allied Powers—who were never completely comfortable with the idea of Japan as an equal coimperialist power—forced Japan's retreat from China. Japan remained on good terms with the West during the 1920s but then, in the wake of the Depression of 1929, Japan resumed its path of conquest by invading Manchuria in September 1931 and creating the puppet state of Manchukuo the following spring.

In 1937 Japan saw a chance to humble China with a decisive blow, before the Communists and Nationalists, who had formed their united front the year before, made common cause in earnest, and while the Allied Powers were still keeping their distance, tacitly if uneasily pro-Japan. Britain and the United States were willing to give the Japanese a free hand to stabilize and control the China scene—so long as they respected the integrity and protected the freedom of British and American financial interests. The farthest thing from any Japanese or Western leader's thinking was the suffering, the interests, or the rights of the Chinese people.

In August 1937 Japanese forces launched an aerial bombing of Shanghai. In December they began their infamous invasion of Nanking, which was then China's seat of government. Their hope was that delivering a knockout blow to the capital would lead to swift Chinese surrender and to Japan's political supremacy. The Soviet and Nazi governments were the only ones to oppose the Japanese juggernaut in any serious and practical manner.[45] The "rape of Nanking" took the lives of an estimated 300,000 Chinese citizens (according to the official Chinese record) but failed to lead to a Japanese victory. The Japanese massacred the population of Nanking, but Chinese resistance consolidated and deepened. Meanwhile, the U.S. view began to change, as the revolution in China developed and the Chinese Communist Party moved to center stage.

The American share in the British Empire had been growing since 1918. By the end of 1938 President Roosevelt was ready to exploit England's weakening grip on its empire and to take a more active stance against the Japanese. That meant tilting toward China, a move the British did not like. The U.S. media was flooded with photos and stories sympathetic to the Chinese. In 1938 Pearl Buck won the Nobel Prize for literature for her portrayal of the Chinese in *The Good Earth*. (Her book later became a major film.) Changing lethargic or hostile American attitudes toward China was now on the agenda. On the level of financial diplomacy, "the first American grant of credit to China [twenty-five million dollars] was announced on December 16, 1938. . . . [This was] construed by the Chinese as indicating the commencement of action by those powers [the United States and Great Britain] to prevent Japan from achieving its aims in the Far East."[46] Coming a full year after the start of the Nanking Massacre, the loan to the Nationalists signaled America's determination to oppose Japan and displace British power in Asia.

In the six years following the U.S. loan, Chiang Kai-shek "was to hound Great Britain and the United States with innuendo and veiled threats. But his meaning was quite clear. Without greater and greater support from the Western Powers, he might find the continued struggle too burdensome for his war-weary nation. He might yield to the counsel he was receiving from various quarters that he cooperate with Japan in achieving an 'Asia for the Asians.'"[47] As the Americans and British worked to keep Nationalist forces from going over to the Japanese side, Mao Zedong and Zhou Enlai were organizing armies of peasants and harassing Japanese forces.

By the summer of 1941 conflict between Japan and the United States was imminent. An oil embargo against Japan and other measures taken by Roosevelt convinced the Japanese that they would have to make a decisive strike against U.S. forces, another instance of their "Nanking" mentality. Japanese war leaders were banking on the strength of American isolationist sentiment to limit Roosevelt's options. But the Japanese had gone too far. Roosevelt would never agree to the extent of control in China that the Japanese wanted. In 1942 Roosevelt sent General Stilwell to China to train and organize Chinese forces and bring them actively into military alliance with the United States against the Japanese.

Conclusion

Beginning with its wrongful engagement in China's civil war in 1945 and ending in 1991 with the civil war in Cambodia, for which it bears considerable responsibility, the U.S. government waged war in Asia—sometimes unilaterally and unlawfully (without congressional consent), sometimes in concert with the United Nations or other allies. The term "Cold War," if valid in Europe, was never applicable in Asia. The death toll in Asia's many wars has never been calculated, but estimates are that the total in all of the region's killing fields could easily amount to two or three holocausts; i.e., twelve to eighteen million. In the postwar period, America played God in Asia . . . and failed. Some Americans may comfort themselves with the thought that after 1945 the United States was simply continuing to fight their "good war" (World War II) in Asia or that if mistakes were made Washington's motives were good. But there is little good to be found in these Asian wars. In fact, U.S. military involvement in Asia in the post-1945 period was far more like the Philippine War from the turn of the century being fought over and over and over again.[48]

As the late, great senator from Arkansas, J. William Fulbright, was reported to have said, "Most Americans can never remember what most people can never forget."

Afterword

What are the pedagogical responsibilities of teachers in the fields of area studies and foreign relations? Above all, I would say, to search for the voice of the Other and thus to discover ourselves. To ask the questions so rarely raised: How does U.S. power affect the lives of those on the receiving end? How does the idle bombing by U.S. missiles of a pharmaceutical factory in Sudan affect the people living there? What happened to the districts of Panama City bombed in 1989 by U.S. planes allegedly in an effort to capture the U.S. asset and drug-lord Manuel Noriega? No U.S. media asked such questions or brought to American viewers footage of those who had to suffer and live with the consequences of these acts of force.

For Asia we have yet to compute the death toll. Beginning in 1945, U.S., Western, and Japanese aggressors in China, Korea, Indonesia, Vietnam, Laos, and Cambodia killed directly and indirectly many millions of Asians, far more of them civilian than military. "The souls of our dead are floating in the heaven imploring to be put to rest," says a Korean farmer demanding justice for his mother, shot to death in 1951 by American forces. The victim's words were conveyed in December 1999—almost fifty years too late—by *Far Eastern Economic Review* reporter Shim Jae Hoon, who adds, "Comforting the souls of the dead lies at the core of efforts to gain official acknowledgement of the massacres [in Korea by U.S. forces], a process of catharsis the Koreans call han or the act of righting the wrongs committed against them. Han must be dealt with by the living to appease the souls of those who died unjust deaths."

This demand for justice and redress is an attempt to pick up the unfinished business that Robert McNamara spoke of when he said, "We were wrong, terribly wrong." Other nations have tried, however imperfectly, to acknowledge their crimes and thus redeem their honor; official America, like official Japan, has yet to step up to that minimal standard of morality and religion. And our media, by controlling and shaping our information, stand in the way.

It is often argued that American leaders have merely "made mistakes" in

Asia, mistakes that arose from inadequate knowledge of the history and culture of Asian nations. This is doubtful. Crimes and mistakes are two different things. And faulty knowledge of Asia is a problem, but not the main problem. Faulty knowledge of our own culture, and our history of easy resort to violence under the mantle of religion and morality, is more to the point. Perhaps we can understand our own official history best through the eyes and voices of those we have wronged. Did any U.S. media bring us the voice of the Korean farmer on the day of his loss? It is not enough even now for McNamara to have said, "We were wrong." For in this phrase the reference remains only to ourselves. "We have wronged others," is what remains to be said, to be understood, and to be overcome. Otherwise, we acquiesce and forego responsibility.

Notes

I wish to thank Marilyn Young, Kristin Pelzer, Alvin So, Tom Fenton, and two anonymous *BCAS* readers for their thoughtful criticisms and valuable suggestions. A slightly different version of this essay originally appeared in the *Bulletin of Concerned Asian Scholars* 32(3) (July–Sept. 2000), and is reprinted here with permission.

1   Robert S. McNamara, with Brian Vandemark, *In Retrospect: The Tragedy and Lessons of Vietnam* (New York: Times Books, 1995), xvi. This book may be read in conjunction with Paul Hendrickson's masterful portrait of McNamara, *The Living and the Dead: Robert McNamara and Five Years of a Lost War* (New York: Knopf, 1996).

2   Robert S. McNamara, *Argument without End: In Search of Answers to the Vietnam Tragedy* (New York: Public Affairs, 1999).

3   For the author's view of (and further references on) the problem of government-agency influence on the China studies field, see "Contra Ideocracy," in the symposium proceedings of "Asia, Asian Studies, and the National Security State," *Bulletin of Concerned Asian Scholars* 29(1) (1997): 47–49.

4   Estimates of the death toll are not only vague they also seldom distinguish fatalities before April 1975 (for reasons discussed later in this essay). Moreover, the losses suffered by minority or religious communities (Vietnamese, Chinese, Chams, Buddhists) are not broken down. See Ben Kiernan, "The Genocide in Cambodia, 1975–79," *Bulletin of Concerned Asian Scholars* 22(2) (1990): 35–40. Kiernan's article discusses the extermination of minorities, which is at the heart of the legal definition of genocide.

   On the question of how many Cambodian fatalities resulted from famine rather than from liquidation: In 1979 Noam Chomsky and Edward S. Herman wrote, "[William] Goodfellow also correctly assigns the responsibility for the impending famine: it was caused primarily by the U.S. bombing campaign which 'shattered' the agrarian economy—an unquestionable fact that has since been quietly forgotten" (*After the Cataclysm: Postwar Indochina and the Reconstruction of Imperial Ideology* [Boston: South End Press, 1979], 160–61). There is more evidence on this point: "In 1980,

UNICEF and the International Committee of the Red Cross (ICRC) began a lifesaving relief operation in Cambodia . . . in order to prevent mass starvation resulting from a poor 1979 harvest and the economic dislocation of war and the Pol Pot regime" (Jay Peterzell, "Reagan's Covert Action Policy [II]," *First Principles* 7(4) [February 1982]: 7 [published by the Center for National Security Studies]). Environmental stress and famine have to be factored in to any assessment of Khmer Rouge atrocities.

5 Kiernan, "The Genocide in Cambodia."

6 Ben Kiernan, *The Pol Pot Regime: Race, Power, and Genocide in Cambodia under the Khmer Rouge, 1975–79* (New Haven: Yale University Press, 1996), 128. See also "The Lesser Evil," an interview with Norodom Sihanouk, published in the *New York Review of Books*, 14 March 1985, 21–26. "Pol Pot took power in 1975 to 1977," Sihanouk is quoted as saying. For the shredding of official files for the early Reagan years, see Patrick Tyler, "The (Ab)normalization of U.S.-China Relations," *Foreign Affairs* 78(5) (September-October 1999): 93–122 (citation on 97).

7 Details may be found in Nayan Chanda, *Brother Enemy: The War after the War* (New York: Harcourt, Brace, Jovanovich, 1986), 17.

8 Peterzell, "Reagan's Covert Action Policy (II)," 7. Displacing responsibility for U.S. backing for the Khmer Rouge, an editorial in the *New York Times* on 1 September 1975, says delicately, "The Chinese [are the] prime friends of the present Cambodian ruling group."

9 In February 1979 China attacked Vietnam, inflicting and suffering heavy casualties; the Americans warned Moscow not to aid Hanoi. Within weeks the Chinese, bloodied, terminated the action.

10 Derek Davies, "Caught in History's Vice," *Far Eastern Economic Review* 25 (December 1981): 17–21.

11 Chanda, *Brother Enemy*, 68.

12 Marilyn Young, *The Vietnam Wars, 1945–1990* (New York: HarperCollins, 1991), 236.

13 A rare and striking counter-example may be found in an "Open Forum" essay by Rick Rowden published in the *San Francisco Chronicle* on 14 August 1997.

14 William Shawcross, *Sideshow: Kissinger, Nixon, and the Destruction of Cambodia* (New York: Simon and Schuster, 1979), 219. Shawcross writes: "It could be argued that this use of [American] air power constitutes a prima-facie case of breach of international law. Article 6(b) of the Charter of the International Military Tribunal following World War II defined 'war crimes' as 'violations of the laws or customs of war. Such violations shall include . . . wanton destruction of cities, towns or villages, or devastation not justified by military necessity.'"

15 Young, *The Vietnam Wars*, 283.

16 Kiernan, *The Pol Pot Regime*, 19.

17 For discussion of the U.S. role pre-1969, see "The Prince," chapter 3 in Shawcross, *Sideshow*.

18 Shawcross, *Sideshow*, 85–86.

19 Gordon Chang, *Friends and Enemies* (Stanford: Stanford University Press, 1990), 58.

20 Shawcross attributes this interpretation to Frank Snepp, chief CIA analyst in the Saigon station, though there are as yet no substantiating documents (and may never be).

(See Shawcross, *Sideshow*, 114.) The Snepp interpretation is circumstantially warranted. For further information on U.S. involvement in the coup see Kiernan, *The Pol Pot Regime*, 15 n. 35.

21 Cambodia coverage is not a unique case. Splitting the picture to displace culpability is a recurring pattern in the ideological treatment of events in Asia. As dividing nations is the hallmark of post-World War II Western colonialist rule, so divided histories are a staple of colonialist ideology. World War I is divided from World War II; the China War (1931–1941) is divided from the Pacific War (1941–1945); pre-1949 Chinese history is divided from post-1949. In the public media basic information is withheld, in effect marked "off limits" *as a warning* that exploring the wider picture, above all the role of U.S. agencies, is professionally unwise.

22 George Kennan argues against the American habit of "overpersonalizing" relations with foreign governments (see "The United States and the World: An Interview with George Kennan," *New York Review of Books*, 12 August 1999, 4–6).

23 Revealingly, the U.S. media gave no credit to the Vietnamese for their "humanitarian assistance" to the Cambodian people, nor did the media seriously investigate the commendable "moral commitment" the Vietnamese had made toward rescuing and stabilizing Cambodia and limiting the atrocities committed by U.S.-backed Khmer Rouge forces. In the Orwellian discourse of the *New York Times* and most domestic media, only U.S. foreign policy qualifies as moral and humanitarian.

24 Seymour Hersh, *The Price of Power* (New York: Pantheon, 1983), 442.

25 The *Wall Street Journal* series "Ten Years After," published in 1985, discusses the benefits to the United States of losing the Vietnam War and what would have been the liabilities of victory.

26 Mao Zedong, *The Chinese Revolution and the Chinese Communist Party*, December 1939, in *Selected Works of Mao Tse-t'ung*, vol. 2 (Peking: Foreign Language Press, 1965), 310.

27 Barbara Tuchman's *Stilwell and the American Experience in China, 1911–1945* (New York: Macmillan, 1970) is a forthright introduction to the subject. For original documents, see Joseph W. Esherick's *Lost Chance in China: The World War II Despatches of John S. Service* (New York: Random House, 1974). Joseph Alsop served as political adviser to General Claire Chennault, Stilwell's rival in China, as Service served Stilwell. Stilwell and Service were, however, U.S. government employees, Chennault and Alsop worked for the Chiang regime. Alsop gives his account of the period in three articles published in the *Saturday Evening Post*, 7, 14, and 21 January 1950. The exclusion of John Service from all public and academic discussion of China for twenty-five years (1945–1970), taken together with the privileged access of Joseph Alsop to all forums, is one way to measure the limits placed on U.S. citizens' freedom to learn about China.

28 Owen Lattimore, *China Memoirs: Chiang Kai-shek and the War against Japan* (Tokyo: University of Tokyo Press, 1991), 25.

29 Chang, *Friends and Enemies*, 46.

30 Ibid., 27, 40.

31 For an original survey of the issues, see James Peck, *Ideal Illusions: China, Globalism, and the National Security World, 1947–1968* (Ph.D. diss., New York University, May 1996).

32 "Rethinking the Lost Chance in China," *Diplomatic History* 21(1) (1997): 71–75.

33 Warren I. Cohen, introduction to the symposium (ibid., 75).

34 Ibid., 80.

35 Ibid., 82.

36 Ibid.

37 The views of the symposium participants are conventional. Over the past fifty years few American accounts of U.S.-China relations in the year 1949 have been able to rise above nationalist imperatives to give a balanced account of how things did (or must have) looked to the other side. In the early 1970s, concomitant with improved Sino-American relations, John Service was rehabilitated and a few balanced accounts of the year 1949 appeared.

38 Chiang Kai-shek, leader of the Kuomintang, had an abiding anxiety that after the war the Western powers would not treat China as an equal. One of his purposes in hiring Lattimore was to convey this concern to President Roosevelt. Chiang to Lattimore, 31 July 1941: "What guarantee would there be when the war comes to an end that the other democracies would not [*sic*] treat her [China] on the basis of equality? This is something which has been troubling the minds of the Chinese people. . . . The Japanese have been conducting an intensive propaganda to the effect that white men are still treating China as a colony and would not hesitate to sacrifice her interests for the purpose of ensuring their continual [*sic*] domination in the Far East." From Lattimore's transcribed notes in Robert Newman, *Owen Lattimore and the Loss of China* (Berkeley: University of California Press, 1992), 61–62.

39 Chen Jian, "The Myth of America's 'Lost Chance' in China: A Chinese Perspective in the Light of New Evidence," in *Diplomatic History* 21(1) (1997): 77–86. A dubious suggestion found in the symposium is that the rejection of the "lost chance" thesis has some added authenticity when coming from the Chinese themselves. Why claim special authority for a Chinese perspective? Do Jews have superior authority on Middle East or holocaust questions? Blacks on African history or slavery or ghettos? In addition to indulging in identity politics, the symposium is suited to a particular ideological moment of official correctness, namely sanitizing the murky U.S. foreign policy record in the early Cold War years. The symposium contains no contrary or balancing view, nor did its members make use of (or solicit) the views of John Service, who, judging by E. J. Kahn's profile in the *New Yorker* (8 April 1972), would have contributed a different interpretation. Even in 1996 an informed witness of Service's integrity and credibility was not utilized by such scholars as a resource.

40 "Despite a fairly widespread anti-colonial sentiment prevailing in the United States, sometimes mirrored in the public rhetoric of its officials, the actions of the Truman administration during the first postwar years were not supportive of the Indonesian struggle for independence. The administration's actions, while discreet and largely indirect, were in fact heavily beneficial to the Dutch effort for re-conquest" (Audrey R. and George McT. Kahin, *Subversion as Foreign Policy: The Secret Eisenhower and Dulles Debacle in Indonesia* [Seattle: University of Washington Press, 1995], 29).

41 Ronald L. McGlothlen, *Controlling the Waves: Dean Acheson and U.S. Foreign Policy in Asia* (New York: W. W. Norton, 1993), 21–22. Perhaps unknown to the meta-

phorist, "controller of the waves" was the title held by Ma Yuan (Ma Vien) who subdued the Trung Sisters revolt in Vietnam in A.D. 43–44.

42 *Vital Speeches of the Day* 17(17) (15 June 1951): 515. Cited in Peck, *Ideal Illusions*, 88. As Peck observes, the domestic counterpart of such excommunications was the denunciation of liberals and leftists as un-American. In May 1951, Dean Rusk had acquired no new sophistication in his definitive formulation of the China problem: "The Peiping regime may be a colonial Russian government—a Slavic Manchukuo on a larger scale. It is not the Government of China. It does not pass the first test. It is not Chinese."

43 Some might see an analogy to American support for the Philippine nationalist leader Aguinaldo against Spain, support that quickly turned to hostility: with Spanish power in the Philippines destroyed, President McKinley moved to bring the islands under American dominion. (This goal was accomplished at the cost of years of fighting that was as ruthless as the fighting in Vietnam.)

44 Bruce Cumings, *Parallax Visions: Making Sense of American–East Asian Relations at the End of the Century* (Durham, N.C.: Duke University Press, 1999), 41.

45 The Nazis had important economic and military interests in China. Their support for the Chiang regime lasted until early 1938. The Nazi foreign office had made strenuous diplomatic efforts to limit Japanese aggression, but in February 1938 the Reichstag agreed at last to recognize Manchukuo. This meant that Germany would henceforth focus on Europe and no longer hinder Japanese expansion in China. It takes nothing away from the personal heroism of the Nazi John Rabe, who saved many Chinese during the Nanking Massacre, to recognize that he was conforming to his government's policy. Rabe was recalled to Germany in February 1938 and told to keep his mouth shut.

46 John Hunter Boyle, *China and Japan at War, 1937–1945* (Stanford: Stanford University Press, 1972), 223.

47 Ibid., 222.

48 Those interested in the deeper origins of the events discussed in this essay may benefit from reading Robert Beisner, *Twelve against Empire: The Anti-Imperialists, 1898–1900* (1968; Chicago: University of Chicago Press, 1985). Many eminent men of that era raised prophetic warnings against the damage to American political institutions that the Philippine War would cause. Their near-forgotten voices are immediately and urgently relevant to the crisis of our own time.

From Politics to Culture: Modern Japanese Literary Studies in the Age of Cultural Studies
James A. Fujii

Introduction

In the U.S., the study of Japan had been shaped by and housed in area studies departments designed to generate knowledge of regions with strategic significance for the State Department. Most scholars of East Asian area studies went about their work more or less oblivious to the foundational logic of their departments, while a small minority made critical engagement of these circumstances an abiding concern in their scholarship. Today, many in my own discipline of Japanese literary studies continue their work as if changes in worldly conditions and the institutions they helped shape have no bearing on the work that they produce, but an increasing minority have begun to shed their disciplinary restrictions (in many cases, this meant text-centered work) as they actively eschew what has become in many ways an anachronistic structure. However, as they have come to produce work that resembles cultural studies, two things strike me. First, with few exceptions, these works do not seem to "qualify" as cultural studies—by which I mean that they are not widely read by its more prominent practitioners. Second, most of these essays, like the high-profile works that helped constitute cultural studies, do not address the consequences of an academic landscape that, at least in the U.S., has shifted from one centered by imperatives of global state-driven politics (area studies) to a logic of mega-corporate economics and finance (cultural studies).[1] This essay focuses on two concerns: the logic of commodity culture and the role assumed by "global English" as implicit arbiter of what passes as an unbounded, non-hierarchic non-discipline (cultural studies), and how what still remains a marginal part of the humanities, Japanese literary studies, might find a significant role to play within these contexts. If on the one hand the very unbounded nature of cultural studies has rightly been touted as a salutary feature of a practice that comes marked with the intention of overcoming the limits of textuality (both as object of study and as method of comprehension and analysis), on the other hand the imprint of a free-market logic that sees no boundaries or impediments to inclusion must at least give us reason to pause. Put differently, what is lost or gained in displacing area studies with an explicitly non-disciplinary practice (cultural studies)? And what might it mean when disciplinary protocols are replaced by a cultural-linguistic one? For in our eagerness to attend to class, gender, race, sexual orientation, and other means of denominating otherness, we can still miss seeing the capacity for just about anything—in this case language and culture— to function as gatekeeper.

In exploring the effects of the discursive shift from area to cultural studies, I take as a starting point the polarization of critical theory into scornful disregard of material/realpolitik by high theory at one end, and an economistic denigration of high theoretical deconstruction that destabilizes "reality" at the other end. In what some will see as a questionable leap of faith, I am attributing to both a concern for transformational politics (which may or may not also be linked to commercial gain, for a pure politics is as much fiction as is unalloyed profit). There are existing materialist critiques of global economic realities that at the same time admit to the limits of such approaches and simultaneously affirm the material consequences of non-material forces through the use of such concepts as the virtual, the simulacural, or the hyperreal. In a moment when culture, like all other realms of human activity, is realized almost always within circuits of commercial exchange, how do we guard against its use for displacing politics altogether? Even as materialist critique seeks to identify and transform the thorough commoditization of the world today, such efforts, and for that matter poststructuralist thought, cannot escape inscription within circuits of commodification. This is the kind of space that I think informs John Frow's observation about the state: "Any serious cultural politics today must confront the non-identity of capital and the state (as well as of the state, consumers, or the 'public'), and thus understand the political ambiguity of the state as the major support both of regimes of private property and of the public sector."[2] We would have to inflect our understanding of such categories as commodity, virtuality, and economy, with a similar admittance of ambiguities. In addressing such worldly and "real" matters as the assault on labor, uneven development, the articulation of corporate power, or the destruction of wilderness, Frow challenges unreflective empiricisms from a "discursive position" without a hint of apology for his "literariness."

I approach these questions obliquely, in a spirit of deep distrust of the realist genres of sociological, economic, and political description. I am by training a literary theorist, and what expertise I possess lies in the study of genres—that is, in the study of the way effects of the real and the authority to speak it are constituted by generic conventions and a generic frame.[3]

Let me begin then, by briefly revisiting the Gulf War in relation to the more recent war in Kosovo, in an effort to negotiate this split within the Humanities in a way similar to that proposed by Frow.

"They Practice Ethnic Cleansing, We Do Crisis Management": The English Language and Capitalist Expansion

For most Americans "Kosovo" was a three-month-long episode presented by the mainstream media as a humanitarian intervention by U.S.-led NATO Forces to stop Serbian atrocities directed at ethnic Albanian Kosovars. If in the past "ethnic cleansing" served as a euphemism to mask an unthinkably harsh reality, in this instance it was deployed by the U.S. media for the opposite effect—to vastly hyperbolize the conflicts that up until the NATO bombings had resulted in about 2,000 deaths and 500,000 refugees on all sides—as Chomsky notes, tragic, but still a very small-scale domestic civil war as such conflicts go.[4] Available information from all sides makes clear that the U.S. and NATO deliberately avoided negotiations in all forms—by circumventing the UN, driving out the existing OSCE peacekeepers, and adding new demands to the Rambouillet Agreements at the eleventh hour that no sovereign country would accept.[5] The resulting unprecedented bombing attacks on military and mostly civilian targets (hospitals, water supplies, electrical stations, apartment buildings, bridges, markets) was a capital-intensive war where the primary motives were to consume high-ticket military hardware and to destabilize Yugoslavia by a broad array of measures—IMF-led restructuring of loans to promote the secession of first Slovenia and then Croatia and other kindred economic measures, selling of military training and arms to groups urged to break up this former non-capitalist nation—in short, strategies pursued in Latin America, Asia and throughout the world by the U.S. in weakening nations that do not cater to the largest State-capital interests. How do we reconcile NATO's "humanitarian" reasons for intervention with NATO official predictions made just prior to the bombings that their entry into this conflict would surely result in a steep rise in the number of dead and refugees created?

Bombardment of Serbia and Kosovo by NATO was turned into another television program that was called "Crisis in Kosovo" (surprisingly, this rubric was not hastily patented as have been such terms as "Three-peat" to describe the

Chicago Bull's three-year reign atop the NBA). And, in line with the simplistic character types that network brass appear determined to keep offering to its viewers, the show was unambiguously narrativized to have a good guy (NATO), bad guys (Milosevic and Serbs), and victims (Albanian refugees, the KLA as freedom fighters). Accordingly, the illegal and unprecedented destructive fire-power unleashed by NATO upon largely civilian targets that would destroy far more lives and create many more refugees than the ten years of ethnic conflict in Kosovo ever did; the efforts by German and U.S. forces that over the years have systematically balkanized the former Republic of Yugoslavia; the "Great Powers" struggle to establish control over the flow of petroleum from the oil-rich Caspian fields to the area east of the Balkans that was once part of the Soviet Union but quickly "destabilized" in the wake of the dissolution of the Soviet Union; the failure of the U.S. or NATO to intervene in any number of areas in the world where far more people had been killed and made refugees during this same period; the very clear, direct, strong ties between the Albanian Mafia controlling drugs in the region and the KLA; economic policies enforced by the World Bank and the IMF that would lead to the quick secession of Slovenia and Croatia from what was then Yugoslavia; the waging of what Chomsky called a capital-intensive war whose purpose was to expend or consume high-priced weaponry highly profitable for the corporations that manufacture them—all of these matters went largely unreported, for they didn't conform to the simple script that would justify our intervention in Kosovo, which was to rescue ethnic Albanians from Milosevic and his bad guys. For the Western capitalist powers (the Cold War–era NATO members) in the aftermath of the Cold War, the Former Republic of Yugoslavia (FRY) was one of the few relatively large, potentially threatening non-capitalist nations that happened to occupy an important geographic site within the compass of the Western powers' economic interests (oil fields, transfer routes). Throughout the 1990s a combination of economic "restructuring" initiatives, behind-the-scenes maneuverings, and outright military force would be deployed in varying measure to ensure the breakup of Yugoslavia.[6] The successive dissolution was faithfully attributed to ethnic conflicts, as if they were divorced from political, material, capital-based initiatives that had been launched largely by the U.S. and Germany.

The speciousness of U.S.-NATO action still evades large sectors of the U.S. public, not only because its mainstream corporate media had a direct vested interest in representing this as a just intervention (they profited directly as in the case of G.E.-owned NBC, and "indirectly" in "added value" to the news; and besides, mainstream media have almost always worked hand in hand with state-defined interests in times of such conflict), but because such acts as high-tech bombing of an adversary unable to defend itself, forwarding economic inden-turedness, etc., defy our capacity to understand. We may recognize the expan-sive nature of capitalism, but the viciousness of its methods defy comprehen-sion; we still tend to be baffled by the connection of atrocities to so-called enlightened societies. But there seems to be another explanation for our incom-prehension. In the world today, the theoretical recognition of the impossibility of being "outside of anything" finds stunning corroboration by our own com-plicity in damaging nature and society—through our own investment portfo-lios, the nature of the institutions we work for, the choices we make as con-sumers that inevitably seem to result in destruction of old-growth forests, the torture of laboratory animals, encouragement of sweatshop labor, and the kill-ing of indigenous folks that come from "structural" reorganizations of nations. Could it be not so much the increased complexity of the present world but our own complicity in its pernicious effects that accounts for our blindness?

If war once spelled for the nation-state a series of far-reaching mobiliza-tions, like the Gulf War, war against Serbia/Kosovo did nothing to alter the rhythms of everyday life in the U.S.[7] Even as critics and commentators noted the ominous appropriation of the war as a "representational event" (as with the Gulf War, both in the way the U.S. military completely controlled what would pass as "news" for the viewing public and the video-game figures of tracer lights, bomb and aircraft trails that dominated visual representations of the war), the campaign against Iraq was at least still called a war. Kosovo, on the other hand, would never be referred to by that term, as the mainstream media would toe the State Department line and call it a "conflict" or a "crisis"—something that could be handled by the crisis management team called NATO, equipped to po-lice the world with deadly robotic force.[8] This recent war was reminiscent of the 1991 U.S. attacks on Iraq also in the way analysis and representation of the events split along deeply divided lines within the humanities: high-theoretical meditations, represented by the well known series of essays written by Jean Bau-drillard on the Gulf War on one side, and on the other side its critics such as Christopher Norris who saw as profoundly problematic Baudrillard's reduction of the real to the virtual. Discernible in this dispute is a shift from a framework that assumes the division of the world into strategically important regions to a paradigm of indifference to a geopolitically differentiated landscape. Ideological slogans matter little to expanding capital. This difference in critical perspective seems very much like the morphing of what was in earlier decade's conten-tiousness surrounding theory and practice in the scholarly enterprise.

As the U.S.-led multinational forces were waging war against Iraq late in January of 1991, Jean Baudrillard would publish what has become a well-known series of articles beginning with "The Gulf War Will Not Take Place," followed by "The Gulf War: Is It Really Taking Place?" and culminating in "The Gulf War Did Not Take Place."[9] The ferocious bombings and the loss of mostly civilian lives seemed to belie Baudrillard's counterintuitive and glib-sounding extended pronouncements, and Christopher Norris would lead the charge from the left in an essay entitled "Baudrillard and the War that Never Happened."[10] His well-known criticism is summed up like this:

> We have lost all sense of the difference—the ontological or epistemological difference—between truth and the various true-seeming images, analogues and fantasy-substitutes which currently claim that title. So the Gulf War figures as one more example in Baudrillard's extensive and varied catalogue of postmodern "hyperreality."[11]

While the point of contention has been widely held to revolve around the issue of reality and its representation, the disagreement just as significantly turns on the prevalence of mass indifference, malaise, or disinterest.[12] If we somewhat charitably recognize this as the subtext of Baudrillard's essays, then they can be read as *provocations*, which Norris chooses to take for truth claims (e.g., that there really was no war).[13] Just as the people of the U.S. were not asked to sacrifice, mobilize, and in any tangible way alter their daily routines, after the initial congressional debate over Iraq (which was very nearly a 50–50 split) and following the decision to deploy U.S. military force, the mainstream media was able to help transform whatever reality might have been into a stupor of mass indifference, generating in its place a kind of "interest" one displays toward a computer game. As I turn to the realm of Japanese literary study (below), I hope to show more persuasively the importance of negotiating an unblinking materialism with what has been defined (incorrectly, I hope to show) as its opposite, or "discursive" understanding—that is, to forge a critical understanding that does not get preempted by an anachronistic but nonetheless frequently invoked paradigm that insists upon the separation of representation and reality.

Form and Power

"Kosovo" cannot be read simply as presented to us by the corporate press as manifest content divorced from globalization, a practice that subjugates vast sectors of the world not just through warfare but also through large-scale financial initiatives (e.g., coercive and usurious loan sharking, forced "economic restructuring"). The specific aspect that stands as a kind of empty signifier, what might be called the increased Anglification of global social relations reduced to commerce, is not only a significant feature of everyday life but also figures in shaping the global articulation of cultural studies as a "field" that has displaced disciplines in an era where the humanities stand imperiled. The English at issue is a language evacuated of culture and reduced to an instrument of communication, but its culturalist function is what concerns me.[14] Frantz Fanon was surely right in noting that "to speak a language is to take on a world, a culture,"[15] but if the age of England as an imperial power has long ended, recent decades have seen the hegemonic rise of its language released from its cultural moorings. If the global articulation of English as a lingua franca speaks to a language pressed into service for its de-localized communicative function, in relation to the issue of cultural studies, it is precisely this "cultural" dimension—an Anglicentrism which I use to denote England and the whole of its settler and settled colonies and even less-intense "contact points" (e.g., Shanghai)—that demands our attention. To enlist a well-worn example, in the way that almost without exception Western cinema can only treat non-Western societies when it inserts a Western protagonist (into it), British, Australian, and North American cultural studies venture beyond their domestic spheres but only to lands that have adopted this common linguistic culture. Thus we see India, the Caribbean, and Hong Kong as constitutive of cultural studies, but not Korea, Japan, Russia, Iran, or other nations where English has never insinuated itself as a first, official, or even viable second language (i.e., never became colonies).[16] And perhaps more important, what is at issue is the capacity to recognize and to overcome the signifier's ability to hold dominion over societies that have achieved what Guy Debord had the prescience to recognize back in the sixties. For as surely as visuality was the object of his critical project, the target of his *Society of the Spectacle* was ultimately the triumph of form in postindustrial society. And that is how I read the global practice of English, including its capacity to arbitrate, shape, and determine a cultural studies—an exclusionary politics of form.

We are accustomed to recognizing capital as the currency (literally and metaphorically) that denominates and differentiates nation, class, etc. In a very similar way, English serves as the standard by which we differentiate, exclude, mark, and represent. Henri Lefebvre's work shows us how everyday life (like space) is not given to us but rather worked and acted upon. Language (in this case, English), like capital, shapes, constructs, and transforms what might better be designated the conditions of everyday life. To use another example of the determining power of what we conventionally see as symbolic representations (like currency and language which denominate exchange value and referents respectively), most economists attribute institutional reasons for the now decade-long poor performance of the Japanese economy. Recent literature has amply demonstrated how such tools of global finance and trade as the IMF, WTO, the World Bank, and GATT have been used to effectively "manage" a nation's or region's economic health (Japan or Asia, for example). It is quite clear that these mechanisms have been manipulated to affect the economies of Brazil, Russia, etc., and to impoverish many nations in the world (often deployed together with such measures as economic sanctions, covert activities, and overt military force; see their effects on Cuba, Chile, Iraq, Somalia, Brazil, Bolivia, North Korea, etc.).[17] But I have digressed a bit by referring to the larger picture of global contest that is inscribed in globalization, and I would like to return to the point that if computers have played a significant role in realizing what is primarily the "virtuality of globality" (e.g., fiscal transactions that are fleeting figures on a screen rather than the transfer of actual currency), they are a technology built around the English language. Japan's decade-long economic malaise is in part a result of its linguistic alterity in this regard.[18]

From States to Corporate Space: Area Studies — MBA Programs — Cultural Studies

In an essay written a few years ago on cultural studies, Stuart Hall noted that we still tend to view the superstructural (including culture) as lesser, supplemental, and secondary:

> [I]f you work on culture . . . you have to recognize that you will always be working in an area of displacement. There's always something decentred about the medium of culture, about language, textuality, and signification, which always escapes and evades the attempt to link it, directly and immediately, with other structures.[19]

This is not to deny the "culturalist" fashion that has swept academia over the last decade or two, as the fact that what Immanuel Wallerstein calls the nomothetic disciplines—economics, political science, and sociology—have increasingly turned to culture reveals a pronounced tension underwriting the rules that constitute academic production today.[20] But at the same time implicit protocols of higher learning designate the pecking order of disciplines that more or less reflect Stuart Hall's observation that opened this section, placing the study of national or global politics, economics, and history above disciplines centrally concerned with culture. Their association to "real life" has always distinguished the nomothetic discipline, be it politics, economic policies, or social studies. In contrast, the humanities or the study of culture is perceived to be separate from matters of "governance" or commerce, although many specific practices within such fields as anthropology and history, for instance, were conceived and held in more direct relation to such worldly and increasingly corporate concerns.[21] This very convergence has spelled the rise of an "interested" (rather than an "objective") practice used to forward policy issues and political agendas. In research focusing on a foreign country there is inevitably the coalescence of scholars whose work becomes shaped by alliance politics (the Japanese term for scholars whose work serves the ends of government policy is *goyō gakusha*; or, witness the separation of Japan bashers and apologists), and in the U.S. area studies was anchored by the nomothetic disciplines. Much-needed challenges to this order have come through the work of scholars from E. H. Norman to Harootunian, Dower, and Cumings, but if their critiques have received relatively little attention outside of East Asian studies, the literary and cultural realms within East Asian studies have been almost completely neglected.[22] While the study of literature has come to cling even more noticeably to the nation-state—the paradox of "world" literature as a framework is to reinforce just such national identity—cultural studies has given us a de-, trans-, or multi-nationalized landscape. And, whereas literary study was content to examine visual representation, multiculturalism and ethnic studies, class conflict, sexual orientation, etc. as the content of literature, it is as if the sheer urgency of these worldly matters had to seek more unrestrained address, giving rise to queer studies, colonial and postcolonial studies, diasporic studies, subaltern studies which, together with text-centered studies, would be seen as constituting cultural studies.

The inclusive, richly varied content, and the non- or multi-disciplinary nature of cultural studies[23]—that is, the practice of making connections, analyzing, and coming to know phenomena unencumbered by disciplinary protocols—clearly all this gives it unusual power. But, as if to mimic the way capitalism has become naturalized as a universal when it is, of course, a particular way of organizing economic relations, the apparent inclusiveness of cultural studies serves to mask its particularities.[24] Cultural studies has effectively expanded beyond its own borders, and in the absence of traditional disciplinary requirements it foregrounds what might be better identified as a practice than something like a "method." This practice signifies the conjuncture of topicality and political agenda, where the main imperative seems to be its capacity to sell itself. The absence of disciplinary and other structures seems to require some other way of valuing such work, and not surprisingly such work must summon the attention not of specialists (as discipline-based practice did in the past) but of a broadly-based fellow-consumer/producer to whom it must appeal. But, if that describes the general logic within which such work circulates, there is also the Anglicentricity that arbitrates values. As noted earlier, unless a topic has some direct or significant contact points with Anglo-, and perhaps even Euro-America, it does not quite belong to cultural studies. Accordingly, ethnic studies, which in the U.S. does count as cultural studies, is neatly separated from Asian studies, albeit differently from its separation in the Cold War years. And to supplement my earlier references, former colonies of Euro-America such as India, nations with francophone literature, Caribbean and Latin American nations multiply colonized by European powers "count," while the study of lands that have remained more or less separated from the Euro-American metropoles—particularly at the level of linguistic influence—be they Korea, Japan, even China (clearly a "mixed" case in such former colonial spaces as Hong Kong and Singapore), or Slavic nations, typically do not.

Subaltern studies represents a singular and notable subset within cultural studies, diverging from ethnic studies by considering subjecthood not on transplanted terrain, but within once-colonized space ("local" insofar as it lies at some remove from the dominant metropolitan). Perhaps the genesis of subaltern studies as a category of identity politics (much needed, in this context) prevented their engagement with longtime critics of area studies who had covered some of the ground they would come to claim in their own work. The ascendance of subaltern studies, which I would like to affirm as a particularly vigorous and important constituent of cultural studies, might be seen, nonetheless, as a practice that reflects an Anglicentric aporia.[25] While quick to recognize the postcolonial critics for sensitively addressing "operations of domination and power," H. D. Harootunian observes that subaltern histories tend to instate an essentialized "authentic" local history, but in affirming the centrality of the Other, end up leaving untouched the very structure of domination that engendered oppositional writing in the first place—i.e., of (transnational) capitalism. "The search for the excluded voice . . . often leads to the dead-end pursuit for authenticity," he continues, "and restores precisely the Eurocentric claims of the sovereign subject it wishes to eliminate."[26]

For years, a few oppositional figures who work in East Asian studies such as H. D. Harootunian[27] have been contesting similar practices of native identification which to be sure belonged to a somewhat different arrangement of power relations but which nonetheless defined the mainstream practice of East Asian area studies.[28] Interestingly, it took another East Asianist to address what he called the "Chicago School of Japanese Studies;" he would credit its members for producing "without doubt, the majority of the most innovative and interesting scholarship on Japan in the Anglophone world." John Lie, however, ultimately criticized them like this: "Despite their theoretical sophistication, methodological rigor, and progressive politics, they work almost exclusively in the discursive realm."[29] The familiar opposition of discourse to real-life materialities was invoked in this instance to affirm Ahmad's economism in the latter's criticism of Said, but in the process the author of this essay misrecognizes the accomplishments of the "Chicago School," particularly the seminal figures he names: Harootunian, Miyoshi, and Najita. Together they had pioneered the use of critical theory in analyzing and challenging the ideological underpinnings of area studies and particularly the difficult nativist-orientalist binary that otherwise went unexamined.

The dissolution of the Cold War has not spelled the complete irrelevance of area studies. The 1980s saw a proliferation of programs linking Asian studies, especially language study, to international studies—a "field" which more and more came to mean not diplomatic procedures and its history but business-related curricula. If East Asian studies was nested in national security concerns during the Cold War era, today it is the MBA program, sometimes yoked together with international relations and foreign language study that most directly expresses the driving force of these programs. We should note that now in the late 1990s, the reasoning that brought area studies to "international relations" has virtually disappeared from college campuses with the apparently secure entrenchment of English as the currency of international business.

Any current consideration of Japanese literary study must run through cultural studies.[30] The by-now familiar trajectory of cultural studies, especially its British heritage, hardly needs rehearsing. The work of E. P. Thompson and Raymond Williams occupies the discursive center of work which takes on institutional force in such figures as Richard Hoggart and Stuart Hall and the Birmingham Centre for Contemporary Cultural Studies in the late 1960s, and is further inflected with neo-Marxist and poststructuralist theories before sending forth a new generation of culturalist scholars dispersed throughout the English-speaking parts of the globe.[31] In the U.S., diasporic transplantation of people be they from postcolonial origins or migrants engendered by global corporate policies (including those of GATT, WTO, and the World Bank) have helped engender study of people who at times seem reduced by the demographic signifier of "multiculturalism," flourishing together with such other areas as popular culture. But whether we refer to American, British, or Australian practices, as John Frow remarks, cultural studies "doesn't have the sort of secure definition of its object that would give it the thematic coherence and the sense of a progressive accumulation of knowledge."[32] Unlike a discipline such as English (literature), which in institutional settings tends to dominate other linguistic-literary fields (from French on out to ever-more exotic languages), the threat of totalization as embodied in cultural studies issues from its very non-unified, non-discipline-bound expansiveness—a trait appearing all the more ominous when these existing marginal disciplines seem marked for obsolescence. But, if the elimination of professional-disciplinary requirements is neither unambiguously good nor bad, the logic of "free market" appeal to arbitrate academic production we seem left with is problematic.

Cultural Studies and Japanese Literary Studies

Even if an inchoate transdisciplinarity makes cultural studies difficult to define, it is nonetheless approach, method, or theory that distinguishes its practice, especially from many of its neighboring (social science) disciplines, which share its topics. Among the many recent works which take cultural studies to task precisely for its "approach" is the work of Norma Field, who engages the issue from the position of overlapping marginalities—area studies and Japanese literature. Norma Field's thoughtful study of Japanese literary study in the postwar era[33] expresses unease with both the theoretical excesses of cultural studies and the likelihood that it might completely displace literary studies. She is especially concerned with the baneful effects of "deconstruction, with its thematics of decentering, playful mobility of the signifier," and work concerned only with what she calls "discursive formation,"[34] which appears to be defined in contrast to theory that explicitly addresses worldly conditions and material realities.[35] The Japanese cultural theorist and literary critic Karatani Kōjin is singled out as the most influential figure who exemplifies such work. His roundtable discussion with Asada Akira, Hasumi Shigehiko, and Miura Masashi is roundly—and not without justification—dismissed with the assertion that "there is no reflection on how the theory relates to its contexts."[36] Whereas Norma Field cites Masao Miyoshi's 1974 book, *Accomplices of Silence*, in laudatory terms as a work of contestatory energy and spirited critique, the intervening effects of "poststructuralism, especially deconstruction" is cause for reservations about his more recent *Off Center*, described as a work enthusiastically embracing "joyous, oral, Third World plenitude." While she is right in noting significant formal differences between the two books, as I peruse such essays as "Bashers and Bashing in the World" as well as "The 'Great Divide' Once Again" (both from *Off Center*), it is difficult to ignore just how Miyoshi led the way, and more or less alone within Japanese studies at one point, in making the political economy a major subject of study within humanistic inquiry.[37]

If the urgency of worldly conditions lent to materialist approaches the imperative to wed theory to practice, poststructuralist theory problematized the ontological separation of reality from representation. However, the recognition of effects in representation, the signifier, or discourse that hitherto were attributed only to their putative other—the real—does not have to be read as a simple dismissal of "real life." There is ample evidence of "discursive work," even in the Japan field, which is pointedly attentive to the material conditions of the world.[38] One of its most compelling illustrations can be found in Field's own (justly) acclaimed *In the Realm of the Dying Emperor*, which achieves some of its meaningfulness from decades of preceding theoretical work which has helped engender and invigorate such hybrid cultural exposition and study.[39] In a more recent article entitled "War and Apology: Japan, Asia, the Fiftieth, and After,"[40] Norma Field provides an even more compelling example of work which itself might be characterized as "discursive" work that is also firmly moored in the everyday world. Her insightful and provocative meditation on Japan and the responsibilities attendant a nation-state that forged itself an aggressive and violent part in the geopolitics of half a century ago is introduced this way:

> I survey the long- and short-term history of ways in which Japanese have addressed their role in World War II, specifically, the shifting economy of self-understanding as victims and aggressors. I sketch the overlapping and competing diplomatic, politico-economic, and moral discourses through which the pursuit and avoidance of apology have been enacted. . . . I attempt a philosophico-linguistic excursus to broach the implications of the textualist, antifoundationalist views of the world that are influential with humanists and nonpositivistic social scientists in the last decades of the twentieth century for addressing the nightmares of the twentieth century. This genre of apology is a nodal point for the individual and the collectivity, the past and the present, the rational and the emotional, the particular and the structural.[41]

And, as Field proceeds to deliver what is promised, as we see in this excerpt, she demonstrates just how "literature" might inform subject matter that would surely be treated very differently in the "genres" belonging to the social sciences. Whereas Field has made both "discussion of discursive formation" and theory divorced from the material conditions of life the object of her criticism, her own practice suggests how the two realms defy easy separation.

The problem, as we saw in the instance where Miyoshi's work was discussed, revolves around the conjuncture of literary study, theory, and cultural studies. If I am to read the recent works by Field and Miyoshi, for example, I cannot see "attentiveness to the real world" as the divide. Instead, I see similarity in the form of a divide that both have increasingly observed: a deep split between work that is "literary" and work that is "worldly." Field, in particular, has noted with alarm the status of the literary (diminished, increasingly ignored) in the academy today. In a recent essay on postwar Japanese literary study, as a corrective to this state of affairs she urges "focused study and translation, which themselves are of course not atheoretical."[42] Her longstanding wariness regarding the self-containedness of theory is coupled with a more temporally urgent fear expressed this way: "If Japanese literature . . . has had one kind of constrained yet varied existence within area studies, its release into cultural studies may be so transformational as to signify its evaporation as object of study."[43]

But, just as surely as the contours of "literature" have changed over the years, literary study itself has assumed radically different forms. Leaving in abeyance for now the question of literature as a moribund form of cultural expression, might we not admit the contours of literary study today as being virtually unrecognizable in relation to some of its earlier practices? Though the following two examples do not mark the limits of such new possibilities, Miyoshi's discussion of orality and Japanese literature, and Field's own production of hybrid genres, might both be seen in varying relations to "literature proper." And, within the context of the steep rise of cultural studies, in spite of their differences, the recent work of both of these scholars are likely to be seen as belonging to "cultural studies"—even if the two may disavow such belonging for reasons of their own—in part because these works have considered Japan as an effect of American or "global" capitalist practices (which is an "outcome" far likelier to be recognized or "produced" by their theoretically inflected interventions on the political economy as scholars of literature and culture that conventional social science is likely to miss).

Norma Field looks to Rey Chow who has addressed the beleaguered status of literature from another angle. Chow, who warns against the instrumentalization of literature to what she calls "other disciplinary controls," noting that "the instrumentalist, reflectionist assumptions about language and representation, which literature challenges as part of its critical project, remain entirely unexamined."[44] Most of us will agree that the reduction of knowledge to information is problematic, but Rey Chow's observation regarding literature's capacity to challenge such reduction of language and representation is in fact an affirmation not simply of literature but of its theoretical gains. At the same time that I affirm Norma Field's insistence upon the value of translation and close reading, I wish to point to her own, determinedly committed work—work that is often powerfully discursive. I see this discursivity as a distinct feature of "literary practice" that, among other things permits, as Rey Chow notes, the demystification of concealed ideologies upon which societies operate.[45]

My intention is not to echo either the endorsements of theory or the critiques which fault theory's disregard of the real. But the critics who see "discourse" as displacing "the real" need not, it seems, ignore the transformative power that frequently links discursive understanding and analysis to realities no more stable or material than the former. While I do not wish to suggest a passive complacency, the way we view things does indeed come inscribed with evaluation, criticism, in short, ingredients for change. Nomothetic scholars can study the very same subject or topic as the discursive analyst, and the result is a significantly different study. (My own interests in Japanese modernity have led me to attribute the canonization of Natsume Sōseki's *Kokoro*, for instance, in part to its role in helping to naturalize the identity of the self as a privatized, bourgeois being deflected from concerns about sociality or a nation's imperialist behavior.)

A similar "discursive" methodology might also permit one to understand, for example, recent shifts in social priorities for redirecting income and resources from public to private and corporate realms. Conventional wisdom has money, capital, and resources in various forms as the proprietary "creation" of corporate practices, but foundational criticism—particularly as expressed in Marxist and "post-Marxist" critiques—allows us to discern hidden connections, aporias, inversions so that, in the case at hand, the real subject of material objects and means of exchange can be identified with networks of collective labor, hidden from view by systems of laws meant to obscure such perceptions. The "naturalness" of industry and corporations as creators of wealth requires continual and renewed unmasking as itself a "cultural" creation, a kind of discursive fiction that runs unbridled through the transnational collective psyche. Our ability to challenge the widely held view of private claims to the generation of wealth, money, and capital requires what might be called a "discursive mediation"—a method of "reading" that can help us see the networks of institutionalized thought, legal practices, and prevailing views concerning indigenous rights in relation to transnational (corporate) rights, which together conspire to insist upon the verity of "private" ownership as unquestioned truth. But that we have to recognize it as such through the lens of discursivity makes the reality of its hegemony, not to mention the consequences of these practices (the exploitation of workers throughout the globe as short-term, replaceable labor), no less pernicious. Discourse analysis is a literary practice par excellence, albeit with a twist that undoubtedly reflects its own birth—an astute self-consciousness regarding the limits of an insistent empiricism that seeks neat separation between the real and the representational. And, it ought to be recognized as perhaps a mutation of literature itself, neither "fictional" nor subject-centered as in Western European standards of high literature in the last two centuries, but rather as a way of perceiving or making sense of semiotic comprehension that is profoundly literary because of its ostensibly "theoretical" roots.

Colonizing Japan

Travel to just about anywhere in the world, from France to Taiwan, Japan, or Brazil, and you will encounter at least two streams of popular music. One fits our ideas of "traditional" popular music (e.g., *enka* in Japan) while the other is more a local version of rock-pop music catering to a younger demographic slice. Though one is rooted in local ethno-musical characteristics and the other not, decades of popular acceptance suggests that both now function as "native" popular forms. Against these "local" veins of popular music, take a recent example, the culture of hip hop with its musical expression, rap, which has been widely embraced by youth around the globe who listen to rap music from artists in the U.S., as well as being able to play or hear locally produced rap delivered in Chinese, Japanese, French, or Portuguese, inflected to capture life on the streets and neighborhoods of their own nations. Cultural studies may not carry all the signs of a popular medium like rap music, but it seems to mimic the popular diffusion of music, film, and tastes and habits of urban consumers that flow outwardly from the U.S., the metropole of global culture. And cultural studies may not have taken root as widely away from its Anglo-American roots as has rap music, but it has become the hottest intellectual practice or commodity in recent years, particularly in the industrialized countries of Asia.

Karuchuraru sutadeizu (*karu-suta* to its detractors; the homophone "karu" suggesting the meaning of "light studies" to this dismissive referent) had arrived in Japan with focused, commercial intensity in the mid-1990s (though there were certainly earlier examples of works that might have been called that). When I returned to Tokyo in the summer of 1999 to participate in a workshop on 1920s Japan, cultural studies was being niche marketed, competing with and in some cases overtaking the bookstore spaces formerly reserved for thought (shisō), tetsugaku (philosophy), or the works associated with the contributors to the journal *Gendai shisō* (Contemporary Thought). A decade or two earlier, Japan enjoyed an Edo-būmu, when books, artifacts, public lectures, etc. that focused on the many aspects of urban society in the Tokugawa era were all the rage. In contrast, cultural studies is a boomlet that is largely restricted to the academic community, but it also happens to have begun flourishing as literary study, and indeed the humanities as a whole (which would include cultural studies) are in a state of crisis as they are facing curricular elimination and prospects of being made an adjunct to other realms like international studies.

Amidst the steady stream of Western cultural studies works that get translated into Japanese stand two noteworthy milestones. In 1996, the Iwanami journal *Shisō* (Thought) published a special issue titled "Karuchuraru sutadeizu: Atarashii bunka hihan to tame ni" (Cultural Studies: Toward a New Critique of Culture).[46] Contributors included David Roediger ("From the Social Construction of Race to the Abolition of Whiteness"), Dipesh Chakrabarty ("Subaltern Studies: Writings on South Asian Culture and Society"), Lisa Lowe ("Asian American: Hybridity, Multiplicity, Difference"), Megan Morris ("Luncheon Directed at Republicanism: Australian Debates on Feminism, Media, Identity Politics"), an interview of Stuart Hall, Chungmoo Choi ("Transnational Capitalism, National Imaginary, and the Protest Theater in South Korea"), Rey Chow (Where Have All the Natives Gone"), and Naoki Sakai ("Distinguishing 'Literature' and the Labor of Translation: Theresa Han Kyun Sha's *Dictée* and Repetition Without Return"). Here cultural studies is preponderantly a critique and interrogation of imperialism and identity formations. In the same year a symposium was jointly sponsored by the University of Tokyo Center for Social Research (Shakai jōhō kenkyū-jo) and the British Council entitled "A Dialogue with Cultural Studies" (Karuchuraru sutadeizu to no taiwa).[47] The subsequent conference volume that was published in 1999 includes a nod of recognition toward two native sons who Satō Takeshi claims to have prefigured the arrival of Western culture studies in the 1990s: Tsurumi Shunsuke and Katō Shūichi.[48] Both well known to those of us in the West who study modern Japanese literature and culture, here Satō cites Tsurumi for his notion of "discommunication" as a central feature of social relations that reveals relations of power, while Katō's essay on the hybridity of Japanese culture (Nihon bunka no zasshu-sei) is cited as a seminal piece that challenged a Japanese discourse of singular culturalism in the 1950s. To Satō's brief account I would like to add Maeda Ai, whose engagement with Western critics and theorists (Benjamin, Marx, Poulet, Bakhtin, Foucault, and Derrida, to name a few) and a broad spectrum of work that spanned social history, explorations of visuality, theories of space and everyday life in the city, and film and literature reception anticipated the practice of what looks in retrospect very similar to much of what passes as cultural studies today.[49]

I strayed a bit in mentioning Maeda Ai because Yoshimi, Komori, and Narita, arguably the most prominent figures in Japanese cultural studies today, are indebted more to Maeda (and for that matter, other culturalist predecessors as Minami Hiroshi and Tsurumi Shunsuke) than to, say, British cultural studies,

360   James A. Fujii

particularly in the way their work focuses on Japanese modernity rather than matters of contemporary social interest. If Naoki Sakai of Cornell orchestrated the *Shisō* volume of 1996, Yoshimi and Komori together with Narita play the role of native practitioner as well as host to Stuart Hall and others in the 1996 conference held at Tokyo University under the auspices of the British Council and Tokyo University in March of 1996. This second milestone in Japanese cultural studies saw among its invitees Stuart Hall, Angela McRobbie, Colin Sparks, and David Morley. They were brought in congress with those who have become key figures in the practice of cultural studies in Japan—Narita Ryūichi, Yoshimi Shun'ya, Kawamura Minato, Ueno Chizuko, Komori Yōichi, and Hanada Tatsurō, together with more transnational intellectuals like Naoki Sakai and Sangjung Kang. Theory and fashion travel in interesting ways. As has been true in the U.S., in Japan British cultural studies is authentic, real, and more highly valued. And like in the U.S., Japanese academics who were engaged in communication studies are among the first to seize upon Western cultural studies.

Yoshimi and Hanada's introductory comments to the conference volume carefully articulate the contexts and histories that bring cultural studies to its own scene, and it is clear that whatever gaps there may be between the ambitious problematics, approaches, and agendas that are ushered in by cultural studies in Japan, it serves primarily as a rich menu for the Japanese academic. Gender studies, ethnographic approaches, the eliding of high and low culture, ethnicity as a topic of academic inquiry—surely they have consequences within the Japanese context of rethinking the place given to knowledge, education, disciplines, etc. that revolve around higher education in the West. In that sense, that a mediating figure like Naoki Sakai stands so prominently in Japanese cultural studies, attests to the notably "de-nationalized" transformation of academic practices as they once played out in area studies. Back then Japan was the source of information, where the native informant and appropriate objects of study were to be found by the North American and European student of Japanese society and culture. In the last ten years or so, overlapping greatly the influx of theory and cultural studies from West to East, this commerce has changed drastically. Students from North American universities still go to study with these Japanese specialists whose knowledge of literature, history, or thought are to be imparted to their "blue-eyed" charges. But, in the 1990s, the most sought-after figures in the realm of humanistic inquiry—Komori, Yoshimi, Narita, Karatani—look steadfastly Westward in knowing what their own agendas are to be. (Cyberspace is now replete with gossip about which American graduate student first introduced Eve Sedgwick's work to Professor so-and-so.) While this hardly means that Japanese academics have nothing to teach the foreign student of Japan, like the ambiguities of auto-parts and car company identities, it is getting difficult to say that knowledge about Japanese texts or cultural practices is the domain of the specialist in Japan.

I would like to conclude by bringing back the position from which and about which I write—the study of modern Japanese literature in the age of cultural studies. At the most "local" of concerns is the transformation of what was once a model that was virtually a universal: the West sought to understand the non-West, and the former brought to bear its superior technologies of understanding ("methods") upon other societies made accessible by native informants. Now the agendas, the topics, the subjects of inquiry and the methods— in effect everything—are determined by a practice without a common subject or approach. This formlessness substitutes a linguistic unity for disciplinary protocols that once upon a time determined objects of study. Put differently, if cultural studies might tritely be represented as the all-encompassing software for academic production in the humanities today, we are apt to miss seeing that the constituent "language" of that software is unmistakably English. And while we recognize as self-serving fiction the view that academic work used to be immune from academic fashion, there can be no mistake in recognizing the intensification of the essentially "commercial" imperatives that drive academic production at this century's end. Neither forms of Marxist critique nor poststructuralist thought stand outside that system. That does not deny them the capacity to engage its effects, but it also does not diminish the importance of recognizing and challenging them.

Of course it is not as if the age of area studies as it played out in academia was devoid of practices that we might identify as commercial, as the requirements for all the familiar activities of academic practice and exchange under capitalism clearly underwrote, not to mention predated the "logic" of area studies. Under that kind of academic structure, critical, oppositional work was produced, as mentioned above. Technology-aided new permutations of capital flow, new non-national structures like the wto, and other developments have produced "realities" that require appropriately fresh means of understanding and criticizing their effects. In rebutting Arif Dirlik's broadside against postcolonial critics, Stuart Hall refers to the Gulf War as an example of contemporary realities that defy analysis with a nostalgic return to "clear-cut politics of binary oppositions." [50] The implication of a past of commensurately clear-cut realities seems misleading, however. Hall notes the mixed motives of the un Alliance working against the atrocities committed by Saddam Hussein against Kurds and Marsh Arabs and the Alliance's defense of Western oil interests, and character-

362   James A. Fujii

izes it as a new complexity reflective of the world today, calling it "characteristic of a certain kind of political event of our 'new times' in which *both* the crisis of the uncompleted struggle for 'decolonisation' *and* the crisis of the 'post-independence' state are deeply inscribed."[51] In my view, earlier conflicts were also multiply inflected with contradictory aims, motives, and effects, and perhaps in different ways, every bit as elusive and complex. How we represent and understand them, however, *have* changed. In Hall's essay that once again runs into the deep fault line that separates what he calls a nostalgic and "clear-cut politics of binary oppositions" (Dirlik's materialist attack on postcolonial critics) against his own ratification of post-structuralist orientations, he urges us to "keep these two ends of the chain in play at the same time—over-determination and difference, condensation and dissemination," warning against falling into "the trap of assuming that, because essentialism has been deconstructed *theoretically*, therefore it has been displaced *politically*."[52] In pointing to the mutation of English into both a culturally delinked lingua franca of a "global" world and the concomitant effect of both English-speakingness and Euro-English culture as a hegemonic determinant, I have tried to show how such culturalism makes doing what Hall urges far more difficult to practice than to assert.

Notes

1   For a perceptive essay that addresses area and cultural studies around issues of visuality, see Joe Murphy's "Problems in Incorporating Film into an Area Studies Framework," forthcoming in *positions*.

2   See his "Metacapital: A Response to Pierre Bourdieu," in *Polygraph: an International Journal of Culture and Politics* 10 (1998): 34.

3   John Frow, *Time and Commodity Culture: Essays in Cultural Theory and Postmodernity* (Clarendon Press, Oxford, 1997), 11.

4   The April 3, 1999, issue of the *Los Angeles Times* carried a chart of the "World's Ethnic Crises" which listed deaths and refugees claimed in different regions over the past year. Of the eleven countries listed, Kosovo (a region in the province of Serbia, not a country) was lowest by far in terms of lives lost (2,000) and people uprooted (459,000). The chart is reproduced below:

Country	Uprooted	Killed
Afghanistan	6.2 million	1,050,000
Algeria	105,000	80,000–100,000
Colombia	1 million	+40,000–250,000
India/Kashmir	213,000	30,000–50,000
Iraq	1.5 million	+100,000–250,000
Kosovo	459,000 (before NATO)	2,000

Myanmar	1 million +	130,000–500,000
Rwanda	3.5 million +	500,000–800,000
Sierra Leone	1.45 million	15,000–20,000
Sri Lanka	900,000 +	55,000–70,000
Sudan	4.3 million +	1.5 million

Despite some comparably high figures, left off the list was Turkey, which happens to be a NATO ally. According to the UNHCR, Turkey has created in excess of 350,000 internal refugees in recent years; and we must not forget Palestinians as one of the largest group of displaced people in the world. The website for the United Nations High Commission on Refugees can be found at http://www.unhcr.ch/refworld/refworld/country/country.htm.

5 This included the massive occupation of U.S. and NATO forces not just in Kosovo, but within all of Yugoslavia, with full immunity from any legal or other challenge to the conduct of its forces, making Yugoslavia bear the costs of such occupation, and making Kosovo an effective free trade zone with separate "free market" economic practices for Kosovo, a province of Serbia and what remains of Yugoslavia (Serbia and Montenegro).

6 See, for example, Michel Collon, *Poker Menteur: Les grandes puissances, la Yougoslavie et les prochaines guerres* (Anvers, Belgium: EPO, 1998); Michel Choussodovsky, *The Globalization of Poverty: Impacts of IMF and World Bank Reforms* (Penang, Malaysia: Third World Network, 1997); and Noam Chomsky, *Profit Over People: Neoliberalism and Global Order* (New York: Seven Stories Press, 1999).

7 Most readers will likely not remember that the eleven weeks of bombings lasted from March through much of June 1999.

8 Manuel de Landa identifies the development of what he calls "machinic phylum" into the realm of warfare and computers. Computer circuitry and response mechanisms built into elaborate networks of computers that manage separate realms—military armaments in specific locations, overarching command centers, systems of release mechanisms—whose responses and activities constitute a non-human "intelligence." See his *War in the Age of Intelligent Machines* (New York: Swerve Editions, 1991).

9 The chronology is outlined in the introduction to the U.S. edition, published by Indiana University Press. Jean Baudrillard, *The Gulf War Did Not Take Place*, translated and with an introduction by Paul Patton (Bloomington: Indiana University Press, 1995).

10 It appears as chapter 1 in his book *Uncritical Theory: Postmodernism, Intellectuals, and the Gulf War* (Amherst: University of Massachusetts Press, 1992).

11 Ibid., 15.

12 Paul Patton who writes the introduction to the English language edition, is a bit too eager to rescue Baudrillard from the likes of Norris's criticism, referring to Baudrillard's essays as not so much irony as a kind of "black humour which seeks to subvert what is being said by pursuing its implicit logic to extremes: so you want us to believe that this was a clean, minimalist war, with little collateral damage and few Allied casualties. Why stop there: War? What war?" (7).

13 At the same time that I credit Baudrillard's text with such intent, I can simultaneously feel outrage at both the U.S. bombings and economic sanctions directed against the people of Iraq. The latter, ostensibly gentler tactic of sanctions alone are

largely responsible for over a million civilian lives lost, mostly among children and the sick and elderly.

14 According to David Crystal, "there are estimates that perhaps 80 per cent of the world's 6,000 or so living languages will die out within the next century" (David Crystal, *English as a Global Language* [Cambridge: Cambridge University Press, 1997], 17). The situation at hand might also benefit from the following loose analogy to the strategy pursued by corporations such as Microsoft which has made "Windows" into the common medium of computer-based exchange as well as the centerpiece to a strategy which seeks to vertically capture everything from platforms to language software to communications software, thereby shaping and even determining the very "content" of what is transmitted through their medium (the Windows platform). We might point to the many other analogies including the paper industry and how it is involved in driving what in fact are its "secondary" or tertiary concerns—magazine publishers, the book industry, the newspaper industry, etc. The simple "medium" of paper might be seen here as exceeding its apparently neutral function as a medium for transmitting text and image, acquiring a certain "agency" of its own that is driven by the interest to expand the use of paper.

15 Joseph Buttigieg quotes from Frantz Fanon who links language to power in colonial relations where "to speak a language is to take on a world, a culture." Quoted from Fanon's *Black Skin, White Masks*, 38, 47, in Joseph A. Buttigieg, "Teaching English and Developing a Critical Knowledge of the Global," *boundary 2* 26(2) (summer 1999).

16 For a discussion of Arabic as it negotiates such realities, see Ronald Judy, "On the Politics of Global Language, or Unfungible Local Value, *boundary 2* 24(2) (summer 1997): 101–43.

17 See, for example, Michel Choussodovsky, *The Globalisation of Poverty*, and Jeremy Brecher and Tim Costello, *Global Village or Global Pillage: Economic Reconstruction from the Bottom Up*, 2nd ed. (Cambridge, Mass.: South End Press, 1998).

18 Language has been viewed as an impediment to Japanese modernization well back in the early Meiji period as the debates in the pages of the *Meiroku zasshi* show. The development and especially the relative low rates of computer use throughout Japanese society in comparison to the U.S. reflect language-related lags more than anything.

19 Stuart Hall, "Cultural Studies and Its Theoretical Legacies," in *Stuart Hall: Critical Dialogues in Cultural Studies*, ed. David Morley and Kuan-Hsing Chen (London: Routledge, 1996), 271.

20 Wallerstein, "The Unintended Consequences of Cold War Area Studies," 198, in *The Cold War and the University: Toward an Intellectual History of the Postwar Years*, ed. Noam Chomsky et al. (New York: The New Press, 1997).

21 The subject of Said's orientalism and John Dower's discussion of American anthropologists and the Pacific War come immediately to mind.

22 It should be noted that the work of the critics mentioned here is distinguished by its attentiveness to cultural dimensions of society.

23 Stuart Hall, Gayatri Spivak, and Iain Chambers, among others, have approvingly noted the non- or adisciplinarity of cultural studies.

24 Detractors might use the term "symptomatic" (of the capacity of global capitalism to assume, engender, even promote multiplicity), supporters perhaps "emblematic" (of the multiple fronts needed to take on the infinite proliferation of capitalism) in situat-

ing cultural studies in its own moment. See also Naoki Sakai's essay "Karuchuraru sutadeizu no genzai" (Cultural Studies Today), in *Gurōbarizeeshon no naka no ajia: Karuchuraru sutadeizu no genzai* (Tokyo: Poesis sōsho, 1998), where he affirms the importance of multi-lingual (non-English) articulations of cultural studies.

25 A rather extended critique of subaltern studies by Arif Dirlik from a different angle (which is forcefully challenged by Stuart Hall) appears as "The Postcolonial Aura: Third World Criticism in the Age of Global Capitalism," *Critical Inquiry* (winter 1994); Stuart Hall, "When Was 'the Post-Colonial'? Thinking at the Limit," in *The Postcolonial Question: Common Skies, Divided Horizons,* ed. Iain Chambers and Lidia Curti (New York: Routledge, 1996).

26 See his essay "Tracking the Dinosaur: Area Studies in a Time of 'Globalism,'" in *History's Disquiet: Modernity, Cultural Practice, and the Question of Everyday Life* (New York: Columbia University Press, 2000) (the Wellek Library lectures at the University of California, Irvine, 1997).

27 As critical as Harootunian has been about the reproduction of cultural essentialisms found in the latter, he has also helped to pioneer critical theoretical approaches to the study of East Asia. His work in particular problematizes the facile separation of "representations" from "the real" in precisely the way that nomothetic practices typically cannot.

28 For a critique of the practice, see Rey Chow, "The Politics of Pedagogy of Asian Literatures in American Universities," in *Writing Diaspora: Tactics of Intervention in Contemporary Cultural Studies* (Bloomington: Indiana University Press, 1993).

29 John Lie, "Enough Said, Ahmad: Politics and Literary Theory" *positions* 2(2) (summer 1994): 421.

30 Figures in the *MLA Bulletin* suggest that institutional hiring categories have largely remained unchanged, even as demand for those working in cultural studies increases, whether it be determined by opportunity for publication or class "demand."

31 Anthologies with narrative accounts of this history can be found in *What Is Cultural Studies? A Reader,* edited by John Storey; *The Cultural Studies Reader,* edited by Simon During; *Cultural Studies,* edited by Lawrence Grossberg, Cary Nelson, and Paula Treichler; *Stuart Hall: Critical Dialogues in Cultural Studies,* edited by David Morley and Kuan-Hsing Chen; *The Post-Colonial Question: Common Skies, Divided Horizons,* edited by Iain Chambers and Lidia Curti. John Frow's *Cultural Studies and Cultural Value* treats it in more inclusive fashion, as well as *British Cultural Studies: An Introduction,* by Graeme Turner.

32 John Frow, *Cultural Studies and Cultural Value* (Oxford: Oxford University Press, 1995), 7.

33 "'The Way of the World': Japanese Literary Studies in the Postwar United States," in *The Postwar Developments of Japanese Studies in the United States* (Leiden: Brill, 1998), 227–93.

34 Field, "Japanese Literary Studies," 261.

35 Norma Field's criticism of "discursive work" seems closely echoed in Teresa Ebert's materialist critique of ludic feminism (which she argues centers language, representation, etc., that displaces concern for actual conditions of inequality). See Teresa Ebert, *Ludic Feminism and After: Postmodernism, Desire, and Labor in Late Capitalism* (Ann Arbor: University of Michigan Press, 1996).

36 Field, "Japanese Literary Studies," 264.

37 In his chapter "The Great Divide Again," for example, in discussing orality in relation to modern Japanese literature, Miyoshi's criticism of Derrida, for example ("language is always already a writing"), is precisely a criticism of what might be called "discursive formalism."

38 See, for example, Takashi Fujitani's *Splendid Monarchy: Power and Pageantry in Modern Japan* (Berkeley: University of California Press, 1996); Kevin Doak's *Dreams of Difference: The Japan Romantic School and the Crisis of Modernity* (Berkeley: University of California Press, 1994); Leslie Pincus's *Authenticating Culture in Imperial Japan: Kuki Shuzo and the Rise of National Aesthetics* (Berkeley: University of California Press, 1995); and Sandra Buckley, *Broken Silence: Voices of Japanese Feminism* (Berkeley: University of California Press, 1997).

39 Such other works as Sara Suleri's *Salad Days* (Chicago: University of Chicago Press, 1989), and Alice Kaplan's *French Lessons: A Memoir* (Chicago: University of Chicago Press, 1993) come to mind.

40 Norma Field, "War and Apology: Japan, Asia, the Fiftieth, and After," in *positions* 5(1) (spring 1997): 1–50.

41 Field, "War and Apology," 3.

42 Field, "'Japanese Literary Studies," 265.

43 Ibid., 268.

44 Rey Chow, "The Politics of Pedagogy of Asian Literature," in *Writing Diaspora: Tactics of Intervention in Contemporary Cultural Studies* (Bloomington: Indiana University Press, 1993), 132.

45 Rey Chow makes the observation with these words: "Concern with social reality must be accompanied with a close attention to how language works—not so much in the creation of formal beauty as in the concealment of ideology" (135).

46 "Karuchuraru sutadeizu: Atarashii bunka hihan to tame ni" (Cultural Studies: Toward a New Critique of Culture), *Shisō* 859 (January 1996).

47 Invited participants included Stuart Hall, Ali Rattansi, Angela McRobbie, Naoki Sakai, Colin Sparks, Charlotte Mary Brunsdon, and David Morley. Participants from Japan read like a list of those most closely associated with cultural studies in Japan today: Yoshimi Shun'ya, Narita Ryūichi, Ueno Chizuko, Kawamura Minato, and Komori Yōichi. The conference volume was published in 1999 by Shin'yō-sha, edited by Tatsurō Hanada, Yoshimi Shun'ya, and Colin Sparks.

48 Ibid., 258–75.

49 Among Maeda's impressive oeuvre are studies of the rise of popular literature and women's magazines in the 1920s and 1930s, the transformation of reading practices in modern Japan (wherein he also identifies the significant homosociality of what was a transformative moment of heterogeneous reading practices), the advent of movie theatres and other modern visual mass media, the signification of light and shadow in Kiyochika's prints, and the mutation of social relations through the re-spatialization of urban space in literature, to mention just a few.

50 Stuart Hall, "When Was 'the Post-Colonial'?" 244.

51 Ibid.

52 Ibid., 249.

Questions of Japanese Cinema: Disciplinary Boundaries and the Invention of the Scholarly Object
Mitsuhiro Yoshimoto

Disciplines are now experiencing a legitimation crisis. The notion of what constitutes the rightful territories of disciplines is radically being put to the test. Questions such as what should be studied, how it should be studied, and for what purpose it should be studied are no longer self-evident. The increasingly unsettling vagueness of disciplines makes the boundaries between them the contested terrains and overdetermined spaces rather than the unambiguously fixed outlines. Film studies is one of these disciplines facing a formidable challenge of refashioning or reinventing themselves to survive the legitimation crisis of academic knowledge and the university. In the 1970s and 1980s, film studies secured its legitimacy by its focus on theory and radical interdisciplinarity. Yet after more than two decades of rapid institutional expansion and consolidation, these characteristics of film studies are no longer so distinctive. When so many other humanities and social science departments have climbed on the bandwagon of interdisciplinary studies and critical theory, film studies' attempt to maintain its territorial boundaries and control the academic production of knowledge of film sometimes appears more oppressive and reactionary than oppositional and liberating.

The institutional vicissitudes of film studies and other humanistic disciplines can be discussed from a number of different perspectives. In this essay, we will examine the scholarship on Japanese cinema as a symptomatic manifestation of the current disciplinary crisis. More specifically, to come to grips with the problem of disciplines, we will scrutinize film studies and Japanese studies, another institutional site of academic discourse that makes a claim to Japanese cinema as its own scholarly property. Both film studies and Japanese studies are undergoing their own identity crises due to superficially different yet ultimately common reasons. In each case, the way Japanese cinema has been treated as an object of knowledge reveals the constitutive blindness and limitation of the disciplinary assumptions, regulations, and practices. In the case of film studies, it is important to note at the outset that Japanese cinema was not simply added to the disciplinary canon some time after the successful legitimation of film as an object of serious academic research; on the contrary, Japanese cinema played a significant role in the establishment of film studies as a discrete discipline. The position of Japanese cinema is inseparable from the question of how film studies has constituted itself, legitimated its existence, and maintained its institutional territoriality through a double process of inclusion and exclusion. Very schematically, the history of the U.S. scholarship on Japanese cinema, which will be examined closely in the pages following, can be divided into three phases: 1) humanistic appreciation of the great auteurs and Japanese culture in the 1960s; 2) formalistic and/or Marxist celebration of Japanese cinema as an alternative to the classical Hollywood cinema in the 1970s; and 3) the critical reexamination of the preceding approaches through the introduction of the discourse of Otherness and cross-cultural analysis in the 1980s. Instead of being confined within the subfield of Japanese cinema studies, as we shall see, these stages were an integral part of the expansion and consolidation of film studies as a discrete discipline from the late 1960s onward. In contrast, Japanese studies' treatment of Japanese cinema is characterized by a history of systematic neglect and strategic containment. It is only recently that the insularity of Japanese studies is being challenged to some extent by the emergence of a new generation of Japan scholars working on film and other types of popular culture. This is therefore probably an appropriate moment for us to take stock of the historical development of Japanese studies as an area studies and see whether there is any structural correlation between the invisibility of Japanese cinema and the self-legitimation of Japanese studies.

A Brief History of Japanese Cinema Scholarship

Japanese cinema burst upon the American film scene when Kurosawa's *Rashomon* was unexpectedly awarded a grand prix at the Venice Film Festival in 1951. This unique period film was extensively reviewed in the major newspapers and highbrow magazines, and its critical and commercial success aroused American curiosity about other Japanese films. Parallel to Hollywood depictions of Japanese life and culture in the 1950s,[1] many of these journalistic writings relied on stereotyped images of Japan, or fixated specific aspects of Japanese culture and social customs as the Japanese essence. For Hollywood and the predominantly journalistic film criticism of the 1950s, Japan was often nothing more than a land of exoticism and alien culture.[2]

As Japanese cinema began to be treated as a distinct object of knowledge in the 1960s, the production of critical discourses on Japanese cinema was also transformed into a more specialized activity. The first significant text that contributed to this transformation was *The Japanese Film: Art and Industry* by Joseph L. Anderson and Donald Richie, published in 1960. Intended for a serious yet general audience, *The Japanese Film* is a highly informative overview of the Japanese film history combined with separate sections on major film directors and actors, generic types, and industrial structure. The publication of this book did not immediately engender the field of Japanese cinema in academia; however, over the years, this pioneering work by Anderson and Richie has firmly established itself as the most basic reference book for film scholars conducting research on Japanese cinema.[3] In addition to *The Japanese Film*, Donald Richie has published, as the most authoritative voice in the West and in Japan, numerous articles and books on Japanese cinema.

The 1960s discourse on Japanese cinema, exemplified by the works of Donald Richie, is a type of humanist criticism, which sees film as a repository of universal values. The best films, humanists argue, can teach audiences, without overtly being didactic, important moral lessons regarding human dignity, freedom, and the unity of the human race. But these universal ideals are most effectively conveyed to audiences when they are represented through the concrete images of a particular nation, history, or culture. According to humanist criticism, what makes a film a great artistic achievement is therefore not the abstract presentation of universal values but the complex interplay of the universal and the particular, in which the latter embodies the former.

One of the most enduring legacies of the 1960s humanist criticism on Japanese cinema is the use of "national character" as the particular, through which the humanistic ideals of universal significance are said to be represented concretely. This focus on national character as a determinate factor in analysis and interpretation has led to an unfortunate situation in which stereotypes on the Japanese national character and cultural essence are routinely used to explain thematic motifs, formal features, and contextual backgrounds of Japanese films. Thus, in American scholarship on Japanese cinema, the Japanese are often presented as the homogeneous, ahistorical collective essence called the "Japanese mind." ("To the Japanese mind, the self-sacrificing hero is the most admirable hero of all.")[4] It is argued that "Japanese culture and consciousness are marked by a valuing of the irrational," and this is why "one finds in Japanese culture a deeply embedded notion called *yugen*, which entails the presence of mystery and incomprehensibility in all things."[5] Many sweeping statements on Japanese culture are made without any consideration for its relationship to social practices and history. ("The Buddhist view of the world as transitory and full of pain has suffused the entire culture, inducing a sense of resignation in the presence of political brutality"; "Zen has infiltrated all aspects of Japanese culture, including the cinema"; "Although the codas [the uncharacted shots that begin and end most sequences] have narrative significance, Ozu's privileging them over simply following the action of the characters suggests an aesthetic attitude that places the individual as a mere element in the universe, the 'void', rather than at the center, as in Western, Greco-Roman thought.")[6] Japanese films are said to be worth studying because of "what they reveal of the Japanese character."[7] The ubiquitous presence in Japanese cinema of the traditional aesthetic is simply assumed without any critical analysis of that aesthetic. ("The black and white becomes an aesthetic device, which in this case reflects the Japanese ideal of *wabi* [poverty, the prizing of that which looks simple].")[8]

It is of course not possible to precisely determine where this valorization of the Japanese national character came from. But we cannot ignore two possible sources of the proliferation of stereotypes and clichés: auteurism in film criticism and the legacy of the American military intelligence activity during and after World War II. Japanese films' appeal to the audiences in and outside of Japan led many critics to conclude that there was some kind of universal value in those films. While the exotic appeal of Japanese cultural specificity was acknowledged, the critical acclaim that certain Japanese films—particularly *gendai-geki* or films set in contemporary Japan—earned at international film festivals was regarded as a living proof of Japanese cinema's ability to go beyond the parochial context of Japanese society. The gap between universality and particularity was believed to be filled by "humanity," which was posited as the most common denominator among diverse groups of people transcending national and cultural differences. And it was the role of auteurs to mediate the specificity of cultural tradition and the universality of films' messages. Therefore, in the context of 1960s auteurism, the most important book on Japanese cinema was not Anderson and Richie's *The Japanese Film* but Richie's *The Films of Akira Kurosawa* (1965), since the latter was not only the first comprehensive study of the work of a Japanese film director but also one of the earliest examples of serious film books devoted to *any* auteur's work.[9]

Auteurism has, according to Janet Staiger, three basic criteria to determine the value of filmmakers as auteurs: "Transcendence of time and place, a personal vision of the world, and consistency and coherence of statement." In their pursuit of "universality" and "endurance," the auteurist critics find history transcended in the works of great filmmakers.[10] These basic characteristics of auteurism make it an ideal system of critical discourse that has created a space for

Japanese cinema in the American academia. Whether explicitly stated or not, the idea of universality of shared humanity is indispensable for making Japanese films intelligible to the American audience. Because of the great auteurs' putative ability to transcend the specificity of history and cultural context, the seemingly exotic films of Kurosawa, Mizoguchi, and other Japanese directors can be easily incorporated into a canon of the "world cinema." However, to the extent that history and cultural tradition cannot but play a significant role in the formation of a "personal vision," what is supposedly transcended sneaks back into the auteurs' works. The humanist studies of Japanese cinema typically try to resolve this ambivalent relationship of the universal and the particular through recourse to Zen and the idea of religious transcendence.

Auteurism as a critical discourse enabled critics to transcend contradiction of universalism and particularlism. Another set of discursive practice which also shaped the field of Japanese cinema was the ethnographic study of Japanese national character promoted by the U.S. government during and after World War II.[11] The extensive wartime collaboration of anthropologists, sociologists, and psychologists with the U.S. military intelligence produced a significant body of works on Japanese national character. The "fundamental premise of the national-character approach was," writes John Dower, " 'the psychic unity of humankind'—the assumption, as Margaret Mead later expressed it, that 'all human beings share in a basic humanity.' "[12] This combination of the universality of a basic humanity and the particularity of national character is not as strange as it might seem at first, since the notion of national character was evoked in part to discredit the racist theories of biological determinism. Researchers engaged in the study of national character argued that instead of race, "integrated cultural patterns, the unconscious logic of sentiments and assumptions, and the processes of 'enculturation' were the keys to understanding all people participating in a common milieu."[13] In other words, the national character study was first promoted as a way of dislodging race from the status of a final determinant in the production of differences. However, despite its anti-racist impetus, it is no secret that the national character study was quickly appropriated by and contributed to the racist discourse of wartime propaganda.

The most influential work on the Japanese national character is Ruth Benedict's *The Chrysanthemum and the Sword* (1946),[14] which opens with the following sentences: "The Japanese were the most alien enemy the United States had ever fought in an all-out struggle. In no other war with a major foe had it been necessary to take into account such exceedingly different habits of acting and thinking."[15] As her opening remark shows, Benedict approaches Japan as the most complete Other to the United States. Drawing on diverse sources of information including Japanese films, Benedict tries to find deep-seated cultural patterns in seemingly contradictory manifestations of the Japanese daily life. Benedict especially focuses on such categories of social and moral obligations as *on*, *chu*, *ko*, and *giri* in order to demonstrate how the cultural patterns of the Japanese are fundamentally different not only from those in the Occident but also from those in the Orient. As the Japanese ethnographer Yanagita Kunio points out, Benedict's "theory of culture patterns . . . seems to be concerned with those patterns which are permanently attached to a nation or a race, and which are not modified by changes in environment and by the power of time."[16] Race recedes from the foreground of discussion, yet to the extent that "cultural patterns" are permanently fixed to a particular race without any real possibility for their fundamental changes, Benedict's argument is as problematic as a more overtly racist theory. Benedict's view of Japanese society is too totalizing, and not enough attention is paid to various kinds of differences in class, gender, region, and so on. Her sweeping claim on Japanese patterns of thought and behavior is ahistorical, "guilty of ignoring meaningful temporal distinctions, e.g., using materials of Tokugawa period currency to draw generalizations about present-day behavior."[17]

During WWII, Japanese cinema was studied as part of the military intelligence activities to grasp the Japanese national character and their thought and behavioral patterns.[18] The final result of this type of research was then used to aid policy-makers in deciding how to deal with Japan during and after the war. In the 1950s and 1960s, this relationship between national character and cinema was reversed by film critics. Instead of analyzing Japanese cinema as a key to unlock the mystery of the Japanese national character they started using the Japanese national character as a means of "correctly" appreciating Japanese cinema. The ideas of *on*, *giri*, *ninjo*, etc., which Benedict had laboriously analyzed, were blithely used in analyses of Japanese films without being put into a critical scrutiny. The fundamental operative principle of humanist criticism of Japanese cinema is the inversion of question and answer; that is, what should be scrutinized through a careful analysis of films is used precisely as the answer to interpretive questions raised by those films. This inversion corresponds to what Tetsuo Najita calls "Japanese inversion of Benedict." Najita argues that the postwar Japanese social scientists and critics such as Nakane Chie and Doi Takeo "proceed from the presumption that the Japanese are 'unknowable' except to Japanese, and that the role of social science is to mediate and define their self-knowledge in terms accessible to the world of others. . . . The 'scientifically' reduced structural forms and relational axes explained the distinctiveness of a Japanese culture which outsiders could not directly know or participate in, and could at best approach through the mediations of social-scientific interpreters. Just how effective this Japanese 'inversion' of Benedict has been can be appreciated by the consistent use of this perception of Japanese exceptionalism (unknowable but not inscrutable) in terms of group harmony and vertical loyalty to explain Japanese technological and organizational proficiency."[19] In the humanistic study of Japanese cinema, through this process of inversion, the difference of Japanese cinema is attributed to that elusive entity called "Japan."

The axiomatic characteristics of the humanist scholarship on Japanese cinema basically preclude possibilities of political intervention. The fixated notions of national character, the Japanese mind, the Japanese way of life, etc. make an attempt to intervene in the status quo of society simply superfluous. Even when some attempt is made to introduce politics and ideology into criticism, the haunting effect of the essentialized Japaneseness often reinforces the national stereotypes. When, on rare occasions, humanist critics call for a political change, they still end up reaffirming national stereotypes, thus creating adverse political effects. A plethora of claims on the feudal remnants in modern Japanese society, like Benedict's argument, virtually eliminate historical specificity from what is supposed to be a historical study of Japanese cinema.[20]

The success of film studies as a newly emerging discipline was inseparable from a certain spirit of contestation in the 1960s against the way knowledge was produced in the traditional humanities. For a younger generation of scholars who were increasingly unsatisfied with the limits of academic disciplines, film was not just another type of art deserving serious scholarly attention. The radical critics of the late 1960s and early 1970s turned to film in order to question the ideological underpinnings of what was considered constituting "scholarly seriousness." The study of Japanese cinema did not remain outside this trend of theoretical radicalization. The 1970s saw the rise of the second wave of scholarship on Japanese cinema characterized by its oppositional politics of aesthetic and form. The single most important work of this radicalized scholarship is Noël Burch's *To the Distant Observer: Form and Meaning in the Japanese Cinema* (1979),[21] which introduced for the first time the ideology of film form as a central question in the study of Japanese cinema.

One of the axiomatic premises of Burch's work is that there is the "essential difference between the dominant modes of Western and Japanese cinema."[22] Throughout his book, Burch constantly contrasts the cinema and culture of Japan with those of the West. The operative principle of Burch's theory is very much akin to Benedict's paradigm of "Us/Not-Us";[23] that is, the absolute dichotomy of the West and Japan. What Burch is ultimately interested in is not the latter but the former, since Burch's study "is intended . . . as a step in the direction of a critical analysis of the ideologically and culturally determined system of representation from which the film industries of Hollywood and elsewhere derive their power and profit."[24] And some critics have confirmed Burch's objective by finding in *To the Distant Observer* one of the most lucid descriptions of the formal system of the classical Hollywood cinema.[25]

Because in his theory the significance of Japanese cinema is completely dependent on the hegemonic system of Western cinema, Burch has been accused of being engaged in an Orientalist project. For Burch, Japanese cinema has a meaning only to the extent that it functions as a model of a new cinema which critiques the bourgeois ideological assumptions of the dominant Western cinema. Or as one critic puts it, Burch uses "Japanese cinema as a rod with which to beat the back of Western bourgeois transparent cinema."[26] Burch's theoretical bias—understanding of the West mediated by a "detour through the East"—is not by itself a fatal flaw. Nor is there anything inherently wrong with an attempt to search for some alternative system of representation and textuality in Japanese cinema (or for that matter in the emerging moment of the cinema in the early twentieth century West),[27] provided "Japanese cinema" utilized for this purpose is not a mere mirage of the critic's desire. Conversely, the critic can "also . . . isolate somewhere in the world (*faraway*) a certain number of features . . . , and out of these features deliberately form a system," and decide to call this system "Japan" as long as this "Japan"[28] always remains an imaginary construct, not a reality. The problem with *To the Distant Observer* is precisely the confounding of Japan as a fictitious construct and as a reality. As Dana Polan argues, there is a fundamental contradiction in Burch's project,[29] a contradictory split between the fictional status of "Japan" he constructs and his claim that his "approach is . . . historical in every sense."[30] Burch is most misleading when he tries to develop a historical argument because to substantiate his point, he often tailors the modern Japanese history to fit his Orientalist view of Japanese cinema's essential difference. Burch's view of non-synchronous development of aesthetic form, political ideology, and capitalist economic system may be complex with full of nuances;[31] however, the sheer complexity of a historical model guarantees neither the historical accuracy nor the anti-ethnocentricity of that model. What makes Burch's Orientalism particularly troubling is his critical stance on the dominant mode of filmic representation in the West. As he indicts the ideology of the dominant Western cinema, Burch falls prey to the Orientalist trap, and despite his avowed intention, ends up affirming that same ideology which he criticizes.

Despite its critical success, Burch's work failed to create a "theoretical turn" in the study of Japanese cinema. Why did the humanistic studies of Japanese cinema continue to thrive even after the publication of Burch's pioneering work? To understand the institutional politics of Japanese cinema scholarship, it is imperative to recognize that a theoretical study of Japanese cinema initiated by Burch was not simply interrupted or abandoned by scholars more interested in contextualizing Japanese cinema historically and culturally. Despite their apparent differences, there is in the end no absolute disjunction between the humanism of the 1960s and the ideological criticism of the 1970s. Both schools of criticism start from the premise that Japanese cinema is essentially different from Hollywood cinema; what has changed is the system of explanation to account for Japanese cinema's Otherness and how that system breaks down because of internal inconsistency and contradiction. Despite their apparent differences, there is a complicity between auteur-centered humanism and Burch's radical theorization. Instead of theoretically reexamining the critical premises of humanist criticism, Burch develops his poststructuralist/Marxist approach to Japanese cinema based on those premises. Instead of introducing a theoretical turn in the field of Japanese cinema, because of the inseparability of his theoretical claim and Orientalism, Burch's theoretical intervention ends up authorizing the continuation of more traditional humanistic studies.

Burch's book has been extensively reviewed and discussed since its original appearance in 1979. Out of these discussions have grown two types of trends in the field of Japanese cinema. On the one hand, those who see excessive theorization and lack of attention to historical context in Burch's project try to produce more contextualized accounts of auteurs' works, aesthetics, movements, and limited periods of Japanese film history.[32] On the other hand, what is called cross-cultural analysis tries to continue theorization of Japanese cinema and simultaneously construct a new historical narrative of intercultural exchange. What Burch does in his first major theoretical work on the non-Western cinema is symptomatically represented by its title, *To the Distant Observer: Form and Meaning in the Japanese Cinema*. After briefly justifying his critical position as a "distant observer" who is not too familiar with Japanese history, culture, and language, Burch concentrates on his ideological and formalist analysis of "form and meaning in the Japanese cinema." Cross-cultural analysis reverses this hierarchical relationship of the critical premise and the main body of argument in Burch's book; that is, instead of treating the position of the critic as a significant yet ultimately secondary methodological issue, cross-cultural analysis foregrounds it as a central point of contention in the study of Japanese cinema by American academics.

Scott Nygren develops an argument on cross-cultural influence, misrecognition, and exchange in his two articles "Reconsidering Modernism: Japanese Film and the Postmodern Context" and "Doubleness and Idiosyncrasy in Cross-

Cultural Analysis."[33] The former tries to construct a large-scale historical model of cross-cultural exchange between the West and Japan; the latter is more concerned with the role of the critic's identity in cross-cultural analysis. One of Nygren's main theses in both texts is that modern Japan and the West are in a certain sense the inverted mirror image of each other. "Humanism and anti-humanism," writes Nygren, "play inverse roles in the conflict of tradition and modernism in Japan and the West: each culture turns to the other for traditional values which function to deconstruct its own dominant ideology. Japan borrows humanism from the West as a component of Japanese modernism, just as the West borrows anti-humanist elements from Japanese tradition to form Western modernism. At points of cross-cultural exchange between Japan and the West, traditional and modernist values are likely to seem paradoxically inter-twined."[34] What makes him realize this inverted relationship is the emergence of postmodernism, which "is conceived in the West as a non-progressivist freeplay of traditionalist and modernist signification without progressivist de-terminism."[35]

There are a number of problems in what Nygren presents as cross-cultural analysis, but first and foremost it is the ambiguity of certain key terms used by him. For instance, although he wavers between different usages of the phrase "Western modernism," what he means by it is fairly clear. The most consistent examples of Western modernism mentioned are various artistic movements of the late 19th century and early 20th century (e.g., Impressionism, Cubism, Sur-realism, Futurism, etc.). In contrast, it is difficult to pinpoint what he calls Japa-nese modernism. He neither defines the term clearly nor provides a coherent set of examples of Japanese modernists or modernist works.[36] Strangely, there is no explicit reference to various modernist movements in Japanese literature, art, theater, architecture, and even film.[37] Granted that it is never possible to analyze comprehensively every aspect of Japanese modernism in a single article or book, it is still necessary to specify what kind of modernist movement is examined and what others are excluded from a particular study. Without some kind of de-limitation, the word "modernism" remains nothing more than an empty signi-fier, and the discussion becomes indistinguishable from a mere word play.

Why is it the case that while mentioning different kinds of modernism in the West, Nygren fails to differentiate various modernist movements in Japan? It is because any specific examination of Japanese modernism would make it im-possible to establish the relationship of inversion between Japan and the West. Nygren's claim that there is a correspondence between what the "modern" meant for the Japanese of the Meiji period and Western humanism and individu-alism is highly contestable. Even if we accept his claim for argument's sake, it still does not automatically lead to the conclusion that Japanese modernists were most influenced by Western humanism, not modernism, even in the 1920s, 1950s, or 1960s. To support his thesis, Nygren keeps insisting on Japanese artists' preference of humanism over modernism, yet some of the examples illustrating his point are simply not convincing. It is difficult to understand why Japanese artists' alleged preference of Impressionism and Post-Impressionism over such avant-garde movements as Cubism, Surrealism, and Dadaism can be construed as evidence of the "deconstructive role of the Western humanist tradition in a Japanese context."[38]

"Cross-cultural reading is always at least double, and articulates both cultural situations, that of the reader and that of the read, unavoidably and simultaneously."[39] Yet, instead of presenting "both cultural situations, that of the reader and that of the read," Nygren's essays only play with the reader's construction of the West and Japan. His description of the cultural situation of the read is full of stereotypes and clichés about Japanese society, institutions, and the "psychoanalytic formation of the Japanese subject," in other words, fixated images of the Japanese essence produced by Nihonjinron (Discourse on Japaneseness).[40] When what is articulated as Japanese "reality" is only a stereotype or cliché constructed by the "Western" reader from the very beginning, how can cross-cultural analysis take place as an event? Can cross-cultural analysis be developed with a false sense of reciprocity? Nygren writes: "If we as Westerners can only conceive of the Orient by speaking or writing through the Other of Western ideology, then it is also true that the West appears to the East in terms of its own Other. Japan's view of the West through its Other is as valid, as problematic, and as unavoidable as the West's conception of Japan through its own Other."[41] Yet, history shows otherwise. In 1854, Commodore Perry and the shogunate officials signed a diplomatic treaty between the United States and Japan, both of which had vastly different interpretations of the same treaty. The United States, however, immediately took action to enforce its own version of interpretation, and faced by the infinitely superior military power Japan did not have any other choice but to accept it. H. D. Harootunian finds in this historical event a paradigmatic pattern of the U.S.-Japan interaction in the last century and a half: "It might be argued, on the basis of this inaugural misrecognition, that Japanese/American relations derived from and were set upon their course by an act of interpretation, whereby the United States jumped to occupy the 'enunciative voice' to determine the meaning of a statement before the Japanese were able to press their own claim. On their part, the Japanese appeared to have been assigned to the status of second-term, or silent, interlocutors whose interests, hereafter, were to be represented to themselves by another. Sometimes the interaction has resembled the relationship between ventriloquist and dummy."[42] What is erased in Nygren's equivocal conflation of Japan's and the West's views is precisely the historical specificity of the geopolitical hierarchy and power relationship evident in the U.S.-Japan interaction since the mid-nineteenth century.

The cross-cultural analysis's valorization of theory over history is only a veneer, since there is nothing particularly theoretical about cross-cultural analysis. The real dichotomy in cross-cultural analysis is not established between theory and history but between the identity of Japanese and that of Westerners. While trying to decenter the hierarchical relationship of Japan and the West, cross-cultural analysis ends up reaffirming the fixed identities of both. To this extent, cross-cultural analysis is in a complementary relation to mono-cultural analysis promoted by native Japanese scholars such as Keiko I. McDonald. Because her book on Japanese cinema and classical theater "is not a book on film theory," writes McDonald, "it disavows any absolute theoretical stance or ideological commitment of the sort seen in the second semiology (Marxist-psychoanalytic-semiology)": "My own approach has most to do with that basic question about cultural specificity which I seek time and again as a teacher and scholar of Japanese cinema to answer: How does a person coming from the Japanese tradition see a Japanese film for what it is?"[43] Thus, in both cross-cultural and mono-cultural analysis, the question of theory's role in interpretation is displaced by identity politics.

Film Studies: Its Institutionalization and Constitutive Ethnocentrism

The critical and methodological problems with the scholarship on Japanese cinema cannot be discussed merely as an internal problem of the field of Japanese cinema. To understand them fully, we must broaden a horizon of our examination to include the larger institutional context. Since the field of Japanese cinema is not an autonomous entity but an integral part of film studies' disciplinary formation, a brief examination of the history of film studies as an academic discipline is in order.

Film has been part of the American university curricula for many years,[44] yet it was only in the late 1950s and early 1960s that film studies finally came into existence as an academic discipline. Many new courses on film were created in the 1960s, and they were gradually consolidated into coherent programs and curricula. The increasing popularity of film as an academic subject meant a great demand for survey books on film. New film history books (e.g., Arthur Knight's *The Liveliest Art* [1957]) were published and widely used in the classroom,[45] and the classical works on film history were also reprinted in a new paperback edition or under a new title.[46] In the late 1960s and throughout the 1970s, film studies experienced an extraordinary period of rapid expansion. As the study of film was firmly established as an academic discipline, the institutional centers of film study shifted from museums and archives to universities. There was a dramatic increase in not only the number of film courses but also that of universities offering them.[47] In addition to such established journals as *Film Quarterly* and *Cinema Journal,* new film journals were created for film scholars to publish peer-reviewed articles which were essential for tenure and promotion.[48] As the need for legitimating the study of film as a serious academic endeavor increased, the formation of a professional society became necessary. In 1957 and 1958, the Museum of Modern Art in New York organized meetings of film teachers at American universities. Out of these meetings was born the Society of Cinematologists, which later became the Society for Cinema Studies,[49] the most influential organization of film academics.

What made film studies one of the fastest-growing academic disciplines in the late 1960s and the 1970s? The influx of art films in the 1950s and 1960s mainly from Europe dramatically changed the image of cinema in the United States. Fellini, Bergman, Antonioni, and others were celebrated as serious artists, and in the eyes of many intellectuals and professors their films were as important as the canonical works of English literature, music, and fine arts. As the prestigious status of these filmmakers as auteurs was firmly established, Hollywood cinema was reappraised, too. French film critics' enthusiasm over American cinema was brought back to the U.S., and through the works of critics like Andrew Sarris, such directors as Ford, Hitchcock, Houston, and Wyler were all elevated to the status of auteurs. The romantic conception of filmmakers as serious artists who imprint their films with their unique signatures (e.g., stylistic and thematic motifs consistently found in their oeuvres) became orthodoxy not only in academia but also in the world of journalistic film criticism.[50]

Because of the constitutive hybridity of film as a medium, film courses were initially offered by such a wide variety of departments as motion pictures, radio and television, theater, art, English, sociology, political science, business, etc. But the disciplines which most eagerly appropriated film as a new object of analysis were the humanities, which desperately needed new courses to accommodate the rapid expansion of university enrollments and to cope with the effects of the 1960s university reform and democratization of higher education. Already in the pioneering days of film studies when education department offered the largest number of film courses, the "courses dealing with film history, criticism, or appreciation . . . were usually attached to literature or drama departments."[51] The inroad of film into the American university system in the 1960s reinforced this connection between film studies and the humanities, or more specifically, literary studies. In terms of the sheer number, more universities and colleges offered film courses in speech, communication, and film/television than in English and language departments.[52] But even in the non-language departments, the critical paradigm of the study of film was a humanistic, interpretive one. The specific institutional locations of film programs and curricula were less important than the emergence of a new institutional paradigm of film criticism that readily crossed departmental boundaries.

If the combination of auteurism and art cinema launched film studies as a respectable academic field in the 1960s, it was theory that made film studies a cutting-edge discipline in the 1970s. A number of humanities scholars took their cues from European cultural criticism and theoretical thinking. For these radical critics, the study of film was more than just an introduction of a new object of research into the humanities. They saw it as an "opportunity to help shift the ground of the whole realm of humanities."[53] Semiotics, Lacanian psychoanalysis, and Althusserian Marxism were enthusiastically studied and used to theorize subject positions, spectatorship, and textual unconscious; the results of theorization and critical pieces which applied theory to specific films were constantly published in journals on film, literary studies, critical theory, and cultural studies. In the rapidly expanding field of film studies, theory occupied a privileged position; to some extent, theory and methodology were more important than what was being theorized or analyzed.

In the 1970s and early 1980s, film studies experienced a research boom, and there was a genuine sense of newness and excitement. Yet by definition a boom does not last forever, and now there seems to be a consensus that the field of film studies has reached an impasse. There are probably a number of different ways to discuss the state of the discipline, but I find Robert Ray's and David Bordwell's assessment of the situation particularly illuminating. Although they have very different agendas and solutions to remedy the problem at hand, in general both seem to agree that a major source of the stalemate is the hegemonic status of theory-inspired film criticism in the discipline.

In *Making Meaning*, Bordwell argues that we can construct only four types of meanings out of a film—referential, explicit, implicit, and symptomatic meanings (the first two together constituting so-called literal meanings)—and that film criticism basically falls into either thematic explication (constructing implicit meanings) or symptomatic interpretation (symptomatic meanings).[54] Although these two types of interpretive activity are normally regarded as very different from each other by film scholars, Bordwell sees otherwise. He examines numerous examples of explicatory and symptomatic criticism to demonstrate that there is no such radical disjunction between the two, not even between auteur criticism as explication and Lacanian/Althusserian ideological critique as symptomatic interpretation. Through a careful analysis of interpretive rhetoric, Bordwell tries to demonstrate that poststructuralist film criticism owes much less to poststructuralist theory than to the set of inferential patterns and rhetorical devices that have been widely used by film critics of various persuasions since the Second World War. From Bordwell's standpoint, poststructuralist film criticism's emergence in the 1970s and its dominance in the 1980s did not introduce anything particularly new in film studies; on the contrary, its proliferation ensured the continuation of routine interpretive practices to such an extent that film criticism has become totally repetitive and uninteresting. Thus, Bordwell proclaims: "Film interpretation is in no crisis; it is in stagnation";[55] "the great days of interpretation-centered criticism are over; . . . the basic strategies and tactics have all been tried."[56]

Robert Ray also contests the current state of film studies. He points out the futility of producing interpretive pieces based on the mechanically repeatable procedures and reusable theoretical jargons as follows:

> The extraordinary contagiousness of contemporary theory lies precisely in its generalizing power: the old model of scholarship, which relied on a specialized, scrupulous coverage of a field of study, insisted that the right to speak about, for example, fiction or narrative accrued only to those who had read all the major novels in a given literature (hence such books as Wayne Booth's *The Rhetoric of Fiction*, which seems to mention every important English novel). Contemporary theory, on the other hand, finds its representative model in Barthes's S/Z, which uses one Balzac novella (and a minor one at that) to make an argument about narrative in general. Having seen that approach in action, academics have ignored its lesson and insisted on using it as a new model for case-by-case analyses. But if you understand Barthes's points about storytelling, you do not need to see them worked out with a hundred other examples: that procedure may be useful for beginning students, as a way of apprehending Barthes's approach, but surely it should not be the model for advanced scholarly work. . . . Having committed itself to a particular way of doing business (which we might call 'semiotic', using that term to stand for the amalgam of structuralist, psychoanalytic, ideological, and feminist methodologies), film studies has, since 1970, constructed an enormously powerful theoretical machine for exposing the ideological

abuse hidden by the apparently natural stories and images of popular culture. That machine, however, now runs on automatic pilot, producing predictable essays and books on individual cases.[57]

While criticizing, like Bordwell, the mass-producibility of theoretical interpretation of individual films, Ray also recognizes the significance of theory introducing discontinuity in the development of film studies. According to Ray, the impasse of film studies is not created by poststructuralist theory's inherent flaws but by the discrepancy between the radical potential of theory as practice and the sterile thematization of theory in the routine, streamlined interpretation.

Film studies' development briefly described above has not only shaped the Japanese film scholarship but also used Japanese cinema for its own purposes. As Ray argues, at the early stage of its institutionalization film studies transgressed both national and disciplinary boundaries: "Because its subject matter was international, [film studies] could never have respected the university's linguistic divisions: the movies, after all, were not just 'French' or 'American' or 'German' or 'Japanese'; they constituted a new language which similarly disregarded the old, neat distinctions between music, dance, painting, and the plastic arts. Inevitably, therefore, film studies found an almost immediate need for interdisciplinarity, and for methods which would guide its activities in the unsponsored, uncharted free zones between official departments."[58] When film studies was struggling to establish itself as a discrete discipline, the international dimension of the cinema was a significant point to emphasize. The international scope of film as a hybrid art form could justify the establishment of a new academic unit because, limited by their focus on either specific nations or artistic media, traditional departments were not particularly suitable for the study of the cinema.

It was in this context of disciplinary power struggle that Japanese cinema played an indispensable role. Film studies as a new intercultural discipline became all the more acceptable with the discovery of other cinemas, such as Japanese cinema, whose unique artistic quality made it simultaneously an instance of particularity and a proof of the cinema's universal appeal. Japanese cinema was an ideal example demonstrating dialectic of the universal and the particular, a widely used rhetorical trope to reconcile contradictory aspects of the cinema as high art and popular culture, as universal language and culturally specific practice, etc.[59] Japanese cinema was also valuable for film studies because it boasted two great auteurs, Mizoguchi and Kurosawa. The idea of individual authorship was essential for the self-legitimation of film studies at its early stage of institutionalization. Without the presence of auteurs like Fellini, Antonioni,

Bergman, et al., it would have been much more difficult for humanities professors in the 1960s to incorporate film into their teaching and research. Japanese cinema continued to play a significant role in film studies' disciplinary and canon formation by steadily supplying other auteurs besides Kurosawa and Mizoguchi (e.g., Ozu, Naruse, Kobayashi, Oshima, and Imamura).

Interpretation gained its hegemonic status not only because film studies was most closely aligned with literary criticism but also because it was remarkably international and cosmopolitan. For film critics who were not familiar with the language, history, and cultural context of Japan, Brazil, or Hungary, the easiest way to deal with the cinemas of these countries would be to interpret—either explicatively or symptomatically—thematic motifs and stylistic aspects of individual films. For the purpose of interpreting unfamiliar national cinemas, film studies has built a powerful interpretive machine, which, by supplying film critics with stock images of national character, tradition, and fixed cultural traits, makes it possible for them to understand and say something intelligible about those cinemas. Thus, to this extent, the disciplinary structure of film studies demands for the concept of national cinema as part of its strategy of containment. Because of this interpretive machine, even those who do not have command of the necessary languages can study non-Western national cinemas, and these studies are justified in the name of cross-cultural analysis.[60] However, the final product of this kind of national cinema criticism is often as equally predictable and repetitious as theoretical criticism, the value of which is seriously questioned by Bordwell, Ray, and others.

The national cinemas Ray mentions in the passage previously quoted—French, American, German, and Japanese cinemas—do not coexist side by side in a non-hierarchical relationship. Each of them does not have the same kind of leverage over the formation of film studies' disciplinary structure, in which theory occupies a privileged position. Despite theory's—explicit or implicit—universalist claim, specific examples used and analyzed in theory are often from American, French, and German films.[61] In contrast, Japanese cinema has never been included in the canon of film theory except when, as in Burch's study, theory is used in order to assert Japanese cinema's essential difference from Western cinema. There is a privileged connection between Western cinema and theory, which is supposed to present a totalized, general view, capable of explaining different aspects of the cinema irrespective of national and cultural differences. This grandiose claim of theory has been criticized by Bordwell, Noël Carroll, and others, who point out theory's internal contradictions and axiomatic claims unsupported by empirical evidence.[62] In addition to these internal critiques, it is also important to note a larger disciplinary context in which the primacy of theory and theoretical criticism has been maintained.

Film studies has constructed a code-switching mechanism which enables theory to legitimate its universal claim by seemingly acknowledging its own limitation. This code-switching mechanism re-presents theory as "Western" theory, which is, according to theorists, not directly applicable to non-Western cinema without inflicting some kind of critical violence upon it. However, when a critical interpretation which "applies" Lacanian psychoanalytic theory to a Japanese, Taiwanese, or Indonesian film turns out to be less than convincing, it does not necessarily show either difficulty or danger of applying Western theory to non-Western text. Instead, it merely foregrounds a shaky ground on which theory can be used in interpretation of any text, whether Western or non-Western. The dichotomy of Western theory and non-Western text is a rhetorical device, the primary purpose of which is not to be attentive to the specificity of non-Western text but to hide a problematic relationship of Western theory and Western text. Another purpose of this dichotomy is to create an alibi for theorists to ignore non-Western cinema on the ground that the former is not applicable to the latter. Thus, there is a process of marginalization going on within an interdisciplinary and international discipline which guards itself against the colonizing power of Western theory. On the one hand, by evoking the dichotomy of Western theory and non-Western text, film studies acknowledges the limitations of theory as a culturally specific discursive activity. On the other hand, by institutionally marginalizing the study of non-Western cinema, film studies in actuality sanctions the universalist claim of theory. And the scholarship on Japanese cinema has been a primary product of this marginalization; at the same time, it has also played a significant role in the promotion and legitimation of the same marginalizing process.

Japanese Studies: Its Marginalization and Fossilization

Jonathan Culler points out that "national literature departments have increasingly become sites where a wide range of cultural objects are studied—not just film and popular culture but discourses of sexuality, conduct books, and any discourse that contributes to the construction of cultures and individuals."[63] Yet, this observation is applicable mostly to European language and literature departments, but not to their Asian counterparts. Unlike English, French, or German departments, East Asian language departments have not been receptive to a general trend of broadening the definition of "text" to include film, popular culture, media, urban space, and so on. Why has film not become part of East Asian departments? Obviously there are no simple answers to this question. But we can still think of several possible reasons why film has not been accepted as a legitimate object of scholarship in Japanese language and literature programs.

The emergence of Japanese studies as an area studies after the Second World War was closely tied to U.S. intelligence activity during the war and its postwar attempt to incorporate Japan into the hegemonic sphere of the U.S. as engaged in the Cold War. This original complicity of the objectives of Japanese studies and those of the American government's policy toward Japan and East Asia has continued to influence the subsequent development of the field. The specific ideological bent of Japanese studies has been actively maintained through teaching, training of young researchers, standards and priorities for publications, tenure, and promotion, control over distribution of research money and scholarships, selection of conference topics and objectives, and so on. Since its inception as an organized field of scholarly inquiry, Japanese studies has produced research helping the State Department and trade negotiators to deal with security questions concerning the protection of American interest in the East Asia region. Another institutional role of Japanese studies has been to provide ideological justification for the American subordination of Japan, which reached after the Second World War "a new stage of imperialism and colonialism without territorialization."[64] As John Dower reports, "many leading American Japan specialists have at one time or another not only worked for the American Government or spoken on its behalf in support of the United States-Japan military and economic relationship, but have also engaged in a sustained endeavor to discredit that sector of the Japanese intelligentsia which has opposed postwar American actions in Asia and Japan's support of those actions."[65]

It must be clear from this brief sketch of the institutional history that the study of Japanese literature does not occupy the central position in Japanese studies. In the American academia where Eurocentrism and Orientalism are still at work at multiple levels of institutional standards and practices, Japanese studies is for the most part marginalized in an academic ghetto. The field of Japanese literature is further marginalized in this already marginal area studies, in which literary scholars have less leverage over the direction of research programs than historians, sociologists, anthropologists, political scientists, or economists. Japanese literature scholars may be able to escape from their doubly marginalized position by interacting with their counterparts specializing in other national literatures rather than by simply intermingling with Japanologists; however, the institutional structure of the university, venues of publications, and topics and structures of conferences do not allow this kind of inter-literary communication to happen as often as it should.

It is important to note that the marginal status of Japanese literature does not necessarily indicate the ideological innocence of the field of Japanese literature. Even though its hierarchical position is subordinate to social sciences, the study of Japanese literature plays a significant role in the self-legitimation of Japanese studies, which is sustained by the division of labor assigning different functions to social science and literary studies. Whereas social science is often used as a direct instrument for the American government determining its foreign policy, literary studies creates a façade hiding the instrumentality of Japanese studies. The field of Japanese literature dissociates itself from the worldliness of Japanese culture, and tries to mold Japanese literature into an instance of high culture, which is ancient, unique, mysterious, and aesthetically refined. As classical Japanese literature is used to affirm the fixed image of Japaneseness, modern Japanese literature is marginalized and devalued. The hierarchy of classical and modern is firmly entrenched in the disciplinary structure of Japanese studies, and the pristine, authentic classical text is valorized over the contaminated, hybrid modern text. Of course modern Japanese literature is not ignored completely; however, it is often studied in order to reaffirm the central significance of classical literature rather than to attend to its historical specificity. By detecting in the modern text the resilient presence of traditional aesthetics and sensibility in spite of the impact of Western influences, the study of modern Japanese literature tends to emphasize the continuity of Japanese literary history and the derivative position of modern literature vis-à-vis classical literature.

At first, it may appear that at a certain level of institutional struggle the hypostatization of Japanese tradition has some strategic value. Through the assertion of the classical text's unique value, Japanese literature is made into an instance of major national literature. Yet, no matter how effective a strategy it might seem, the essentialization of Japanese literary aesthetics as a different tradition does not change the status of Japanese literature as a minor literature in the periphery of the humanities. We must remain wary of the dialectic of fetishism and marginalization, since it is precisely through the fetishism of the classical text as difference that the marginality of Japanese literature is further reinforced. There is nothing inherently liberating about recognition of difference. In fact, Orientalism feeds on it. The fetishism of Japanese tradition makes Japanese literature an object worthy of serious scholarly attention as long as the Eurocentric paradigm recuperates Japanese literature as one term of the East-West dichotomy. Scholars of Japanese literature cannot blame Eurocentrism of academia as the only cause for their institutional marginalization. Instead of challenging the hegemony of Eurocentrism, Japan specialists' fetishistic assertion of the value of classical Japanese literature supplements it.

The coherence of Japanese studies is not maintained by shared theoretical assumptions or research methodologies. What gives Japanese studies a sense of unity is the putative identity of Japan as a strategically important nation or geographical region for the American national interest. The role assigned to literary studies is to depoliticize Japan as a geopolitical entity and re-present it as a sign of unique cultural totality. By equating classical Japanese literature and high culture, Japanese studies tries to hide its political instrumentality and legitimate itself as an ideologically neutral academic enterprise.

To the extent that its main purpose is to create a fixed image of Japanese tradition, the field of Japanese literature does not need any rigorous theory or analytical methods. The mastery of language and the training in reading original manuscripts from hundreds of years ago are by themselves valuable without much regard to what kind of purpose they are put to use. Richard Okada describes the methodological poverty of the study of classical Japanese literature as follows:

> Having begun their careers as translators, many among the critics [of Japanese literature] found in philology the "discipline" needed to write "commentary" and in New Criticism the "method" needed to help execute the addendum, usually called "introduction," to a translation that required the supplying of "background" or "critical" remarks. The actual activity of scholars in the field, however, at times only vaguely resembled the two methodologies. "Philology" too often became yet another act of "translation," not the adaptation of any complex method of philology or text criticism but rather the more mundane (and arbitrary) search for "appropriate" English equivalents to Japanese words. And far from any consistent and rigorous employment of New Critical reading procedures, criticism has meant either summary of Japanese scholarship in terms of historical "background" information and detailed points of descriptive interpretation or an unquestioned (and most often unstated) reliance on the writer's own political and cultural norms for broader interpretive maneuvers.[66]

Although Okada's main target of criticism is the way classical Japanese literature has been studied, what he points out also in general applies to the scholarship on modern Japanese literature, whose dominant topoi include writers' biographies, relationships of sources and influences (e.g., influences of *Tale of Genji* on the works of Kawabata, or influences of Western naturalism on Japanese *Shizenshugi*), themes and symbols in the work of a particular writer, and so on.

Given this institutional background of the field of Japanese literature, there is nothing surprising about its unresponsiveness toward Japanese cinema. Undoubtedly the lack of attention to Japanese cinema by Japan specialists is related to the valorization of classical literature over modern literature and to the fetishism of ancient culture. For Japanese studies, film is far more dangerous than modern literature, since as popular culture it poses a direct threat to the institutional legitimation of Japanese literature programs and Japanese studies. As long as they speak from the position of authority on Japanese literature and culture, literary scholars' occasional excursion into film criticism is acceptable. But the wholesale incorporation of film into Japanese studies is out of the question because it will erode the luster of Japanese culture as high culture. To the extent that film studies and poststructuralist film theory are inseparable, Japanese studies' refusal to take film seriously is also a sign of its aversion to theory. Furthermore, Japanese studies' indifference or outright hostility toward Japanese film is testimony to complicity between Japanologists in the U.S. and the official ideology of the Japanese government. Even though there were periods when certain government agencies showed interest in marketing Japanese film abroad, in general, the Japanese government has been reluctant to support Japanese cinema. Despite many filmmakers' and film critics' complaint, the Japanese government has refused to admit the cinema as a significant part of Japanese culture and has kept its condescending attitude toward Japanese film.

The dubious status of film in the field of Japanese studies is also related to the fact that at a certain level research language competency of the researcher plays a less crucial role for the study of cinema than for that of literature. In film, language is directly present as spoken dialogue, lyrics, intertitles, and visual image on the screen, and to this extent it is certainly an important part of filmic experience. Yet, unlike for literature, the role of language is less essential for film because of its audio-visual nature. There is a definite difference in the degree of mediation between a translated Japanese novel and a Japanese film with English subtitles. While in the former almost no aspect of the novel escapes from the effect of translation, in the latter the original sound and image remain intact. This is why it is possible for non-Japanese speaking scholars to watch and study Japanese films in the academic context of film studies and to produce a significant body of scholarly works. However, precisely for the same reason, film has never been an object worthy of receiving Japan specialists' serious scholarly attention. If anybody can seemingly understand Japanese film without specialized training in Japanese language, history, and culture, why is it necessary for Japanese studies to acknowledge it as a legitimate object of scholarship? The absence of Japanese cinema in Japanese studies is closely related to the latter's institutional history and the question of what constitutes scholarly expertise. Japanese cinema is a threat to Japanese studies because it problematizes a type of identity politics underlying the field of Japanese literary studies. The specialists of Japanese literature are clearly differentiated from two groups of people: non-specialists who cannot read Japanese, and native informers who have not gone through a rigorous training in learning Japanese as a foreign language, and are thus regarded as naïve readers of their own culture. To the extent that film presumably does not require Japan specialists' expert knowledge and mastery of language to be made into an intelligible object, the study of Japanese cinema challenges the distinction between non-native experts, native informants, and non-specialists. It puts into question the seemingly objective notions of professional training and expertise, which are in reality often used as an excuse for protecting the vested interests of so-called specialists and for excluding issues that might put the legitimacy of their scholarship in jeopardy.

Comparative Studies: Neo-Ethnocentrism in the Age of Globalization

In the humanities, comparative literature seems to be the closest to film studies in terms of its disciplinary structure, expectations, and objectives. Both film studies and comparative literature go beyond the boundary of a single nation. Regardless of their specialization in any particular national cinema, film scholars are first and foremost expected to be students of film as a medium of art and industry in general; similarly, scholars of comparative literature try to study literature as a human activity unrestricted by national boundaries. It is in part these transnational characteristics that have made both film studies and comparative literature a stronghold of literary and critical theory in academia. This focus on theory has been a major factor in the distinction of film studies and comparative literature from foreign language and national literature departments.

Despite their similarities, comparative literature and film studies have different positions on the question of foreign language competency. Many film scholars are competent in French and German, two languages in which theoretical texts on film and relevant topics are extensively published. Yet, generally speaking, film studies as a discipline does not particularly lay special emphasis on foreign language skill. In contrast, comparative literature strongly stresses the significance of reading literary texts in the original languages. For comparatists and other literary scholars, language is not a research tool. A major purpose of studying literature is precisely to critique an instrumental view of language as a transparent medium of communicating information. For comparative literature, the competency in foreign languages is a core of its disciplinary identity. And this is where comparative literature has more affinities with Japanese studies than with film studies. While in film studies the majority of books and articles on Japanese cinema have been written by those who do not know Japanese, a good command of Japanese is an essential prerequisite for any comparatist who claims to have expertise in Japanese literature.

To the extent that it combines two strong points of film studies and Japanese studies, i.e., focus on theory and language, comparative literature seems like a better discipline in which research on Japanese cinema can be pursued. Once housed in comparative literature, the study of Japanese cinema will not suffer at least from the researchers' lack of facility in the language and critical methodologies. Comparative literature can train students to become "Japanese-speaking scholars" who are also conversant in film theory and critical issues in interpretation, formal analysis, and historiography. But before jumping to these conclusions, we must first examine the current state of comparative literature, the legitimacy and identity of which have become no less problematic than those of either film studies or Japanese studies. Comparative literature is not immune from the same institutional forces that have prompted film studies to search for its new disciplinary identity and objective.

As René Wellek reports in his often-quoted statement made in 1958, comparative literature as a discipline has never had a clear and stable identity. ("The most serious sign of the precarious state of our study is the fact that it has not been able to establish a distinct subject matter and a specific methodology.")[67] Other distinguished comparatists have expressed a similar sense of uncertainty about comparative literature: "Although I hold a Ph.D. in comparative literature, I have never been sure I deserved it, since I've never been sure what the field, or the discipline, is and never sure that I could really claim to be teaching it or working in it";[68] "Let's not kid ourselves: I am not a comparatist. I am not even entirely sure what a comparatist is or does."[69] What makes comparatists particularly nervous now is the emergence of cultural studies as a post-disciplinary discursive activity of academics. Cultural studies has attracted many comparatists as a way of renewing or refashioning comparative literature as a viable discipline of the age of globalization, while it simultaneously alarmed others who do not see it as a solution but as a major cause of comparative literature's crisis. The nervous tension between comparative literature and cultural studies is not a unique phenomenon but part of a sea change in the university where so many other disciplines and departments are experiencing the similar kinds of crisis or going through the intense process of self-examination. The sig-

nificance of the debate on cultural studies does not always lie in what proponents and opponents say about cultural studies but in what they say about other
disciplines. According to Fredric Jameson, cultural studies is not really a theory
or a "floor plan for a new discipline"; instead, cultural studies, a symptom of the
crisis of the university, "came into the world as the result of dissatisfaction with
other disciplines, not merely their contents but also their very limits as such."[70]
Cultural studies is often perceived as an external threat invading the boundaries
of already existing disciplines; at the same time, it is also a projection of those
disciplines' internal contradictions and deficiencies. By attacking, embracing,
or selectively appropriating cultural studies, other disciplines reaffirm their legitimacy, test their coherence, or expand and redraw their limits and boundaries.

Many prominent comparatists defend the literariness of literature against
the onslaught of cultural studies by arguing that "literature can be taught 'as literature' . . . , with its 'invariant features' . . . , without worrying about the historical contingency of this category. That worry belongs with cultural studies,
which for these critics constitutes an approach to literature from without, not a
theory of reading but an ideologization of aesthetic values for the purpose of political critique."[71] Peter Brooks defends the specificity of (comparative) literature against the generality of cultural studies, which in his argument seems
to be equated to "contextualization."[72] Jonathan Culler calls for transformation
of comparative literature into a "real" comparative literature department, in
which comparatists study the aesthetic features of literariness without being
hampered by such non-literary contingent factors as national differences.[73]
Trying to defend the specificity of literature, some comparatists attack the
vagueness of "culture" as an all-inclusive term.[74]

It does not seem to be particularly interesting to decide who the best readers
are, comparatists or cultural studies critics. Nor does it seem to be fruitful to discuss which term, literature or culture, is too all-inclusive to be a viable notion
around which to build a discrete discipline. On the one hand, it is ludicrous to
deny literature any specificity or to construe it as a type of textual discourse no
different from a medical treatise, advertising pamphlet, or camcorder manual.
On the other hand, it seems futile to try to stop the erosion of comparative literature's disciplinary identity by espousing the notion of literariness. First, the idea
of literature upheld by opponents of cultural studies is very restricted and narrow in its scope. This does not mean that literature should be studied only
"as one discursive practice among many others in a complex, shifting, and often contradictory field of cultural production."[75] The problem with the narrow
definition of literature does not lie in its rejection of contemporary cultural theory but its refusal to acknowledge the historicity of the idea of literature. I am

much more sympathetic to the position of Lionel Gossman whose "allegiance is probably to a far older conception of 'literature' than that current in present-day university departments of literature, comparative or otherwise. . . . That older conception of literature embraced a wide range of discourses, extending from philosophical and political argument, to sermons, eulogies, and works of erudition. . . . It is a conception completely antithetical to the restrictive and purist post-Romantic idea of literature that has become generally accepted in our culture—and in departments of Comparative Literature certainly no less than anywhere else."[76] Second, if what comparatists are supposed to study is literariness of literature, then it is more appropriate to call this new discipline "literature" rather than "comparative literature." The exclusive focus on the notion of "literature," which is chosen as a strategy to defend comparative literature against cultural studies, cannot but lead to the dissolution of *comparative* literature as a discipline.

What is not clearly elucidated in the debate on comparative literature is the notion of "comparative." As Rey Chow argues, "the 'comparative' in comparative literature is equally, if not more, crucial a factor in considering the future of comparative literature: exactly what constitutes 'comparison'—what kinds of relations, critical formations, analytical perspectives are relevant?"[77] Regardless of whether comparatists actually compare anything, there is always a hierarchy created among different national literatures, and this hierarchy is either explicitly delineated or implicitly accepted as a natural order. Even when comparison of literature is carried out by crossing national boundaries, new boundaries are created at a higher level, whereby the imagined unity of the nation is replaced by that of the larger geopolitical entity: "Europe." Like "literature," "comparative" is not an ideologically neutral term. "Comparatists" refer to those who specialize in certain European literatures, whereas those who study Chinese and Japanese are called "Asiatic comparatists."[78] Eurocentrism still guides comparative literature even when it tries to adapt itself to institutional changes in the university and the post-Cold War world of globalization. The displacement of comparison as a central activity merely masks the ingrained Eurocentric bias of the discipline instead of grappling with it.

In the final instance, the identity of comparative literature has never been determined by its emphasis on theory, multilingualism, comparison, or literature as a transnational art form. Instead, at the disciplinary core of comparative literature has always been the idea of Europe. I would even venture to argue that comparative literature is less a discipline of literature than a type of area studies, a counterpart to East Asian studies, Middle Eastern studies, Latin American studies, etc. It is therefore no accident that some prominent comparatists find an alternative model of comparative literature in area studies.[79] To this extent, as an alternative institutional space for the study of Japanese cinema, comparative literature is at least as equally problematic as Japanese studies and film studies.

Conclusion

Japan has produced one of the most remarkable body of films in the history of the cinema. For this reason alone, Japanese cinema deserves serious scholarly attention. But as we have examined in the previous sections, Japanese cinema does not legitimately belong to any established discipline. Film studies, which for many years was the center of the Japanese film scholarship, no longer pays much attention to Japanese cinema. The increasingly popular idea of globalization, which often reduces individual national cinemas or film culture to mere sightseeing spots on a package tour, ends up further reinforcing the monocultural tendency of film studies as an academic discipline. In general, Japanese studies is still too stagnant to accept film as an object worthy of scholarly attention in any serious way, while trapped in its Eurocentric cage, comparative literature is at a loss to deal with Japanese literature, let alone Japanese cinema. It is therefore urgent for us to establish a new institutional space or culture in which Japanese cinema can be studied as a legitimate object of knowledge. We must discuss not only the teaching of Japanese film courses but also the training of future teachers and scholars of Japanese cinema, the formation and expansion of a scholarly community and a forum for serious debates where new ideas are produced and exchanged on a regular basis.

Yet all these things are ultimately meaningless if they merely lead to the reestablishment of Japanese cinema studies as an academic field or territory with fixed boundaries. We must reject any attempt by existing disciplines and programs to appropriate Japanese film and popular culture for their survival without confronting the sources of their impasse and demise. The hiring of a token Japanese film or anime expert in the East Asian studies department is not a sign of progress but one of desperation and confusion. So is the presence of an Asian cinema specialist in the film department. Far from an obstacle to be overcome, in the current climate of disciplinary uncertainty, the lack of Japanese cinema's clear disciplinary affiliation gives us a unique opportunity for critical intervention. When the institutional identities of well-established disciplines are not self-evident any more, we should capitalize on the free-floating status of Japanese cinema as an effective means of problematizing the idea of autonomous discipline. Whether Japanese film's formal system, industrial structure, or position in the cultural history of modern Japan is analyzed, the object of study in each case needs to be invented against various kinds of disciplinary constraints and in alliance with disciplines, fields, and theories that are regarded as irrelevant for the study of Japanese cinema by so-called experts of all kinds. Whatever institutionally recognized discipline we happen to belong to, we cannot study Japanese cinema seriously without simultaneously questioning the basic premises of the discipline. The new study of Japanese cinema in the post-disciplinary age must be political; that is, beyond its specificity it must be conceived as a tactical intervention in the structures and practices of the established yet slowly vanishing disciplines.

Notes

An earlier version of this essay appeared in my *Kurosawa: Film Studies and Japanese Cinema* (Durham: Duke University Press, 2000).

1   The list of the 1950s Hollywood films in which Japan is featured prominently includes: *Japanese War Bride* (King Vidor, 1952), *House of Bamboo* (Samuel Fuller, 1955), *Teahouse of the August Moon* (1956), *Sayonara* (Joshua Logan, 1957), *The Barbarian and the Geisha* (1958), *Geisha Boy* (1958), *The Crimson Kimono* (Samuel Fuller, 1959), etc. For detailed analyses of these films, see Gina Marchetti, *Romance and the "Yellow Peril": Race, Sex, and Discursive Strategies in Hollywood Fiction* (Berkeley: University of California Press, 1993) and Murakami Yumiko, *Iero feisu: Hariuddo eiga ni miru ajia jin no shōzō* (Tokyo: Asahi shinbunsha, 1993).

2   See, for instance, newspaper and magazine reviews of *Rashomon* published when the film was originally released in the U.S. and the U.K. Some of these reviews are reprinted in Donald Richie, ed., *Rashomon* (New Brunswick: Rutgers University Press, 1987). Yet, not all writings on Japanese cinema in the 1950s were so blatantly ethnocentric or reductive. There were a number of articles and reviews whose main purpose was to introduce Japanese cinema to American audiences. Written by both Japanese film critics and American specialists on Japan, these texts discussed not only specific Japanese films but also the history and current condition of Japanese cinema, major directors, genres, stars, the state of Japanese film criticism, and so on. Some of these informative articles on Japanese cinema are: Masayoshi Iwabutchi, "1954 in Japan," *Sight and Sound* (spring 1955): 202–205; Akira Iwasaki, "Japan's New Screen Art: More Real Than 'Rashomon,'" *Nation* (May 12, 1956): 398–401; Earl Miner, "Japanese Film Art in Modern Dress," *Quarterly of Film, Radio, and Television* 10(4) (1956); Donald Richie, "The Unexceptional Japanese Films Are More Preferred in Japan than Those That Intrigue the West," *Films in Review* (June-July 1955): 273–277.

3   Other books on Japanese cinema published in the 1960s include the following two works by Donald Richie, *The Japanese Movies: An Illustrated History* (Tokyo: Kodansha International, 1966) and *Japanese Movies* (Tokyo: Japan Travel Bureau, 1961). Neither particularly academic nor comprehensive, unlike *The Japanese Film*, these books have hardly been mentioned in American scholarship on Japanese cinema.

4 Desser, "Toward a Structural Analysis of the Postwar Samurai Film" in *Reframing Japanese Cinema: Authorship, Genre, History*, ed. Arthur Nolletti and David Desser (Bloomington: Indiana University Press, 1992), p. 147.

5 Allan Casebier, "Images of Irrationality in Modern Japan: The Films of Shohei Imamura," *Film Criticism* 7(1) (fall 1983): 42–43.

6 Joan Mellen, *The Waves at Genji's Door: Japan Through Its Cinema* (New York: Pantheon Books, 1976), pp. 396–397; Desser, "Toward a Structural Analysis," p. 155; Kathe Geist, "Buddhism in *Tokyo Story*," in *Ozu's Tokyo Story*, ed. David Desser (Cambridge: Cambridge University Press, 1997), p. 110.

7 Desser, "Toward a Structural Analysis," p. 156.

8 Ibid., p. 149.

9 Another pioneering auteurist study, *Hitchcock's Films* by Robin Wood, was also published in 1965.

10 Janet Staiger, "The Politics of Film Canons," *Cinema Journal*, 24(3) (1985): 12.

11 For instance, to justify the use of Zen as the most pertinent cultural context for his study of Ozu's films, Paul Schrader refers to a report prepared by the Allied Powers' Religious and Cultural Division during the Occupation of Japan: "The type of conduct usually expressed by the words, 'Japanese spirit' is essentially Zen in nature." And he does not forget to add that this characterization of Japanese culture is "echoed by both Alan Watts and Langdon Warner," Western authorities on Zen and Japanese art respectively (Schrader, *Transcendental Style in Film* [Berkeley: University of California Press, 1972], p. 27).

12 John Dower, *War without Mercy: Race and Power in the Pacific War* (New York: Pantheon, 1986), p. 119.

13 Ibid., p. 121.

14 On Benedict's relation to the wartime collaboration of the military and social scientists, see, for instance, Clifford Geertz, *Works and Lives: The Anthropologist as Author* (Stanford: Stanford University Press, 1988), pp. 123–126.

15 Ruth Benedict, *The Chrysanthemum and the Sword: Patterns of Japanese Culture* (Boston: Houghton Mifflin Company, 1946), p. 1.

16 Yanagita Kunio, "Jinjojin no jinseikan," *Minzokugaku Kenkyū* 14(4) (1949): 290, quoted in John W. Bennett and Michio Nagai, "The Japanese Critique of the Methodology of Benedict's 'Chrysanthemum and the Sword,'" *American Anthropologist* 55(3) (August 1953): 407–408.

17 Bennett and Nagai, "The Japanese Critique of the Methodology of Benedict's 'Chrysanthemum and the Sword,'" p. 408. For a deconstructive reading of Benedict's book, see Geertz, *Works and Lives*.

18 Donald Keene reports that in 1942 at the U.S. Navy Japanese Language School in Boulder, Colorado, he and other students were required to watch Japanese films every week to improve their spoken Japanese. The films he saw were all so dreadful that he did not see a single Japanese film for nine years until *Rashomon* won the grand prix at the Venice Film Festival (Donald Keene, "Kurosawa," *Grand Street* 1(4) [summer 1982]: 140–141). Is the U.S. military's instrumental use of Japanese films during the Second World War partially responsible for the neglect of film by Japanese studies whose founding members were mostly trained by the military and/or worked for the Occupation government?

19 Tetsuo Najita, "On Culture and Technology in Postmodern Japan," in *Postmodernism and Japan*, ed. Masao Miyoshi and H. D. Harootunian (Durham: Duke University Press, 1989), p. 14.

20 For instance, see Joan Mellen, *The Waves at Genji's Door: Japan through Its Cinema* (New York: Pantheon Books, 1976). Her seemingly historical argument is sometimes nothing more than the simple imposition of two essentialized stereotypes onto Japanese history, traditional Japan ("feudalism") and the modern West ("modernity").

21 Prior to the publication of *To the Distant Observer: Form and Meaning in the Japanese Cinema*, ed. Annette Michelson (Berkeley: University of California Press, 1979), Burch published an article outlining the basic theoretical premises of his Japanese cinema project. Noel Burch, "To the Distant Observer: Towards a Theory of Japanese Film," *October* 1 (spring 1976): 32–46.

22 Burch, *To the Distant Observer*, p. 11.

23 This is the title of the chapter on Benedict in Geertz's *Works and Lives*.

24 Burch, *To the Distant Observer*, p. 11.

25 "Of most general value . . . are," writes Bordwell, "his insights into Western filmmaking. Like Debussy and other avant-garde artists, Burch returns from his contemplation of Eastern art with a critical vision of our own traditions. . . . *To the Distant Observer* succeeds in imposing a sense of a unified representational scheme at work in Western film style" (David Bordwell, "Review of *To the Distant Observer*," *Wide Angle*, 3(4) [1985]: 73). Phil Rosen also develops a similar argument: "Burch compares Japanese practices to patterns of editing, camerawork, narrative articulation, etc. common in dominant western practices, the IMR [Institutional Mode of Representation]. The compulsive return to such comparisons is as central to Burch's method of film-textual description as the sensitivity to intertextual vicissitudes of motifs is to Kracauer's. Indeed, a carefully chosen collection of excerpts from Burch's book on Japanese cinema could supply us with one of his fullest descriptions of the IMR" (Phil Rosen, "History, Textuality, Nation: Kracauer, Burch, and Some Problems in the Study of National Cinemas," *Iris* 2(2) [1984]: 75–76).

26 Sheila Whitaker, "Review of *To the Distant Observer: Form and Meaning in the Japanese Cinema* by Noël Burch," *Framework* 11 (autumn 1979): 48.

27 Noël Burch, *Life to Those Shadows* (Berkeley: University of California Press, 1990).

28 Roland Barthes, *Empire of Signs*, trans. Richard Howard (New York: Hill and Wang, 1982), p. 3. After quoting the same passage, Burch asserts that he does "share the basic premises of this opening statement of *L'Empire des signes*" (*To the Distant Observer*, p. 16).

29 Dana Polan, "Formalism and Its Discontents," *Jump Cut* 26 (1981): 64–65.

30 Burch, *To the Distant Observer*, p. 11.

31 Because his view of the history of class dynamics in Japan is more complex than his view of that history in the West, there is less linearity and teleology in Burch's descriptions of the development of Japanese filmic representation" (Rosen, "History, Textuality, Nation," p. 79).

32 Examples of this type include Noletti and Desser, *Reframing Japanese Cinema*; Linda C. Ehrlich and David Desser, eds., *Cinematic Landscapes: Observations on the Vi-*

sual Arts and Cinema of China and Japan (Austin: University of Texas Press, 1994); David Desser, *Eros plus Massacre: An Introduction to the Japanese New Wave Cinema* (Bloomington: Indiana University Press, 1988); Kyoko Hirano, *Mr. Smith Goes to Tokyo: Japanese Cinema under the American Occupation, 1945–1952* (Washington, D.C.: Smithsonian Institution Press, 1992).

33 Scott Nygren, "Reconsidering Modernism: Japanese Film and the Postmodern Context," *Wide Angle* 11(3) (July 1989): 6–15; "Doubleness and Idiosyncrasy in Cross-Cultural Analysis," *Quarterly Review of Film and Video* 13(1–3) (1991): 173–187.

34 Nygren, "Reconsidering Modernism," p.14.

35 Ibid., p. 7.

36 Nygren refers to the painter Saeki Yuzō and the I-novel as two exemplary cases showing how Japanese modernism aligned itself with the Western humanist tradition. But it is far from clear why the case of Saeki is mentioned, since the only significant information given is the fact of Saeki's suicide in 1928. The misleading characterization of the I-novel as a "Japanese response to Western naturalism" also does not tell us much about Japanese modernism (Nygren, "Reconsidering Modernism," p. 10).

37 There are a number of modernist groups, trends, and movements in modern Japan: the Shinkankaku-ha (New Sensibility school) writers of the 1920s, Dadaism, the Jun eiga-geki undō (Pure Film movement), the Shōchiku Kamata modanizumu, the 1950s kindaishugi led by the director Masumura Yasuzō, etc. In architecture, various modernist movements existed contemporaneously in Japan and in the West, and there is nothing which suggests Japanese modernist architects somehow "misunderstood" modernism as an extension of Western humanism.

38 Nygren, "Reconsidering Modernism," p. 13.

39 Nygren, "Doubleness and Idiosyncrasy," p. 184.

40 Nygren writes: "Within the framework of *giri*, obligations to larger social groups 'naturally' precede those of smaller social units. As a result, obligation to the Emperor was paramount, since the Emperor represented in his body or person the entirety of Japanese culture. After the Emperor, any position of social authority follows along the same principle, so that feudal lord or corporate/*zaibatsu* director become interchangeable, and the patriarch within the family is owed duty as the person responsible for that social group" (Nygren, "Doubleness and Idiosyncrasy," pp. 179–180.) The explanation of *giri* in this passage is very misleading. For instance, the size of the social unit does not directly correspond to the degree of obligation. In fact, one's *giri* to a single individual can easily force him or her to reject the demand of a larger social unit such as family, school, or nation. It is also problematic to use the concept of *giri* when we talk about Japanese "obligation to the Emperor." Rather than a general principle of the Japanese social system from time immemorial, the "obligation to the Emperor" was manufactured at different historical moments for specific ideological purposes that cannot be reduced to the idea of *giri*. In short, the image of Japanese social structure presented by Nygren is nothing more than a caricature.

41 Nygren, "Doubleness and Idiosyncrasy," p. 179.

42 H. D. Harootunian, "America's Japan/Japan's Japan," in *Japan in the World*, ed. Masao Miyoshi and H. D. Harootunian (Durham: Duke University Press, 1993), pp. 197–198.

43 Keiko I. McDonald, *Japanese Classical Theater in Films* (Rutherford N.J.: Fairleigh Dickinson University Press, 1994), pp. 12–13.

44 For instance, in 1929 the Department of Cinema was established at the University of Southern California, and in 1932 it granted the B.A in Cinema for the first time in the U.S. ("University Film Teaching in the United States," *Film Quarterly* 16(3) [spring 1963]: 45).

45 Besides Knight's book, other popular survey books include: Richard Griffith and Arthur Mayer, *The Movies* (1957); A. R. Fulton, *Motion Pictures: The Development of an Art* (1960); and Kenneth MacGowan, *Behind the Screen* (1965).

46 These refurbished books on film history include: Terry Ramsaye's *A Million and One Nights* (1965[1926 originally]); Lewis Jacobs' *The Rise of the American Film* (1968/1939); and Benjamin Hampton's *History of the American Film Industry* (1970), which was first published as *A History of the Movies* in 1931 (Robert C. Allen and Douglas Gomery, *Film History: Theory and Practice* [New York: Knopf, 1985], p. 28).

47 A dramatic growth of film studies in the 1960s and 1970s can be glimpsed in the following statistics. According to Jack C. Ellis, in the 1952–53 catalogues of the hundred largest American universities there were 575 film-related courses. In 1964–65, the number of film courses at the same hundred schools increased to 846, an increase of 47% (Jack C. Ellis, "Ruminations of an Ex-Cinematologist," *Cinema Journal* 24(2) [winter 1985]: 48). "In 1967 some 200 colleges offered courses in film. Ten years later the number had passed 1000, an increase of more than 500 percent. In 1978 the American Film Institute counted nearly 4200 separate courses in film studies being offered in American colleges and nearly 150 schools offered degrees in film" (Allen and Gomery, *Film History*, pp. 27–28).

48 For example, such leading film journals as *Camera Obscura*, *Film Criticism*, *Quarterly Review of Film Studies*, and *Wide Angle* were all established in 1976.

49 Ellis, "Ruminations of an Ex-Cinematologist," p. 49.

50 Robert E. Kapsis, *Hitchcock: The Making of Reputation* (Chicago: University of Chicago Press, 1992), p. 101.

51 Ellis, "Ruminations of an Ex-Cinematologist," p. 48.

52 According to Harold W. Schneider, in the early 1970s, about 20 to 25 percent of the college film courses were taught in literature and language departments (Schneider, "Literature and Film: Marking Out Some Boundaries," *Literature/Film Quarterly* 3(1) [winter 1975]: 30).

53 Andrew, *Concepts in Film Theory* (Oxford: Oxford University Press, 1984), p. 6.

54 David Bordwell, *Making Meaning: Inference and Rhetoric in the Interpretation of Cinema* (Cambridge: Harvard University Press, 1989).

55 David Bordwell, "Film Interpretation Revisited," *Film Criticism* 17(2–3) (winter-spring 1993): 113.

56 Bordwell, *Making Meaning*, p. xiii.

57 Robert B. Ray, *The Avant-Garde Finds Andy Hardy* (Cambridge: Harvard University Press, 1995), pp. 6–7.

58 Ray, "Film Studies/Crisis/Experimentation," p. 57.

59 See, for instance, the following passage from the editor's foreword to the 1968 reprint of Lewis Jacobs's classic, *The Rise of the American Film*: "Here must surely be one more confrontation of an essential paradox of art: that its potential universality and timeliness grow out of immersion in its own place and time. The truest universals are

details of particular existences; the deliberate universals, confected of generalities of whatever grandeur of purpose, dwindle to unfleshed symbols, without roots in life except in slogans and theories. In the cinema, as in all art, the paradox may be observed as a truly Heraclitean mutuality of opposites: particular and universal having an essential unity, being phases in the experiences of audiences. In the process of experience, in a dynamic obeying mysterious laws, the organic tension of particular and universal drives the works of cultures towards Culture" (Martin S. Dworkin, "General Editor's Foreword," in Lewis Jacobs, *The Rise of the American Film: A Critical History* [New York: Teachers College Press, 1968], pp. x-xi).

60 However, the reverse is hardly accepted as a legitimate academic practice; that is, no reciprocal privilege is granted to non-Western scholars in the U.S. studying German or French cinema without a good command of German or French. This asymmetrical relationship between Western scholars' study of non-Western cinemas and non-Western scholars' study of Western cinemas reminds us of "unequal treaties" in the age of imperialism.

61 The Soviet and Italian cinemas are also part of the canon of film theory. Their significance in the canon is heavily dependent on the presence of specific theorists (Eisenstein, Kuleshov, Pudovkin, etc.) and schools or movements (Soviet montage school, Italian neorealism, etc.).

62 See, for instance, David Bordwell and Noël Carroll, eds., *Post-Theory: Reconstructing Film Studies* (Madison: University of Wisconsin Press, 1996).

63 Jonathan Culler, "Comparative Literature, At Last!" in *Comparative Literature in the Age of Multiculturalism*, ed. Charles Bernheimer (Baltimore: Johns Hopkins University Press, 1995), p. 119.

64 Harootunian, "America's Japan/Japan's Japan," p. 200.

65 Dower, "E. H. Norman, Japan, and the Uses of History," in *Origins of the Modern Japanese State*, ed. John Dower (New York: Pantheon Books, 1975), p. 33.

66 H. Richard Okada, *Figures of Resistance: Language, Poetry, and Narrating in "The Tale of Genji" and Other Mid-Heian Texts* (Durham: Duke University Press, 1991), pp. 9–10. Since film cannot be either "translated" or "annotated," the traditionally trained literary scholars do not probably know what to do with Japanese cinema. The best they can do is to deal with film scripts or to transcribe films; however, there is little analogy between these activities and translation of literary texts.

67 René Wellek, "The Crisis of Comparative Literature," in *Concepts of Criticism*, ed. Stephen Nichols (New Haven: Yale University Press, 1963), p. 282.

68 Peter Brooks, "Must We Apologize?" in *Comparative Literature*, ed. Bernheimer, p. 97.

69 Thomas G. Rosenmeyer, "Am I a Comparatist?" in *Building a Profession: Autobiographical Perspectives on the History of Comparative Literature in the United States*, ed. Lionel Grossman and Mihai I. Spariosu (Albany: State University of New York Press, 1994), p. 49.

70 Fredric Jameson, "On *Cultural Studies*," in *The Identity in Question*, ed. John Rajchman (Routledge: New York, 1995), pp. 251–253.

71 Charles Bernheimer, "Introduction: The Anxieties of Comparison," in *Comparative Literature*, ed. Bernheimer, pp. 10–11.

72　Brooks, "Must We Apologize?," pp. 97–106.

73　Jonathan Culler, "Comparative Literature, at Last!" pp. 117–121.

74　Marjorie Perloff, "'Literature' in the Expanded Field," in *Comparative Literature*, ed. Bernheimer, pp. 175–186.

75　Charles Bernheimer, et al., "The Bernheimer Report, 1993: Comparative Literature at the Turn of the Century," in *Comparative Literature*, ed. Bernheimer, p. 42.

76　Lionel Gossman, "Out of a Gothic North," in *Building a Profession*, ed. Gossman and Spariosu, p. 203.

77　Rey Chow, "In the Name of Comparative Literature," in *Comparative Literature*, ed. Bernheimer, p. 107.

78　Harry Levin, *Grounds for Comparison* (Cambridge: Harvard University Press, 1972), p. 84.

79　"It may be . . . that the Ph.D. in comparative literature will be replaced by a Ph.D. in one of many area studies—European studies, Latin American studies, Asian studies, and so on—as well as in different time frames: medieval studies, Renaissance studies, eighteenth-century studies, modernism, postmodernism" (Perloff, "'Literature' in the Expanded Field," p. 183). Perhaps following Perloff's suggestions, Charles Bernheimer also proposes period studies and area studies as two possible "new disciplinary configurations with a multicultural comparative outlook" (Bernheimer, "Introduction," p. 14). In his scenario, studies of non-Western literatures and cultures are valorized as useful supplement to research projects in medieval studies, Renaissance studies, and eighteenth-century studies. In this newly configured period studies, the non-West is still only a supplement, an aid which facilitates a deeper understanding of Western cultures. Bernheimer writes: "If the research groups were to explore the dynamics of the elliptical approach, their comparative work could intersect with that of scholars of non-Western cultures in the same or similar periods, and the result could be a broadened and revitalized conception of literary and cultural history, still centered in Europe but also crucially decentered. . . . Still, the area studies model could be reconceptualized to foreground literature and to undo, via an elliptical bifocus, the notion of a stable geographical area" (p. 14). But it is not clear how literature can be foregrounded suddenly when it has never been a primary focus of area studies dominated by social scientists.

Contributors

PAUL A. BOVÉ is Professor of English at the University of Pittsburgh.

REY CHOW is Andrew W. Mellon Professor of the Humanities at Brown University.

BRUCE S. CUMINGS is Norman and Edna Freehling Professor of History at the University of Chicago.

JAMES A. FUJII teaches Japanese literature and contemporary geopolitics at the University of California, Irvine.

H. D. HAROOTUNIAN is Chair of the East Asian Studies Department and Professor of History at New York University.

MASAO MIYOSHI is Hajime Mori Professor of Japanese, English, and Comparative Literature at the University of California, San Diego.

TETSUO NAJITA is Robert S. Ingersoll Distinguished Service Professor of History Emeritus at the University of Chicago.

RICHARD H. OKADA is Associate Professor of Japanese Literature at Princeton University.

BENITA PARRY is honorary professor in the Department of English and Comparative Literature Studies at the University of Warwick, U.K.

MOSS ROBERTS is Professor of Chinese at New York University.

BERNARD S. SILBERMAN is Professor of Political Science at the University of Chicago.

STEFAN TANAKA is Associate Professor of History at the University of California, San Diego.

ROB WILSON is Professor of Literature and Graduate Chair, University of California at Santa Cruz.

SYLVIA YANAGISAKO is Professor of Cultural and Social Anthropology at Stanford University.

MITSUHIRO YOSHIMOTO is Associate Professor of East Asian Studies at New York University.

Index

Japanese cinema studies: auteurism and, 371–72; as discipline, 383; marginalization of, 384–85, 389; and national character study, 370–72, 374, 378; theory and, 374–75; as threat, 390

Japanese literature. *See* New Criticism

Japanese studies: fetish of tradition and, 387–88; and holistic concept of culture, 307, 309; marginalization of, 386; *Nihonteki* procedural norms and, 308, 310

Japan Foundation, 2–3, 159

Johnson, Chalmers, 315

Karatani Kōjin, 355

Kawashima Takeyoshi, 94–95

Khmer Rouge, 323–24; sponsored by United States and China, 323–24; war against Vietnam, 323. *See also* Cambodia; Vietnam War

Kiernan, Ben, 324, 326

Kingston, Maxine Hong, 232–33

Koselleck, Reinhart, 84, 86, 92, 95

Kosovo, 346–47

Krimsky, Sheldon, 36

Lattimore, Owen, 277

Lazarus, Neil, 140, 142

Lefebvre, Henri, 350

Lévi-Strauss, Claude, 41–42

London, Jack, 239; *Sea Wolf*, 240–41

Maeda Ai, 349

Mao Zedong, 328–29

Maruyama Masao, 63, 69, 97

Marx, Karl, 306, 308

Matthiessen, F. O., 210, 212

Mellon Foundation (Andrew W.), 286, 303

Melville, Herman, 237; imperialism and, 238

Mercer, Kobena, 138

Miller, Christopher, 136

Millikan, Max, 279

Miyoshi, Masao, 123, 140, 355–56

Modernization studies, 93, 274; and claims to objectivity, 94–95; conceptual poverty of, 96; and Japan, 158–59

Moore, Barrington, 287–88

Mosely, Philip: and CIA ties, 271–74

Multiculturalism, 43–46, 113, 140, 221

Muzzafar, Chandra, 245

Najita, Tetsuo, 373–74

Nakane Chie, 308, 312

National Endowment for the Humanities (NEH), 207, 212–14

National Security Education Act (NSEA), 280–82, 284

Negri, Antonio, 65

New Criticism: and WWII, 193–94; cleansing of Japanese literature and, 196–97; political essentialism and, 202

Nixon, Richard, 328–29

Norman, E. H., 61–63, 77, 163, 306; *The Anatomy of Japanese Feudalism*, 61

Norris, Christopher, 349

Nygren, Scott, 376–78

Office of Strategic Services (OSS), 263–64, 268

Ogyū Sorai, 69–70

Ohmae, Kenichi, 245

Okada, Richard, 388

Parsons, Talcott, 210

Pol Pot, 323–24. *See also* Cambodia; Khmer Rouge

Poppe, Nikolai, 277–78

Postcoloniality: and authenticity, 154, 169–70; English studies and, 153, 167–68

Prakash, Gyan, 123, 126

Prewitt, Kenneth, 288

Radcliffe-Brown, A. R., 177–78

Ramseyer, Mark J., and Francis McCall Rosenbluth, 314–15

Rational choice theory: critique of, 286–87, 305, 313–15

Ray, Robert, 382–84

Readings, Bill, 199–200

Reischauer, Edwin, 92, 93–94

Rekishigaku kenkyūkai (Rekiken), 80; and concept of nation (*minzoku*), 81–87; and world history (*sekaishi*), 83–86, 90

Ricoeur, Paul, 73

Ritchie, Donald, 370–71

Rizvi, Fazal, 111, 114

Roberts, Moss, 284

Rockefeller Foundation, 156, 215–16, 269

Rothman, Kenneth J., 36

Library of Congress Cataloging-in-Publication Data
Learning places : the afterlives of area studies / edited
by Masao Miyoshi and H. D. Harootunian.
p. cm. — (Asia-Pacific : culture, politics, and society)
Includes bibliographical references and index.
ISBN 0-8223-2826-7 (cloth : alk. paper)
ISBN 0-8223-2840-2 (pbk. : alk. paper)
1. Asia—Study and teaching (Higher)—United States. 2. Area
studies—United States. 3. Area studies. I. Miyoshi, Masao.
II. Harootunian, Harry D., 1929– III. Asia-Pacific.
DS32.9.U5 L43 2002   950'.071'173—dc21   2002004456